OpenGL® Game Programming

PRIMA TECH'S

GAME DEVELOPMENT

D1354563

OpenGL® Game Programming

Kevin Hawkins and Dave Astle

PRIMA TECH'S

GAME DEVELOPMENT

Premier
p
Press™

A Division of Prima Publishing

Prima Publishing and colophon are registered trademarks of Prima Communications, Inc. PRIMA TECH and the Game Development series are trademarks of Prima Communications, Inc., Roseville, California 95661.

Publisher: Stacy L. Hiquet
Associate Marketing Manager: Jennifer Breece
Managing Editor: Sandy Doell
Acquisitions Editor: Jody Kennen
Project Editor: Kelly Talbot
Technical Reviewer: Nathan Beittenmiller
Copy Editor: Kate Welsh
Interior Layout: Bill Hartman
Cover Design: Prima Design Team
Indexer: Sharon Shock
Proofreader: Kim Benbow

ISBN: 0-7615-3330-3

Library of Congress Catalog Card Number: 2001-086796

Printed in the United States of America

02 03 04 05 BH 10 9 8 7 6 5 4 3

For my family and friends
—Kevin Hawkins

For Lissa
—Dave Astle

Acknowledgments

There are many people who helped me in the process of creating this book. I'd like to thank all of my family and friends for the support they've given me. It has helped tremendously. Thank you, Kara, for putting up with me for so many months and staying strong even when times were tough. Thanks to Todd and Tucker for keeping me sane. And to my teammates and coaches, thank you for asking me every day how things were coming along and in your own way keeping me motivated to complete the book. And I especially thank Dave, who I know has less time than I do left in his life to do a huge project like this, for finally agreeing to help me write the book.

I'd like to thank all the good people at Prima and especially Jody Kennen and Kelly Talbot for presenting to me the opportunity to write this book and for their support throughout the whole thing. Thanks to André LaMothe for giving us a direction to follow. Also, thank you to Ernest "TANSTAAFL" Pazera for making me realize that sometimes you only get one chance to do something.

And finally, thank you to all of the people who have enhanced my knowledge over the years, and especially during the development of this book. I'd specifically like to thank Bas Kuenen, Mark Kilgard, Mark DeLoura, André LaMothe, Richard "Keebler" Benson, Chris "kiwidog" Hargrove, Richard Wright, Jordan "jdm" Maynard, Nate Miller, Nate Robins, and Jeff "NeHe" Molofee.

—Kevin Hawkins

A lot of people came together to make this book possible. First and foremost, I'd like to thank Kevin, who was able to put much more time and effort into this than I was. Most of what you now hold in your hands is the result of his dedication. Second, I'd like to thank my wife, who made countless sacrifices to allow me to work on this despite being pregnant the whole time. I'd like to thank my four children, Rebekah, Evan, Elise, and Tyler, sometimes for letting me work, and other times for dragging me away to play with them. I'd thank you too, Nathan, but you just kinda sat in mom's tummy. I especially want to thank Madonna for all the help she's given me over the years.

I'm also indebted to Ernest "TANSTAAFL" Pazera for talking me into writing this in the first place; despite all the stress it's caused me, it's been quite an experience. I'd also like to thank everyone at Prima, especially Jody Kennen and Kelly Talbot for their constant support, and André LaMothe for his feedback on the direction we should take with this.

Finally, I want to thank everyone who has provided me with the knowledge—either directly or indirectly—that allowed me to write this, including Chuck Hansen (my graphics professor at the University of Utah), Jeff "NeHe" Molofee (who did a fabulous job of putting together content for the CD), Mark Kilgard, Nate Robins, Nate Miller, Scott "druid-" Franke, and Rich "Keebler" Benson.

—Dave Astle

About the Authors

Kevin Hawkins is a Computer Science graduate of Embry-Riddle University in Daytona Beach, FL, where he will also be going for his Master's degree in Software Engineering. His programming experience extends back almost seven years and includes development experience with C/C++, OpenGL, DirectX, and a host of other languages and APIs. Kevin is also one of the cofounders and the CEO of GameDev.net (**www.gamedev.net**), the most comprehensive resource for game development on the Internet. On the non-technical side, Kevin plays on Embry-Riddle's intercollegiate baseball team as a pitcher. He also enjoys reading, playing games, playing guitar, and spending time with his girlfriend, Kara.

Dave Astle received his bachelor's degree in Computer Science from the University of Utah, where he specialized in graphics, artificial intelligence, networking, and compiler theory and design. He started programming games almost 20 years ago and is currently a software engineer at WaveLink. He is the cofounder and Executive Producer of GameDev.net, the leading online community for game developers. He is also the owner and lead programmer of Myopic Rhino Games (**www.myopicrhino.com**), an independent game company developing for the mass market. When not absorbing radiation from his monitor, Dave enjoys music, reading, skating, collecting rhinos, trying to attain Jason Hall–like proportions at the gym, and playing with his kids.

CONTENTS AT A GLANCE

CONTENTS

CHAPTER 2

USING WINDOWS WITH OPENGL ● ● ● ● ● ● ● ● ● ● ● ● ● ● 21

CHAPTER 3
AN OVERVIEW OF 3D GRAPHICS THEORY...63

CHAPTER 5
COORDINATE TRANSFORMATIONS AND
OpenGL Matrices ■■■■■■■■■■■■■■■■■■■■■■■■113

CHAPTER 6
ADDING COLORS, BLENDING, AND
LIGHTING ■■■■■■■■■■■■■■■■■■■■■■■■■■■■■■■■■151

CHAPTER 7

BITMAPS AND IMAGES WITH OPENGL....205

CHAPTER 8
TEXTURE MAPPING 229

CHAPTER 9

ADVANCED TEXTURE MAPPING 281

CHAPTER 10

DISPLAY LISTS AND VERTEX ARRAYS 319

CHAPTER 11

DISPLAYING TEXT 341

CHAPTER 14

CURVES AND SURFACES

CHAPTER 15

SPECIAL EFFECTS

PART III
BUILDING A GAME ::::::::::::::::::::::::475

CHAPTER 16
USING DIRECTX: DIRECTINPUT ::::::::::::::477

CHAPTER 17

USING DIRECTX AUDIO ■■■■■■■■■■■■■■■■■■■■■■517

CHAPTER 19

PHYSICS MODELING WITH OPENGL.........631

CHAPTER 20
BUILDING A GAME ENGINE 707

LETTER FROM THE
SERIES EDITOR

OpenGL Game Programming is one of the first books we developed for the Prima Game Development series and probably one of the most ambitious books as well. There are dozens of books on OpenGL programming as well as general 3D graphics, but no one has written a game programming book that uses OpenGL as its target platform. *OpenGL Game Programming* had to simultaneously satisfy these goals and more. First and foremost, the book had to be about game programming. However, OpenGL is like a distant cousin of anything Windows, thus showing how to integrate all the aspects of Windows programming along with OpenGL and then framing it in the context of a game programming book is nothing less than a miracle! Let's all give Kevin Hawkins and Dave Astle (co-founders of GameDev.net) a big round of applause!

Now let me tell you something: I own so many books on OpenGL I can't count them, but as a game programmer there isn't one single book that has met my needs. This is the book that game programmers have been looking for. Even if you're new to game programming, this book will get you started. It starts with a simple overview of gaming along with a comparison of OpenGL vs. DirectX. After you know the score, *OpenGL Game Programming* delves into the black art of Windows programming, but using OpenGL as the graphics system rather than Direct3D. Once the foundation is laid and you know how to get OpenGL and Windows working together, the authors build up your 3D knowledge, illustrating everything you need to know about transformations, lighting, clipping, projection, and texture mapping. If the book stopped right there, it would be worth it, but it goes on to discuss advanced topics such as display lists, curved surfaces, and special effects. The curved surface stuff is especially cool!

At this point, the book switches back into game programming mode and covers what no OpenGL book on earth covers—DirectX! Both DirectInput and DirectSound are covered, which rounds out the software components needed to make a game on a PC. Now with everything in place, *OpenGL Game Programming* finishes off with physics modeling, the design of a complete game engine, and a demo game to illustrate everything the book covers.

In conclusion, this book has been in development for quite some time, but I know that you will appreciate the extra time we and the authors put into the book to make it special and what will surely be the quintessential book on OpenGL and gaming.

Sincerely,

André LaMothe
May 2001

FOREWORD

Let's face it: 3D video games are fun. These games create immersive worlds that challenge our reflexes and wits. Writing these games is a great challenge too. I'm here to tell you that this is the best of all times for learning 3D game programming. If you're thinking about writing a game for the PC or just learning about what game programming is all about, now is the time and this is the book.

In my view, the most incredible aspect of game development today is how much 3D graphics functionality and performance comes jam-packed in a new PC with an up-to-date graphics card. In the past, the best available graphics hardware for gaming was at one of two extremes. At the high end, proprietary UNIX workstations from companies such as Silicon Graphics, my previous employer, provided graphics horsepower for a price, a price that only scientists, engineers, and artists in big organizations could afford. Although cool games exist for these workstations, no one could justify buying one just to play games! At the low end, game consoles provided graphics hardware at the right price for the game-playing public, but console programming was a black art and only professional game programmers had access to the development environments required to make games for consoles.

Unlike inexpensive consoles, high-end graphics workstations were quite expensive, so it was imperative that the 3D programming interface for these machines be both extremely efficient and straightforward to program. Silicon Graphics developed a high-performance, straightforward programming interface called IRIS GL; the GL stands for "graphics library." IRIS GL was the starting point for an improved 3D programming interface called OpenGL that was standardized by all the major UNIX workstation vendors. Thousands of 3D engineering, scientific, medical, and animation applications use OpenGL. Microsoft, too, standardized on OpenGL for its NT Workstation operating system; later, Microsoft added OpenGL support to Windows 95 and subsequent operating systems.

OpenGL is fundamentally designed for hardware-accelerated 3D rendering. Each OpenGL call issued on a high-end Silicon Graphics workstation is relayed directly to the graphics hardware for execution. When OpenGL was first implemented for PCs, OpenGL commands had to be handled by the CPU, so OpenGL was not the speed-demon it was designed to be. Fortunately, it was only a matter of time until PC hardware would catch up with OpenGL. Today, PC graphics hardware such as NVIDIA's GeForce line of graphics chips directly executes OpenGL commands in hardware. Ever-increasing semiconductor densities and clever graphics chip designs have now created a situation where the latest PC graphics chips are several times faster than the best Silicon Graphics systems of only a few years ago (not to mention far cheaper!). And OpenGL had evolved along with PC graphics hardware to incorporate multi-texturing and a host of other game-oriented extensions.

This has created an amazing synergy where the best 3D programming interface for professional 3D applications is also the best 3D programming interface for games. And OpenGL is not just for Windows PCs. OpenGL is now the standard 3D programming interface for the Mac, including Apple's OS X release. OpenGL is available on all UNIX workstations including Sun, HP, IBM, and, of course, Silicon Graphics. OpenGL is also a vital part of the open source software movement; Mesa and the original Silicon Graphics OpenGL sample implementation provide OpenGL support for Linux PCs. I won't be surprised when game consoles embrace OpenGL, too.

If you are familiar with the latest 3D games for the PC, I'm sure that you've heard of and probably played OpenGL-based games. The hall of fame includes all the *Quake* series of games and the much-anticipated *Doom 3* from id Software; *Half Life* from Valve; *Soldier of Fortune* and *Star Trek: Voyager—Elite Force* from Raven Software; *Tribes 2* from Dynamix; and *Serious Sam* from Croteam. Behind all these games was a one-time novice programmer with the passion to learn 3D game programming and realize their game. Maybe you'll add a game to this list!

This book is about the whole task of writing a game. Of course, graphics is the cornerstone of any 3D game, so a practical introduction to OpenGL gets the book started. This book also covers other key aspects of building a PC game: use of DirectX Input for obtaining user input; use of DirectX Audio for sound and music; loading file formats containing textures and 3D character models; basic physics to handle realistic object collisions and interactions; and design of the overall game architecture. This book is really just the beginning. Be sure to check out the accompanying CD-ROM and the resources described in the appendices.

Personally, I'm thrilled to see this book published. It is about time for PC programmers to find a practical resource to learn about 3D game design using OpenGL.

Even if you don't end up writing games for a living, learning about OpenGL and game development will help you better appreciate the technology behind the games you play and help you develop valuable computer programming skills for whatever life has in store for you. The fact that OpenGL is "not just for games" makes it a valuable programming interface for developing other 3D application software. So, let the games begin.

Mark J. Kilgard
Graphics Software Engineer, *NVIDIA Corporation*
Author of *OpenGL Programming for the X Window System*
and the OpenGL Utility Toolkit (also known as GLUT)

INTRODUCTION

Welcome to *OpenGL Game Programming*! In this book, you'll learn how to make a game using high-performance graphics and game libraries. What you have in your hands is the culmination of over a year of work by the authors. We think it will be a tremendous resource, and it will get you well on your way to creating the games you've always wanted to make.

As you can guess from the title, we're going to show you how to use OpenGL for game graphics. Since OpenGL is a graphics-only library and because games also require sound, music, input, and so on, we'll also integrate DirectX into our games.

We see this book as filling a gap in the resources available to prospective game developers. There are many DirectX-based game programming books available. There are also a number of graphics books covering OpenGL. But until now, there has not been a book combining the two.

Although we're going to be covering OpenGL and DirectX, this book is not intended as a complete reference for either. We'll only be covering the components that are needed in the games and demos developed for this book. Toward the end, we'll list some resources for learning more about these rich and powerful libraries.

The book is organized into three parts.

In Part I, we lay the foundation of things to come. We look at the background and history of OpenGL and DirectX, providing a high-level view of how they work. Because we're using Windows as our development platform, we go over Windows programming essentials. We also cover the basics of 3D theory in order to prepare you for using 3D graphics.

In Part II, we cover OpenGL, focusing on those things most applicable to games. All of the chapters include demo programs allowing you to see OpenGL in action. They also provide an opportunity for you to experiment and try new things on your own.

In Part III, we pull everything together to create a framework for your games, using OpenGL for graphics and pulling in DirectSound and DirectInput for sound and input. Finally, you'll witness the creation of a 3D game using this framework and many of the techniques covered throughout the book.

In addition to the information you'll find in these pages, we've included a CD packed with a wealth of knowledge. Included are dozens of demo programs, games, and tutorials, providing an excellent supplement to the book.

What are you still reading the Introduction for? Let's get on with the show!

Part I

Introduction to OpenGL and DirectX

CHAPTER 1

THE EXPLORATION BEGINS! OPENGL AND DIRECTX

Before heading into the meat of game development, you need to develop a good understanding of where your tools come from and how they are designed. Throughout this book, two application programming interfaces (APIs) will be used. You'll use the OpenGL API to create your 3D graphics and other visual content, while the DirectX API will be used to handle the input, sound, and multiplayer capabilities of your games. This chapter starts things off by giving a basic background of each API's history and design and talks a little about what this book will encompass. With that in mind, let's get on with the show!

In this chapter we'll discuss

- What a game is
- The basics of OpenGL
- The components of DirectX
- A comparison of OpenGL and DirectX

WHY MAKE GAMES?

Interactive entertainment has grown by leaps and bounds in the last decade. Computer games, which used to be considered children's toys, have now grown into a multi-billion-dollar market. Recent years have shown a trend of accelerating growth whose end is not in sight. The interactive entertainment industry is an explosive market that pushes the latest computer technologies to the edge and helps drive research in areas such as graphics and artificial intelligence beyond what a research firm alone could manage. It is this relentless drive and growth that attracts many people to the industry, but why do people really make games?

Having talked with many different people throughout the game industry, one thing seems to drive them to learn and succeed at the art of game development: *fun*. Games have come to be known as one of the more creative forms of software development, and the amazing games that have been released in recent years are a testament to that. Games like *Half-Life* by Valve Software have pushed the envelope of game design to the point that the industry will never be the same again. Game developers are drawn into this industry by the idea of creating their own virtual world that thousands, if not millions, of other people will one day experience. The game developer strives to be challenged and to discover new technologies and new worlds. According to Michael Sikora, an independent game developer, "It's like a trip I just can't get off." This is what making games is all about.

THE WORLD OF 3D GAMES

Some 10 years ago, a little game called *Wolfenstein 3D* by id Software was unleashed into the world. *Wolf3D* brought the gaming world to its knees with realtime raycasting 3D graphics and an immersive world that left gamers sitting at their computers for hours upon hours. The game was a new beginning for the industry, and it never looked back. In 1993, the world of *Doom* went on a rampage and pushed 3D graphics technology past yet another limit with its 2.5D engine. The gaming world reveled in the technical achievement brought by id Software in their game *Doom*, but they did not stop there. Several years later, *Quake* changed 3D gaming for good. No longer were enemies "fake 3D," but rather full 3D entities that could move around in a fully polygonal 3D world with 6 degrees of freedom. The possibilities were now limited only by how many polygons the CPU could process and display on the screen. *Quake* also brought multiplayer gaming over a network to reality as hordes of Internet users joined in the fun of death matches with 30 other people.

Since the release of *Quake*, the industry has been blessed by new technological advancements nearly every few months. The 3D gaming sector has brought on 3D accelerator hardware that performs the 3D math right on the silicon itself. Now, new hardware is released every six months that seems to double its predecessor in both raw power and speed. With all these advancements, there could not be a more exciting time than now for 3D game development. Figure 1.1 shows one of the most recent advancements in 3D game development, *Unreal Tournament* by Epic.

Figure 1.1

A screen shot from the smash hit Unreal Tournament.

THE ELEMENTS OF A GAME

You may now be asking, "How is a game made?" In order to fully answer this question, you must understand that games are, at their lowest level, software. Today's software is developed in teams, where each member of a team works on his or her specialty until everyone's work is integrated to create a single, coherent work of art. Games are much the same way, except programming is not the only area of expertise. Artists are required to generate the images and beautiful scenery that are prevalent in so many of today's games. Level designers bring the virtual world to life and use the art provided to them by the artists to create worlds beyond belief. Programmers piece together each element and make sure everything works as a whole. Sound techs and musicians create the audio necessary to provide the gamer with a rich, multimedia, believable, and virtual experience.

With each person working on different areas of expertise, the game must be divided into various elements that will get pieced together in the end. In general, games are divided into these areas:

- Graphics
- Input
- Music and sound
- Game logic and artificial intelligence
- Networking
- User interface and menuing system

Each of these areas can be further divided into more specific systems. For example, game logic would consist of physics and particle systems, while graphics might have a 2D and 3D renderer. Figure 1.2 shows an example of a simplistic game architecture.

As you can see, each element of a game is divided into its own separate piece and communicates with other elements of the game. The game logic element tends to be the hub of the game, where decisions are made for processing input and sending output. The architecture shown in Figure 1.2 is very simplistic; however, Figure 1.3 shows what a more advanced game's architecture might look like.

As you can see in Figure 1.3, a more complex game requires a more complex architectural design. More detailed components are developed and used to implement specific features or functionality that the game software needs to operate smoothly. One thing to keep in mind is that games feature some of the most complex blends of technology and software designs, and as such, game development requires abstract thinking and implementation on a higher level than traditional software development. When you are developing a game, you are developing a work of art, and it needs to be treated as such. Be ready to try new things on your own and redesign existing technologies to suit your needs. There is no set way to develop games, much as there is no set way to paint a painting. Strive to be innovative and set new standards!

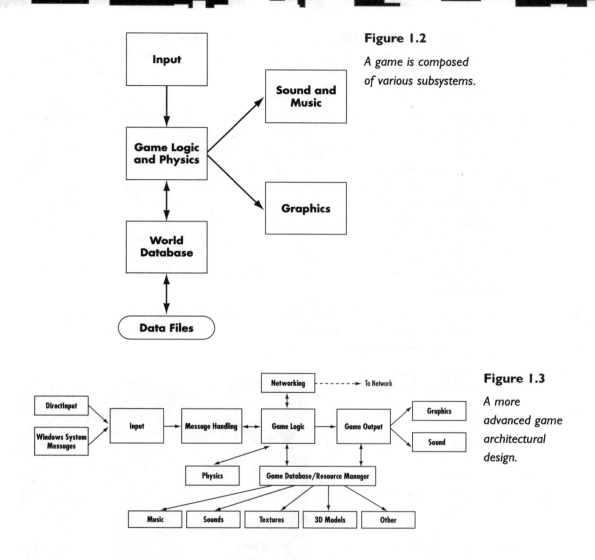

Figure 1.2

A game is composed of various subsystems.

Figure 1.3

A more advanced game architectural design.

YOUR TOOLS

In order to use this book, you're going to need a few things. First off, you'll need a C++ compiler. Because we assume you already know C++, it's probably safe to assume you already have a C++ compiler. All the code samples for this book were written using Microsoft Visual C++, although you should be able to get everything to work with any compiler capable of generating Windows code.

In addition to the compiler, you'll need to have the DirectX and OpenGL libraries and headers installed on your computer with your compiler set up to find them. If you do not already have them installed or aren't sure whether you do, use the following directions to make sure that OpenGL and DirectX are set up correctly.

Because the OpenGL specification doesn't change very frequently, there's a good chance that your compiler already includes the latest version. Visual C++ does, so if that's what you're using, you're set. Otherwise, you'll need to manually check your compiler's directory to see if the appropriate files are there. Your compiler's directory should have a subdirectory for header files called something like "include." It should also have a subdirectory for libraries called something like "lib." Look in the headers directory for a subdirectory called "gl," which should contain the files *gl.h, glu.h,* and *glaux.h.* Then look in the libraries directory for the files *opengl32.lib, glu32.lib,* and *glaux.lib.* In the unlikely event that any of these files are missing, we've included the necessary files on the CD-ROM. Find the file called *opengl95.exe.* Extract this file, and copy the libraries into the library folder for your compiler. Then create a subdirectory called "gl" in your headers directory and copy the headers into it.

Once all of these files are present, the last step is to make sure you have the latest OpenGL drivers for your video card. These can be obtained from your video card manufacturer's Web site or by using the free GLSetup utility available at http://www.glsetup.com.

The CD-ROM accompanying this book includes the DirectX 8.0 SDK. If you do not currently have this or a more recent version of the SDK installed on your system, you will need to install it to use the later examples in this book. If you have an older version of the SDK, you'll have to uninstall it using the control panel before installing this version. To install the DirectX SDK, just run the setup program on the CD-ROM and follow the onscreen instructions, installing the files to whichever directory you like.

> **NOTE**
>
> Because OpenGL is an open architecture, you may find several versions of the libraries and headers floating around the Internet. The two main implementations for Windows are from Silicon Graphics and Microsoft. Because Silicon Graphics is no longer maintaining or supporting its Windows implementation of OpenGL, you should be sure to get Microsoft's implementation, available at the link above.

After both SDKs are installed, you need to verify that your compiler is set up to find the appropriate headers and libraries. If you copied the OpenGL headers and libraries to the default locations described above and if you allowed the DirectX installer to update your compiler automatically, this step is not necessary. Otherwise, in Visual C++, do the following:

1. Open the Tools menu and select the Options command.
2. Scroll to the Directories tab and select it.
3. Add the directories that the headers were installed in to the list of directories that you see. Once added, be sure to move the path to the top of the list so that the most recent headers are found before the older ones that come with Visual C++.
4. Click on the drop-down list at the top of the dialog and choose Library files.
5. Add the library directories in the same way you added the header directories.

Finally, whenever making a new project, you'll have to be sure to add whatever library files you'll be using for the project. There are several ways to do this, but the preferred method is by opening the Project menu, selecting the Settings command, clicking the Link tab, and adding the library to the "Object/library modules" line. As an example, for all programs and demos that use OpenGL, the files *opengl32.lib* and *glu32.lib* will be added to the "Object/library" modules line.

WHAT IS OPENGL?

OpenGL provides the programmer with an interface to graphics hardware. It is a powerful, low-level rendering and modeling software library, available on all major platforms, with wide hardware support. It is designed for use in any graphics applications, from games to modeling to CAD. Many games, such as id Software's *Quake 3*, shown in Figure 1.4, use OpenGL for their core graphics-rendering engines.

Figure 1.4

Quake 3 Arena.

OpenGL intentionally provides only low-level rendering routines, allowing the programmer a great deal of control and flexibility. The provided routines can easily be used to build high-level rendering and modeling libraries, and in fact, the OpenGL Utility Library (GLU), which is included in most OpenGL distributions, does exactly that. Note also that OpenGL is just a graphics library; unlike DirectX, it does not include support for sound, input, networking, or anything else not directly related to graphics.

OpenGL History

OpenGL was originally developed by Silicon Graphics, Inc. (SGI) as a multi-purpose, platform-independent graphics API. Since 1992, the development of OpenGL has been overseen by the OpenGL Architecture Review Board (ARB), which is made up of major graphics vendors and other industry leaders, currently consisting of ATI, Compaq, Evans & Sutherland, Hewlett-Packard, IBM, Intel, Intergraph, nVidia, Microsoft, and Silicon Graphics. The role of the ARB is to establish and maintain the OpenGL specification, which dictates which features must be included when one is developing an OpenGL distribution.

At the time of this writing, the most recent version of OpenGL is Version 1.2. OpenGL has been around for a while, so the fact that it's only at version 1.2 should suggest something: The specification doesn't get updated that often.

Because OpenGL is designed to be used with high-end graphics workstations, it has, until recently, included the power to take full advantage of consumer-level graphics hardware. Furious competition over the last couple of years, however, has brought features once available only on graphics workstations to the consumer level; as a result, there are more and more video cards of which OpenGL can't take full advantage. Fortunately, the video-card manufacturers can and do provide OpenGL *extensions*, which allow you to access advanced hardware–specific features. Eventually, these extensions may become official additions to the OpenGL standard. OpenGL 1.2 was the first version to contain support for features specifically requested by game developers (such as multitexturing), and it is likely that future releases will be influenced by gaming as well.

OpenGL Architecture

OpenGL is a collection of several hundred functions providing access to all the features offered by your graphics hardware. Internally, it acts as a state machine—a collection of states that tell OpenGL what to do. Using the API, you can set various aspects of the state machine, including such things as the current color, lighting, blending, and so on. When rendering, everything drawn is affected by the current settings of the state machine. It's important to be aware of what the various states are, and the effect they have, because it's not uncommon to have unexpected results due to having one or more states set incorrectly. Although we're not going to cover the entire OpenGL state machine, we'll cover everything that's relevant to what we're doing.

At the core of OpenGL is the rendering pipeline, as shown in Figure 1.5. You don't need to understand everything that happens in the pipeline at this point, but you should at least be aware that what you see on the screen results from a series of steps. Fortunately, OpenGL handles most of these steps for you.

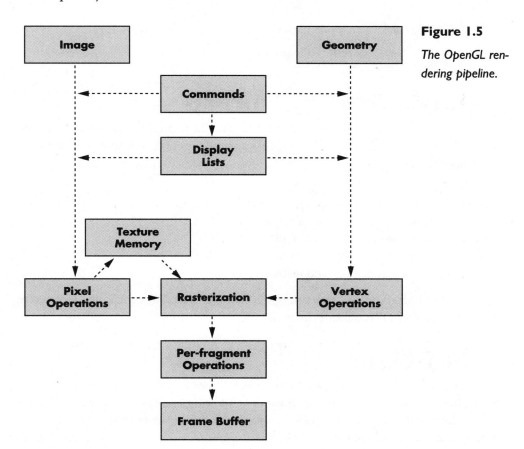

Figure 1.5

The OpenGL rendering pipeline.

Under Windows, OpenGL provides an alternative to using the Graphics Device Interface (GDI). GDI architects designed it to make the graphics hardware entirely invisible to Windows programmers. This provides layers of abstraction that help programmers avoid dealing with device-specific issues. However, GDI is intended for use with applications and thus lacks the speed required for games. OpenGL allows you to bypass GDI entirely and deal directly with graphics hardware. Figure 1.6 illustrates the OpenGL hierarchy under Windows.

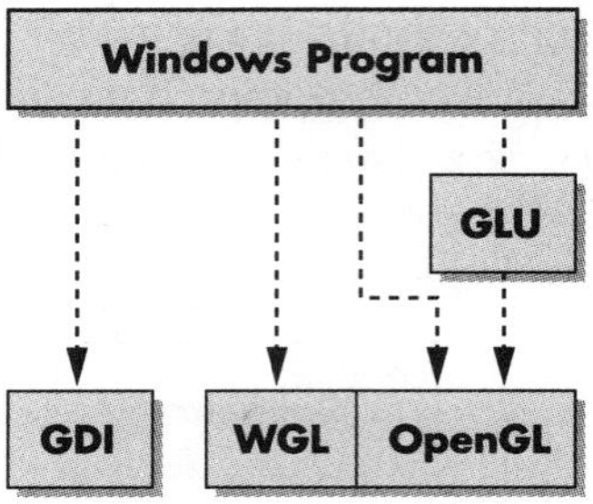

Figure 1.6

OpenGL API hierar-chy under Windows systems.

The OpenGL Utility Library

The OpenGL Utility Library, or GLU, supplements OpenGL by providing higher-level functions. GLU offers features that range from simple wrappers around OpenGL functions to complex components supporting advanced rendering techniques. Its features include:

- 2D image scaling
- Rendering 3D objects including spheres, cylinders, and disks
- Automatic mipmap generation from a single image
- Support for curves surfaces through NURBS
- Support for tessellation of non-convex polygons
- Special-purpose transformations and matrices

If you don't understand what some of those things are, don't worry. We explain the various features of GLU as we use them throughout the book.

What Is GLUT?

GLUT, short for *OpenGL Utility Toolkit*, is a set of support libraries available on every major platform. OpenGL does not directly support any form of windowing, menus, or input. That's where GLUT comes in. It provides basic functionality in all of those areas, while remaining platform independent, so that you can easily move GLUT-based applications from, for example, Windows to UNIX with few, if any, changes.

GLUT is easy to use and learn, and although it does not provide you with all the functionality the operating system offers, it works quite well for demos and simple applications.

Because your ultimate goal is going to be to create a fairly complex game, you're going to need more flexibility than GLUT offers. For this reason, it is not used in the code in the book. However, some of the demos on the accompanying CD-ROM use it; so if you'd like to know more, visit the official GLUT Web page at http://reality.sgi.com/mjk/glut3/.

A Sneak Peek

Let's jump ahead and take a look at some code that you will be using. The example shown in Figure 1.7 shows a rotating, lit, texture-mapped cube reflecting on a surface. The code for this example program can be found on the CD-ROM. Although much of it won't make sense to you yet, it will at least give you an idea of where we are going. Also, note that this code uses GLUT for handling all the operating system–specific stuff. This is just to keep things simple until we can go over some Windows programming. If you decide to build this example on your own, be sure to copy the GLUT headers and libraries from the CD-ROM to your compiler's directory, just as you did with the OpenGL headers and libraries.

Figure 1.7

A simple OpenGL example program.

WHAT IS DIRECTX?

DirectX is Microsoft's attempt at a set of APIs that provide "direct" access to hardware in the Windows operating system environment. Each API controls a set of low-level functions that access the hardware or provide hardware emulation if no hardware exists. These functions include support for 2D and 3D graphics acceleration, control over myriad input devices, functions for mixing and sampling sound and music output, control over networking and multiplayer gaming, and control over various multimedia streaming formats. The component APIs that handle these functions are the following:

- DirectDraw
- Direct3D
- DirectInput
- DirectSound
- DirectMusic
- DirectPlay
- DirectShow

Microsoft's philosophy with DirectX is to make a fast, device-independent, and feature-rich multimedia solution for the Windows operating system. Now at DirectX 7, Microsoft is beginning to break the entry-level barriers posed by earlier versions of DirectX, and hardware vendors are beginning to work out hardware conflicts that have plagued this versatile API. Along with the usual bug fixes, DirectX 7 introduces a few helper libraries such as D3DX, which take away the repetitive initialization functions that made DirectX difficult to use for first-timers. The next step, DirectX 8, is slated to provide a slew of new features to the API, including an overall architecture redesign. Let's take a look at the history of DirectX to get a grasp of where it's headed.

DirectX History

When DOS was the operating system of choice, game developers enjoyed direct access to the hardware for which they were developing. With this access to interrupts, sound cards, input devices, and the VGA controller, developers could get the hardware to do exactly what they wanted it to do. In fact, when Windows 3.1 was released, developers stayed away because nobody wanted to deal with the overhead that Windows created.

DOS, however, was not without problems. Hardware device support in DOS became a nightmare, as hundreds of PC configurations became possible with the ever-growing list of hardware available on the market. More time was being spent programming support for the hardware to work with the game than programming for the game itself!

Then Microsoft unleashed Windows 95 into the world with promises of a new and different operating system. Windows 95 had much to offer over its DOS-based Windows 3.1 predecessor. Plug and Play was introduced to make it simple for the consumer to install the latest hardware, be that a video card, input device, or sound card. The operating system introduced a new resource-handling system that made device management easier and device independence more of a reality. Windows 95 alone, however, still did not bring the performance enhancements needed for game developers to develop for the Windows platform.

DirectX set out to change all this. The original developers began with the simple goal of making Microsoft Windows a desirable platform for game development. They determined that in order to do this, they would need to create DirectX through fast, low-level libraries that allowed the developer to maintain creative freedom over his games. Next, the DirectX developers aimed at shifting the burden of hardware support from the game developer to the hardware manufacturer. This made much more sense, as hardware manufacturers are more qualified to write drivers for their products than the game developer is. Another important feature of DirectX would be the capability to coexist peacefully with other Windows components, including the ability to run a normal Windows application while a DirectX application ran in the background. Lastly, DirectX would have the performance capable in DOS while meeting all the above specifications. With this in mind, development of DirectX has taken off the last several years as Microsoft has created one of the top APIs currently available for developers. Now let's take a look at how the DirectX developers have actually put this API together.

DirectX Architecture

DirectX uses two drivers, the hardware abstraction layer (HAL) and the hardware emulation layer (HEL), to send requests to the hardware device. When DirectX is initialized, it checks the hardware to see if the hardware supports certain capabilities. If the hardware does support a certain capability, then the HAL will be used to access that hardware function; otherwise, the HEL will be used to emulate the capability through software. Figure 1.8 shows this a little better.

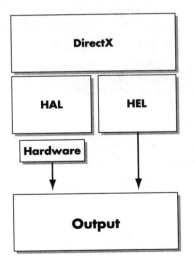

Figure 1.8

The DirectX HAL/HEL archi-tecture.

As you can see, the HAL directly uses the hardware functionality for output while the HEL bypasses the hardware and implements its own functionality. This architecture allows for easier expandability in future hardware. For example, let's say you have a graphics card that supports 3D bump mapping, but it doesn't support 3D environment mapping. You just bought the latest game that has both bump mapping and environment mapping in its 3D engine's feature list. In this case, the DirectX HAL would take advantage of the bump-mapping capabilities while the HEL would provide the functionality needed for environment mapping. If in the future you decide to get a new 3D graphics card that supports both of these capabilities in its hardware, the DirectX HAL will take control and you will experience the effects in the same game through hardware acceleration.

Another aspect of DirectX's architecture is the various component APIs that comprise it. These APIs have already been listed for you, so now let's take a more detailed look at each one and figure out which ones you will be using in this book.

DirectX Graphics

DirectX Graphics is the complete integration of DirectDraw and Direct3D from previous DirectX versions. Because we're using OpenGL for graphics, we have no need to discuss DirectX Graphics.

DirectX Audio

This is the audio component of DirectX. Now a combination of DirectSound and DirectMusic in DirectX 8, DirectX Audio provides a complete system for implementing a dynamic soundtrack that takes care of hardware acceleration, Downloadable Sounds (DLS), DirectX Media Objects (DMOs), and advanced 3D positioning effects. This component of the API is basically a mixing engine, allowing for endless possibilities in 3D sound positioning and effects in games and other multimedia. This book covers DirectX Audio for implementing audio in your demos and games.

DirectInput

DirectInput provides the developer with an interface to myriad input devices, including support for force feedback. This component bypasses the Windows messaging system by working directly with device drivers, which in turn provides the faster responsiveness required in games. You will be using DirectInput to handle the input for all of your demos and games.

DirectPlay

DirectPlay is a set of tools that simplify communications across networks, the Internet, or modems. The tools allow game players to find game sessions easily to help manage the flow between hosts and players. This book does not cover DirectPlay.

DirectShow

DirectShow provides multimedia support for video files such as AVIs and MPGs. This component of DirectX that was once an outside API will be integrated with the release of DirectX 8. This book does not cover DirectShow.

DirectSetup

DirectSetup provides a simple API for installing DirectX from your customized application. With DirectX being a complex product, this component greatly simplifies the process of installation. This book does not cover DirectSetup.

OPENGL VERSUS DIRECTX

Many flame wars have occurred over this topic, and it most likely won't end any time soon. What we're going to do right now is take a look at both APIs and compare what each offers.

The first difference is that DirectX has more than just the graphics component; it includes tools for sound, input, music, networking, and multimedia. OpenGL, on the other hand, is strictly a graphics API. So what is it that separates OpenGL from the graphics component of DirectX?

To start things off, both APIs use the traditional graphics pipeline. This is the same pipeline design that has graced 3D graphics since the early days of computer graphics, and although it has been modified somewhat with the advancements of hardware, the basic idea still has not changed.

Both APIs also describe vertices as a set of data consisting of coordinates in space that define the vertex location and any other vertex-related data. Graphics primitives (points, lines, and triangles) are defined as an ordered set of vertices. However, the difference in the APIs comes with how vertices are combined to form primitives, as each API handles that differently.

There is a slew of other differences; to make it easier to see what each API has to offer, we've listed each API's features in Table 1.1.

Table 1.1 OpenGL versus DirectX: A Comparison

Feature	OpenGL	DirectX 8
Vertex blending	N/A	Yes
Multiple operating systems	Yes	No
Extension Mechanism	Yes	Yes
Development	Multiple-member board	Microsoft
Thorough specification	Yes	No
Two-sided lighting	Yes	No
Volume Textures	Yes	No
Hardware independent Z-buffers	Yes	No
Accumulation buffers	Yes	No
Full-Screen Antialiasing	Yes	Yes
Motion Blur	Yes	Yes
Depth of Field	Yes	Yes
Stereo Rendering	Yes	No
Point-size/line-width attributes	Yes	No
Picking	Yes	No, but has utility functions
Parametric curves and surfaces	Yes	No
Cache geometry	Display lists	Vertex buffers
Software emulation	Hardware not present	Lets application determine
Interface	Procedure calls	COM
Updates	Yearly ARB or extensions	Yearly update
Source-code availability	Sample implementation	Starting point in Microsoft DDK

SUMMARY

In this chapter you took a look at the OpenGL and DirectX APIs. You will be using the OpenGL API to create the 3D graphics for your games and demos while you use DirectX for sound and input.

DirectX was created to give Windows applications more "direct access" to the hardware. The HAL and HEL work together to give the developer access to all API features regardless of whether or not hardware is present. You will be using the DirectX Audio and DirectInput components of DirectX in this book.

Now that you have an overview of the APIs you will be using, you can get into the fun part of actual development!

CHAPTER 2

USING WINDOWS WITH OpenGL

People who have not yet taken a good look at Windows programming tend to think it's a horrible mess. Well, maybe it is, but once you understand what is happening within the operating system and exactly what each function is doing, programming for Windows is as easy as anything else out there. So in this chapter, you are going to explore the world of Windows by going step by step through what is happening in each line of code. If you didn't like Windows before, maybe you will after reading this chapter! Here's what you'll cover:

- Overview of Windows architecture
- The windows procedure
- Window classes
- Resources
- The main Windows message loop
- The WGL "wiggle" functions
- Pixel formats
- Using OpenGL with Windows
- Full-screen OpenGL

INTRODUCTION TO WINDOWS PROGRAMMING

Now it's time to take a peek at the wonderful world of Microsoft Windows. Since you'll be developing your games and demos on the Windows platform, you should know the mechanics and structure of Windows application programming. This chapter will give you a good enough grasp on Windows programming that you can create simplistic Windows applications to wrap around your framework and OpenGL, or even allow you to create your own simplistic applications such as game-editing tools.

Microsoft Windows is a multitasking operating system that allows multiple applications or *processes* to run at one time. Each process is given a certain amount of time, called a *time slice*, where the application is allowed to have control of the system without interruption from other processes. The time slice is determined by the *scheduler*, which allocates time and sets runtime priority for each process. It is basically the time manager of the multitasking operating system, as it makes sure each process is given the time and priority it needs depending on the current state of the system. Figure 2.1 shows how Windows multitasking works with multiple processes.

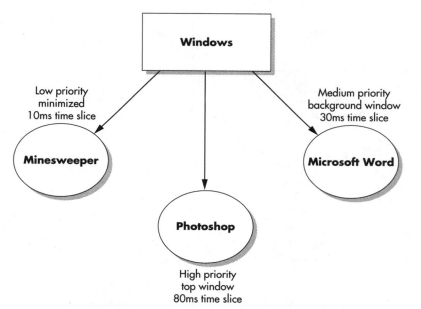

Figure 2.1

Windows multitasking between processes.

A feature of interest to game developers is *multithreading*. Processes can be broken down into what are called *threads*, where each thread can execute its own code to allow for multitasking within a single application. Threads are scheduled in the same way as processes through different priorities and time slices, except threads are what make up the processes. So in your games, you can have multiple threads running that can perform multiple calculations at once and provide your game with a sense of multitasking within itself. But wait! You can go even further with this.

In the latest versions of Windows 98, NT, and ME, an even lower-level execution object has been introduced called a *fiber*. Each thread of your process can have multiple fibers that perform multiple operations at once—all within a single thread! This can get confusing, so Figure 2.2 attempts to show the whole breakdown of processes, threads, and fibers within the multitasking environment of Windows.

Aside from multitasking, Microsoft Windows is what is called an *event-driven* operating system. This means that processes execute based on the events they receive from the operating system. For example, an application might sit idle and wait for a user to press a key. Once a key is pressed, Windows registers an event and sends out an event to your application that a key is down. It is then up to your application to process the event and handle the situation accordingly. Event handling is accomplished through the *windows procedure*, discussed shortly. At the beginning of each application loop, the application's *event queue* is checked to determine whether there are any events to be processed. If there are, then the application processes them and performs whatever action it needs to take before starting the whole process over again.

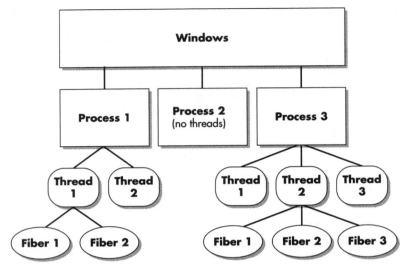

Figure 2.2

The breakdown of processes, threads, and fibers within the Windows operating system.

This is the gist of how an application runs in Windows. As you can see, event handling is something that you will need to take care of in your own applications. Now that you have this background information, you can better understand what a real Windows program does.

The Basic Windows Application

As we said, Windows programming is not difficult at all. In fact, you'll start with the most common and basic program in this world: the Hello, World! program. If you've seen any elementary DOS-based C or C++ book, chances are that you've seen this code:

```
// Hello, world! program
#include <stdio.h>

void main()
{
    printf("Hello, world!\n");
}
```

You're now going to take this basic DOS-based program and convert it into "Hello, World!" Windows style.

```
#define WIN32_LEAN_AND_MEAN         // trim down the libraries used

#include <windows.h>                // main Windows headers
```

```
// the main entry point to your program
int WINAPI WinMain(HINSTANCE hInstance, HINSTANCE hPrevInstance, LPSTR lpCmdLine,
                   int nShowCmd)
{
    // show a very simple message box with the text "Hello, world!" displayed
    MessageBox(NULL, "\tHello, world!", "My First Windows Application", NULL);
    return 0;
}
```

That's it! This is probably the simplest Windows application you will ever see. All it does is display a message box with the message "Hello, world!" printed inside.

Now let's take a look at what you need to do to create your own Windows application so you can develop something a little more robust.

Getting Started with WinMain()

The primary entry point into a non-Windows program is through the main() function. In retrospect, the people who designed Windows decided to be a little creative and called the main entry point for Windows programs WinMain(). Here's the WinMain() function's prototype:

```
int WINAPI WinMain(HINSTANCE hInstance, HINSTANCE hPrevInstance, LPSTR lpCmdLine,
                   int nShowCmd);
```

As you can see, the return type of WinMain() is always int. WINAPI is a calling convention that all 32-bit Windows operating systems use. Normally your functions use the C calling convention, which you do not have to specify. However, for a Windows application and in particular WinMain(), you need to use the WINAPI calling convention to distinguish the function as the entry point for your application.

WinMain() uses four parameters that are passed to it by Windows when the application starts:

- The first, *hInstance*, is a handle to your application's instance, where an instance can be considered a single run of your application. The instance is used by Windows as a reference to your application for event handling, message processing, and various other operating-system duties.
- The second parameter, *hPrevInstance*, will always be NULL. This parameter's use dates back to the days of Windows 3.1, when the parameter would be non-zero if other instances of the program were running in the background.
- The third parameter, *lpCmdLine*, is a pointer to a string that is used to hold any command-line arguments that may have been specified when the application began. For

example, if the user opened the Run application, and typed `myapp.exe myparameter 1`, then `lpCmdLine` will be `myparameter 1`.

- Lastly, *nShowCmd* is the parameter that determines how your application's window will be displayed once it begins executing.

The Windows Procedure

Your Windows program will need a way to handle the messages that Windows sends to it. Messages like `WM_CREATE`, `WM_SIZE`, and `WM_MOVE` are just a few of the countless messages that Windows might send your program. To allow Windows to communicate with your application, a function called a *windows procedure* (commonly called `WndProc`) must be created and used to determine how your application responds to various Windows events. The Windows procedure is also called the *event handler* because of the response to Windows events. This function receives a message from Windows, processes it, and then takes the desired course of action.

Here's the function prototype for the Windows procedure:

```
LRESULT CALLBACK WndProc(HWND hwnd, UINT message, WPARAM wParam, LPARAM lParam);
```

The `WndProc` is declared with a return type of `LRESULT CALLBACK`. The type `LRESULT` is used by Windows to define a long integer. `CALLBACK` is the calling convention used with functions that are called by Windows. One thing to keep in mind here is that the windows procedure is a *function pointer*. You can call the function whatever you want because the function's address will be assigned as a function pointer when you create the window class.

The first parameter for the `WndProc` is a window handle, *hwnd*. This parameter is only important if there are multiple windows open at the same time with the same window class. In this case, you would want to check which window *hwnd* pointed to before deciding which action the message should trigger.

The second parameter, *message*, is the actual message identifier that the `WndProc` will be handling. It can be a variety of windows messages, most starting with the WM_ prefix.

Your third and fourth parameters, *wParam* and *lParam*, are actually extensions of the *message* parameter. They give more information and point to specifics that *message* alone cannot.

Handling Messages

In order to handle the messages and perform the necessary actions, the typical `WndProc` uses a switch statement to redirect execution to the proper message-handling code. Windows might send several hundred different messages to your application at any time, but you only need to provide functionality for the messages that your application should care about and perform actions for. For those messages you do not care about, the default action is carried out and in most cases handled by Windows. The code shown here is a sample WndProc that handles messages through a switch statement.

```
LRESULT CALLBACK WndProc(HWND hwnd, UINT message, WPARAM wParam, LPARAM lParam)
{
    PAINTSTRUCT ps;
    switch (message)
    {
        case WM_CREATE:                    // window creation
        {                                  // do stuff on window creation
            return 0;                      // return to message loop
        }
        case WM_CLOSE:                      // close message
        {
            PostQuitMessage(0);            // send quit message
            return 0;
        }
        case WM_PAINT:                      // paint in window
        {
            BeginPaint(hwnd, &ps);         // validate window
            EndPaint(hwnd, &ps);           // do painting here
        }

        default:
            break;
    }

    // pass all unhandled messages to DefWindowProc
    return DefWindowProc(hwnd,message,wParam,lParam);
}
```

In its current state, the WinProc doesn't do much. In fact, all it really does is post a quit message to the message queue if it's time to quit. Despite this, however, you can get a good feel of how these messages are handled through the switch statement. Your first message-handling code is for WM_CREATE, which is sent on the creation of the window. This message is best handled by placing initialization code before the return statement, or as in your case, just using the return statement immediately. Some people place application initialization code for this event, while others don't; it's up to you.

The next message you handle is WM_CLOSE. This is sent when the window pointed to by hwnd is closed. The most common action to take with this message is to post a quit message (WM_QUIT) to the message queue with the PostQuitMessage() function.

Lastly, the WM_PAINT message is sent when the window needs repainting. This message is best handled by doing your own painting to the window, and in your example, you tell Windows that you did through the BeginPaint and EndPaint functions. By calling these two functions, you validate the window and fill the background with the background brush specified in the window class.

Another thing that should be mentioned is the DefWindowProc() function, which is the default message handler. The default message handler will handle whatever messages you do not handle explicitly in your windows procedure. Having this function in the return statement at the end guarantees that if you do not handle the message, then Windows will handle it for you.

Window Classes

A *window class* is defined as a set of attributes that the system uses as a template to create and define a window. Each window is a member of a window class, and each window class is associated with a windows procedure that is shared by all members of the same class. In this way, each window can process Windows messages and perform their own actions based on the windows procedure their window class defines. In Windows, everything is a class: buttons, windows, list boxes, edit boxes, and so on. The values of the members stored in the window class are what differentiate a dialog box from an edit box or a list box from a button. If you compare Windows to the C++ programming language, you might think of a window class as the overloading feature, where the parameters change the behavior of the class.

An application must define and register a window class before it can create a window of that class. You will use the WNDCLASSEX structure to define your window class. This is an extension of the older WNDCLASS structure, to which two additions have been made. The first is a variable that holds the size of the structure, and the second is the addition of a small icon handle that holds the value of the window class's small icon. The WNDCLASSEX structure looks like this:

```
typedef struct _WNDCLASSEX {
    UINT       cbSize;          // size of the WNDCLASSEX structure
    UINT       style;           // style of the window
    WNDPROC    lpfnWndProc;     // address to the windows procedure
    int        cbClsExtra;      // extra class Information
    int        cbWndExtra;      // extra window Information
    HANDLE     hInstance;       // handle of application Instance
    HICON      hIcon;           // handle of application large Icon
    HCURSOR    hCursor;         // handle of mouse cursor
    HBRUSH     hbrBackground;   // window background color
    LPCTSTR    lpszMenuName;    // main menu name
    LPCTSTR    lpszClassName;   // window class name
    HICON      hIconSm;         // handle of application small Icon
} WNDCLASSEX;
```

So to create your window class variable, you simply define:

```
WNDCLASSEX windowClass;                    // your window class
```

Setting the Windows Class Attributes

Filling out the window class structure is fairly straightforward. The cbSize field is assigned the size of the WNDCLASSEX structure like so:

```
windowClass.cbSize = sizeof(WNDCLASSEX);
```

The hInstance field holds the current application instance handle, which is available from WinMain(). Also make sure to assign the address of the windows procedure to lpfnWndProc. If you use the windows procedure discussed earlier, you can assign lpfnWndProc like this:

```
windowClass.lpfnWndProc = WndProc;
```

The style field describes the general properties of the window that you fill with predefined flags. With these flags, you can draw any type of window you desire through the use of the bitwise OR operator. Table 2.1 lists the flags that you might need to use.

You have all these flags available for you, but you're only going to pick two of them for now: CS_HREDRAW and CS_VREDRAW. To assign these flags to the style field, you type this:

```
windowClass.style = CS_VREDRAW | CS_HREDRAW;
```

The cbClsExtra and cbWndExtra fields will be set to 0. The cbClsExtra field specifies the number of extra bytes to allocate following the window-class structure, and the cbWndExtra field specifies the number of extra bytes to allocate following the window instance. You have no use for either functionality, so you'll leave them alone.

Loading Icons and Mouse Pointers

Your application's mouse pointer and icons will also need to be defined in the window class structure. These resources can be custom made, or you can use one of the built-in resource styles that Windows provides. Let's take a quick look at how to handle both mouse pointers and icons.

Two icons can be created for a window class: a large icon and a small icon. The small icon is usually 16×16, and is used in the system menu or displayed on the taskbar when the application is minimized. Windows uses the large icon for the visual representation of files, folders, and the desktop. The function LoadIcon() is used to load both types of icons and is defined as

```
HICON LoadIcon (HINSTANCE hInst, LPCSTR lpszName);
```

This function loads the icon resource specified by lpszName and returns a handle to the icon. The parameter hInst specifies the handle of the module that contains the icon. To use one of the built-in icons that Windows provides, you use NULL for the hInst parameter and then you can give

Table 2.1 Window Class Style Flags

Flag	Action
CS_DBLCLKS	Sends double-click messages to the windows procedure when the user double-clicks the mouse while the cursor is within a window belonging to the class.
CS_CLASSDC	Allocates one device context to be shared by all windows in the class.
CS_GLOBALCLASS	Allows an application to create a window of the class regardless of the value of the hInstance parameter passed to the CreateWindowEx function.
CS_HREDRAW	Redraws the entire window if a movement or size adjustment changes the width of the client area.
CS_NOCLOSE	Disables the Close command on the system menu.
CS_OWNDC	Allocates a unique device context for each window in the class.
CS_PARENTDC	Sets the clipping region of the child window to that of the parent window so that the child can draw on the parent.
CS_SAVEBITS	Saves, as a bitmap, the portion of the screen image obscured by a window. This style is useful for small windows (for example, menus or dialog boxes) that are displayed briefly and then removed before other screen activity takes place.
CS_VREDRAW	Redraws the entire window if a movement or size adjustment changes the height of the client area.

one of the icon macros that Windows has provided for its default resources. For your purposes, the IDI_APPLICATION macro will be used. This is the default application icon. Table 2.2 gives a list of some icon macros that are available from the system.

To actually assign the value of hIcon to an icon resource, you do the following:

```
winClass.hIcon = LoadIcon(NULL, IDI_APPLICATION);
```

Table 2.2 Icon Types

Value	Description
IDI_APPLICATION	Default application
IDI_ASTERISK	Asterisk
IDI_ERROR	Hand-shaped
IDI_EXCLAMATION	Exclamation point
IDI_HAND	Hand-shaped
IDI_INFORMATION	Asterisk
IDI_QUESTION	Question mark
IDI_WARNING	Exclamation point
IDI_WINLOGO	Windows logo

This will assign the main icon of the window class to the default application icon. Loading an icon resource for the hIconSm field is essentially the exact same thing:

```
winClass.hIconSm = LoadIcon(NULL, IDI_WINLOGO);
```

Instead of the default application icon, that statement will load the Windows logo and assign it to the small icon field of the window class.

Loading a mouse cursor for the hCursor field is very similar to loading an icon. You can load the mouse cursor resource through the LoadCursor() function defined as

```
HCURSOR LoadCursor (HINSTANCE hInst, LPCSTR lpszName);
```

This function loads the cursor resource specified by lpszName and returns a handle to the cursor. Like LoadIcon(), the parameter hInst specifies the handle of the module that contains the cursor resource. Using NULL for the hInst parameter will cause your application to use one of the default cursors defined by Windows. You will use the default macro IDC_ARROW so you use the default arrow pointer provided by Windows. For other cursor types, take a look at Table 2.3.

To assign hCursor to your desired cursor type, do this:

```
windowClass.hCursor = LoadCursor(NULL, IDC_ARROW);
```

Table 2.3 Cursor Types

Value	Description
IDC_APPSTARTING	Standard arrow with small hourglass
IDC_ARROW	Standard arrow
IDC_CROSS	Crosshair
IDC_HELP	Arrow and question mark
IDC_IBEAM	I-beam
IDC_NO	Slashed circle
IDC_SIZEALL	Four-pointed arrow
IDC_SIZENESW	Double-pointed arrow pointing northeast and southwest
IDC_SIZENS	Double-pointed arrow pointing north and south
IDC_SIZENWSE	Double-pointed arrow pointing northwest and southeast
IDC_SIZEWE	Double-pointed arrow pointing east and west
IDC_UPARROW	Vertical arrow
IDC_WAIT	Hourglass

This will assign the standard arrow cursor to the window class. Now that you've covered a majority of the fields in the window class, take a look at a full listing of a window class being assigned values:

```
WNDCLASSEX windowClass;                                    // the window class

windowClass.cbSize = sizeof(WNDCLASSEX);                   // get size of struct
windowClass.style = CS_HREDRAW | CS_VREDRAW;               // redraw on size
windowClass.lpfnWndProc = (WNDPROC)WndProc;                // assign function pointer
windowClass.cbClsExtra = 0;
windowClass.cbWndExtra = 0;
windowClass.hInstance = hInstance;                         // application's hInstance
windowClass.hIcon = NULL;                                  // no Icon
windowClass.hCursor = LoadCursor(NULL, IDC_ARROW);         // load the default arrow cursor
windowClass.hbrBackground = NULL;                          // no background brush
```

```
windowClass.lpszMenuName = NULL;            // no menu
windowClass.lpszClassName = "MyClass";      // window class name
windowClass.hIconSm = NULL;                 // no small Icon

RegisterClassEx(&windowClass);              // register your window class
```

That's it! Rather simple, isn't it?

Registering the Class

After you have fully specified the fields in the window class, you need to register it with Windows using the function RegisterClassEx(). The function prototype is defined as

```
ATOM RegisterClassEx (CONST WNDCLASSEX *lpWClass);
```

And is used like this

```
RegisterClassEx(&windowClass);
```

Note that this function is only for the WNDCLASSEX data type and not for the old WNDCLASS type. After you register the class, you can create your window with the assigned class name.

Window Creation

With the window class set and registered, you can begin creating windows. Window creation is accomplished through the CreateWindow() or CreateWindowEx() function. In your programs you'll be using the CreateWindowEx() function because it's the latest and greatest version of the window-creation functions. This is also when you get to see the real use of the window class you created earlier. First, let's take a look at the CreateWindowEx() prototype:

```
HWND CreateWindowEx(
     DWORD dwExStyle,          // extended window style
     LPCTSTR lpClassName,      // pointer to registered class name
     LPCTSTR lpWindowName,     // pointer to window name
     DWORD dwStyle,            // window style
     int x,                    // horizontal position of window
     int y,                    // vertical position of window
     int nWidth,               // window width
     int nHeight,              // window height
     HWND hWndParent,          // handle to parent or owner window
     HMENU hMenu,              // handle to menu, or child-window identifier
     HINSTANCE hInstance,      // handle to application instance
     LPVOID lpParam);          // pointer to window-creation data
```

Take a look at the comments to the right of each parameter to see what they mean. Then take a look at a few of the more discrete parameters:

- The first would be the `lpClassName` parameter. You set this parameter to the name of the window class you want to use on this window. For example, using the window class you created earlier, this parameter would be equal to `"MyClass"`.
- The `lpWindowName` parameter is basically the text that will go at the top bar of your application's window. Values such as `My First Application` are not uncommon with those first learning windows programming.
- Ah, the big one—`dwStyle`. This is a style flag that tells `CreateWindowEx()` how the window should behave and what it should look like. Table 2.4 lists possible values for this parameter.

Table 2.4 Window Styles

Style	Description
WS_BORDER	Creates a window that has a thin-line border.
WS_CAPTION	Creates a window that has a title bar (includes the WS_BORDER style).
WS_CHILD	Creates a child window. This style cannot be used with the WS_POPUP style.
WS_HSCROLL	Creates a window that has a horizontal scrollbar.
WS_ICONIC	Creates a window that is initially minimized. Same as the WS_MINIMIZE style.
WS_MAXIMIZE	Creates a window that is initially maximized.
WS_MAXIMIZEBOX	Creates a window that has a Maximize button. Cannot be combined with the WS_EX_CONTEXTHELP style. The WS_SYSMENU style must also be specified.
WS_MINIMIZE	Creates a window that is initially minimized. Same as the WS_ICONIC style.
WS_MINIMIZEBOX	Creates a window that has a Minimize button. Cannot be combined with the WS_EX_CONTEXTHELP style. The WS_SYSMENU style must also be specified.

The CreateWindowEx() function returns a NULL value if the function is unsuccessful. If the function *is* successful, it returns a handle to the newly created window.

Now that you know the parameters, take a look at how you actually use this function:

```
hwnd = CreateWindowEx(NULL,                      // not using extended style
                      "MyClass",                 // the class name
                      "My Windows Application!", // window title
                      WS_OVERLAPPEDWINDOW |      // window style
                      WS_CLIPSIBLINGS |
                      WS_CLIPCHILDREN,
```

Table 2.4 Window Styles (continued)

Style	Description
WS_OVERLAPPED	Creates an overlapped window. An overlapped window has a title bar and a border. Same as the WS_TILED style.
WS_OVERLAPPEDWINDOW	Creates an overlapped window with the WS_OVERLAPPED, WS_CAPTION, WS_SYSMENU, WS_THICKFRAME, WS_MINIMIZEBOX, and WS_MAXIMIZEBOX styles. Same as the WS_TILEDWINDOW style.
WS_POPUP	Creates a pop-up window. This style cannot be used with the WS_CHILD style.
WS_POPUPWINDOW	Creates a pop-up window with WS_BORDER, WS_POPUP, and WS_SYSMENU styles. The WS_CAPTION and WS_POPUPWINDOW styles must be combined to make the window menu visible.
WS_SIZEBOX	Creates a window that has a sizing border. Same as the WS_THICKFRAME style.
WS_SYSMENU	Creates a window that has a window menu on its title bar. The WS_CAPTION style must also be specified.
WS_VISIBLE	Creates a window that is initially visible.
WS_VSCROLL	Creates a window that has a vertical scrollbar.

```
        0, 0,                           // x, y coordinate
        200, 200,                       // window width, height
        NULL,                           // handle to parent (no parent)
        NULL,                           // handle to menu (no menu)
        hInstance,                      // application instance
        NULL);                          // no extra creation parameters
```

This code will create a 200×200 window located in the top left corner of the screen. When the window is created, it will not be immediately visible. You could remedy this by adding WS_VISIBLE to the window style parameter, but in case you don't want that parameter as the sample code has it, you will need to call the ShowWindow() function like this:

```
ShowWindow(hwnd, nCmdShow);
```

The nCmdShow variable comes from the WinMain() parameter back at the entry point of the program. Now that you have the window showing, you need to force Windows to update the window's contents and send a WM_PAINT message to the windows procedure. To do this, you call

```
UpdateWindow();
```

And that's it! You have created and displayed your application's window. Now let's wrap things up with a discussion of the message loop.

The Message Loop

Your application communicates with Windows by retrieving messages from a queue to which Windows adds when an event occurs. Because of this queue, all Windows applications must set up a *message loop* in the WinMain() function. The loop checks and reads a pending message from the queue and dispatches the message back to Windows, where any operating system processing is performed before sending the message to the application's windows procedure with the message as a parameter. As you can see in Figure 2.3, the message loop follows a pattern of peek, translate, and dispatch functions on messages received in the message queue.

You use the PeekMessage() function to check the message queue for pending messages. Here is the PeekMessage() function prototype:

```
BOOL PeekMessage (LPMSG lpMsg, HWND hWnd, UINT wMsgFilterMin, UINT wMsgFilterMax,
                  UINT wRemoveMsg);
```

If a message is pending, it is removed from the queue and placed in the lpMsg parameter. Specifying NULL for the hWnd parameter tells PeekMessage() to check the current application's message queue. Both wMsgFilterMin and wMsgFilterMax will be set to NULL for our purposes. The last parameter, wRemoveMsg is assigned the value PM_REMOVE, which tells PeekMessage() to remove messages from the queue after they are processed.

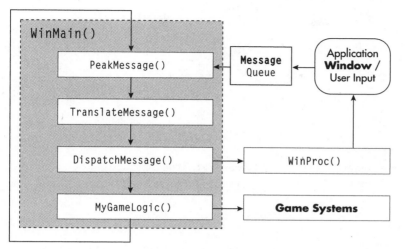

Figure 2.3

The message loop in action.

The TranslateMessage() function is used to translate virtual-key messages into character messages. The character messages are posted to the calling thread's message queue to be read the next time the thread calls the PeekMessage() function. It looks like this:

```
BOOL TranslateMessage (CONST MSG *lpMsg);
```

The parameter *lpMsg* is a message that will be translated by the TranslateMessage() function.

The last function in the message loop is DispatchMessage(). This function dispatches a message specified as its only parameter back to

NOTE

There is also a function called GetMessage() that does the same thing as PeekMessage(); if there are no messages in the queue, however, GetMessage() stalls your application until one shows up. You are using the runtime function PeekMessage() because it lets the application continue if there are no messages in the queue. This is perfect for games.

Windows, where it is processed and then sent to the application's windows procedure. The DispatchMessage() function prototype is

```
LONG DispatchMessage (CONST MSG *lpMsg);
```

The message loop will terminate after a set condition has been reached, typically with the receipt of a WM_QUIT message. WinMain() terminates by returning the value of msg.wParam to Windows.

Let's take a look at a sample message loop:

```
// message loop, loop until you receive a quit message
while (!done)
{
```

```
        if (PeekMessage(&msg, NULL, 0, 0, PM_REMOVE))      // pending message?
        {
                if (msg.message == WM_QUIT)        // If a quit message has been received
                {                                  // you want to quit the application
                    done = TRUE;
                }
                else
                {
                    // do stuff
                    TranslateMessage(&msg);        // translate the message
                    DispatchMessage(&msg);         // dispatch the message to Windows

                }
        }
}
return msg.wParam;                                 // return termination code
```

When the loop is entered, PeekMessage() checks to see whether a message is waiting in the message queue. If a message is found and it is not a quit message, then the application calls your application-specific code. After that is complete, the message is translated and then dispatched back to Windows before heading to the windows-procedure function for processing by the application. As you can see, the message loop provides a rather simple and effective way to handle the large amount of messages that Windows might send to your application.

A Complete Windows Application

Now that you've seen the bits and pieces that make up a Windows application, you can actually build a complete one. What follows is an entire code listing of another type of "Hello, World!" Windows application, except this time the text is blue and is shown inside a white background window:

```
#define WIN32_LEAN_AND_MEAN                        // trim the excess fat from Windows

#include <windows.h>                               // standard Windows app include

// the Windows Procedure event handler
LRESULT CALLBACK WndProc(HWND hwnd, UINT message, WPARAM wParam, LPARAM lParam)
{
    PAINTSTRUCT paintStruct;
    HDC hDC;                                        // device context
    char string[] = "Hello, world!";                // text to be displayed
```

```
        switch(message)
        {
            case WM_CREATE:                      // window is being created
                return 0;
                break;

            case WM_CLOSE:                       // windows is closing
                PostQuitMessage(0);
                return 0;
                break;

            case WM_PAINT:                       // window needs updating
                hDC = BeginPaint(hwnd, &paintStruct);

                // set text color to blue
                SetTextColor(hDC, COLORREF(0x00FF0000));

                // display text in middle of window
                TextOut(hDC, 150, 150, string, sizeof(string)-1);

                EndPaint(hwnd, &paintStruct);
                return 0;
                break;

            default:
                break;
        }

        return (DefWindowProc(hwnd, message, wParam, lParam));
}

// The application entry point
int WINAPI WinMain(HINSTANCE hInstance, HINSTANCE hPrevInstance, LPSTR lpCmdLine,
                int nShowCmd)
{
    WNDCLASSEX windowClass;                   // window class
    HWND       hwnd;                          // window handle
    MSG        msg;                           // message
    bool       done;                          // flag saying when your app is complete
```

```
        // fill out the window class structure
        windowClass.cbSize = sizeof(WNDCLASSEX);
        windowClass.style = CS_HREDRAW | CS_VREDRAW;
        windowClass.lpfnWndProc = WndProc;
        windowClass.cbClsExtra = 0;
        windowClass.cbWndExtra = 0;
        windowClass.hInstance = hInstance;
        windowClass.hIcon = LoadIcon(NULL, IDI_APPLICATION);
        windowClass.hCursor = LoadCursor(NULL, IDC_ARROW);
        windowClass.hbrBackground = (HBRUSH)GetStockObject(WHITE_BRUSH);
        windowClass.lpszMenuName = NULL;
        windowClass.lpszClassName = "MyClass";
        windowClass.hIconSm     = LoadIcon(NULL, IDI_WINLOGO);

        // register the window class
        if (!RegisterClassEx(&windowClass))
            return 0;

        // class registered, so now create your window
        hwnd = CreateWindowEx(NULL,                             // extended style
                        "MyClass",                              // class name
                        "A REAL Windows Application!",  // app name
                        WS_OVERLAPPEDWINDOW |                   // window style
                        WS_VISIBLE |
                        WS_SYSMENU,
                        100, 100,                               // x,y coordinate
                        400, 400,                               // width, height
                        NULL,                                   // handle to parent
                        NULL,                                   // handle to menu
                        hInstance,                              // application instance
                        NULL);                                  // no extra params

        // check if window creation failed (hwnd would equal NULL)
        if (!hwnd)
            return 0;

        done = false;              // initialize the loop condition variable
```

```
    // main message loop
    while (!done)
    {
        PeekMessage(&msg, hwnd, NULL, NULL, PM_REMOVE);

        if (msg.message == WM_QUIT)         // do you receive a WM_QUIT message?
        {
            done = true;                    // if so, time to quit the application
        }
        else
        {
            TranslateMessage(&msg);         // translate and dispatch to event queue
            DispatchMessage(&msg);
        }
    }

    return msg.wParam;
}
```

That's your basic Windows application. Now let's dissect it and figure out what's happening.

The first thing you'll notice is the statement #define WIN32_LEAN_AND_MEAN. This keeps Visual C++ from linking extraneous modules that you will not need for your application.

Next, you #include <windows.h>, which includes all the Windows headers that you'll need for this application. Another header file you might want to include is <windowsx.h>, which gives you some useful macros to use for Windows development.

The WndProc is the first function you'll see. For simplicity, you use the same function as the one we talked about earlier (refer to the section titled "The Windows Procedure") with a few additions. The first of these additions is the following lines:

```
HDC hDC;                                // device context
char string[] = "Hello, world!";        // text to be displayed
```

These lines declare the device context you're going to use to output to the window and the string you're using to store the text you're going to display.

Device Context

We have not yet discussed a device context, so maybe now is a good time. Essentially, a *device context* is used as a data structure for output. In your case, the output is for graphics rendering in a window, but you can have a device context for a printer. All output to the window goes through the graphics device context, which can be created with the GetDC() function:

```
hDC = GetDC(hwnd);
```

This statement would retrieve the graphics context for the window pointed to by hwnd and assign it to hDC. You could then use hDC to output to the window. So with that out of the way, you can now see why you declare a device context— you need to output graphics to the window.

Next begins the switch statement that determines the type of message being passed to the windows procedure. Of interest here is the WM_PAINT block:

```
case WM_PAINT:                          // window needs updating
    hDC = BeginPaint(hwnd, &paintStruct);

    // set text color to blue
    SetTextColor(hDC, COLORREF(0x00FF0000));

    // display text in middle of window
    TextOut(hDC, 150, 150, string, sizeof(string)-1);

    EndPaint(hwnd, &paintStruct);
    return 0;
    break;
```

Again, this block is run when the window needs updating from a move, resize, or other event that affects the window display. The first difference you'll notice here is that the hDC device context is being used. The Win32 function BeginPaint() returns the graphics device context for the hwnd passed to it. You can then use this hDC to set the text color with SetTextColor() and display the text with the function TextOut(). For the time being, you will leave these two functions alone, but if you want to know more about them, be sure to check the Win32 API Reference in MSDN.

Next up is the main entry point we all know and love: WinMain(). Everything you see in WinMain() should be fairly straightforward, but there are of course a few things to point out. The msg variable is used to hold the message received by `PeekMessage()` from the queue, as it will then be sent to `TranslateMessage()` and `DispatchMessage()`. The boolean variable `done` is used by your message loop and will equal `true` when a `WM_QUIT` message is received from the queue to indicate that your application is about to close.

Be sure to note the order in which each Windows setup task is accomplished. In fact, you can break it up into this list:

1. Window-class setup
2. Window-class registration
3. Window creation
4. Message loop with event handler

Well, that's it! You have a fully working Windows application that is now ready to be modified to your liking. Now you can move on to the next step of incorporating OpenGL into your Windows application. This is when the real fun begins.

INTRODUCTION TO WGL

Because OpenGL is only a graphics API, any user interaction or screen/window issues will need to be handled by the host operating system. To make life easier on the programmer, each operating system usually has a set of extensions that tie OpenGL together with the user interaction and window management of the host environment. In UNIX systems, this is accomplished through GLX. In Microsoft Windows, however, you use a set of functions called the *wiggle* functions. Each of these functions are prefixed with *wgl*, hence the "wiggle." Windows also has a set of its own Win32 API functions that are used to interface with OpenGL.

The Rendering Context

In order to maintain portability with OpenGL, each operating system must supply functionality for specifying the rendering window before OpenGL can use it. In Windows, the Graphics Device Interface uses a device context to remember settings about drawing modes and commands, but for OpenGL, the *rendering context* is used to remember OpenGL settings and commands. Keep in mind that a device context is *not* a rendering context. The device context must be specified in a GDI call, while the rendering context is implicit in an OpenGL call. You do need to set a device context's pixel format before creating the rendering context.

Multiple rendering contexts are allowed if you wish to render to more than one window at once. All you need to do is make sure to set the current rendering context to the window on which you wish to render. Another concept to keep in mind is that OpenGL is thread-safe. You can have multiple threads rendering to the same device context at once. One benefit of this is that you can have one thread render the world while another thread handles the user interface. Another thread could even render to another window that gives another viewpoint of the world. The possibilities are endless.

Using WGL

As already mentioned, the wiggle functions bring Windows API support to OpenGL. Without them, OpenGL on the Windows platform would be next to nonexistent. Let's take a look at three of the common wiggle functions:

- `wglCreateContext()`
- `wglDeleteContext()`
- `wglMakeCurrent()`

wglCreateContext()

The `wglCreateContext()` function creates a handle to the OpenGL rendering context while being passed a handle to a GDI device context. The `wglCreateContext()` function prototype is

```
HGLRC wglCreateContext(HDC hDC);
```

You should call this function only after the pixel format for the device context has been set. (We'll talk about setting the pixel format shortly.)

wglDeleteContext()

Keep in mind that as with a device context, a rendering context must be deleted after you finish using it. This is accomplished through the `wglDeleteContext()` function shown here:

```
BOOL wglDeleteContext(HGLRC hRC);
```

wglMakeCurrent()

`wglMakeCurrent()` does exactly as it says: It makes the rendering context passed to it the current rendering context to which OpenGL will render. The device context used must have the same pixel format characteristics as the device context that was used to create the rendering context. That means that the device context used to create the rendering context does not need to be the same device context made that is assigned to wglMakeCurrent(). The wglMakeCurrent() function prototype is

```
BOOL wglMakeCurrent(HDC hDC, HGLRC hRC);
```

You need to make sure both the device context and rendering context you pass to wglMakeCurrent() have the same pixel format for the function to work. If you wish to deselect the rendering context, you can pass NULL for the hRC parameter, or you can simply pass another rendering context.

The wglCreateContext() and wglMakeCurrent() functions should be called upon window creation, such as when the WM_CREATE message is passed to the windows procedure. The wglDeleteContext() function should be called after sending a NULL hRC parameter to the wglMakeCurrent() function when the window is being destroyed, such as with a WM_DESTROY message.

Here's a code snippet to demonstrate this concept:

```
LRESULT CALLBACK WndProc (HWND hwnd, UINT message, WPARAM wParam, LPARAM lParam)
{
    static HGLRC    hRC;          // rendering context
    static HDC      hDC;          // device context

    switch(message)
    {
        case WM_CREATE:            // window Is being created
            hDC = GetDC(hwnd);                  // get device context for window
            hRC = wglCreateContext(hDC);        // create rendering context
            wglMakeCurrent(hDC, hRC);           // make rendering context current
            break;

        case WM_DESTROY:                        // window Is being destroyed
            wglMakeCurrent(hDC, NULL);          // deselect rendering context
            wglDeleteContext(hRC);              // delete rendering context
            PostQuitMessage(0);                 // send WM_QUIT
            break;
    }  // end switch
}      // end WndProc
```

This little bit of code will create and destroy your OpenGL window. You use static variables for the rendering and device contexts so you don't have to re-create them every time the windows procedure is called. This helps speed WndProc up by eliminating unnecessary calls. The rest of the code is fairly straightforward as the comments tell exactly what is going on. Before you can actually create your OpenGL window, though, we need to discuss pixel formats and the PIXELFORMATDESCRIPTOR.

PIXEL FORMATS

The *pixel format* is another extension to the Win32 API that is provided for support of OpenGL functionality. Several properties are assigned in the pixel format setup process, including color mode, depth buffer, bits per pixel, and whether the window is double-buffered. Before creating a rendering context, the pixel format must be set up and created.

The first thing you need to do is use the PIXELFORMATDESCRIPTOR structure to define the characteristics and behavior you desire for the window. This structure is defined as

```
typedef struct tagPIXELFORMATDESCRIPTOR {
    WORD nSize;              // size of the structure
    WORD nVersion;          // always set to 1
    DWORD dwFlags;          // flags for pixel buffer properties
    BYTE iPixelType;        // type of pixel data
    BYTE cColorBits;        // number of bits per pixel
    BYTE cRedBits;          // number of red bits
    BYTE cRedShift;         // shift count for red bits
    BYTE cGreenBits;        // number of green bits
    BYTE cGreenShift;       // shift count for green bits
    BYTE cBlueBits;         // number of blue bits
    BYTE cBlueShift;        // shift count for blue bits
    BYTE cAlphaBits;        // number of alpha bits
    BYTE cAlphaShift;       // shift count for alpha bits
    BYTE cAccumBits;        // number of accumulation buffer bits
    BYTE cAccumRedBits;     // number of red accumulation bits
    BYTE cAccumGreenBits;   // number of green accumulation bits
    BYTE cAccumBlueBits;    // number of blue accumulation bits
    BYTE cAccumAlphaBits;   // number of alpha accumulation bits
    BYTE cDepthBits;        // number of depth buffer bits
    BYTE cStencilBits;      // number of stencil buffer bits
    BYTE cAuxBuffers;       // number of auxiliary buffers
    BYTE iLayerType;        // no longer used
    BYTE bReserved;         // number of overlay and underlay units
    BYTE dwLayerMask;       // no longer used
    BYTE dwVisibleMask;     // index of underlay plane
    BYTE dwDamageMask;      // no longer used
} PIXELFORMATDESCRIPTOR;
```

Let's take a look at the more important fields in this structure.

nSize

The first of the more important fields in the structure is `nSize`. This field should always be set equal to the size of the structure, like this:

```
pfd.nSize = sizeof(PIXELFORMATDESCRIPTOR);
```

This is fairly straightforward and is a common requirement for data structures that get passed as pointers. Often, a structure will need to know its size and how much memory has been allocated for it when performing various operations. A size field allows easy and accurate access to this information with a quick dereference to the size field.

dwFlags

The next field, `dwFlags`, specifies the pixel-buffer properties. Table 2.5 shows the more common values that you will need for `dwFlags`.

iPixelType

The `iPixelType` field specifies the type of pixel data. You can set this field to one of the following values:

- **PFD_TYPE_RGBA.** RGBA pixels. Each pixel has four components in this order: red, green, blue, and alpha.
- **PFD_TYPE_COLORINDEX.** Color-index pixels. Each pixel uses a color-index value.

For our purposes, the `iPixelType` field will always be set to `PFD_TYPE_RGBA`. This allows you to use the standard RGB color model with an alpha component for effects like transparency.

cColorBits

The `cColorBits` field specifies the bits per pixel available in each color buffer. At the present time, this value can be set to 8, 16, 24, or 32. If the requested color bits are not available on the hardware present in the machine, then the highest setting closest to the one you chose will be used. For example, if you set `cColorBits` to 24 and the graphics hardware does not support 24-bit rendering, but it does support 16-bit rendering, then the device context that is created will be 16 bit.

After you have the `PIXELFORMATDESCRIPTOR` structure established, the next step is to pass the structure to the `ChoosePixelFormat()` function. This function attempts to match an appropriate pixel format supported by a device context to the `PIXELFORMATDESCRIPTOR` passed to it. An integer

Table 2.5 dwFlags Constants

Value	Meaning
PFD_DRAW_TO_WINDOW	The buffer can draw to a window or device surface.
PFD_SUPPORT_OPENGL	The buffer supports OpenGL drawing.
PFD_DOUBLEBUFFER	The buffer is double buffered. This flag and PFD_SUPPORT_GDI are mutually exclusive in the current generic implementation.
PFD_SWAP_LAYER_BUFFERS	Indicates whether a device can swap individual layer planes with pixel formats that include double-buffered overlay or underlay planes. Otherwise all layer planes are swapped together as a group. When this flag is set, wglSwapLayerBuffers is supported.
PFD_DEPTH_DONTCARE	The requested pixel format can either have or not have a depth buffer. To select a pixel format without a depth buffer, you must specify this flag. The requested pixel format can be with or without a depth buffer. Otherwise, only pixel formats with a depth buffer are considered.
PFD_DOUBLEBUFFER_DONTCARE	The requested pixel format can be either single or double buffered.

representing an index to an available pixel format for the device context is returned by ChoosePixelFormat(), and this index is then passed to the SetPixelFormat() function. The call to the SetPixelFormat() function completes your quest and sets the pixel format for the device context.

The following listing gives a short sample of how it might look to set the values of the PIXELFORMATDESCRIPTOR:

```
int nPixelFormat;                          // your pixel format index

static PIXELFORMATDESCRIPTOR pfd = {
    sizeof(PIXELFORMATDESCRIPTOR),         // size of the structure
```

```
        1,                                    // version, always set to 1
        PFD_DRAW_TO_WINDOW |                  // support window
        PFD_SUPPORT_OPENGL |                  // support OpenGL
        PFD_DOUBLEBUFFER,                     // support double buffering
        PFD_TYPE_RGBA,                        // RGBA color mode
        32,                                   // go for 32 bit color mode
        0, 0, 0, 0, 0, 0,                     // ignore color bits, not used
        0,                                    // no alpha buffer
        0,                                    // ignore shift bit
        0,                                    // no accumulation buffer
        0, 0, 0, 0,                           // ignore accumulation bits
        16,                                   // 16 bit z-buffer size
        0,                                    // no stencil buffer
        0,                                    // no auxiliary buffer
        PFD_MAIN_PLANE,                       // main drawing plane
        0,                                    // reserved
        0, 0, 0 };                            // layer masks ignored

// choose best matching pixel format, return index
nPixelFormat = ChoosePixelFormat(hDC, &pfd);

// set pixel format to device context
SetPixelFormat(hDC, nPixelFormat, &pfd);
```

One of the first things you might notice about that snippet is the number of zeroes that are assigned to the fields of the PIXELFORMATDESCRIPTOR structure. This simply means that there are several fields that you don't even need in order to set the pixel format. At times you may need these other fields, but for now you can just set them equal to zero.

THE OPENGL WINDOW APPLICATION

You have the tools, now let's apply them. In this section of the chapter, you will piece together the previous sections to give you a basic framework for creating the OpenGL-enabled window. What follows is a complete listing of an OpenGL window application that simply displays a window with a red rotating triangle on a black background.

```
#define WIN32_LEAN_AND_MEAN           // trim the excess fat from Windows

////// Includes
#include <windows.h>                  // standard Windows app include
#include <gl/gl.h>                    // standard OpenGL include
```

```c
#include <gl/glu.h>                        // OpenGL utilities
#include <gl/glaux.h>                       // OpenGL auxiliary functions

////// Global Variables
float angle = 0.0f;                         // current angle of the rotating triangle
HDC g_HDC;                                   // global device context

// function to set the pixel format for the device context
void SetupPixelFormat(HDC hDC)
{
    int nPixelFormat;               // your pixel format index

    static PIXELFORMATDESCRIPTOR pfd = {
        sizeof(PIXELFORMATDESCRIPTOR),              // size of the structure
        1,                                          // version, always set to 1
        PFD_DRAW_TO_WINDOW |                        // support window
        PFD_SUPPORT_OPENGL |                        // support OpenGL
        PFD_DOUBLEBUFFER,                           // support double buffering
        PFD_TYPE_RGBA,                              // RGBA color mode
        32,                                         // go for 32 bit color mode
        0, 0, 0, 0, 0, 0,                           // ignore color bits, not used
        0,                                          // no alpha buffer
        0,                                          // ignore shift bit
        0,                                          // no accumulation buffer
        0, 0, 0, 0,                                 // ignore accumulation bits
        16,                                         // 16-bit z-buffer size
        0,                                          // no stencil buffer
        0,                                          // no auxiliary buffer
        PFD_MAIN_PLANE,                             // main drawing plane
        0,                                          // reserved
        0, 0, 0 };                                  // layer masks ignored

    // choose best matching pixel format, return index
    nPixelFormat = ChoosePixelFormat(hDC, &pfd);

    // set pixel format to device context
    SetPixelFormat(hDC, nPixelFormat, &pfd);
}

// the Windows Procedure event handler
LRESULT CALLBACK WndProc(HWND hwnd, UINT message, WPARAM wParam, LPARAM lParam)
```

```c
{
    static HGLRC hRC;                   // rendering context
    static HDC hDC;                     // device context
    char string[] = "Hello, world!";    // text to be displayed
    int width, height;                  // window width and height

    switch(message)
    {
        case WM_CREATE:                 // window is being created

            hDC = GetDC(hwnd);          // get current window's device context
            g_HDC = hDC;
            SetupPixelFormat(hDC);      // call your pixel format setup function

            // create rendering context and make it current
            hRC = wglCreateContext(hDC);
            wglMakeCurrent(hDC, hRC);

            return 0;
            break;

        case WM_CLOSE:                  // windows is closing

            // deselect rendering context and delete it
            wglMakeCurrent(hDC, NULL);
            wglDeleteContext(hRC);

            // send WM_QUIT to message queue
            PostQuitMessage(0);

            return 0;
            break;

        case WM_SIZE:
            height = HIWORD(lParam);    // retrieve width and height
            width = LOWORD(lParam);

            if (height==0)              // don't want a divide by zero
            {
                height=1;
            }
```

```
                // reset the viewport to new dimensions
                glViewport(0, 0, width, height);
                glMatrixMode(GL_PROJECTION);          // set projection matrix
                glLoadIdentity();                     // reset projection matrix

                // calculate aspect ratio of window
                gluPerspective(45.0f,(GLfloat)width/(GLfloat)height,1.0f,1000.0f);

                glMatrixMode(GL_MODELVIEW);           // set modelview matrix
                glLoadIdentity();                     // reset modelview matrix

                return 0;
                break;

            default:
                break;
        }

        return (DefWindowProc(hwnd, message, wParam, lParam));
}

// the main Windows entry point
int WINAPI WinMain(HINSTANCE hInstance, HINSTANCE hPrevInstance, LPSTR lpCmdLine,
                    int nShowCmd)
{
        WNDCLASSEX windowClass;        // window class
        HWND       hwnd;               // window handle
        MSG        msg;                // message
        bool       done;              // flag saying when your app is complete

        // fill out the window class structure
        windowClass.cbSize            = sizeof(WNDCLASSEX);
        windowClass.style             = CS_HREDRAW | CS_VREDRAW;
        windowClass.lpfnWndProc       = WndProc;
        windowClass.cbClsExtra        = 0;
        windowClass.cbWndExtra        = 0;
        windowClass.hInstance         = hInstance;
        windowClass.hIcon             = LoadIcon(NULL, IDI_APPLICATION);  // default icon
        windowClass.hCursor           = LoadCursor(NULL, IDC_ARROW);      // default arrow
        windowClass.hbrBackground     = NULL;                    // don't need background
        windowClass.lpszMenuName      = NULL;                    // no menu
```

```
windowClass.lpszClassName    = "MyClass";
windowClass.hIconSm          = LoadIcon(NULL, IDI_WINLOGO);    // small icon

// register the window class
if (!RegisterClassEx(&windowClass))
    return 0;

// class registered, so now create your window
hwnd = CreateWindowEx(NULL,                             // extended style
                "MyClass",                              // class name
                "The OpenGL Window Application",        // app name
                WS_OVERLAPPEDWINDOW | WS_VISIBLE |      // style
                WS_SYSMENU | WS_CLIPCHILDREN |
                WS_CLIPSIBLINGS,
                100, 100,               // x,y coordinate
                400, 400,               // width, height
                NULL,                   // handle to parent
                NULL,                   // handle to menu
                hInstance,              // application instance
                NULL);                  // no extra params

// check if window creation failed (hwnd would equal NULL)
if (!hwnd)
    return 0;

ShowWindow(hwnd, SW_SHOW);               // display the window
UpdateWindow(hwnd);                      // update the window

done = false;                            // initialize the loop condition variable

// main message loop
while (!done)
{
    PeekMessage(&msg, hwnd, NULL, NULL, PM_REMOVE);

    if (msg.message == WM_QUIT)          // do you receive a WM_QUIT message?
    {
        done = true;                     // if so, time to quit the application
    }
    else
    {
```

```
                // do rendering here
                // clear screen and depth buffer
                glClear(GL_COLOR_BUFFER_BIT | GL_DEPTH_BUFFER_BIT);
                glLoadIdentity();           // reset modelview matrix

                angle = angle + 0.1f;       // increase your rotation angle counter
                if (angle >= 360.0f)        // reset angle counter
                    angle = 0.0f;
                glTranslatef(0.0f,0.0f,-5.0f);        // move back 5 units
                glRotatef(angle, 0.0f,0.0f,1.0f);     // rotate along z-axis

                glColor3f(1.0f,0.0f,0.0f);            // set color to red
                glBegin(GL_TRIANGLES);                // draw the triangle
                    glVertex3f(0.0f,0.0f,0.0f);
                    glVertex3f(1.0f,0.0f,0.0f);
                    glVertex3f(1.0f,1.0f,0.0f);
                glEnd();

                SwapBuffers(g_HDC);                   // bring back buffer to foreground

                TranslateMessage(&msg);               // translate/dispatch to event queue
                DispatchMessage(&msg);
            }
        }

        return msg.wParam;
}
```

The bulk of the Windows code comes from the Windows application example presented earlier in this chapter, and you should notice that the two sample programs are fairly similar. Let's take a look at this example piece by piece and figure out what makes it different.

The first difference you might notice is the addition of two global variables: angle and g_HDC.

```
////// Global Variables
float angle = 0.0f;                 // current angle of the rotating triangle
HDC g_HDC;                          // global device context
```

The variable angle lets you keep track of the rotating triangle's current angle. Rotation will be discussed in more detail in Chapter 7, "Bitmaps and Images with OpenGL," but this demo includes it so you can see some sample OpenGL code.

The next variable, g_HDC, is a handle to a device context that you will use to render your OpenGL graphics.

The next thing you might notice is the addition of the SetupPixelFormat() function. This function initializes a PIXELFORMATDESCRIPTOR structure and sets the pixel format described in that structure to the device context, hDC, which is passed as a parameter to the function. As you can see, setup of the pixel format is exactly as described in the previous section.

After initializing the PIXELFORMATDESCRIPTOR, the device context is used to determine the best matching pixel format through the ChoosePixelFormat() function. After the best pixel format has been chosen and stored as an index, you use SetPixelFormat() to finally assign the pixel format to the chosen device context, and voilà! You've set up the pixel format and are now ready to do some rendering.

Now take a look at the windows procedure WndProc(). Here you can see where you actually use all these OpenGL window setup functions. The first block of code to look at is WM_CREATE:

```
case WM_CREATE:                     // window is being created

    hDC = GetDC(hwnd);              // get current window's device context
    g_HDC = hDC;                    // assign the global device context
    SetupPixelFormat(hDC);          // call your pixel format setup function

    // create rendering context and make it current
    hRC = wglCreateContext(hDC);
    wglMakeCurrent(hDC, hRC);

    return 0;
    break;
```

WM_CREATE is the message sent to the windows procedure when your window is being created. So naturally, the best thing to do here is to go ahead and set up your OpenGL window! As you can see, the first step to accomplishing this is to get your window's device context with the GetDC() function. In order to make your life easier, use a global device context variable, g_HDC, that you will use to swap the front and back buffers of the current window since your pixel format describes a device context with a back buffer. After this, you call your SetupPixelFormat() function that we discussed earlier, which completes the setup of the pixel format for your window.

The next two lines of the WM_CREATE block of code create the rendering context of your OpenGL window. After the wglCreateContext() function creates the rendering context, the wglMakeCurrent() function sets the rendering context to be the current one.

This completes your OpenGL window setup code, so let's take a look at the window support and rendering code.

The other block of code in WndProc() is the WM_SIZE block:

```
case WM_SIZE:
     height = HIWORD(lParam);                 // retrieve width and height
     width = LOWORD(lParam);

     if (height==0)                           // don't want a divide by zero
     {
          height=1;
     }

     glViewport(0, 0, width, height);   // reset the viewport
     glMatrixMode(GL_PROJECTION);       // set projection matrix x
     glLoadIdentity();                  // load identity matrix

     // calculate aspect ratio of window
     gluPerspective(45.0f,(GLfloat)width/(GLfloat)height,1.0f,1000.0f);

     glMatrixMode(GL_MODELVIEW);        // set modelview matrix
     glLoadIdentity();                  // reset modelview matrix

     return 0;
     break;
```

The WM_SIZE message is passed after a window's size has changed. When this happens, the OpenGL window becomes distorted, so you need to rescale it to fit the new window size. The first thing you should do is retrieve the new width and height of the window by using the lParam parameter that is passed to the WndProc() function. The lParam variable is of the LPARAM type, a 32-bit double word that, in this case, is the width and height in a package of two 16-bit words. In order to retrieve the width and height, you use two macros, LOWORD and HIWORD, which are defined here:

```
WORD LOWORD(DWORD dwValue);     // value from which low-order word is retrieved
WORD HIWORD(DWORD dwValue);     // value from which high-order word is retrieved
```

The low-order word is the width, and the high-order word is the height. After retrieving the two values, you can then determine how your viewport should be rescaled.

First you need to make sure that the height does not equal zero. If it does, then you would get a divide-by-zero error when you set up what is called the *perspective projection*. So in order to prevent such a nasty error from occurring, you must set the height to the minimum of one.

The glViewport() function actually resets the OpenGL viewport to the new width and height dimensions. You should skip the rest of the OpenGL code until we talk about matrices and projections in Chapter 5. Just understand that the code resets your 3D viewing world as well, since the viewport has changed.

The last bit of code that you will look at for this example program is the new code that has been introduced in the main message loop:

```
// do rendering here
// clear screen and depth buffer
glClear(GL_COLOR_BUFFER_BIT | GL_DEPTH_BUFFER_BIT);
glLoadIdentity();                          // reset modelview matrix

angle = angle + 0.1f;                      // increase your rotation angle counter
if (angle >= 360.0f)                       // reset angle counter
    angle = 0.0f;
    glTranslatef(0.0f,0.0f,-5.0f);         // move back 5 units
    glRotatef(angle, 0.0f,0.0f,1.0f);      // rotate along z-axis

    glColor3f(1.0f,0.0f,0.0f);             // set color to red
    glBegin(GL_TRIANGLES);                 // draw the triangle
        glVertex3f(0.0f,0.0f,0.0f);
        glVertex3f(1.0f,0.0f,0.0f);
        glVertex3f(1.0f,1.0f,0.0f);
    glEnd();

    SwapBuffers(g_HDC);                    // bring back buffer to foreground

    TranslateMessage(&msg);               // translate/dispatch to event queue
    DispatchMessage(&msg);
```

This code snippet is placed after the PeekMessage() function in the loop. The glClear() function clears out the color buffer and depth buffer, effectively clearing the window to a black background. The OpenGL code that follows draws and rotates a red triangle on the screen. You should go ahead and compile this program to see exactly what it does. Then you can tweak the values passed to the OpenGL functions to see how your changes affect what is displayed.

After the OpenGL code comes the primary use of your global device context variable, g_HDC. After OpenGL has rendered to the back buffer, you call the SwapBuffers() function, which takes the g_HDC device context and swaps the front and back buffers to give you a smooth frame-by-frame animation look to the scene. Figure 2.4 shows how this works.

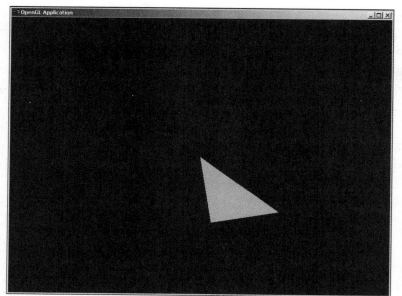

Figure 2.4

A screenshot of the windowed OpenGL application.

That's it! You've completed the setup of your OpenGL window and are now ready to move on to bigger and better things. The best part is that you can use this base Windows application as a framework for the games and demos you will be creating later on. There is, however, one more thing we should cover about creating OpenGL windows: using full-screen OpenGL.

FULL-SCREEN OPENGL

Not everyone wants to play your games in a window, so you need a way to create a full-screen version for a more mind-numbing experience. Nearly all 3D games created nowadays are displayed in full-screen mode. There is no reason why your games and demos cannot support it as well. You'll take the sample program you just created and modify it to give it full-screen capabilities, but rather than rewrite the entire sample program, let's take a look at only the key parts that you need to change.

To start things off, you want to create a global boolean variable that you will call `fullScreen`. If `fullScreen` is equal to true, then you are in full-screen mode and need to react accordingly. You declare your `fullScreen` boolean variable like so:

```
bool fullScreen = TRUE;                  // start off in full-screen mode
```

Keep in mind that this is a global variable, and it will be used throughout the program to determine whether or not the application is in full-screen or windowed mode.

The next thing that needs to be added is the code to actually switch to full-screen mode. In order to do this, you must use the DEVMODE data structure, which contains information about the device initialization and environment of an output device. There are, of course, some things you need to keep in mind when switching to full-screen mode. The first is that you need to make sure that the width and height you use to create the window is the same width and height you specify in the DEVMODE data structure. Also, you need to be sure to change the display settings *before* creating the window; otherwise, you'll run into some major problems. In any case, one way to combat this is to simply use the width and height variables that your application has already defined.

The code for setting the display to full-screen mode is rather simple. You just fill out a few fields of the DEVMODE data structure and call the ChangeDisplaySettings() function:

```
DEVMODE devModeScreen;
memset(&devModeScreen, 0, sizeof(devModeScreen));     // clear the DEVMODE structure
devModeScreen.dmSize = sizeof(devModeScreen);         // size of the structure
devModeScreen.dmPelsWidth = screenWidth;              // set the width
devModeScreen.dmPelsHeight = screenHeight;            // set the height
devModeScreen.dmBitsPerPel = screenBpp;               // set the bits per pixel
devModeScreen.dmFields  = DM_PELSWIDTH | DM_PELSHEIGHT | DM_BITSPERPEL;

if (ChangeDisplaySettings(&devModeScreen, CDS_FULLSCREEN) != DISP_CHANGE_SUCCESSFUL)
    // change has failed, you'll run in windowed mode
    fullScreen = false;
```

The ChangeDisplaySettings() function changes the settings of the default display device to the graphics mode described in the DEVMODE data structure that is passed to the function. The CDS_FULLSCREEN parameter is used to remove the taskbar from the screen and to force Windows to leave the rest of the screen alone when resizing and moving windows around in the new display mode. If the function is successful, it returns the DISP_CHANGE_SUCCESSFUL code and you can continue setting up for a full-screen application; if the function is unsuccessful, however, you need to change your fullScreen boolean variable to false so you set up in windowed mode.

After setting the display mode, you need to actually create the window. The style settings for full-screen modes differ from those of regular windows, so you need to be able to handle both cases. If you are not in full-screen mode, you will use the same style settings as described in the sample program for the regular window. If you are in full-screen mode, you need to use the WS_EX_APP-WINDOW flag for the extended style and the WS_POPUP flag for the normal window style. The WS_EX_APPWINDOW flag forces a top-level window down to the taskbar once your own window is visible. The WS_POPUP flag creates a window without a border, which is exactly what you want with a full-screen application. Another thing you want to do for full-screen is remove the mouse cursor from the screen. This can be accomplished with the ShowCursor() function. The following code demonstrates the style settings and cursor hiding for both full-screen and windowed modes:

```
if (fullScreen)
{
    extendedWindowStyle = WS_EX_APPWINDOW;      // hide top level windows
    windowStyle = WS_POPUP;                     // no border on your window
    ShowCursor(FALSE);                          // hide the cursor
}
else
{
    extendedWindowStyle = NULL;                 // same as earlier example
    windowStyle = WS_OVERLAPPEDWINDOW | WS_VISIBLE |
                  WS_SYSMENU | WS_CLIPCHILDREN | WS_CLIPSIBLINGS;
}
```

The next addition we are going to talk about has nothing to do with full-screen mode, but rather gives a better display in the windowed applications. The AdjustWindowRectEx() function calculates the required size of the window rectangle, based on the desired client-rectangle size. This means that after this function is called, the window borders will not overlap your OpenGL rendering area; essentially, you get the maximum drawing area that you have requested. You pass a RECT structure to this function along with both the regular and extended window styles. The variable windowRect is another addition to the program and should be defined in the variable section. Here is the code you use:

```
RECT windowRect;              // client area coordinates of the window
windowRect.top = 0;           // top left
windowRect.left = 0;
windowRect.bottom = screenHeight;        // bottom right
windowRect.right = screenWidth;

// readjust your window
AdjustWindowRectEx(&windowRect, windowStyle, FALSE, extendedWindowStyle);
```

Rather than pouring out another code dump here, take a look at the OpenGLWindow2 program on the CD-ROM to see how you integrate the full-screen mode into your programs. As you can see, you don't need to modify your program too much to add the capability to use full-screen mode. With a little extra Windows programming, you can even ask the user if he or she would like full-screen or windowed mode before the program even starts. Throughout the rest of the book, you will develop games and demos that will have the option of running in either mode.

SUMMARY

The Microsoft Windows platform is a multitasking, process-based operating system. Each process is given a time slice per cycle in which the program is allowed to run. All of this is handled by the scheduler, which keeps all the applications running at optimal performance based on priorities and application requirements.

Each process can be divided into threads that allow the process to multitask within itself. The latest versions of Windows include a new feature called *fibers* that allow even more detailed multitasking within each thread.

The WinMain() function is the main entry point of all Windows applications. In order to handle events and messages that are passed by Windows to the application, the windows procedure is created. Messages are typically passed to the windows procedure and sent through a switch statement that determines the type of message and ensures that the application properly handles that message.

The WNDCLASSEX structure is used to define the window class, which is a set of attributes used to define a window. This window class must be defined and registered before the window can be created, or the application will terminate with an error.

The message loop is the part of WinMain() that keeps the application running. There are three main steps in the message loop:

1. Retrieve message from message queue using PeekMessage()
2. Translate message
3. Dispatch message

You also took a look at a sample Windows application that showed how you use message handling and window creation.

The WGL, or *wiggle*, functions are a set of extensions to the Win32 API that were created specifically for OpenGL. Several of the main functions involve the rendering context, which is used to remember OpenGL settings and commands. You can use several rendering contexts at once.

The PIXELFORMATDESCRIPTOR is the structure that is used to describe a device context that will be used to render with OpenGL. This structure must be specified and defined before any OpenGL code will work on a window.

Lastly, full-screen OpenGL is used by most 3D games that are being developed. You took a look at how you can implement full-screen mode into your OpenGL applications, and the OpenGLWindow2 program on the included CD-ROM gives a clear picture of how to integrate the full-screen code.

CHAPTER 3

AN OVERVIEW OF 3D GRAPHICS THEORY

Now we are going to take a brief look at several topics in 3D graphics to get an idea of what you are going to be playing with as you start making your demos and games. Having a good background in 3D theory is not absolutely necessary to get started with OpenGL, but it sure helps. Keep in mind, however, that this chapter is only the tip of the iceberg. There is much more to learn about 3D graphics theory than what can be taught in a chapter. We suggest you check out the resources in the appendixes if you wish to learn more details about 3D theory. But until then, let's take a look at some of the basics that will get you started on the rest of your journey.

In this chapter, you'll learn the following:

- Scalar and vector math
- Matrices and matrix math
- Transformations
- Projections
- Lighting
- Texture Mapping

SCALARS, POINTS, AND VECTORS

In 3D computer graphics, you need a way to represent the geometric objects that make up a 3D world. Although each world is different and can have a variety of different objects, each of these objects can be broken down into three simple types:

- **Scalars.** Although a scalar is not a geometric type, you need to use it as a unit of measurement. A scalar is a value that represents only the magnitude. For example, the temperature on a thermometer is a scalar value, as is the length of a line segment, or the amount of ambient light in a 3D scene.
- **Points.** A point is the fundamental geometric object and represents a location in 3D space. In our case, the location is defined as a set of three scalar values representing the distance along each of the three axes, or coordinates, in a 3D scene: x, y, and z.
- **Vectors.** A vector is described in physics as a quantity with both direction and magnitude. For example, when you roll a ball across the floor, the ball has both a direction and a speed, or magnitude. Vectors in 3D graphics are described the same way. To represent a vector, you use a directed line segment where the length of the line segment is equal to

the length of the vector. You can see this in Figure 3.1. Notice that each of the vectors is of equal length and direction. When this happens, you say that the vectors are identical because vectors do not have a fixed location in space. This would be analogous to two people rolling two different balls at different positions on the floor, but they roll the balls at the same speed and in the same direction. Although each of the balls might have a different location, or point, their velocity vectors are identical.

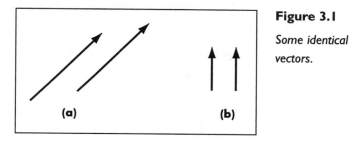

Figure 3.1

Some identical vectors.

Vector Magnitude

If you have a vector, you're going to need to calculate the magnitude of the vector at some point. Determining the magnitude is basically finding out the length of the vector, or the *norm*. The length is represented mathematically by two vertical bars around the vector. For example, the "length of A" is shown as

$|A|$

Length is a distance measurement, which means that you can use the standard Pythagorean theorem to compute it. Because you are in 3D, you need to extend the theorem a little by adding the z-value to the equation. This means that the length of A would be defined as

$|A| = \text{sqrt}(A_x^2 + A_y^2 + A_z^2)$

Vector Normalization

Now that you know how to get the length of a vector, you can *normalize* it. When you normalize a vector, you are reducing the vector size to a length of 1.0. This presents a couple of properties that are useful in 3D mathematics, but we'll talk about them later. To calculate the normal of a vector, you divide the vector by the length of the vector like this:

$n = N / |N|$

This is simply saying that the normalized vector *n* is equal to the vector *N* divided by the magnitude of vector *N*.

Vector Addition

You can also do mathematical operations on vectors just as you would do with scalars. The two basic operations are vector addition and vector-scalar multiplication. If you define a vector as $V(x,y,z)$, then the sum of two vectors $A(x_a,y_a,z_a)$ and $B(x_b,y_b,z_b)$ would be

> **NOTE**
>
> Vector subtraction is identical to vector addition except that it uses the subtraction operation.

$$A(x_a,y_a,z_a) + B(x_b,y_b,z_b) = C(x_a + x_b, \ y_a + y_b, \ z_a + z_b)$$

This equation would translate to the pictorial shown in Figure 3.2. All of vector A's components are added to vector B's components to form vector C.

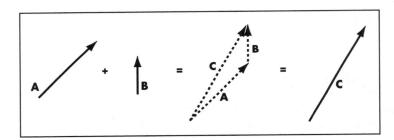

Figure 3.2

Vector addition.

Vector-Scalar Multiplication

You can also multiply a vector by a scalar value to create another vector whose magnitude or direction is changed, but whose orientation remains the same. For example, if you were to multiply vector A by a scalar value of 4, the direction and orientation of A would remain the same, but its magnitude would quadruple. Similarly, if you multiply vector A by a scalar value of -1, then the vector would have the same magnitude, but it would point in the opposite direction. This operation is accomplished through the following equation:

$$s \cdot A(x_a,y_a,z_a) = B(s \cdot x_b, \ s \cdot y_b, \ s \cdot z_b)$$

As you can see, to do vector-scalar multiplication, you just multiply the scalar value by each component of the vector. The resulting vector contains the result of the multiplications in its own components. Figure 3.3 illustrates vector-scalar multiplication.

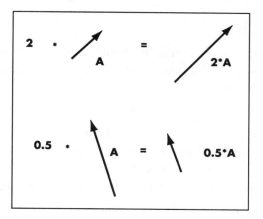

Figure 3.3

Vector-scalar multiplication.

The Dot Product

Both the dot product and the cross product are operations that are used throughout 3D graphics. The dot product, also called the *inner product*, is useful for calculating the angle between two vectors. To compute the dot product, you add the products of each vector component. The result you receive from the operation is a scalar value. You can use two equations to find the dot product of vectors A and B:

$A . B = A_x \cdot B_x + A_y \cdot B_y$

$A . B = |A| \cdot |B| \cdot \cos \theta$

The first equation shows that the dot product is calculated by adding the products of each vector component. With some algebraic rearranging, you can find the angle between two vectors with the equation

$\cos \theta = (A . B) / (|A| \cdot |B|)$

From there you just compute the inverse of $\cos \theta$ to get your angle. Another interesting fact is that if the length of vectors A and B are 1.0, then $|A| * |B|$ is equal to 1.0, and the formula can be simplified to

$\cos \theta = A . B$

This is an obvious shortcut and is important to 3D graphics. There are also a few properties of the dot product of which you should be aware:

- $A . B = 0$, if the angle between A and B is 90 degrees
- $A . B > 0$, if the angle between A and B is < 90 degrees
- $A . B < 0$, if the angle between A and B is > 90 degrees
- $A . B = |A|^2 = |B|^2$, if A and B are equal

The Cross Product

The cross product is another important operation in 3D graphics and will be used in many different areas including collision detection, lighting, and physics. Given two 3D vectors A and B, the cross product of the two vectors is defined as

$$A \times B = |A| \cdot |B| \cdot \sin \theta \cdot n$$

Taking a look at the equation, the $\sin \theta$ is equal to the angle between the two vectors A and B. Recognize n? It's the normal vector we talked about before, and it's the perpendicular vector to A and B. From this equation, you can gather information about the angle between A and B and the normal vector of A and B, but there is another way for you to find the cross product.

Because the previous equation is not used very often in practice and requires some matrix manipulation to really do anything with it, let's take a look at the other equation to find the cross product between two vectors A and B:

$$C = A \times B = (A_y \cdot B_z - A_z \cdot B_y, \ A_z \cdot B_x - A_x \cdot B_z, \ A_x \cdot B_y - A_y \cdot B_x)$$

Remember that the cross-product operation returns a normal vector. With this equation you calculate each component of the new vector by "crossing out" the component in vectors A and B that relate to the current calculation. For example, when calculating the C_x component you leave out both the A_x and B_x components and only use the A_y, A_z, B_y, and B_z components in the calculation. Hopefully that doesn't confuse you more; just understand that the cross product is a very important tool that you will need to use often in 3D game programming.

MATRICES

Now we get to talk about the matrix—no, not the movie, but rather the mathematical concept! In a nutshell, a matrix is just a two-dimensional array of numbers with a set number of rows and columns. Actually, matrices can be three dimensions as well, but you don't need to use three-dimensional matrices for 3D graphics. So sticking with the 2D matrix, you can define the dimension of a matrix as $m \times n$, which says that a matrix has m rows and n columns. If you had a matrix with 3 rows and 2 columns, you would say you had a 3×2 matrix. Here is a 3×3 matrix M:

$$M = \begin{vmatrix} 1 & 2 & 3 \\ 4 & 5 & 6 \\ 7 & 8 & 9 \end{vmatrix}$$

You can retrieve a value from a particular position in a matrix by using the row and column values often denoted as the ith row and jth column. For example, using matrix M above, the value of 5 would be located in the (1,1) location. You might be wondering why it isn't the (2,2) location. Well, matrices are defined as two-dimensional arrays when you actually implement them, and because the language you are using is C/C++, the arrays start at location $(0,0)$. So with that in mind, the value 1 will be located at $(0,0)$, 2 is at $(0,1)$, 4 at $(1,0)$, and so on. Take a look at the labeling of a 3×3 matrix:

$$M = \begin{vmatrix} m_{00} & m_{01} & m_{02} \\ m_{10} & m_{11} & m_{12} \\ m_{20} & m_{21} & m_{22} \end{vmatrix}$$

Remember this representation for matrices, because it's the same representation you will be using when accessing the two-dimensional arrays in your actual matrix code. We will also use this representation whenever we discuss matrices.

Now that you have an idea of what a matrix actually is, let's discuss how you can actually do some math with them.

The Identity Matrix

There is one particular matrix that is rather useful in matrix mathematics. Called the *identity matrix*, ones are placed in the main diagonal of the matrix while zeroes are placed elsewhere. Identity matrices may be of any size, but they must be square, or $m \times m$. Here's an example 3×3 identity matrix:

$$M = \begin{vmatrix} 1 & 0 & 0 \\ 0 & 1 & 0 \\ 0 & 0 & 1 \end{vmatrix}$$

An interesting property of the identity matrix is that when you multiply an identity matrix by another matrix, the result you receive is the original matrix. We'll cover matrix multiplication shortly.

The Zero Matrix

Although you really won't need to ever use zero matrices, we might as well discuss them briefly. Essentially, the *zero matrix* is filled with zeroes in every element. When you add or multiply a zero matrix with another matrix, it is the same as multiplying or adding 0 to a scalar value. Here is a 3×3 zero matrix:

$$M = \begin{vmatrix} 0 & 0 & 0 \\ 0 & 0 & 0 \\ 0 & 0 & 0 \end{vmatrix}$$

Matrix Addition and Subtraction

Matrix addition and subtraction is fairly straightforward. Each element of the two matrices are added to or subtracted from each other with the result being placed in the same (i,j) location as the elements that have been operated on. Here is an example of adding two 3×3 matrices M and N:

$$M = \begin{vmatrix} 2 & 2 & 2 \\ 0 & 1 & 4 \\ 7 & 3 & 1 \end{vmatrix} \qquad N = \begin{vmatrix} 1 & 2 & 3 \\ 4 & 5 & 6 \\ 7 & 8 & 9 \end{vmatrix}$$

$$M+N = \begin{vmatrix} 2 & 2 & 2 \\ 0 & 1 & 4 \\ 7 & 3 & 1 \end{vmatrix} + \begin{vmatrix} 1 & 2 & 3 \\ 4 & 5 & 6 \\ 7 & 8 & 9 \end{vmatrix} = \begin{vmatrix} (2+1) & (2+2) & (2+3) \\ (0+4) & (1+5) & (4+6) \\ (7+7) & (3+8) & (1+9) \end{vmatrix} = \begin{vmatrix} 3 & 4 & 5 \\ 4 & 6 & 10 \\ 14 & 11 & 10 \end{vmatrix}$$

$$M-N = \begin{vmatrix} 2 & 2 & 2 \\ 0 & 1 & 4 \\ 7 & 3 & 1 \end{vmatrix} - \begin{vmatrix} 1 & 2 & 3 \\ 4 & 5 & 6 \\ 7 & 8 & 9 \end{vmatrix} = \begin{vmatrix} (2-1) & (2-2) & (2-3) \\ (0-4) & (1-5) & (4-6) \\ (7-7) & (3-8) & (1-9) \end{vmatrix} = \begin{vmatrix} 1 & 0 & -1 \\ -4 & -4 & -2 \\ 0 & -5 & -8 \end{vmatrix}$$

As you can see, $M(0,0)$ is added to $N(0,0)$ to get the result $M+N(0,0)$. Each element of the result is computed this way for both addition and subtraction. Also, when doing matrix addition and subtraction, you need to make sure that the matrices involved have the same $m \times n$ dimension. Otherwise the operations just will not work. There are also a few properties for adding and subtracting matrices.

Matrix addition and subtraction are associative, meaning that $M + (N + X) = (M + N) + X$. Subtraction is not commutative however, as $(M–N)$ might not equal $(N–M)$.

Matrix Multiplication

There are two ways to do matrix multiplication. The first is called *scalar matrix multiplication*, and it involves multiplying a matrix by a scalar value. This operation is very simple and just involves multiplying the scalar value by each element of the matrix. As an example, you can multiply this 2×2 matrix by the scalar value of 2:

$$M = \begin{vmatrix} 1 & 3 \\ 2 & 0 \end{vmatrix} \qquad k = 2$$

$$C = k*M = 2*\begin{vmatrix} 1 & 3 \\ 2 & 0 \end{vmatrix} = \begin{vmatrix} (2*1) & (2*3) \\ (2*2) & (2*0) \end{vmatrix} = \begin{vmatrix} 2 & 6 \\ 4 & 0 \end{vmatrix}$$

Scalar matrix multiplication is rather straightforward. For those who like the more general mathematical description, here is one for a 3×3 matrix being multiplied by a constant scalar value k.

$$\text{Let } M = \begin{vmatrix} m_{00} & m_{01} & m_{02} \\ m_{10} & m_{11} & m_{12} \\ m_{20} & m_{21} & m_{22} \end{vmatrix}$$

$$\text{Then } k*M = k* \begin{vmatrix} m_{00} & m_{01} & m_{02} \\ m_{10} & m_{11} & m_{12} \\ m_{20} & m_{21} & m_{22} \end{vmatrix} = \begin{vmatrix} k*m_{00} & k*m_{01} & k*m_{02} \\ k*m_{10} & k*m_{11} & k*m_{12} \\ k*m_{20} & k*m_{21} & k*m_{22} \end{vmatrix}$$

The simplicity of scalar matrix multiplication really comes out with the general mathematical description. One of this operation's uses is scaling, which we will discuss later in this chapter.

The other type of matrix multiplication is the "real" type where you multiply two matrices together. This particular operation might be a little more difficult for someone new to matrices as the whole process can be somewhat confusing at first. The first thing you need to know before diving in is that not all matrices are created equal when multiplication is involved. In fact, in order to multiply two matrices together, the *inner dimension* of each matrix must be the same. The inner dimension applies to the column value of the first matrix and the row value of the second matrix. For example, let's say you have two matrices, A and B, where A is a 3×2 matrix and B is a 3×3 matrix. You cannot multiply A and B together because A has two columns while B has three rows. Now, if A were a 2×3 matrix, then you could multiply it by B. Another way to look at it is since the 2 from matrix A and the 3 from matrix B are not the same, the two matrices A and B cannot be multiplied together. Looking at this idea in a more general form, if A is $m \times n$, then B must be $n \times r$, but m and r do not have to be equal to each other.

Before multiplying two matrices, you can determine what dimensions the resulting matrix should have. Quite simply, the dimensions of the resulting matrix are equal to the *outer dimensions* of the two matrices. For example, if A is a 3×1 matrix and B is a 1×3 matrix, then the resulting matrix C will be a 3×3 matrix. In other words, (3×1) × (1×3) results in a 3×3 matrix. Using the general form just described, the resulting matrix C will be equal to $m \times r$.

So what about the actual multiplication? Well, given two matrices A and B, the idea is to take a row from A and multiply it by the corresponding column of B. Each element that is multiplied from the A row and B row are then added together to give the new element of the resulting matrix. This may seem somewhat confusing right now, so take a look at Figure 3.4, which gives an easier-to-understand look at the whole matrix multiplication process.

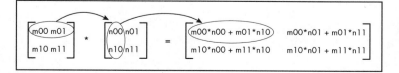

Figure 3.4

Step-by-step matrix multiplication.

The following example multiplies a 2×3 matrix with a 3×3 matrix:

```
A = | 1   3   4 |                 | 3   1   2 |
    | 2   0   2 |       B =       | 0   1   2 |
                                  | 1   4   3 |
```

$$A \times B = \begin{vmatrix} (1*3 + 3*0 + 4*1) & (1*1 + 3*1 + 4*4) & (1*2 + 3*2 + 4*3) \\ (2*3 + 0*0 + 2*1) & (2*1 + 0*1 + 2*4) & (2*2 + 0*2 + 2*3) \end{vmatrix}$$

```
A x B = | 7   20   20 |
        | 8   10   10 |
```

The general description of multiplication for a 1×3 and a 3×3 matrix goes like this:

$$\text{Let } M = \begin{vmatrix} m_{00} & m_{01} & m_{02} \end{vmatrix} \qquad \text{Let } N = \begin{vmatrix} n_{00} & n_{01} & n_{02} \\ n_{10} & n_{11} & n_{12} \\ n_{20} & n_{21} & n_{22} \end{vmatrix}$$

$$M \times N = \begin{vmatrix} (m_{00}*n_{00} + m_{01}*n_{10} + m_{02}*n_{20}) & (m_{00}*n_{01} + m_{01}*n_{11} + m_{02}*n_{21}) & (m_{00}*n_{02} + m_{01}*n_{12} + m_{02}*n_{22}) \end{vmatrix}$$

Also, it would be good to note that matrix multiplication is not a commutative operation. This simply means that

$$(M*N) \mathrel{!=} (N*M)$$

Or that multiplying two matrices in a certain order is not the same as multiplying them together in the reverse order. The exceptions to this statement occur when either matrix is an identity matrix, a zero matrix, or when both are the same.

Putting It Together

You now know how matrices work, but how do you implement this stuff? There are several different ways people can implement matrices. What you are going to do is create a special type that is just a 3×3 matrix, and then you will create a function for each matrix operation.

To start things off, here is some code for the 3×3 matrix type definition:

```
// the 3x3 matrix type
typedef struct
{
    float mat[3][3];          // the rows and columns
} matrix3x3_t;
```

Now you can use that definition for each of the matrix operation functions:

```
void MatrixAdd(matrix3x3_t* matrixA, matrix3x3_t* matrixB, matrix3x3_t* resultMatrix)
{
    // add two matrices, A and B, together and store result in resultMatrix

    // loop through all the elements of each matrix
    for (int row = 0; row < 3; row++)
    {
        for (int col = 0; col < 3; col++)
        {
            // add the current element of each matrix
            resultMatrix->m[row][col] = matrixA->m[row][col] +
                                        matrixB->m[row][col];

        } // end for col
    } // end for row
} // end MatrixAdd

void ScalarMatrixMult(float scalarValue,
                      matrix3x3_t* matrixA,
                      matrix3x3_t* resultMatrix)
{
    // perform scalar-matrix multiplication, return resultMatrix

    // loop through entire matrix
    for (int row = 0; row < 3; row++)
    {
        for (int col = 0; col < 3; col++)
        {
            // multiply scalar and current element
            resultMatrix->m[row][col] = scalarValue*matrixA->m[row][col];

        } // end for col
    } // end for row
} // end ScalarMatrixMult


void MatrixMult(matrix3x3_t* matrixA, matrix3x3_t* matrixB, matrix3x3_t* resultMatrix)
{
    // multiply two matrices together and return resultMatrix
```

```
    float sum;        // used to store sum of multiplications

    for (int row = 0; row < 3; row++)
    {
        for (int col = 0; col < 3; col++)
        {
            sum = 0;       // reset to zero

            // multiply the row of A by the column of B
            for (int k = 0; k < 3; k++)
            {
                sum += matrixA->m[row][k] * matrixB->m[k][col];
            } // end for k
            resultMatrix->m[row][col] = sum;       // store sum of multiples
        } // end for col
    } // end for row
} // end MatrixMult
```

Well that about does it for matrices. Now you can actually see where these things are useful in 3D through transformations. They're up next.

TRANSFORMATIONS

Transformations are what make 3D worlds come alive. They allow you to move objects, rotate them, make them bigger or smaller, and even manipulate how an object looks. As we will discuss in Chapter 5, transformations operate in what is called a local coordinate system. If the local coordinate system is located at the origin, then all of the transformations will be performed about the origin, but if the local coordinate system is located at the point (0, 10, 4), then the transformations will be performed with the point (0, 10, 4) representing the origin of the coordinate system.

To do transformations, you basically multiply the point you want to transform by the desired transformation matrix. The result you receive is the newly transformed point. If you have a point p and transformation matrix M, then to transform p using M with return result p', you would do

$p' = M*p$

For transformations, you are going to use what is called *homogeneous coordinates*. Although these are not of any super mathematical importance, using homogeneous coordinates allows translations in transformations while also allowing you to scale any transformation. This can be useful later on. To create homogeneous coordinates, you place the value of 1 in the final diagonal element in each transformation matrix. This will become more apparent when you look at each transformation matrix separately.

Translation

Translation can be thought of as moving a point from one coordinate in 3D space to another. To perform translation on a point, you simply add each axis's delta values, or the amount the translation is occurring along each axis, to the original values of the point being translated. For example, here is the translation matrix:

$$MT = \begin{vmatrix} 1 & 0 & 0 & dx \\ 0 & 1 & 0 & dy \\ 0 & 0 & 1 & dz \\ 0 & 0 & 0 & 1 \end{vmatrix}$$

If you want to translate a point using this matrix, you multiply the translation matrix by the vector matrix like this:

$$p = \begin{vmatrix} x \\ y \\ z \\ 1 \end{vmatrix}$$

$$MT*p = \begin{vmatrix} 1 & 0 & 0 & dx \\ 0 & 1 & 0 & dy \\ 0 & 0 & 1 & dz \\ 0 & 0 & 0 & 1 \end{vmatrix} * \begin{vmatrix} x \\ y \\ z \\ 1 \end{vmatrix} = \begin{vmatrix} (1*x) + (0*y) + (0*z) + (dx*1) \\ (0*x) + (1*y) + (0*z) + (dy*1) \\ (0*x) + (0*y) + (1*z) + (dz*1) \\ (0*x) + (0*y) + (0*z) + (1*1) \end{vmatrix} = \begin{vmatrix} x+dx \\ y+dy \\ z+dz \\ 1 \end{vmatrix}$$

This effectively means that

$x' = x+dx$
$y' = y+dy$
$z' = z+dz$

And there you have it. You can now translate a point or vector from one position in 3D space to another. Note how the homogeneous value in the point vector is equal to 1. If it were equal to 0, you would not be able to perform the translation. If the value were equal to anything else, then the scaling of the translation would be different.

Rotation

The next transformation is rotation. What makes this transformation matrix more difficult than the others is that it uses trigonometry and that each axis of rotation has a different set of values in its matrix elements.

The matrix for rotation about the x axis is defined as

$$
M\_RX = \begin{vmatrix} 1 & 0 & 0 & 0 \\ 0 & \cos \theta & -\sin \theta & 0 \\ 0 & \sin \theta & \cos \theta & 0 \\ 0 & 0 & 0 & 1 \end{vmatrix}
$$

As you can see, when rotating about the x axis, the *x* values are left unchanged. The same goes for rotation about the y axis: You leave the *y* values unchanged as seen here:

$$
M\_RY = \begin{vmatrix} \cos \theta & 0 & \sin \theta & 0 \\ 0 & 1 & 0 & 0 \\ -\sin \theta & 0 & \cos \theta & 0 \\ 0 & 0 & 0 & 1 \end{vmatrix}
$$

And for rotation about the z axis, you leave the *z* values alone:

$$
M\_RZ = \begin{vmatrix} \cos \theta & -\sin \theta & 0 & 0 \\ \sin \theta & \cos \theta & 0 & 0 \\ 0 & 0 & 1 & 0 \\ 0 & 0 & 0 & 1 \end{vmatrix}
$$

If you want to rotate a point about the origin along a desired axis, you multiply the desired axis rotation matrix by the point. For example, to rotate a point about the z axis, do the following:

$$
p = \begin{vmatrix} x \\ y \\ z \\ 1 \end{vmatrix}
$$

$$
M\_RZ*p = \begin{vmatrix} \cos \theta & -\sin \theta & 0 & 0 \\ \sin \theta & \cos \theta & 0 & 0 \\ 0 & 0 & 1 & 0 \\ 0 & 0 & 0 & 1 \end{vmatrix} * \begin{vmatrix} x \\ y \\ z \\ 1 \end{vmatrix} = \begin{vmatrix} (x*\cos \theta) - (y*\sin \theta) + (0*z) + (0*1) \\ (x*\sin \theta) + (y*\cos \theta) + (0*z) + (0*1) \\ (0*x) + (0*y) + (1*z) + (0*1) \\ (0*x) + (0*y) + (0*z) + (1*1) \end{vmatrix}
$$

$$
= \begin{vmatrix} (x*\cos \theta) - (y*\sin \theta) \\ (x*\sin \theta) + (y*\cos \theta) \\ z \\ 1 \end{vmatrix}
$$

Naturally, this vector column matrix would translate to meaning

$x' = (x*\cos \theta) - (y*\sin \theta)$
$y' = (x*\sin \theta) + (y*\cos \theta)$
$z' = z$

Use of the rotation matrix brings up an issue called *concatenation of transformations*. The idea here is that you combine matrices, so that instead of having several matrices by which to multiply a point, you can combine the matrices to form a single matrix. Because matrix multiplication is not a commutative operation, the order in which matrices are combined and multiplied does matter. With rotation, you first do a rotation about the z axis, followed by a rotation about the y axis, and ending with a rotation about the x axis. Matrix multiplication is a right-hand operation, meaning we proceed from right to left when performing the multiplication. Knowing this, and given that R is the final desired rotation matrix, then the notation for the concatenated rotation matrix is

$R = R_z * R_y * R_x$

Now if you actually multiply the three rotation matrices together, then after several steps of algebra you reach this set of equations, where α is equal to the rotation angle for the z axis, γ is the angle for the y axis, and β is the angle for the x axis:

$x' = x*[(\cos \alpha)*(\cos \gamma)] +$
$\quad y*[(\cos \alpha)*(\sin \gamma)*(\sin \beta) - (\sin \alpha)*(\cos \beta)] +$
$\quad z*[(\cos \alpha)*(\sin \gamma)*(\sin \beta) - (\sin \alpha)*(\cos \beta)]$

$y' = x*[(\sin \alpha)*(\cos \gamma)] +$
$\quad y*[(\sin \alpha)*(\sin \gamma)*(\sin \beta) - (\cos \alpha)*(\cos \beta)] +$
$\quad z*[(\sin \alpha)*(\sin \gamma)*(\cos \beta) - (\cos \alpha)*(\sin \beta)]$

$z' = -x*(\sin \alpha) + z*[(\cos \gamma)*(\sin \beta)]$

If you translate this set of equations to matrix form, you get

$$R = \begin{vmatrix} x' \\ y' \\ z' \\ 1 \end{vmatrix}$$

Essentially, this new matrix gives you a single matrix to perform all of your rotations in one pass rather than passing the point to several rotation matrices one at a time. Which method you use is up to you, and you can even come up with other matrix concatenations to form different customized matrices.

Scaling

You can scale vertices by multiplying them by a scaling factor. In 3D graphics, because you use the three coordinates x, y, and z, you can use the scaling factors of sx, sy, and sz. The scaling matrix looks like this:

$$MS = \begin{vmatrix} sx & 0 & 0 & 0 \\ 0 & sy & 0 & 0 \\ 0 & 0 & sz & 0 \\ 0 & 0 & 0 & 1 \end{vmatrix}$$

When you multiply this matrix with a vector matrix, you get

$$p = \begin{vmatrix} x \\ y \\ z \\ 1 \end{vmatrix}$$

$$MS*p = \begin{vmatrix} sx & 0 & 0 & 0 \\ 0 & sy & 0 & 0 \\ 0 & 0 & sz & 0 \\ 0 & 0 & 0 & 1 \end{vmatrix} * \begin{vmatrix} x \\ y \\ z \\ 1 \end{vmatrix} = \begin{vmatrix} (sx*x) + (0*y) + (0*z) + (0*1) \\ (0*x) + (sy*y) + (0*z) + (0*1) \\ (0*x) + (0*y) + (sz*z) + (0*1) \\ (0*x) + (0*y) + (0*z) + (1*1) \end{vmatrix} = \begin{vmatrix} x*sx \\ y*sy \\ z*sz \\ 1 \end{vmatrix}$$

And then by extracting each component out of the resulting matrix, you get these equations for scaling:

$x' = x*sx$
$y' = y*sy$
$z' = z*sz$

That completes your look at matrices. Get used to them now, because they are central to the 3D graphics you will be doing, particularly with OpenGL. If you still have trouble with them at this point, you might want to take a look at Appendix A for some online resources with great tutorials on this subject.

PROJECTIONS

Although the world you are creating is 3D, your viewing portal into this world is a 2D display. To handle this problem, you rely on the concept of *projection*. Projection is essentially the process of "projecting" 3D world coordinates onto a 2D screen display.

Two types of projections concern you in 3D graphics. The first, called *parallel projection*, is a projection in which all objects remain the same size on the projection plane no matter how far away they are in the world. The *projection plane* could be considered the camera lens of the 3D world. It is the 2D plane to which all viewable 3D points are projected.

The next projection, called *perspective projection,* determines object sizes based on the object's distance from the projection plane. With this projection, all the light rays bouncing off the objects in the 3D space converge on a single point for the viewer's eye. Figure 3.5 shows how this works.

Let's take a look at each of these projections in more detail.

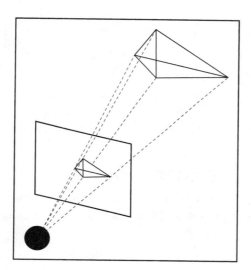

Figure 3.5

Light rays bounce off objects in 3D space and converge at the viewer's eye.

Parallel Projection

Parallel projections are often used by CAD engineers to portray different viewing angles of objects in their drawings. These viewing angles are also called *orthographic projections.* In CAD, the top, front, and side views are the most common orthographic projections because they give the viewer enough information to visualize what the object looks like.

Parallel projection can be accomplished in two steps. The first step is that you need to transform the projection plane to match the *xy* plane of the 3D space. This transformation allows you to complete the second step, which is to remove the *z* component of all viewable points. By doing this, you remove all depth information from the objects in the world, which makes the objects' projection the same size regardless of their distance from the viewer.

Although parallel projections might be good for CAD applications, they do not produce the realistic effect that perspective projections do because of the loss of depth information (see Figure 3.6). For this reason, you will want to primarily use perspective projection in your 3D games and demos.

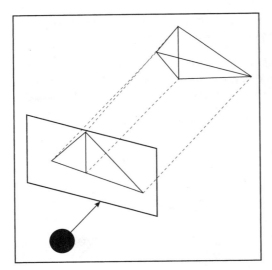

Figure 3.6

Parallel projection from a 3D space onto a projection plane.

Perspective Projection

As mentioned previously, perspective projection produces a view where the object's size in the view depends on the object's distance from the viewer. For example, an object that is farther from the viewer will be smaller than an object that is closer.

To accomplish perspective projection, the viewer's eye becomes the single point where all light rays reflected by the world's objects converge. This is very much like the how the human eye sees. Now, think of the projection plane as the outside of the eyeball. As light rays come into the viewer's eye, they intersect the projection plane where you can plot a set of points. This set of points is the illusion of the 3D world on a 2D plane. Figure 3.5 showed how this works.

The idea in perspective projection is to determine where the reflected light rays intersect the projection plane. You can accomplish this through a *perspective transformation matrix*, but first you need to take a look at the focus distance.

The *focus distance* is defined as the distance between the viewer's eye and the projection plane, as shown in Figure 3.7. The focus is particularly important in 3D graphics when it comes to determining the field of view (FOV) angle. The FOV is shown in Figure 3.8. As the focus distance increases, the FOV becomes smaller, or narrower. When the focus decreases, the FOV becomes larger. When developing your 3D games or demos, you often need to experiment with different focus distances in order to get a more realistic-looking view. This comes from distortions that might occur from use of the perspective transformation.

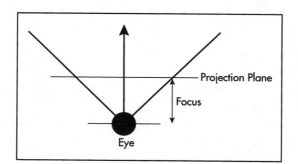

Figure 3.7

The focus distance is the distance between the viewer's eye and the projection plane.

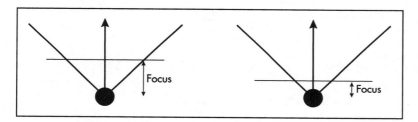

Figure 3.8

The field of view (FOV) with different focus distances.

Speaking of the perspective transformation, it's time you took a look at the matrix. First, though, understand that in order to do perspective transformations, you must use *homogeneous coordinates*. This means the value of 1 is placed in the point vector after the *x*, *y*, and *z* components, and after a transformation has occurred, this value should remain equal to 1. If you take a look back at the transformations we have already discussed, you can see that you have already been using homogeneous coordinates throughout. Now, should this value change from 1 to another value, the vector needs to be *renormalized*. You accomplish this by multiplying each entry by the same value to make the last entry in the point vector equal to 1 again. The perspective transformation matrix is equal to

$$
M\_P \ = \ \begin{vmatrix} 1 & 0 & 0 & 0 \\ 0 & 1 & 0 & 0 \\ 0 & 0 & 0 & 1/focus \\ 0 & 0 & -1 & 0 \end{vmatrix}
$$

By multiplying this matrix by a point vector, you receive this:

$$
p \ = \ \begin{vmatrix} x \\ y \\ z \\ 1 \end{vmatrix}
$$

$$
M\_P*p = \begin{vmatrix} 1 & 0 & 0 & 0 \\ 0 & 1 & 0 & 0 \\ 0 & 0 & 0 & 1/focus \\ 0 & 0 & -1 & 0 \end{vmatrix} * \begin{vmatrix} x \\ y \\ z \\ 1 \end{vmatrix} = \begin{vmatrix} x \\ y \\ -1 \\ z/focus \end{vmatrix}
$$

As you can see by the result, the last component of the resulting point vector is not equal to 1. This means that you need to renormalize the vector by multiplying each component by the reciprocal of the last component value, focus/z.

$$
focus/z * \begin{vmatrix} x \\ y \\ -1 \\ z/focus \end{vmatrix} = \begin{vmatrix} x*(focus/z) \\ y*(focus/z) \\ -focus/z \\ 1 \end{vmatrix}
$$

One important thing to note is that if z is ever equal to 0, then you would get a division-by-zero error. To prevent this from happening, you "clip" points that would cause errors from being transformed into the perspective transformation, discussed next.

3D CLIPPING

When world coordinates of objects exceed the screen viewing boundaries, you might run into errors when using the perspective transformation. This happens in particular when z is equal to 0, but there also is no reason to transform objects that are behind the viewer when z would be negative. These errors can go to the point of crashing the program, so you need a way to prevent them from occurring.

The common approach to this problem is to create a view volume. A *view volume* is essentially a section of 3D space that is visible from the viewer (camera). Anything outside the view volume cannot be seen by the camera, and should therefore not be sent to the projection transformation. When using perspective projection, the view volume has a pyramid shape. This is illustrated in Figure 3.9.

LIGHTING

If you were to go into a room with no windows and turn out the light, you would see exactly what a 3D world on your computer screen would look like without light: nothing! Now you can see (or, in this case, cannot see) why lighting is so important in 3D graphics. Just being able to see things is not the only reason lighting is important though; lighting also provides 3D graphics with more realistic worlds, complete with shadows, reflective surfaces, color, and various other effects. We will get into more theory later on, but for now let's take a look at the three different types of light: ambient, diffuse, and specular.

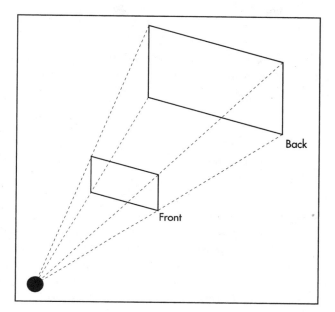

Figure 3.9

The view volume of a perspective projection is in the shape of a pyramid.

Back

Front

Ambient Light

Ambient light is the type of light that fills a room until the light rays no longer have direction. This essentially means that the light does not come from any particular direction, or at least it appears that way. Ambient light does in fact have a source, but objects illuminated by it are lit on all sides and at the same intensity. If you were to consider a room filled with an infinite number of light bulbs that were all turned on at once, then a box placed in the middle of that room would be totally lit on all sides without any hint of shadows or gradients. Figure 3.10 gives a better look at ambient light.

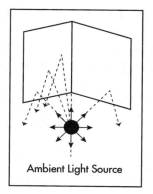

Figure 3.10

Illumination of a surface using ambient light.

Ambient Light Source

If you know that ambient light uniformly illuminates all points of a scene, you can determine an *ambient intensity* at each point. Although we will not be getting into the detailed mathematics of lighting and reflection, know that you can apply the red, green, and blue components of the ambient light to each point in a scene to determine the illumination at each of those points through a series of equations.

Diffuse Light

Diffuse light is probably the type of lighting to which you are accustomed in your everyday life. It comes from a particular direction and is reflected evenly across a surface. You can, however, have two surfaces that reflect light differently if the angle at which the light hits them is different. For example, light that is pointed directly at a surface will be reflected much more brightly than light that is pointed at a sharp angle to another surface. Sunlight is similar to diffuse light in that it comes from one direction and is evenly distributed across the earth. If you were in space looking at the earth as it spun around, you would see varying levels of reflection from the sun off the surface of the earth. A bright spot would be located where the sun is directly above the surface, while a darker shade would be seen at the edges of the visible earth. Because a sphere is made up of a bunch of smaller surfaces, this makes sense. Figure 3.11 gives an example of diffuse light.

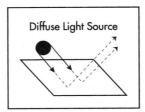

Figure 3.11

Illumination of a surface using diffuse light.

Specular Light

Specular light is another directional light, except it is heavily reflected, and it reflects in a particular direction. Often if a light is highly specular, it will create a bright spot on the surface it points to. This bright spot is called the *specular highlight.* Specular lighting can be used to create "shiny" surfaces or even spotlights. Take a look at Figure 3.12 for a better idea of how specular light works.

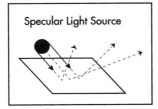

Figure 3.12

Illumination of a surface using specular light.

TEXTURE MAPPING

Texture mapping is the technique that turns 3D worlds from a bunch of colored triangles into potentially photo realistic scenes. Nowadays, virtually every 3D game uses *textures*, or *texture maps*, so there is no reason why you shouldn't as well.

At their lowest level, textures are patterns that can range from stripes and shapes to natural patterns that can be generated by a programmer or drawn by an artist. Sometimes actual photos are used as textures, particularly in simulations.

When viewing objects in the world, you can differentiate the many objects by their size, shape, and texture. You can do the same thing for your 3D virtual world by specifying object size, shape, and the type of texture that covers the object.

We are going to focus on two-dimensional (2D) texture, although you can have 1D, 3D, and 4D textures as well. The 2D texture is typically loaded from an image or picture file that was drawn by an artist or that comes from a scanned photo; *procedural textures*, however, which are textures generated during runtime, are starting to become more common.

First, let's get some terminology out of the way. If you apply a coordinate system to a 2D texture, then each point on that texture could be referenced and manipulated. Each point is called a *texture coordinate*, which is often referenced as the point (s,t), as shown in Figure 3.13. When a texture map is loaded into texture memory as an array of $n \times m$ texture elements, you refer to each element as a *texel*.

When you apply a texture map to a surface, you need a way to define the orientation of the texture on the surface. In order to do this, you use what are called *parametric coordinates*, which are defined as (u,v) and shown in Figure 3.14. For normal texture mapping, the values of u and v lie

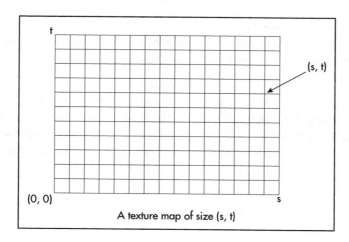

Figure 3.13

The texture coordinates (s,t) on a texture map.

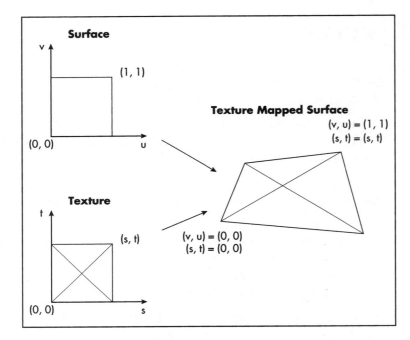

Figure 3.14

Parametric coordinates determine how a texture map is applied to a surface.

between the values of 0 and 1, or (0,1). The minimum and maximum values of both u and v on the texture-mapped surface determine where the extents of the texture map lie. Changing these values can generate different effects, but we will discuss more about how you can play with the parametric coordinates in Chapter 8 when we discuss texture mapping.

SUMMARY

Geometric objects represented in 3D worlds can be broken down to three main components: points, scalars, and vectors. Scalars are essentially measurements such as temperature, distance, and width and do not have any sort of direction. Vectors, on the other hand, have both a direction and a magnitude. Points are just a location in 3D space.

Matrices are used to represent vectors and to perform operations on them. These operations, called *transformations*, include translation, rotation, and scaling. Translation allows you to move from one point to another, rotation allows you to rotate about a specified axis, and scaling increases or decreases the distance between a set of vertices, which in turn allows an object to increase or decrease in size.

The two projections you are concerned with are parallel and perspective projections. Parallel projection causes your view to be orthogonal, or like a CAD application where the object remains the same size no matter how far away it is from the viewer. Prospective projection provides the distortion necessary to cause objects farther away to appear smaller than objects closer to the viewer.

The view volume is the 3D space that your viewer can "see." Anything outside the view volume is clipped and not drawn. This saves on rendering time and potential errors that might arise from division when calculating the perspective.

There are three types of light that you will be using. Ambient light is light reflected in all directions in a room. Diffuse light comes from a particular direction and is reflected evenly off a surface. Specular light is reflected heavily and in a particular direction.

Texture mapping allows you to create more realistic 3D worlds by placing an image on a polygon. Just like in the real world, textures help you identify objects and distinguish them from other objects.

Part II

Using OpenGL

CHAPTER 4

OpenGL
States and
Primitives

ell, here you are, four chapters in, and you're finally getting to the meat of OpenGL! To begin to unlock the power of OpenGL, you need to start with the basics, and that means understanding primitives. But before we cover that, we need to discuss something that is going to come up as we cover primitives and pretty much everything else from this point on: the OpenGL state machine.

The OpenGL state machine consists of hundreds of settings that affect various aspects of rendering. Because the state machine will play a role in everything you do, it's important to understand what the default settings are, how you can get information about the current settings, and how to change those settings. Numerous general-purpose functions are used to control the state machine, so we'll look at those here, and then deal with specific functions as they come up.

As you read this chapter, you'll learn the following:

- How to change and access values in the OpenGL state machine
- What primitives are and the types of primitives available in OpenGL
- How to modify the way primitives are handled and displayed

STATE FUNCTIONS

In general, OpenGL contains a lot of general-purpose functions that can affect a wide range of settings depending on the values passed to them. Nowhere is that more true than with the state machine functions we'll be discussing in this section.

The first function you'll look at is glGet(), which is used to query the state machine for its current settings. glGet() comes in four different versions, listed below:

```
void glGetBooleanv(GLenum pname, GLboolean *params);

void glGetDoublev(GLenum pname, GLdouble *params);

void glGetFloatv(GLenum pname, GLfloat *params);

void glGetIntegerv(GLenum pname, GLint *params);
```

params is an array with sufficient space to hold all the values associated with the setting about which you're inquiring. The parameter pname specifies the state setting you're querying, and it can be any of the values listed below. Note that we'll be discussing the specific meaning of each of these as they come up because most of them won't make much sense yet (unless you're already an OpenGL guru, in which case, what are you doing reading this?).

GL_ACCUM_ALPHA_BITS
GL_ACCUM_BLUE_BITS
GL_ACCUM_CLEAR_VALUE
GL_ACCUM_GREEN_BITS
GL_ACCUM_RED_BITS
GL_ALPHA_BIAS
GL_ALPHA_BITS
GL_ALPHA_SCALE
GL_ALPHA_TEST
GL_ALPHA_TEST_FUNC
GL_ALPHA_TEST_REF
GL_ATTRIB_STACK_DEPTH
GL_AUTO_NORMAL
GL_AUX_BUFFERS
GL_BLEND
GL_BLEND_DST
GL_BLEND_SRC
GL_BLUE_BIAS
GL_BLUE_BITS
GL_BLUE_SCALE
GL_CLIENT_ATTRIB_STACK_DEPTH
GL_CLIP_PLANEn (n ranges from 0 to GL_MAX_CLIP_PLANES $- 1$)
GL_COLOR_ARRAY
GL_COLOR_ARRAY_SIZE
GL_COLOR_ARRAY_STRIDE
GL_COLOR_ARRAY_TYPE
GL_COLOR_CLEAR_VALUE
GL_COLOR_LOGIC_OP
GL_COLOR_MATERIAL
GL_COLOR_MATERIAL_FACE
GL_COLOR_MATERIAL_PARAMETER
GL_COLOR_WRITEMASK
GL_CULL_FACE
GL_CULL_FACE_MODE
GL_CURRENT_COLOR
GL_CURRENT_INDEX
GL_CURRENT_NORMAL
GL_CURRENT_RASTER_COLOR
GL_CURRENT_RASTER_DISTANCE
GL_CURRENT_RASTER_INDEX
GL_CURRENT_RASTER_POSITION
GL_CURRENT_RASTER_POSITION_VALID
GL_CURRENT_RASTER_TEXTURE_COORDS
GL_CURRENT_TEXTURE_COORDS
GL_DEPTH_BIAS
GL_DEPTH_BITS
GL_DEPTH_CLEAR_VALUE
GL_DEPTH_FUNC
GL_DEPTH_RANGE

```
GL_DEPTH_SCALE
GL_DEPTH_TEST
GL_DEPTH_WRITEMASK
GL_DITHER
GL_DOUBLEBUFFER
GL_DRAW_BUFFER
GL_EDGE_FLAG
GL_EDGE_FLAG_ARRAY
GL_EDGE_FLAG_ARRAY_STRIDE
GL_FOG
GL_FOG_COLOR
GL_FOG_DENSITY
GL_FOG_END
GL_FOG_HINT
GL_FOG_INDEX
GL_FOG_MODE
GL_FOG_START
GL_FRONT_FACE
GL_GREEN_BIAS
GL_GREEN_BITS
GL_GREEN_SCALE
GL_INDEX_ARRAY
GL_INDEX_ARRAY_STRIDE
GL_INDEX_ARRAY_TYPE
GL_INDEX_BITS
GL_INDEX_CLEAR_VALUE
GL_INDEX_LOGIC_OP
GL_INDEX_MODE
GL_INDEX_OFFSET
GL_INDEX_SHIFT
GL_INDEX_WRITEMASK
GL_LIGHTn (n ranges from 0 to GL_MAX_LIGHTS − 1)
GL_LIGHTING
GL_LIGHT_MODEL_AMBIENT
GL_LIGHT_MODEL_LOCAL_VIEWER
GL_LIGHT_MODEL_TWO_SIDE
GL_LINE_SMOOTH
GL_LINE_SMOOTH_HINT
GL_LINE_STIPPLE
GL_LINE_STIPPLE_PATTERN
GL_LINE_STIPPLE_REPEAT
GL_LINE_WIDTH
GL_LINE_WIDTH_GRANULARITY
GL_LINE_WIDTH_RANGE
GL_LIST_BASE
GL_LIST_INDEX
GL_LIST_MODE
GL_LOGIC_OP
GL_LOGIC_OP_MODE
GL_MAP1_COLOR_4
```

```
GL_MAP1_GRID_DOMAIN
GL_MAP1_GRID_SEGMENTS
GL_MAP1_INDEX
GL_MAP1_NORMAL
GL_MAP1_TEXTURE_COORD_1
GL_MAP1_TEXTURE_COORD_2
GL_MAP1_TEXTURE_COORD_3
GL_MAP1_TEXTURE_COORD_4
GL_MAP1_VERTEX_3
GL_MAP1_VERTEX_4
GL_MAP2_COLOR_4
GL_MAP2_GRID_DOMAIN
GL_MAP2_GRID_SEGMENTS
GL_MAP2_INDEX
GL_MAP2_NORMAL
GL_MAP2_TEXTURE_COORD_1
GL_MAP2_TEXTURE_COORD_2
GL_MAP2_TEXTURE_COORD_3
GL_MAP2_TEXTURE_COORD_4
GL_MAP2_VERTEX_3
GL_MAP2_VERTEX_4
GL_MAP_COLOR
GL_MAP_STENCIL
GL_MATRIX_MODE
GL_MAX_CLIENT_ATTRIB_STACK_DEPTH
GL_MAX_ATTRIB_STACK_DEPTH
GL_MAX_CLIP_PLANES
GL_MAX_EVAL_ORDER
GL_MAX_LIGHTS
GL_MAX_LIST_NESTING
GL_MAX_MODELVIEW_STACK_DEPTH
GL_MAX_NAME_STACK_DEPTH
GL_MAX_PIXEL_MAP_TABLE
GL_MAX_PROJECTION_STACK_DEPTH
GL_MAX_TEXTURE_SIZE
GL_MAX_TEXTURE_STACK_DEPTH
GL_MAX_VIEWPORT_DIMS
GL_MODELVIEW_MATRIX
GL_MODELVIEW_STACK_DEPTH
GL_NAME_STACK_DEPTH
GL_NORMAL_ARRAY
GL_NORMAL_ARRAY_STRIDE
GL_NORMAL_ARRAY_TYPE
GL_NORMALIZE
GL_PACK_ALIGNMENT
GL_PACK_LSB_FIRST
GL_PACK_ROW_LENGTH
GL_PACK_SKIP_PIXELS
GL_PACK_SKIP_ROWS
GL_PACK_SWAP_BYTES
```

```
GL_PERSPECTIVE_CORRECTION_HINT
GL_PIXEL_MAP_A_TO_A_SIZE
GL_PIXEL_MAP_B_TO_B_SIZE
GL_PIXEL_MAP_G_TO_G_SIZE
GL_PIXEL_MAP_I_TO_A_SIZE
GL_PIXEL_MAP_I_TO_B_SIZE
GL_PIXEL_MAP_I_TO_G_SIZE
GL_PIXEL_MAP_I_TO_I_SIZE
GL_PIXEL_MAP_I_TO_R_SIZE
GL_PIXEL_MAP_R_TO_R_SIZE
GL_PIXEL_MAP_S_TO_S_SIZE
GL_POINT_SIZE
GL_POINT_SIZE_GRANULARITY
GL_POINT_SIZE_RANGE
GL_POINT_SMOOTH
GL_POINT_SMOOTH_HINT
GL_POLYGON_MODE
GL_POLYGON_OFFSET_FACTOR
GL_POLYGON_OFFSET_UNITS
GL_POLYGON_OFFSET_FILL
GL_POLYGON_OFFSET_LINE
GL_POLYGON_OFFSET_POINT
GL_POLYGON_SMOOTH
GL_POLYGON_SMOOTH_HINT
GL_POLYGON_STIPPLE
GL_PROJECTION_MATRIX
GL_PROJECTION_STACK_DEPTH
GL_READ_BUFFER
GL_RED_BIAS
GL_RED_BITS
GL_RED_SCALE
GL_RENDER_MODE
GL_RGBA_MODE
GL_SCISSOR_BOX
GL_SCISSOR_TEST
GL_SHADE_MODEL
GL_STENCIL_BITS
GL_STENCIL_CLEAR_VALUE
GL_STENCIL_FAIL
GL_STENCIL_FUNC
GL_STENCIL_PASS_DEPTH_FAIL
GL_STENCIL_PASS_DEPTH_PASS
GL_STENCIL_REF
GL_STENCIL_TEST
GL_STENCIL_VALUE_MASK
GL_STENCIL_WRITEMASK
GL_STEREO
GL_SUBPIXEL_BITS
GL_TEXTURE_1D
```

```
GL_TEXTURE_2D
GL_TEXTURE_COORD_ARRAY
GL_TEXTURE_COORD_ARRAY_SIZE
GL_TEXTURE_COORD_ARRAY_STRIDE
GL_TEXTURE_COORD_ARRAY_TYPE
GL_TEXTURE_ENV_COLOR
GL_TEXTURE_ENV_MODE
GL_TEXTURE_GEN_Q
GL_TEXTURE_GEN_R
GL_TEXTURE_GEN_S
GL_TEXTURE_GEN_T
GL_TEXTURE_MATRIX
GL_TEXTURE_STACK_DEPTH
GL_UNPACK_ALIGNMENT
GL_UNPACK_LSB_FIRST
GL_UNPACK_ROW_LENGTH
GL_UNPACK_SKIP_PIXELS
GL_UNPACK_SKIP_ROWS
GL_UNPACK_SWAP_BYTES
GL_VERTEX_ARRAY
GL_VERTEX_ARRAY_SIZE
GL_VERTEX_ARRAY_STRIDE
GL_VERTEX_ARRAY_TYPE
GL_VIEWPORT
GL_ZOOM_X
GL_ZOOM_Y
```

See what we mean by general purpose? You can do a lot with this function!

Of course, determining the current state machine settings is interesting, but not nearly as interesting as being able to change the settings. Contrary to what you might expect, there is no glSet() or similar general-purpose function for setting state machine values. Instead, there are numerous more-specific functions, which we'll discuss as they become relevant.

Often, you just want to query a boolean value, the purpose being to find out whether a particular OpenGL capability is enabled. Although this can be done with glGet(), it's usually easier to use glIsEnabled(), which has the following prototype:

```
GLboolean glIsEnabled(GLenum cap);
```

GLboolean() can be called with any of the values in the following list. It returns GL_TRUE if the capability is enabled, and GL_FALSE otherwise. Again, we'll wait to explain the meaning of the various values as they come up.

```
GL_ALPHA_TEST
GL_AUTO_NORMAL
GL_BLEND
GL_CLIP_PLANEn (n ranges from 0 to GL_MAX_CLIP_PLANES − 1)
GL_COLOR_ARRAY
```

```
GL_COLOR_LOGIC_OP
GL_COLOR_MATERIAL
GL_CULL_FACE
GL_DEPTH_TEST
GL_DITHER
GL_FOG
GL_INDEX_ARRAY
GL_INDEX_LOGIC_OP
GL_LIGHTn (n ranges from 0 to GL_MAX_LIGHTS − 1)
GL_LIGHTING
GL_LINE_SMOOTH
GL_LINE_STIPPLE
GL_LOGIC_OP
GL_MAP1_COLOR_4
GL_MAP1_INDEX
GL_MAP1_NORMAL
GL_MAP1_TEXTURE_COORD_1
GL_MAP1_TEXTURE_COORD_2
GL_MAP1_TEXTURE_COORD_3
GL_MAP1_TEXTURE_COORD_4
GL_MAP1_VERTEX_3
GL_MAP1_VERTEX_4
GL_MAP2_COLOR_4
GL_MAP2_INDEX
GL_MAP2_NORMAL
GL_MAP2_TEXTURE_COORD_1
GL_MAP2_TEXTURE_COORD_2
GL_MAP2_TEXTURE_COORD_3
GL_MAP2_TEXTURE_COORD_4
GL_MAP2_VERTEX_3
GL_MAP2_VERTEX_4
GL_NORMAL_ARRAY
GL_NORMALIZE
GL_POINT_SMOOTH
GL_POLYGON_OFFSET_FILL
GL_POLYGON_OFFSET_LINE
GL_POLYGON_OFFSET_POINT
GL_POLYGON_SMOOTH
GL_POLYGON_STIPPLE
GL_SCISSOR_TEST
GL_STENCIL_TEST
GL_TEXTURE_1D
GL_TEXTURE_2D
GL_TEXTURE_COORD_ARRAY
GL_TEXTURE_GEN_Q
GL_TEXTURE_GEN_R
GL_TEXTURE_GEN_S
GL_TEXTURE_GEN_T
GL_VERTEX_ARRAY
```

We'll frequently refer to glGet() and glIsEnabled(), but there are many more state machine functions (in fact, most OpenGL functions affect the state machine in some way). We'll cover several specific state functions in this chapter and many of the remaining ones in following chapters.

Handling Primitives

So, what are primitives? If you pull out your copy of *Merriam-Webster*'s, you'll find that a primitive is "an unsophisticated person." Well, that doesn't help much, so we'll give it a shot: Simply put, *primitives* are basic geometric entities such as points, lines, triangles, and the like.

You'll be using thousands and thousands of these primitives to make your games, so it's important to know how they work. Before we get into specific primitive types, though, we need to talk about a couple of OpenGL functions that you're going to be using a lot. The first is glBegin(), which has the following prototype:

```
void glBegin (GLenum mode);
```

You use glBegin() to tell OpenGL that you're ready to start drawing and to specify the primitive type you want to draw. You specify the primitive type with the mode parameter, which can take on any of the values in Table 4.1.

Table 4.1 Valid glBegin() Parameters

Parameter	Definition
GL_POINTS	Single points
GL_LINES	Non-connected lines
GL_LINE_STRIP	Series of connected lines
GL_LINE_LOOP	Closed loop of connected lines
GL_TRIANGLES	Single triangles
GL_TRIANGLE_STRIP	Series of connected triangles
GL_TRIANGLE_FAN	Set of triangles containing a common central vertex
GL_QUADS	Quadrilaterals
GL_QUAD_STRIP	Series of connected quadrilaterals
GL_POLYGON	Polygon with an arbitrary number of vertices

The rest of this chapter provides a detailed look at each of these primitive types.

Each call to glBegin() needs to be accompanied by a call to glEnd(), which has the following form:

```
void glEnd();
```

As you can see, glEnd() takes no parameters. There really isn't much to say about glEnd(), other than that it tells OpenGL that you're finished rendering the type of primitive you specified in glBegin(). Note that glBegin()/glEnd() pairs can't be nested, i.e. you can't place a call to glBegin() or glEnd() inside another glBegin()/glEnd() block.

Not all OpenGL functions can be used inside a glBegin()/glEnd() pair. In fact, only variations of glVertex(), glColor(), glIndex(), glNormal(), glTexCoord(), glEvalCoord(), glEvalPoint(), glMaterial(), glEdgeFlag(), glCallList(), and glCallLists() are valid; using any other OpenGL calls will generate an error. Each of these functions will be discussed in detail later.

There is one other function—or actually, family of functions—we need to talk about before moving on to primitive types: namely, the glVertex() functions. These functions are called within glBegin()/glEnd() pairs to specify a point in space, which is then interpreted appropriately depending on the value passed to glBegin(). There are a lot of variations of glVertex() functions, and they take the form

```
void glVertex[2,3,4][d,f,i,s][v](...);
```

The number indicates how many dimensions you are specifying. The first letter indicates the type of data you're using, which can be doubles, floats, integers, or shorts. The v (which is optional) indicates that the parameters will be passed as a vector (that is, in an array) rather than individually. The number and type of parameters are determined by the name of the function. The version of glVertex() you'll be using most often is glVertex3f(), which takes three floating-point values representing the *x*, *y*, and *z* coordinates of the vertex.

That about does it for the basics, so let's look at some of the most common primitive types that you'll be using.

Drawing Points in 3D

It doesn't get any more primitive than a point, so that's what we'll look at first. Drawing a point in 3D is simple, and really quite powerful. After all, if you can draw a single pixel on the screen, you can draw anything! So without further ado, here's how to draw a point in OpenGL:

```
glBegin(GL_POINTS);
  glVertex3f(0.0, 0.0, 0.0);
glEnd();
```

In the first line, you tell OpenGL that you're going to be drawing points by passing GL_POINTS to glBegin(). In the next line, you tell it to draw a single point at the origin. Finally, you let OpenGL know you are finished drawing points for now. Note that indenting the code within the glBegin()/glEnd() pair is optional, but it's a common practice among OpenGL programmers because it makes the code a bit easier to read.

What if you want to draw a second point, this one at (0.0, 1.0, 0.0)? Well, you could use

```
glBegin(GL_POINTS);
  glVertex3f(0.0, 0.0, 0.0);
glEnd();
glBegin(GL_POINTS);
  glVertex3f(0.0, 1.0, 0.0);
glEnd();
```

However, that would be horribly inefficient. If you notice, GL_POINTS is plural (in fact, many of the values you can pass to glBegin() are plural), which should suggest that within a single glBegin()/glEnd() block, you can render more than one point, and that's exactly the case. So the code above would become:

```
glBegin(GL_POINTS);
  glVertex3f(0.0, 0.0, 0.0);
  glVertex3f(0.0, 1.0, 0.0);
glEnd();
```

Ah…shorter, faster, better. You can make as many calls to glVertex() as you want within the glBegin()/glEnd() block, and each will be rendered as a single point.

OpenGL includes functions to modify exactly how primitives are drawn, and points are no exception. There are two things you can modify: the size of the points, and whether they are antialiased.

Modifying Point Size

To change the point size, you use

```
void glPointSize(GLfloat size);
```

The default size is 1.0. If point antialiasing is disabled (which it is by default) the point size will be rounded to the nearest integer (with 0 being treated as 1) indicating the pixel dimensions of the point. If you like, you can use glGet() with GL_POINT_SIZE to find out the currently selected size.

Antialiasing Points

Although you can specify primitives with almost infinite precision, there are a finite number of pixels on the screen. This can cause the edges of primitives to look jagged. Antialiasing provides a means of smoothing out the edges to give them a more realistic look. If you want to use antialiasing, you can turn it on by passing GL_POINT_SMOOTH to glEnable() (it can be turned off again by passing the same parameter to glDisable()). If you're unsure whether point antialiasing is currently enabled or disabled, you find out by calling glGet() with GL_POINT_SMOOTH, or with glIsEnabled(GL_POINT_SMOOTH).

When antialiasing is enabled, not all point sizes are enabled. The only size for which the OpenGL specification requires support with antialiasing is 1.0. If an unsupported size is used, it will be rounded to the nearest supported value. To find out the range of sizes your implementation supports, you can call glGet() with GL_POINT_SIZE_RANGE, and you can use GL_POINT_SIZE_GRANULARITY to find the size difference between adjacent supported sizes. The following code shows how to do both:

```
GLfloat sizes[2];
GLfloat granularity;

glGetFloatv(GL_POINT_SIZE_RANGE, sizes);
GLfloat minPointSize = sizes[0];
GLfloat maxPointSize = sizes[1];

glGetFloatv(GL_POINT_SIZE_GRANULARITY, &granularity);
```

With antialiasing on, the current point size will be used as the diameter of a circle centered at the x and y window coordinates of the point you specified. OpenGL will determine how much of each adjacent pixel is covered by the point and adjust the pixel color accordingly.

Now that you have points down, let's move on to something a little more interesting.

Drawing Lines in 3D

Drawing a line in 3D isn't all that different from drawing two points, and because you already know how to do that, let's just dive right in:

```
glBegin(GL_LINES);
  glVertex3f(-2.0, -1.0, 0.0);
  glVertex3f(3.0, 1.0, 0.0);
glEnd();
```

This time, you start off by passing GL_LINES to glBegin() so that OpenGL knows how to interpret the two vertices you're about to specify. After it has both vertices, it knows to draw a line connecting the two of them.

Just as with points, you can draw as many lines as you want to between the calls to glBegin()/glEnd(). Each pair is treated as the endpoints of a new line. If you don't specify an even number of vertices, the last one will just be discarded.

As with points, OpenGL allows you to change several parameters to affect how lines are drawn. In addition to setting the line width and turning on antialiasing, you can specify a stipple pattern.

Modifying Line Width

The default line width is 1.0. To change it, you can call glLineWidth() like so:

```
void glLineWidth(GLfloat width);
```

To find out the currently selected line width, simply call glGet() with GL_LINE_WIDTH.

Antialiasing Line Width

Antialiasing for lines works very much like it does with points. You can turn it on and off by passing GL_LINE_SMOOTH to glEnable() and glDisable(), and the current state can be determined by passing GL_LINE_SMOOTH to glGet() or glIsEnabled(). It is disabled by default.

Again, when using antialiasing, an OpenGL implementation is only required to support the default line width of 1.0. To determine the range and granularity of supported sizes, you can use glGet() with GL_LINE_WIDTH_RANGE and GL_LINE_WIDTH_GRANULARITY, respectively. Here's an example of how to do that:

```
GLfloat sizes[2];
GLfloat granularity;

glGetFloatv(GL_LINE_WIDTH_RANGE, sizes);
GLfloat minLineWidth = sizes[0];
GLfloat maxLineWidth = sizes[1];

glGetFloatv(GL_LINE_WIDTH_GRANULARITY, &granularity);
```

Looks a lot like the points sample above, doesn't it?

Specifying a Stipple Pattern

You can specify a stipple pattern with which to draw the lines. The stipple pattern specifies a mask that will determine which portions of the line get drawn, and it can thus be used for things like dashed lines. Before using stippling, you need to enable it by passing GL_LINE_STIPPLE to glEnable(). Then, you set the stipple pattern using glLineStipple(), which looks like this:

```
void glLineStipple(GLint factor, GLushort pattern);
```

The factor parameter defaults to 1 and is clamped to fall in the range 1–256. It is used to determine how many times each bit in the pattern is repeated in the pattern before moving on to the next bit.

The pattern parameter specifies a 16-bit pattern. Any bits that are set in the pattern will result in the corresponding pixels being set; otherwise they are not drawn. Something to be aware of is that the bits in the integer are applied in reverse order, so that the low-order bit affects the leftmost pixel; then, as the line progresses to the right, higher-order bits are used. This is illustrated in Figure 4.1.

The following code enables line stippling and then specifies a pattern of alternating dashes and dots:

```
glEnable(GL_LINE_STIPPLE);
GLushort stipplePattern = 0xFAFA;

glLineStipple(2, stipplePattern);
```

You can determine the currently selected stipple pattern and repeat factor by calling glGet() with GL_LINE_STIPPLE_PATTERN and GL_LINE_STIPPLE_REPEAT.

Now that you have a handle on lines, let's move on to the heart and soul of almost every 3D game in existence: the all-mighty polygon.

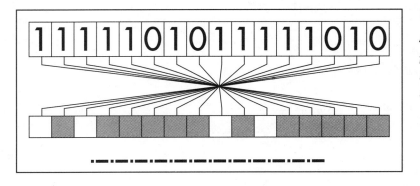

Figure 4.1

A sample stipple pattern demonstrating how the bit order is interpreted.

Drawing Polygons in 3D

Although you can (and will) do some interesting things with points and lines, there's no doubt that polygons give you the most power to create immersive 3D worlds, so that's what we'll spend the rest of the chapter on. Before we get into specific polygon types supported by OpenGL (that is, triangles, quadrilaterals, and polygons), we need to discuss a few things that pertain to all polygon types.

You draw all polygons by specifying several points in 3D space. These points specify a region that is then filled with color. At least, that's the default behavior. However, as you'd probably expect by now, the state machine controls the way in which the polygon is drawn, and you're free to change the default behavior. To change the way polygons are drawn, you use

```
void glPolygonMode(GLenum face, GLenum mode);
```

As you'll learn in the next subsection, OpenGL handles the front and back faces of polygons separately; as a result, when you call glPolygonMode(), you need to specify the face to which the change should be applied. You do this by setting the face parameter to GL_FRONT for front-facing polygons, GL_BACK for back-facing polygons, or GL_FRONT_AND_BACK for both.

The mode parameter can take on any of the values in Table 4.2.

If, for example, you want to set the front-facing polygons to be drawn filled and the back-facing ones to be rendered as a wire frame (as lines), you could use the following code:

```
glPolygonMode(GL_FRONT, GL_FILL);
glPolygonMode(GL_BACK, GL_LINE);
```

Table 4.2 Polygon Modes

Value	Definition
GL_POINT	Each vertex specified is rendered as a single point, which can be controlled by the point states discussed earlier. This basically produces the same effect as calling glBegin() with GL_POINTS.
GL_LINE	This will draw the edges of the polygon as a set of lines. Any of the line states discussed previously will affect how the lines are drawn. This is similar to calling glBegin() with GL_LINE_LOOP.
GL_FILL	This is the default state, which renders the polygon with the interior field. This is the only state in which polygon stipple and polygon smoothing (see the following sections) will take effect.

Note that unless you have changed the mode for front-facing polygons elsewhere, the first line is unnecessary, because polygons are drawn filled by default.

To find out the current mode for drawing polygons, you can call glGet() with GL_POLYGON_MODE.

Polygon Face Culling

Although polygons are infinitely flat, they have two sides, implying that they can be seen from either side. Sometimes, it makes sense to have each side displayed differently, and this is why some of the functions presented here require you to specify whether you're modifying the front face, back face, or both. In any case, both sides of the polygon are drawn separately. When you know that the viewer will only be able to see one side of the polygon, it is not necessary to draw both. For example, with an object that is completely enclosed, like a ball, the inside will never be seen. Through a process known as *culling*, you can tell OpenGL not to render one side of the polygon. To use culling you first need to enable it by passing GL_CULL_FACE to glEnable(). Then, you need to specify which face you want culled, which is done with glCullFace():

```
void glCullFace(GLenum mode);
```

mode can be GL_FRONT to cull front-facing polygons, GL_BACK to cull back-facing polygons, or GL_FRONT_AND_BACK to cull them both. Choosing the latter causes polygons not to be drawn at all, which doesn't seem particularly useful. GL_BACK is the default setting.

The next step is telling OpenGL how to determine whether a polygon is front-facing or back-facing. It does this based on *polygon winding*, which is the order in which you specify vertices. Looking at a polygon head-on, you can choose any vertex with which to begin describing it. To finish describing it, you have to proceed either clockwise or counterclockwise around its vertices. It is important to be consistent about how you specify your polygons so that OpenGL can automatically determine whether a polygon face is front- or back-facing using the winding. By default, OpenGL treats polygons with counterclockwise ordering as front-facing and polygons with clockwise ordering as back-facing. The default behavior can be changed using glFrontFace():

```
void glFrontFace(GLenum mode);
```

mode should be GL_CCW if you want to use counterclockwise orientation for front-facing polygons, and GL_CW if you want to use clockwise orientation.

Hiding Polygon Edges

It's not uncommon to want to render something in wire-frame mode, and sometimes you may not want to have all the edges of your polygons show up. For example, if you're drawing a square using two triangles, you may not want the viewer to see the diagonal line. This is illustrated in Figure 4.2.

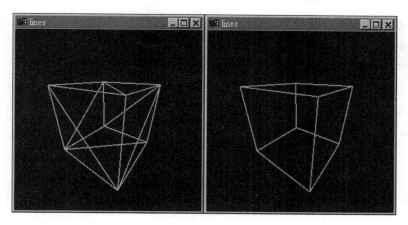

Figure 4.2

Hiding polygon edges you don't want the user to see.

You can tell OpenGL whether a particular edge of a polygon should be included when rendering it as lines by calling `glEdgeFlag()`, which can take on one of the two following forms:

```
void glEdgeFlag(GLboolean isEdge);
```

```
void glEdgeFlag(const GLboolean *isEdge);
```

The only difference between these two forms is that the first takes a single boolean value as its parameter, and the second takes a pointer to an array containing a single boolean value. (The OpenGL designers must have had a good reason to want to pass a single value in an array, but I can't think of one myself!) Either way, these functions are used to set the edge flag. If the flag is set to `GL_TRUE` (the default), the edges you specify are drawn; if it is set to `GL_FALSE`, they are not. Pretty simple.

Antialiasing Polygons

As with points and lines, you can also choose to antialias polygons. You control polygon antialiasing by passing `GL_POLYGON_SMOOTH` to `glEnable()` and `glDisable()`, and the current state can be determined by passing the same parameter to `glGet()` or `glIsEnabled()`. As you might expect, it is disabled by default.

Specifying a Stipple Pattern

The last general polygon attribute you need to look at is polygon stippling, which is similar to line stippling. Rather than filling in a polygon with a solid color, you can set a stipple pattern to fill the polygon. If you've ever set a pattern for your Windows wallpaper, you'll have some idea of the effect.

Polygon stippling is off by default, but you can turn it on by passing GL_POLYGON_STIPPLE to glEnable(). Once it's enabled, you need to specify a stipple pattern, which you do using the following:

```
void GlPolygonStipple(const GLubyte *mask);
```

The mask parameter in this call is a pointer to an array containing a 32×32 pattern. This mask will be used to determine which pixels show up (for bits that are turned on) and which ones don't. Unlike line-stipple patterns, which show up in reverse, polygon-stipple patterns show up as they are specified. Note that the stipple pattern is applied to screen coordinates in 2D. Thus, rotating a polygon doesn't rotate the pattern as well.

Now that we've discussed some general polygon properties, we can look at specific polygonal primitives supported by OpenGL.

Triangles

Triangles are generally the preferred polygon form. There are several reasons for this:

- The vertices of a triangle are always coplanar, because three points define a plane.
- A triangle can never be concave.
- A triangle can't cross over itself.

If you try to render a polygon that violates any of these three properties, unpredictable behavior will result. Because any polygon can be broken down into a number of triangles, it makes sense to work with them.

Not surprisingly, drawing a triangle in 3D isn't any harder than drawing a point or a line. You just need to change the value passed to glBegin(), and then specify three vertices:

```
glBegin(GL_TRIANGLES);
  glVertex3f(-2.0, -1.0, 0.0);
  glVertex3f(3.0, 1.0, 0.0);
  glVertex3f(0.0, 3.0, 0.0);
glEnd();
```

Just as with points and lines, you can draw multiple triangles at one time. OpenGL will treat every vertex triple as a separate triangle. If the number of vertices defined isn't a multiple of 3, then the extra vertices will be discarded.

OpenGL also supports a couple of primitives related to triangles that can improve performance. To understand why you might want to use these, consider Figure 4.3.

Here, you have two connected triangles, which have vertices A and C in common. If you render these using GL_TRIANGLES, you'll have to specify a total of six vertices (A, B, and C for triangle 1 and A, D, and C for triangle 2). You'll send A and C down the pipeline twice, performing the same

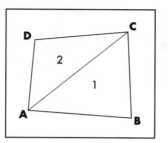

Figure 4.3

Two polygons with shared vertices.

geometrical operations on them each time. Obviously, this is wasteful; compounding this, you can have vertices shared by many triangles in more complex models. If you can cut down the number of times you're transforming each vertex, you can improve performance, which is always good.

One way you can do this is by using triangle strips. Simply call glBegin() with GL_TRIANGLE_STRIP, followed by a series of vertices. OpenGL handles this by drawing the first three vertices as a single triangle; after that, it takes every vertex specified and combines it with the previous two vertices to create another triangle. This means that after the first triangle, each additional triangle only costs a single vertex. In general, every set of n triangles you can reduce to a triangle strip reduces the number of vertices from $3n$ to $n + 2$.

Triangle fans are a similar concept; you can visualize them as a series of triangles around a single central vertex. You draw fans by calling glBegin() with GL_TRIANGLE_FAN. The first vertex specified is the central vertex, and every following adjacent pair of vertices is combined with the center vertex to create a new polygon. Like strips, fans allow you to draw n triangles while specifying only $n + 2$ vertices. However, the number of triangles that can be represented as a single fan is usually considerably fewer than the number that can be represented as a strip because in most cases, any given vertex won't be shared by a huge number of triangles.

The challenge with either method is in identifying strips and fans, which is relatively easy with simple models but becomes increasingly difficult as the complexity of your models grows. Doing so effectively is beyond the scope of our current discussion. Besides, you won't be using strips or fans very much because later, as performance becomes more of an issue, we'll introduce meshes as a means of avoiding repeated transformation of shared vertices.

Quadrilaterals

Quadrilaterals, or quads, can be convenient when you want to draw a square or rectangle. You create them by calling glBegin() with GL_QUADS, and then specifying four or more vertices. Like triangles, you can draw as many quads as you want at a time.

OpenGL provides quad strips as a means of improving the speed of rendering quads. They are specified using GL_QUAD_STRIP. Each pair of vertices specified after the first pair defines a new quad.

Polygons

OpenGL also supports polygons with an arbitrary number of vertices, but in such cases, only one polygon can be drawn within a glBegin()/glEnd() block. The parameter passed is GL_POLYGON (notice that it's not plural), and once glEnd() is reached, the last vertex will automatically be connected to the first. If fewer than three vertices are specified, nothing is drawn.

Using Primitives

Well, we've presented all the primitive types supported by OpenGL and some code snippets for handling them, and even covered some ways in which you can modify how the primitives are rendered. It's time to pull everything together and see it all in action. The demo application for this chapter, shown in Figure 4.4, displays most of the primitive types we've covered. You can use the keyboard to change the type of primitive being drawn and to change the way in which it's being drawn. The commands available to you are listed in Table 4.3.

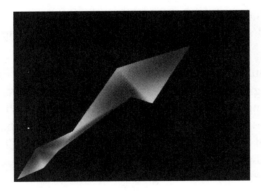

Figure 4.4

A triangle strip being displayed in the example program.

Table 4.3 Demo Controls

Key	Action	Key	Action
1	Draw points	6	Draw quads
2	Draw lines	7	Draw a polygon
3	Draw triangles	A	Toggle antialiasing
4	Draw a triangle strip	S	Toggle stippling
5	Draw a triangle fan	P	Rotate through polygon modes

Spend some time looking at and modifying the source code for this demo on the CD to be sure you're comfortable with it. You'll be using primitives in every application from here on out, so you'd better understand them well!

SUMMARY

In this chapter, you learned a little more about the OpenGL state machine. You know how to use `glGet()` and `glIsEnabled()` to query the values of parameters within the state machine. You've also seen some specialized functions for altering the state machine, and you should now have an idea of how it works. You'll be looking at other aspects of the state machine as you move on.

You also learned about the primitive types supported by OpenGL and how to modify properties pertaining to them. You should now have no trouble putting points, lines, triangles, and other primitives on the screen. Now that you have state machine basics and primitives under your belt, you can safely move on to more interesting things.

CHAPTER 5

COORDINATE TRANSFORMATIONS AND OPENGL MATRICES

N ow it's time to take a short break from learning how to *create* objects in the world, and focus on learning how to *move* the objects around the world. This is a vital ingredient to generating realistic 3D gaming worlds; without it, the 3D scenes you create would be static, boring, and totally non-interactive. OpenGL makes it easy for the programmer to move objects around through the use of various *coordinate transformations*, discussed in this chapter. You will also take a look at how to use your own matrices with OpenGL, which is a feature that is often used to create special-effect transformations on objects.

In this chapter, you'll learn the following:

- The basics of coordinate transformations
- The camera and viewing transformations
- OpenGL matrices and matrix stacks
- Projections
- Using your own matrices with OpenGL

Understanding Coordinate Transformations

Transformations allow us to move, rotate, and manipulate entities in a 3D world. One use of transformations is the capability to project 3D coordinates on a 2D screen. Another use was discussed in Chapter 3, "An Overview of 3D Graphics Theory," which covered the theory side of translate, rotate, and scale. Although it may seem that these transformations modify the objects directly, in reality, they modify the coordinate systems of the objects being transformed. For example, when you rotate a model's coordinate system, the model will appear to be rotated when it is drawn. Similarly, when you translate a model from the origin to a point 100 units away, the model will appear to be 100 units away from the camera when it is drawn.

When rendering 3D scenes, vertices pass through three types of transformations before they are finally rendered on the screen:

- **Viewing transformation.** Specifies the location of the camera.
- **Modeling transformation.** Moves objects around the scene.
- **Projection transformation.** Defines the viewing volume and clipping planes.

There is an additional transformation called the viewport transformation, which maps the two-dimensional projection of the scene into the window on your screen. You don't count the viewport transformation as a transformation that the vertices pass through because it relates strictly to the rendering window. Additionally, there is one other transformation that we will discuss: the modelview transformation. It can be considered a combination of the viewing and modeling transformation. Table 5.1 shows a summary of all these transformations.

Table 5.1 OpenGL Transformations

Transformation	Description
Viewing	Specifies the location of the camera
Modeling	Handles moving objects around the scene
Projection	Defines the viewing volume and clipping planes
Viewport	Maps the 2D projection of the scene into the rendering window
Modelview	Combination of the viewing and modeling transformations

When you are actually implementing these transformations, they must be executed in a specific order. The viewing transformations must execute before the modeling transformations; however, the projection and viewport transformations can be executed at any point before rendering. Figure 5.1 shows the general order that these vertex transformations are executed.

The Camera and Eye Coordinates

One of the most critical concepts to transformations and viewing in OpenGL is the concept of the *camera,* or *eye, coordinates.* Eye coordinates come strictly from the Cartesian coordinate system applied to the camera. In OpenGL, the default camera always looks down the negative z axis, as shown in Figure 5.2.

Eye coordinates remain the same no matter what transformations have been applied to them. For example, when rotating an object, you are in effect rotating the coordinate system of the object with respect to the eye's coordinate system. If you were to rotate a triangle 45 degrees counterclockwise, you would be transforming the triangle's coordinate system by 45 degrees counterclockwise. Figure 5.3 shows this transformation.

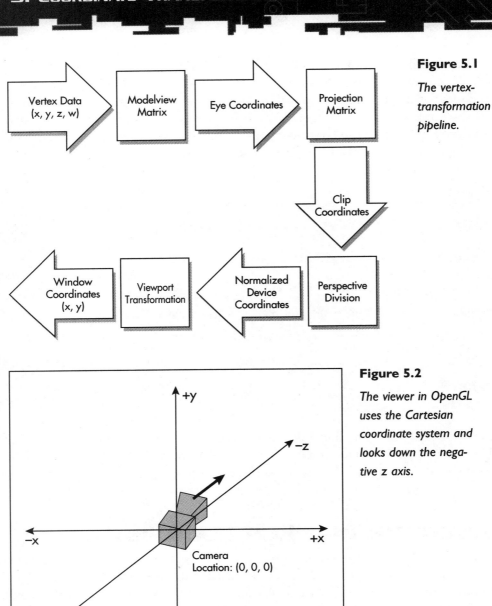

Figure 5.1

The vertex-transformation pipeline.

Figure 5.2

The viewer in OpenGL uses the Cartesian coordinate system and looks down the negative z axis.

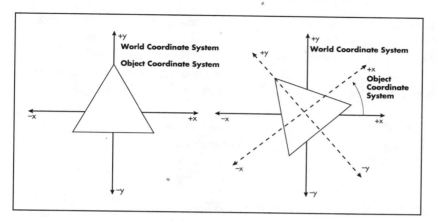

Figure 5.3

Rotating a triangle actually rotates its coordinate system with respect to eye coordinates.

Understanding eye coordinates is essential to understanding OpenGL transformations. We'll be taking a look at how you can modify the current coordinates to transform objects all over your 3D world.

Viewing Transformations

The viewing transformation is the first transformation applied to the scene and is used to position and aim the camera. As already stated, the camera's default orientation is to point down the negative z axis while positioned at the origin (0,0,0). You can move and change the camera's orientation through translation and rotation commands, which in effect manipulate the viewing transformation.

Remember that the viewing transformation must be completed before any other transformations. This is because it moves the current coordinate system with respect to the eye-coordinate system. Any other transformations that you do are based on the modified current coordinate system.

So how do you create the viewing transformation? Well, first you need to clear the *current matrix*. You accomplish this through the glLoadIdentity() command, specified as

```
void glLoadIdentity(void);
```

This sets the current matrix equal to the identity matrix and is necessary because most transformation commands manipulate the current matrix and set it to their own values. This can cause unexpected results, so you need to remember to clear the matrix.

After initializing the current matrix, you can create the viewing matrix in several different ways. One way is to just set the viewing matrix equal to the identity matrix. This will result in the default location and orientation of the camera, which would be at the origin and looking down the negative z axis. Other ways include the following:

- Using the `gluLookAt()` function to specify a line of sight that extends from the camera. This is a function that encapsulates a set of translation and rotation commands.
- Using the translation and rotation modeling commands `glTranslate*()` and `glRotate*()`. These commands are discussed in more detail later in this chapter; for now, suffice it to say that this method moves the objects in the world relative to a stationary camera.
- Creating your own routines that use the translation and rotation routines for your own coordinate system (for example, polar coordinates for a camera orbiting around an object).

Using the gluLookAt() Function

Because we have not yet talked about the modeling transformations, let's take a look at the `gluLookAt()` function, defined as

```
void gluLookAt(GLdouble eyex, GLdouble eyey, GLdouble eyez, GLdouble centerx, GLdouble centery, GLdouble centerz, GLdouble upx, GLdouble upy, GLdouble upz);
```

You can use this function to define the camera's location and orientation. The first set of three parameters (*eyex, eyey, eyez*) specifies the location of the camera. The value (0,0,0) would naturally specify the origin. The next set of parameters (*centerx, centery, centerz*) specifies where the camera is pointing, also called the *line of sight*. This typically specifies a point somewhere in the middle of the scene that is currently being examined. The last set of parameters (*upx, upy, upz*) is a vector that tells which direction is up. Figure 5.4 shows how all of these parameters work on the camera with the `gluLookAt()` function.

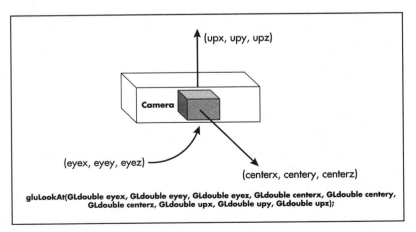

Figure 5.4

The `gluLookAt()` *parameters specify the location and orientation of the camera.*

Here is a short code snippet that uses the gluLookAt() function. Don't worry about any code you don't understand yet. You will get to it at some point. In any case, here is the code:

```
void DisplayScene()
{
    glClear(GL_COLOR_BUFFER_BIT);        // clear the color buffer
    glColor3f(1.0f, 0.0f, 0.0f);         // set color to red
    glLoadIdentity();                    // clear the current matrix

    // Now we set the viewing transformation with the gluLookAt() function.
    // This sets the camera at the position (0,0,10) and looking down the
    // negative z axis (0.0, 0.0, -100.0).
    // (eyex, eyey, eyez) = (0.0, 0.0, 10.0)
    // (centerx, centery, centerz) = (0.0, 0.0, -100.0)
    // (upx, upy, upz) = (0.0, 1.0, 0.0)
    gluLookAt(0.0f, 0.0f, 10.0f, 0.0f, 0.0f, -100.0f, 0.0f, 1.0f, 0.0f);

    // draw a triangle at the origin
    glBegin(GL_TRIANGLE);
        glVertexf(10.0f, 0.0f, 0.0f);
        glVertexf(0.0f, 10.0f, 0.0f);
        glVertexf(-10.0f, 0.0f, 0.0f);
    glEnd();

    // flush the buffer
    glFlush();
}
```

As you can see, the gluLookAt() function is rather easy to use. By manipulating the parameters, you can move the camera to any position and orientation that you want.

Using the glRotate*() and glTranslate*() Functions

A drawback to the gluLookAt() function, however, is that you must link the GLU library with your application. What if you don't want to use the GLU library? Well, one solution is to simply use the glRotate*() and glTranslate*() modeling-transformation functions. These functions modify the location of the objects in the world relative to a stationary camera. So rather than move the actual camera coordinates, you move the entire world around the camera. If you do not already understand the modeling-transformation functions, you might want to skip ahead to that section before looking at the following code. This code uses the modeling functions to produce the same effect on the camera as the gluLookAt() code.

```
void DisplayScene()
{
     glClear(GL_COLOR_BUFFER_BIT);        // clear the color buffer
     glColor3f(1.0f, 0.0f, 0.0f);         // set color to red
     glLoadIdentity();                    // clear the current matrix

     // Now we set the viewing transformation with the glTranslatef() function.
     // We move the modeling transformation to (0.0, 0.0, -10.0), which effectively
     // moves the camera to the position (0.0, 0.0, 10.0).
     glTranslatef(0.0f, 0.0f, -10.0f);

     // draw a triangle at the origin
     glBegin(GL_TRIANGLE);
         glVertexf(10.0f, 0.0f, 0.0f);
         glVertexf(0.0f, 10.0f, 0.0f);
           glVertexf(-10.0f, 0.0f, 0.0f);
     glEnd();

     // flush the buffer
     glFlush();
}
```

In this case, there isn't a serious difference in code from the gluLookAt() function because all you are doing is moving the camera along the z axis. But if you were orienting the camera at an odd angle, you would need to use the glRotate() function as well, which leads to the next way of manipulating the camera: your own custom routines.

Creating Your Own Custom Routines

Suppose you want to create your own flight simulator. In a typical flight simulator, the camera is positioned in the pilot's seat, so it moves and is oriented in the same manner as the plane. Plane orientation is defined by pitch, yaw, and roll, which are rotation angles relative to the center of gravity of the plane (in your case, the pilot/camera position). Using the modeling-transformation functions, you could create the following function to create the viewing transformation:

```
void PlaneView(GLfloat planeX, GLfloat planeY, glFloat planeZ, // the plane's position
               GLfloat roll, GLfloat pitch, GLfloat yaw)         // orientation
{
     // roll is rotation about the z axis
     glRotatef(roll, 0.0f, 0.0f, 1.0f);
```

```
    // yaw, or heading, is rotation about the y axis
    glRotatef(yaw, 0.0f, 1.0f, 0.0f);

    // pitch is rotation about the x axis
    glRotatef(pitch, 1.0f, 0.0f, 0.0f);

    // move the plane to the plane's world coordinates
    glTranslatef(-planeX, -planeY, -planeZ);
}
```

Using this function would place the camera in the pilot's seat of your airplane regardless of the orientation or location of the plane. This is just one of the uses of your own customized routines. Other uses include applications of polar coordinates, such as rotation about a fixed point and use of the modeling-transformation functions to create what is called "*Quake*-like movement," where the mouse and keyboard can be used to control the camera.

Modeling Transformations

The modeling transformations allow you to manipulate the position and set the orientation of a model by moving, rotating, and scaling it. You can perform these operations one at a time or as a combination of events. Figure 5.5 illustrates the three operations that you can use on objects:

- **Translation.** This operation is the act of moving an object along a specified axis.
- **Rotation.** This is where an object is rotated about one of the axes.
- **Scaling.** This is when you increase or decrease the size of an object. With scaling, you can specify different values for different axes. This gives you the ability to stretch and shrink objects non-uniformly.

The order that you specify modeling transformations is very important to the final rendition of your scene. For example, as shown in Figure 5.6, rotating and then translating an object has a completely different effect than translating and then rotating the object. Let's say you have an arrow located at the origin, and the first transformation you apply is a rotation of 30 degrees around the z axis. You then apply a translation transformation of 5 units along the x axis. The final position of the triangle would be (5, 4.33) with the arrow pointing at a 30-degree angle from the positive x axis. Now, let's say you translate the arrow by 5 units along the x axis instead of rotating it first. After the translation, the arrow would be located at (5,0). When you apply the rotation transformation, the arrow would still be located at (5,0), but it would be pointing at a 30-degree angle from the x axis.

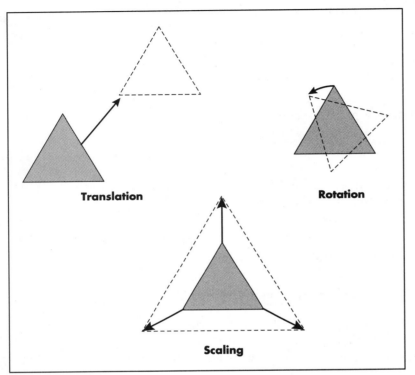

Figure 5.5

The three modeling transformations.

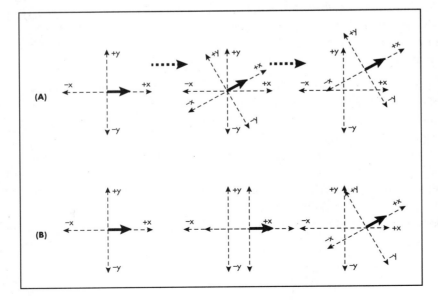

Figure 5.6

(a) Performing rotation before translation; (b) Performing translation before rotation.

Projection Transformations

The projection transformation defines the viewing volume and clipping planes. It is performed after the modelview transformation, which we have not yet covered in detail. You can think of the projection transformation as determining which objects belong in the viewing volume and how they should look. It is very much like choosing a camera lens that is used to look into the world. The field of view you choose when creating the projection transformation determines what type of lens you have. For instance, a wider field of view would be like having a wide-angle lens, where you could see a huge area of the scene without much detail. With a smaller field of view, which would be similar to a telephoto lens, you would be able to look at objects as though they were closer to you than they actually are.

OpenGL offers two types of projections:

- **Perspective projection.** This type of projection shows 3D worlds exactly how you see things in real life. With perspective projection, objects that are farther away appear smaller than objects that are closer to the camera.
- **Orthographic projection.** This type of projection shows objects on the screen in their true size, regardless of their distance from the camera. This projection is useful for CAD software, where objects are drawn with specific views to show the dimensions of an object.

The Viewport Transformation

The last transformation is the *viewport transformation*. This transformation maps the two-dimensional scene created by the perspective transformation onto your window's rendering surface. You can think of the viewport transformation as determining whether the final image should be enlarged or shrunk, depending on the size of the rendering surface.

OPENGL AND MATRICES

Now that you've learned about the various transformations involved in OpenGL, let's take a look at how you actually use them. Transformations in OpenGL rely on the *matrix* for all mathematical computations. As you will soon see, OpenGL has what is called the *matrix stack*, which is useful for constructing complicated models composed of many simple objects. You will be taking a look at each of the transformations and look more into the matrix stack in this section.

The Modelview Matrix

The modelview matrix defines the coordinate system that is being used to place and orient objects. It is a 4×4 matrix that is multiplied by vertices and transformations to create a new matrix that reflects the result of any transformations that have been applied to the vertices.

You can specify that you want to modify the modelview matrix through the OpenGL command glMatrixMode(), which is defined as

```
void glMatrixMode(GLenum mode);
```

Before calling any transformation commands, you must specify whether you want to modify the modelview matrix or the projection matrix. In order to modify the modelview matrix, you use the argument GL_MODELVIEW. This will set the modelview matrix to the current matrix, which means that it can be modified with subsequent transformation commands. Doing this would look like

```
void glMatrixMode(GL_MODELVIEW);
```

Other arguments for glMatrixMode include GL_PROJECTION and GL_TEXTURE. GL_PROJECTION is used to specify the projection matrix, and GL_TEXTURE is used to indicate the texture matrix, which we will discuss in Chapter 8, "Texture Mapping."

In most cases, you will want to reset the modelview matrix after you set it to the current matrix. To do this, you call the glLoadIdentity() function, discussed earlier. Calling this function will set the modelview matrix equal to the identity matrix and reset the current coordinate system to the origin. Here's a snippet of how you would reset the modelview matrix:

```
// ...
glMatrixMode(GL_MODELVIEW);
glLoadIdentity();                    // reset the modelview matrix

// ... do transformations

glBegin(GL_POINTS);
    glVertex3f(0.0f, 0.0f, 0.0f);
glEnd();

// ... continue with program
```

Translation

Translation allows you to move an object from one place to another in the 3D world. You can accomplish this with OpenGL using the functions glTranslatef() and glTranslated(), which are defined as follows:

```
void glTranslatef(GLfloat x, GLfloat y, GLfloat z);
void glTranslated(GLdouble x, GLdouble y, GLdouble z);
```

The only difference between these two functions is their parameter types. You pass float parameters to glTranslatef() and double parameters to glTranslated(). Which one you decide to use depends on the level of precision you desire.

The parameters x, y, and z specify the amount to translate along the x, y, and z axes. For example, if you execute the command

```
glTranslatef(3.0f, 1.0f, 8.0f);
```

your object will move three units along the positive x axis, one unit along the positive y axis, and eight units along the positive z axis.

Suppose you want to move a cube from the origin to the position (5, 5, 5). You first load the modelview matrix and reset it to the identity matrix. Then you translate the current matrix to the position (5,5,5) before calling your DrawCube() function. In code, this looks like

```
glMatrixMode(GL_MODELVIEW);       // set current matrix to modelview
glLoadIdentity();                 // reset modelview to identity matrix
glTranslatef(5.0f, 5.0f, 5.0f);   // move to (5,5,5)
DrawCube();                       // draw the cube
```

Figure 5.7 illustrates how this code executes.

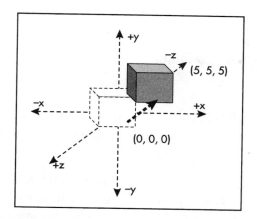

Figure 5.7

Translating a cube from the origin to (5,5,5).

Rotation

Rotation in OpenGL is accomplished through the glRotate*() function, which is defined as

```
void glRotatef(GLfloat angle, GLfloat x, GLfloat y, GLfloat z);
void glRotated(GLdouble angle, GLdouble x, GLdouble y, GLdouble z);
```

Again, you can use either doubles or floats for your parameters. With this function, you are performing a rotation around the vector specified by the x, y, and z parameters. The angle of rotation is specified by *angle* and is measured in degrees in the counterclockwise direction.

For example, if you wanted to rotate around the y axis 135 degrees in the counterclockwise direction, you would use the following code:

```
glRotatef(135.0f, 0.0f, 1.0f, 0.0f);
```

The value of 1.0f for the y argument specifies a unit vector pointing in the direction of the y axis. When doing the rotation, you only need to specify unit vectors to rotate about the axis you desire. Figure 5.8 illustrates how the glRotate*() function works.

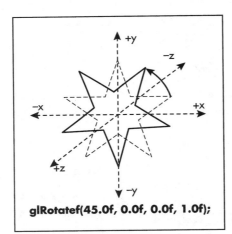

glRotatef(45.0f, 0.0f, 0.0f, 1.0f);

Figure 5.8

The glRotate*() *function takes the angle of rotation and a unit vector for the axis of rotation as parameters.*

If you wanted to rotate clockwise, you would set the angle of rotation as a negative number. To rotate around the y axis 135 degrees in the clockwise direction, you use the following code:

```
glRotatef(-135.0f, 0.0f, 1.0f, 0.0f);
```

What if you wanted to rotate around an arbitrary axis? You can accomplish this by specifying the arbitrary axis vector in the x, y, and z parameters. By drawing a line from the origin to the point represented by (x,y,z), you can see the arbitrary axis around which you will rotate. For instance, if you rotate 90 degrees about the axis specified by the vector (1,1,0), you rotate about the axis that goes from the origin to the point (1,1,0). In code, this looks like the following:

```
glRotatef(90.0f, 1.0f, 1.0f, 0.0f);
```

Figure 5.9 illustrates how it works.

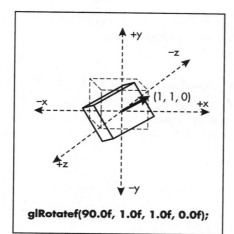

Figure 5.9

Rotation about an arbitrary axis.

glRotatef(90.0f, 1.0f, 1.0f, 0.0f);

And now a quick snippet of code that rotates a cube 60 degrees along the x axis and 45 degrees along the y axis:

```
glMatrixMode(GL_MODELVIEW);              // set matrix to modelview and reset
glLoadIdentity();

glRotatef(60.0f, 1.0f, 0.0f, 0.0f);      // rotate 60 degrees around x axis
glRotatef(45.0f, 0.0f, 1.0f, 0.0f);      // rotate 45 degrees around y axis
DrawCube();                              // draw the cube
```

Scaling

Scaling is when you increase or decrease the size of an object. Vertices of an object are expanded or shrunk along the three axes depending on the scaling factor for each axis. You perform scaling through the OpenGL function glScale*(), which is defined as

```
void glScalef(GLfloat x, GLfloat y, GLfloat z);
void glScaled(GLdouble x, GLdouble y, GLdouble z);
```

The values passed to the *x*, *y*, and *z* parameters specify the scale factor along each axis. For example, the following line doubles the current size of an object:

```
glScalef(2.0f, 2.0f, 2.0f);
```

Now, let's say you had a cube, and you wanted to double its width (the x axis) without changing its height (the y axis) and depth (the z axis). You would use the following:

```
glScalef(2.0f, 1.0f, 1.0f);
```

What if you wanted to shrink an object? Well, because the scaling factors are each multiplied by the vertices, you simply choose a value less than one, like this:

```
glScalef(0.5f, 0.5f, 0.5f);
```

This line will shrink an object by half its original size. A value of 0.2 would shrink it by one-fifth, 0.1 by one-tenth, and so on. Now, if you set a scaling factor to 1.0, then the axis it belongs to will not be scaled. This is equivalent to multiplying a number by 1.0. Otherwise, values less than 1.0 will shrink the object, and values greater than 1.0 will enlarge the object. Figure 5.10 illustrates the glScale*() function.

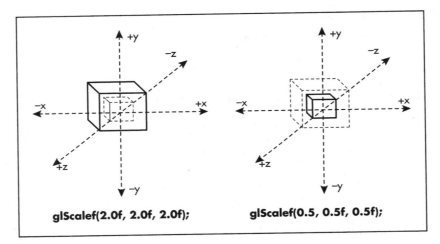

Figure 5.10

The glScale() function.*

Here is some code that will double the size of a cube:

```
glMatrixMode(GL_MODELVIEW);          // set matrix to modelview and reset
glLoadIdentity();

glScalef(2.0f, 2.0f, 2.0f);          // double the size
DrawCube();                          // draw the cube
```

Matrix Stacks

The modelview matrix we've been playing with so far is actually only the top of a stack of matrices, which is naturally called the OpenGL matrix stack. There are three types of matrix stacks in OpenGL:

- The modelview matrix stack
- The projection matrix stack
- The texture matrix stack

The modelview matrix is actually the top of the modelview matrix stack, and as you will see, the projection matrix is the top of the projection matrix stack. Figure 5.11 gives some more information about these matrix stacks. The texture matrix stack is used for the transformation of coordinates.

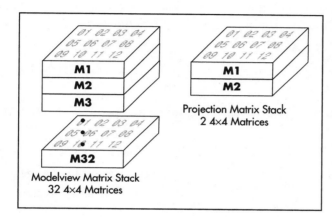

Figure 5.11

The modelview and projection matrix stacks are made up of 32 4×4 matrices and two 4×4 matrices, respectively, for the Microsoft OpenGL implementation.

The modelview matrix stack is used to construct complicated models out of more-simple ones. For example, consider how a robot might be built out of boxes. If you divide the robot into individual components, you have the torso, two arms, one head, and two legs. So in our program, we'd have a function to draw the torso, a function for one arm, a function for the head, and one for the legs. Each of these functions draws its respective component centered around the origin and at a normal orientation.

When you draw the robot, you would first draw the torso. Then, to draw the left arm, you would call the arm-drawing routine after translating to the position of the left arm relative to the torso. To draw the right arm, you would translate to the position of the right arm, again relative to the torso. Likewise, the legs and head would be drawn in their respective positions relative to the torso.

Matrix stacks provide this type of functionality in OpenGL. You can move object *A* relative to object *B*'s origin, draw object *A* around its own origin, and then throw away the whole transformation so you are again relative to object *B*'s origin. Two stack operations make this possible: glPushMatrix() and glPopMatrix().

The glPushMatrix() function copies the current matrix and places it as the second matrix in the stack after pushing all the other matrices in the current stack down one level. Using this function is like telling OpenGL to remember the current position in the world for a few moments while you visit another portion of the world. glPushMatrix() is defined as

```
void glPushMatrix(void);
```

If you push too many matrices onto the stack, then OpenGL gives a GL_STACK_OVERFLOW error.

The glPopMatrix() function discards the top matrix on the stack, destroying its contents, and places the second matrix at the top of the stack. All other matrices in the stack are moved up one. Using this function is like telling OpenGL to take you back to your original position after you've been visiting another portion of the world. glPopMatrix() is defined as

```
void glPopMatrix(void);
```

If you try to use this function when there is only one matrix in the stack, OpenGL will give a GL_STACK_UNDERFLOW error.

Figure 5.12 shows how the glPushMatrix() and glPopMatrix() functions operate on the matrix stack.

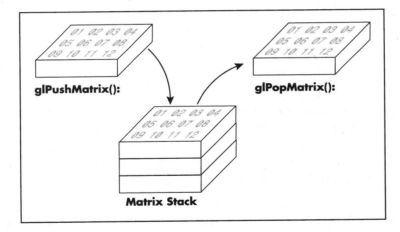

glPushMatrix():

glPopMatrix():

Matrix Stack

Figure 5.12

Pushing and popping on the matrix stack.

The Robot Example

Let's take a break and look at an example that uses everything we've talked about so far in this chapter. The source code on the following pages is for a small OpenGL demo that shows a walking robot around which the camera rotates. The robot is constructed of cubes that you scale to different shapes and sizes to give it the arms, legs, torso, and head. Take special note of how you use the glPushMatrix() and glPopMatrix() functions to place and move the robot.

Without further ado, here is the code:

```
#define WIN32_LEAN_AND_MEAN                 // trim the excess fat from Windows

////// Includes
#include <windows.h>                        // standard Windows app include
#include <gl/gl.h>                          // standard OpenGL include
#include <gl/glu.h>                         // OpenGL utilities
#include <gl/glaux.h>                       // OpenGL auxiliary functions

////// Global Variables
float angle = 0.0f;                         // current angle of the camera
HDC g_HDC;                                  // global device context
bool fullScreen = false;

////// Robot Variables
float legAngle[2] = { 0.0f, 0.0f };    // each leg's current angle
float armAngle[2] = { 0.0f, 0.0f };    // each arm's current angle

// DrawCube
// desc: since each component of the robot is made up of
//       cubes, we will use a single function that will
//       draw a cube at a specified location.
void DrawCube(float xPos, float yPos, float zPos)
{
    glPushMatrix();
        glTranslatef(xPos, yPos, zPos);
        glBegin(GL_POLYGON);
            glVertex3f(0.0f, 0.0f, 0.0f);  // top face
            glVertex3f(0.0f, 0.0f, -1.0f);
            glVertex3f(-1.0f, 0.0f, -1.0f);
            glVertex3f(-1.0f, 0.0f, 0.0f);
            glVertex3f(0.0f, 0.0f, 0.0f);  // front face
            glVertex3f(-1.0f, 0.0f, 0.0f);
            glVertex3f(-1.0f, -1.0f, 0.0f);
            glVertex3f(0.0f, -1.0f, 0.0f);
            glVertex3f(0.0f, 0.0f, 0.0f);   // right face
            glVertex3f(0.0f, -1.0f, 0.0f);
            glVertex3f(0.0f, -1.0f, -1.0f);
            glVertex3f(0.0f, 0.0f, -1.0f);
            glVertex3f(-1.0f, 0.0f, 0.0f);  // left face
            glVertex3f(-1.0f, 0.0f, -1.0f);
            glVertex3f(-1.0f, -1.0f, -1.0f);
```

```
                        glVertex3f(-1.0f, -1.0f, 0.0f);
                        glVertex3f(0.0f, 0.0f, 0.0f);   // bottom face
                        glVertex3f(0.0f, -1.0f, -1.0f);
                        glVertex3f(-1.0f, -1.0f, -1.0f);
                        glVertex3f(-1.0f, -1.0f, 0.0f);
                        glVertex3f(0.0f, 0.0f, 0.0f);   // back face
                        glVertex3f(-1.0f, 0.0f, -1.0f);
                        glVertex3f(-1.0f, -1.0f, -1.0f);
                        glVertex3f(0.0f, -1.0f, -1.0f);
                glEnd();
        glPopMatrix();
}


// DrawArm
// desc: draws one arm
void DrawArm(float xPos, float yPos, float zPos)
{
        glPushMatrix();
                glColor3f(1.0f, 0.0f, 0.0f);        // red
                glTranslatef(xPos, yPos, zPos);
                glScalef(1.0f, 4.0f, 1.0f);         // arm is a 1x4x1 cube
                DrawCube(0.0f, 0.0f, 0.0f);
        glPopMatrix();
}


// DrawHead
// desc: draws the robot head
void DrawHead(float xPos, float yPos, float zPos)
{
        glPushMatrix();
                glColor3f(1.0f, 1.0f, 1.0f);        // white
                glTranslatef(xPos, yPos, zPos);
                glScalef(2.0f, 2.0f, 2.0f);         // head is a 2x2x2 cube
                DrawCube(0.0f, 0.0f, 0.0f);
        glPopMatrix();
}


// DrawTorso
// desc: draws the robot torso
void DrawTorso(float xPos, float yPos, float zPos)
```

```
{
    glPushMatrix();
        glColor3f(0.0f, 0.0f, 1.0f);      // blue
        glTranslatef(xPos, yPos, zPos);
        glScalef(3.0f, 5.0f, 2.0f);       // torso is a 3x5x2 cube
        DrawCube(0.0f, 0.0f, 0.0f);
    glPopMatrix();
}


// DrawLeg
// desc: draws a single leg
void DrawLeg(float xPos, float yPos, float zPos)
{
    glPushMatrix();
        glColor3f(1.0f, 1.0f, 0.0f);      // yellow
        glTranslatef(xPos, yPos, zPos);
        glScalef(1.0f, 5.0f, 1.0f);       // leg is a 1x5x1 cube
        DrawCube(0.0f, 0.0f, 0.0f);
    glPopMatrix();
}


// DrawRobot
// desc: draws the robot located at (xPos,yPos,zPos)
void DrawRobot(float xPos, float yPos, float zPos)
{
    static bool leg1 = true;          // robot's leg states
    static bool leg2 = false;          // true = forward, false = back

    static bool arm1 = true;
    static bool arm2 = false;

    glPushMatrix();

        glTranslatef(xPos, yPos, zPos);      // draw robot at desired coordinates

        // draw components
        DrawHead(1.0f, 2.0f, 0.0f);
        DrawTorso(1.5f, 0.0f, 0.0f);
        glPushMatrix();
```

```
            // if leg is moving forward, increase angle, else decrease angle
            if (arm1)
                armAngle[0] = armAngle[0] + 1.0f;
            else
                armAngle[0] = armAngle[0] - 1.0f;

            // once leg has reached its maximum angle in a direction,
            // reverse it
            if (armAngle[0] >= 15.0f)
                arm1 = false;
            if (armAngle[0] <= -15.0f)
                arm1 = true;

            // move the leg away from the torso and rotate it to give
            //"walking" effect
            glTranslatef(0.0f, -0.5f, 0.0f);
            glRotatef(armAngle[0], 1.0f, 0.0f, 0.0f);
            DrawArm(2.5f, 0.0f, -0.5f);
    glPopMatrix();

    glPushMatrix();
            // if leg is moving forward, increase angle, else decrease angle
            if (arm2)
                armAngle[1] = armAngle[1] + 1.0f;
            else
                armAngle[1] = armAngle[1] - 1.0f;

            // once leg has reached its maximum angle in a direction,
            // reverse it
            if (armAngle[1] >= 15.0f)
                arm2 = false;
            if (armAngle[1] <= -15.0f)
                arm2 = true;

            // move the leg away from the torso and rotate it to give
            //"walking" effect
            glTranslatef(0.0f, -0.5f, 0.0f);
            glRotatef(armAngle[1], 1.0f, 0.0f, 0.0f);
            DrawArm(-1.5f, 0.0f, -0.5f);
    glPopMatrix();
```

```
// we want to rotate the legs relative to the robot's position in the
//world. this is leg 1, the robot's right leg
glPushMatrix();

    // if leg is moving forward, increase angle, else decrease angle
    if (leg1)
        legAngle[0] = legAngle[0] + 1.0f;
    else
        legAngle[0] = legAngle[0] - 1.0f;

    // once leg has reached its maximum angle in a direction,
    // reverse it
    if (legAngle[0] >= 15.0f)
        leg1 = false;
    if (legAngle[0] <= -15.0f)
        leg1 = true;

    // move the leg away from the torso and rotate it to give
    //"walking" effect
    glTranslatef(0.0f, -0.5f, 0.0f);
    glRotatef(legAngle[0], 1.0f, 0.0f, 0.0f);

    // draw the leg
    DrawLeg(-0.5f, -5.0f, -0.5f);

    glPopMatrix();

    // do the same as above with leg 2, the robot's left leg
    glPushMatrix();

    if (leg2)
        legAngle[1] = legAngle[1] + 1.0f;
    else
        legAngle[1] = legAngle[1] - 1.0f;

    if (legAngle[1] >= 15.0f)
        leg2 = false;
    if (legAngle[1] <= -15.0f)
        leg2 = true;
```

```
                glTranslatef(0.0f, -0.5f, 0.0f);
                glRotatef(legAngle[1], 1.0f, 0.0f, 0.0f);
                DrawLeg(1.5f, -5.0f, -0.5f);

            glPopMatrix();
        glPopMatrix();
}


// Render
// desc: handles drawing of scene
void Render()
{
    glEnable(GL_DEPTH_TEST);                        // enable depth testing

    // do rendering here
    glClearColor(0.0f, 0.0f, 0.0f, 0.0f);           // clear to black
    glClear(GL_COLOR_BUFFER_BIT | GL_DEPTH_BUFFER_BIT);  // clear color/depth buffer
    glLoadIdentity();                               // reset modelview matrix

    angle = angle + 1.0f;          // increase our rotation angle counter
    if (angle >= 360.0f)           // if we've gone in a circle, reset counter
        angle = 0.0f;

    glPushMatrix();                // put current matrix on stack
        glLoadIdentity();          // reset matrix
        glTranslatef(0.0f, 0.0f, -30.0f);    // move to (0, 0, -30)
        glRotatef(angle, 0.0f, 1.0f, 0.0f);  // rotate the robot on its y axis
        DrawRobot(0.0f, 0.0f, 0.0f);         // draw the robot
    glPopMatrix();                           // dispose of current matrix

    glFlush();
    SwapBuffers(g_HDC);            // bring back buffer to foreground
}

// function to set the pixel format for the device context
void SetupPixelFormat(HDC hDC)
{
    int nPixelFormat;                       // our pixel format index
```

```c
        static PIXELFORMATDESCRIPTOR pfd = {
            sizeof(PIXELFORMATDESCRIPTOR),  // size of structure
            1,                              // default version
            PFD_DRAW_TO_WINDOW |            // window-drawing support
            PFD_SUPPORT_OPENGL |            // OpenGL support
            PFD_DOUBLEBUFFER,               // double-buffering support
            PFD_TYPE_RGBA,                  // RGBA color mode
            32,                             // 32-bit color mode
            0, 0, 0, 0, 0, 0,               // ignore color bits, non-palletized mode
            0,                              // no alpha buffer
            0,                              // ignore shift bit
            0,                              // no accumulation buffer
            0, 0, 0, 0,                     // ignore accumulation bits
            16,                             // 16-bit z-buffer size
            0,                              // no stencil buffer
            0,                              // no auxiliary buffer
            PFD_MAIN_PLANE,                 // main drawing plane
            0,                              // reserved
            0, 0, 0 };                      // layer masks ignored

        // choose best-matching pixel format
        nPixelFormat = ChoosePixelFormat(hDC, &pfd);

        // set pixel format to device context
        SetPixelFormat(hDC, nPixelFormat, &pfd);
}

// the Windows Procedure event handler
LRESULT CALLBACK WndProc(HWND hwnd, UINT message, WPARAM wParam, LPARAM lParam)
{
        static HGLRC hRC;           // rendering context
        static HDC hDC;             // device context
        int width, height;          // window width and height

        switch(message)
        {
            case WM_CREATE:          // window is being created

                hDC = GetDC(hwnd);           // get current window's device context
                g_HDC = hDC;
                SetupPixelFormat(hDC);       // call our pixel format setup function
```

```
            // create rendering context and make it current
            hRC = wglCreateContext(hDC);
            wglMakeCurrent(hDC, hRC);

            return 0;
            break;

    case WM_CLOSE:              // Windows is closing

            // deselect rendering context and delete it
            wglMakeCurrent(hDC, NULL);
            wglDeleteContext(hRC);

            // send WM_QUIT to message queue
            PostQuitMessage(0);

            return 0;
            break;

    case WM_SIZE:
            height = HIWORD(lParam);         // retrieve width and height
            width = LOWORD(lParam);

            if (height==0)                   // don't want a divide by zero
            {
                height=1;
            }

            // reset the viewport to new dimensions
            glViewport(0, 0, width, height);
            glMatrixMode(GL_PROJECTION); // set projection matrix current matrix
            glLoadIdentity();               // reset projection matrix

            // calculate aspect ratio of window
            gluPerspective(54.0f,(GLfloat)width/(GLfloat)height,1.0f,1000.0f);

            glMatrixMode(GL_MODELVIEW);  // set modelview matrix
            glLoadIdentity();               // reset modelview matrix

            return 0;
            break;
```

```cpp
                default:
                    break;
        }

        return (DefWindowProc(hwnd, message, wParam, lParam));
}

// the main Windows entry point
int WINAPI WinMain(HINSTANCE hInstance, HINSTANCE hPrevInstance, LPSTR lpCmdLine,
                    int nShowCmd)
{
    WNDCLASSEX windowClass;            // windows class
    HWND        hwnd;                  // window handle
    MSG         msg;                   // message
    bool        done;                  // flag saying when our app is complete
    DWORD       dwExStyle;             // window extended style
    DWORD       dwStyle;               // window style
    RECT        windowRect;

    // screen/display attributes
    int width = 800;
    int height = 600;
    int bits = 32;

    windowRect.left=(long)0;           // set left value to 0
    windowRect.right=(long)width;      // set right value to requested width
    windowRect.top=(long)0;            // set top value to 0
    windowRect.bottom=(long)height;    // set bottom value to requested height

    // fill out the windows class structure
    windowClass.cbSize                 = sizeof(WNDCLASSEX);
    windowClass.style                  = CS_HREDRAW | CS_VREDRAW;
    windowClass.lpfnWndProc            = WndProc;
    windowClass.cbClsExtra             = 0;
    windowClass.cbWndExtra             = 0;
    windowClass.hInstance              = hInstance;
    windowClass.hIcon                  = LoadIcon(NULL, IDI_APPLICATION);
    windowClass.hCursor                = LoadCursor(NULL, IDC_ARROW);
    windowClass.hbrBackground          = NULL;
    windowClass.lpszMenuName           = NULL;
```

```
windowClass.lpszClassName          = "MyClass";
windowClass.hIconSm                = LoadIcon(NULL, IDI_WINLOGO);

// register the windows class
if (!RegisterClassEx(&windowClass))
    return 0;

if (fullScreen)         // full screen?
{
    DEVMODE dmScreenSettings;              // device mode
    memset(&dmScreenSettings,0,sizeof(dmScreenSettings));
    dmScreenSettings.dmSize = sizeof(dmScreenSettings);
    dmScreenSettings.dmPelsWidth = width;          // screen width
    dmScreenSettings.dmPelsHeight = height;        // screen height
    dmScreenSettings.dmBitsPerPel = bits;          // bits per pixel
    dmScreenSettings.dmFields=DM_BITSPERPEL|DM_PELSWIDTH|DM_PELSHEIGHT;

    if (ChangeDisplaySettings(&dmScreenSettings, CDS_FULLSCREEN) !=
                        DISP_CHANGE_SUCCESSFUL)
    {
        // setting display mode failed, switch to windowed
        MessageBox(NULL, "Display mode failed", NULL, MB_OK);
        fullScreen=FALSE;
    }
}

if (fullScreen)                       // are we still in full-screen mode?
{
    dwExStyle=WS_EX_APPWINDOW;        // window extended style
    dwStyle=WS_POPUP;                 // Windows style
    ShowCursor(FALSE);                // hide mouse pointer
}
else
{
    dwExStyle=WS_EX_APPWINDOW | WS_EX_WINDOWEDGE;  // window extended style
    dwStyle=WS_OVERLAPPEDWINDOW;                   // Windows style
}

AdjustWindowRectEx(&windowRect, dwStyle, FALSE, dwExStyle);
```

```
// class registered, so now create our window
hwnd = CreateWindowEx(NULL, "MyClass",          // class name
                      "OpenGL Robot",            // app name
                      dwStyle | WS_CLIPCHILDREN |
                      WS_CLIPSIBLINGS,
                      0, 0,                       // x,y coordinate
                      windowRect.right - windowRect.left,
                      windowRect.bottom - windowRect.top, // width, height
                      NULL,                       // handle to parent
                      NULL,                       // handle to menu
                      hInstance,                  // application instance
                      NULL);                      // no extra params

// check if window creation failed (hwnd would equal NULL)
if (!hwnd)
     return 0;

ShowWindow(hwnd, SW_SHOW);          // display the window
UpdateWindow(hwnd);                 // update the window

done = false;                       // initialize the loop condition variable

// main message loop
while (!done)
{
     PeekMessage(&msg, hwnd, NULL, NULL, PM_REMOVE);

     if (msg.message == WM_QUIT)     // do we receive a WM_QUIT message?
     {
          done = true;               // if so, time to quit the application
     }
     else
     {
          Render();
          TranslateMessage(&msg);
          DispatchMessage(&msg);
     }
}
```

```
    if (fullScreen)
    {
        ChangeDisplaySettings(NULL,0);        // if so switch back to the desktop
        ShowCursor(TRUE);                      // show mouse pointer
    }
    return msg.wParam;
}
```

Wow! That was a lot of code, but you're just now beginning to get into the fun stuff. If you trace through to the DrawRobot() function, you will see how you can build and animate a hierarchical model, which is obviously in this case a robot-like figure. Pay careful attention to how you use the glPushMatrix() and glPopMatrix() functions to place the robot's arms, legs, torso, and head relative to the robot's local coordinate system origin. You could get really fancy and add hands, feet, or other body parts by using the push/pop functions to place the other body parts relative to existing parts. We'll leave that as an exercise for when we get bored. In the meantime, Figure 5.13 shows a screenshot of the robot demo.

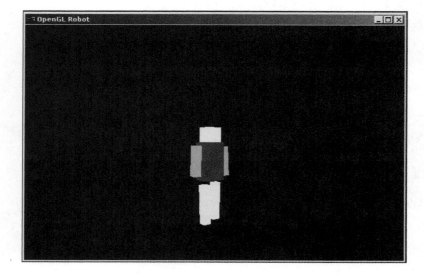

Figure 5.13

A screenshot of the OpenGL robot demo.

PROJECTIONS

We've mentioned projection transformations several times now, and even used it in code, so it's high time we discussed how they work. As we've pointed out, there are two general classes of projection transformations available in OpenGL: orthographic (or parallel) and perspective. We'll look at both of these in detail.

Setting a projection transformation creates a viewing volume, which serves two purposes. The first is that it specifies a number of clipping planes, which determine which portion of your 3D world is visible at any given time. Objects that are outside this volume are not transformed or rendered. The second purpose of the viewing volume is to determine how objects are drawn. This depends on the shape of the viewing volume, which is the primary difference between orthographic and perspective projections.

Before specifying any kind of projection transformation, though, you need to make sure that the projection matrix stack is currently selected. As with the modelview matrix, this is done with a call to glMatrixMode():

```
glMatrixMode(GL_PROJECTION);
```

In most cases, you'll want to follow this up with a call to glLoadIdentity() to clear out anything that may be stored in the matrix stack, so that previous transformations don't get accumulated. Unlike with the modelview matrix, it is very rare to make a lot of changes to the projection matrix.

Once the projection matrix stack is selected, you're ready to specify your projection. We'll look at orthographic projections first, and then at the more commonly used perspective transformations.

Orthographic

As we mentioned before, orthographic, or parallel, projections are those that involve no perspective correction. In other words, no adjustment for distance from the camera is made; objects appear the same size on screen whether they are close or far away. Although this may not look as realistic as perspective projections, it has a number of uses. Traditionally, orthographic projections are included in OpenGL for things like CAD.

NOTE

Although orthographic projections can be used for isometric games, this is rarely done in practice due to the fact that a higher level of detail can be obtained using conventional 2D methods. This could very well change in the future, however.

Orthographic projections can also be used for 2D games or for creating isometric games.

OpenGL provides the glOrtho() function to set up orthographic projections:

```
glOrtho(GLdouble left, GLdouble right, GLdouble bottom, GLdouble top, GLdouble near,
        GLdouble far);
```

left and *right* specify the x-coordinate clipping planes, *bottom* and *top* specify the y-coordinate clipping planes, and *near* and *far* specify the distance to the z-coordinate clipping planes. Together, these coordinates specify a box-shaped viewing volume. More precisely, opposite planes are parallel to each other, and adjacent planes are perpendicular.

Because orthographic projections are commonly used to create 2D scenes, the Utility Library provides an additional routine to set up orthographic projections for scenes in which you won't really be using the z coordinate:

```
gluOrtho2D(GLdouble left, GLdouble right, GLdouble bottom, GLdouble top);
```

`left`, `right`, `bottom`, and `top` are as with `glOrtho()` above. Using `gluOrtho2D` is equivalent to calling `glOrtho()` with near set to `-1.0` and far set to `1.0`. When using `gluOrtho2D()`, you'll normally want to use a version of `glVertex()` that takes only two parameters (the x and y coordinates) because the z coordinate will be ignored anyway. It's common in this case to use integer coordinates and to set the view volume to match the x and y coordinates of the viewport.

Perspective

Although orthographic projections can be interesting, perspective projections create more realistic-looking scenes, so that's what you'll likely be using more often. In perspective projections, as an object gets farther from the viewer, it appears smaller on the screen—an effect commonly referred to as *foreshortening*. The viewing volume for a perspective projection is a *frustum*, which looks like a pyramid with the top cut off, with the narrow end toward the viewer. That the far end of the frustum is larger than the near end is what creates the foreshortening effect. The way this works is that OpenGL transforms the frustum so that it becomes a cube. This transformation affects the objects inside the frustum as well, so objects at the wide end of the frustum get compressed more than objects at the narrow end. The greater the ratio between the wide and narrow ends, the more objects will be shrunk. If the ends of the frustum are close in size, there won't be much perspective correction (if they are the same, there will be no correction at all, which is what happens with orthographic projections).

There are a couple ways you can set up the view frustum, and thus the perspective projection. The first we'll look at is the following:

```
void glFrustum(GLdouble left, GLdouble right, GLdouble bottom, GLdouble top,
               GLdouble near, GLdouble far);
```

`left`, `right`, `top`, and `bottom` together specify the x and y coordinates on the near clipping plane, and `near` and `far` specify the distance to the near and far clipping planes. Thus, the top-left corner of the near clipping plane is at (`left`, `top`, `-near`), and the bottom-right corner is at (`right`, `bottom`, `-near`). The corners of the far clipping plane are determined by casting a ray from the viewer through the corners of the near clipping plane and intersecting them with the far clipping plane. So, the closer the viewer is to the near clipping plane, the larger the far clipping plane will be, and the more foreshortening will be apparent.

Using glFrustum() enables you to specify an asymmetrical frustum, which may be useful in some instances, but it's not typically what you'll want to do. In addition, thinking about what the viewer can see in terms of a frustum is not particularly intuitive. Instead, it's easier to think about their field of view—that is, how wide of an angle they can see. The OpenGL Utility Library provides a function that allows you to directly specify the field of view, and then calculates the frustum for you. This function is

```
void gluPerspective(GLdouble fov, GLdouble aspect, GLdouble near, GLdouble far);
```

fov specifies, in degrees, the angle in the y direction that is visible to the user. *aspect* is the aspect ratio of the scene, which is the width divided by the height. This determines the field of view in the x direction. *near* and *far* have the same meanings as they've had in the other projection functions in this section.

One thing we haven't mentioned in our discussion of setting up a frustum is how to determine an appropriate ratio between the width of the far and near end (that is, how wide the field of view is). The appropriate field of view is highly application dependent. If you want to create a fish-eye effect, a very wide field of view may be appropriate. For a realistic perspective, something around 90 degrees will probably work best. In general, you'll want to experiment to see what looks right for your particular application.

Setting the Viewport

Some of the projection functions we've just discussed are closely related to the size of the viewport (for example, the aspect ratio in gluPerspective). You know that the viewport transformation happens after the projection transformation, so now is as good a time as any to discuss it. Although you can't modify the viewport matrix directly, you can set the size of the viewport, which is all you really need to do.

In essence, the viewport specifies the dimensions and orientation of the 2D window into which you'll be rendering. It is set using glViewport():

```
void glViewport(GLint x, GLint y, GLsizei width, GLsizei height);
```

x and *y* specify the coordinates of the lower-left corner of the viewport, and *width* and *height* specify the size of the window, in pixels.

When a rendering context is first created and attached to your window, the viewport is automatically set to match the dimensions of the window. That may be good enough for some applications, but in most cases, you'll want to update your viewport any time the window is resized. Although the viewport will generally match your window size, there is nothing requiring it to be the same size. There may be times when you want to limit rendering to a sub-region of your window, and setting a smaller viewport is one way to do this.

Projection Example

To get a better idea of the differences between the two major projection types, we've included a simple demo that will allow you to view the same scene in each mode. The demo starts off with a perspective projection; pressing the spacebar will enable you to toggle between perspective (shown in Figure 5.14) and orthographic (shown in Figure 5.15).

The relevant portion of this demo is in the ResizeScene and UpdateProjection functions, which are listed here for convenience:

```
/*************************************************************************
ResizeScene()

Updates the viewport and projection based on the screen size.
*************************************************************************/
GLvoid ResizeScene(GLsizei width, GLsizei height)
{
  // avoid divide by zero
  if (height==0)
  {
    height=1;
  }
```

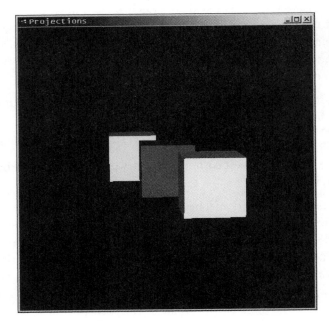

Figure 5.14

Perspective projection.

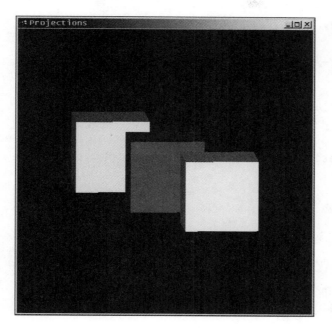

Figure 5.15

Orthographic projection.

```
  // reset the viewport to the new dimensions
  glViewport(0, 0, width, height);

  // set up the projection, without toggling the projection mode
  UpdateProjection();
} // end ResizeScene()


/*****************************************************************************
UpdateProjection()

Sets the current projection mode. If toggle is set to GL_TRUE, then the
projection will be toggled between perspective and orthograpic. Otherwise,
the previous selection will be used again.
*****************************************************************************/
void UpdateProjection(GLboolean toggle = GL_FALSE)
{
  static GLboolean s_usePerspective = GL_TRUE;
```

```
  // toggle the control variable if appropriate
  if (toggle)
    s_usePerspective = !s_usePerspective;

  // select the projection matrix and clear it out
  glMatrixMode(GL_PROJECTION);
  glLoadIdentity();

  // choose the appropriate projection based on the currently toggled mode
  if (s_usePerspective)
  {
    // set the perspective with the appropriate aspect ratio
    glFrustum(-1.0, 1.0, -1.0, 1.0, 5, 100);
  }
  else
  {
    // set up an orthographic projection with the same near clip plane
    glOrtho(-1.0, 1.0, -1.0, 1.0, 5, 100);
  }

  // select modelview matrix and clear it out
  glMatrixMode(GL_MODELVIEW);
} // end UpdateProjection
```

USING YOUR OWN MATRICES

Up until now, we've talked about functions that allow you to modify the matrix stacks without really having to worry about the matrices themselves. This is great, because it allows you to do a lot without having to understand matrix math, and the functions OpenGL provides for you are actually quite powerful and flexible. Eventually, though, you may want to create some advanced effects that are possible only by directly affecting the matrices. This will require that you know your way around matrix math, which we're not going to cover in any more detail than we have already. However, we'll at least show you how to load your own matrix, how to multiply the top of the matrix stack by a custom matrix, and one example of using a custom matrix.

Loading Your Matrix

Before you can load a matrix, you need to specify it. OpenGL matrices are column-major 4×4 matrices of floating point numbers, laid out as in Figure 5.16.

$$\begin{bmatrix} m_0 & m_4 & m_8 & m_{12} \\ m_1 & m_5 & m_9 & m_{13} \\ m_2 & m_6 & m_{10} & m_{14} \\ m_3 & m_7 & m_{11} & m_{15} \end{bmatrix}$$

Figure 5.16

OpenGL's column-major matrix format.

Because the matrices are 4×4, you may be tempted to declare them as two-dimensional arrays, but there is one major problem with this. In C and C++, two-dimensional arrays are row major. For example, to access the bottom-left element of the matrix in Figure 5.16, you might think you'd use `matrix[3][0]`, which is how you'd access the bottom-left corner of a 4×4 C/C++ two-dimensional array. Because OpenGL matrices are column major, however, you'd really be accessing the top-right element of the matrix. To get the bottom-left element, you'd need to use `matrix[0][3]`. This is the opposite of what you're used to in C/C++, making it counterintuitive and error-prone. Rather than using two-dimensional arrays, it's recommended that you use a one-dimensional array of 16 elements. The nth element in the array corresponds to element m_n in Figure 5.16.

As an example, if you want to specify the identity matrix (something you'd never need to do in practice due to the `glLoadIdentity()` function), you could use

```
GLfloat identity[16] = { 1.0, 0.0, 0.0, 0.0, 0.0, 1.0, 0.0, 0.0, 0.0, 0.0, 1.0, 0.0,
0.0, 0.0, 0.0, 1.0 };
```

That's easy enough. So, now that you've specified a matrix, the next step is to load it. This is done by calling `glLoadMatrix()`, which has two flavors:

```
void glLoadMatrixd(const GLdouble *matrix);
```

```
void glLoadMatrixf(const GLfloat *matrix);
```

The only difference between these functions is that one takes an array of `doubles`, and the other takes an array of `floats`. When `glLoadMatrix()` is called, whatever is at the top of the currently selected matrix stack is replaced with the values in the `matrix` array, which is a 16-element array as specified previously.

Multiplying Matrices

In addition to loading new matrices onto the matrix stack (and thus losing whatever information was previously in it), you can multiply the contents of the active matrix by a new matrix. Again, you'd specify your custom matrix as above, and then call one of the following:

```
void glMultMatrixd(const GLdouble *matrix);
```

```
void glMultMatrixf(const GLfloat *matrix);
```

Again, *matrix* is an array of 16 elements. If the active matrix before the call to glMultMatrix() is M_{old}, and the new matrix is M_{new}, then the new matrix will be $M_{old} \times M_{new}$. Note that the ordering is important; because matrix multiplication is not commutative, $M_{old} \times M_{new}$ is not likely to have the same result as $M_{new} \times M_{old}$.

Custom Matrix Example

For an example of using your own matrices, refer to the sample program from Chapter 1, "The Exploration Begins: OpenGL and DirectX." In this program, we used a custom matrix to generate shadows in real time. The code we're interested in for the purposes of the current discussion follows:

```
GLfloat shadowMatrix[16] = { lightPos[1], 0.0,   0.0, 0.0, -lightPos[0], 0.0,
                            -lightPos[2],  -1.0, 0.0, 0.0,  lightPos[1], 0.0, 0.0,
                            0.0,   0.0, lightPos[1] };

...
// project the cube through the shadow matrix
glMultMatrixf(shadowMatrix);
DrawCube();
```

This matrix projects any vertices passed through it onto the y = 0 plane. If you set the current drawing color to black (along with some alpha blending and use of the stencil buffer, which are beyond the scope of this chapter), this has the effect of creating a shadow of the objects being drawn. You store the matrix into the modelview matrix stack by using glMultMatrix() rather than glLoadMatrix() because you want to preserve other transformations that have been used to orient the scene and position the cube.

One final note needs to be made in regard to using your own matrices: Whenever possible, you should use OpenGL's built-in transformation functions. In many cases, they are able to take advantage of hardware acceleration that you will not have access to.

SUMMARY

In this chapter, you have seen how to manipulate objects in your scene by using transformations. You've also examined how to change the way in which the scene itself is viewed through setting up projections. In the process, you've learned about the projection and modelview matrices and how to manipulate them using both built-in functions and matrices you define yourself. You now have the means to place objects in a 3D world, to move and animate them, and to move around the world. Hmm…sounds like the beginnings of a game!

CHAPTER 6

ADDING COLORS, BLENDING, AND LIGHTING

world without color would be pretty boring, not to mention confusing and depressing. Likewise, moving around in a 3D world drawn in shades of black and white on a computer screen would get to be rather monotonous for most people. Fortunately, you can take care of this problem with a little OpenGL magic.

But wait, color isn't the only thing you can add to generate a little excitement to your 3D scenes. With OpenGL, you can manipulate the lighting and objects in your 3D world to generate many different effects. Add on top of that materials, which you need to get your awesome lighting effects, and you are well on your way to making some incredible 3D worlds for your games.

This chapter begins by taking a look at how colors work both in the world you live in and in OpenGL. Then we'll dive into the world of lighting and materials before moving onto blending and transparency. As you can see, the fun is just beginning!

In this chapter, you'll learn about

- Color in OpenGL
- Shading
- OpenGL lighting
- Light sources
- Blending and transparency

How Does Color Work?

So just how does color work? Well, to find out, you need to take a brief trip to physics class with a discussion of light. As you may or may not remember, light is composed of photons, which are tiny particles that move in their own direction and vibrate at their own frequency. This is why light is viewed as both a wave and a particle and is what physicists refer to as the *wave-particle duality*. As a wave, light is similar to ripples in a pond with a wavelength, crest, and a trough as seen in Figure 6.1. As a particle, light is like a very fast-moving projectile moving through space.

Photons in visible light have wavelengths ranging from approximately 390 nanometers (nm) to 720nm. This range of wavelengths gives you millions of colors, including the colors of the rainbow, often referred to as the *visible spectrum*: violet, indigo, blue, green, yellow, orange, and red. Figure 6.2 shows how the visible spectrum is structured.

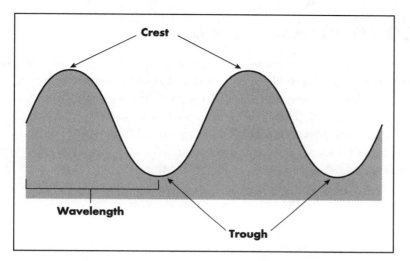

Figure 6.1

A wave is made up of a crest, trough, and wavelength.

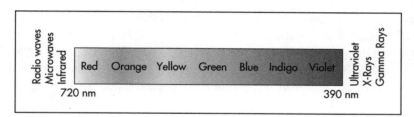

Figure 6.2

The visible light spectrum.

As you know, these colors of the visible spectrum are not the only colors you see with your eyes. You see millions of different shades and combinations every day. So how does this work? Well, the retinas in the back of your eyes hold millions of special cells, called *cones*, that act similarly to photo paper. When photons enter your eyes and strike these cones, the cones become excited and send neural impulses to your brain where the impulses are decoded into an image of light and color.

There are three different types of cone cells: red, green, and blue. Each type of cone cell responds best to the wavelength of its particular light. That is, red cone cells respond best to the wavelength of red light, blue cone cells to the wavelength of blue light, and green cone cells to the wavelength of green light. When the eye receives a mixture of photons with varying wavelengths, then the cone cells translate the photons into varying intensities of light, and you see a mixture of colors.

USING COLORS IN OPENGL

Let's extend this to the computer monitor. The colored pixels you see on the computer monitor are actually a combination of red, green, and blue phosphors that emit at varying intensities. Each pixel on the screen emits different amounts of red, green, and blue light. In computer graphics, these varying intensities are called the *RGB values*, and they are used in *RGB mode*. Sometimes, a fourth value, called the *alpha* value, is added to give you *RGBA mode*. (The alpha value is covered later when we talk about blending in this chapter.) You can also have *color-index mode*, where a color index is stored for each pixel in a table called the *color map*. You can specify the red, green, and blue intensities for each index in the color map such that you have your own set of colors from which to choose. So just how many colors can you use? To figure that out, we need to talk about color depth.

Color Depth

Color depth is how you determine how many colors you can use for a single pixel and is often stored in the *color buffer*. The color buffer is given a size in bits such as 4, 8, 16, and so on. An 8-bit color buffer can store 8 bits of data, which equates to 2^8, or 256, colors. Today's hardware typically supports four different color depths that programmers can use for their applications: 8, 16, 24, and 32. Check out Table 6.1 for a rundown on each of these color depths.

Table 6.1 Common Color Depths

Color Depth	Attributes
8	256 colors; colors indexed with value from 0 to 255 in a palette
16	65,536 colors; RGB bits are usually 565; also, 15-bit depth is 555
24	16,777,216 colors; 8 bits per color component (red, green, blue)
32	Same as 24-bit, but improves performance by 32-bit alignment

The Color Cube

OpenGL specifies color as three separate intensities of red, green, and blue. The values of these intensities can range from 0.0 (no intensity) to 1.0 (full intensity). Looking at the color cube in Figure 6.3, you can see how a combination of these three intensities can produce a wide range of colors. For example, with R = 1.0, G = 0.0, and B = 0.0, you get the highest intensity (brightest) possible red. If R = 0.0, G = 1.0, and B = 1.0, you get the highest intensity possible cyan. If all three components are equal to 0.0, then you get black. If all three components are equal to 1.0, then you get white. Also, if all three components have the same value, you get different shades of gray with the intensity of the shade depending on how close to 0.0 and 1.0 the components' values are. You can use the color cube to help you create the colors you want. The axes of the color cube represent intensities of red, green, and blue; as you move further from the axes, the more the axes' colors are blended.

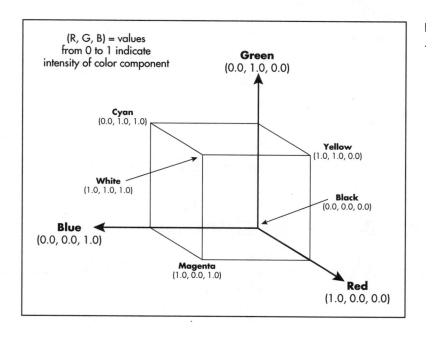

Figure 6.3

The color cube.

RGBA Mode in OpenGL

To specify a color in RGBA mode with OpenGL, you pass the red, green, and blue color-component mixture that you want to the glColor*() functions. There are several glColor*() functions with various suffixes appended to the function name. Here are the functions that you will use most often:

```
void glColor3f(GLfloat r, GLfloat g, GLfloat b);
void glColor4f(GLfloat r, GLfloat g, GLfloat b, GLfloat a);
void glColor3fv(const GLfloat *v);
void glColor4fv(const GLfloat *v);
```

The first function sets the current color to the color combination described by the values of the red, green, and blue color components. The second function is the same as the first with the addition of an alpha value, which deals with blending (discussed later in the chapter). The values for these two functions' parameters should range between 0.0 and 1.0, with 0.0 equaling zero intensity and 1.0 equaling maximum intensity. The third and fourth functions are essentially the same as the first two, except that the parameter passed is a pointer to an array of floating-point values. You will see more of this as you advance through OpenGL.

Using the first function, if you want to set the current color to green, you do the following:

```
void glColor3f(0.0f, 1.0f, 0.0f);
```

Pretty easy, huh? If you wanted to set the current color to magenta, you would use the following:

```
void glColor3f(1.0f, 0.0f, 1.0f);
```

As you can probably tell, specifying the color values with the glColor3f() function is very much like specifying the colors in the color cube. For instance, you can specify gray by using 0.5 for each color component, like this:

```
void glColor3f(0.5f, 0.5f, 0.5f);
```

You will be using RGBA mode as your primary color mode, but let's take a look at color-index mode just so you know what it entails.

Color-Index Mode in OpenGL

Back in the days of DOS, programmers had to create what was called a *color palette*, which was basically a lookup table that held color values that a program or game would be able to use at any given time. This was analogous to a painter's palette where the painter has access to certain colors, but also has a place where he can mix the colors to produce new ones. Palettes are still used in games and applications that use 8-bit color depth.

The size of the *color map*, the name given by OpenGL to the lookup table, determines the number of simultaneously available colors at any given time. Figure 6.4 shows how the color map works. The number of colors available on the color map is always a power of 2, such as 256 or 4096, and is determined by the amount of hardware available for it. In color-index mode, each index, or position, in the color map can be shared by many pixels. When the contents of a color-map entry change, all the pixels that share that entry in the color map change their color.

Index	Intensities		
	R	G	B
0	0	0	0
1	1	1	1
2	3	3	3
3	5	4	6
4	7	6	8
5	8	7	9
6	9	8	10
7	10	11	15
8	20	19	20
9	21	22	25
10	22	23	30
11	30	40	35
•	•	•	•
•	•	•	•
•	•	•	•
255	255	255	255

Figure 6.4

A sample color map.

To use color-index mode, you use the `glIndex*()` command to set the current color index. The most common forms of this function look like this:

```
void glIndexf(GLfloat c);
```

```
void glIndexfv(const GLfloat *c);
```

These functions set the current color index equal to the value in c. Through the suffix v, the second function indicates that the argument is an array of floating-point values; however, the array contains only one value.

You can also clear the color buffer in color-index mode by using the `glClearIndex()` function defined as

```
void glClearIndex(GLfloat cindex);
```

This function sets the color index to use in color-index mode that will clear the color buffers. The default value is 0.0.

SHADING

So far we have talked about drawing OpenGL primitives with one solid color across the entire primitive. This is accomplished by using the same color for each vertex in the primitive. What happens if you use a different color for each vertex of a primitive?

To find out the answer, let's consider a line with two vertices of different colors. We'll keep things simple and say that the first vertex is black, and the second vertex is white. So what is the color of the line itself? This answer comes from what is known as the *shading model*.

Shading can either be *flat* or *smooth*. Flat shading is drawn with a single color, typically with the color of the last vertex (except with OpenGL's GL_POLYGON, which uses the first specified vertex color). Smooth shading, or *Gouraud shading*, is the more realistic of the two and uses interpolation to determine the colors between the vertices of a primitive.

If we use flat shading on our sample line, the line will be white because the last vertex that is drawn is white. However, if we use smooth shading, then our line will progress from the color black at the first vertex, to gray at the middle of the line, to white at the second vertex. This effect is illustrated in Figure 6.5.

Vertex 1   Vertex 2

Figure 6.5

Smooth shading of a line with black at the first vertex and white at the second vertex.

As you can see, interspersed between the first vertex and the middle of the line are progressively lighter shades of gray. The progression continues on the other half of the line as the colors shift through lighter shades of gray until you reach white.

The idea of smooth shading with polygonal primitives is essentially the same as smooth shading with a line. For example, drawing a triangle using smooth shading with a different color for each vertex will yield a triangle where each vertex color progressively changes to the other two vertices' color as it moves across the polygon's surface.

Now that you know what these shading modes are all about, how do you go about implementing them? The glShadeModel() function lets you specify the current shading model before you begin drawing. It is defined as

```
void glShadeModel(GLenum mode);
```

You can specify either GL_SMOOTH, for smooth shading, or GL_FLAT, for flat shading, as the *mode* parameter. The default setting is GL_SMOOTH.

So with this information, you can now create some code that will draw a smooth-shaded triangle:

```
// initialization...
glShadeModel(GL_SMOOTH);
```

```
// some code...

// draw our smooth-shaded triangle
glBegin(GL_TRIANGLES);
    glColor3f(1.0f, 0.0f, 0.0f);          // red vertex
    glVertex3f(-10.0f, -10.0f, -5.0f);
    glColor3f(0.0f, 1.0f, 0.0f);          // green vertex
    glVertex3f(20.0f, -10.0f, -5.0f);
    glColor3f(0.0f, 0.0f, 1.0f);          // blue vertex
    glVertex3f(-10.0f, 20.0f, -5.0f);
glEnd();
```

The output is shown in Figure 6.6. The red, green, and blue colors from each of the vertices progressively change as they move across the triangle's surface. In the middle, the three colors converge to create the color gray, which means that the three colors (RGB) are each at the same intensity.

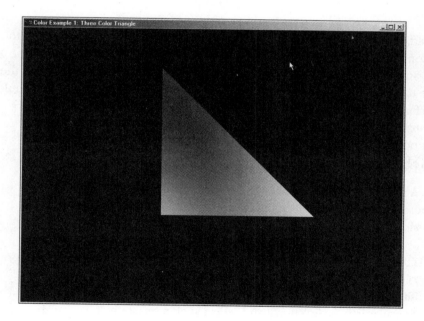

Figure 6.6

A smooth-shaded triangle with red, green, and blue vertices.

LIGHTING IN OPENGL

You have now arrived at one of the most important aspects of 3D graphics: lighting. It is one of the few elements that can make or break the realism of your 3D game. So far you've looked at how to build objects, move objects, put color on objects, and shade them. Now let's look at how to make these objects come to life with materials, lights, and lamps.

OpenGL Lighting and the Real World

Let's take a quick step back and look at how light works in the real world. As we discussed, when you look at an object, the color that you see is based on the distribution of photons that trigger your eyes' cone cells. Obviously these photons must come from some sort of light source that is being reflected, and possibly absorbed, by the object you are viewing. The object itself might be made of a shiny material, in which case it would reflect more light and your eye would receive more photons. On the other hand, the object might be made of a coarse material where more light is absorbed or reflected away from your eye, and it appears to have a darker shade because your eye does not receive many photons.

Similar to the real world, OpenGL calculates light and lighting by approximating the light into red, green, and blue components. This means that the color a light emits is determined by the amount of red, green, and blue light it emits. When the light strikes a surface, OpenGL uses the material of the surface to determine the percentage of the red, green, and blue light that should be reflected by the surface. Even though they are approximations, the equations used by OpenGL can be computed rather quickly. If you would rather have more accurate (and unnecessary) lighting, you can do your own calculations, but this is not recommended.

OpenGL attempts to model real-world lighting through the use of four light components:

- **Ambient light.** Ambient light does not seem to come from any particular direction. Even with a source, this light has been scattered so much that determining a direction is nearly impossible. Surfaces that are illuminated by ambient light reflect it in all directions.
- **Diffuse light.** Diffuse light comes from a certain direction, but once it strikes a surface, it is reflected equally in all directions. To the eye, the surface appears equally bright no matter what position the eye is in.
- **Specular light.** Specular light is directional and reflected off a surface in a particular direction. Specularity is often referred to as shininess.
- **Emissive light.** Objects with an emissive component appear to have light that originates from them, except this light does not affect any other objects in the scene. With OpenGL, emissive color adds intensity to an object, but light sources do not affect it.

Materials

OpenGL approximates material colors based on the red, green, and blue light the material reflects. For example, if you have a surface that is pure green, it reflects all the incoming green light while absorbing all the incoming red and blue light. If you were to place this green surface under a pure red light, the surface would appear to be black. This is because the surface reflects only green light; when it is placed under red light, the surface absorbs the light and reflects nothing—so you see black. If you were to place the green surface under a white light, you would see a green surface because the green component of the white light is being reflected while the red and blue components are being absorbed. Lastly, if the surface were placed in green light, you would see a green surface, because the green light is being reflected back to you.

Materials have three of the same color properties as light: ambient, diffuse, and specular. These properties determine how much light the material reflects. A material with high ambient, low diffuse, and low specular reflectance will reflect only ambient light sources well while absorbing the diffuse and specular light sources. A material with a high specular reflectance will appear shiny while absorbing the ambient and diffuse light sources. The values specified by the ambient and diffuse reflectances typically determine the color of the material and are usually identical in value. In order to make sure that specular highlights end up being the color of the light source's specular intensity, specular reflectance is normally set to be gray or white. A good way to think about this is to think of a bright white light pointing at a shiny blue surface. Although the surface would mostly show up as blue, the specular highlight on the surface would appear as white.

Normals

Before we can go much further in lighting, we need to talk about *surface normals* and how to calculate them. Figure 6.7 illustrates what we mean by surface normal.

As you can see, the surface normal is a vector that is perpendicular to the surface plane. It sounds complicated, but it's not. Before you do your lighting calculations, you need to calculate the normal so you, or OpenGL, can determine what kind of color and shading the polygon should get when it is drawn based on the angle of the lighting to the polygon. Basically, when a light source is specified, it shines light in some specific direction, or all directions if it's ambient. When you draw an object, the light rays from this light source will approach and strike the surfaces of the object's polygons at some angle. Using this angle and the angle that is created when the light rays reflect off the surfaces, combined with lighting and material properties, you can calculate the color of the surface. So with the normal, your goal is to calculate the angle at which the ray of light is striking the surface.

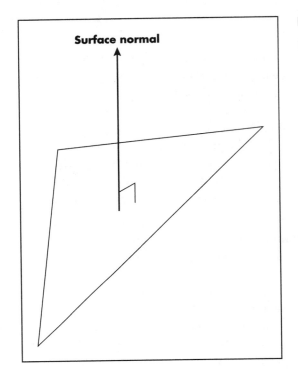

Figure 6.7

The surface normal.

If you were to perform your lighting calculations by using only the surface's normal, then you would get flat-shaded surfaces where each surface is filled with a single color. You don't want that in your 3D graphics, so what you are going to do (and OpenGL does nicely) is specify the normal for each vertex of the surface. This means that the proper color is calculated at each vertex and then smoothly shaded across the polygon with the other vertices to create the illusion of a smoothly lit surface. This is what you want in your 3D graphics! But for now, you need to keep it simple and figure out how to do your lighting with surface normals.

Calculating Normals

Here you get to apply some of that vector math you learned about in Chapter 3, "An Overview of 3D Graphics Theory." If you remember, you discovered how to calculate the cross product, and learned that this helps you calculate normals for things like collision detection, physics, and lighting. The equation for the cross product, given two 3D vectors A and B, is

$$A \times B = (A_y \cdot B_z - A_z \cdot B_y, \ A_z \cdot B_x - A_x \cdot B_z, \ A_x \cdot B_y - A_y \cdot B_x)$$

So, this means that you need two vectors, A and B, to calculate your surface's normal. Where can you find two vectors? Well, think about the definition of a surface and how one is constructed. A surface is not a single vertex; that is a point. A surface is not created from two vertices; that is a line. If you have three vertices, you can make a triangle, which is a surface. If you have four vertices, you have a quadrilateral, another surface. You can keep adding vertices to your heart's content, and you will always have a surface as long as you have three vertices that are in the same plane.

As you can see, if you have three vertices you can calculate your normal. If you have three points, *P1*, *P2*, and *P3*, you can define two vectors *V1* and *V2* that go from *P1* to *P2* and *P1* to *P3*, respectively. Figure 6.8 illustrates this.

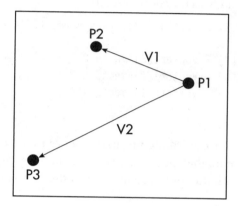

Figure 6.8

You can define two vectors V1 and V2 out of three points.

Now all you have to do is take the cross product of *V1* and *V2*, and you get your normal. You can easily accomplish this with a simple function, as shown here:

```
void CrossProduct(float point1[3], float point2[3], float point3[3], float normal[3])
{
    float vector1[3], vector2[3];

    // calculate the two vectors that we need to calculate the cross product
    vector1[0] = point1[0] - point2[0];
    vector1[1] = point1[1] - point2[1];
    vector1[2] = point1[2] - point2[2];

    vector2[0] = point2[0] - point3[0];
    vector2[1] = point2[1] - point3[1];
    vector2[2] = point2[2] - point3[2];
```

```
    // calculate the cross product of our two vectors and store in normal[3]
    normal[0] = vector1[1]*vector2[2] - vector1[2]*vector2[2];
    normal[1] = vector1[2]*vector2[0] - vector1[0]*vector2[2];
    normal[2] = vector1[0]*vector2[1] - vector1[1]*vector2[0];
}
```

You can use this function to calculate the cross product, given three points that lie on a plane. You pass in your points with the three parameters point1, point2, and point3, and the last parameter, normal, which stores your calculated normal. If you calculate the two vectors before you need to calculate the normal, you can simply use this function instead:

```
void CrossProduct(float vector1[3], float vector2[3],float normal[3])
{
    normal[0] = vector1[1]*vector2[2] - vector1[2]*vector2[1];
    normal[1] = vector1[2]*vector2[0] - vector1[0]*vector2[2];
    normal[2] = vector1[0]*vector2[1] - vector1[1]*vector2[0];
}
```

These generic functions are usually fine for calculating normals, but not in the case of lighting. Lighting calculations are rather intensive mathematically, so you welcome any shortcuts you can get. We will discuss one particular shortcut, the unit normal, soon in this chapter.

Using Normals

You specify vector normals as you would any other vector. For instance, if you have a triangle that was drawn flat on the XZ plane (no variations in the y components of the vertices), and you draw a line perpendicular to this triangle through one of its vertices at (4, 5, 0), then the line defined by the point (4, 10, 0) that extends to this vertex is both perpendicular and the normal to the triangle. Instead of specifying a normal with two points like this, however, you can subtract the x, y, and z components of the two points to get your normal vector, which turns out to be (0, 5, 0). Figure 6.9 illustrates this example.

To specify a normal for a surface in OpenGL, you use the glNormal3f() function, which lets you define the normal to use for the next vertex or set of vertices that are specified to be drawn. Its prototype looks like this:

```
void glNormal3f(GLfloat nx, GLfloat ny, GLfloat nz);
```

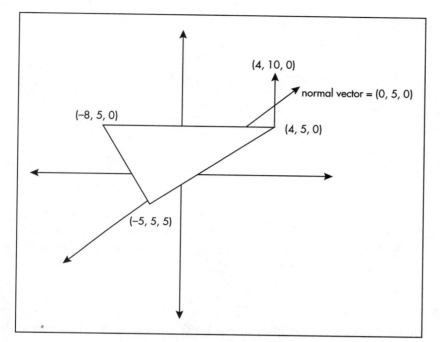

Figure 6.9

This illustration shows how a normal is perpendicular to its surface, and how you can derive the normal vector from two points.

The three parameters passed to this function are the x, y, and z components of the normal vector of the surface. You call this function with the normal vector data right before you call your vertex functions like this:

```
glBegin(GL_TRIANGLES);
    glNormal3f(0.0f, 1.0f, 0.0f);
    glVertex3f(0.0f, 5.0f, 0.0f);
    glVertex3f(4.0f, 5.0f, 0.0f);
    glVertex3f(0.0f, 5.0f, 4.0f);
glEnd();
```

This block of code will draw the triangle in Figure 6.9. The glNormal3f() function defines a normal vector in the positive y direction that is perpendicular to the triangle's surface. This code makes it such that when you apply lighting to your scene, all the lighting calculations that OpenGL performs on this triangle will use the normal vector that points in the positive y direction.

You can also send an array of the normal vector data with the glNormal3fv() function. For instance

```
GLfloat normalVector = { 0.0f, 1.0f, 0.0f };
...
glBegin(GL_TRIANGLES);
    glNormal3fv(normalVector);
    glVertex3f(0.0f, 5.0f, 0.0f);
    glVertex3f(4.0f, 5.0f, 0.0f);
    glVertex3f(0.0f, 5.0f, 4.0f);
glEnd();
```

This code will do the exact same thing as the previous block. The difference is that you send the normal vector as an array of data instead of three separate components. Besides being a common way to define the surface normals, this can be useful if you have a data set of normals that you need to specify when rendering your objects.

The Unit Normal

In order to perform its lighting calculations, OpenGL must convert the normals that you pass to the glNormal3f() function into what are called *unit normals*. Unit normals are simply normal vectors that have a length of 1.

If you remember in Chapter 3, you discovered that you could find the length of vector A with the equation

$$|A| = sqrt(A_x^2 + A_y^2 + A_z^2)$$

Well, normal vectors are in fact vectors, and by applying this equation you can get the length of any normal vectors that you calculate. To calculate the unit vector, called *normalization,* you divide each component of the normal vector by its length. The unit vector you get is in the same direction as your normal vector, but it only has a length of 1.

One way you can ensure that unit normals are used by OpenGL is to call glEnable() with GL_NOR-MALIZE or GL_RESCALE_NORMALIZE as a parameter:

```
glEnable(GL_NORMALIZE);
```

You use GL_RESCALE_NORMALIZE if the normal was scaled uniformly and has a length of 1. Specifying this parameter causes each component of the normal to be multiplied by the same value as determined by the modelview matrix.

The GL_NORMALIZE parameter is more common and tells OpenGL to calculate the unit vector. This basically makes your life easier so you won't have to calculate the normals on your own; using this does, however, bring in some performance issues. It is often better to calculate the unit normals ahead of time on your own instead of having OpenGL do it for you.

So how do you calculate the unit normal? Here are some functions to do it:

```
// calculates and returns the length of vector
double VectorLength(float vector[3])
{
    return sqrt((vector[0]*vector[0]) +
                (vector[1]*vector[1]) +
                (vector[2]*vector[2]) );
}


// normalizes the vector defined by normalVector
void Normalize(float normalVector[3])
{
    double length;          // using double to keep high precision

    length = VectorLength(normalVector);    // calculate the length

    // divide each vector component by the length to get the unit vector
    for (int idx = 0; idx < 3; idx++)
        normalVector[idx] /= length;
}
```

You usually use the Normalize() function after you have already calculated your normal vector. So you can take the CrossProduct() function from earlier and add in the Normalize() function at the end to get your new function CalculateNormal():

```
void CalculateNormal(float point1[3],
                     float point2[3],
                     float point3[3],
                     float normal[3])
{
    // calculate the cross product of the three points
    CrossProduct(point1, point2, point3, normal);

    // normalize our vector so it is a unit vector to speed up lighting
    Normalize(normal);
}
```

As you can see, this function will calculate the cross product of your points and normalize the result of the cross product to give you your unit normal. And yes, to speed things up a little, you can eliminate function-call overhead by putting everything in the `CrossProduct()` and `Normalize()` functions into this `CalculateNormal()` function. For now, however, leave the function like this so you know what is happening when you are calculating a normal.

Using OpenGL Lighting

It's time to turn on the lights and get on with the show! OpenGL lets you have as many as eight lights in your scene at any one time. You shouldn't really need more than eight, and even in worlds that have more than eight lights in their database, you should use some sort of data manipulation routines that will clip out lights that are not currently visible. With this in mind, there are four steps (from the *OpenGL Programming Guide*, by Woo, Neider, Davis, Shreiner, published by Addison-Wesley) that are required to add lighting to your scenes:

1. Calculate normal vectors for each vertex of every object. The normals determine the object's orientation relative to the light source.
2. Create, select, and position all light sources.
3. Create and select a lighting model. The lighting model defines the ambient light and location of the viewpoint for the lighting calculations.
4. Define the material properties for the objects in the scene.

We've already discussed the first step, but how do you "create, select, and position light sources"? Well, first let's take a look at some sample source that displays a rotating lit cube:

```
////// Lighting variables
float ambientLight[] = { 0.3f, 0.5f, 0.8f, 1.0f };    // ambient light
float diffuseLight[] = { 0.25f, 0.25f, 0.25f, 1.0f }; // diffuse light
float lightPosition[] = { 0.0f, 0.0f, 0.0f, 1.0f };   // the light position
```

These variables define your light's properties. The `ambientLight` variable declares an ambient property of 0.3 red, 0.5 green, and 0.8 blue. This means that the global light that reflects off of everything will have a bluish tone to it. The `diffuseLight` is set to 0.25 for the red, green, and blue values. This means that any surface of your cube that the diffuse light hits directly will be lighter than the areas of the cube that the light barely hits, which will be dark. The last value for each of these lights is the alpha value, but you won't need to worry about it right now.

The last lighting variable is the light position. The first three values are basically the same as using the `glTranslatef()` function. Here you are setting the light at the origin of your world (0, 0, 0). The fourth value of the light position tells OpenGL whether the first three coordinates are a position or a vector. In this example, you set the fourth value equal to 1.0, which means that the first three coordinates (0, 0, 0) are the position of the light.

Let's say you changed this value to 0.0. What would happen? OpenGL would interpret this as meaning that your light comes from the direction specified by the vector in the first three values of the light position. With a vector of (0, 0, 0), your light isn't doing much lighting, so you would need to change it to a vector that actually pointed somewhere. Well, considering that your camera is at the origin and looking down the negative z axis, you could set up the light as coming from the positive z axis so it would shine on your cube. To get the same effect as above, but using a vector instead of an absolute position, you would do the following:

```
// light from positive z axis
float lightPosition[] = { 0.0f, 0.0f, 1.0f, 0.0f };
```

This is how you do directional lights. Pretty neat huh? Now what about those materials?

```
////// Material variables
float matAmbient[] = { 1.0f, 1.0f, 1.0f, 1.0f };
float matDiff[] = { 1.0f, 1.0f, 1.0f, 1.0f};
```

The first variable, matAmbient, defines how your surfaces will respond to the ambient component of the light. With each value of matAmbient equal to 1.0, the red, green, and blue components of the ambient light will be fully reflected by the surfaces. The same goes for matDiff, which defines how your surfaces will respond to the diffuse component of the light. All of the red, green, and blue components of the diffuse light will be fully reflected by the surfaces. Next up is your Initialize() function:

```
// Initialize
// desc: initializes OpenGL
void Initialize()
{
    glClearColor(0.0f, 0.0f, 0.0f, 0.0f);   // clear to black
    glShadeModel(GL_SMOOTH);                 // use smooth shading
    glEnable(GL_DEPTH_TEST);                 // hidden surface removal
    glEnable(GL_CULL_FACE);                  // do not calculate inside of polys
    glFrontFace(GL_CCW);                     // counterclockwise polygons are out

    glEnable(GL_LIGHTING);                   // enable lighting

    // Set up the materials for LIGHT0
    glMaterialfv(GL_FRONT, GL_AMBIENT, matAmbient);
    glMaterialfv(GL_FRONT, GL_DIFFUSE, matDiff);
```

```
    // Now set up LIGHT0
    glLightfv(GL_LIGHT0, GL_AMBIENT, ambientLight);    // set up the ambient element
    glLightfv(GL_LIGHT0, GL_DIFFUSE, diffuseLight);    // the diffuse element
    glLightfv(GL_LIGHT0, GL_POSITION, lightPosition);  // place the light in the
                                                       // world


    // Enable the light
    glEnable(GL_LIGHT0);
}
```

Your Initialize() function is pretty straightforward with the comments. First you'll notice that you set the shading mode to GL_SMOOTH, which means that Gouraud shading will be used. You also enable hidden surface removal with the GL_DEPTH_TEST flag.

Something you may not have seen yet is the GL_CULL_FACE flag. Setting this bit means that OpenGL will not be doing any calculations on the inside of your polygons. In order to make sure you know which side is the outside, or front, of your polygons, you set the GL_CCW flag with the glFrontFace() function. The CCW stands for counterclockwise and means that if you are looking at your polygon as you draw it, you must draw it counterclockwise if you want to be able to see it. If you were to draw the polygon clockwise, then you would be seeing the inside, and the inside has been disabled with the GL_CULL_FACE bit.

Next up is the big bit, GL_LIGHTING. By using glEnable() on this value, you tell OpenGL that you are going to be doing some lighting calculations.

You use the glMaterialfv() function to set up the material properties that are used for each light. We'll discuss more about the material functions later in this chapter. In this example, you are setting the ambient and diffuse material properties for the front of the polygons.

The glLightfv() function is how you set up the properties for each light that you use. If you remember, OpenGL lets you use up to eight lights in your scene at any given time. To specify which light you are modifying, you use the notation GL_LIGHTX, where X is a number between 0 and 7. For example, to tell OpenGL that you are modifying the fifth light, you use GL_LIGHT4. We'll discuss this function in more detail soon in this chapter.

And lastly, you use the glEnable() function with the light you want to enable passed as a parameter to tell OpenGL to use that light in your scene. If you did not call this function, your light would never be lit.

And that is the code to get lights in your scene. Now you can actually draw your cube and transform it:

```
// DrawCube
// desc: draws a cube at the specified location in
//       the current coordinate space
void DrawCube(float xPos, float yPos, float zPos)
{
    glPushMatrix();
        glTranslatef(xPos, yPos, zPos);
        glBegin(GL_QUADS);
            glNormal3f(0.0f, 1.0f, 0.0f);          // top face
            glVertex3f(0.5f, 0.5f, 0.5f);
            glVertex3f(0.5f, 0.5f, -0.5f);
            glVertex3f(-0.5f, 0.5f, -0.5f);
            glVertex3f(-0.5f, 0.5f, 0.5f);
        glEnd();
        glBegin(GL_QUADS);
            glNormal3f(0.0f, 0.0f, 1.0f);          // front face
            glVertex3f(0.5f, 0.5f, 0.5f);
            glVertex3f(-0.5f, 0.5f, 0.5f);
            glVertex3f(-0.5f, -0.5f, 0.5f);
            glVertex3f(0.5f, -0.5f, 0.5f);
        glEnd();
        glBegin(GL_QUADS);
            glNormal3f(1.0f, 0.0f, 0.0f);          // right face
            glVertex3f(0.5f, 0.5f, 0.5f);
            glVertex3f(0.5f, -0.5f, 0.5f);
            glVertex3f(0.5f, -0.5f, -0.5f);
            glVertex3f(0.5f, 0.5f, -0.5f);
        glEnd();
        glBegin(GL_QUADS);
            glNormal3f(-1.0f, 0.0f, 0.0f);          // left face
            glVertex3f(-0.5f, 0.5f, 0.5f);
            glVertex3f(-0.5f, 0.5f, -0.5f);
            glVertex3f(-0.5f, -0.5f, -0.5f);
            glVertex3f(-0.5f, -0.5f, 0.5f);
        glEnd();
        glBegin(GL_POLYGON);
            glNormal3f(0.0f, -1.0f, 0.0f);          // bottom face
            glVertex3f(-0.5f, -0.5f, 0.5f);
            glVertex3f(-0.5f, -0.5f, -0.5f);
            glVertex3f(0.5f, -0.5f, -0.5f);
```

```
                glVertex3f(0.5f, -0.5f, 0.5f);
        glEnd();
        glBegin(GL_POLYGON);
                glNormal3f(0.0f, 0.0f, -1.0f);        // back face
                glVertex3f(0.5f, -0.5f, -0.5f);
                glVertex3f(-0.5f, -0.5f, -0.5f);
                glVertex3f(-0.5f, 0.5f, -0.5f);
                glVertex3f(0.5f, 0.5f, -0.5f);
        glEnd();
    glPopMatrix();
}
```

The DrawCube() function does exactly as it says it does: draws a cube at the location specified by its parameters relative to the current transformation matrix. Here you draw the six sides separately to get a 1×1×1 cube with its center at the origin. The real meat here is the glNormal3f() function that we talked about when we discussed normals. It tells OpenGL what the surface normal is for the next set of vertices. In this case, you define a surface normal with the glNormal3f() function each time you draw a face.

As an example, the front face of the cube faces the camera toward the positive z axis. This means that its normal also points toward the positive z axis, or (0, 1, 0). If you look at the bottom face of the cube, you see that its normal points down the negative y axis, or (0, –1, 0). As you can see, you specify unit normals for each of the face's normals to help out OpenGL. If you didn't specify unit normals, you would need to enable the GL_NORMALIZE bit, which tells OpenGL to make sure the normals you pass to it are unit normals, and if they aren't, to calculate them.

Here is the code for the Render() function that uses DrawCube():

```
// Render
// desc: handles drawing of scene
void Render()
{
    // clear screen and depth buffer
    glClear(GL_COLOR_BUFFER_BIT | GL_DEPTH_BUFFER_BIT);
    glLoadIdentity();          // reset modelview matrix

    angle = angle + 0.2f;      // increase our rotation angle counter
    if (angle >= 360.0f)
        angle = 0.0f;

    // perform transformations
    glTranslatef(0.0f, 0.0f, -3.0f);
```

```
        glRotatef(angle, 1.0f, 0.0f, 0.0f);
        glRotatef(angle, 0.0f, 1.0f, 0.0f);
        glRotatef(angle, 0.0f, 0.0f, 1.0f);

        DrawCube(0.0f, 0.0f, 0.0f);          // draw the transformed cube

        glFlush();
        SwapBuffers(g_HDC);                  // bring back buffer to foreground
}
```

Your last function here, Render(), is called each frame to handle your transformations and buffer swapping. There isn't anything here that we haven't covered. Basically, each frame in the current coordinate system is moved to (0, 0, –3) where it is then rotated along all three axes by the same number of degrees, and the cube is drawn. Because your lighting has already been set up and is calculated by OpenGL, you don't have to do anything dealing with lighting here.

You might notice that you didn't use the CalculateNormal() function that you created earlier. Because you were using a cube, you know what direction the surface normals for the cube will be facing, so you can just specify the normals on your own instead of wasting CPU time to calculate them. This method is similar to loading 3D models from certain file formats. Some file formats store the normals in the file along with the object data. When you use these file formats, you don't have to worry about calculating the normals because that has already been done for you. The idea is similar here, where you already know what your object looks like and what direction its normals should be facing. When you get irregular or morphing objects, you will need to calculate the normals in real time.

With all this in mind, Figure 6.10 shows your rotating lit cube.

Creating Light Sources

As the sample program shows, you can define several properties of light sources, including their color, position, and direction. The glLight*() function lets you define these properties. You will most commonly use this form of the glLight*() function when defining your lights:

```
void glLightfv(GLenum light, GLenum pname, TYPE *param);
```

The function takes three parameters: the light for which you are specifying the property, the property itself, and the value of that property. As mentioned before, the light parameter can be GL_LIGHT0, GL_LIGHT1, and so on, up to GL_LIGHT7, which specifies which light you are defining. The characteristic, or the property, you are defining in pname can be anything listed in Table 6.2.

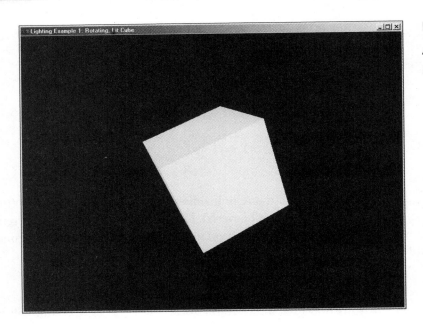

Figure 6.10

A picture of the rotating lit cube.

Table 6.2 `glLight*()` Parameters

Parameter	Meaning
GL_AMBIENT	Ambient intensity of light
GL_DIFFUSE	Diffuse intensity of light
GL_SPECULAR	Specular intensity of light
GL_POSITION	Position of light as point (x, y, z, w)
GL_SPOT_DIRECTION	Direction of spotlight as vector (x, y, z)
GL_SPOT_EXPONENT	Spotlight exponent
GL_SPOT_CUTOFF	Spotlight cutoff angle
GL_CONSTANT_ATTENUATION	Constant attenuation value
GL_LINEAR_ATTENUATION	Linear attenuation value
GL_QUADRATIC_ATTENUATION	Quadratic attenuation value

The values you pass to the last parameter, param, will be an array of floats when you use the glLightfv() function. For example, you can specify a bright white ambient light with these two lines:

```
float ambientLight[] = { 1.0f, 1.0f, 1.0f, 1.0f };    // bright white ambient light
glLightfv(LIGHT0, GL_AMBIENT, ambientLight);          // specify ambient light
```

Keep in mind that when you specify the ambient property of a light source, you are specifying the RGBA intensity of the ambient light that the light source adds to the scene. So the preceding two lines are saying that LIGHT0 will contribute an ambient light with full white-light intensity to the scene. By default, there is no ambient light, as its default value is equal to (0.0, 0.0, 0.0, 1.0).

The GL_DIFFUSE parameter is a little bit different. Think of it as the color of the light that the light source is projecting. The default value for GL_DIFFUSE is (1.0, 1.0, 1.0, 1.0), but only for LIGHT0. The rest of the lights (1–7) have a default diffuse value of (0.0, 0.0, 0.0, 0.0).

The term *specular highlight* refers to that bright reflection you sometimes see on an object under a specifically directed light. The GL_SPECULAR parameter determines the color of this specular highlight, and it is often specified with the same value as the GL_DIFFUSE parameter. This is done to get a more realistic effect, because real-world objects tend to have a specular highlight (GL_SPECULAR) with the same color as the light they are reflecting (GL_DIFFUSE). The default value for GL_SPECULAR is (1.0, 1.0, 1.0, 1.0) for GL_LIGHT0 and (0.0, 0.0, 0.0, 0.0) for the rest of the lights.

As mentioned before, the last component of these values is the alpha value; and you don't need to worry about this value until we talk about blending.

Positioning Light Sources

We briefly discussed light positioning with the sample program, but let's take a deeper look at it now. Light positions are defined with a four-value vector (x, y, z, w) and the GL_POSITION parameter. As you found earlier, if the w value is equal to 0.0, then the value (x, y, z) defines a vector that points in the direction the light is coming from. This is what you call a *directional light source*, where all the light rays are parallel as though the position of the light were far, far away from your objects. Probably the most common example of a directional light source is the sun. By the time the sun's light reaches the earth, the light rays are virtually parallel to each other. Specifying a directional light source for LIGHT0 looks like this:

```
float lightPosition[] = { 0.0f, 0.0f, 1.0f, 0.0f };
glLightfv(GL_LIGHT0, GL_POSITION, lightPosition);
```

These two lines of code will define a directional light that comes from the positive z axis, or out of the screen in the default camera view.

When you specify the *w* value as non-zero (not 0.0), you get what is called a *positional light source*. With a positional light source, the (*x*, *y*, *z*) values define the light's location in homogeneous object coordinates. A lamp and light bulb are both positional lights. In our rotating lit cube demo, you define a positional light at the world origin:

```
float lightPosition[] = { 0.0f, 0.0f, 0.0f, 1.0f };
glLightfv(GL_LIGHT0, GL_POSITION, lightPosition);
```

Attenuation

Attenuation is when the intensity of a light decreases as you get further away from the origin of the light. If you look at a street lamp at night (especially in the fog), you'll actually be able to see how the intensity of the light drops off from the lamp. You can get this same effect in your 3D games by setting the attenuation factor, but only for positional light sources. It wouldn't make sense to try to set the attenuation factor for a directional light, because these light sources are an infinite distance. OpenGL calculates the attenuation of a light source by multiplying the light source's contribution by an attenuation factor. Table 6.3 shows the three attenuation parameters OpenGL lets you specify.

Although Table 6.3 shows the default values for each of the attenuation parameters, you can specify your own by using the glLightf() function:

```
glLightf(GL_LIGHT0, GL_CONSTANT_ATTENUATION, 4.0f);
glLightf(GL_LIGHT0, GL_LINEAR_ATTENUATION, 1.0f);
glLightf(GL_LIGHT0, GL_QUADRATIC_ATTENUATION, 0.25);
```

Table 6.3 OpenGL Attenuation Parameters

Parameter	Default Value
GL_CONSTANT_ATTENUATION	1.0
GL_LINEAR_ATTENUATION	0.0
GL_QUADRATIC_ATTENUATION	0.0

The only values attenuation does not affect are the emission and global ambient light values. Otherwise, attenuation affects all other ambient, diffuse, and specular light properties in the world. There is one drawback to using attenuation, however: Because the equation for calculating the attenuation at a certain distance requires a division, and maybe some additions and multiplications, your game may run slower when you use attenuation.

Spotlights

If you reduce the radiance of the positional light we just talked about from all directions to a specific direction, you get what the world calls a *spotlight*. To create a spotlight, you do the same thing that you do to create a positional light with the addition of a few spotlight-specific parameters: the spotlight cutoff, the spotlight's direction, and the spotlight's focus.

Let's think about what a spotlight looks like for a moment. If you were looking at a spotlight in pure darkness, you would see that the light creates a cone of light in the direction that the spotlight is pointing. With OpenGL, you can define how wide this cone of light should be by specifying the angle between the edge of the cone and its axis with the GL_SPOT_CUTOFF parameter, as illustrated in Figure 6.11.

A GL_SPOT_CUTOFF value of 180 degrees means that the light will radiate in all directions, because 180×2 = 360. Conversely, a GL_SPOT_CUTOFF value of 10 degrees will result in a spotlight with a cone of light that spreads out a total of 20 degrees in the spotlight's direction. OpenGL only lets you specify a value between 0.0 and 90.0 for the GL_SPOT_CUTOFF parameter, unless you use the special 180.0 degrees value. If you want to specify a cone of light that spreads a total of 30.0 degrees, you use the glLightf() function like this:

```
glLightf(GL_LIGHT0, GL_SPOT_CUTOFF, 15.0f);        // 30 degree light cone
```

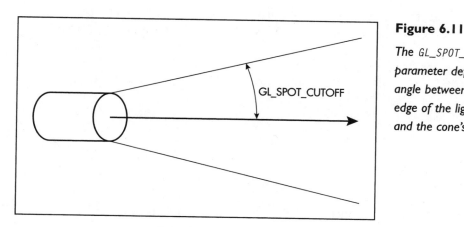

Figure 6.11

The GL_SPOT_CUTOFF parameter defines the angle between the edge of the light cone and the cone's axis.

The next thing you need to do is specify the direction that the spotlight is facing. The parameter you need to do this is GL_SPOT_DIRECTION, which takes a vector of the format (x, y, z). The default value of GL_SPOT_DIRECTION is (0.0, 0.0, –1.0), which points the spotlight down the negative z axis. You can specify your own direction for the spotlight by using the glLightfv() function, like so:

```
float spotlightDirection[] = { 0.0, -1.0, 0.0 };
glLightfv(GL_LIGHT0, GL_SPOT_DIRECTION, spotlightDirection);
```

These two lines will point the spotlight down the negative y axis.

And finally, you can specify the focus of the spotlight, which can be defined as the concentration of the spotlight in the center of the light cone. As you move away from the center of the cone, the light is attenuated until there is no more light at the edge of the cone. You use the GL_SPOT_EXPONENT parameter to set the amount of concentration, with a higher spot exponent proportional to a more focused light source. The following line sets the GL_SPOT_EXPONENT parameter to a value of 10.0:

```
glLightf(GL_LIGHT0, GL_SPOT_EXPONENT, 10.0f);
```

How about an example that uses spotlights? Take a look at this code that shines a spotlight on a rotating sphere:

```
////// Global variables
float angle = 0.0f;                                   // rotation angle


////// Lighting variables
float ambientLight[] = { 0.5f, 0.5f, 0.5f, 1.0f };  // ambient light
float diffuseLight[] = { 0.5f, 0.5f, 0.5f, 1.0f };  // diffuse light


float spotlightPosition[] = { 6.0f, 0.5f, 0.0f, 1.0f };  // spotlight position
float spotlightDirection[] = { -1.0f, 0.0f, -1.0f };     // spotlight direction


////// Material variables
float matAmbient[] = { 1.0f, 1.0f, 1.0f, 1.0f };      // ambient material
float matDiff[] = { 1.0f, 1.0f, 1.0f, 1.0f};          // diffuse material
float matSpecular[] = { 1.0f, 1.0f, 1.0f, 1.0f };     // specular material


// Initialize
// desc: initializes OpenGL
void Initialize()
{
    glClearColor(0.0f, 0.0f, 0.0f, 0.0f);             // clear to black
```

```
        glShadeModel(GL_SMOOTH);              // use smooth shading
        glEnable(GL_DEPTH_TEST);              // hidden surface removal
        glEnable(GL_CULL_FACE);               // do not calculate inside of polys
        glFrontFace(GL_CCW);                  // counterclockwise polygons are out

        glEnable(GL_LIGHTING);                // enable lighting

        // Now set up LIGHT0
        // set up the ambient element
        glLightfv(GL_LIGHT0, GL_AMBIENT, ambientLight);

        // the diffuse element
        glLightfv(GL_LIGHT0, GL_DIFFUSE, ambientLight);

        // place the light in the world
        glLightfv(GL_LIGHT0, GL_POSITION, spotlightPosition);

        // spotlight properties
        glLightf(GL_LIGHT0, GL_SPOT_CUTOFF, 40.0f);        // 80 degree-wide cone
        glLightf(GL_LIGHT0, GL_SPOT_EXPONENT, 30.0f);
        glLightfv(GL_LIGHT0, GL_SPOT_DIRECTION, spotlightDirection);

        // Enable the light
        glEnable(GL_LIGHT0);

        // track the colors set by glColor() for ambient and diffuse light
        glEnable(GL_COLOR_MATERIAL);
        glColorMaterial(GL_FRONT, GL_AMBIENT_AND_DIFFUSE);

        // materials have minimal shine
        glMaterialfv(GL_FRONT, GL_SPECULAR, matSpecular);
        glMaterialf(GL_FRONT, GL_SHININESS, 10.0f);
}

// Render
// desc: handles drawing of scene
void Render()
{
        // clear screen and depth buffer
        glClear(GL_COLOR_BUFFER_BIT | GL_DEPTH_BUFFER_BIT);
        glLoadIdentity();                 // reset modelview matrix
```

```
        angle = angle + 0.1f;              // increase our rotation angle counter
        if (angle >= 360.0f)
            angle = 0.0f;

        // move back 5 units and rotate about the y axis
        glTranslatef(0.0f, 0.0f, -5.0f);
        glRotatef(angle, 0.0f, 1.0f, 0.0f);

        // set color to mid-cyan
        glColor3f(0.0f, 0.5f, 0.5f);

        // draw sphere
        auxSolidSphere(1.0);

        glFlush();
        SwapBuffers(g_HDC);                // bring back buffer to foreground
}
```

This code gives you a rotating sphere that has a spotlight shining on it, as shown in Figure 6.12. You'll probably notice that you use the auxSolidSphere() function. This is a function from the

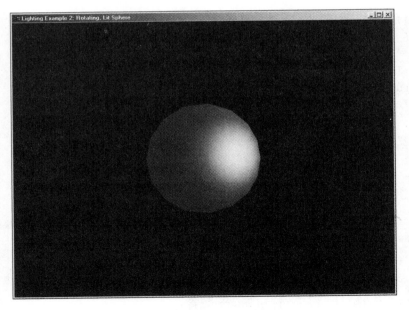

Figure 6.12

The rotating lit sphere.

GLAUX library and is used to draw a sphere with a radius that you pass to it. To use the GLAUX library, you need to link the *GLAUX.LIB* file in the Project Settings of MSVC++. Refer to the Introduction for information on how to do this.

Although you've seen how to do a spotlight, there are several lines in the sample program that we haven't discussed yet. Because these lines primarily deal with materials, let's talk about them now!

Defining Materials

You've looked at a couple examples that defined material properties for objects, but you haven't really looked in depth at the functions you use. Actually, setting a material is fairly similar to creating a light source. The difference is the function that is used:

```
void glMaterialf(GLenum face, GLenum pname, TYPE param);
void glMaterialfv(GLenum face, GLenum pname, TYPE *param);
```

This function defines the current material property that will be used in lighting calculations. The *face* parameter specifies how the material will be applied to the object's polygons. It can be one of three values: GL_FRONT, GL_BACK, or GL_FRONT_AND_BACK. The GL_FRONT value tells OpenGL that only the front of the polygons will use the material. Conversely, the GL_BACK value tells OpenGL that only the back of the polygons will use the material. The GL_FRONT_AND_BACK value applies the material to both the front and back of the polygons. The next parameter, *pname*, tells OpenGL which material properties are being set. This parameter can be any of the values listed in Table 6.4. The last parameter, depending on the function name itself, is either an array (for glMaterialfv) or a scalar value (for glMaterialf).

Table 6.4 glMaterial*() pname Parameters

Parameter	Meaning
GL_AMBIENT	Ambient color of material
GL_DIFFUSE	Diffuse color of material
GL_AMBIENT_AND_DIFFUSE	Ambient and diffuse color of material
GL_SPECULAR	Specular color of material
GL_SHININESS	Specular exponent
GL_EMISSION	Emissive color of material

If you want to set the ambient material color to red, for the front and back of polygons, then you would do this:

```
float red[] = { 1.0f, 0.0f, 0.0f, 1.0f };
glMaterialfv(GL_FRONT_AND_BACK, GL_AMBIENT, red);
```

Similarly, to set both the ambient and diffuse materials to white for the front of polygons, you do this:

```
float white[] = { 1.0f, 1.0f, 1.0f, 1.0f };
glMaterialfv(GL_FRONT, GL_AMBIENT_AND_DIFFUSE, white);
```

Keep in mind that any polygons you draw after calling glMaterial*() will be affected by the material settings until there is another call to glMaterial*().

Another way to set material properties is by what is called *color tracking*. Color tracking allows you to set material properties with calls to the glColor*() function. You can use color tracking by passing the GL_COLOR_MATERIAL parameter to the glEnable() function. Then you use the glColorMaterial() function to specify the material parameters that will be affected by calls to glColor*(). Here is some sample code to set the diffuse property of the fronts of polygons to use color tracking:

```
glEnable(GL_COLOR_MATERIAL);              // enable color tracking
glColorMaterial(GL_FRONT, GL_DIFFUSE);    // front of polygons, diffuse material
glColor3f(1.0f, 0.0f, 0.0f);              // set color to red
glBegin(GL_TRIANGLES);
     // draw triangles
glEnd();
```

As you can see, color tracking is very simple to set up and use. The spotlight sample program used color tracking to get the cyan-like color for the sphere. We will talk more about using materials for lighting effects soon in this chapter.

Lighting Models

The one step we haven't covered that is required to add lighting to your scene is creating and selecting a *lighting model*. The lighting model in OpenGL allows you to define four components that affect your scene:

- The ambient light intensity of the scene
- Whether the location of the viewpoint is local or infinite (affects specular–reflection angle calculation)
- One-sided or two-sided lighting
- Whether specular color is separate from ambient and diffuse

You define the lighting model with the glLightModel*() function, which is defined as

```
void glLightModel[if](GLenum pname, TYPE param);
void glLightModel[if]v(GLenum pname, TYPE param);
```

The first parameter of each of these functions, *pname*, specifies which lighting model property you are going to define. The second parameter, *param*, is the value that you are setting for the lighting model property. It will be either a single float value or an array of values, depending on the version of the function used. The *pname* parameter can be set to any of the values listed in Table 6.5.

The first parameter listed in Table 6.5 is the GL_LIGHT_MODEL_AMBIENT parameter. As you have seen, you can tell a light source to contribute its own ambient light to a scene. When you specify the GL_LIGHT_MODEL_AMBIENT parameter in the lighting model, you are telling OpenGL that there will be an ambient light that doesn't come from any particular light source, which is called *global ambient light*. To set the global ambient light to a medium light, you do the following:

```
float ambientLightModel[] = { 0.5, 0.5, 0.5, 1.0 };          // medium light
glLightModelfv(GL_LIGHT_MODEL_AMBIENT, ambientLightModel);
```

When you have a specular light and OpenGL is calculating a specular highlight for an object, the direction from the vertex being calculated and the viewpoint can affect the intensity of the specular highlight. The GL_LIGHT_MODEL_LOCAL_VIEWER parameter lets you specify whether the viewpoint is local to the objects or an infinite distance away. Having a local viewpoint will increase

Table 6.5 glLightModel*() pname Parameters

Parameter Name	Meaning
GL_LIGHT_MODEL_AMBIENT	Ambient intensity of the scene (RGBA); default value is (0.2, 0.2, 0.2, 1.0)
GL_LIGHT_MODEL_LOCAL_VIEWER	Viewpoint is local or infinite; default value is GL_FALSE (infinite)
GL_LIGHT_MODEL_TWO_SIDE	One-sided or two-sided lighting; default value is GL_FALSE (one-sided)
GL_LIGHT_MODEL_COLOR_CONTROL	Specular color is calculated separate from ambient and diffuse color; default value is GL_SINGLE_COLOR (not separate)

the realism of your scene, but at the same time, performance will decrease because the direction has to be calculated for each vertex. An infinite viewpoint (set with GL_FALSE) is used by default, but you can change it to a local viewpoint with this line:

```
glLightModeli(GL_LIGHT_MODEL_LOCAL_VIEWER, GL_TRUE);
```

The next parameter you can specify is GL_LIGHT_MODEL_TWO_SIDE. This parameter deals with whether you want to calculate the lighting for the back of polygons correctly. For example, if you were to take an enclosed object such as a cube and cut it in half, you would see that the back, or inside, of the polygons are not correctly illuminated. If you want the inside of these polygons to be illuminated correctly, you set the GL_LIGHT_MODEL_TWO_SIDE parameter to GL_TRUE like so:

```
glLightModeli(GL_LIGHT_MODEL_TWO_SIDE, GL_TRUE);
```

When you set this parameter to GL_TRUE, you are telling OpenGL to reverse the surface normals for the back-face of polygons, which results in all of the polygons being illuminated correctly. With this extra calculation, two-sided lighting naturally performs more slowly than one-sided lighting. Again, to switch back to one-sided lighting, set the value to GL_FALSE.

The final light model property you can set is the GL_LIGHT_MODEL_COLOR_CONTROL property. This property is used for when you are using lighting with texture mapping, and the specular high-lighting does not work well with the texture. Rather than add together the ambient, diffuse, specular, and emissive material values as it normally does, OpenGL creates two colors for each vertex of the object being lit: the primary color consisting of the non-specular components and a secondary color that consists of all the specular components. When texture mapping occurs, only the primary color is applied. Then afterwards, the secondary specular color is added to the result. This leads to more visible specular highlights. You tell OpenGL to separate the specular components from the others with this line of code:

```
glLightModeli(GL_LIGHT_MODEL_COLOR_CONTROL, GL_SEPARATE_SPECULAR_COLOR);
```

If you want to combine the specular component with the other components, then you call this function with the value GL_SINGLE_COLOR instead of GL_SEPARATE_SPECULAR_COLOR. You should set this parameter only when texture mapping; if you're not texture mapping, there won't be any reason to separate the specular component from the other components.

Specular Lighting Effects

Although the rotating sphere example showed you how to create and use a spotlight, there are a few other interesting lighting effects dealing with specular light and materials that you need to take a look at. When looking at the example, or even the screenshot, you might have noticed that the spotlight appeared to be shining off the seemingly glossy surface of the sphere. This shininess is the result of a small angle between the angle of incidence for the light, and is called a *specular highlight*. It occurs when almost all the light that strikes a surface is reflected.

Although the spotlight you created in the sample program did not have a specular component, you could add one very easily. As with the other lighting components, adding a specular component to a light source is as simple as setting the value with the glLightfv() function:

```
float specularLight[] = { 1.0f, 1.0f, 1.0f, 1.0f };   // specular light value
float lightPosition[] = { 0.0f, 0.0f, 0.0f, 1.0f };   // light position
...
glEnable(GL_LIGHTING);           // enable lighting
...
// set up LIGHT0
glLightfv(GL_LIGHT0, GL_SPECULAR, specularLight);
glLightfv(GL_LIGHT0, GL_POSITION, lightPosition);
glEnable(GL_LIGHT0);
```

Although you can also add an ambient and diffuse component to LIGHT0, these lines of code will set up the specular component and position of LIGHT0. The specular component has a value of (1.0, 1.0, 1.0, 1.0), which is a very bright white light similar to sunlight.

To get specular lighting effects, however, you also need to define specular material properties. The spinning sphere did this; let's take a look at the code it used:

```
float matSpecular[] = { 1.0f, 1.0f, 1.0f, 1.0f };        // specular material

// materials have minimal shine
glMaterialfv(GL_FRONT, GL_SPECULAR, matSpecular);
glMaterialf(GL_FRONT, GL_SHININESS, 10.0f);
```

The matSpecular variable could also be called the specular reflectance value. This means that with a value of (1.0, 1.0, 1.0, 1.0), any surfaces created after this material is defined will reflect almost all the incident specular light it receives.

The third line in this code fragment sets the GL_SHININESS property, which defines how focused the specular highlight is. You can specify this value anywhere from 1.0 to 128.0, with a value of 0.0 meaning that the specular highlight is unfocused. With a value of 128.0, surfaces are very pronounced and shiny.

Moving and Rotating Lights

You can move and rotate lights just like any other object in the 3D world. When you call glLight*() to define the position or direction of a light, the information you specify is manipulated by the current modelview matrix. As an example, the sample programs you have created thus far in this chapter have all had static light sources because the light position for every light was defined before any transformations occurred.

So what do you need to do to make a light move around? Well, think about how you would make any other object in the world move around. One way is to set the position of the object after you translate or rotate it. You can do the same thing with lights. This next example rotates a point light around a cube. Also included in the example is a way for you to handle input so you can change the scene dynamically. Let's take a look:

```c
////// Includes
#include <windows.h>            // standard Windows app include
#include <gl/gl.h>              // standard OpenGL include
#include <gl/glu.h>             // OpenGL utilities
#include <gl/glaux.h>           // OpenGL auxiliary functions

////// Global Variables
float angle = 0.0f;             // current angle of the rotating triangle
HDC g_HDC;                      // global device context
bool fullScreen = false;        // true = full screen; false = windowed
bool keyPressed[256];           // holds true for keys that are pressed

// Red, Green, and Blue Light Positions
float lightPositionR[] = { 0.0f, 0.0f, 75.0f, 1.0f };
float lightPositionG[] = { 0.0f, 0.0f, 75.0f, 1.0f };
float lightPositionB[] = { 0.0f, 0.0f, 75.0f, 1.0f };

// Red, Green, and Blue Ambient Light Intensities
float ambientLightR[] = { 1.0f, 0.0f, 0.0f, 1.0f };
float ambientLightG[] = { 0.0f, 1.0f, 0.0f, 1.0f };
float ambientLightB[] = { 0.0f, 0.0f, 1.0f, 1.0f };

// Red, Green, and Blue Specular Light Intensities
float specularLightR[] = { 1.0f, 0.0f, 0.0f, 1.0f };
float specularLightG[] = { 0.0f, 1.0f, 0.0f, 1.0f };
float specularLightB[] = { 0.0f, 0.0f, 1.0f, 1.0f };

// Spotlight's Direction
float spotDirection[] = { 0.0f, 0.0f, -1.0f };

// World Light Properties: Diffuse, Specular, Position
float diffuseLight[] = { 0.5f, 0.5f, 0.5f, 1.0f };
float specularLight[] = { 1.0f, 1.0f, 1.0f, 1.0f };
float lightPosition[] = { 0.0f, 0.0f, 100.0f, 1.0f };
```

```cpp
float objectXRot;          // the cube's x rotation
float objectYRot;          // the cube's y rotation
float objectZRot;          // the cube's z rotation

float redXRot;             // red light x rotation
float redYRot;             // red light y rotation

int currentColor = 1;      // 1 = red, 2 = green, 3 = blue
bool spotEnabled = true;   // true = on; false = off

// Initialize()
// desc: initializes OpenGL
void Initialize()
{
    glShadeModel(GL_SMOOTH);      // use smooth shading
    glEnable(GL_DEPTH_TEST);      // hidden surface removal
    glEnable(GL_CULL_FACE);       // do not calculate inside of polys
    glFrontFace(GL_CCW);          // counterclockwise polygons are out

    glEnable(GL_LIGHTING);        // enable lighting

    /* LIGHT0 is the spotlight.
       It points from (0.0, 0.0, 100.0) down the negative z axis. */
    glLightfv(GL_LIGHT0, GL_DIFFUSE, diffuseLight);
    glLightfv(GL_LIGHT0, GL_SPECULAR, specularLight);
    glLightfv(GL_LIGHT0, GL_POSITION, lightPosition);
    glLightf(GL_LIGHT0, GL_SPOT_CUTOFF, 40.0f);
    glLightf(GL_LIGHT0, GL_SPOT_EXPONENT, 80.0f);

    /* LIGHT1 is our moving point light. It starts out as a red light. */
    glLightfv(GL_LIGHT1, GL_DIFFUSE, diffuseLightR);
    glLightfv(GL_LIGHT1, GL_SPECULAR, specularLightR);
    glLightfv(GL_LIGHT1, GL_POSITION, lightPositionR);

    // Enable our lights
    glEnable(GL_LIGHT0);
    glEnable(GL_LIGHT1);

    // Use color tracking for material properties
    glEnable(GL_COLOR_MATERIAL);
    glColorMaterial(GL_FRONT, GL_AMBIENT_AND_DIFFUSE);
```

```
        // We want a very shiny effect on the cube
        glMaterialfv(GL_FRONT, GL_SPECULAR, specularLight);
        glMateriali(GL_FRONT, GL_SHININESS, 128);

        // Clear background to black
        glClearColor(0.0f, 0.0f, 0.0f, 0.0f);
}

// Render()
// desc: handles drawing of scene
void Render()
{
        // clear screen and depth buffer
        glClear(GL_COLOR_BUFFER_BIT | GL_DEPTH_BUFFER_BIT);

        // reset modelview matrix
        glLoadIdentity();

        // Move everything back to (0, 0, -150)
        glTranslatef(0.0f, 0.0f, -150.0f);

        glPushMatrix();
            // rotate along the x and y axes
            glRotatef(redYRot, 0.0f, 1.0f, 0.0f);
            glRotatef(redXRot, 1.0f, 0.0f, 0.0f);

            // place the light in the world
            glLightfv(GL_LIGHT1, GL_POSITION, lightPositionR);

            switch (currentColor)
            {
                case 1:        // red light
                {
                    glLightfv(GL_LIGHT1, GL_DIFFUSE, diffuseLightR);
                    glLightfv(GL_LIGHT1, GL_POSITION, lightPositionR);
                    glLightfv(GL_LIGHT1, GL_SPECULAR, specularLightR);

                    // translate to draw the light's sphere
                    glTranslatef(lightPositionR[0],
                                lightPositionR[1],
                                lightPositionR[2]);
```

```
              glColor3f(1.0f, 0.0f, 0.0f);
              break;
          }
          case 2:        // green light
          {
              glLightfv(GL_LIGHT1, GL_DIFFUSE, diffuseLightG);
              glLightfv(GL_LIGHT1, GL_POSITION, lightPositionG);
              glLightfv(GL_LIGHT1, GL_SPECULAR, specularLightG);

              // translate to draw the light's sphere
              glTranslatef(lightPositionG[0],
                           lightPositionG[1],
                           lightPositionG[2]);
              glColor3f(0.0f, 1.0f, 0.0f);
              break;
          }
          case 3:        // blue light
          {
              glLightfv(GL_LIGHT1, GL_DIFFUSE, diffuseLightB);
              glLightfv(GL_LIGHT1, GL_POSITION, lightPositionB);
              glLightfv(GL_LIGHT1, GL_SPECULAR, specularLightB);

              // translate to draw the light's sphere
              glTranslatef(lightPositionB[0],
                           lightPositionB[1],
                           lightPositionB[2]);
              glColor3f(0.0f, 0.0f, 1.0f);
              break;
          }
      }

      // Save the lighting attributes
      glPushAttrib(GL_LIGHTING_BIT);

          /* Disable lighting when we draw the sphere
             so the sphere is not affected by any lights */
          glDisable(GL_LIGHTING);
          auxSolidSphere(2.5f);
          glEnable(GL_LIGHTING);
```

```
            glPopAttrib();          // restore the lighting attributes
        glPopMatrix();

        // Draw the rotating cube
        glPushMatrix();
            glColor3f(1.0f, 1.0f, 1.0f);
            glRotatef(objectXRot, 1.0f, 0.0f, 0.0f);
            glRotatef(objectYRot, 0.0f, 1.0f, 0.0f);
            glRotatef(objectZRot, 0.0f, 0.0f, 1.0f);
            auxSolidCube(70.0f);
        glPopMatrix();

        glFlush();
        SwapBuffers(g_HDC);             // bring back buffer to foreground

        // increase rotation values
        objectXRot += 0.01f;
        objectYRot += 0.02f;
        objectZRot += 0.01f;

        redXRot += 0.3f;
        redYRot += 0.1f;
    }
```

The following code is inserted into the WndProc() that you have been using:

```
case WM_KEYDOWN:                    // is a key pressed?
    keyPressed[wParam] = true;
    return 0;
    break;

case WM_KEYUP:                      // is a key released?
    keyPressed[wParam] = false;
    return 0;
    break;
```

The following code is the Windows message loop that is a part of WinMain():

```
while (!done)
{
    PeekMessage(&msg, hwnd, NULL, NULL, PM_REMOVE);
```

```cpp
        if (msg.message == WM_QUIT)          // do we receive a WM_QUIT message?
        {
            done = true;                     // if so, time to quit the application
        }
        else
        {
            if (keyPressed[VK_ESCAPE])
                done = true;
            else
            {
                if (keyPressed['R'])
                    currentColor = 1;

                if (keyPressed['G'])
                    currentColor = 2;

                if (keyPressed['B'])
                    currentColor = 3;

                if ((keyPressed['S']) && (spotEnabled))
                {
                    spotEnabled = false;
                    glDisable(GL_LIGHT0);
                }
                else if ((keyPressed['S']) && (!spotEnabled))
                {
                    spotEnabled = true;
                    glEnable(GL_LIGHT0);
                }

                Render();

                // translate and dispatch to event queue
                TranslateMessage(&msg);
                DispatchMessage(&msg);
            }
        }
    }    // end while
```

Keep in mind that this code is definitely not optimized, and with a couple line changes you can easily speed up the application. This is left for you to figure out as an exercise. One such place would be the switch() statement in the Render() function. You *do not* have to set the color of the light every single time you render. In fact, doing so can sometimes dramatically reduce the performance of your application. However, to get your object to move, you *do* need to specify the position of your light after you've completed your transformations, as you can see with the lines

```
// rotate along the x and y axes
glRotatef(redYRot, 0.0f, 1.0f, 0.0f);
glRotatef(redXRot, 1.0f, 0.0f, 0.0f);

// place the light in the world
glLightfv(GL_LIGHT1, GL_POSITION, lightPositionR);
```

If the moving light had spotlight properties, you would also need to specify the GL_SPOT_DIRECTION parameter, but you are using a point of light that emits light in all directions, so you only need to define the GL_POSITION parameter.

To draw the sphere that you use to represent the position of the light, you use the glPushAttrib() function. Although we won't get into detail on this function, just know that along with the projection, modelview, and texture stacks, there is another stack you can use to store the current rendering state. With the GL_LIGHTING_BIT attribute that you pass to the function, you can save all the lighting information for the scene. Doing this gives you a chance to turn off lighting so you can draw your sphere without any lighting effects on it. Once you're finished drawing the sphere, you can turn lighting back on and use the glPopAttrib() function, which will restore the lighting attributes you had just saved to the attribute stack.

Lastly, this example also shows how you can handle some input from the keyboard. To do this, you define an array of 255 boolean values that represent the 255 possible ASCII codes that can be input via the keyboard. So for example, when a user presses the A key on the keyboard, WndProc()'s WM_KEYDOWN code will set the value of keysPressed[65] equal to true, with 65 being the ASCII code of A.

With this type of functionality, you can check which keys have been pressed while you're in the Windows message loop and react accordingly. In this example, you can change the color of the positional light depending on what key is pressed. You can also turn off the spotlight if the S key is pressed. For the color of the positional light, R changes it to red, G changes it to green, and B changes it to blue. Figure 6.13 is a screenshot of this example.

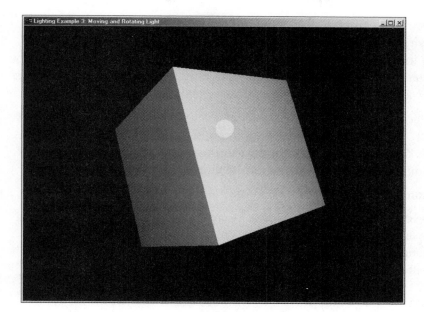

Figure 6.13

A screenshot of the moving and rotating lights example.

A common item in 3D games nowadays is a flashlight. Flashlights, or headlights, are simply another way to position and move a light around the world. This problem is often referred to as having a light position stay fixed relative to the eye, or camera, position. To achieve this effect, you need to specify the light position in eye-coordinate space. First you set the modelview matrix to the identity matrix, and then you define your light position at the origin. If you do not specify a direction, then you get the effect of a lantern or lamp located at the position of the camera. If you want a headlight or flashlight effect, you need to set the light direction to point down the negative z axis. Because your light position is fixed, you can specify it only when you initialize your application, which will eliminate the need to redefine the light position every time you render a frame.

BLENDING

Color blending in OpenGL allows you to introduce effects such as transparency into your scenes. With transparency you can simulate water, windows, glass, and other objects in the world that you can see through.

Remember the alpha value we've been ignoring all this time? Well, now that we're talking about blending, you need to learn how to use it. When you enable blending, you are telling OpenGL to combine the color of the incoming primitive with the color that is already in the frame buffer and store the result back in the frame buffer. Blending operations are typically viewed with the RGB values representing the color and the alpha value representing the opacity. A lower opacity, or lower alpha value, results in higher transparency and translucency. From now on, we will refer to the incoming primitive as the *source*, and the currently stored pixel as the *destination*.

To enable blending in OpenGL, you call the glEnable() function with the GL_BLEND parameter. You then call the glBlendFunc() where you define the source and destination blending functions. The default glBlendFunc() arguments are GL_ONE for the source and GL_ZERO for the destination. Table 6.6 shows the blending functions you can use for the source argument.

Table 6.7 shows the blending functions you can use for the destination argument.

Typically, applications use only a small number of these to create blending effects. For example, as you will see with transparency, you use the GL_SRC_ALPHA function for the source and the GL_ONE_MINUS_SRC_ALPHA function for the destination. Experimentation with different blending-function combinations will help you find new effects to use.

Table 6.6 Source Blending Functions

Function	Description
GL_ZERO	The source color is equal to (0, 0, 0, 0).
GL_ONE	Use the current source color.
GL_DST_COLOR	Multiply the source color by the destination color.
GL_ONE_MINUS_DST_COLOR	Multiply the source color by [(1, 1, 1, 1) − destination color].
GL_SRC_ALPHA	Multiply the source color by the source alpha value.
GL_ONE_MINUS_SRC_ALPHA	Multiply the source color by (1 − source alpha value).
GL_DST_ALPHA	Multiply the source color by the destination alpha value.
GL_ONE_MINUS_DST_ALPHA	Multiply the source color by (1 − destination alpha value).
GL_SRC_ALPHA_SATURATE	Multiply the source color by the minimum of the source and (1 − destination).

Table 6.7 Destination Blending Functions

Function	Description
GL_ZERO	Destination color is equal to (0, 0, 0, 0).
GL_ONE	Use the current destination color.
GL_SRC_COLOR	Multiply the destination color by the source color.
GL_ONE_MINUS_SRC_COLOR	Multiply the destination color by [(1, 1, 1, 1) − source color].
GL_SRC_ALPHA	Multiply the destination color by the source alpha value.
GL_ONE_MINUS_SRC_ALPHA	Multiply the destination color by (1 − source alpha value).
GL_DST_ALPHA	Multiply the destination color by the destination alpha.
GL_ONE_MINUS_DST_ALPHA	Multiply the destination color by (1 − destination alpha value).
GL_SRC_ALPHA_SATURATE	Multiply the destination color by the minimum of the source and (1 − destination).

Transparency

As mentioned, transparency comes from the combination of a source function of GL_SRC_ALPHA and a destination function of GL_ONE_MINUS_SRC_ALPHA. The following lines of code set up blending for transparency:

```
glEnable(GL_BLEND);
glBlendFunc(GL_SRC_ALPHA, GL_ONE_MINUS_SRC_ALPHA);
```

With this blending function, a certain amount of the source color (determined by its alpha value) is overlaid onto the pixel in the frame buffer.

Let's take a look at a quick example of transparency. The following code displays two overlapping polygons with an alpha value of 0.6. As you will see, the order in which the polygons are drawn will affect the final outcome:

```cpp
bool leftFirst = true;          // true = draw left poly first; false = right first

// Initialize
// desc: initializes OpenGL
void Initialize()
{
    glEnable(GL_BLEND);                    // enable blending

    // transparency blending function
    glBlendFunc(GL_SRC_ALPHA, GL_ONE_MINUS_SRC_ALPHA);

    glShadeModel(GL_SMOOTH);               // use smooth shading

    // Clear background to black
    glClearColor(0.0f, 0.0f, 0.0f, 0.0f);
}

// DrawLeftPoly()
// desc: draws the left polygon
void DrawLeftPoly()
{
    glColor4f(0.8f, 0.9f, 0.7f, 0.6);      // set alpha value = 0.6
    glBegin(GL_QUADS);
        glVertex3f(-10.0f, -10.0f, 0.0f);
        glVertex3f(0.0f, -10.0f, 0.0f);
        glVertex3f(0.0f, 10.0f, 0.0f);
        glVertex3f(-10.0f, 10.0f, 0.0f);
    glEnd();
}

// DrawRightPoly()
// desc: draws the right polygon
void DrawRightPoly()
{
    glColor4f(0.0f, 0.5f, 0.5f, 0.6);      // set alpha value = 0.6
    glBegin(GL_QUADS);
        glVertex3f(0.0f, -10.0f, 0.0f);
        glVertex3f(10.0f, -10.0f, 0.0f);
        glVertex3f(10.0f, 10.0f, 0.0f);
        glVertex3f(0.0f, 10.0f, 0.0f);
    glEnd();
}
```

```
// Render
// desc: handles drawing of scene
void Render()
{
     // clear screen and depth buffer
     glClear(GL_COLOR_BUFFER_BIT | GL_DEPTH_BUFFER_BIT);
     glLoadIdentity();

     if (angle >= 359.9f)
          angle = 0.0f;

     angle += 0.1;              // increase rotation angle

     glTranslatef(0.0f, 0.0f, -40.0f);

     // rotate and draw the opaque polygon
     glPushMatrix();
          glRotatef(angle, 0.0f, 0.0f, 1.0f);
          if (leftFirst)
               DrawLeftPoly();
          else
               DrawRightPoly();
     glPopMatrix();

     // rotate and draw the transparent polygon
     glPushMatrix();
          glRotatef(angle, 0.0f, 0.0f, -1.0f);
          if (leftFirst)
               DrawRightPoly();
          else
               DrawLeftPoly();
     glPopMatrix();

     glFlush();
     SwapBuffers(g_HDC);          // bring back buffer to foreground
}
```

As you can see from the example shown in Figure 6.14, adding blending to a scene is not very difficult when all the objects are located at the same distance from the camera.

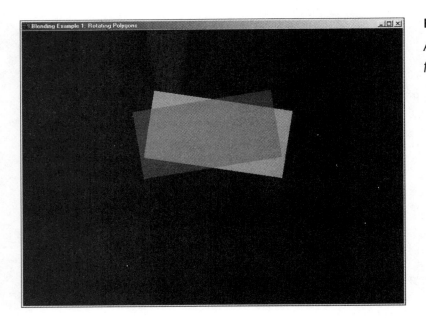

Figure 6.14

A screenshot of our first blending example.

With 3D, however, there are a few more things you need to take care of to ensure proper blending and drawing of your scene. The most important thing is to turn depth testing on with the command

```
glEnable(GL_DEPTH_TEST);
```

You enable depth testing because you want to hide objects located behind other objects. Now you have a decision to make. The depth buffer is used to keep track of the distance between the viewpoint and a pixel of an object that occupies a position in the window. When another color arrives for that pixel, the pixel is only replaced if the new pixel's object is closer to the viewpoint. If a replacement occurs, the new pixel's depth value is placed in the depth buffer. This allows for OpenGL to hide objects behind closer opaque objects.

The correct way to do blending in OpenGL involves turning the depth buffer on and off when you are drawing your scene. To use this method, you first draw all the opaque objects with the depth buffer in its normal mode. Then you can use the glDepthMask() function to set the depth buffer to read-only. This protects the depth values set when you were drawing the opaque objects. With the depth buffer in read-only mode, you can draw translucent objects without affecting the already-drawn opaque objects because the depth buffer cannot be altered. Keep in mind, however, that the translucent objects are still compared to the depth buffer and will not be drawn if they are located behind opaque ones. If they are in front of the opaque objects, the translucent objects will be blended with them. To use the glDepthMask() function, you pass GL_FALSE if you want to set read-only mode, while GL_TRUE sets the normal mode.

The following sample program shows how you perform these steps. Figure 6.15 is a screenshot of the program, which displays one opaque sphere and one transparent sphere that rotate around another, smaller sphere. The smaller sphere denotes the location of a positional light that is reflected by the spheres.

```
float lightPosition[] = { 0.0f, 0.0f, 1.0f, 0.0f };  // global light is directional

float diffuseLight[] = { 1.0f, 1.0f, 1.0f, 1.0f };   // diffuse light
float diffuseMat[] = { 1.0f, 1.0f, 1.0f, 1.0f };     // diffuse material

float ballDiffuse[] = { 0.5f, 0.5f, 0.0f, 1.0f };    // ball diffuse
float ballSpecular[] = { 1.0f, 1.0f, 1.0f, 1.0f };   // ball specular
float ballPosition[] = { 0.0f, 0.0f, 0.0f, 1.0f };   // ball position

// Initialize
// desc: initializes OpenGL
void Initialize()
{
    // enable lighting, depth buffer, and back-face culling
    glEnable(GL_LIGHTING);
    glEnable(GL_DEPTH_TEST);
    glEnable(GL_CULL_FACE);

    // set properties for global diffuse light
    glLightfv(GL_LIGHT0, GL_DIFFUSE, diffuseLight);
    glLightfv(GL_LIGHT0, GL_POSITION, lightPosition);
    glEnable(GL_LIGHT0);

    // set properties for the "sun" ball light
    glLightfv(GL_LIGHT1, GL_DIFFUSE, ballDiffuse);
    glLightfv(GL_LIGHT1, GL_SPECULAR, ballSpecular);
    glEnable(GL_LIGHT1);

    // set diffuse material for objects
    glMaterialfv(GL_FRONT, GL_DIFFUSE, diffuseMat);
```

```
        // enable color tracking
        glEnable(GL_COLOR_MATERIAL);

        // use smooth shading
        glShadeModel(GL_SMOOTH);

        // clear background to black
        glClearColor(0.0f, 0.0f, 0.0f, 0.0f);
}

// Render
// desc: handles drawing of scene
void Render()
{
        // clear screen and depth buffer
        glClear(GL_COLOR_BUFFER_BIT | GL_DEPTH_BUFFER_BIT);
        glLoadIdentity();

        // both spheres use the same rotation speed
        if (angle >= 359.9f)
                angle = 0.0f;
        angle += 0.1;

        // move back 15 units
        glTranslatef(0.0f, 0.0f, -15.0f);

        // set the position of the light for the "sun" ball
        glLightfv(GL_LIGHT1, GL_POSITION, ballPosition);

        // draw the "sun" ball
        glPushMatrix();
                glColor3f(1.0f, 1.0f, 0.0f);
                glTranslatef(ballPosition[0], ballPosition[1], ballPosition[2]);
                auxSolidSphere(0.5f);
        glPopMatrix();

        // draw opaque sphere
      ! glPushMatrix();
                glRotatef(angle, 0.0f, 1.0f, 0.0f);
                glTranslatef(0.0f, 0.0f, 6.0f);
```

```
        glColor4f(1.0f, 0.2f, 0.2f, 1.0f);
        auxSolidSphere(2.0f);
    glPopMatrix();

    // enable blending
    glEnable(GL_BLEND);

    // enable read-only depth buffer
    glDepthMask(GL_FALSE);

    // set the blend function to what we use for transparency
    glBlendFunc(GL_SRC_ALPHA, GL_ONE);

    // draw transparent sphere
    glPushMatrix();
        glRotatef(angle, 0.0f, 1.0f, 0.0f);
        glTranslatef(0.0f, 0.0f, -6.0f);
        glColor4f(0.0f, 0.5f, 0.5f, 0.3f);
        auxSolidSphere(2.0f);
    glPopMatrix();

    // set back to normal depth buffer mode (writeable)
    glDepthMask(GL_TRUE);

    // disable blending
    glDisable(GL_BLEND);

    glFlush();
    SwapBuffers(g_HDC);                 // bring back buffer to foreground
}
```

As you can see in the code, you draw the opaque objects before enabling blending, setting the depth buffer to read-only, and drawing your transparent objects. This example also brings back some lighting effects to show how it mixes with blending and transparency.

Because you set the alpha value for the transparent sphere equal to 0.3, more light can pass through it because it is more transparent. If the yellow "ball" light were not included, the sphere would be very dim. Remember that as the alpha value gets closer to 1.0, the more opaque the object is. When the alpha value gets closer to 0.0, the more transparent the object is. In fact, an alpha value of 0.0 gives you a perfectly clear object, while an alpha value of 1.0 gives a completely solid and opaque object.

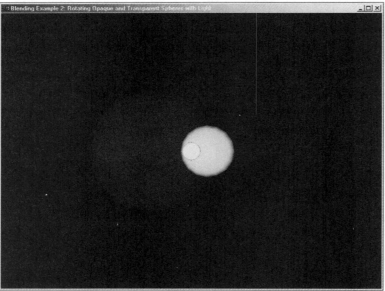

Figure 6.15

Screenshot of our second blending sample program, which shows how you can use the glDepthMask() *function.*

SUMMARY

Light is considered both a particle and a wave. The cones in your eyes translate light into combinations of red, green, and blue light. Similarly, computer monitors emit various intensities of red, green, and blue phosphors.

The color depth is how you determine how many colors you can use and is often stored in the *color buffer*. The color buffer is given a size in bits such as 4, 8, 16, and so on. An 8-bit color buffer can store 8 bits of data, which equates to 2^8, or 256, colors. Today's hardware typically supports four different color depths that programmers can use for their applications: 8, 16, 24, and 32.

OpenGL specifies color as three separate intensities of red, green, and blue. The values of these intensities can range from 0.0 (no intensity) to 1.0 (full intensity).

Shading can either be *flat* or *smooth*. Flat shading is drawn with a single color, typically with the color of the last vertex. Smooth shading, or *Gouraud shading*, is the more realistic of the two and uses interpolation to determine the colors between the vertices of a primitive.

OpenGL attempts to model real-world lighting through the use of four components: ambient, diffuse, specular, and emissive. OpenGL approximates material colors based on the red, green, and blue light the material reflects.

Normals are used to calculate the amount of light that strikes a surface. You convert normals to unit normals before submitting them to OpenGL for speed purposes.

There are four steps to setting up lighting in OpenGL as defined in the *OpenGL Programming Guide*:

1. Calculate normal vectors for each vertex of every object. The normals determine the object's orientation relative to the light source.
2. Create, select, and position all light sources.
3. Create and select a lighting model. The lighting model defines the ambient light and location of the viewpoint for the lighting calculations.
4. Define the material properties for the objects in the scene.

You can move and rotate lights just like any other object in OpenGL. When you call `glLight*()` to define the position or direction of a light, the information you specify is manipulated by the current modelview matrix.

Color blending in OpenGL allows you to introduce effects such as transparency into your scenes. You can get transparency when blending with the combination `GL_SRC_ALPHA` for the source and `GL_ONE_MINUS_SRC_ALPHA` for the destination.

You use the `glDepthMask()` function to set the depth buffer to read-only when you are drawing translucent objects.

CHAPTER 7

Bitmaps and Images with OpenGL

Now it's time to break off from the world of 3D graphics and take a look at the world of *raster graphics,* which are two-dimensional arrays of color. In this chapter you'll be looking specifically at how you can use OpenGL to perform various functions on bitmaps and images. We'll also be discussing how to load and save two image file formats: the Windows BMP (*.bmp*) and the Targa (*.tga*) image file format.

In this chapter you'll cover

- Bitmaps with OpenGL
- The Windows bitmap
- Targa image files

THE OPENGL BITMAP

The term *bitmap* in the context of OpenGL is defined as a rectangular array of pixels, where a single bit of information (a 0 or 1) is stored about each pixel. They are treated as drawing masks for a rectangular area of the window and are typically used for characters in fonts. As an example, let's say you have a 16×16 bitmap, and you divide the bitmap into a 16×16 grid as shown in Figure 7.1. When you draw this bitmap, a pixel in the current raster color (remember glColor3f()?) will be drawn if the pixel's grid location has a value of 1. When a value of 0 is encountered, nothing is drawn.

Although we will discuss more about fonts in Chapter 11, "Displaying Text," let's take a look at how you can display a single character to the screen using the OpenGL bitmap functions glBitmap() and glRasterPos*().

Positioning the Bitmap

The glRasterPos*() function lets you specify the screen position where your bitmap or image will be drawn. The coordinates that are sent to the function define the bottom-left corner of the bitmap. For example, passing the coordinates (30, 10) to the glRasterPos*() function will draw the next bitmap with its bottom-left corner at (30, 10). The function is defined as

```
void glRasterPos[234][sifd](TYPE x, TYPE y, TYPE z, TYPE w);
void glRasterPos[234][sifd]v(TYPE *coords);
```

1	0	0	0	0	0	0	0	0	0	0	0	0	0	0	1
0	1	0	0	0	0	0	0	0	0	0	0	0	0	1	0
0	0	1	0	0	0	0	0	0	0	0	0	0	1	0	0
0	0	0	1	0	0	0	0	0	0	0	0	1	0	0	0
0	0	0	0	1	0	0	0	0	0	0	1	0	0	0	0
0	0	0	0	0	1	0	0	0	0	1	0	0	0	0	0
0	0	0	0	0	0	1	0	0	1	0	0	0	0	0	0
0	0	0	0	0	0	0	1	1	0	0	0	0	0	0	0
0	0	0	0	0	0	0	1	1	0	0	0	0	0	0	0
0	0	0	0	0	0	1	0	0	1	0	0	0	0	0	0
0	0	0	0	0	1	0	0	0	0	1	0	0	0	0	0
0	0	0	0	1	0	0	0	0	0	0	1	0	0	0	0
0	0	0	1	0	0	0	0	0	0	0	0	1	0	0	0
0	0	1	0	0	0	0	0	0	0	0	0	0	1	0	0
0	1	0	0	0	0	0	0	0	0	0	0	0	0	1	0
1	0	0	0	0	0	0	0	0	0	0	0	0	0	0	1

Figure 7.1

A 16×16 bitmap divided into a grid of zeroes and ones.

With this example, you would call the function like this:

```
glRasterPos2i(30, 10);
```

Unless you specify the modelview and projection matrices for 2D rendering, the coordinates sent to the glRasterPos*() function are converted to screen coordinates. You can define a 2D rendering viewport with a simple change to your viewport setup code. Instead of using the gluProjection() function to define a 3D viewport, you can use the glOrtho() or gluOrtho2D() functions to define a 2D viewport. This is how you would define a simple 2D viewport using the glOrtho() function, with width and height defining the width and height of the window:

```
glViewport(0, 0, width, height);      // reset the viewport to new dimensions
glMatrixMode(GL_PROJECTION);          // set projection matrix current matrix
glLoadIdentity();                     // reset projection matrix

// define 2D viewport
glOrtho(0.0f, width - 1.0, 0.0, height - 1.0, -1.0, 1.0);

glMatrixMode(GL_MODELVIEW);           // set modelview matrix
glLoadIdentity();                     // reset modelview matrix
```

You can find out if the raster position you passed to the function is a valid raster position by passing the GL_CURRENT_RASTER_POSITION_VALID parameter to the glGetBooleanv() function. If the function returns false, the position is invalid.

Drawing the Bitmap

After you have set the current raster position, you actually draw your bitmap with the `glBitmap()` function, which is defined as

```
void glBitmap(GLsizei width, GLsizei height, GLfloat xOrigin, GLfloat yOrigin,
              GLfloat xIncrement, GLfloat yIncrement, const GLubyte *bitmap);
```

This function will draw a bitmap with the specified width and height at the (*xOrigin, yOrigin*) coordinates relative to the current raster position. The (*xIncrement, yIncrement*) coordinates specify the increments that are added to the current raster position after the bitmap has been drawn. Figure 7.2 shows how a bitmap would be affected by these parameters.

> **NOTE**
>
> One drawback to OpenGL bitmaps is that you can neither rotate nor zoom them, but you can do these operations with pixel maps, or images, as you will see.

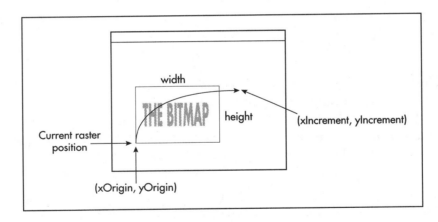

Figure 7.2

The effect of `glBitmap()` *parameters when drawing a bitmap.*

An OpenGL Bitmap Example

As we discussed, we are going to take a look at an example of how you actually use the OpenGL bitmaps and their functions. The following example displays 50 16×16 bitmaps in random locations during each frame. The end result is a window with 50 letter *A*s popping up and disappearing randomly.

First, you need to define your character *A* as an array of bit information:

```
unsigned char letterA[] = {
                    0xC0, 0x03,
                    0xC0, 0x03,
                    0xC0, 0x03,
                    0xC0, 0x03,
                    0xC0, 0x03,
                    0xDF, 0xFB,
                    0x7F, 0xFE,
                    0x60, 0x06,
                    0x30, 0x0C,
                    0x30, 0x0C,
                    0x18, 0x18,
                    0x18, 0x18,
                    0x0C, 0x30,
                    0x0C, 0x30,
                    0x07, 0xE0,
                    0x07, 0xE0
};
```

These bits translate to the bitmap you see in Figure 7.3. Keep in mind that you are storing the bitmap upside down, but Figure 7.3 is how the bitmap will be displayed.

	0	1	2	3	4	5	6	7	8	9	10	11	12	13	14	15
0	0	0	0	0	0	1	1	1	1	1	1	0	0	0	0	0
1	0	0	0	0	0	1	1	1	1	1	1	0	0	0	0	0
2	0	0	0	0	1	1	0	0	0	0	1	1	0	0	0	0
3	0	0	0	0	1	1	0	0	0	0	1	1	0	0	0	0
4	0	0	0	1	1	0	0	0	0	0	0	1	1	0	0	0
5	0	0	0	1	1	0	0	0	0	0	0	1	1	0	0	0
6	0	0	1	1	0	0	0	0	0	0	0	0	1	1	0	0
7	0	0	1	1	0	0	0	0	0	0	0	0	1	1	0	0
8	0	1	1	0	0	0	0	0	0	0	0	0	0	1	1	0
9	0	1	1	1	1	1	1	1	1	1	1	1	1	1	1	0
10	1	1	0	1	1	1	1	1	1	1	1	1	1	0	1	1
11	1	1	0	0	0	0	0	0	0	0	0	0	0	0	1	1
12	1	1	0	0	0	0	0	0	0	0	0	0	0	0	1	1
13	1	1	0	0	0	0	0	0	0	0	0	0	0	0	1	1
14	1	1	0	0	0	0	0	0	0	0	0	0	0	0	1	1
15	1	1	0	0	0	0	0	0	0	0	0	0	0	0	1	1

Figure 7.3

The bit-by-bit definition of our letter A.

You then create your Render() function:

```
void Render()
{
    // clear screen and depth buffer
    glClear(GL_COLOR_BUFFER_BIT | GL_DEPTH_BUFFER_BIT);
    // set alignment to 1 byte
    glPixelStorei(GL_UNPACK_ALIGNMENT, 1);

    // set color to white
    glColor3f(1.0f, 1.0f, 1.0f);

    // display 50 16x16 letter As randomly on the 800x600 screen
    for (int numA = 0; numA < 50; numA++)
    {
        glRasterPos2i(rand() % 800, rand() % 600);
        glBitmap(16, 16, 0.0, 0.0, 0.0, 0.0, letterA);
    }

    glFlush();
    SwapBuffers(g_HDC);                   // bring back buffer to foreground
}
```

In this function, set your raster color to white before randomly displaying your letter *A* bitmaps on the screen. As you can see in the glBitmap() function, the origin for the bitmap is the same location as the position you set with glRasterPos2i(), and there are no increment values for after the bitmap is rendered.

Lastly, you set your viewport with the function glOrtho() like this:

```
glViewport(0, 0, width, height); // reset the viewport to new dimensions
glMatrixMode(GL_PROJECTION);        // set projection matrix current matrix
glLoadIdentity();                    // reset projection matrix

// set 2D orthographic projection
glOrtho(0.0f, width - 1.0, 0.0, height - 1.0, -1.0, 1.0);

glMatrixMode(GL_MODELVIEW);         // set modelview matrix
glLoadIdentity();                    // reset modelview matrix
```

As you can see, this is a very short and simple example. The end result, or a single frame anyway, is shown in Figure 7.4.

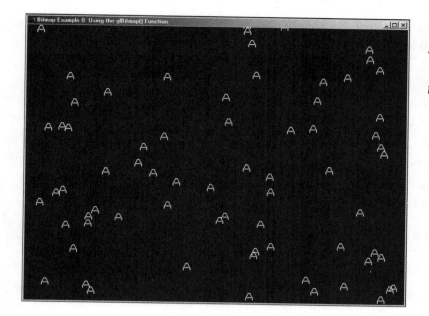

Figure 7.4

A screenshot of the glBitmap() sample program.

Using Images

Typically, developers use *images* instead of the OpenGL bitmap when performing raster graphics. Images are similar to the bitmap, except images hold more information for a pixel than a single bit, such as the RGB values for each pixel.

You use OpenGL to manipulate images pixel by pixel. Sometimes images are referred to as *pixel maps* or *pixmaps*. Although we will be talking about displaying images on the screen in this chapter, you can also use images as texture maps to put the images on your 3D polygons. We'll discuss texture mapping in Chapter 8, "Texture Mapping."

Drawing Image Data

Assuming you already have your image data loaded into memory, you can use the OpenGL function glDrawPixels() to display the image data at a specified raster position in the window. Like glBitmap(), you specify the raster position by using the glRasterPos*() function. The glDrawPixels() function looks like this:

```
void glDrawPixels(GLsizei width, GLsizei height, GLenum format, GLenum type,
                  const GLvoid *pixels);
```

You specify the width and height of the image along with the pixel format and pixel type of the pixel data that is passed to the function. The pixel format can be any of the formats listed in Table 7.1. Typically, you'll use the GL_RGB pixel format to tell OpenGL that the pixel data is the red, green, and blue values for each pixel in the image.

The pixel type can be any of the types listed in Table 7.2. This parameter defines the data type of each pixel element.

Here is some code that uses the glDrawPixels() function to draw an image at the screen position (300, 300) that you have stored in the variable imageData:

```
unsigned char *imageData;
int            imageWidth, imageHeight;
...
glRasterPos2i(300, 300);
glDrawPixels(imageWidth, imageHeight, GL_RGB, GL_UNSIGNED_BYTE, imageData);
```

Table 7.1 Pixel Formats

Pixel Format	Description
GL_ALPHA	Alpha color pixels
GL_BGR	Pixels ordered as blue, green, red
GL_BGRA	Pixels ordered as blue, green, red, alpha
GL_BLUE	Blue pixels
GL_COLOR_INDEX	Color-index pixels
GL_GREEN	Green pixels
GL_RED	Red pixels
GL_RGB	Pixels ordered as red, green, blue
GL_RGBA	Pixels ordered as red, green, blue, alpha

Table 7.2 Pixel Types

Pixel Type	Description
GL_BITMAP	A single bit (0 or 1)
GL_BYTE	Signed 8-bit integer (2 bytes)
GL_UNSIGNED_BYTE	Unsigned 8-bit integer (2 bytes)
GL_SHORT	Signed 16-bit integer (4 bytes)
GL_UNSIGNED_SHORT	Unsigned 16-bit integer (4 bytes)
GL_INT	Signed 32-bit integer (8 bytes)
GL_UNSIGNED_INT	Unsigned 32-bit integer (8 bytes)

Reading from the Screen

There may be times when you want to read the pixels already on the screen so you can save them to disk as an image file or so you can manipulate them for special effects. To do this, OpenGL provides you with the glReadPixels() function, which is defined as

```
void glReadPixels(GLint x, GLint y, GLsizei width, GLsizei height, GLenum format,
                  GLenum type, GLvoid *pixels);
```

With glReadPixels() you see essentially the same parameters that you see with glDrawPixels() with the addition of an (x, y) coordinate. The (x, y) coordinate specifies the lower-left corner of the rectangle with dimensions defined by width and height that will be read from the screen and stored in the pixels parameter. The format and type parameters work the same way as glDrawPixels() and can be the same values as those defined in Tables 7.1 and 7.2.

If you want to read the top half of your window into an RGB buffer, you use the glReadPixels() function like this:

```
void *imageData;
int  screenWidth, screenHeight;
...
glReadPixels(0, screenHeight/2, screenWidth, screenHeight/2, GL_RGB, GL_UNSIGNED_BYTE,
             imageData);
```

Copying Screen Data

Aside from reading and writing to the screen, OpenGL also lets you copy pixels from one portion of the screen to another with the glCopyPixels() function, defined as

glCopyPixels(GLint x, GLiny y, GLsizei *width*, GLsizei *height*, GLenum *buffer*);

This function copies the pixel data in the frame buffer with a rectangle whose lower-left corner is at the screen location (x, y) and has dimensions defined by *width* and *height* to the current raster position. The *buffer* parameter can be any of the values defined in Table 7.3.

One application of glCopyPixels() for games is a magnifying glass or a sniper gun scope. By copying a specific portion of the screen and using your next function, glPixelZoom(), you can zoom in on areas of your world.

Magnification, Reduction, and Flipping

OpenGL lets you enlarge, reduce, and flip images with the glPixelZoom() function, defined as

void glPixelZoom(GLfloat *xZoom*, GLfloat *yZoom*);

By default, the *xZoom* and *yZoom* parameters are 1.0, meaning a normal image. Values greater than 0.0 and less than 1.0 reduce the image; values greater than 1.0 magnify the image. When you specify negative values, the image is reflected about the current raster position. Here are some examples, and their effects in comments:

```
glPixelZoom(-1.0f, -1.0f);      // flip image horizontally and vertically
glPixelZoom(0.5f, 0.5f);         // reduce image to half its original size
glPixelZoom(5.0f, 5.0f);         // magnify the image 5 times in all directions
```

Table 7.3 glCopyPixels() Buffer Values

Buffer Value	Description
GL_COLOR	Copy from the color buffer
GL_DEPTH	Copy from the depth buffer
GL_STENCIL	Copy from the stencil buffer

MANAGING PIXEL STORAGE

You may find that when you move the project you're developing from one machine to another, such as from your desktop machine to your laptop, your project runs more slowly. Although there are many factors that could contribute to this, the one we are concerned with here is data alignment in memory. Some machines might move data more quickly if the data is aligned in memory on 2-, 4-, or 8-byte boundaries. When this is the case, you can control your data alignment with pixel storage by using the glPixelStorei() function:

```
void glPixelStorei(GLenum pname, TYPE param);
```

For our uses, the *pname* parameter can be either GL_PACK_ALIGNMENT or GL_UNPACK_ALIGNMENT. The *param* parameter can be set to 1, 2, 4, or 8. When you specify the GL_PACK_ALIGNMENT parameter, you are telling OpenGL how data is packed into memory. When you specify the GL_UNPACK_ALIGN-MENT parameter, you are telling OpenGL how data is unpacked from memory. By default, both parameters are equal to 4.

As an example, the following line of code tells OpenGL to use the next available byte since the alignment is set to 1:

```
glPixelStorei(GL_UNPACK_ALIGNMENT, 1);
```

THE WINDOWS BITMAP

Now that you know the functions you can use and how you can get images to the screen, let's talk about applying these functions to some real image data. The first image type we're going to look at is the Microsoft Windows BMP file.

The great thing about BMP files is that they can be created, edited, and viewed by anyone using the Microsoft Windows operating system. On the downside, BMP files do not use any compression schemes, so they can grow to be quite large in size; however, the lack of compression scheme also means the file format is easy to read and use.

The BMP File Format

As Figure 7.5 shows, BMP files are structured into three parts: the bitmap file header, the bitmap information header, and the actual bitmap data.

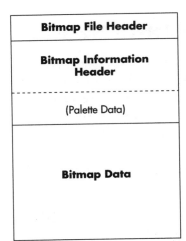

| Bitmap File Header |
| Bitmap Information Header |
| (Palette Data) |
| Bitmap Data |

Figure 7.5

The BMP file structure.

You use the BITMAPFILEHEADER structure to load in the bitmap file header data. This structure is defined as

```
typedef struct tagBITMAPFILEHEADER
{
    WORD  bfType;          // specifies the file type; must be BM (0x4D42)
    DWORD bfSize;          // specifies the size in bytes of the bitmap file
    WORD  bfReserved1;     // reserved; must be zero
    WORD  bfReserved2;     // reserved; must be zero
    DWORD bOffBits;        // specifies the offset, in bytes, from the
                           // BITMAPFILEHEADER structure to the bitmap bits
} BITMAPFILEHEADER;
```

One thing to note about this structure is that when you are reading in the BMP file data, you'll check the *bfType* field of the BITMAPFILEHEADER structure to verify that you are in fact loading a Windows BMP file. This field should be equal to the hexadecimal value of 0x4D42.

The next part of a bitmap file holds the information specific to the bitmap data. This part will be composed of one or two structures, depending on whether the bitmap is 8-bit and has a palette. You won't be loading BMP files with palettes, so all you will read in is the BITMAPINFOHEADER structure:

```
typedef struct tagBITMAPINFOHEADER
{
    DWORD biSize;          // specifies number of bytes required by the structure
    LONG  biWidth;         // specifies the width of the bitmap, in pixels
    LONG  biHeight;        // specifies the height of the bitmap, in pixels
```

```
    WORD   biPlanes;            // specifies the number of color planes, must be 1
    WORD   biBitCount;          // specifies the number of bits per pixel; must be 1, 4,
                                // 8, 16, 24, or 32
    DWORD biCompression;        // specifies the type of compression
    DWORD biSizeImage;          // size of image in bytes
    LONG   biXPelsPerMeter;     // specifies the number of pixels per meter in x axis
    LONG   biYPelsPerMeter;     // specifies the number of pixels per meter in y axis
    DWORD biClrUsed;            // specifies the number of colors used by the bitmap
    DWORD biClrImportant;       // specifies the number of colors that are important
} BITMAPINFOHEADER;
```

This structure is rather self-explanatory, but the biCompression field might cause a few problems. Although the BMP files you will be using do not use any sort of compression, there are different forms of the BMP file that can use what is called RLE compression, which stands for *run length encoding*. In-depth discussion of RLE is beyond the scope of this book, so when you look at the biCompression field, you should find the field equal to BI_RGB, which means that the BMP is uncompressed.

The final part of the BMP file is the actual image data. This data is stored as a series of bytes that define the pixels of the image and can be in 1-, 4-, 8-, 16-, or 24-bit format.

Loading BMP Files

To load a BMP into memory, you just need to read these three parts in order. Once you have the BITMAPINFOHEADER loaded, you can use the information stored there to determine how much memory to allocate for the image data. After you have read the image data into memory, you must swap the red and blue values of each pixel so OpenGL will display the proper colors. Let's take a look at the function to load a 24-bit BMP file:

```
unsigned char *LoadBitmapFile(char *filename, BITMAPINFOHEADER *bitmapInfoHeader)
{
    FILE                *filePtr;           // the file pointer
    BITMAPFILEHEADER    bitmapFileHeader;   // bitmap file header
    unsigned char       *bitmapImage;       // bitmap image data
    int                 imageIdx = 0;       // image index counter
    unsigned char        tempRGB;           // swap variable

    // open filename in "read binary" mode
    filePtr = fopen(filename, "rb");
    if (filePtr == NULL)
        return NULL;
```

```c
// read the bitmap file header
fread(&bitmapFileHeader, sizeof(BITMAPFILEHEADER), 1, filePtr);

// verify that this is a bitmap by checking for the universal bitmap id
if (bitmapFileHeader.bfType != BITMAP_ID)
{
    fclose(filePtr);
    return NULL;
}

// read the bitmap information header
fread(bitmapInfoHeader, sizeof(BITMAPINFOHEADER), 1, filePtr);

// move file pointer to beginning of bitmap data
fseek(filePtr, bitmapFileHeader.bfOffBits, SEEK_SET);

// allocate enough memory for the bitmap image data
bitmapImage = (unsigned char*)malloc(bitmapInfoHeader->biSizeImage);

// verify memory allocation
if (!bitmapImage)
{
    free(bitmapImage);
    fclose(filePtr);
    return NULL;
}

// read in the bitmap image data
fread(bitmapImage, 1, bitmapInfoHeader->biSizeImage, filePtr);

// make sure bitmap image data was read
if (bitmapImage == NULL)
{
    fclose(filePtr);
    return NULL;
}

// swap the R and B values to get RGB since the bitmap color format is in BGR
for (imageIdx = 0; imageIdx < bitmapInfoHeader->biSizeImage; imageIdx+=3)
{
    tempRGB = bitmapImage[imageIdx];
```

```
            bitmapImage[imageIdx] = bitmapImage[imageIdx + 2];
            bitmapImage[imageIdx + 2] = tempRGB;
    }


    // close the file and return the bitmap image data
    fclose(filePtr);
    return bitmapImage;
}
```

As you can see, loading the BMP is rather straightforward. Here's how you can use this function:

```
BITMAPINFOHEADER        bitmapInfoHeader;       // bitmap info header
unsigned char*          bitmapData;             // the bitmap data
...
bitmapData = LoadBitmapFile("test.bmp", &bitmapInfoHeader);
glPixelStorei(GL_UNPACK_ALIGNMENT, 4);                 // set memory alignment
glRasterPos2i(100,100);                                // set raster position
glDrawPixels(bitmapInfoHeader.biWidth, bitmapInfoHeader.biHeight, GL_RGB,
            GL_UNSIGNED_BYTE, bitmapImage);    // draw the bitmap
```

Writing BMP Files

What if you want to save the current image you just received from the glReadPixels() function to a BMP file? Simple. You write the data to a file instead of reading it, and this time, you'll be setting all the values yourself for the BITMAPFILEHEADER and BITMAPINFOHEADER structures.

Here's a function to write image data to a BMP file with dimensions specified by width and height:

```
int WriteBitmapFile(char *filename, int width, int height, unsigned char *imageData)
{
    FILE                *filePtr;           // file pointer
    BITMAPFILEHEADER    bitmapFileHeader;   // bitmap file header
    BITMAPINFOHEADER    bitmapInfoHeader;   // bitmap info header
    int                 imageIdx;           // used for swapping RGB->BGR
    unsigned char       tempRGB;            // used for swapping

    // open file for writing binary mode
    filePtr = fopen(filename, "wb");
    if (!filePtr)
        return 0;
```

```c
    // define the bitmap file header
    bitmapFileHeader.bfSize = sizeof(BITMAPFILEHEADER);
    bitmapFileHeader.bfType = 0x4D42;
    bitmapFileHeader.bfReserved1 = 0;
    bitmapFileHeader.bfReserved2 = 0;
    bitmapFileHeader.bfOffBits = sizeof(BITMAPFILEHEADER) + sizeof(BITMAPINFOHEADER);

    // define the bitmap information header
    bitmapInfoHeader.biSize = sizeof(BITMAPINFOHEADER);
    bitmapInfoHeader.biPlanes = 1;
    bitmapInfoHeader.biBitCount = 24;                        // 24-bit
    bitmapInfoHeader.biCompression = BI_RGB;                 // no compression
    bitmapInfoHeader.biSizeImage = width * abs(height) * 3;  // w * h * (RGB bytes)
    bitmapInfoHeader.biXPelsPerMeter = 0;
    bitmapInfoHeader.biYPelsPerMeter = 0;
    bitmapInfoHeader.biClrUsed = 0;
    bitmapInfoHeader.biClrImportant = 0;
    bitmapInfoHeader.biWidth = width;                        // bitmap width
    bitmapInfoHeader.biHeight = height;                      // bitmap height

    // switch the image data from RGB to BGR
    for (imageIdx = 0; imageIdx < bitmapInfoHeader.biSizeImage; imageIdx+=3)
    {
        tempRGB = imageData[imageIdx];
        imageData[imageIdx] = imageData[imageIdx + 2];
        imageData[imageIdx + 2] = tempRGB;
    }

    // write the bitmap file header
    fwrite(&bitmapFileHeader, 1, sizeof(BITMAPFILEHEADER), filePtr);

    // write the bitmap info header
    fwrite(&bitmapInfoHeader, 1, sizeof(BITMAPINFOHEADER), filePtr);

    // write the image data
    fwrite(imageData, 1, bitmapInfoHeader.biSizeImage, filePtr);

    // close the file
    fclose(filePtr);

    return 1;
}
```

If you use this function with glReadPixels(), then you can have a simple screenshot function to save the window contents to a 24-bit BMP. Here is a function to do just that:

```
unsigned char *imageData;
...
void SaveScreenshot(int winWidth, int winHeight)
{
    imageData = malloc(winWidth*winHeight*3);    // allocate memory for the imageData
    memset(imageData, 0, winWidth*winHeight*3); // clear imageData memory contents

    // read the image data from the window
    glReadPixels(0, 0, winWidth-1, winHeight-1, GL_RGB, GL_UNSIGNED_BYTE, imageData);

    // write the image data to a file
    WriteBitmapFile("writeout.bmp", winWidth, winHeight, (unsigned char*)imageData);

    // free the image data memory
    free(imageData);
}
```

TARGA IMAGE FILES

The next image file we're going to talk about is the Targa image format. This format is fairly simple to work with, and it brings the added bonus of an alpha channel over the BMP format. With the addition of the alpha channel, you can perform cool special effects when you load Targa files and use them as textures.

The Targa File Format

The Targa format is divided into two parts: the header and the data. The header consists of 12 fields that are arranged in this structure:

```
typedef struct tagTARGAFILEHEADER
{
    unsigned char imageIDLength;      // number of characters in identification field;
                                      // 0 denotes no identification field is included
    unsigned char colorMapType;       // type of color map; always 0
    unsigned char imageTypeCode;      // uncompressed RGB is 2;
                                      // uncompressed grayscale is 3
    short int colorMapOrigin;         // origin of color map (lo-hi); always 0
```

```
    short int colorMapLength;      // length of color map (lo-hi); always 0
    short int colorMapEntrySize;   // color map entry size (lo-hi); always 0
    short int imageXOrigin;        // x coordinate of lower-left corner of image
                                   // (lo-hi); always 0
    short int imageYOrigin;        // y coordinate of lower-left corner of image
                                   // (lo-hi); always 0
    short int imageWidth;          // width of image in pixels (lo-hi)
    short int imageHeight;         // height of image in pixels (lo-hi)
    unsigned char bitCount;        // number of bits; 16, 24, 32
    unsigned char imageDescriptor; // 24 bit = 0x00; 32-bit = 0x08
} TARGAFILEHEADER;
```

The Targa image data starts directly after the header ends. The first field out of the header that you are concerned about is the imageTypeCode. This field tells you what type of Targa file you're dealing with. Some of the possible values for imageTypeCode are listed in Table 7.4, although you will only be dealing with types 2 and 3.

The last four fields of the Targa header help you determine how much memory the image data will require and how you should read the data into memory. Also, like the BMP, the Targa format stores the image data in either BGR or BGRA format, depending on whether it is 24-bit or 32-bit, respectively.

Loading Targa Files

Now let's take a look at how you can load the Targa image data into memory. For this format, you're going to create a structure that will hold all the pertinent image information that you will need to load the data properly into memory.

Table 7.4 Targa File Types

Code	Description
2	Uncompressed RGB images
3	Uncompressed black-and-white images
10	Run-length encoded RGB images
11	Compressed black-and-white images

```c
typedef struct
{
    unsigned char imageTypeCode;
    short int     imageWidth;
    short int     imageHeight;
    unsigned char bitCount;
    unsigned char *imageData;
} TGAFILE;
```

With this basic structure, you can then create a function that will load your necessary Targa data:

```c
int LoadTGAFile(char *filename, TGAFILE *tgaFile)
{
    FILE           *filePtr;    // the file pointer
    unsigned char  ucharBad;    // garbage unsigned char data
    short int      sintBad;     // garbage short int data
    long           imageSize;   // size of the TGA image
    int            colorMode;   // 4 for RGBA or 3 for RGB
    long           imageIdx;    // counter variable
    unsigned char  colorSwap;   // swap variable

    // open the TGA file
    filePtr = fopen(filename, "rb");
    if (!filePtr)
        return 0;

    // read first two bytes of data we don't need
    fread(&ucharBad, sizeof(unsigned char), 1, filePtr);
    fread(&ucharBad, sizeof(unsigned char), 1, filePtr);

    // read in the image type
    fread(&tgaFile->imageTypeCode, sizeof(unsigned char), 1, filePtr);

    // for our purposes, the image type should be either a 2 or a 3
    if ((tgaFile->imageTypeCode != 2) && (tgaFile->imageTypeCode != 3))
    {
        fclose(filePtr);
        return 0;
    }

    // read 13 bytes of data we don't need
    fread(&sintBad, sizeof(short int), 1, filePtr);
    fread(&sintBad, sizeof(short int), 1, filePtr);
```

```
        fread(&ucharBad, sizeof(unsigned char), 1, filePtr);
        fread(&sintBad, sizeof(short int), 1, filePtr);
        fread(&sintBad, sizeof(short int), 1, filePtr);

        // read image dimensions
        fread(&tgaFile->imageWidth, sizeof(short int), 1, filePtr);
        fread(&tgaFile->imageHeight, sizeof(short int), 1, filePtr);

        // read image bit depth
        fread(&tgaFile->bitCount, sizeof(unsigned char), 1, filePtr);

        // read 1 byte of data we don't need
        fread(&ucharBad, sizeof(unsigned char), 1, filePtr);

        // colorMode -> 3 = BGR, 4 = BGRA
        colorMode = tgaFile->bitCount / 8;
        imageSize = tgaFile->imageWidth * tgaFile->imageHeight * colorMode;

        // allocate memory for image data
        tgaFile->imageData = (unsigned char*)malloc(sizeof(unsigned char)*imageSize);

        // read in image data
        fread(tgaFile->imageData, sizeof(unsigned char), imageSize, filePtr);

        // change BGR to RGB so OpenGL can read the image data
        for (imageIdx = 0; imageIdx < imageSize; imageIdx += colorMode)
        {
            colorSwap = tgaFile->imageData[imageIdx];
            tgaFile->imageData[imageIdx] = tgaFile->imageData[imageIdx + 2];
            tgaFile->imageData[imageIdx + 2] = colorSwap;
        }

        // close the file
        fclose(filePtr);

        return 1;
}
```

To use this function, you could do something like this:

```
TGAFILE *myTGA;
...
myTGA = (TGAFILE*)malloc(sizeof(TGAFILE));
LoadTGAFile("test.tga", myTGA);
```

Then, you can use the `glDrawPixels()` function in the same way you used it for the BMP format:

```
glPixelStorei(GL_UNPACK_ALIGNMENT, 4);
glRasterPos2i(200,200);
glDrawPixels(myTGA->imageWidth, myTGA->imageHeight, GL_RGB, GL_UNSIGNED_BYTE,
             myTGA->imageData);
```

Writing Targa Files

Writing a Targa file is just as easy as reading one. All you need to do is make sure you specify the type of Targa file, the bit depth, and the color mode for RGB or RGBA. For the Targa structure fields that are unimportant, you can just put values of 0. Also, you need to remember to convert the image data from RGB(A) to BGR(A). Let's take a look at the `WriteTGAFile()` function:

```
int WriteTGAFile(char *filename, short int width, short int height,
                 unsigned char* imageData)
{
    unsigned char byteSkip;          // used for byte garbage data
    short int     shortSkip;         // used for short int garbage data
    unsigned char imageType;         // type of image we're writing to file
    int           colorMode;         // color mode of image
    unsigned char colorSwap;         // used for BGR-to-RGB conversion
    int           imageIdx;          // counter for BGR-to-RGB conversion
    unsigned char bitDepth;          // bit depth of the image
    long          imageSize;         // size of the image data
    FILE          *filePtr;          // pointer to file

    // create file for writing binary mode
    filePtr = fopen(filename, "wb");
    if (!filePtr)
    {
        fclose(filePtr);
        return 0;
    }
```

```c
imageType = 2;           // RGB, uncompressed
bitDepth = 24;           // 24-bitdepth
colorMode = 3;           // RGB color mode

byteSkip = 0;            // garbage data for byte data
shortSkip = 0;           // garbage data for short int data

// write blank data
fwrite(&byteSkip, sizeof(unsigned char), 1, filePtr);
fwrite(&byteSkip, sizeof(unsigned char), 1, filePtr);

// write imageType
fwrite(&imageType, sizeof(unsigned char), 1, filePtr);

// write blank data
fwrite(&shortSkip, sizeof(short int), 1, filePtr);
fwrite(&shortSkip, sizeof(short int), 1, filePtr);
fwrite(&byteSkip, sizeof(unsigned char), 1, filePtr);
fwrite(&shortSkip, sizeof(short int), 1, filePtr);
fwrite(&shortSkip, sizeof(short int), 1, filePtr);

// write image dimensions
fwrite(&width, sizeof(short int), 1, filePtr);
fwrite(&height, sizeof(short int), 1, filePtr);
fwrite(&bitDepth, sizeof(unsigned char), 1, filePtr);

// write 1 byte of blank data
fwrite(&byteSkip, sizeof(unsigned char), 1, filePtr);

// calculate the image size
imageSize = width * height * colorMode;

// change image data from RGB to BGR
for (imageIdx = 0; imageIdx < imageSize ; imageIdx += colorMode)
{
     colorSwap = imageData[imageIdx];
     imageData[imageIdx] = imageData[imageIdx + 2];
     imageData[imageIdx + 2] = colorSwap;
}
```

```
    // write the image data
    fwrite(imageData, sizeof(unsigned char), imageSize, filePtr);

    // close the file
    fclose(filePtr);

    return 1;
}
```

Like the BMP file format, you can use the glReadPixels() function to create a screen-capture function that will save the current window contents to a Targa file. Here is that function:

```
unsigned char *imageData;
...
void SaveScreenshot()
{
    imageData = malloc(800*600*3);              // allocate memory for the imageData
    memset(imageData, 0, 800*600*3);            // clear imageData memory contents

    // read the image data from the window
    glReadPixels(0, 0, 799, 599, GL_RGB, GL_UNSIGNED_BYTE, imageData);

    // write the image data to a file
    WriteTGAFile("writeout.tga", 800, 600, (unsigned char*)imageData);

    // free the image data memory
    free(imageData);
}
```

SUMMARY

The term *bitmap* in the context of OpenGL is defined as a rectangular array of pixels, where a single bit of information (a 0 or 1) is stored about each pixel. They are treated as drawing masks for a rectangular area of the window and are typically used for characters in fonts.

The glRasterPos*() function lets you specify the screen position where your bitmap or image will be drawn. The coordinates that are sent to the function define the bottom-left corner of the bitmap.

After you have set the current raster position, you actually draw your bitmap with the `glBitmap()` function.

Assuming you already have your image data loaded into memory, you can use the OpenGL function `glDrawPixels()` to display the image data at a specified raster position in the window. Like `glBitmap()`, you specify the raster position by using the `glRasterPos*()` function.

Sometimes you might want to read the pixels already on the screen so you can save them to disk as an image file or so you can manipulate them for special effects. You can do this with the OpenGL function `glReadPixels()`.

The `glCopyPixels()` function lets you copy pixel data from one portion of the screen to another.

OpenGL also lets you enlarge, reduce, and flip images with the `glPixelZoom()` function.

The Windows BMP file and the Truevision Targa image file are two simple-to-use and -understand image files that you can load into memory and display using OpenGL.

CHAPTER 8

TEXTURE MAPPING

othing we have discussed so far can bring as much realism to a 3D scene as texture mapping. Lighting comes close, but it doesn't have near the impact that a simple texture map can have when applied to an object. Instead of having multicolored polygons that seemingly come together to form a recognizable object, you can create photo-realistic worlds with texture mapping that can almost persuade the user that the objects being viewed on the screen are real. In this chapter, you'll learn how to achieve a high level of realism through an introduction to the concept and implementation of texture-mapping techniques in OpenGL.

In this chapter, you'll learn about the following:

- The basics of texture mapping
- Texture objects
- Repeating and clamping textures
- Mipmaps and level of detail
- Two fun texture mapping examples

AN OVERVIEW OF TEXTURE MAPPING

In a nutshell, *texture mapping* allows you to attach images to polygons in a nice, realistic manner. As an example, you could apply an image of the front of this book to a rectangular polygon; afterward, the polygon would appear to be a 3D virtual representation of the front of the book. Another example would be to take a map of Earth and texture-map it onto a sphere. You could then say that you had a 3D virtual representation of Earth, merely because you glued an image of Earth onto a sphere. Nowadays, texture maps are used everywhere in 3D graphics. In fact, texture mapping brings the realism and authenticity desired in today's games.

Texture maps are composed of rectangular arrays of data; each piece of data is called a *texel*. Although they are rectangular arrays of data, texture maps can be mapped to nonrectangular objects, such as spheres, cylinders, and other 3D object models.

Usually, developers use the two-dimensional texture in their graphics; however, using one-dimensional and three-dimensional textures is not unheard of. The two-dimensional texture has both a width and a height, as seen in Figure 8.1. One-dimensional textures have a width and a height equal to only 1 pixel. Three-dimensional textures have a width, height, and depth, and are sometimes called *volume textures*. In this chapter, we will be primarily concerned with two-dimensional textures.

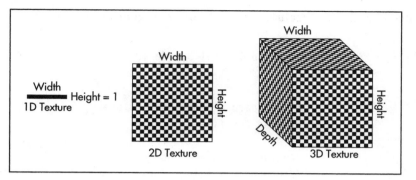

Figure 8.1

The difference between one-, two-, and three- dimensional textures.

When you map a texture onto a polygon, the texture will be transformed as the polygon is transformed. In other words, if you rotate the Earth example we just talked about, the texture map will rotate with the sphere and give the effect of a rotating Earth. Similarly, if you use translation and another rotation to rotate the Earth image around a sphere we'll call "Sun," then the texture map will stay on the Earth sphere as it rotates around the Sun sphere. You can think of texture mapping as applying a sort of skin to a 3D object or polygon. You can move this skin around the object, stretch it, or shrink it, but no matter what, the skin, or texture map, stays with the polygons to which you apply it. Let's take a quick look at an example before we go into more detail.

The Checkered-Cube Example

The example we're going to look at right now displays the old rotating cube you've seen before, except this time, the cube is texture mapped with the checkerboard texture shown in Figure 8.2.

Figure 8.2

The checkerboard texture.

Because this texture is a Windows BMP file, you will be using the LoadBitmapFile() function you created in Chapter 7, "Bitmaps and Images with OpenGL," to load the texture data into memory. Also, the texture you load must have dimensions of the power of 2. For example, you can load a 64×64 texture, because 64 is equal to 2^6. Similarly, you can load a texture with the dimensions 256×256, because 256 is the same as 2^8. The texture you're loading in this example is a 64×64 texture.

The first bit of code you need has the file #includes, #defines, and your global variables:

```
////// Defines
#define BITMAP_ID 0x4D42                     // the universal bitmap ID

////// Includes
#include <windows.h>                         // standard Windows app include
#include <stdio.h>                           // used for file i/o
#include <stdlib.h>
#include <gl/gl.h>                           // standard OpenGL include
#include <gl/glu.h>                          // OpenGL utilities library

////// Global Variables
HDC g_HDC;                                   // global device context
bool fullScreen = false;                     // true = full screen; false = windowed
bool keyPressed[256];                        // holds true for keys that are pressed
float angle = 0.0f;                          // rotation angle

////// Texture Information
BITMAPINFOHEADER    bitmapInfoHeader;        // bitmap info header
unsigned char*            bitmapData;        // the texture data
unsigned int               texture;          // the texture object
```

Most of these declarations should look familiar. The newest variable you declare is the texture object. These objects are used to reference and store texture data in memory and are often the fastest way to apply textures.

The next block of code you have is the LoadBitmapFile() function. You may remember this function from Chapter 7; with it, you pass the bitmap filename and a BITMAPINFOHEADER variable that will give you pertinent information about the bitmap. This function returns a pointer to the bitmap data, which is stored as a stream of unsigned char, also called a stream of bytes.

```
unsigned char *LoadBitmapFile(char *filename, BITMAPINFOHEADER *bitmapInfoHeader)
{
        FILE                *filePtr;              // the file pointer
        BITMAPFILEHEADER    bitmapFileHeader;      // bitmap file header
        unsigned char       *bitmapImage;          // bitmap image data
        int                 imageIdx = 0;          // image index counter
        unsigned char       tempRGB;               // swap variable

        // open filename in "read binary" mode
        filePtr = fopen(filename, "rb");
```

```c
    if (filePtr == NULL)
        return NULL;

    // read the bitmap file header
    fread(&bitmapFileHeader, sizeof(BITMAPFILEHEADER), 1, filePtr);

    // verify that this is a bitmap by checking for the universal bitmap id
    if (bitmapFileHeader.bfType != BITMAP_ID)
    {
        fclose(filePtr);
        return NULL;
    }

    // read the bitmap information header
    fread(bitmapInfoHeader, sizeof(BITMAPINFOHEADER), 1, filePtr);

    // move file pointer to beginning of bitmap data
    fseek(filePtr, bitmapFileHeader.bfOffBits, SEEK_SET);

    // allocate enough memory for the bitmap image data
    bitmapImage = (unsigned char*)malloc(bitmapInfoHeader->biSizeImage);

    // verify memory allocation
    if (!bitmapImage)
    {
        free(bitmapImage);
        fclose(filePtr);
        return NULL;
    }

    // read in the bitmap image data
    fread(bitmapImage, 1, bitmapInfoHeader->biSizeImage, filePtr);

    // make sure bitmap image data was read
    if (bitmapImage == NULL)
    {
        fclose(filePtr);
        return NULL;
    }
```

```
        // swap the R and B values to get RGB since the bitmap color format is in BGR
        for (imageIdx = 0; imageIdx < bitmapInfoHeader->biSizeImage; imageIdx+=3)
        {
            tempRGB = bitmapImage[imageIdx];
            bitmapImage[imageIdx] = bitmapImage[imageIdx + 2];
            bitmapImage[imageIdx + 2] = tempRGB;
        }

        // close the file and return the bitmap image data
        fclose(filePtr);
        return bitmapImage;
}
```

Next up is the function that will draw your textured cube. This function is very much like the previous cube drawing functions, except this function also defines the texture coordinates for each vertex. We'll talk more about texture coordinates in this chapter, but for now take a look:

```
void DrawTextureCube(float xPos, float yPos, float zPos)
{
    glPushMatrix();
        glTranslatef(xPos, yPos, zPos);

        glBegin(GL_QUADS);          // top face
            glTexCoord2f(0.0f, 0.0f); glVertex3f(-0.5f, 0.5f, 0.5f);
            glTexCoord2f(1.0f, 0.0f); glVertex3f(0.5f, 0.5f, 0.5f);
            glTexCoord2f(1.0f, 1.0f); glVertex3f(0.5f, 0.5f, -0.5f);
            glTexCoord2f(0.0f, 1.0f); glVertex3f(-0.5f, 0.5f, -0.5f);
        glEnd();

        glBegin(GL_QUADS);          // front face
            glTexCoord2f(0.0f, 0.0f); glVertex3f(0.5f, -0.5f, 0.5f);
            glTexCoord2f(1.0f, 0.0f); glVertex3f(0.5f, 0.5f, 0.5f);
            glTexCoord2f(1.0f, 1.0f); glVertex3f(-0.5f, 0.5f, 0.5f);
            glTexCoord2f(0.0f, 1.0f); glVertex3f(-0.5f, -0.5f, 0.5f);
        glEnd();

        glBegin(GL_QUADS);          // right face
            glTexCoord2f(0.0f, 0.0f); glVertex3f(0.5f, 0.5f, -0.5f);
            glTexCoord2f(1.0f, 0.0f); glVertex3f(0.5f, 0.5f, 0.5f);
            glTexCoord2f(1.0f, 1.0f); glVertex3f(0.5f, -0.5f, 0.5f);
            glTexCoord2f(0.0f, 1.0f); glVertex3f(0.5f, -0.5f, -0.5f);
        glEnd();
```

```
        glBegin(GL_QUADS);      // left face
            glTexCoord2f(0.0f, 0.0f); glVertex3f(-0.5f, -0.5f, 0.5f);
            glTexCoord2f(1.0f, 0.0f); glVertex3f(-0.5f, 0.5f, 0.5f);
            glTexCoord2f(1.0f, 1.0f); glVertex3f(-0.5f, 0.5f, -0.5f);
            glTexCoord2f(0.0f, 1.0f); glVertex3f(-0.5f, -0.5f, -0.5f);
        glEnd();

        glBegin(GL_QUADS);      // bottom face
            glTexCoord2f(0.0f, 0.0f); glVertex3f(0.5f, -0.5f, 0.5f);
            glTexCoord2f(1.0f, 0.0f); glVertex3f(-0.5f, -0.5f, 0.5f);
            glTexCoord2f(1.0f, 1.0f); glVertex3f(-0.5f, -0.5f, -0.5f);
            glTexCoord2f(0.0f, 1.0f); glVertex3f(0.5f, -0.5f, -0.5f);
        glEnd();

        glBegin(GL_QUADS);      // back face
            glTexCoord2f(0.0f, 0.0f); glVertex3f(0.5f, 0.5f, -0.5f);
            glTexCoord2f(1.0f, 0.0f); glVertex3f(0.5f, -0.5f, -0.5f);
            glTexCoord2f(1.0f, 1.0f); glVertex3f(-0.5f, -0.5f, -0.5f);
            glTexCoord2f(0.0f, 1.0f); glVertex3f(-0.5f, 0.5f, -0.5f);
        glEnd();
    glPopMatrix();
}
```

So now you have a function to load the texture data into memory, and a function to draw a texture-mapped cube. Next you need an initialization function that will set up the OpenGL scene and handle the texture data. You accomplish this with the Initialize() function:

```
void Initialize()
{
    glClearColor(0.0f, 0.0f, 0.0f, 0.0f);       // clear background to black
    glShadeModel(GL_SMOOTH);                     // use smooth shading
    glEnable(GL_DEPTH_TEST);                      // hidden surface removal
    glEnable(GL_CULL_FACE);                       // do not calculate inside of polys
    glFrontFace(GL_CCW);                          // counterclockwise polygons are out
    glEnable(GL_TEXTURE_2D);                      // enable 2D texturing

    // load our bitmap file
    bitmapData = LoadBitmapFile("checker.bmp", &bitmapInfoHeader);

    glGenTextures(1, &texture);                   // generate texture object
    glBindTexture(GL_TEXTURE_2D, texture);        // bind the texture
```

```
glTexParameteri(GL_TEXTURE_2D, GL_TEXTURE_MAG_FILTER, GL_NEAREST);
glTexParameteri(GL_TEXTURE_2D, GL_TEXTURE_MIN_FILTER, GL_NEAREST);

// load the texture image
glTexImage2D(GL_TEXTURE_2D, 0, GL_RGB, bitmapInfoHeader.biWidth,
            bitmapInfoHeader.biHeight, 0, GL_RGB, GL_UNSIGNED_BYTE, bitmapData);
}
```

The first line of interest here is where you enable texturing with the GL_TEXTURE_2D parameter.
This line tells OpenGL that you are going to be putting textures on your polygons. You can also
disable texturing by using the glDisable() function and passing GL_TEXTURE_2D as the parameter.

After you have loaded your texture data from the BMP file, you use the glGenTextures() function
to assign a name to the texture object. The glBindTexture() function "binds" the texture object to
be the current texture that you will use when rendering the cube. If you want to use multiple texture objects, you use the glBindTexture() function each time you want to use a different texture.

The glTexParameteri() function tells OpenGL how you want your texture to be filtered. We'll talk
about filtering later in this chapter.

Lastly, you load your image data into memory as a texture with the glTexImage2D() function. This
function specifies the size, type, location, and format of the data.

Next up is your Render() function, which performs the transformations and calls the
DrawTextureCube() function:

```
void Render()
{
    // clear screen and depth buffer
    glClear(GL_COLOR_BUFFER_BIT | GL_DEPTH_BUFFER_BIT);
    glLoadIdentity();

    glTranslatef(0.0f, 0.0f, -3.0f);          // perform transformations
    glRotatef(angle, 1.0f, 0.0f, 0.0f);       // place cube at (0,-3) and rotate it
    glRotatef(angle, 0.0f, 1.0f, 0.0f);
    glRotatef(angle, 0.0f, 0.0f, 1.0f);

    DrawTextureCube(0.0f, 0.0f, 0.0f);            // draw the textured cube

    if (angle >= 360.0f)
        angle = 0.0f;
    angle += 0.2f;
```

```
        glFlush();
        SwapBuffers(g_HDC);                        // bring back buffer to foreground
}
```

And that's it! After you plug all this code into the Windows framework we've been using so far, you will have a rotating textured cube on your hands. Take a look at the screenshot in Figure 8.3.

Now that you've seen how some basic texturing is done, let's take a more in-depth look at how OpenGL texturing is performed.

Figure 8.3

A screenshot of your rotating, checkerboard-textured cube.

APPLYING THE TEXTURE MAP

After you load your texture-image data into memory from a file, you need to define it as a texture map with OpenGL. The dimensions of the texture map determine which function you use to accomplish this. If you have a 2D texture map, you use the glTexImage2D() function. 1D texture maps use the glTexImage1D() function, and 3D texture maps use the glTexImage3D() function. The following sections describe how you use these functions.

2D Textures

As mentioned, you use the `glTexImage2D()` function to define a 2D texture map with OpenGL. This function is defined as

```
void glTexImage2D(GLenum target, GLint level, GLint internalFormat, GLsizei width,
                  GLsizei height, GLint border, GLenum format, GLenum type,
                  const GLvoid* texels)
```

The *target* parameter can be equal to either GL_TEXTURE_2D or GL_PROXY_TEXTURE_2D. For our purposes, this parameter will be equal to GL_TEXTURE_2D. The *level* parameter specifies the resolution of the texture map. Because we have not yet discussed multiple resolutions, this parameter will be equal to 0, which means that you are using only one resolution.

The *internalFormat* parameter describes the format of the texels that you are passing to the function. This parameter can either equal an integer value from 1 to 4, or can equal any one of 38 constants. Rather than listing all these constants, we'll just mention the ones that will interest you most: GL_LUMINANCE, GL_LUMINANCE_ALPHA, GL_RGB, GL_RGBA.

The *width* and *height* parameters define the width and height of the texture map. These parameters must be equal to a power of 2. The *border* parameter indicates whether there is a border around the texture. This parameter is equal to either 0, for no border, or 1.

The *format* parameter defines the format of the texture-image data. It can be equal to any of the following values: GL_COLOR_INDEX, GL_RGB, GL_RGBA, GL_RED, GL_GREEN, GL_BLUE, GL_ALPHA, GL_LUMINANCE, or GL_LUMINANCE_ALPHA.

The *type* parameter defines the data type of the texture-image data. This parameter can be equal to GL_BYTE, GL_UNSIGNED_BYTE, GL_SHORT, GL_UNSIGNED_SHORT, GL_INT, GL_UNSIGNED_INT, GL_FLOAT, or GL_BITMAP.

texels, the last parameter, is a pointer to the actual texture image data that you either generated or loaded from an image file.

Let's say you've loaded an RGBA image into the variable *textureData* that has a width and height of *textureWidth* and *textureHeight*, respectively. You use the `glTexImage2D()` function like this:

```
glTexImage2D(GL_TEXTURE_2D, 0, GL_RGBA, textureWidth, textureHeight, 0,
             GL_RGBA, GL_UNSIGNED_BYTE, textureData);
```

After this function is called, the texture is loaded and ready to use.

1D Textures

1D textures are essentially 2D textures with a height equal to 1. These textures are often used for drawing color bands or for performing shading techniques that would otherwise require an excessive amount of polygons. To create a 1D texture, you use the `glTexImage1D()` function, which is defined as

```
void glTexImage1D(GLenum target, GLint level, GLint internalFormat, GLsizei width,
                  GLint border, GLenum format, GLenum type, const GLvoid *texels);
```

All of the parameters for `glTexImage1D()` are the same as those for `glTexImage2D()`. The only difference between the two functions is the *height* parameter, which is not present in the `glTexImage1D()` function. Also, the *texels* parameter is now a one-dimensional array, as opposed to a two-dimensional array with `glTexImage2D()`. And for the *target* parameter, you now specify the value `GL_TEXTURE_1D`, which tells OpenGL that you are creating a 1D texture.

Here is a short code snippet using the `glTexImage1D()` function:

```
unsigned char imageData[128];
...
glTexImage1D(GL_TEXTURE_1D, 0, GL_RGBA, 32, 0, GL_RGBA, GL_UNSIGNED_BYTE, imageData);
```

3D Textures

3D textures can produce some amazing visual effects, but they consume an enormous amount of memory for even the smallest textures. Although the medical field already uses 3D textures for applications such as MRI, widespread usage in 3D gaming remains to be seen. With advancements in graphics hardware, however, 3D textures might become more commonplace.

To create a 3D texture, you use the `glTexImage3D()` function:

```
glTexImage3D(GLenum target, GLint level, GLint internalFormat, GLsizei width,
             GLsizei height, GLsizei depth, GLint border, GLenum format, GLenum type,
             const GLvoid *texels);
```

The parameters for this function are essentially the same as those for `glTexImage1D()` and `glTexImage2D()`. The difference here is the *depth* parameter, which specifies the third dimension of the texture. Also, the *texels* parameter now points to a three-dimensional array of image data instead of a one- or two-dimensional array.

Here is a short code snippet using the glTexImage3D() function:

```
unsigned char imageData[16][16][16][3];
...
glTexImage3D(GL_TEXTURE_3D, 0, GL_RGB, 16, 16, 16, 0, GL_RGB,
             GL_UNSIGNED_BYTE, imageData);
```

TEXTURE OBJECTS

Texture objects allow you to store texture data and keep it readily available for usage. Using texture objects, you can load many textures into memory at once and have the ability to reference any of those textures at any time during the scene rendering. Using this technique dramatically increases performance, because the textures do not have to be loaded into memory each time they are used.

Generating the Texture Name

The first thing you have to do when using texture objects is generate a texture name. Texture names can be any non-zero unsigned integer. To make sure you never use the same texture name twice, you use the glGenTextures() function:

```
void glGenTextures(GLsizei n, GLuint *textureNames);
```

The parameter *n* specifies how many texture names will be generated and placed in the *textureNames* array. For instance, if you have size-3 array in which to store texture names, you can use the glGenTextures() function like this:

```
unsigned int textureNames[3];
...
glGenTextures(3, textureNames);
```

Creating and Using Texture Objects

After you've generated the texture names, you need to "bind" the texture names to texture data. You accomplish this with the glBindTexture() function:

```
void glBindTexture(GLenum target, GLuint textureName);
```

The first time you use this function, a new texture object is created with default values for the texture image and texture properties. Any OpenGL texture function calls after this initial binding will redefine the default values and store them in the texture object. The target parameter for this function can be equal to GL_TEXTURE_1D, GL_TEXTURE_2D, or GL_TEXTURE_3D.

After you have bound a texture object to its data, you can then use the glBindTexture() function to set the texture object to the current texture state. For example, suppose you have created some texture objects and bound each of them to their texture data and properties. When you are rendering the polygons in the scene, you can tell OpenGL which texture to use by specifying it with the glBindTexture() function. The following code will tell OpenGL to set the second texture object to the current texture after defining the texture properties:

```
unsigned int textureNames[3];
...
glGenTextures(3, textureNames);
...
glBindTexture(GL_TEXTURE_2D, textureNames[1]);
// set texture data and properties
glBindTexture(GL_TEXTURE_2D, textureNames[1]);
// draw object
```

TEXTURE FILTERING

Because of the distorted nature of texture maps after they have been applied to a transformed polygon, a single pixel can represent only a small portion of a texel or a collection of texels from the texture map. You use *texture filtering* to tell OpenGL how these pixels and texels should be calculated for the final image.

In texture filtering, *magnification* refers to when a pixel represents a small portion of a texel. *Minification* refers to when a pixel represents a collection of texels. You can tell OpenGL how you want it to handle both of these filtering cases with the glTexParameteri() function:

```
void glTexParameteri(GLenum target, GLenum pname, GLint param);
```

The value of the *target* parameter depends on the textures you are using and can be equal to GL_TEXTURE_1D, GL_TEXTURE_2D, or GL_TEXTURE_3D. For magnification or minification filtering, the *pname* parameter is equal to GL_TEXTURE_MAG_FILTER or GL_TEXTURE_MIN_FILTER. Table 8.1 lists the possible values for the *param* parameter.

Note that you can only use the mipmap values when you are using the GL_TEXTURE_MIN_FILTER parameter. Don't worry too much about mipmaps just yet because we'll be discussing mipmaps and level of detail soon in this chapter.

Here is an example of setting the magnification and minification filters using the glTexParameteri() function:

```
glTexParameteri(GL_TEXTURE_2D, GL_TEXTURE_MAG_FILTER, GL_LINEAR);
glTexParameteri(GL_TEXTURE_2D, GL_TEXTURE_MIN_FILTER, GL_LINEAR);
```

Table 8.1 Texture Filter Values

Filter	Description
GL_NEAREST	Use the texel nearest to the center of the pixel being textured.
GL_LINEAR	Use linear interpolation (weighted average) with the four texels that are closest to the center of the pixel being rendered.
GL_NEAREST_MIPMAP_NEAREST	Use the image closest to the polygon resolution and use GL_NEAREST filtering.
GL_NEAREST_MIPMAP_LINEAR	Use the image closest to the polygon resolution and use GL_LINEAR filtering.
GL_LINEAR_MIPMAP_NEAREST	Use linear interpolation between the two mipmaps closest to the polygon resolution and use GL_NEAREST filtering.
GL_LINEAR_MIPMAP_LINEAR	Use linear interpolation between the two mipmaps closest to the polygon resolution and use GL_LINEAR filtering.

TEXTURE FUNCTIONS

As with color blending, OpenGL also lets you specify the behavior of texture-map colors through texture functions. For each texture, you can choose from four texture functions with the glTexEnvi() function:

void glTexEnvi(GLenum *target*, GLenum *pname*, GLint *param*);

The *target* parameter must be equal to GL_TEXTURE_ENV. You must also set the *pname* parameter equal to GL_TEXTURE_ENV_MODE, which tells OpenGL that you will be specifying how textures are going to be combined with colors in the frame buffer. You can then assign *param* to any of the values listed in Table 8.2.

Table 8.2 Texture Modes

Mode	Description
GL_BLEND	Texture color multiplied by pixel color and combined with a constant color
GL_DECAL	Texture replaces existing pixels
GL_MODULATE	Texture color multiplied by pixel color

The default value for glTexEnvi() is GL_MODULATE. Here is a line of code that will set the texture function to GL_DECAL:

```
glTexEnvi(GL_TEXTURE_ENV, GL_TEXTURE_ENV_MODE, GL_DECAL);
```

TEXTURE COORDINATES

When you actually render your scene, you have to specify the texture coordinates of each vertex. Texture coordinates are used to determine where each texel in the texture map belongs on an object. A texture coordinate of (0, 0) specifies the lower-left corner of a texture, while a texture coordinate of (1, 1) specifies the upper-right corner.

When you render a polygon, you need to make sure you specify the texture coordinates for each vertex of the polygon. With 2D textures, these coordinates are of the form (s, t), where s and t are equal to a value from 0 to 1. Figure 8.4 shows the texture coordinates for each vertex of a polygon. These texture coordinates must be specified before each of their respective vertices are rendered.

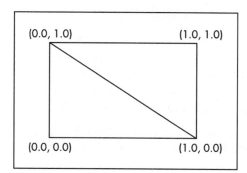

Figure 8.4

A polygon with texture coordinates.

As an example of how OpenGL interpolates the texture coordinates, consider what the texture coordinates would be for a vertex in the exact center of the polygon. With the texture coordinates for the upper-right corner of the polygon equal to (1, 1) and the lower-left corner of the polygon equal to (0, 0), an imaginary vertex in the middle of the polygon would have texture coordinates of (0.5, 0.5). OpenGL calculates this for you automatically, so all you have to worry about is specifying the texture coordinates of each vertex.

You specify texture coordinates by using the glTexCoord2f() function. Other forms of this function are available, but for our purposes, you'll be using either one of the following:

```
void glTexCoord2f(float s, float t);
void glTexCoord2fv(float *coords);
```

This function will set the current 2D texture coordinates. When you specify your vertex with the glVertex*() function, the vertex will be assigned the texture coordinates that you specify with the glTexCoord2f() function.

Looking back at our example from earlier in this chapter, here is some code that uses the glTexCoord2f() function:

```
glBegin(GL_QUADS);
    glTexCoord2f(0.0f, 0.0f); glVertex3f(-0.5f, 0.5f, 0.5f);    // lower left
    glTexCoord2f(1.0f, 0.0f); glVertex3f(0.5f, 0.5f, 0.5f);     // lower right
    glTexCoord2f(1.0f, 1.0f); glVertex3f(0.5f, 0.5f, -0.5f);    // upper right
    glTexCoord2f(0.0f, 1.0f); glVertex3f(-0.5f, 0.5f, -0.5f);   // upper left
glEnd();
```

Although texture coordinates are generally in the range of 0 to 1, they can be assigned values outside this range. Doing this results in textures being repeated or clamped. Let's take a look at how this works.

Repeating and Clamping

When you specify texture coordinates outside the range of 0–1, you can tell OpenGL to either repeat or clamp the texture coordinates in the texture map. (*Repeating* is sometimes referred to as *tiling*). If you specify the texture coordinates (2.0, 2.0), then the texture will be tiled four times, as shown in Figure 8.5. Similarly, if you specify the texture coordinates (1.0, 2.0), then the texture will be tiled two times in the t direction, while the texture remains "normal" in the s direction.

OpenGL performs clamping by setting any texture coordinate values greater than 1.0 to 1.0, and any texture coordinate values less than 0.0 to 0.0. Figure 8.6 shows the result of clamping with the texture coordinates (2.0, 2.0). As you can see, clamping results in one copy of the texture appearing in the lower-left corner of the polygon.

Figure 8.5

The result of repeating a texture using the texture coordinates (2.0, 2.0) on the checkered-cube example.

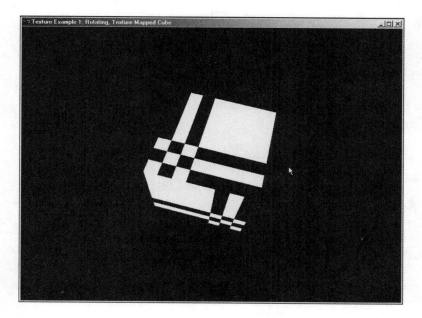

Figure 8.6

The result of clamping a texture using the texture coordinates (2.0, 2.0) on the checkered-cube example.

So how do you tell OpenGL whether to perform repeating or clamping? You use the glTexParameteri() function we discussed for texture filtering, except this time you use GL_TEXTURE_WRAP_S and GL_TEXTURE_WRAP_T as the values for the target parameter. The GL_TEXTURE_WRAP_S value refers to the s direction, and the GL_TEXTURE_WRAP_T value refers to the t direction. You can then specify which wrapping mode you want to use for each direction by specifying either GL_REPEAT, GL_CLAMP, or GL_CLAMP_TO_EDGE. (The GL_CLAMP_TO_EDGE value is used when you have borders for your texture and you want OpenGL to ignore the border.)

Here's some code that will tell OpenGL to repeat the texture in each direction:

```
glTexParameteri(GL_TEXTURE_2D, GL_TEXTURE_WRAP_S, GL_REPEAT);
glTexParameteri(GL_TEXTURE_2D, GL_TEXTURE_WRAP_T, GL_REPEAT);
```

You can also tell OpenGL to clamp in one direction while repeating in the other direction. Here is some code that will clamp in the s direction and repeat in the t direction:

```
glTexParameteri(GL_TEXTURE_2D, GL_TEXTURE_WRAP_S, GL_CLAMP);
glTexParameteri(GL_TEXTURE_2D, GL_TEXTURE_WRAP_T, GL_REPEAT);
```

MIPMAPS AND LEVEL OF DETAIL

When rendering a textured object, you might notice some visual artifacts, or problem areas, when the object moves closer or farther away from the camera. These artifacts are the result of OpenGL trying to compensate for the moving texture by filtering the texture map down to a size that fits the object. You can help to eliminate these artifacts by controlling the level of detail with *mipmaps*, which are shown in Figure 8.7.

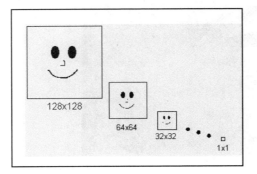

Figure 8.7

Mipmaps help control the level of detail for textured objects.

OpenGL performs mipmapping by determining which texture image to use based on the resolution of the object. So when an object is close to the camera, it will take up more pixels on the screen and have a higher resolution, which means the larger texture map is used. When the object is farther away, it will use fewer pixels on the screen and have a lower resolution, resulting in the smaller texture map being used.

You define mipmaps just like you do normal textures with the glTexImage2D() function, except each mipmap texture resolution is assigned its own level value. When you define normal textures, you set the level parameter of the glTexImage2D() function to 0. With mipmapped textures, a value of 0 for the level parameter means that the texture is the primary, or highest-resolution, image. The level-1 image has half the resolution of the level-0 image. As the level value increases, the resolution of the image is equal to one-half the resolution of the previous level.

When creating your mipmap texture, you need to make sure you keep all the different sizes of the texture in powers of 2 from the largest size of the texture to a 1×1 texture map. For example, if the largest texture map is 64×64, then you also need to create sizes 32×32, 16×16, 8×8, 4×4, 2×2, and 1×1. When applied to the glTexImage2D() function, the 64×64 map would be the level-0 image, the 32×32 map would be the level-1 image, the 16×16 map would be the level-2 image, and so on. In code, it looks like this:

```
glTexParameteri(GL_TEXTURE_2D, GL_TEXTURE_MAG_FILTER, GL_LINEAR);
glTexParameteri(GL_TEXTURE_2D, GL_TEXTURE_MIN_FILTER, GL_NEAREST_MIPMAP_LINEAR);
glTexImage2D(GL_TEXTURE_2D, 0, GL_RGB, 64,64,0, GL_RGB, GL_UNSIGNED_BYTE, texImage0);
glTexImage2D(GL_TEXTURE_2D, 1, GL_RGB, 32,32,0, GL_RGB, GL_UNSIGNED_BYTE, texImage1);
glTexImage2D(GL_TEXTURE_2D, 2, GL_RGB, 16,16,0, GL_RGB, GL_UNSIGNED_BYTE, texImage2);
glTexImage2D(GL_TEXTURE_2D, 3, GL_RGB, 8, 8, 0, GL_RGB, GL_UNSIGNED_BYTE, texImage3);
glTexImage2D(GL_TEXTURE_2D, 4, GL_RGB, 4, 4, 0, GL_RGB, GL_UNSIGNED_BYTE, texImage4);
glTexImage2D(GL_TEXTURE_2D, 5, GL_RGB, 2, 2, 0, GL_RGB, GL_UNSIGNED_BYTE, texImage5);
glTexImage2D(GL_TEXTURE_2D, 6, GL_RGB, 1, 1, 0, GL_RGB, GL_UNSIGNED_BYTE, texImage6);
```

Also keep in mind that when you are using mipmaps, you need to make sure you set the minification filter defined by GL_TEXTURE_MIN_FILTER to the proper value. Table 8.3 lists the values you can use.

Automatically Generating Mipmaps

The GLU library provides a nice set of functions that allow you to build mipmaps automatically. For 2D textures, the gluBuild2DMipmaps() function replaces the set of calls you would normally make to the glTexImage2D() function and is defined as

```
int gluBuild2DMipmaps(GLenum target, GLint internalFormat, GLint width, GLint height,
                      GLenum format, GLenum type, void *texels);
```

Table 8.3 Filter Values for Mipmaps

Filter	Description
GL_NEAREST_MIPMAP_NEAREST	Use the image closest to the polygon resolution, and use GL_NEAREST filtering.
GL_NEAREST_MIPMAP_LINEAR	Use the image closest to the polygon resolution, and use GL_LINEAR filtering.
GL_LINEAR_MIPMAP_NEAREST	Use linear interpolation between the two mipmaps closest to the polygon resolution, and use GL_NEAREST filtering.
GL_LINEAR_MIPMAP_LINEAR	Use linear interpolation between the two mipmaps closest to the polygon resolution, and use GL_LINEAR filtering.

This function will create a series of mipmaps automatically by calling the glTexImage2D() function internally. All you have to worry about is passing in the primary, or level-0, texture to the function, and your mipmapped texture will be generated. Pretty simple, huh?

Here's code using the gluBuild2DMipmaps() function that does the exact same thing as our previous mipmap example:

```
glTexParameteri(GL_TEXTURE_2D, GL_TEXTURE_MAG_FILTER, GL_LINEAR);
glTexParameteri(GL_TEXTURE_2D, GL_TEXTURE_MIN_FILTER, GL_NEAREST_MIPMAP_LINEAR);
gluBuild2DMipmaps(GL_TEXTURE_2D, GL_RGB, 64, 64, GL_RGB, GL_UNSIGNED_BYTE, texImage0);
```

THE WAVING-FLAG EXAMPLE

The example you're going to look at here will display a dynamic, waving American flag. Sound complicated? Don't worry; we'll go through this one step by step.

The Explanation

To start things off, you'll be using a 128×64 texture of the U.S. flag in 24-bit Windows BMP format. You'll be applying this texture to a set of GL_QUADS arranged in a 35×20 rectangular object.

This dimension is being used to try to maintain the realistic dimensions of the flag. In order to get the wavy effect from the texture, you will need to generate texture coordinates for every vertex inside the flag object, as shown in Figure 8.8.

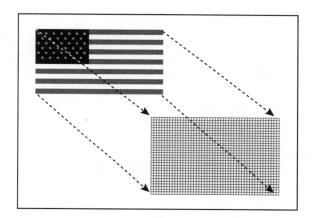

Figure 8.8

You will be applying the flag texture map to a 35×20 grid of GL_QUADS.

So just how *do* you get the wavy effect? Well, think back to trigonometry class for a moment. Remember anything from that class that had to do with waves? Does sine and cosine sound familiar? Ah yes, remember now? You will be using the `sin()` function to initialize the flag to a wave pattern. After initialized, you can keep track of the vertex coordinates frame by frame to move the wave along the flag's length. By determining the wave pattern before you actually execute the wave, you save processing time that you would otherwise have to use up frame by frame. This doesn't sound so hard now, does it?

Also, your flag object will be located along the x and y axis, which means that all the flag waving will be done along the z axis. Figure 8.9 illustrates how the waving effect will work.

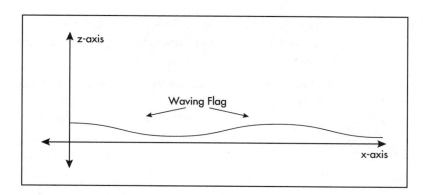

Figure 8.9

The flag will be waving along the z axis.

The Implementation

Rather than have a huge code dump, let's go through the program step by step:

```
////// Defines
#define BITMAP_ID 0x4D42                // the universal bitmap ID
#define PI 3.14159f

////// Includes
#include <windows.h>                    // standard Windows app include
#include <stdio.h>
#include <stdlib.h>
#include <math.h>
#include <gl/gl.h>                      // standard OpenGL include
#include <gl/glu.h>                     // OpenGL utilities

////// Global Variables
HDC g_HDC;                              // global device context
bool fullScreen = false;               // true = full screen; false = windowed
bool keyPressed[256];                  // holds true for keys that are pressed

////// Texture Information
BITMAPINFOHEADER    bitmapInfoHeader;   // bitmap info header
unsigned char*      bitmapData;         // the texture data
unsigned int        texture;            // the texture object

////// Flag Data
float flagPoints[36][20][3];           // flag is 36×20 (in points)
float wrapValue;                       // used to wrap point data
```

This first bit of code shows the header files you're including and the global variables you'll be using. Most of this should be familiar by now, but let's see what is new here. As you should know, you include the math.h header file because you are using the sin() function.

You can also see that you'll be storing your flag data as a two-dimensional 36×20 array of points. Points in this array will be accounting for 35 quadrilaterals in the x direction and 19 quadrilaterals in the y direction, all of which you will be assigning texture coordinates to so your flag texture displays properly.

As you will see, the variable wrapValue is used to help move the flag's wave data from the end of the flag to the beginning, such that, in effect, you are using the same wave during the entire rendering process.

Next up is the `InitializeFlag()` function, which initializes the points of your flag with the `sin()` wave function:

```
void InitializeFlag()
{
    int xIdx;                 // counter index for x plane
    int yIdx;                 // counter index for y plane
    float sinTemp;            // temp variable used for sin calculation

    // loop through all of the flag points and calculate the sin wave
    // for the z coordinate. x and y coordinates equal to counter indices
    for (xIdx = 0; xIdx < 36; xIdx++)
    {
        for (yIdx = 0; yIdx < 20; yIdx++)
        {
            flagPoints[xIdx][yIdx][0] = (float)xIdx;
            flagPoints[xIdx][yIdx][1] = (float)yIdx;

            sinTemp = ((float)xIdx*20.0f / 360.0f)*2.0f*PI;
            flagPoints[xIdx][yIdx][2] = (float)sin(sinTemp);
        }
    }
}
```

This function is pretty simple and straightforward. What you do here is loop through all the points in the flag database and calculate the sine wave based on your location along the x axis of the wave. You can change the wave's characteristics by changing how `sinTemp` is calculated. After this function is complete, you get something like the image shown in Figure 8.10.

Next up is the function you use to initialize OpenGL and the rest of your application:

```
void Initialize()
{
    glClearColor(0.0f, 0.0f, 0.0f, 0.0f);    // clear to black
    glEnable(GL_DEPTH_TEST);                  // hidden surface removal
    glEnable(GL_CULL_FACE);                   // do not calculate inside of polys
    glFrontFace(GL_CCW);                      // counterclockwise polygons are out

    glEnable(GL_TEXTURE_2D);                  // enable 2D texturing

    // load our bitmap file
    bitmapData = LoadBitmapFile("usflag.bmp", &bitmapInfoHeader);
```

Figure 8.10

After the `InitializeFlag()`
*function is complete, you get
a set of points arranged as a
wave in the x direction.*

```
glGenTextures(1, &texture);                // generate texture object
glBindTexture(GL_TEXTURE_2D, texture);   // enable our texture object

glTexParameteri(GL_TEXTURE_2D, GL_TEXTURE_MAG_FILTER, GL_NEAREST);
glTexParameteri(GL_TEXTURE_2D, GL_TEXTURE_MIN_FILTER, GL_NEAREST);

    // generate the texture image
glTexImage2D(GL_TEXTURE_2D, 0, GL_RGB, bitmapInfoHeader.biWidth,
                  bitmapInfoHeader.biHeight, 0, GL_RGB, GL_UNSIGNED_BYTE,
                  bitmapData);

    InitializeFlag();
}
```

This function should look pretty familiar by now as well. As you can see, you use the
`LoadBitmapFile()` function that you created in Chapter 7 to load your BMP file into memory
so you can use it as a texture.

After you load the BMP file into memory, you generate your texture object with the
`glGenTextures()` function and enable the texture object with the `glBindTexture()` function. You
then give the texture object its texture data with the `glTexImage2D()` function.

Next is the DrawFlag() function, which handles the rendering of the textured flag per frame:

```
void DrawFlag()
{
    int xIdx;                   // counter index for x direction
    int yIdx;                   // counter index for y direction
    float texLeft;              // left texture coordinate for quads
    float texBottom;            // bottom texture coordinate for quads
    float texTop;               // top texture coordinate for quads
    float texRight;             // right texture coordinate for quads

    glPushMatrix();
        glBindTexture(GL_TEXTURE_2D, texture);          // bind our texture
        glBegin(GL_QUADS);                              // draw flag using quads

        // loop through the flag's points, minus the last 2 in each direction
        // since we only use them to draw the last GL_QUAD in each direction
        for (xIdx = 0; xIdx < 36; xIdx++)               // x direction
        {
            for (yIdx = 0; yIdx < 18; yIdx++)           // y direction
            {
                // calculate texture coordinates for current quad
                texLeft = float(xIdx) / 35.0f;          // left texture coordinate
                texBottom = float(yIdx) / 18.0f;        // bottom texture coordinate
                texRight = float(xIdx+1) / 35.0f;       // right texture coordinate
                texTop = float(yIdx+1) / 18.0f;         // top texture coordinate

                // bottom left
                glTexCoord2f(texLeft, texBottom);
                glVertex3f(flagPoints[xIdx][yIdx][0], flagPoints[xIdx][yIdx][1],
                        flagPoints[xIdx][yIdx][2]);

                // bottom right
                glTexCoord2f(texRight, texBottom);
                glVertex3f(flagPoints[xIdx+1][yIdx][0],
                        flagPoints[xIdx+1][yIdx][1],
                        flagPoints[xIdx+1][yIdx][2]);

                // top right
                glTexCoord2f(texRight, texTop);
                glVertex3f(flagPoints[xIdx+1][yIdx+1][0],
```

```
                        flagPoints[xIdx+1][yIdx+1][1],
                        flagPoints[xIdx+1][yIdx+1][2]);

                // top left
                glTexCoord2f(texLeft, texTop);
                glVertex3f(flagPoints[xIdx][yIdx+1][0],
                        flagPoints[xIdx][yIdx+1][1],
                        flagPoints[xIdx][yIdx+1][2] );
        }
    }
    glEnd();

    /*
      Now we do the flag movement:
      We go to each point in the flag by row and move the z coordinate
      of each point one point to the right to simulate the movement of a
      a wave.
    */
    for( yIdx = 0; yIdx < 19; yIdx++ )                  // loop for y plane
    {
        // store the furthest-right point's z-coordinate value for this row
        wrapValue = flagPoints[35][yIdx][2];

        for( xIdx = 35; xIdx >= 0; xIdx--)       // loop for x plane
        {
            // current point z coordinate is set to the
            // previous point's z coordinate
            flagPoints[xIdx][yIdx][2] = flagPoints[xIdx-1][yIdx][2];
        }

        // set the furthest-left point's z coordinate to the stored wrapValue
        flagPoints[0][yIdx][2] = wrapValue;
    }

    glPopMatrix();
}
```

The comments in this function really help explain what's happening as the code executes. First
you bind your flag texture as the current texture. Then you tell OpenGL that you will be drawing
using GL_QUADS.

When you actually render the flag, you start at the bottom-left corner and traverse through the vertices such that you draw one GL_QUAD at a time. Before you draw each GL_QUAD, however, you must calculate the texture coordinates for each vertex of the GL_QUAD in relation to the entire flag object so the overall flag texture is properly displayed on the object. You calculate each texture coordinate by dividing the point's x and y coordinates by the total number of points across the flag's axes.

After the texture coordinates are calculated you draw the GL_QUAD using the glTexCoord2f() and glVertex3f() functions. You draw each GL_QUAD with its vertices in counterclockwise order.

After drawing the entire flag, you need to manipulate the flag data so you get the effect of waves traveling across the flag. To do this, you go through each row of points and move the z-coordinate data for each point on that row to its neighboring point to the right, but you do this after you first store the right-most point's z coordinate in the variable wrapValue. After you have traversed the row, you store the value held in wrapValue into the left-most point's z coordinate so you get a wrap-around effect.

The Render() function here is very similar to all the other Render() functions you've seen thus far, except this time you call the DrawFlag() function once per frame after moving the view into an area where you can see the flag a little better:

```
void Render()
{
    // clear screen and depth buffer
    glClear(GL_COLOR_BUFFER_BIT | GL_DEPTH_BUFFER_BIT);
    glLoadIdentity();

    glTranslatef(-15.0f, -10.0f, -50.0f);      // perform transformations

    DrawFlag();                                // draw flag

    glFlush();
    SwapBuffers(g_HDC);                         // bring back buffer to foreground
}
```

Here is the rest of the code for this example (by now, none of this code should be new):

```
unsigned char *LoadBitmapFile(char *filename, BITMAPINFOHEADER *bitmapInfoHeader)
{
    FILE                *filePtr;          // the file pointer
    BITMAPFILEHEADER    bitmapFileHeader;  // bitmap file header
    unsigned char       *bitmapImage;      // bitmap image data
```

```c
int                 imageIdx = 0;          // image index counter
unsigned char       tempRGB;               // swap variable

// open filename in "read binary" mode
filePtr = fopen(filename, "rb");
if (filePtr == NULL)
    return NULL;

// read the bitmap file header
fread(&bitmapFileHeader, sizeof(BITMAPFILEHEADER), 1, filePtr);

// verify that this is a bitmap by checking for the universal bitmap id
if (bitmapFileHeader.bfType != BITMAP_ID)
{
    fclose(filePtr);
    return NULL;
}

// read the bitmap information header
fread(bitmapInfoHeader, sizeof(BITMAPINFOHEADER), 1, filePtr);

// move file pointer to beginning of bitmap data
fseek(filePtr, bitmapFileHeader.bfOffBits, SEEK_SET);

// allocate enough memory for the bitmap image data
bitmapImage = (unsigned char*)malloc(bitmapInfoHeader->biSizeImage);

// verify memory allocation
if (!bitmapImage)
{
    free(bitmapImage);
    fclose(filePtr);
    return NULL;
}

// read in the bitmap image data
fread(bitmapImage, 1, bitmapInfoHeader->biSizeImage, filePtr);

// make sure bitmap image data was read
if (bitmapImage == NULL)
```

```
        {
            fclose(filePtr);
            return NULL;
        }

        // swap the R and B values to get RGB since the bitmap color format is in BGR
        for (imageIdx = 0; imageIdx < bitmapInfoHeader->biSizeImage; imageIdx+=3)
        {
            tempRGB = bitmapImage[imageIdx];
            bitmapImage[imageIdx] = bitmapImage[imageIdx + 2];
            bitmapImage[imageIdx + 2] = tempRGB;
        }

        // close the file and return the bitmap image data
        fclose(filePtr);
        return bitmapImage;
}

void SetupPixelFormat(HDC hDC)
{
        int nPixelFormat;                       // our pixel format index

        static PIXELFORMATDESCRIPTOR pfd = {
            sizeof(PIXELFORMATDESCRIPTOR),      // size of structure
                1,                              // default version
                PFD_DRAW_TO_WINDOW |            // window-drawing support
                PFD_SUPPORT_OPENGL |            // OpenGL support
                PFD_DOUBLEBUFFER,               // double-buffering support
                PFD_TYPE_RGBA,                  // RGBA color mode
                32,                             // 32-bit color mode
                0, 0, 0, 0, 0, 0,               // ignore color bits, non-palletized mode
                0,                              // no alpha buffer
                0,                              // ignore shift bit
                0,                              // no accumulation buffer
                0, 0, 0, 0,                     // ignore accumulation bits
                16,                             // 16-bit z-buffer size
                0,                              // no stencil buffer
                0,                              // no auxiliary buffer
                PFD_MAIN_PLANE,                 // main drawing plane
                0,                              // reserved
                0, 0, 0 };                      // layer masks ignored
```

```
        nPixelFormat = ChoosePixelFormat(hDC, &pfd);      // choose matching pixel format
        SetPixelFormat(hDC, nPixelFormat, &pfd);          // set pixel format to DC
}

LRESULT CALLBACK WndProc(HWND hwnd, UINT message, WPARAM wParam, LPARAM lParam)
{
        static HGLRC hRC;           // rendering context
        static HDC hDC;             // device context
        int width, height;          // window width and height

        switch(message)
        {
                case WM_CREATE:          // window is being created
                        hDC = GetDC(hwnd);      // get current window's device context
                        g_HDC = hDC;
                        SetupPixelFormat(hDC); // call our pixel format setup function

                        // create rendering context and make it current
                        hRC = wglCreateContext(hDC);
                        wglMakeCurrent(hDC, hRC);
                        return 0;
                        break;

                case WM_CLOSE:          // windows is closing
                        // deselect rendering context and delete it
                        wglMakeCurrent(hDC, NULL);
                        wglDeleteContext(hRC);

                        // send WM_QUIT to message queue
                        PostQuitMessage(0);

                        return 0;
                        break;

                case WM_SIZE:
                        height = HIWORD(lParam);                // retrieve width and height
                        width = LOWORD(lParam);

                        if (height==0)                          // don't want a divide by zero
                                height=1;
```

```
                glViewport(0, 0, width, height);      // reset the viewport
                glMatrixMode(GL_PROJECTION);          // set projection matrix
                glLoadIdentity();                     // reset projection matrix

                // calculate aspect ratio of window
                gluPerspective(54.0f,(GLfloat)width/(GLfloat)height,1.0f,1000.0f);
                glMatrixMode(GL_MODELVIEW);           // set modelview matrix
                glLoadIdentity();                     // reset modelview matrix

                return 0;
                break;

        case WM_KEYDOWN:                              // is a key pressed?
                keyPressed[wParam] = true;
                return 0;
                break;

        case WM_KEYUP:
                keyPressed[wParam] = false;
                return 0;
                break;

        default:
                break;
    }
    return (DefWindowProc(hwnd, message, wParam, lParam));
}


int WINAPI WinMain(HINSTANCE hInstance, HINSTANCE hPrevInstance,
                LPSTR lpCmdLine, int nShowCmd)
{

    WNDCLASSEX windowClass;           // window class
    HWND       hwnd;                  // window handle
    MSG        msg;                   // message
    bool       done;                  // flag saying when our app is complete
    DWORD      dwExStyle;             // Window extended style
    DWORD      dwStyle;               // Window style
    RECT       windowRect;
```

```cpp
// temp var's
int width = 800;
int height = 600;
int bits = 32;

windowRect.left=(long)0;              // Set left value to 0
windowRect.right=(long)width;         // Set right value to requested width
windowRect.top=(long)0;               // Set top value to 0
windowRect.bottom=(long)height;       // Set bottom value to requested height

// fill out the windows class structure
windowClass.cbSize                  = sizeof(WNDCLASSEX);
windowClass.style                   = CS_HREDRAW | CS_VREDRAW;
windowClass.lpfnWndProc             = WndProc;
windowClass.cbClsExtra              = 0;
windowClass.cbWndExtra              = 0;
windowClass.hInstance               = hInstance;
windowClass.hIcon                   = LoadIcon(NULL, IDI_APPLICATION);
windowClass.hCursor                 = LoadCursor(NULL, IDC_ARROW);
windowClass.hbrBackground           = NULL;
windowClass.lpszMenuName            = NULL;
windowClass.lpszClassName           = "MyClass";
windowClass.hIconSm                 = LoadIcon(NULL, IDI_WINLOGO);

// register the windows class
if (!RegisterClassEx(&windowClass))
    return 0;

if (fullScreen)                     // fullscreen?
{
    DEVMODE dmScreenSettings;       // device mode
    memset(&dmScreenSettings,0,sizeof(dmScreenSettings));
    dmScreenSettings.dmSize = sizeof(dmScreenSettings);
    dmScreenSettings.dmPelsWidth = width;           // screen width
    dmScreenSettings.dmPelsHeight = height;         // screen height
    dmScreenSettings.dmBitsPerPel = bits;           // bits per pixel
    dmScreenSettings.dmFields = DM_BITSPERPEL|DM_PELSWIDTH|DM_PELSHEIGHT;
    if (ChangeDisplaySettings(&dmScreenSettings, CDS_FULLSCREEN) !=
        DISP_CHANGE_SUCCESSFUL)
    {
```

```
            // setting display mode failed, switch to windowed
            MessageBox(NULL, "Display mode failed", NULL, MB_OK);
            fullScreen=FALSE;
        }
    }

    if (fullScreen)                     // Are we still in full-screen mode?
    {
        dwExStyle=WS_EX_APPWINDOW;      // Window extended style
        dwStyle=WS_POPUP;               // Windows style
        ShowCursor(FALSE);              // Hide mouse pointer
    }
    else
    {
        dwExStyle=WS_EX_APPWINDOW | WS_EX_WINDOWEDGE;      // Window extended style
        dwStyle=WS_OVERLAPPEDWINDOW;                       // Windows style
    }
    AdjustWindowRectEx(&windowRect, dwStyle, FALSE, dwExStyle);

    // class registered, so now create our window
    hwnd = CreateWindowEx(NULL,                     // extended style
                        "MyClass",                  // class name
                        "Texture Example 2: The Waving Flag Example", // app name
                        dwStyle | WS_CLIPCHILDREN |
                        WS_CLIPSIBLINGS,
                        0, 0,                        // x,y coordinate
                        windowRect.right - windowRect.left,
                        windowRect.bottom - windowRect.top,     // width, height
                        NULL,                        // handle to parent
                        NULL,                        // handle to menu
                        hInstance,                   // application instance
                        NULL);                       // no extra params

    // check if window creation failed (hwnd would equal NULL)
    if (!hwnd)
        return 0;

    ShowWindow(hwnd, SW_SHOW);               // display the window
    UpdateWindow(hwnd);                      // update the window
```

```
    done = false;                          // initialize the loop condition variable
    Initialize();                          // initialize OpenGL

    // main message loop
    while (!done)
    {
        PeekMessage(&msg, hwnd, NULL, NULL, PM_REMOVE);
        if (msg.message == WM_QUIT)        // do we receive a WM_QUIT message?
        {
            done = true;                   // if so, time to quit the application
        }
        else
        {
            if (keyPressed[VK_ESCAPE])
                done = true;
            else
            {
                Render();
                TranslateMessage(&msg);    // translate and dispatch to event queue
                DispatchMessage(&msg);
            }
        }
    }
    free(bitmapData);
    if (fullScreen)
    {
        ChangeDisplaySettings(NULL,0);      // If so switch back to the desktop
        ShowCursor(TRUE);                   // Show mouse pointer
    }
    return msg.wParam;
}
```

That example wasn't too bad, was it? Your final result is shown in Figure 8.11.

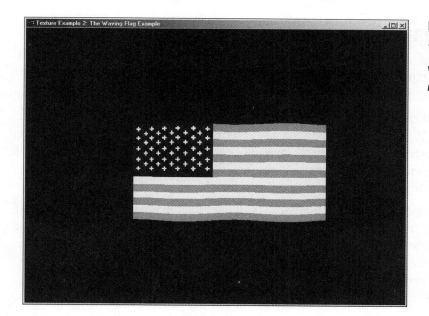

Figure 8.11

The final result of the waving texture-mapped flag example.

THE TEXTURED HEIGHTFIELD TERRAIN EXAMPLE

The next example you're going to look at is what is known in the computer-graphics industry as a *heightfield terrain*, which is a landscape, or terrain system, that is divided into a grid of height values. When you draw all these height values on the screen, you get a mesh that resembles a world's landscape.

Keep in mind that the method you're going to look at here is only one way to develop a simple landscape. There are quite a few methods out there that could be used to make this example work much faster or to even look better. Also, you will be using some simple camera movement so you can rotate your view around the terrain.

The terrain itself is texture mapped with a simple texture to represent grass. You also use a texture for water to give the scene more realism, even though you set the water to a transparent blue color. With this in mind, let's take a look at how you develop the terrain example.

The Explanation

Keeping in mind our definition of *heightfield terrain*, you're going to create a grid of vertices that are spaced evenly apart but have varying heights based on the height of the terrain data at the vertex's grid location.

You'll be determining the height of each grid location by loading a 32×32 grayscale bitmap into memory with each bit of the bitmap representing a grid location in the heightfield. You can then use the color value of each bit to determine the height of each grid location. In a 24-bit grayscale bitmap, the color values will range from 0 to 255, which means that the heights for the heightfield will range from 0.0 to 255.0.

After you load all of these grid values into memory, you'll have a set of data points that represent the height of the terrain at specific intervals, but how do you determine these intervals? To set the intervals, or the distance between each height vertex, you use what is called a *map scale*. If you remember, *scaling* is where you increase or decrease the size of an object based on a scale factor. The same idea applies here: To increase the interval between each height data point, you increase the value of the map scale factor.

When you assign the vertex coordinates for each grid location, you'll need to multiply the map scale factor by the grid location index based on the coordinate element you are defining. For example, when you're defining the x coordinate for a vertex, you'll take the grid location along the x axis and multiply it by the scale factor.

This brings us to how you will represent the terrain map. Well, you know that the map is a grid of height values, so why don't you create a 2D array of vertex coordinates? This grid will extend along the x and z axes, with the y axis representing the terrain height.

After you load in your data points for the terrain grid, you get a heightfield like the one shown in Figure 8.12.

To render the terrain map, you'll use a GL_TRIANGLE_STRIP for each row of grid values along the z axis. Because you're rendering the terrain this way, you'll need to specify the points in a specific order so you get proper rendering. Basically what you will do is start at one end of the row and move along the positive x axis by drawing the vertices in a Z pattern, as shown in Figure 8.13. In order to get proper texture mapping, you'll send four vertices at a time to OpenGL. After you reach the end of the row, you move on to the next row and do the same thing. The process is repeated until you've processed all of the rows.

Figure 8.14 shows how the Z pattern looks when it is rendered using the data points in Figure 8.12.

Figure 8.12

A set of heightfield data points.

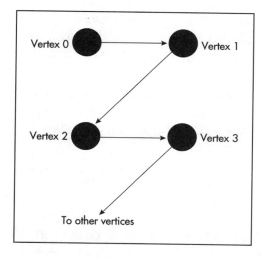

Figure 8.13

Process the vertices for each row in a Z pattern.

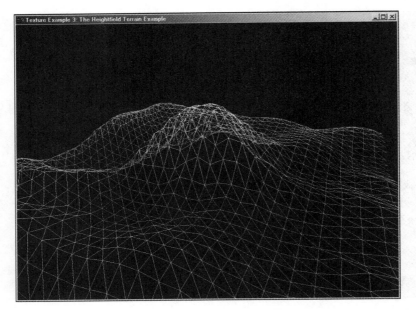

Figure 8.14

The heightfield data points drawn with lines using the Z pattern.

If you apply grayscale coloring to the terrain, you get a shaded heightfield like the one shown in Figure 8.15. The lighter shades represent higher elevations, while the darker shades represent lower elevations. You can leave this shading in the scene to add another level of realism to the terrain when you texture-map it.

You're going to texture-map the terrain by specifying one texture for every four vertices, because four vertices will define a quadrilateral made up of two triangles, and your textures are in the shape of a rectangle. So when you define the texture coordinates, you will set them equal to the values shown in Figure 8.16.

With a texture for every quadrilateral, you get a nice, smooth-looking terrain, as shown in Figure 8.17.

Wow, looks pretty cool doesn't it?

Next up for discussion is the water that you'll add to the scene. To do this part, you need to think about how things are done in nature. For example, consider the term *sea level*. Sea level defines the average height of the oceans on the Earth. If you raise or lower the sea level, then you increase or decrease the amount of water coverage on the Earth. A lower sea level results in more land being available, while a higher sea level results in less land being available. If you think of the Earth's landmasses as heightfield terrain, then you might be able to see where we're going with the water in this example.

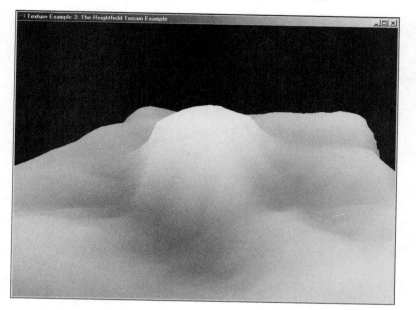

Figure 8.15

The heightfield data points with grayscale color applied to each vertex.

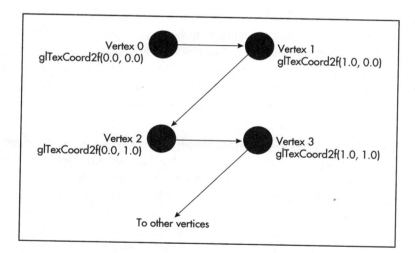

Figure 8.16

Texture coordinates applied to the Z pattern.

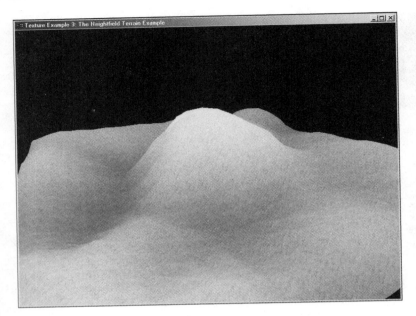

Figure 8.17

The resulting height-field data points with texturing applied.

You're going to define a certain height in your scene as the "sea level" for your water. At this sea level will be a single quadrilateral that you will set to a transparent blue color to represent the water. Then you'll apply a water texture to this quadrilateral so you have a more realistic look and feel to the scene. And then, to really impress your friends, you're going to make the quadrilateral move up and down in a small interval to make the water appear to move and "wash upon the shores" of the terrain. After you add this water to the scene, you get something like that shown in Figure 8.18.

But looking at this terrain from one angle is boring. To spice things up, you're going to add some simple camera movement using the mouse. Basically, the camera will rotate around the terrain left or right when the mouse is moved left or right, respectively, and you will move the camera closer or further away from the center of the terrain when the mouse is moved forward or backward. The camera will always point toward a predetermined point that you will hard-code into the sample program. You'll move the camera by checking for the WM_MOUSEMOVE message in the WndProc() and calculating the new location of the camera using sine and cosine based on how much the mouse has moved from the previous WM_MOUSEMOVE message.

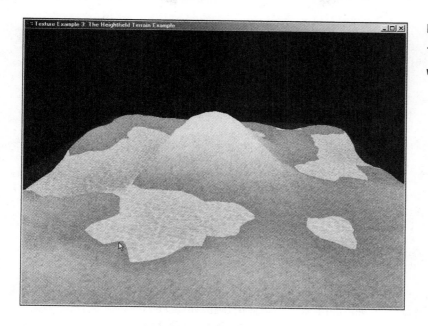

Figure 8.18

The heightfield terrain with water added.

The Implementation

Let's look at this beast one piece at a time. This first block of code declares your constants and variables:

```
////// Defines
#define BITMAP_ID      0x4D42        // the universal bitmap ID
#define MAP_X          32            // size of map along x axis
#define MAP_Z          32            // size of map along z axis
#define MAP_SCALE      20.0f         // the scale of the terrain map
#define PI             3.14159       // the constant value for PI

////// Includes
#include <windows.h>                 // standard Windows app include
#include <stdio.h>
#include <stdlib.h>
#include <math.h>
#include <gl/gl.h>                   // standard OpenGL include
#include <gl/glu.h>                  // OpenGL utilities
```

```
////// Global Variables
HDC g_HDC;                              // global device context
bool fullScreen = false;               // true = full screen; false = windowed
bool keyPressed[256];                  // holds true for keys that are pressed

float angle = 0.0f;                    // camera angle
float radians = 0.0f;                  // camera angle in radians
float waterHeight = 154.0f;            // height of water
bool waterDir = true;                  // used to animate water
                                       // true = up, false = down


////// Mouse/Camera Variables
int mouseX, mouseY;                    // mouse coordinates
float cameraX, cameraY, cameraZ;       // camera coordinates
float lookX, lookY, lookZ;             // camera look-at coordinates

////// Texture Information
BITMAPINFOHEADER    bitmapInfoHeader;  // temp bitmap info header
BITMAPINFOHEADER    landInfo;          // land texture info header
BITMAPINFOHEADER    waterInfo;         // water texture info header

unsigned char*      imageData;         // the map image data
unsigned char*      landTexture;       // land texture data
unsigned char*      waterTexture;      // water texture data
unsigned int        land;              // the land texture object
unsigned int        water;             // the water texture object

////// Terrain Data
float terrain[MAP_X][MAP_Z][3];        // heightfield terrain data
```

Quite a bit more code in this part of the example than you're used to! The block of defines is filled with constants that you use for determining the size of the map along the x and z axes and the map scale. You also define a constant for pi, which you use when you're calculating the current camera position.

Most of the variables declared here are rather self-explanatory. As you can see, you define a water height for the quadrilateral that represents the sea level of the terrain. You also have a variable that determines whether the water is rising or falling. Next are the variables for holding the current mouse position in the window, along with the variables for the current camera coordinates.

The imageData variable is used to hold the map-image data that you load from a 32×32 grayscale Windows BMP file. The landTexture and waterTexture variables are used to hold the land- and water-texture data, respectively. To speed up the texturing process, you use texture objects for the land and water textures by declaring the land and water variables.

Last is the two-dimensional array of terrain data that holds the vertex coordinates for each point in the heightmap terrain. You determine the size of the terrain through the MAP_X and MAP_Z constants.

Although it is not shown here, you also include the LoadBitmapFile() function that you have been using in previous examples to load 24-bit Windows BMP files into memory.

The next block of code is the InitializeTerrain() function:

```
void InitializeTerrain()
{
    // loop through all of the heightfield points, calculating
    // the coordinates for each point
    for (int z = 0; z < MAP_Z; z++)
    {
        for (int x = 0; x < MAP_X; x++)
        {
            terrain[x][z][0] = float(x)*MAP_SCALE;
            terrain[x][z][1] = (float)imageData[(z*MAP_Z+x)*3];
            terrain[x][z][2] = -float(z)*MAP_SCALE;
        }
    }
}
```

Basically all this function does is calculate the vertex coordinates for each point in the heightfield terrain grid. The easiest calculations are for the x and z axes. For the x axis, you just multiply the index of the grid point by the map scale to get the x component of the coordinate. To calculate the coordinate for the z axis, you multiply the index of the grid point by the map scale, but you also negate the result so the terrain lies along the negative-z axis. Using this method is merely personal preference and is not required; however, if you change how the coordinates are calculated, you will also need to change how the camera is moved and its orientation is determined.

The y component of each grid coordinate is the interesting part of this function. In actuality, all you're doing is extracting the corresponding grayscale pixel value from the grayscale bitmap that represents your terrain, but calculating which pixel corresponds to the current grid value is the tricky part. As you can see, you use the following equation to calculate the location of the corresponding pixel:

```
(z*MAP_Z+x)*3
```

When looking at this equation, keep in mind that the bitmap data is arranged in a one-dimensional array of RGB values, where the red, green, and blue components of each pixel are all equal to the same value.

Next up is the LoadTextures() function, which you use to load and bind all your textures into memory:

```
bool LoadTextures()
{
    // load the land-texture data
    landTexture = LoadBitmapFile("green.bmp", &landInfo);
    if (!landTexture)
        return false;

    // load the water-texture data
    waterTexture = LoadBitmapFile("water.bmp", &waterInfo);
    if (!waterTexture)
        return false;

    // generate the land texture as a mipmap
    glGenTextures(1, &land);
    glBindTexture(GL_TEXTURE_2D, land);
    glTexParameteri(GL_TEXTURE_2D, GL_TEXTURE_MAG_FILTER, GL_NEAREST);
    glTexParameteri(GL_TEXTURE_2D, GL_TEXTURE_MIN_FILTER, GL_NEAREST);
    gluBuild2DMipmaps(GL_TEXTURE_2D, GL_RGB, landInfo.biWidth, landInfo.biHeight,
                      GL_RGB, GL_UNSIGNED_BYTE, landTexture);

    // generate the water texture as a mipmap
    glGenTextures(1, &water);
    glBindTexture(GL_TEXTURE_2D, water);
    glTexParameteri(GL_TEXTURE_2D, GL_TEXTURE_MAG_FILTER, GL_NEAREST);
    glTexParameteri(GL_TEXTURE_2D, GL_TEXTURE_MIN_FILTER, GL_NEAREST);
    glTexParameteri(GL_TEXTURE_2D, GL_TEXTURE_WRAP_S, GL_REPEAT);
    glTexParameteri(GL_TEXTURE_2D, GL_TEXTURE_WRAP_T, GL_REPEAT);
    gluBuild2DMipmaps(GL_TEXTURE_2D, GL_RGB, waterInfo.biWidth, waterInfo.biHeight,
                      GL_RGB, GL_UNSIGNED_BYTE, waterTexture);

    return true;
}
```

After loading the texture image data into memory using the `LoadBitmapFile()` function, you first create the land-texture object and set the magnification filters before building the mipmaps for the texture. You then generate the water-texture object and set its magnification filters. You also set the water texture to repeat itself when wrapping is involved before building mipmaps for this texture. The wrapping is purposely defined here, as you will be using texture wrapping when you render the water:

```
void Render()
{
    radians =  float(PI*(angle-90.0f)/180.0f);

    // calculate the camera's position
    cameraX = lookX + sin(radians)*mouseY;   // multiplying by mouseY makes the
    cameraZ = lookZ + cos(radians)*mouseY;   // camera get closer/
                                             // farther away with mouseY

    cameraY = lookY + mouseY / 2.0f;

    // calculate the camera look-at coordinates as the center of the terrain map
    lookX = (MAP_X*MAP_SCALE)/2.0f;
    lookY = 150.0f;
    lookZ = -(MAP_Z*MAP_SCALE)/2.0f;

    // clear screen and depth buffer
    glClear(GL_COLOR_BUFFER_BIT | GL_DEPTH_BUFFER_BIT);
    glLoadIdentity();

    // set the camera position
    gluLookAt(cameraX, cameraY, cameraZ, lookX, lookY, lookZ, 0.0, 1.0, 0.0);

    // set the current texture to the land texture
    glBindTexture(GL_TEXTURE_2D, land);

    // we are going to loop through all of our terrain's data points,
    // but we only want to draw one triangle strip for each set along the x axis.
    for (int z = 0; z < MAP_Z-1; z++)
    {
        glBegin(GL_TRIANGLE_STRIP);
        for (int x = 0; x < MAP_X-1; x++)
        {
            // for each vertex, we calculate the grayscale shade color,
            // we set the texture coordinate, and we draw the vertex.
```

```
/*
    the vertices are drawn in this order:

    0  ---> 1
           /
          /
       |/
       2  ---> 3
*/

// draw vertex 0
glColor3f(terrain[x][z][1]/255.0f, terrain[x][z][1]/255.0f,
          terrain[x][z][1]/255.0f);
glTexCoord2f(0.0f, 0.0f);
glVertex3f(terrain[x][z][0], terrain[x][z][1], terrain[x][z][2]);

// draw vertex 1
glTexCoord2f(1.0f, 0.0f);
glColor3f(terrain[x+1][z][1]/255.0f, terrain[x+1][z][1]/255.0f,
          terrain[x+1][z][1]/255.0f);
glVertex3f(terrain[x+1][z][0], terrain[x+1][z][1],
          terrain[x+1][z][2]);

// draw vertex 2
glTexCoord2f(0.0f, 1.0f);
glColor3f(terrain[x][z+1][1]/255.0f, terrain[x][z+1][1]/255.0f,
          terrain[x][z+1][1]/255.0f);
glVertex3f(terrain[x][z+1][0], terrain[x][z+1][1],
          terrain[x][z+1][2]);

// draw vertex 3
glColor3f(terrain[x+1][z+1][1]/255.0f, terrain[x+1][z+1][1]/255.0f,
          terrain[x+1][z+1][1]/255.0f);
glTexCoord2f(1.0f, 1.0f);
glVertex3f(terrain[x+1][z+1][0], terrain[x+1][z+1][1],
          terrain[x+1][z+1][2]);
    }
  glEnd();
}
```

```
// enable blending
glEnable(GL_BLEND);

// enable read-only depth buffer
glDepthMask(GL_FALSE);

// set the blend function to what we use for transparency
glBlendFunc(GL_SRC_ALPHA, GL_ONE);

glColor4f(0.5f, 0.5f, 1.0f, 0.7f);          // set color to a transparent blue
glBindTexture(GL_TEXTURE_2D, water);        // set texture to the water texture

// draw water as one large quad surface
glBegin(GL_QUADS);
    glTexCoord2f(0.0f, 0.0f);               // lower-left corner
    glVertex3f(terrain[0][0][0], waterHeight, terrain[0][0][2]);

    glTexCoord2f(10.0f, 0.0f);              // lower-right corner
    glVertex3f(terrain[MAP_X-1][0][0], waterHeight,
               terrain[MAP_X-1][0][2]);

    glTexCoord2f(10.0f, 10.0f);             // upper-right corner
    glVertex3f(terrain[MAP_X-1][MAP_Z-1][0], waterHeight,
               terrain[MAP_X-1][MAP_Z-1][2]);

    glTexCoord2f(0.0f, 10.0f);              // upper-left corner
    glVertex3f(terrain[0][MAP_Z-1][0], waterHeight,
               terrain[0][MAP_Z-1][2]);
glEnd();

// set back to normal depth buffer mode (writeable)
glDepthMask(GL_TRUE);

// disable blending
glDisable(GL_BLEND);

// animate the water
if (waterHeight > 155.0f)
    waterDir = false;
else if (waterHeight < 154.0f)
    waterDir = true;
```

```
    if (waterDir)
        waterHeight += 0.01f;
    else
        waterHeight -= 0.01f;

    glFlush();
    SwapBuffers(g_HDC);                     // bring back buffer to foreground
}
```

This function starts off by calculating the camera angle in radians. This radian value is used to calculate the new camera coordinates by taking the sine of the angle for the x axis and cosine of the angle for the z axis. Then, by using the map constants, you calculate the coordinates for the middle of the terrain because you want the camera to point there.

Next, you set the camera position and orientation by using the gluLookAt() function.

Before drawing the terrain, you first tell OpenGL that you are going to use the land texture through the glBindTexture() function. You use a triangle strip for each row of data points along the z axis. So when you draw the triangle strip, you move along the x axis until you reach the last data point for that row. For each vertex, you set the grayscale color (by dividing the vertex height by 255.0 for 255 grayscale shades) and the texture coordinates in the order of the Z pattern that we discussed before.

Next up is the code to draw the transparent water. You might recognize the code from Chapter 6, "Adding Colors, Blending, and Lighting," to set up transparency before you start drawing the water quadrilateral. You also use the glBindTexture() function to set the water texture to the current texture. You render the quadrilateral by sending the vertices to OpenGL in counterclockwise order. Transparency is then turned off before you get to the code that controls the direction that the water moves.

Your Initialize() function looks like this:

```
void Initialize()
{
    glClearColor(0.0f, 0.0f, 0.0f, 0.0f);       // clear to black

    glShadeModel(GL_SMOOTH);                    // use smooth shading
    glEnable(GL_DEPTH_TEST);                    // hidden surface removal
    glEnable(GL_CULL_FACE);                     // do not calculate inside of polys
    glFrontFace(GL_CCW);                        // counterclockwise polygons are out

    glEnable(GL_TEXTURE_2D);                    // enable 2D texturing
```

```
        imageData = LoadBitmapFile("terrain2.bmp", &bitmapInfoHeader);

        // initialize the terrain data and load the textures
        InitializeTerrain();
        LoadTextures();
}
```

This function sets up and initializes your sample program. After setting up OpenGL, you load the terrain data into memory with the LoadBitmapFile() function. Then you initialize the terrain data and load the textures into memory.

Because you're moving the camera around with the mouse, you need to make some modifications to the WndProc() function, displayed here:

```
LRESULT CALLBACK WndProc(HWND hwnd, UINT message, WPARAM wParam, LPARAM lParam)
{
        static HGLRC hRC;                       // rendering context
        static HDC hDC;                         // device context
        int width, height;                      // window width and height
        int oldMouseX, oldMouseY;               // old mouse coordinates

        switch(message)
        {
                case WM_CREATE:                 // window is being created

                        hDC = GetDC(hwnd);      // get current window's device context
                        g_HDC = hDC;
                        SetupPixelFormat(hDC);  // call our pixel format setup function

                        // create rendering context and make it current
                        hRC = wglCreateContext(hDC);
                        wglMakeCurrent(hDC, hRC);

                        return 0;
                        break;

                case WM_CLOSE:                  // window is closing

                        // deselect rendering context and delete it
                        wglMakeCurrent(hDC, NULL);
                        wglDeleteContext(hRC);
```

```
                // send WM_QUIT to message queue
                PostQuitMessage(0);

                return 0;
                break;

        case WM_SIZE:
                height = HIWORD(lParam);                // retrieve width and height
                width = LOWORD(lParam);

                if (height==0)                          // don't want a divide by zero
                {
                        height=1;
                }

                // reset the viewport to new dimensions
                glViewport(0, 0, width, height);

                // set projection matrix current matrix
                glMatrixMode(GL_PROJECTION);
                glLoadIdentity();                       // reset projection matrix

                // calculate aspect ratio of window
                gluPerspective(54.0f,(GLfloat)width/(GLfloat)height,1.0f,1000.0f);

                glMatrixMode(GL_MODELVIEW);             // set modelview matrix
                glLoadIdentity();                       // reset modelview matrix

                return 0;
                break;

        case WM_KEYDOWN:                                // is a key pressed?
                keyPressed[wParam] = true;
                return 0;
                break;

        case WM_KEYUP:
                keyPressed[wParam] = false;
                return 0;
                break;
```

```
        case WM_MOUSEMOVE:
            // save old mouse coordinates
            oldMouseX = mouseX;
            oldMouseY = mouseY;

            // get mouse coordinates from Windows
            mouseX = LOWORD(lParam);
            mouseY = HIWORD(lParam);

            // these lines limit the camera's range
            if (mouseY < 200)
                mouseY = 200;
            if (mouseY > 450)
                mouseY = 450;

            if ((mouseX - oldMouseX) > 0)         // mouse moved to the right
                angle += 3.0f;
            else if ((mouseX - oldMouseX) < 0)  // mouse moved to the left
                angle -= 3.0f;

            return 0;
            break;
        default:
            break;
    }

    return (DefWindowProc(hwnd, message, wParam, lParam));
}
```

The only change to this function from previous examples is the WM_MOUSEMOVE case. In this block of code, you first save the old mouse coordinates so you can use them to determine which direction the mouse is moving. Then you grab the new mouse coordinates from the lParam variable. In order to help keep control over what the user can see, you limit how far you will let the mouse coordinates move. Finally, you determine which way the mouse moved, and you increase or decrease the camera angle accordingly.

Well that's all for this example! As you can see, you can develop some pretty cool-looking graphics if you just take things apart and analyze the problem piece by piece.

SUMMARY

Texture mapping is the process of placing images on a polygon and brings another level of realism to 3D graphics.

After you load your texture-image data into memory from a file, you need to define it as a texture map with OpenGL. The dimensions of the texture map determine which function you use to accomplish this. If you have a 2D texture map, you use the `glTexImage2D()` function. 1D texture maps use the `glTexImage1D()` function, and 3D texture maps use the `glTexImage3D()` function.

Texture objects allow you to store texture data and keep it readily available for usage. Using texture objects, you can load many textures into memory at once and have the ability to reference any of those textures at any time during the scene rendering.

When rendering a textured object, you might notice some visual artifacts when the object moves closer to or farther away from the camera. These artifacts are the result of OpenGL trying to compensate for the moving texture by filtering the texture map down to a size that fits the object. You can help to eliminate these artifacts by controlling the level of detail with mipmaps.

CHAPTER 9

ADVANCED
TEXTURE
MAPPING

Now we're going to take a look at some of the more advanced techniques you can use with texture mapping to bring another level of realism to your scenes. In this chapter, we'll discuss the following:

- Multitexturing
- Environment mapping
- The texture matrix
- Lightmapping
- Multipass multitexturing

Using any of these advanced effects can greatly enhance the look and realism of your 3D graphics, so let's start discussing them!

MULTITEXTURING

Normally when you texture-map a polygon, you apply one texture to the polygon only one time. With OpenGL, however, you can apply several textures to the same polygon through a series of texture operations. This is called *multitexturing*. This feature is what is called an *extension* to OpenGL. The governing body, the OpenGL Architectural Review Board (ARB), must approve extensions to the API. Because multitexturing is not supported in every implementation of OpenGL, it is considered an optional extension.

You perform multitexturing through a series of *texture units*. We'll discuss more about texture units in this chapter, but understand for now that each texture unit represents a single texture, and when you perform multitexturing, each texture unit passes its results to the next texture unit until all the texture units have been gone through for the final resulting texture. Figure 9.1 illustrates how multitexturing works.

You can divide multitexturing into four major steps:

1. Verifying that multitexturing is supported
2. Locating the pointer to the extension function (because you're using MS Windows)
3. Establishing the texture units
4. Specifying the texture coordinates

Let's take a look at each of these steps in detail.

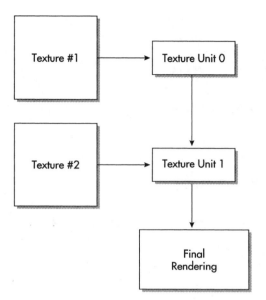

Figure 9.1

Multitexturing is performed by applying more than one texture at a time to a polygon through the use of texture units.

Verifying Multitexture Support

The first step you need to take to perform multitexturing is to verify that your implementation of OpenGL supports multitexturing. Because multitexturing is an extension to the OpenGL API that has been approved by the OpenGL ARB, you need to use the glGetString() function with the GL_EXTENSIONS parameter to retrieve a list of all the extensions supported in the current OpenGL implementation. The list is in the form of a string, with each supported extension listed in the string separated by spaces. You will search the string for the string "GL_ARB_multitexture", which tells you that the implementation supports multitexturing.

If you want to use GLU, you can use the gluCheckExtension() function to determine whether an extension is supported. This function is defined as

```
GLboolean gluCheckExtension(char *extName, const GLubyte *extString);
```

The function will return true if *extName* is found in *extString*; otherwise, it will return false.

Your other option is to search through the string returned by glGetString() for the "GL_ARB_multitexture" string by yourself. Here is a function that you can use to accomplish this task:

```
bool InStr(char *searchStr, char *str)
{
    char *extension;                    // start of an extension in the list
```

```
        char *endOfStr;                // pointer to last string element
        int   idx = 0;                 // index for spaces

        endOfStr = str + strlen(str);  // find the last character in str

        // loop while we haven't reached the end of the string
        while (str < endOfStr)
        {
            // find where a space is located
            idx = strcspn(str, " ");

            // we found searchStr
            if ( (strlen(searchStr) == idx) && (strncmp(searchStr, str, idx) == 0))
            {
                return true;
            }

            // we didn't find searchStr, move pointer to the next string to search
            str += (idx + 1);
        }

        return false;
}
```

This function will return true if the string passed into searchStr is somewhere in str, where str is filled with strings separated by spaces. So when you want to verify that your OpenGL implementation supports multitexturing, you can do this:

```
char *extensionStr;        // list of available extensions

// retrieve a list of the available extensions
extensionStr = (char*)glGetString(GL_EXTENSIONS);

if (InStr("GL_ARB_multitexture", extensionStr))
{
    // multitexturing is supported
}
```

Now that you have verified that the OpenGL implementation you are using supports multitexturing, you can move on to locating pointers to the extension functions.

Accessing Extension Functions

When using extensions with Microsoft Windows platforms, you are required to obtain access to extension functions that allow you to actually use the extensions. This is not as difficult as it sounds; it merely involves using the `wglGetProcAddress()` function to obtain a function pointer to the extension function you want. Each extension function has a data type that is specifically defined for it. Six functions are available for you to use:

- **glMultiTexCoord*i*fARB (where *i* = 1..4).** As you will see, these functions set the texture coordinates for multitexturing.
- **glActiveTextureARB.** Sets the current texture unit.
- **glClientActiveTextureARB.** Sets the current texture unit for pointer-array commands.

After verifying that your OpenGL implementation supports multitexturing, you can use the following code to access the extension functions:

```
PFNGLMULTITEXCOORD2FARBPROC       glMultiTexCoord2fARB       = NULL;
PFNGLACTIVETEXTUREARBPROC         glActiveTextureARB         = NULL;
PFNGLCLIENTACTIVETEXTUREARBPROC glClientActiveTextureARB = NULL;

glMultiTexCoord2fARB = (PFNGLMULTITEXCOORD2FARBPROC)
                    wglGetProcAddress("glMultiTexCoord2fARB");

glActiveTextureARB = (PFNGLACTIVETEXTUREARBPROC)
                    wglGetProcAddress("glActiveTextureARB");

glClientActiveTextureARB = (PFNGLCLIENTACTIVETEXTUREARBPROC)
                    wglGetProcAddress("glClientActiveTextureARB");
```

After this code is executed, you can use the functions `glMultiTexCoord2fARB()` and `glActiveTextureARB()` to perform multitexturing.

Establishing the Texture Units

As mentioned before, you perform multitexturing by establishing texture units that are combined to give you a new texture. Each texture unit is made up of a texture image, filtering parameters, a texture environment, a texture matrix stack, and the capability for automatic texture-coordinate generation.

You use the `glActiveTextureARB()` function to select the current texture unit to which you will assign texture parameters. It is defined as

```
void glActiveTextureARB(GLenum texUnit);
```

After this function is called, all calls to glTexImage*(), glTexParameter*(), glTexEnv*(), glTexGen*(), and glBindTexture() affect the texture unit defined in *texUnit*. The *texUnit* parameter is of the form GL_TEXTURE*i*_ARB, where *i* is equal to any integer between 0 and one less than the maximum number of texture units allowed. For example, GL_TEXTURE0_ARB is for the first texture unit available. You can find out how many texture units are supported by your OpenGL implementation with these lines:

```
int maxTexUnits;              // holds the maximum number of supported texture units
glGetIntegerv(GL_MAX_TEXTURE_UNITS_ARB, &maxTexUnits);
```

If glGetIntegerv() returns 1, then the OpenGL implementation does not support multitexturing.

To make your life easier, you can set up textures with texture objects and then bind those texture objects to texture units. All the texture information stored in the texture object is automatically stored with the texture unit. So to establish your texture units, all you need to do is create the texture objects as you have been doing and then activate each texture unit with the glActiveTextureARB() function. Then you can bind each of your texture objects to their respective texture units. Here's an example:

```
// the texture objects
int texObjects[2];
...
glGenTextures(2, texObjects);                    // generate the two texture objects

// create the first texture
glBindTexture(GL_TEXTURE_2D, texObjects[0]);
glTexParameteri(GL_TEXTURE_2D, GL_TEXTURE_MIN_FILTER, GL_LINEAR);
glTexParameteri(GL_TEXTURE_2D, GL_TEXTURE_MAG_FILTER, GL_LINEAR);
glTexParameteri(GL_TEXTURE_2D, GL_TEXTURE_WRAP_S, GL_REPEAT);
glTexParameteri(GL_TEXTURE_2D, GL_TEXTURE_WRAP_T, GL_REPEAT);
gluBuild2DMipmaps(GL_TEXTURE_2D, GL_RGB, 64, 64, GL_RGB, GL_UNSIGNED_BYTE, texOne);
...
// create the second texture
glBindTexture(GL_TEXTURE_2D, texObjects[1]);
glTexParameteri(GL_TEXTURE_2D, GL_TEXTURE_MIN_FILTER, GL_NEAREST);
glTexParameteri(GL_TEXTURE_2D, GL_TEXTURE_MAG_FILTER, GL_NEAREST);
glTexParameteri(GL_TEXTURE_2D, GL_TEXTURE_WRAP_S, GL_REPEAT);
glTexParameteri(GL_TEXTURE_2D, GL_TEXTURE_WRAP_T, GL_REPEAT);
glTexImage2D(GL_TEXTURE_2D, 0, GL_RGB, 32, 32, 0, GL_RGB, GL_UNSIGNED_BYTE, texTwo);
...
// now we use the two texture objects we created to create two texture units for
// multitexturing
```

```
glActiveTextureARB(GL_TEXTURE0_ARB);
glEnable(GL_TEXTURE_2D);
glBindTexture(GL_TEXTURE_2D, texObjects[0]);
glTexEnvi(GL_TEXTURE_ENV, GL_TEXTURE_ENV_MODE, GL_REPLACE);
glActiveTextureARB(GL_TEXTURE1_ARB);
glEnable(GL_TEXTURE_2D);
glBindTexture(GL_TEXTURE_2D, texObjects[1]);
glTexEnvi(GL_TEXTURE_ENV, GL_TEXTURE_ENV_MODE, GL_MODULATE);
...
```

This code will set up two texture objects and use those texture objects to create texture units that you can use in multitexturing.

Specifying the Texture Coordinates

Now that you know how to load the textures to get set up for multitexturing, you need to figure out how to apply all the textures to polygons. Because you are applying more than one texture to a single polygon, you obviously need to define more than one set of texture coordinates to the polygon as well. In fact, you'll need one set of texture coordinates for each texture unit that you create, and you have to apply them to each vertex. To specify the texture coordinates for a 2D texture, you use the function glMultiTexCoord2fARB(), which is defined as

```
void glMultiTexCoord2fARB(GLenum texUnit, float coords);
```

You can also use other forms of the function so it can take in coordinates for 1D, 3D, or 4D textures, and other data types such as floats. An example would be glMultiTexCoord3dARB(), which would take in coordinates for a 3D texture in the double data type. To use this function, you supply the texture unit for which you are specifying the texture coordinates, and then you supply the texture coordinates themselves. Here's an example:

```
glMultiTexCoord2fARB(GL_TEXTURE0_ARB, 0.0f, 0.0f);
```

This line assigns the texture coordinates (0.0, 0.0) for the first texture unit to the current vertex. As when you use the glTexCoord2f() function, you assign the coordinates for the current vertex for all the texture units with which you want to use multitexturing before you specify the vertex. The following code demonstrates this:

```
glBegin(GL_QUADS);
    // lower-left vertex
    glMultiTexCoord2fARB(GL_TEXTURE0_ARB, 0.0f, 0.0f);
    glMultiTexCoord2fARB(GL_TEXTURE1_ARB, 0.0f, 0.0f);
    glVertex3f(-5.0f, -5.0f, -5.0f);
```

```
    // lower-right vertex
    glMultiTexCoord2fARB(GL_TEXTURE0_ARB, 1.0f, 0.0f);
    glMultiTexCoord2fARB(GL_TEXTURE1_ARB, 1.0f, 0.0f);
    glVertex3f(5.0f, -5.0f, -5.0f);

    // upper-right vertex
    glMultiTexCoord2fARB(GL_TEXTURE0_ARB, 1.0f, 1.0f);
    glMultiTexCoord2fARB(GL_TEXTURE1_ARB, 1.0f, 1.0f);
    glVertex3f(5.0f, 5.0f, -5.0f);

    // upper-left vertex
    glMultiTexCoord2fARB(GL_TEXTURE0_ARB, 0.0f, 1.0f);
    glMultiTexCoord2fARB(GL_TEXTURE1_ARB, 0.0f, 1.0f);
    glVertex3f(-5.0f, 5.0f, -5.0f);
glEnd();
```

This code will draw a basic, multitextured square. As you can see, you specify all the texture units and their texture coordinates for each vertex of the object.

Keep in mind that if you set the texture coordinates with `glTexCoord2f()` when multitexturing, you will be setting the texture coordinates for the first texture unit only. This gives the same effect as calling `glMultiTexCoord2f(GL_TEXTURE0_ARB, ...)`.

Putting It Together

Let's look at an example that performs multitexturing on a cube with two textures. The two textures you are going to use are shown in Figure 9.2.

Figure 9.2

The two textures you are going to use for the multitexturing example.

Now for the code:

```
////// Defines
#define BITMAP_ID 0x4D42        // the universal bitmap ID
#define PI 3.14195              // the pi constant
```

```c
////// Includes
#include <windows.h>                // standard Windows app include
#include <stdio.h>
#include <stdlib.h>
#include <math.h>
#include <gl/gl.h>                  // standard OpenGL include
#include <gl/glu.h>                 // OpenGL utilities
#include "glext.h"                  // header file for OpenGL extensions

////// Types
typedef struct                      // structure to hold texture info/data
{
    int width;                  // width of texture
    int height;                 // height of texture
    unsigned int texID;         // the texture object id of this texture
    unsigned char *data;        // the texture data
} texture_t;

////// Global Variables
HDC g_HDC;                          // global device context
bool fullScreen = false;            // true = full screen; false = windowed
bool keyPressed[256];               // holds true for keys that are pressed
float angle = 0.0f;                 // camera angle
float radians = 0.0f;               // camera angle in radians

////// Mouse/Camera Variables
int mouseX, mouseY;                 // mouse coordinates
float cameraX, cameraY, cameraZ;    // camera coordinates
float lookX, lookY, lookZ;          // camera look-at coordinates

////// Texture Information
texture_t *smileTex;                // the smile texture
texture_t *checkerTex;              // the checkerboard texture

////// Multitexturing Info
PFNGLMULTITEXCOORD2FARBPROC        glMultiTexCoord2fARB = NULL;
PFNGLACTIVETEXTUREARBPROC          glActiveTextureARB = NULL;
PFNGLCLIENTACTIVETEXTUREARBPROC glClientActiveTextureARB = NULL;
int maxTextureUnits = 0;            // the maximum texture units we are allowed
```

Notice the line that includes "glext.h"? You need to include this file whenever you use any sort of ARB extension. This file is from Silicon Graphics and includes all the necessary definitions for you to use any ARB extensions. A copy of this file is included on the CD.

This example also demonstrates how to use a struct to keep texture information and data in a single data block. The *texture_t* type is used to store the object, width, height, and data for a texture. Using this method will simplify the process of loading and using textures with OpenGL.

You'll be using a camera-movement system much like the terrain example from Chapter 8, "Texture Mapping." When the mouse moves along the x axis, the cube will be rotated around the y axis. When the mouse moves along the y axis, the camera will zoom in and out.

The first function you see is the InStr() function you created earlier. This function returns true if *searchStr* is located in *str*, which is a string of words separated by spaces:

```
bool InStr(char *searchStr, char *str)
{
    char *extension;        // start of an extension in the list
    char *endOfStr;         // pointer to last string element
    int idx = 0;

    endOfStr = str + strlen(str);       // find the last character in str

    // loop while we haven't reached the end of the string
    while (str < endOfStr)
    {
        // find where a space is located
        idx = strcspn(str, " ");

        // we found searchStr
        if ( (strlen(searchStr) == idx) && (strncmp(searchStr, str, idx) == 0))
        {
            return true;
        }

        // we didn't find searchStr, move pointer to the next string to search
        str += (idx + 1);
    }

    return false;
}
```

You also create a function to initialize the multitexturing environment in OpenGL. The InitMultiTex() function determines whether the "GL_ARB_multitexture" extension is available and sets up the multitexturing functions if it is. The function returns false if multitexturing is not supported.

```
bool InitMultiTex()
{
    char *extensionStr;          // list of available extensions

    extensionStr = (char*)glGetString(GL_EXTENSIONS);

    if (extensionStr == NULL)
        return false;

    if (InStr("GL_ARB_multitexture", extensionStr))
    {
        // retrieve the maximum number of texture units allowed
        glGetIntegerv(GL_MAX_TEXTURE_UNITS_ARB, &maxTextureUnits);

        // retrieve addresses of multitexturing functions
        glMultiTexCoord2fARB = (PFNGLMULTITEXCOORD2FARBPROC)
                            wglGetProcAddress("glMultiTexCoord2fARB");
        glActiveTextureARB = (PFNGLACTIVETEXTUREARBPROC)
                            wglGetProcAddress("glActiveTextureARB");
        glClientActiveTextureARB = (PFNGLCLIENTACTIVETEXTUREARBPROC)
                                wglGetProcAddress("glClientActiveTextureARB");

        return true;
    }
    else
        return false;
}
```

The next function loads a single texture into memory and stores it in a *texture_t* struct, to which the function returns a pointer. LoadTextureFile() takes in a texture filename as a parameter, calls the LoadBitmapFile() function, and stores all the image information in the *texture_t* struct. LoadTextureFile() also generates a texture object for the texture.

```c
texture_t *LoadTextureFile(char *filename)
{
    BITMAPINFOHEADER texInfo;
    texture_t *thisTexture;

    // allocate memory for the texture structure
    thisTexture = (texture_t*)malloc(sizeof(texture_t));
    if (thisTexture == NULL)
        return NULL;

    // load the texture data and check validity
    thisTexture->data = LoadBitmapFile(filename, &texInfo);
    if (thisTexture->data == NULL)
    {
        free(thisTexture);
        return NULL;
    }

    // set width and height info for this texture
    thisTexture->width = texInfo.biWidth;
    thisTexture->height = texInfo.biHeight;

    // generate the texture object for this texture
    glGenTextures(1, &thisTexture->texID);

    return thisTexture;
}
```

Now that you have code to load textures, you'll create a larger function to load all your textures into memory and set them up with OpenGL multitexturing. The following function, LoadAllTextures(), will load the textures into memory; set the texture parameters, environment, and mipmap generation; and then bind each texture to its own texture unit. Take a look:

```c
bool LoadAllTextures()
{
    // load the smile texture data
    smileTex = LoadTextureFile("smile.bmp");
    if (smileTex == NULL)
        return false;
```

```
    // load the checker texture data
    checkerTex = LoadTextureFile("chess.bmp");
    if (checkerTex == NULL)
        return false;

    // set up the smile texture as a mipmap with bilinear filtering
    glBindTexture(GL_TEXTURE_2D, smileTex->texID);

    // use bilinear filtering
    glTexParameteri(GL_TEXTURE_2D, GL_TEXTURE_MAG_FILTER, GL_LINEAR);
    glTexParameteri(GL_TEXTURE_2D, GL_TEXTURE_MIN_FILTER, GL_LINEAR);
    glTexEnvi(GL_TEXTURE_ENV, GL_TEXTURE_ENV_MODE, GL_REPLACE);
    gluBuild2DMipmaps(GL_TEXTURE_2D, GL_RGB, smileTex->width, smileTex->height,
                    GL_RGB, GL_UNSIGNED_BYTE, smileTex->data);

  // set up the checkerboard texture as a mipmap with bilinear filtering
    glBindTexture(GL_TEXTURE_2D, checkerTex->texID);
    glTexParameteri(GL_TEXTURE_2D, GL_TEXTURE_MAG_FILTER, GL_LINEAR);
    glTexParameteri(GL_TEXTURE_2D, GL_TEXTURE_MIN_FILTER, GL_LINEAR);
    glTexParameteri(GL_TEXTURE_2D, GL_TEXTURE_WRAP_S, GL_REPEAT);
    glTexParameteri(GL_TEXTURE_2D, GL_TEXTURE_WRAP_T, GL_REPEAT);
    glTexEnvi(GL_TEXTURE_ENV, GL_TEXTURE_ENV_MODE, GL_MODULATE);
    gluBuild2DMipmaps(GL_TEXTURE_2D, GL_RGB, checkerTex->width, checkerTex->height,
                    GL_RGB, GL_UNSIGNED_BYTE, checkerTex->data);

    // set active texture unit to 0
    glActiveTextureARB(GL_TEXTURE0_ARB);
    glEnable(GL_TEXTURE_2D);
    glBindTexture(GL_TEXTURE_2D, smileTex->texID);    // bind smile texture to TU 0

    // set active texture unit to 1
    glActiveTextureARB(GL_TEXTURE1_ARB);
    glEnable(GL_TEXTURE_2D);
    glBindTexture(GL_TEXTURE_2D, checkerTex->texID); // bind checker texture to TU 1

    return true;
}
```

Like a good `Initialize()` function should, this one initializes the program data:

```
void Initialize()
{
    glClearColor(0.0f, 0.0f, 0.0f, 0.0f);        // clear to black

    glShadeModel(GL_SMOOTH);              // use smooth shading
    glEnable(GL_DEPTH_TEST);              // hidden surface removal
    glEnable(GL_CULL_FACE);               // do not calculate inside of polys
    glFrontFace(GL_CCW);                  // counterclockwise polygons are out

    glEnable(GL_TEXTURE_2D);              // enable 2D texturing

    InitMultiTex();                       // initializes multitexturing
    LoadAllTextures();                    // loads and initializes textures
}
```

Now for a function with some real meat! Remember the `DrawCube()` function from earlier examples? Well, it's making a reappearance, except this time it's much bigger and cooler than before. Instead of using the single-texture `glTexCoord2f()` function, `DrawCube()` has graduated to the `glMultiTexCoord2fARB()` function! As mentioned before, to perform multitexturing, you need to define the texture coordinates for each texture unit for each vertex:

```
void DrawCube(float xPos, float yPos, float zPos)
{
    glPushMatrix();
        glTranslatef(xPos, yPos, zPos);
        glBegin(GL_QUADS);
            glNormal3f(0.0f, 1.0f, 0.0f);  // top face

            glMultiTexCoord2fARB(GL_TEXTURE0_ARB, 1.0f, 0.0f);
            glMultiTexCoord2fARB(GL_TEXTURE1_ARB, 1.0f, 0.0f);
            glVertex3f(0.5f, 0.5f, 0.5f);

            glMultiTexCoord2fARB(GL_TEXTURE0_ARB, 1.0f, 1.0f);
            glMultiTexCoord2fARB(GL_TEXTURE1_ARB, 1.0f, 1.0f);
            glVertex3f(0.5f, 0.5f, -0.5f);

            glMultiTexCoord2fARB(GL_TEXTURE0_ARB, 0.0f, 1.0f);
            glMultiTexCoord2fARB(GL_TEXTURE1_ARB, 0.0f, 1.0f);
            glVertex3f(-0.5f, 0.5f, -0.5f);
```

```
            glMultiTexCoord2fARB(GL_TEXTURE0_ARB, 0.0f, 0.0f);
            glMultiTexCoord2fARB(GL_TEXTURE1_ARB, 0.0f, 0.0f);
            glVertex3f(-0.5f, 0.5f, 0.5f);
    glEnd();
    glBegin(GL_QUADS);
            glNormal3f(0.0f, 0.0f, 1.0f);  // front face

            glMultiTexCoord2fARB(GL_TEXTURE0_ARB, 1.0f, 1.0f);
            glMultiTexCoord2fARB(GL_TEXTURE1_ARB, 1.0f, 1.0f);
            glVertex3f(0.5f, 0.5f, 0.5f);

            glMultiTexCoord2fARB(GL_TEXTURE0_ARB, 0.0f, 1.0f);
            glMultiTexCoord2fARB(GL_TEXTURE1_ARB, 0.0f, 1.0f);
            glVertex3f(-0.5f, 0.5f, 0.5f);

            glMultiTexCoord2fARB(GL_TEXTURE0_ARB, 0.0f, 0.0f);
            glMultiTexCoord2fARB(GL_TEXTURE1_ARB, 0.0f, 0.0f);
            glVertex3f(-0.5f, -0.5f, 0.5f);

            glMultiTexCoord2fARB(GL_TEXTURE0_ARB, 1.0f, 0.0f);
            glMultiTexCoord2fARB(GL_TEXTURE1_ARB, 1.0f, 0.0f);
            glVertex3f(0.5f, -0.5f, 0.5f);
    glEnd();
    glBegin(GL_QUADS);
            glNormal3f(1.0f, 0.0f, 0.0f);  // right face

            glMultiTexCoord2fARB(GL_TEXTURE0_ARB, 0.0f, 1.0f);
            glMultiTexCoord2fARB(GL_TEXTURE1_ARB, 0.0f, 1.0f);
            glVertex3f(0.5f, 0.5f, 0.5f);

            glMultiTexCoord2fARB(GL_TEXTURE0_ARB, 0.0f, 0.0f);
            glMultiTexCoord2fARB(GL_TEXTURE1_ARB, 0.0f, 0.0f);
            glVertex3f(0.5f, -0.5f, 0.5f);

            glMultiTexCoord2fARB(GL_TEXTURE0_ARB, 1.0f, 0.0f);
            glMultiTexCoord2fARB(GL_TEXTURE1_ARB, 1.0f, 0.0f);
            glVertex3f(0.5f, -0.5f, -0.5f);

            glMultiTexCoord2fARB(GL_TEXTURE0_ARB, 1.0f, 1.0f);
            glMultiTexCoord2fARB(GL_TEXTURE1_ARB, 1.0f, 1.0f);
            glVertex3f(0.5f, 0.5f, -0.5f);
    glEnd();
```

```
glBegin(GL_QUADS);
     glNormal3f(-1.0f, 0.0f, 0.0f);  // left face

     glMultiTexCoord2fARB(GL_TEXTURE0_ARB, 1.0f, 1.0f);
     glMultiTexCoord2fARB(GL_TEXTURE1_ARB, 1.0f, 1.0f);
     glVertex3f(-0.5f, 0.5f, 0.5f);

     glMultiTexCoord2fARB(GL_TEXTURE0_ARB, 0.0f, 1.0f);
     glMultiTexCoord2fARB(GL_TEXTURE1_ARB, 0.0f, 1.0f);
     glVertex3f(-0.5f, 0.5f, -0.5f);

     glMultiTexCoord2fARB(GL_TEXTURE0_ARB, 0.0f, 0.0f);
     glMultiTexCoord2fARB(GL_TEXTURE1_ARB, 0.0f, 0.0f);
     glVertex3f(-0.5f, -0.5f, -0.5f);

     glMultiTexCoord2fARB(GL_TEXTURE0_ARB, 1.0f, 0.0f);
     glMultiTexCoord2fARB(GL_TEXTURE1_ARB, 1.0f, 0.0f);
     glVertex3f(-0.5f, -0.5f, 0.5f);
glEnd();
glBegin(GL_QUADS);
     glNormal3f(0.0f, -1.0f, 0.0f);  // bottom face

     glMultiTexCoord2fARB(GL_TEXTURE0_ARB, 1.0f, 0.0f);
     glMultiTexCoord2fARB(GL_TEXTURE1_ARB, 1.0f, 0.0f);
     glVertex3f(-0.5f, -0.5f, 0.5f);

     glMultiTexCoord2fARB(GL_TEXTURE0_ARB, 1.0f, 1.0f);
     glMultiTexCoord2fARB(GL_TEXTURE1_ARB, 1.0f, 1.0f);
     glVertex3f(-0.5f, -0.5f, -0.5f);

     glMultiTexCoord2fARB(GL_TEXTURE0_ARB, 0.0f, 1.0f);
     glMultiTexCoord2fARB(GL_TEXTURE1_ARB, 0.0f, 1.0f);
     glVertex3f(0.5f, -0.5f, -0.5f);

     glMultiTexCoord2fARB(GL_TEXTURE0_ARB, 0.0f, 0.0f);
     glMultiTexCoord2fARB(GL_TEXTURE1_ARB, 0.0f, 0.0f);
     glVertex3f(0.5f, -0.5f, 0.5f);
glEnd();
glBegin(GL_QUADS);
     glNormal3f(0.0f, 0.0f, -1.0f);  // back face
```

```
            glMultiTexCoord2fARB(GL_TEXTURE0_ARB, 0.0f, 0.0f);
            glMultiTexCoord2fARB(GL_TEXTURE1_ARB, 0.0f, 0.0f);
            glVertex3f(0.5f, -0.5f, -0.5f);

            glMultiTexCoord2fARB(GL_TEXTURE0_ARB, 1.0f, 0.0f);
            glMultiTexCoord2fARB(GL_TEXTURE1_ARB, 1.0f, 0.0f);
            glVertex3f(-0.5f, -0.5f, -0.5f);

            glMultiTexCoord2fARB(GL_TEXTURE0_ARB, 1.0f, 1.0f);
            glMultiTexCoord2fARB(GL_TEXTURE1_ARB, 1.0f, 1.0f);
            glVertex3f(-0.5f, 0.5f, -0.5f);

            glMultiTexCoord2fARB(GL_TEXTURE0_ARB, 0.0f, 1.0f);
            glMultiTexCoord2fARB(GL_TEXTURE1_ARB, 0.0f, 1.0f);
            glVertex3f(0.5f, 0.5f, -0.5f);
        glEnd();
    glPopMatrix();
}
```

Next up is the Render() function. The majority of this function should be familiar ground by now. In this function, you set up your camera orientation, and you actually draw the cube.

```
void Render()
{
    radians =  float(PI*(angle-90.0f)/180.0f);

    // calculate the camera's position
    cameraX = lookX + sin(radians)*mouseY;
    cameraZ = lookZ + cos(radians)*mouseY;
    cameraY = lookY + mouseY / 2.0f;

    // point camera at (0,0,0)
    lookX = 0.0f;
    lookY = 0.0f;
    lookZ = 0.0f;

    // clear screen and depth buffer
    glClear(GL_COLOR_BUFFER_BIT | GL_DEPTH_BUFFER_BIT);
    glLoadIdentity();
```

```
    // set the camera position
    gluLookAt(cameraX, cameraY, cameraZ, lookX, lookY, lookZ, 0.0, 1.0, 0.0);

    // make the cube a 15x15x15 cube
    glScalef(15.0f, 15.0f, 15.0f);

    // draw the cube with its center at (0,0,0)
    DrawCube(0.0f, 0.0f, 0.0f);

    glFlush();
    SwapBuffers(g_HDC);                 // bring back buffer to foreground
}
```

When you plug all these functions into your basic Windows framework, you get the effect shown in Figure 9.3.

As you can see, multitexturing can produce a very cool and realistic texturing effect. Experiment with this technique to try to find ways to perform even more effects. But for now, let's take a look at another awesome effect: environment mapping.

Figure 9.3

A screenshot of the multitextured-cube example.

ENVIRONMENT MAPPING

Environment mapping is the process of rendering an object that entirely reflects its environment. For example, if you took a polished, shiny, silver ball outside, you would see the clouds, sky, ground, trees, and yourself in the reflection off the ball. This is the type of effect you're trying to achieve with environment mapping. The trick is, however, that you don't actually reflect the environment that the object is in to get the effect. With OpenGL, all you have to do is create a texture map that represents the environment the object is in and then use OpenGL to automatically generate the texture coordinates for you. You need to generate new texture coordinates as the object moves to give it the effect of the environment reflection moving with the object.

The best texture maps to use for environment maps are those that look like they have been created using a fish-eye lens. Although having this type of texture map is not absolutely necessary, using one greatly improves the effect and realism of the environment mapping. Also, you *could* calculate the texture coordinates for the environment map on your own, but chances are that doing so would dramatically decrease performance.

To use environment mapping in OpenGL, you simply use these lines:

```
glTexGenf(GL_S, GL_TEXTURE_GEN_MODE, GL_SPHERE_MAP);
glTexGenf(GL_T, GL_TEXTURE_GEN_MODE, GL_SPHERE_MAP);
glEnable(GL_TEXTURE_GEN_S);
glEnable(GL_TEXTURE_GEN_T);
// bind the environment texture
// draw object
```

Yes, that's all you have to do! Let's take a look at a full-blown example.

The Torus in the Sky

The example you're going to look at here renders an environment-mapped torus using the code we just discussed to perform environment mapping. Figure 9.4 shows the end result of this example.

The first thing you need to do is create the environment texture. For the environment map, you're going to use a sky texture that was converted into a fish-eye view with an image-editing program. Figure 9.5 shows the resulting environment map.

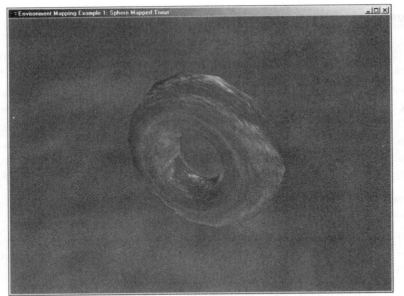

Figure 9.4

The environment-mapped torus.

Figure 9.5

The sky environment map.

Now let's take a look at some of the code. For this example, you're only going to look at the code relevant to the texturing and rendering of the scene.

```
typedef struct
{
    int width;              // width of texture
    int height;             // height of texture
    unsigned int texID;     // the texture object id of this texture
    unsigned char *data;    // the texture data
} texture_t;

...
```

```c
float angle = 0.0f;              // torus rotation angle
texture_t *envTex;               // the environment map
texture_t *skyTex;               // texture for the sky background

...

bool LoadAllTextures()
{
    // load the environment texture data
    envTex = LoadTextureFile("sky-sphere.bmp");
    if (envTex == NULL)
        return false;

    skyTex = LoadTextureFile("sky.bmp");
    if (skyTex == NULL)
        return false;

    // set up the environment texture as a mipmap with bilinear filtering
    glBindTexture(GL_TEXTURE_2D, envTex->texID);
    glTexParameteri(GL_TEXTURE_2D, GL_TEXTURE_MAG_FILTER, GL_LINEAR);
    glTexParameteri(GL_TEXTURE_2D, GL_TEXTURE_MIN_FILTER, GL_LINEAR);
    glTexParameteri(GL_TEXTURE_2D, GL_TEXTURE_WRAP_S, GL_REPEAT);
    glTexParameteri(GL_TEXTURE_2D, GL_TEXTURE_WRAP_T, GL_REPEAT);
    gluBuild2DMipmaps(GL_TEXTURE_2D, GL_RGB, envTex->width, envTex->height, GL_RGB,
                      GL_UNSIGNED_BYTE, envTex->data);

    // set up the background sky texture
    glBindTexture(GL_TEXTURE_2D, skyTex->texID);
    glTexParameteri(GL_TEXTURE_2D, GL_TEXTURE_MAG_FILTER, GL_LINEAR);
    glTexParameteri(GL_TEXTURE_2D, GL_TEXTURE_MIN_FILTER, GL_LINEAR);
    glTexParameteri(GL_TEXTURE_2D, GL_TEXTURE_WRAP_S, GL_REPEAT);
    glTexParameteri(GL_TEXTURE_2D, GL_TEXTURE_WRAP_T, GL_REPEAT);
    gluBuild2DMipmaps(GL_TEXTURE_2D, GL_RGB, skyTex->width, skyTex->height, GL_RGB,
                      GL_UNSIGNED_BYTE, skyTex->data);

    return true;
}

...
```

```cpp
void Render()
{
    // increase rotation angle
    if (angle > 360.0f)
        angle = 0.0f;

    angle = angle + 0.2f;

    // clear screen and depth buffer
    glClear(GL_COLOR_BUFFER_BIT | GL_DEPTH_BUFFER_BIT);
    glLoadIdentity();

    // draw the background sky texture
    glBindTexture(GL_TEXTURE_2D, skyTex->texID);
    glBegin(GL_QUADS);
        glTexCoord2f(0.0f, 0.0f);
        glVertex3f(-200.0f, -200.0f, -120.0f);
        glTexCoord2f(1.0f, 0.0f);
        glVertex3f(200.0f, -200.0f, -120.0f);
        glTexCoord2f(1.0f, 1.0f);
        glVertex3f(200.0f, 200.0f, -120.0f);
        glTexCoord2f(0.0f, 1.0f);
        glVertex3f(-200.0f, 200.0f, -120.0f);
    glEnd();

    // move object back and rotate on all three axes
    glTranslatef(0.0f, 0.0f, -100.0f);
    glRotatef(angle, 1.0f, 0.0f, 0.0f);
    glRotatef(angle, 0.0f, 1.0f, 0.0f);
    glRotatef(angle, 0.0f, 0.0f, 1.0f);

    // set up environment mapping
    glTexGenf(GL_S, GL_TEXTURE_GEN_MODE, GL_SPHERE_MAP);
    glTexGenf(GL_T, GL_TEXTURE_GEN_MODE, GL_SPHERE_MAP);
    glEnable(GL_TEXTURE_GEN_S);
    glEnable(GL_TEXTURE_GEN_T);

    // bind the environment texture
    glBindTexture(GL_TEXTURE_2D, envTex->texID);
```

```
    // solid torus: inner radius of 10, outer radius of 20
    auxSolidTorus(10.0f, 20.0f);

    glFlush();
    SwapBuffers(g_HDC);             // bring back buffer to foreground
}
```

As you can see, environment mapping with OpenGL is very simple as long as you want to let OpenGL automatically calculate the texture coordinates for you. You can calculate the texture coordinates on your own to get a different type of effect, but we won't be discussing it here.

THE TEXTURE MATRIX

In Chapter 5, "Coordinate Transformations and OpenGL Matrices," we talked about how you can transform vertices with translation, rotation, and scaling by modifying the modelview matrix. We also mentioned the matrix stack, and how you can push and pop matrices to achieve hierarchical modeling.

You can do these same things with textures through the use of texture matrices and the *texture matrix stack*. For instance, you can use the glTranslatef() function to move a texture across a surface. Similarly, you can use the glRotatef() function to rotate texture coordinates on a surface, which, in effect, rotates the texture. The game *American McGee's Alice*, by Electronic Arts and Rogue Entertainment, made great use of the effects produced by manipulating the texture matrix when they created the psychedelic world of Wonderland.

Manipulating the texture matrix is very easy. You can use any of the standard matrix-manipulation functions that OpenGL provides, such as glMultMatrix(), glPushMatrix(), glPopMatrix(), and the transformation functions. The first thing you need to do is tell OpenGL that you want to enter texture matrix mode through the following command:

```
glMatrixMode(GL_TEXTURE);
```

Then you can perform any transformations you want on the texture matrix and the texture matrix stack. After you're finished with the texture transformations, you need to tell OpenGL to go back to the modelview matrix mode so you can perform transformations on your objects.

Following is some sample code that shows how you can rotate a texture on a surface:

```
// clear screen and depth buffer
glClear(GL_COLOR_BUFFER_BIT | GL_DEPTH_BUFFER_BIT);
glLoadIdentity();
```

```
// set current matrix mode to texture matrix mode
glMatrixMode(GL_TEXTURE);
glLoadIdentity();
glRotatef(angle, 0.0f, 0.0f, 1.0f);        // rotate the texture
glMatrixMode(GL_MODELVIEW);                 // go back to modelview matrix

glBindTexture(GL_TEXTURE_2D, texID);        // set current texture

// draw textured quad
glBegin(GL_QUADS);
    glTexCoord2f(0.0f, 0.0f);
    glVertex3f(-20.0f, -20.0f, -40.0f);
    glTexCoord2f(1.0f, 0.0f);
    glVertex3f(20.0f, -20.0f, -40.0f);
    glTexCoord2f(1.0f, 1.0f);
    glVertex3f(20.0f, 20.0f, -40.0f);
    glTexCoord2f(0.0f, 1.0f);
    glVertex3f(-20.0f, 20.0f, -40.0f);
glEnd();
```

As you can see, you set the current matrix mode to the texture matrix mode. You then load the identity matrix, which is the default texture matrix to begin with (before you apply the glRotatef() function to the texture matrix), which will rotate your texture at some angle around the positive z axis. After you've performed your rotation, you tell OpenGL to go back to the modelview matrix mode, where you draw a textured quadrilateral. Not too difficult, is it?

Now you might run into a problem with this code; if you draw more objects after the quadrilateral, then their textures will be rotated as well. One solution to this is to do the following:

```
// clear screen and depth buffer
glClear(GL_COLOR_BUFFER_BIT | GL_DEPTH_BUFFER_BIT);
glLoadIdentity();

// set current matrix mode to texture matrix mode
glMatrixMode(GL_TEXTURE);
glLoadIdentity();
glRotatef(angle, 0.0f, 0.0f, 1.0f);        // rotate the texture
glMatrixMode(GL_MODELVIEW);                 // go back to modelview matrix

glBindTexture(GL_TEXTURE_2D, texID);        // set current texture
```

```
// draw textured quad
glBegin(GL_QUADS);
    glTexCoord2f(0.0f, 0.0f);
    glVertex3f(-20.0f, -20.0f, -40.0f);
    glTexCoord2f(1.0f, 0.0f);
    glVertex3f(20.0f, -20.0f, -40.0f);
    glTexCoord2f(1.0f, 1.0f);
    glVertex3f(20.0f, 20.0f, -40.0f);
    glTexCoord2f(0.0f, 1.0f);
    glVertex3f(-20.0f, 20.0f, -40.0f);
glEnd();

// reset the texture matrix for following objects
glMatrixMode(GL_TEXTURE);
glLoadIdentity();
glMatrixMode(GL_MODELVIEW);

// draw other objects
...
```

That's it! Just add a call to glLoadIdentity() so the texture matrix is reset, and the previous texture transformations won't affect any of the following objects. Try playing around with the texture matrix stack on your own. You might find some awesome effects to use in your games!

LIGHTMAPPING

Lightmapping is the process of applying a lightmap to a surface in order to simulate the effect of static lighting on the surface. A *lightmap* is a texture map that represents how a light strikes a surface. Lightmapping has become a rather common technique, especially with the advent of multitexturing support in hardware. Although lightmapping is primarily used for static lighting effects, keep in mind that you can also use it for creating static shadow effects.

Figure 9.6 shows a lightmap texture that simulates a spotlight that points straight at the texture. When applied to a polygon, you get the effect of a spotlight shining directly at the polygon.

Notice that the lightmap texture is a grayscale bitmap, and that the lighter parts of the texture are where the spotlight shines. You'll blend this texture with the texture already on the polygon to get your lighting effect.

Figure 9.6

A sample lightmap.

Using the Lightmap

You know what a lightmap is, so now let's use it. You're going to texture-map a cube with the checkerboard texture from earlier in this chapter. Then you'll apply the lightmap texture to each side of the cube to get the scene shown in Figure 9.7.

Figure 9.7

The lightmapped cube.

When loading lightmaps into memory, you need to make sure you are loading only the grayscale value of each bit. For example, here is a modified version of the LoadBitmapFile() function that you have been using. The difference in this function is that it loads a 24-bit bitmap as a grayscale image:

```c
unsigned char *LoadGrayBitmap(char *filename, BITMAPINFOHEADER *bitmapInfoHeader)
{
    FILE *filePtr;                              // the file pointer
    BITMAPFILEHEADER bitmapFileHeader;          // bitmap file header
    unsigned char *bitmapImage;                 // bitmap image data
    int imageIdx = 0;                           // image index counter
    unsigned char tempRGB;                      // swap variable

    unsigned char *grayImage;                   // grayscale image
    int grayIdx;                                // index for gray image

    // open filename in "read binary" mode
    filePtr = fopen(filename, "rb");
    if (filePtr == NULL)
        return NULL;

    // read the bitmap file header
    fread(&bitmapFileHeader, sizeof(BITMAPFILEHEADER), 1, filePtr);

    // verify that this is a bitmap by checking for the universal bitmap id
    if (bitmapFileHeader.bfType != BITMAP_ID)
    {
        fclose(filePtr);
        return NULL;
    }

    // read the bitmap information header
    fread(bitmapInfoHeader, sizeof(BITMAPINFOHEADER), 1, filePtr);

    // move file pointer to beginning of bitmap data
    fseek(filePtr, bitmapFileHeader.bfOffBits, SEEK_SET);

    // allocate enough memory for the bitmap image data
    bitmapImage = (unsigned char*)malloc(bitmapInfoHeader->biSizeImage);

    // allocate enough memory for the grayscale image data
    // divide by 3 since the grayscale image is not RGB
    // (only need 1/3 of bitmap data
    grayImage = (unsigned char*)malloc(bitmapInfoHeader->biSizeImage / 3);
```

```
        // verify memory allocation
        if (!bitmapImage)
        {
            free(bitmapImage);
            fclose(filePtr);
            return NULL;
        }


        // read in the bitmap image data
        fread(bitmapImage, 1, bitmapInfoHeader->biSizeImage, filePtr);

        // make sure bitmap image data was read
        if (bitmapImage == NULL)
        {
            fclose(filePtr);
            return NULL;
        }


        // save the grayscale values for the bitmap into the grayscale data block
        grayIdx = 0;
        for (imageIdx = 0; imageIdx < bitmapInfoHeader->biSizeImage; imageIdx+=3)
        {
            grayImage[grayIdx] = bitmapImage[imageIdx];
            grayIdx++;
        }


        // free the bitmap image data
        free(bitmapImage);

        // close the file and return the grayscale bitmap image data
        fclose(filePtr);
        return grayImage;
}
```

This function will load a 24-bit lightmap texture for you. After you have the lightmap loaded into memory, you can set it up just like a regular texture with one exception: Instead of defining the format of the texture as GL_RGB, you must define it as GL_LUMINANCE. Here's an example:

```
// build lightmap as a mipmap
gluBuild2DMipmaps(GL_TEXTURE_2D, GL_LUMINANCE, width, height, GL_LUMINANCE,
                  GL_UNSIGNED_BYTE, lightmapData);
```

```
// build lightmap as a single texture
glTexImage2D(GL_TEXTURE_2D, 0, GL_LUMINANCE, width, height, 0, GL_LUMINANCE,
             GL_UNSIGNED_BYTE, lightmapData);
```

That's the hard part. Now you just use multitexturing to apply the lightmap to the polygon (or polygons). Because you're using multitexturing, you need to make sure to set the texture environment mode for the lightmap to GL_MODULATE. Let's look at the important and new functions of this example:

```
typedef struct
{
    int width;                  // width of texture
    int height;                 // height of texture
    unsigned int texID;         // the texture object id of this texture
    unsigned char *data;        // the texture data
} texture_t;


// Texture maps
texture_t *lightmapTex;         // the lightmap texture
texture_t *checkerTex;          // the checkerboard texture


// Multitexturing functions
PFNGLMULTITEXCOORD2FARBPROC    glMultiTexCoord2fARB = NULL;
PFNGLACTIVETEXTUREARBPROC      glActiveTextureARB = NULL;
PFNGLCLIENTACTIVETEXTUREARBPROC glClientActiveTextureARB = NULL;
int maxTextureUnits = 0;

bool InitMultiTex()
{
    char *extensionStr;         // list of available extensions

    extensionStr = (char*)glGetString(GL_EXTENSIONS);

    if (extensionStr == NULL)
        return false;

    if (strstr(extensionStr, "GL_ARB_multitexture"))
    {
        // retrieve the maximum number of texture units allowed
        glGetIntegerv(GL_MAX_TEXTURE_UNITS_ARB, &maxTextureUnits);
```

```
                // retrieve addresses of multitexturing functions
                glMultiTexCoord2fARB = (PFNGLMULTITEXCOORD2FARBPROC)
                                    wglGetProcAddress("glMultiTexCoord2fARB");
                glActiveTextureARB = (PFNGLACTIVETEXTUREARBPROC)
                                  wglGetProcAddress("glActiveTextureARB");
                glClientActiveTextureARB = (PFNGLCLIENTACTIVETEXTUREARBPROC)
                                      wglGetProcAddress("glClientActiveTextureARB");

            return true;
        }
        else
            return false;
}
```

Here you have the InitMultiTex() function, which checks for the extensions that the current implementation of OpenGL supports. This time, however, you use the strstr() function, which returns NULL if the second parameter is not found in the first parameter.

Next is the LoadGrayBitmap() function that we have already discussed:

```
unsigned char *LoadGrayBitmap(char *filename, BITMAPINFOHEADER *bitmapInfoHeader)
{
    FILE *filePtr;                      // the file pointer
    BITMAPFILEHEADER bitmapFileHeader;  // bitmap file header
    unsigned char *bitmapImage;         // bitmap image data
    int imageIdx = 0;                   // image index counter
    unsigned char tempRGB;              // swap variable

    unsigned char *grayImage;           // grayscale image
    int grayIdx;                        // index for gray image

    // open filename in "read binary" mode
    filePtr = fopen(filename, "rb");
    if (filePtr == NULL)
        return NULL;

    // read the bitmap file header
    fread(&bitmapFileHeader, sizeof(BITMAPFILEHEADER), 1, filePtr);

    // verify that this is a bitmap by checking for the universal bitmap id
    if (bitmapFileHeader.bfType != BITMAP_ID)
    {
```

```c
        fclose(filePtr);
        return NULL;
    }

    // read the bitmap information header
    fread(bitmapInfoHeader, sizeof(BITMAPINFOHEADER), 1, filePtr);

    // move file pointer to beginning of bitmap data
    fseek(filePtr, bitmapFileHeader.bfOffBits, SEEK_SET);

    // allocate enough memory for the bitmap image data
    bitmapImage = (unsigned char*)malloc(bitmapInfoHeader->biSizeImage);

    // allocate enough memory for the grayscale image data
    // divide by 3 since the grayscale image is not RGB
    // (only need 1/3 of bitmap data
    grayImage = (unsigned char*)malloc(bitmapInfoHeader->biSizeImage / 3);

    // verify memory allocation
    if (!bitmapImage)
    {
        free(bitmapImage);
        fclose(filePtr);
        return NULL;
    }

    // read in the bitmap image data
    fread(bitmapImage, 1, bitmapInfoHeader->biSizeImage, filePtr);

    // make sure bitmap image data was read
    if (bitmapImage == NULL)
    {
        fclose(filePtr);
        return NULL;
    }

    grayIdx = 0;
    for (imageIdx = 0; imageIdx < bitmapInfoHeader->biSizeImage; imageIdx+=3)
    {
        grayImage[grayIdx] = bitmapImage[imageIdx];
        grayIdx++;
    }
```

```
        free(bitmapImage);

        // close the file and return the bitmap image data
        fclose(filePtr);
        return grayImage;
}
```

The next function, LoadLightmap() is basically the same as the LoadTextureFile() function from previous examples, except this function is geared more toward lightmaps because it calls the LoadGrayBitmap() function:

```
texture_t *LoadLightmap(char *filename)
{
        BITMAPINFOHEADER texInfo;
        texture_t *thisTexture;

        // allocate memory for the texture structure
        thisTexture = (texture_t*)malloc(sizeof(texture_t));
        if (thisTexture == NULL)
            return NULL;

        // load the texture data and check validity
        thisTexture->data = LoadGrayBitmap(filename, &texInfo);
        if (thisTexture->data == NULL)
        {
            free(thisTexture);
            return NULL;
        }

        // set width and height info for this texture
        thisTexture->width = texInfo.biWidth;
        thisTexture->height = texInfo.biHeight;

        // generate the texture object for this texture
        glGenTextures(1, &thisTexture->texID);

        return thisTexture;
}
```

The LoadAllTextures() function below has been changed to support loading the lightmap into OpenGL with the GL_LUMINANCE value. You then assign the main checkerboard texture and the lightmap to texture units for multitexturing. The lightmap is set to texture unit 1.

```
bool LoadAllTextures()
{
    // load the smile texture data
    checkerTex = LoadTextureFile("chess.bmp");
    if (checkerTex == NULL)
        return false;

    // load the checker texture data
    lightmapTex = LoadLightmap("lmap.bmp");
    if (lightmapTex == NULL)
        return false;

    // set up the checkerboard texture
    glBindTexture(GL_TEXTURE_2D, checkerTex->texID);
    glTexParameteri(GL_TEXTURE_2D, GL_TEXTURE_MAG_FILTER, GL_LINEAR);
    glTexParameteri(GL_TEXTURE_2D, GL_TEXTURE_MIN_FILTER, GL_LINEAR);
    glTexParameteri(GL_TEXTURE_2D, GL_TEXTURE_WRAP_S, GL_REPEAT);
    glTexParameteri(GL_TEXTURE_2D, GL_TEXTURE_WRAP_T, GL_REPEAT);
    glTexEnvi(GL_TEXTURE_ENV, GL_TEXTURE_ENV_MODE, GL_REPLACE);
    gluBuild2DMipmaps(GL_TEXTURE_2D, GL_RGB, checkerTex->width, checkerTex->height,
                      GL_RGB, GL_UNSIGNED_BYTE, checkerTex->data);

    // set up the lightmap
    glBindTexture(GL_TEXTURE_2D, lightmapTex->texID);
    glTexParameteri(GL_TEXTURE_2D, GL_TEXTURE_MAG_FILTER, GL_LINEAR);
    glTexParameteri(GL_TEXTURE_2D, GL_TEXTURE_MIN_FILTER, GL_LINEAR);
    glTexEnvi(GL_TEXTURE_ENV, GL_TEXTURE_ENV_MODE, GL_MODULATE);
    gluBuild2DMipmaps(GL_TEXTURE_2D, GL_LUMINANCE, lightmapTex->width,
                      lightmapTex->height, GL_LUMINANCE, GL_UNSIGNED_BYTE,
                      lightmapTex->data);

    // set active texture unit to 0
    glActiveTextureARB(GL_TEXTURE0_ARB);
    glEnable(GL_TEXTURE_2D);
    glBindTexture(GL_TEXTURE_2D, checkerTex->texID);         // bind checkerboard
```

```
    // set active texture unit to 1
    glActiveTextureARB(GL_TEXTURE1_ARB);
    glEnable(GL_TEXTURE_2D);
    glBindTexture(GL_TEXTURE_2D, lightmapTex->texID);        // bind lightmap

    return true;
}
```

The rest of the example is essentially the same as the multitexture example that you developed earlier in this chapter. Also, keep in mind with these examples that the point is to simplify things for you. Feel free to experiment with the code, add more flexibility, and so on, in order to develop a more robust system for your games.

MULTIPASS MULTITEXTURING

What are you supposed to do when multitexturing is not supported? You can't just stop the game from running! What you need to do is find a way to use the blending functions so you can simulate multitexturing—called *multipass rendering*. Although this is slower than the normal multitexturing (using hardware acceleration), this method does allow your less-powerful users to see the great effects you originally intended.

Multipass rendering involves drawing the scene multiple times. However, each time you render the scene, you change the depth buffer and blending modes to get the effect you want. In the case of multipass multitexturing, you do the following:

```
// render first pass
glBindTexture(GL_TEXTURE_2D, tex1);
DrawTexturedCube(0.0f, 0.0f, 0.0f);

// render second pass with blending enabled
glEnable(GL_BLEND);                  // enable blending
glDepthMask(GL_FALSE);               // disable writing to depth buffer
glDepthFunc(GL_EQUAL);
glBlendFunc(GL_ZERO, GL_SRC_COLOR);

    glBindTexture(GL_TEXTURE_2D, tex2);
    DrawTexturedCube(0.0f, 0.0f, 0.0f);

// reset modes
glDepthMask(GL_TRUE);
glDepthFunc(GL_LESS);
glDisable(GL_BLEND);
```

By changing the blending mode, you can change the effect of multitexturing. The following code listing is essentially the same code from the first multitexturing example, except this listing includes changes you needed to make to include multipass multitexturing.

```
bool LoadAllTextures()
{
    // load the smile texture data
    smileTex = LoadTextureFile("smile.bmp");
    if (smileTex == NULL)
        return false;

    // load the checker texture data
    checkerTex = LoadTextureFile("chess.bmp");
    if (checkerTex == NULL)
        return false;

    // set up the smile texture as a mipmap with bilinear filtering
    glBindTexture(GL_TEXTURE_2D, smileTex->texID);
    glTexParameteri(GL_TEXTURE_2D, GL_TEXTURE_MAG_FILTER, GL_LINEAR);
    glTexParameteri(GL_TEXTURE_2D, GL_TEXTURE_MIN_FILTER, GL_LINEAR);
    glTexEnvi(GL_TEXTURE_ENV, GL_TEXTURE_ENV_MODE, GL_REPLACE);
    gluBuild2DMipmaps(GL_TEXTURE_2D, GL_RGB, smileTex->width, smileTex->height,
                      GL_RGB, GL_UNSIGNED_BYTE, smileTex->data);

    // generate the water texture as a mipmap
    glBindTexture(GL_TEXTURE_2D, checkerTex->texID);
    glTexParameteri(GL_TEXTURE_2D, GL_TEXTURE_MAG_FILTER, GL_LINEAR);
    glTexParameteri(GL_TEXTURE_2D, GL_TEXTURE_MIN_FILTER, GL_LINEAR);
    glTexParameteri(GL_TEXTURE_2D, GL_TEXTURE_WRAP_S, GL_REPEAT);
    glTexParameteri(GL_TEXTURE_2D, GL_TEXTURE_WRAP_T, GL_REPEAT);
    glTexEnvi(GL_TEXTURE_ENV, GL_TEXTURE_ENV_MODE, GL_MODULATE);
    gluBuild2DMipmaps(GL_TEXTURE_2D, GL_RGB, checkerTex->width, checkerTex->height,
                      GL_RGB, GL_UNSIGNED_BYTE, checkerTex->data);

    return true;
}


void DrawTexturedCube(float xPos, float yPos, float zPos)
{
    glPushMatrix();
    glTranslatef(xPos, yPos, zPos);
```

```
glBegin(GL_QUADS);
    glNormal3f(0.0f, 1.0f, 0.0f);  // top face

    glTexCoord2f(1.0f, 0.0f); glVertex3f(0.5f, 0.5f, 0.5f);
    glTexCoord2f(1.0f, 1.0f); glVertex3f(0.5f, 0.5f, -0.5f);
    glTexCoord2f(0.0f, 1.0f); glVertex3f(-0.5f, 0.5f, -0.5f);
    glTexCoord2f(0.0f, 0.0f); glVertex3f(-0.5f, 0.5f, 0.5f);
glEnd();
glBegin(GL_QUADS);
    glNormal3f(0.0f, 0.0f, 1.0f);  // front face

    glTexCoord2f(1.0f, 1.0f); glVertex3f(0.5f, 0.5f, 0.5f);
    glTexCoord2f(0.0f, 1.0f); glVertex3f(-0.5f, 0.5f, 0.5f);
    glTexCoord2f(0.0f, 0.0f); glVertex3f(-0.5f, -0.5f, 0.5f);
    glTexCoord2f(1.0f, 0.0f); glVertex3f(0.5f, -0.5f, 0.5f);
glEnd();
glBegin(GL_QUADS);
    glNormal3f(1.0f, 0.0f, 0.0f);  // right face

    glTexCoord2f(0.0f, 1.0f); glVertex3f(0.5f, 0.5f, 0.5f);
    glTexCoord2f(0.0f, 0.0f); glVertex3f(0.5f, -0.5f, 0.5f);
    glTexCoord2f(1.0f, 0.0f); glVertex3f(0.5f, -0.5f, -0.5f);
    glTexCoord2f(1.0f, 1.0f); glVertex3f(0.5f, 0.5f, -0.5f);
glEnd();
glBegin(GL_QUADS);
    glNormal3f(-1.0f, 0.0f, 0.0f); // left face

    glTexCoord2f(1.0f, 1.0f); glVertex3f(-0.5f, 0.5f, 0.5f);
    glTexCoord2f(0.0f, 1.0f); glVertex3f(-0.5f, 0.5f, -0.5f);
    glTexCoord2f(0.0f, 0.0f); glVertex3f(-0.5f, -0.5f, -0.5f);
    glTexCoord2f(1.0f, 0.0f); glVertex3f(-0.5f, -0.5f, 0.5f);
glEnd();
glBegin(GL_QUADS);
    glNormal3f(0.0f, -1.0f, 0.0f);  // bottom face

    glTexCoord2f(1.0f, 0.0f); glVertex3f(-0.5f, -0.5f, 0.5f);
    glTexCoord2f(1.0f, 1.0f); glVertex3f(-0.5f, -0.5f, -0.5f);
    glTexCoord2f(0.0f, 1.0f); glVertex3f(0.5f, -0.5f, -0.5f);
    glTexCoord2f(0.0f, 0.0f); glVertex3f(0.5f, -0.5f, 0.5f);
glEnd();
```

```
    glBegin(GL_QUADS);
        glNormal3f(0.0f, 0.0f, -1.0f);  // back face

        glTexCoord2f(0.0f, 0.0f); glVertex3f(0.5f, -0.5f, -0.5f);
        glTexCoord2f(1.0f, 0.0f); glVertex3f(-0.5f, -0.5f, -0.5f);
        glTexCoord2f(1.0f, 1.0f); glVertex3f(-0.5f, 0.5f, -0.5f);
        glTexCoord2f(0.0f, 1.0f); glVertex3f(0.5f, 0.5f, -0.5f);
    glEnd();
    glPopMatrix();
}

void Render()
{
    radians =  float(PI*(angle-90.0f)/180.0f);

    // calculate the camera's position
    cameraX = lookX + sin(radians)*mouseY;  // multiplying by mouseY makes the
    cameraZ = lookZ + cos(radians)*mouseY;  // camera get closer/farther away
    cameraY = lookY + mouseY / 2.0f;

    // point camera at (0,0,0)
    lookX = 0.0f;
    lookY = 0.0f;
    lookZ = 0.0f;

    // clear screen and depth buffer
    glClear(GL_COLOR_BUFFER_BIT | GL_DEPTH_BUFFER_BIT);
    glLoadIdentity();

    // set the camera position
    gluLookAt(cameraX, cameraY, cameraZ, lookX, lookY, lookZ, 0.0, 1.0, 0.0);

    // make the cube a 15x15x15 cube
    glScalef(15.0f, 15.0f, 15.0f);

    // render first pass
    glBindTexture(GL_TEXTURE_2D, smileTex->texID);
    DrawTexturedCube(0.0f, 0.0f, 0.0f);
```

```
        // render second pass
        glEnable(GL_BLEND);              // enable blending
            glDepthMask(GL_FALSE);       // disable writing to depth buffer
            glDepthFunc(GL_EQUAL);

            glBlendFunc(GL_ZERO, GL_SRC_COLOR);
                glBindTexture(GL_TEXTURE_2D, checkerTex->texID);
                DrawTexturedCube(0.0f, 0.0f, 0.0f);

            // reset modes
            glDepthMask(GL_TRUE);
            glDepthFunc(GL_LESS);
            glDisable(GL_BLEND);

    glFlush();
    SwapBuffers(g_HDC);                  // bring back buffer to foreground
}
```

That's all there is to it! You should reach the same result with this code as you did with the multi-texturing example. The only difference is that this example will run more slowly than the hard-ware-accelerated multitexturing example. In any case, you should experiment with different blend functions to see what types of effects result.

SUMMARY

With OpenGL, you can apply several textures to the same polygon through a series of texture operations. This is called *multitexturing*.

You can divide multitexturing into four major steps: verifying that multitexturing is supported, locating the pointer to the extension function (because you're using Windows), establishing the texture units, and specifying the texture coordinates.

Environment mapping is the process of rendering an object that entirely reflects its environment, as would be the case if you took a polished, shiny silver ball outside. You would see the clouds, sky, ground, trees, and us in the reflection off the ball.

By manipulating the *texture matrix stack,* you can move, rotate, and scale textures on a surface to create different effects.

Lightmapping is the process of applying a lightmap to a surface in order to simulate the effect of stat-ic lighting on the surface. A *lightmap* is a texture map that represents how a light strikes a surface.

CHAPTER 10

DISPLAY LISTS
AND VERTEX
ARRAYS

In many graphics applications, and in virtually all games, maintaining an interactive frame rate and smooth animation is of utmost importance. Although rapid advancements in graphics hardware have lessened the need to optimize every single line of code, programmers still need to focus on writing efficient code that, through the graphics API, harnesses the full power of the underlying hardware. In this chapter, we'll be discussing a couple features that OpenGL provides to help accomplish this task:

- **Display lists.** These provide a means to precompile commonly used sets of commands, allowing them to be used at a lower cost.
- **Vertex arrays.** These allow you to more efficiently store and manipulate vertex data, such as position and color.

DISPLAY LISTS

After you've been writing OpenGL code for a while, you'll probably notice that there are sections of code that you are calling frequently, with the same state machine settings every time. Wouldn't it be nice if you could process those commands in advance (maybe at initialization), and then send the preprocessed commands down the graphics pipeline, rather than processing them all from scratch every time? That's exactly the idea behind OpenGL's display lists.

As you'll see momentarily, display lists are quite easy to create and use; the only catch to using them is that it's not always obvious when they will help improve performance. In addition, some vendors do a better job than others in the implementation of display lists, so your mileage may vary. In the worst case, though, they should never hurt performance.

To see how display lists are created and used, let's look at an example. Suppose you have a program in which you draw a bunch of pyramids, which you're representing as four triangles (the bottom isn't drawn, because you can't see it). You'd probably create a function to do it, and it might look something like this (because all four triangles share a single common central point, you can use a triangle fan):

```
void DrawPyramid()
{
  glBegin(GL_TRIANGLE_FAN);
    glVertex3f(0.0, 1.0, 0.0);
```

```
    glVertex3f(-1.0, 0.0, 1.0);
    glVertex3f(1.0, 0.0, 1.0);
    glVertex3f(1.0, 0.0, -1.0);
    glVertex3f(-1.0, 0.0, -1.0);
  glEnd();
}
```

Because this function is getting called all the time, it's a good candidate to consider for a display list (in truth, it probably won't benefit much from being in a display list, because it's not doing anything else particularly expensive, but it illustrates the point). So, how do you put these calls into a display list?

Creating a Display List

First of all, before you can place items in a display list, you must get a name for one, much like you got a name for a texture object in Chapter 8, "Texture Mapping." This is done by using glGenLists():

```
GLuint glGenLists(GLsizei range);
```

Here, range is the number of display lists you need. The function returns an unsigned integer representing the first display list in the range requested. The next list in the range can be accessed by adding one to this value, and so on. You can think of the values returned by glGenLists() as the names, or IDs, of your display lists. They just provide a unique identifier that allows you to tell OpenGL which display list you are currently working with.

You should always check the return value of glGenLists() to make sure that it is not 0. This is not a valid list name, and it indicates that some error has occurred, such as there not being range contiguous names available. As an additional precaution, at any time you can check to see whether a list name is valid by using glIsList():

```
GLboolean glIsList(GLuint listName);
```

This function returns GL_TRUE if listName is a valid name for a display list, and GL_FALSE otherwise.

Filling a Display List with Commands

After you have a valid list name, the next step is to place commands in the display list associated with it. This is done in a manner very similar to the way you use glBegin()/glEnd() to surround primitive drawing commands. First, you call a function that specifies the display list you want to fill, and when you're finished, you call another function completing the list. These functions are glNewList() and glEndList(), respectively:

```
void glNewList(GLuint listName, GLenum mode);
void glEndList();
```

Here, listName is the name of the display list you want to fill. Note that it can either be a new list you just created with glGenLists(), or it can be a list that you've been using but are ready to clear out and fill with new commands. mode is the compilation mode, and it can either be GL_COMPILE or GL_COMPILE_AND_EXECUTE. The second option executes the commands as it compiles them, where the first just compiles them. Under most circumstances, you'll create your display lists at initialization, and you won't want the commands to execute, so you'll use GL_COMPILE.

Although you can place any OpenGL commands you want between glNewList() and glEndList(), some commands cannot be compiled into a display list. These will instead be executed immediately. These functions are listed here:

```
glColorPointer
glDeleteLists
glDisableClientState
glEdgeFlagPointer
glEnableClientState
glFeedbackBuffer
glFinish
glFlush
glGenLists
glIndexPointer
glInterleavedArrays
glIsEnabled
glIsList
glNormalPointer
glPopClientAttrib
glPixelStore
glPushClientAttrib
glReadPixels
glRenderMode
glSelectBuffer
glTexCoordPointer
glVertexPointer
```

In addition, each of the glGet() commands will execute immediately, as will the glTexImage() functions if a proxy texture is being created (if you're not using a proxy texture, you can safely use the glTexImage() functions, though there are better ways to handle textures, as we'll discuss later).

Executing Display Lists

After you have a display list, you can then use it in any place you would have used the code compiled into it. This is done with

```
void glCallList(GLuint listName);
```

This causes the commands in the list indicated by listName to immediately be executed, in order, just as if they were inserted into your code.

So, what if you want to call several display lists at once? Well, conveniently, OpenGL provides direct support for this:

```
void glCallLists(GLsizei num, GLenum type, const GLvoid *lists);
```

Here, num is the total number of lists to be executed, and lists is a pointer to an array of display-list names. Although the value returned by glGenLists() is an unsigned integer, and that's the type expected by most other display list functions, in reality, you could cast the name to some other data type that's more convenient for your use. And that's why lists is a void pointer, and why the type member is present to indicate the actual data type stored in the array. It can be any of the values in Table 10.1.

When glCallLists() is used, OpenGL will iterate over list, from 0 to num-1, calling the display-list name indicated at each index in the iteration. If any of the display lists' names in the list array are not valid, they'll simply be ignored.

There may be times in doing this (such as when using display lists for text output) that you don't want the iteration to start at zero, but rather at some offset. You can set the offset at which the iteration begins using the following.

```
void glListName(GLuint offset);
```

This will cause the iteration to begin at offset and end at offset + num-1. The value of the offset is 0 by default. Remember, because OpenGL is a state machine, if you change the offset, it will remain at the value you set it until you change it again. If you want to restore it to its original value after you're finished, before changing the offset, you can use glGet() with GL_LIST_BASE to find the original offset value.

Display-List Issues

There are a number of things to be aware of when using display lists. For starters, you can use glCallList() or glCallLists() within display lists—it's perfectly legal to include them within a glNewList()/glEndList() block. To prevent the possibility of infinite recursion caused by two lists calling each other, however, the commands within the display list executed by glCallList() are not made part of the new display list.

Table 10.1 GlCallLists() Types

Constant	Type
GL_BYTE	Signed 1-byte integer
GL_UNSIGNED_BYTE	Unsigned 1-byte integer
GL_SHORT	Signed 2-byte integer
GL_UNSIGNED_SHORT	Unsigned 2-byte integer
GL_INT	Signed 4-byte integer
GL_UNSIGNED_INT	Unsigned 4-byte integer
GL_FLOAT	4-byte floating-point value
GL_2_BYTES	lists is treated as array of bytes, with each pair of bytes designating a display-list name. The value of the name is found by multiplying the unsigned value of the first byte by 2^8 and adding it to the unsigned value of the second byte.
GL_3_BYTES	lists is treated as array of bytes, with each triplet of bytes designating a display-list name. The value of the name is found by summing the unsigned value of the first byte multiplied by 2^{16}, the unsigned value of the second byte multiplied by 2^8, and the unsigned value of the third byte.
GL_4_BYTES	lists is treated as array of bytes, with each pair of bytes designating a display-list name. The value of the name is found by summing the unsigned value of the first byte multiplied by 2^{24}, the unsigned value of the second byte multiplied by 2^{16}, the unsigned value of the third byte multiplied by 2^8, and the unsigned value of the fourth byte.

Another thing to keep in mind is that display lists can contain calls that change the current OpenGL state, and there is no built-in mechanism to save and restore the state over display-list calls. Therefore, you want to be sure to save and restore state information yourself using glPush/PopMatrix() and/or glPush/PopAttrib().

Destroying Display Lists

Creating a display list allocates memory in which to store the commands, so after you are finished using a display list—either at program termination or beforehand—you need to explicitly destroy it to avoid resource leaks. Doing so is quite straightforward via glDeleteLists():

```
void glDeleteLists(GLuint listName, GLsizei range);
```

This will free the memory associated with the display lists starting with listName and proceeding to listName + range-1. If any name within the range refers to a non-existent list, it will simply be ignored. If range is 0, the call will be ignored, and if range is negative, it will generate an error.

Now that you know how to create, fill, call, and destroy display lists, let's see what you have to do to rewrite the pyramid routine above using them. First, of course, you need to create the list, as follows:

```
GLuint pyramidList;

pyramidList = glGenLists(1);
```

Next, you need to fill this list with commands. To do this, you'll rewrite the DrawPyramid() function from earlier. Because you'll only be calling it once now (at startup) you'll rename it InitializePyramid(). Because the list creation also needs to happen only once, you'll move the creation code into the function as well, and have it take a reference to a GLuint as a parameter (so that you can pass pyramidList in). The new function appears here:

```
void InitializePyramid(GLuint &pyramidList)
{
  pyramidList = glGenLists(1);

  glNewList(pyramidList, GL_COMPILE);
  glBegin(GL_TRIANGLE_FAN);
    glVertex3f(0.0, 1.0, 0.0);
    glVertex3f(-1.0, 0.0, 1.0);
    glVertex3f(1.0, 0.0, 1.0);
    glVertex3f(1.0, 0.0, -1.0);
    glVertex3f(-1.0, 0.0, -1.0);
  glEnd();
  glEndList();
}
```

Now, when you need to draw a pyramid, you just translate, rotate, and scale as needed, and then use

```
glCallList(pyramidList);
```

to actually draw the pyramid. When you finish using the pyramid list (probably when exiting the program), you free the list with

```
glDeleteLists(pyramidList, 1);
```

And that's it. Again, remember that in this example, you're probably not going to gain much from using a display list, but you should at least have a pretty good idea of how to use them now.

Display Lists and Textures

Because any of the texture functions can be used within display lists, you might be tempted to create lists that encapsulate the process of defining texture parameters and loading texture data into them. If texture objects didn't exist, this would probably be a good way to go about it. Texture objects do exist, however, and in addition to being quite easy to use, they provide a much greater performance boost than you could get by using display lists for the same purpose. The best approach, then, is to create and initialize your textures once, bind them to a texture object, and then when you need them, select them with appropriate calls to glBindTexture(). Note that there is nothing wrong with putting the calls to glBindTexture(), glTexCoord(), and even glTexEnv() within display lists, because these are involved with using the texture as opposed to creating it.

Example: Robot Demo with Display Lists

To demonstrate using display lists, we've rewritten the robot demo from Chapter 5, "Coordinate Transformations and OpenGL Matrices." Instead of drawing each component of the robot directly every frame, we've compiled each part of the robot into a display list. As much as possible, we've included the transformations within these lists, but a few had to be omitted because the robot is in motion. The new demo, which you'll find on the CD, creates all the display lists at startup, and then calls them every frame. The following code shows the function that creates the display lists. Note that the demo uses nested display lists. One of the lists draws a simple cube, and this list is then used in turn by the lists for the torso, head, arms, and legs after first performing some scaling and translation operations.

```
void InitializeLists()
{
  // allocate 5 lists
  g_cube = glGenLists(5);

  glNewList(g_cube, GL_COMPILE);
  glBegin(GL_POLYGON);
```

```
    glVertex3f(0.0f, 0.0f, 0.0f);    // top face
    glVertex3f(0.0f, 0.0f, -1.0f);
    glVertex3f(-1.0f, 0.0f, -1.0f);
    glVertex3f(-1.0f, 0.0f, 0.0f);
    glVertex3f(0.0f, 0.0f, 0.0f);    // front face
    glVertex3f(-1.0f, 0.0f, 0.0f);
    glVertex3f(-1.0f, -1.0f, 0.0f);
    glVertex3f(0.0f, -1.0f, 0.0f);
    glVertex3f(0.0f, 0.0f, 0.0f);    // right face
    glVertex3f(0.0f, -1.0f, 0.0f);
    glVertex3f(0.0f, -1.0f, -1.0f);
    glVertex3f(0.0f, 0.0f, -1.0f);
    glVertex3f(-1.0f, 0.0f, 0.0f);   // left face
    glVertex3f(-1.0f, 0.0f, -1.0f);
    glVertex3f(-1.0f, -1.0f, -1.0f);
    glVertex3f(-1.0f, -1.0f, 0.0f);
    glVertex3f(0.0f, 0.0f, 0.0f);    // bottom face
    glVertex3f(0.0f, -1.0f, -1.0f);
    glVertex3f(-1.0f, -1.0f, -1.0f);
    glVertex3f(-1.0f, -1.0f, 0.0f);
    glVertex3f(0.0f, 0.0f, 0.0f);    // back face
    glVertex3f(-1.0f, 0.0f, -1.0f);
    glVertex3f(-1.0f, -1.0f, -1.0f);
    glVertex3f(0.0f, -1.0f, -1.0f);
  glEnd();
glEndList();

g_head = g_cube + 1;
glNewList(g_head, GL_COMPILE);
  glPushMatrix();
    glColor3f(1.0f, 1.0f, 1.0f);    // white
    glTranslatef(1.0f, 2.0f, 0.0f);
    glScalef(2.0f, 2.0f, 2.0f);     // head is a 2x2x2 cube
    glCallList(g_cube);
  glPopMatrix();
glEndList();

g_torso = g_cube + 2;
glNewList(g_torso, GL_COMPILE);
  glPushMatrix();
    glColor3f(0.0f, 0.0f, 1.0f);    // blue
```

```
        glTranslatef(1.5f, 0.0f, 0.0f);
        glScalef(3.0f, 5.0f, 2.0f);       // torso is a 3x5x2 cube
        glCallList(g_cube);
      glPopMatrix();
   glEndList();

   g_arm = g_cube + 3;
   glNewList(g_arm, GL_COMPILE);
      glColor3f(1.0f, 0.0f, 0.0f);        // red
      glScalef(1.0f, 4.0f, 1.0f);         // arm is a 1x4x1 cube
      glCallList(g_cube);
   glEndList();

   g_leg = g_cube + 4;
   glNewList(g_leg, GL_COMPILE);
      glColor3f(1.0f, 1.0f, 0.0f);        // yellow
      glScalef(1.0f, 5.0f, 1.0f);         // leg is a 1x5x1 cube
      glCallList(g_cube);
   glEndList();
} // end InitializeLists()
```

Because this is such a simple program, the conversion to display lists doesn't provide a huge speedup. On some of the machines we tested it on, there was a 5–10 percent increase in the frame rate, but on machines with faster hardware, the frame rates were almost identical. In any case, the demo should at least help you understand how display lists are used.

VERTEX ARRAYS

The pyramid-drawing example really only involves rendering vertices, and in practice, you may find that you frequently process massive amounts of vertex or vertex-related data. To this point, we've been using relatively simple objects in our demos, and thus, we've been able to describe them explicitly in the code. In a real game, however, you'll be working with models containing hundreds or even thousands of polygons, and describing such complicated models directly in the code just isn't practical—even if you manage to create decent-looking results, it's going to be a nightmare to maintain. Instead, one of the following two approaches is usually taken:

- **Generate the model procedurally.** Some things you want to represent can be implicitly described with equations due to patterns they contain or because they possess some random properties that you can generate on the fly. A good example of this is fractals. Geometric data for fractals can be created by a procedure that produces the same values every frame.

- **Load the model from a file.** Dozens of great modeling packages enable you to create a model visually and then export the geometric data to a file, which can be read by your program. This approach offers the greatest flexibility. Model loading will be discussed in much greater detail later in the book.

Whichever approach is used, it should be fairly obvious that you don't want to repeat all the work every frame—you certainly don't want to be constantly reading a model from disk, and even procedural methods can have enough overhead to have an adverse effect on performance. Instead, you'll take the geometric data these methods generate and store it in buffers, which you can then access as needed. This is the whole idea behind vertex arrays.

This process can be summarized in the following steps:

1. Generate the data you need, either procedurally or from a model file on disk.
2. Save this data in an array or set of arrays (for example, you could put the position of each vertex in one array, the vertex normal in another, color in another, and so on).
3. When the data is needed, iterate over this array (or these arrays), making appropriate OpenGL calls for each element of the array. Alternatively, you might access some subset or just a few elements of the array.

Assuming you know how to work with arrays and loops in C, you know enough OpenGL by now that you could do all of this yourself, without having to learn any new OpenGL commands. However, because this approach is so widely used, OpenGL includes built in support for vertex arrays, which can provide performance improvements well worth taking advantage of.

Enabling Vertex Arrays

Like most OpenGL features, to be able to use vertex arrays, you must first enable them. You might expect this to be done with glEnable(), but it's not. OpenGL provides a separate pair of functions to control vertex array support:

```
void glEnableClientState(GLenum array);
void glDisableClientState(GLenum array);
```

The array parameter is a flag indicating which type of array you're enabling (or disabling). You need to create a separate array for each type of data you want to use (for example, position, normal, color), and so you need to explicitly enable support for whichever data types you'll be using. The flags to pass to enable for each of these types are listed in Table 10.2.

It is common in OpenGL documentation to refer to all these array types collectively as *vertex arrays*, which can be confusing because there is also a specific array type that is called a vertex array. That said, they are collectively referred to as *vertex arrays* because each array contains data that is referenced on a per-vertex basis. The array type containing positional information is

Table 10.2 Array Type Flags

Flag	Meaning
GL_COLOR_ARRAY	Enables an array containing color information for each vertex
GL_EDGE_FLAG_ARRAY	Enables an array containing edge flags for each vertex
GL_INDEX_ARRAY	Enables an array containing indices to a color palette for each vertex
GL_NORMAL_ARRAY	Enables an array containing the vertex normal for each vertex
GL_TEXTURE_COORD_ARRAY	Enables an array containing the texture coordinate for each vertex
GL_VERTEX_ARRAY	Enables an array containing the position of each vertex

specifically called a *vertex array* because the data stored in it is used internally as if calls to glVertex() were being made. If you'll notice, the name of each array type roughly corresponds to the name of the OpenGL call that will be made on the data it contains (color arrays are used with glColor(), texture coordinate arrays are used with glTexCoord(), and so on).

Working with Arrays

After you have enabled the array types that you will be using, the next step is to give OpenGL some data to work with. It's up to you to create arrays and fill them with the data you will be using (either procedurally, from files, or by any other means, as we've already discussed). You then just need to tell OpenGL about these arrays so it can use them. The function used to do this depends on the type of array you're using. Let's look at each function in detail.

```
void glColorPointer(GLint size, GLenum type, GLsizei stride, const GLvoid *array);
```

This specifies the color array. size is the number of components per color, which should be either 3 or 4. type is the data type of the array (and thus the data type of each color component); it can be GL_BYTE, GL_UNSIGNED_BYTE, GL_SHORT, GL_UNSIGNED_SHORT, GL_INT, GL_UNSIGNED_INT, GL_FLOAT, or GL_DOUBLE. stride is the number of bytes between consecutive colors; if there are no extra bytes between colors, this should be 0. array is the pointer to the array itself (or, more specifically, a pointer to the first element you want to use within that array).

```
void glEdgeFlagPointer(GLsizei stride, const GLboolean *array);
```

Edge flags become important when displaying polygons as lines, and this array allows you to spec-ify which lines are edges. `stride` is the number of bytes between entries in `array`, which should consist of boolean values.

```
void glIndexPointer(GLenum type, GLsizei stride, const GLvoid *array);
```

This array represents color indices for use with palletized display modes. `type` is the data type of `array`, and it can be set to `GL_SHORT`, `GL_INT`, `GL_FLOAT`, or `GL_DOUBLE`. `stride` is the byte offset between adjacent entries in the array.

```
void glNormalPointer(GLenum type, GLsizei stride, const GLvoid *array);
```

This array should contain normal vectors for each vertex, with each element in the array repre-senting a single coordinate. Thus, there should be three elements in the array composing a single normal vector for each vertex you are working with. `type` is the data type of the coordinates, and it can be `GL_BYTE`, `GL_SHORT`, `GL_INT`, `GL_FLOAT`, or `GL_DOUBLE`. `stride` is, again, the offset between sub-sequent normals, and `array` is a pointer to the array itself.

```
void glTexCoordPointer(GLint size, GLenum type, GLsizei stride, const GLvoid *array);
```

This array contains texture coordinates for each vertex. `size` is the number of coordinates per vertex, and it must be 1, 2, 3, or 4. `type` is the data type of each coordinate, and it can be set to `GL_SHORT`, `GL_INT`, `GL_FLOAT`, or `GL_DOUBLE`. `stride` is the offset between consecutive elements, and `array` is, of course, the array itself.

```
void glVertexPointer(GLint size, GLenum type, GLsizei stride, cont GLvoid *array);
```

Finally, this array contains positional data for the vertices. `size` is the number of coordinates per vertex, and it must be 2, 3, or 4. `type` is the data type of the coordinates; it should be `GL_SHORT`, `GL_INT`, `GL_FLOAT`, or `GL_DOUBLE`. `stride` is the byte offset between vertices (set to 0 if the vertices are tightly packed), and `array` is a pointer to the array.

After you've specified which arrays OpenGL should use for each data type, you can begin to have it access that data for rendering. There are several functions that you can choose from.

NOTE

For each data type, you can only have a single array specified at any one time. This means that if you want to represent more than one object in your game with vertex arrays, you either have to combine all the data for them into a single set of arrays, or have each object have its own set of arrays that you switch between using gl*Pointer(). Although the former may be slightly faster because it doesn't require a lot of state changes, the latter is going to be easier to manage.

glDrawArrays()

When this function is called, OpenGL will iterate over each of the currently enabled arrays, rendering primitives as it goes. To understand how it works, you need to look at the prototype:

```
void glDrawArrays(GLenum mode, GLint first, GLsizei count);
```

mode serves the same basic function as the parameter passed to glBegin(): It specifies which type of primitive the vertex data should be used to create. Valid values are GL_POINTS, GL_LINE_STRIP, GL_LINE_LOOP, GL_LINES, GL_TRIANGLE_STRIP, GL_TRIANGLE_FAN, GL_TRIANGLES, GL_QUAD_STRIP, GL_QUADS, and GL_POLYGON. first specifies the index at which the iteration should start, and count specifies the number of indices to process. It should be noted that after a call to glDrawArrays(), states related to the array types being used are undefined. For example, if using normal arrays, the current normal will be undefined.

glDrawElements()

This function is very similar to glDrawArrays(), but in some ways it is even more powerful. With glDrawArrays(), your only option is to iterate sequentially over the list; glDrawElements(), on the other hand, allows you to specify the array elements in any order. Let's look at the prototype:

```
void glDrawElements(GLenum mode, GLsizei count, GLenum type, const GLvoid *indices);
```

mode is used just as in glDrawArrays().count indicates the number of indices to be processed. type is the data type of the values in indices, and it should be GL_UNSIGNED_BYTE, GL_UNSIGNED_SHORT, or GL_UNSIGNED_INT. indices is an array containing the vertices you want to render.

To understand the value of this method, it must be pointed out that not only can you specify the indices in any order, you can also specify the same vertex repeatedly in the series. In games, most vertices will be shared by more than one polygon; by storing the vertex once and accessing it repeatedly by its index, you can save a substantial amount of memory. In addition, good OpenGL implementations will only perform operations on the vertex once and keep the results around so that all references after the first are virtually free. The performance advantages of this should be obvious. See the section titled "Locking Arrays" at the end of this chapter for more information.

glDrawRangeElements()

This function (it's new to OpenGL 1.2, so it can't be used with older implementations) is similar in use to glDrawElements(). The primary difference is that the values in the vertex array that you will be accessing fall within a limited range. For example, if you have a vertex array containing 1,000 vertices, but you know that the object you're about to draw only accesses the first 100 vertices, you can use glDrawRangeElements() to tell OpenGL that you're not using the whole array at the moment. This provides an opportunity for optimization because OpenGL may be able to move those elements into memory that can be accessed more quickly. The prototype is as follows:

```
void glDrawRangeElements(GLenum mode, GLuint start, GLuint end, GLsizei count,
                         GLenum type, const GLvoid *indices);
```

mode, count, type, and indices have the same purpose as the corresponding parameters. start and end correspond to the lower and upper bounds of the vertex indices contained in indices.

glArrayElement()

This is perhaps the least efficient method of accessing vertex array data. Rather than calling upon a range of data, it allows you to evaluate and render a single vertex, as follows:

```
void glArrayElement(GLint index);
```

index is, naturally, the vertex you want to render.

To fully understand how vertex arrays work, let's recap. First, you need the data with which you will fill the arrays, which can be loaded from a file, generated procedurally, or defined by some other method. This data consists of a set of vertices describing some object in your world. Each vertex can include information about its position, color, texture coordinates, edge flags, and/or normal vectors. In addition to storing this data in one or more arrays, you need to enable vertex arrays for each data type you will be using. Then, you tell OpenGL to use each array with corresponding calls to gl*Pointer().

When you want to evaluate and render the data stored in these arrays, you make a call to one of the functions listed above. For each vertex, OpenGL takes the data associated with each data type, and, in essence, uses that data with the appropriate OpenGL call. For example, the color array data is used with glColor(), the normal data is used with glNormal(), and so on. Note that these functions are not necessarily actually called (after all, you could do that yourself and avoid the whole concept of vertex arrays entirely), but the effect is the same.

Vertex Arrays and Multitexturing

Using multitexturing (see Chapter 9, "Advanced Texture Mapping") with vertex arrays requires some additional setup beyond what we have discussed so far. Each texture unit has its own set of states, and thus, vertex arrays can be enabled and disabled for them individually, and each has its own texture coordinate vertex array pointer.

In OpenGL implementations supporting multitexturing, the texture unit that is active by default is the first one. Calls to glTexCoordPointer() and glEnableClientState()/glDisableClientState()

with GL_TEXTURE_COORD_ARRAY affect only the currently active texture unit, so to use vertex arrays with other texture units, you have to activate them. This is done with the following function:

```
void glClientActiveTextureARB(enum texture);
```

texture is a constant corresponding to the unit that you wish to make active, and it must be of the form GL_TEXTURE*i*_ARB, where *i* ranges from 0 to GL_MAX_TEXTURE_UNITS_ARB - 1.

After you have activated the texture unit you wish to modify, you can then make calls to glTexCoordPointer() to assign an array of values or glEnableClientState()/glDisableClientState() to turn vertex arrays on or off for the current unit. Vertex arrays for all texture units are disabled by default. So, to set up vertex arrays for the first two texture stages, you'd use something like the following:

```
// Enable texture coordinate vertex arrays for texture unit 0
glEnableClientState(GL_TEXTURE_COORD_ARRAY);

// Specify an array (defined previously) to use with texture unit 0
glTexCoordPointer(2, GL_FLOAT, 0, (GLvoid *)texUnit0Vertices);

// Select texture unit 1
glClientActiveTextureARB(GL_TEXTURE1_ARB);

// Enable texture coordinate vertex arrays for texture unit 1
glEnableClientState(GL_TEXTURE_COORD_ARRAY);

// Specify an array (defined previously) to use with texture unit 1
glTexCoordPointer(2, GL_FLOAT, 0, (GLvoid *)texUnit1Vertices);
```

After you've enabled and specified vertex arrays for each of the texture units with which you want to use them, there is nothing else you need to do. Subsequent calls to glDrawArrays(), glDrawElements(), and so on, will use them just like any other vertex arrays.

Locking Arrays

Many OpenGL implementations provide an extension that allows you to lock and unlock arrays. Locking the arrays lets the system know that, until unlocked, you won't be modifying the data in the arrays. Rather than transforming a vertex each time it is used, OpenGL will transform it the first time and cache the results. This can result in big speed increases, especially when there are many shared vertices or when multiple passes are being made through the same data. Because the vertex data is, in effect, compiled, the name of this extension is GL_EXT_compiled_vertex_array. The functions associated with this extension are

```
void glLockArraysEXT(GLint first, GLsizei count);
void glUnlockArraysEXT();
```

The first parameter is the index of the first vertex you want to lock, and count is the total number of vertices to lock, starting at the first index.

See the demo in the following section for sample code checking for and using this extension.

Example: Terrain Demo Revisited

In Chapter 8, you saw a terrain demo generated from a height map. Here, you'll revisit that demo, changing it to use vertex arrays. The complete source code is on the CD; we'll look only at the relevant parts here. As you can see from Figures 10.1 and 10.2, the only visual difference between the two demos is the frame rate.

First, you declare the arrays you'll be using:

```
GLuint   g_indexArray[MAP_X * MAP_Z * 6];   // vertex index array
float    g_terrain[MAP_X * MAP_Z][3];       // heightfield terrain data (0-255); 256x256
float    g_colorArray[MAP_X * MAP_Z][3];    // color array
float    g_texcoordArray[MAP_X * MAP_Z][2]; // tex coord array
```

Figure 10.1

The terrain demo from Chapter 8.

Figure 10.2

*The vertex array
version of this
demo*

g_terrain holds the vertex-position data, g_colorArray contains the colors for each vertex, and g_texcoordArray holds the texture coordinates. g_indexArray contains indices describing the terrain date; it will be used with glDrawElements().

Next, you need to place data into each of these arrays, and enable vertex arrays. This is done in the InitializeArrays() function:

```
void InitializeArrays()
{
  // used to track current entry in the index array
  int index = 0;
  int currentVertex;

  // loop over all vertices in the terrain map
  for (int z = 0; z < MAP_Z; z++)
  {
    for (int x = 0; x < MAP_X; x++)
    {
      // vertices are numbered left to right, top to bottom
      currentVertex = z * MAP_X + x;
```

```
        // set the values in the color array
        g_colorArray[currentVertex][0] = g_colorArray[currentVertex][1] =
          g_colorArray[currentVertex][2] = g_terrain[x + MAP_X * z][1]/255.0f;

        // set the values in the texture coordinate array. since the texture
        // is tiled over each "square", we can use texture wrapping
        g_texcoordArray[currentVertex][0] = (float) x;
        g_texcoordArray[currentVertex][1] = (float) z;
      }
    }

    for (z = 0; z < MAP_Z - 1; z++)
    {
      for (int x = 0; x < MAP_X; x++)
      {
        currentVertex = z * MAP_X + x;
        g_indexArray[index++] = currentVertex + MAP_X;
        g_indexArray[index++] = currentVertex;
      }
    }

    // enable the vertex arrays being used
    glEnableClientState(GL_VERTEX_ARRAY);
    glEnableClientState(GL_COLOR_ARRAY);
    glEnableClientState(GL_TEXTURE_COORD_ARRAY);

    // pass the pointers to OpenGL
    glVertexPointer(3, GL_FLOAT, 0, g_terrain);
    glColorPointer(3, GL_FLOAT, 0, g_colorArray);
    glTexCoordPointer(2, GL_FLOAT, 0, g_texcoordArray);
} // end InitializeArrays()
```

The arrays are now ready to use, but there is one last thing you need to do at initialization. Because you'd like to use the GL_EXT_compiled_vertex_arrays extension, you need to check to see whether it's supported. The following code does exactly that, and if the extension exists, pointers to the glEXTLockArrays() and glEXTUnlockArrays() functions are obtained.

```
// check for the compiled array extensions
char *extList = (char *) glGetString(GL_EXTENSIONS);
```

```
if (extList && strstr(extList, "GL_EXT_compiled_vertex_array"))
{
  // get the address of the compiled array extensions
  glLockArraysEXT = (PFNGLLOCKARRAYSEXTPROC)
    wglGetProcAddress("glLockArraysEXT");
  glUnlockArraysEXT = (PFNGLUNLOCKARRAYSEXTPROC)
    wglGetProcAddress("glUnlockArraysEXT");
}
```

Using the vertex array data with the locks is then quite easy. In this demo, since you won't be modifying the terrain data, you can lock the arrays once they've been initialized:

```
// if the compiled arrays extension is available, lock the arrays
if (glLockArraysEXT)
  glLockArraysEXT(0, MAP_X * MAP_Z);
```

To clean up properly, you need to be sure to unlock the arrays before the program exits:

```
// if the compiled arrays extension is available, unlock the arrays
if (glUnlockArraysEXT)
  glUnlockArraysEXT();
```

The data is then displayed using glDrawElements(). Because the data is set up as triangle strips for optimal performance, you need to make several calls to glDrawElements(), each time specifying a different range to extract the vertex data from:

```
// loop through all the triangle strips
for (int z = 0; z < MAP_Z-1; z++)
{
  // draw the triangles in this strip
  glDrawElements(GL_TRIANGLE_STRIP, MAP_X * 2, GL_UNSIGNED_INT, &g_indexArray[z *
MAP_X * 2]);
}
```

That's all there is to it. Pretty simple, isn't it?

Converting this demo to use vertex arrays provided about a 10–15 percent speedup over the original version. That translated into between 5 and 10 additional frames per second on your test machines, which is a significant gain. The best part about it is that the conversion was completed in less than an hour; there's no question that vertex arrays can provide a substantial performance gain with minimal investment in time and effort.

Summary

In this chapter, you've looked at two powerful techniques provided by OpenGL to help get the maximum performance out of your application. There is some overlap in functionality between the two, so the question is, which one should you use? For the most part, if your game uses a lot of vertex data and not many state changes, vertex arrays are a natural choice; if there are a lot of state changes, display lists work well. But, because you can use both of them together, it's really up to you to experiment and determine which combination works for your game. Regardless of what combination you choose, you should be able to get a performance boost, even if it's minor. As you become more experienced through experimentation and practice, you'll be able to use them together for maximum efficiency and speed.

CHAPTER 11

Displaying Text

Chances are, at some point you'll want to display text on the screen in some way. You might use text for menus, screensavers, or just cool effects. In this chapter you'll look at some of the more common techniques for displaying text on the screen through OpenGL. The techniques you'll be looking at include bitmap fonts, outline fonts, and textured fonts.

In this chapter, we'll discuss the following:

- Bitmap fonts
- Outline fonts
- Texture-mapped fonts

BITMAP FONTS

Bitmap fonts are the first type of text you will put on the screen using OpenGL and offer what is probably the cleanest and best looking way to display text. At the same time, they are very simple to create through the use of the "wiggle" function `wglUseFontBitmaps()`, which generates bitmaps from font files loaded on the system.

To use bitmap fonts, the first thing you need to do is to create a display list of 96 OpenGL display list IDs to hold the character bitmaps that you're going to create. You accomplish this by using the `glGenLists()` function:

```
unsigned int base;

base = glGenLists(96);
```

After you've created the display list, you can create your font by using the Windows function `CreateFont()`, which is defined as

```
HFONT CreateFont(
    int nHeight,            // logical height of font
    int nWidth,             // logical average character width
    int nEscapement,        // angle of escapement
    int nOrientation,       // base-line orientation angle
    int fnWeight,           // font weight
    DWORD fdwItalic,        // italic attribute flag
    DWORD fdwUnderline,     // underline attribute flag
```

```
        DWORD fdwStrikeOut,          // strikeout attribute flag
        DWORD fdwCharSet,            // character set identifier
        DWORD fdwOutputPrecision,    // output precision
        DWORD fdwClipPrecision,      // clipping precision
        DWORD fdwQuality,            // output quality
        DWORD fdwPitchAndFamily,     // pitch and family
        LPCTSTR lpszFace             // pointer to typeface name string
);
```

This function will return a handle to the Windows font object. You can then select a device context for this font object and use the device context as a parameter for the wglUseFontBitmaps() function:

```
HFONT hFont;            // windows font

// create a 14pt Courier font
hFont = CreateFont(14, 0, 0, 0, FW_BOLD, FALSE, FALSE, FALSE, ANSI_CHARSET,
                   OUT_TT_PRECIS, CLIP_DEFAULT_PRECIS, ANTIALIASED_QUALITY,
                   FF_DONTCARE | DEFAULT_PITCH, "Courier");

// verify font creation
if (!hFont)
    return 0;

// select a device context for the font
SelectObject(g_HDC, hFont);

// prepare the bitmap font
wglUseFontBitmaps(g_HDC, 32, 96, base);
```

This block of code will build your bitmap font display list with a 14 point Courier bold font.

So you know how to create fonts, but how do you display them? Displaying text with bitmap fonts is actually easier than setting them up. You simply call the glListBase() and glCallLists() functions like this:

```
char *str;

glPushAttrib(GL_LIST_BIT);
    glListBase(base - 32);
    glCallLists(strlen(str), GL_UNSIGNED_BYTE, str);
glPopAttrib();
```

After the `glListBase()` function defines the base display list ID, the `glCallLists()` function calls the display lists needed based on the array of characters (the text string) passed to it.

With all of this base code for using bitmap fonts, you can now develop a set of functions to use these fonts more easily. Let's look at a simple example that displays a text string in the center of the window, as shown in Figure 11.1.

First, you need to keep track of the display list base ID, so you create the variable `listBase`:

```
unsigned int listBase;
```

Next is the function that will create the bitmap font using the `CreateFont()` function:

```
unsigned int CreateBitmapFont(char *fontName, int fontSize)
{
    HFONT hFont;                   // windows font
    unsigned int base;

    base = glGenLists(96);         // create storage for 96 characters

    if (stricmp(fontName, "symbol") == 0)
    {
```

```
            hFont = CreateFont(fontSize, 0, 0, 0, FW_BOLD, FALSE, FALSE, FALSE,
                               SYMBOL_CHARSET, OUT_TT_PRECIS, CLIP_DEFAULT_PRECIS,
                               ANTIALIASED_QUALITY, FF_DONTCARE | DEFAULT_PITCH,
                               fontName);
        }
        else
        {
            hFont = CreateFont(fontSize, 0, 0, 0, FW_BOLD, FALSE, FALSE, FALSE,
                               ANSI_CHARSET, OUT_TT_PRECIS, CLIP_DEFAULT_PRECIS,
                               ANTIALIASED_QUALITY, FF_DONTCARE | DEFAULT_PITCH,
                               fontName);
        }

        if (!hFont)
            return 0;

        SelectObject(g_HDC, hFont);
        wglUseFontBitmaps(g_HDC, 32, 96, base);

        return base;
}
```

The CreateBitmapFont() function first generates the display list for 96 characters. Then it checks whether the desired fontName is a symbol font. If it is, then the CreateBitmapFont() function calls the CreateFont() function with the SYMBOL_CHARSET value for the fdwCharSet parameter. If the function is not a symbol font, then the ANSI_CHARSET value is set. After setting up the bitmap font for use with Windows through the wglUseFontBitmaps() function, the CreateBitmapFont() function returns the base ID for the character display list.

Next is the PrintString() function, which displays a string of text using the current bitmap font at the current raster position:

```
void PrintString(unsigned int base, char *str)
{
    if ((base == 0) || (str == NULL))
        return;

    glPushAttrib(GL_LIST_BIT);
        glListBase(base - 32);
        glCallLists(strlen(str), GL_UNSIGNED_BYTE, str);
    glPopAttrib();
}
```

You also create a function to clean up the display list after you're finished with the application:

```
void ClearFont(unsigned int base)
{
    if (base != 0)
        glDeleteLists(base, 96);
}
```

This function simply calls the glDeleteLists() function, which deletes all the display list elements from the value indicated by base to 96.

For this example, we'll use a 48 point Comic Sans MS font for our text. The Initialize() function sets this up:

```
void Initialize()
{
    glClearColor(0.0f, 0.0f, 0.0f, 0.0f);              // clear to black

    glShadeModel(GL_SMOOTH);                           // use smooth shading
    glEnable(GL_DEPTH_TEST);                           // hidden surface removal

    listBase = CreateBitmapFont("Comic Sans MS", 48);  // create the bitmap font
}
```

Last is the Render() function, which renders your bitmap font text to the center of the screen:

```
void Render()
{
    // clear screen and depth buffer
    glClear(GL_COLOR_BUFFER_BIT | GL_DEPTH_BUFFER_BIT);
    glLoadIdentity();

    // move one unit into the screen
    glTranslatef(0.0f, 0.0f, -1.0f);

    // set color to white
    glColor3f(1.0f, 1.0f, 1.0f);

    // set raster position to (-.35, 0)
    glRasterPos2f(-0.35f, 0.0f);
```

```
    // display text
    PrintString(listBase, "OpenGL Bitmap Fonts!");

    glFlush();
    SwapBuffers(g_HDC);              // bring back buffer to foreground
}
```

You use the `glRasterPos2f()` function to position the text in the window and the `glColor3f()` function to set the drawing color to white. Because you're drawing in perspective mode, as opposed to orthogonal, the raster position is affected by the perspective transformations. To combat this, you first translate into the screen one unit. Then, because you've moved the coordinate system one unit along the z axis, the window's x axis dimensions now extend from about –0.6 to 0.6. You choose –0.35 for the x coordinate because this closely approximates a centering of the text.

Well that's all for bitmap fonts! Let's look at another technique for putting text on the screen: outline fonts.

OUTLINE FONTS

Outline fonts are very similar to the bitmap fonts we just discussed, but they are much more fun to play around with! For instance, you can move outline font text around the screen in 3D, give the font text some thickness, and essentially turn any font on the current system into a 3D font with all the functionality of other 3D objects.

To use outline fonts, you first need to declare an array of 256 GLYPHMETRICSFLOAT variables, which hold information about the placement and orientation of a glyph in a character cell. The GLYPH-METRICSFLOAT structure is a special structure created specifically for using text with OpenGL. It is defined as

```
typedef struct _GLYPHMETRICSFLOAT { // gmf
    FLOAT       gmfBlackBoxX;
    FLOAT       gmfBlackBoxY;
    POINTFLOAT  gmfptGlyphOrigin;
    FLOAT       gmfCellIncX;
    FLOAT       gmfCellIncY;
} GLYPHMETRICSFLOAT;
```

You'll pass the GLYPHMETRICSFLOAT variable you create to the `wglUseFontOutlines()` function. This function creates a set of display lists, one for each glyph of the current outline font, which you can use to render text to the screen. This function is defined as

```
BOOL wglUseFontOutlines(
    HDC hdc,                     // device context of the outline font
    DWORD first,                 // first glyph to be turned into a display list
    DWORD count,                 // number of glyphs to be turned into display lists
    DWORD listBase,              // specifies the starting display list
    FLOAT deviation,             // specifies the maximum chordal deviation from the
                                 // true outlines
    FLOAT extrusion,             // extrusion value in the negative-z direction
    int format,                  // specifies line segments or polygons in display lists
    LPGLYPHMETRICSFLOAT lpgmf    // address of buffer to receive glyph metric data
);
```

Creation of the outline font is essentially the same as the bitmap font with the addition of these two items. For instance, compare the CreateBitmapFont() function you created earlier with this CreateOutlineFont() function:

```
unsigned int CreateOutlineFont(char *fontName, int fontSize, float depth)
{
    HFONT hFont;                 // windows font
    unsigned int base;

    base = glGenLists(256);      // create storage for 256 characters

    if (stricmp(fontName, "symbol") == 0)
    {
        hFont = CreateFont(fontSize, 0, 0, 0, FW_BOLD, FALSE, FALSE, FALSE,
                           SYMBOL_CHARSET, OUT_TT_PRECIS, CLIP_DEFAULT_PRECIS,
                           ANTIALIASED_QUALITY, FF_DONTCARE | DEFAULT_PITCH,
                           fontName);
    }
    else
    {
        hFont = CreateFont(fontSize, 0, 0, 0, FW_BOLD, FALSE, FALSE, FALSE,
                           ANSI_CHARSET, OUT_TT_PRECIS, CLIP_DEFAULT_PRECIS,
                           ANTIALIASED_QUALITY, FF_DONTCARE | DEFAULT_PITCH,
                           fontName);
    }

    if (!hFont)
        return 0;
```

```
        SelectObject(g_HDC, hFont);
        wglUseFontOutlines(g_HDC, 0, 255, base, 0.0f, depth, WGL_FONT_POLYGONS, gmf);

        return base;
}
```

As you can see, this function is very similar to the `CreateBitmapFont()` function you created earlier, but there are a few differences. The first difference you might notice is the addition of the `depth` parameter, which is used by the `wglUseFontOutlines()` function to define the length of the outline font text along the z axis. The next difference is that you create 256 display lists instead of 96. This is because you want to provide support for all the 256 available ASCII codes. And lastly, you use the `wglUseFontOutlines()` function to finalize the setup of the outline fonts for OpenGL.

Displaying outline font text is exactly the same as displaying bitmap font text. Because you used all 256 ASCII codes when initializing the outline font, here is how the display code would look:

```
glPushAttrib(GL_LIST_BIT);
    glListBase(base);
    glCallLists(strlen(str), GL_UNSIGNED_BYTE, str);
glPopAttrib();
```

Pretty simple, eh? Let's take a look at some functions from an example that draws rotating text in the window, similar to some popular screensavers. This example uses the `CreateOutlineFont()` function you just created, so we won't list that function in the code here. We also won't list anything that deals with the core Windows application code.

To start with, you need to declare your variables:

```
HDC g_HDC;                          // global device context
float angle = 0.0f;                 //
unsigned int listBase;              // display list base
GLYPHMETRICSFLOAT gmf[256];         // holds orientation and placement
                                    // info for display lists
```

Next you have the `ClearFont()` function, which is almost exactly the same as the `ClearFont()` function you created earlier. This function, however, is set up to use 256 display lists:

```
void ClearFont(unsigned int base)
{
    glDeleteLists(base, 256);
}
```

The PrintString() function for outline fonts includes some code that will center the text on the point in space to which the text is being drawn. This is accomplished through a loop that goes through each character in the text string that you are displaying. During each iteration of the loop, you add the character's width, which you obtain from the GLYPHMETRICSFLOAT variable, to a variable that stores the sum of all the characters' widths. You then translate your coordinate system along the negative-x axis by half the total length of the text string.

```
void PrintString(unsigned int base, char *str)
{
    float length = 0;
    int idx;

    if ((str == NULL))
        return;

    // center the text
    for (idx = 0; idx < strlen(str); idx++)     // find length of text
    {
        length += gmf[str[idx]].gmfCellIncX; // increase length by character's width
    }
    glTranslatef(-length/2.0f, 0.0f, 0.0f);            // translate to center text

    // draw the text
    glPushAttrib(GL_LIST_BIT);
        glListBase(base);
        glCallLists(strlen(str), GL_UNSIGNED_BYTE, str);
    glPopAttrib();
}
```

In order for outline fonts to be properly displayed, you need to enable lighting. For the sake of simplicity, you're also going to enable GL_COLOR_MATERIAL, so the color you specify will act as the material for the text. All of this is done in the Initialize() function shown here:

```
void Initialize()
{
    glClearColor(0.0f, 0.0f, 0.0f, 0.0f);          // clear to black

    glShadeModel(GL_SMOOTH);                        // use smooth shading
    glEnable(GL_DEPTH_TEST);                        // hidden surface removal
    glEnable(GL_LIGHT0);                            // enable light0
```

```
    glEnable(GL_LIGHTING);                    // enable lighting
    glEnable(GL_COLOR_MATERIAL);              // enable color for material

    listBase = CreateOutlineFont("Arial", 10, 0.25f);  // load 10pt Arial font
}
```

Next you have the Render() function, which shows off the great part of outline fonts: the capability to move around in a 3D world. As you can see, you treat the outline font text the same as a regular 3D object by performing a translation and three rotations:

```
void Render()
{
    // clear screen and depth buffer
    glClear(GL_COLOR_BUFFER_BIT | GL_DEPTH_BUFFER_BIT);
    glLoadIdentity();

    // move 15 units into the screen and rotate along all axes
    glTranslatef(0.0f, 0.0f, -15.0f);
    glRotatef(angle*0.9f, 1.0f, 0.0f, 0.0f);
    glRotatef(angle*1.5f, 0.0f, 1.0f, 0.0f);
    glRotatef(angle, 0.0f, 0.0f, 1.0f);

    // set color to cyan
    glColor3f(0.0f, 1.0f, 1.0f);

    // display the text
    PrintString(listBase, "OpenGL Outline Fonts!");

    angle += 0.1f;

    glFlush();
    SwapBuffers(g_HDC);                       // bring back buffer to foreground
}
```

After you plug all of this code into your Windows framework, you get a rendering similar to the one shown in Figure 11.2.

Figure 11.2

A screenshot of the outline font example.

TEXTURE-MAPPED FONTS

Because outline fonts are composed of polygons and treated as regular 3D objects by OpenGL, you can enhance their look by applying a texture to them to get texture-mapped fonts. You don't even need to worry about calculating or determining the texture coordinates on the polygon text, because you can get OpenGL to do that through automatic texture-coordinate generation. Sound easy? Let's look at an example.

The example you're going to look at will display texture-mapped text on the screen that rotates around a fixed point. The example also offers users the ability to zoom in and out of the scene by pressing the A and Z keys, respectively.

```
////// Defines
#define BITMAP_ID 0x4D42          // the universal bitmap ID

////// Includes
#include <windows.h>              // standard Windows app include
#include <stdio.h>
#include <stdlib.h>
#include <math.h>
#include <gl/gl.h>                // standard OpenGL include
```

```c
#include <gl/glu.h>                        // OpenGL utilities
#include <gl/glaux.h>

////// Types
typedef struct
{
    int width;                             // width of texture
    int height;                            // height of texture
    unsigned int texID;                    // the texture object id of this texture
    unsigned char *data;                   // the texture data
} texture_t;

////// Global Variables
HDC g_HDC;                                 // global device context
bool fullScreen = false;                   // true = full screen; false = windowed
bool keyPressed[256];                      // holds true for keys that are pressed

float angle = 0.0f;                        // angle of rotation
unsigned int listBase;                     // display list base
GLYPHMETRICSFLOAT gmf[256];                // holds orientation and placement
                                           // info for display lists
float zDepth = -10.0f;                     // control position along the z axis

////// Texture Variables
texture_t *texture;

/*
    The LoadBitmapFile() function was taken out of this code dump to prevent
    redundancy.
*/

texture_t *LoadTextureFile(char *filename)
{
    BITMAPINFOHEADER texInfo;
    texture_t *thisTexture;

    // allocate memory for the texture structure
    thisTexture = (texture_t*)malloc(sizeof(texture_t));
    if (thisTexture == NULL)
        return NULL;
```

```
        // load the texture data and check validity
        thisTexture->data = LoadBitmapFile(filename, &texInfo);
        if (thisTexture->data == NULL)
        {
            free(thisTexture);
            return NULL;
        }

        // set width and height info for this texture
        thisTexture->width = texInfo.biWidth;
        thisTexture->height = texInfo.biHeight;

        // generate the texture object for this texture
        glGenTextures(1, &thisTexture->texID);

        return thisTexture;
}

bool LoadAllTextures()
{
        // load the water texture
        texture = LoadTextureFile("water.bmp");
        if (texture == NULL)
            return false;

        // set up the texture parameters
        glBindTexture(GL_TEXTURE_2D, texture->texID);
        glTexParameteri(GL_TEXTURE_2D, GL_TEXTURE_MAG_FILTER, GL_LINEAR_MIPMAP_LINEAR);
        glTexParameteri(GL_TEXTURE_2D, GL_TEXTURE_MIN_FILTER, GL_LINEAR_MIPMAP_LINEAR);
        glTexParameteri(GL_TEXTURE_2D, GL_TEXTURE_WRAP_S, GL_REPEAT);
        glTexParameteri(GL_TEXTURE_2D, GL_TEXTURE_WRAP_T, GL_REPEAT);
        gluBuild2DMipmaps(GL_TEXTURE_2D, GL_RGB, texture->width, texture->height,
                          GL_RGB, GL_UNSIGNED_BYTE, texture->data);

        // we want OpenGL to automatically generate the texture coordinates for the text
        glTexGeni(GL_S, GL_TEXTURE_GEN_MODE, GL_OBJECT_LINEAR);
        glTexGeni(GL_T, GL_TEXTURE_GEN_MODE, GL_OBJECT_LINEAR);
        glEnable(GL_TEXTURE_GEN_S);
        glEnable(GL_TEXTURE_GEN_T);
```

```
        return true;
    }

unsigned int CreateOutlineFont(char *fontName, int fontSize, float depth)
{
        HFONT hFont;                    // windows font
        unsigned int base;

        base = glGenLists(256);   // create storage for 96 characters

        if (stricmp(fontName, "symbol") == 0)
        {
            hFont = CreateFont(fontSize, 0, 0, 0, FW_BOLD, FALSE, FALSE, FALSE,
                              SYMBOL_CHARSET, OUT_TT_PRECIS, CLIP_DEFAULT_PRECIS,
                              ANTIALIASED_QUALITY, FF_DONTCARE | DEFAULT_PITCH,
                              fontName);
        }
        else
        {
            hFont = CreateFont(fontSize, 0, 0, 0, FW_BOLD, FALSE, FALSE, FALSE,
                              ANSI_CHARSET, OUT_TT_PRECIS, CLIP_DEFAULT_PRECIS,
                              ANTIALIASED_QUALITY, FF_DONTCARE | DEFAULT_PITCH,
                              fontName);
        }

        if (!hFont)
            return 0;

        SelectObject(g_HDC, hFont);
        wglUseFontOutlines(g_HDC, 0, 255, base, 0.0f, depth, WGL_FONT_POLYGONS, gmf);

        return base;
    }

void ClearFont(unsigned int base)
{
        glDeleteLists(base, 256);
    }
```

```c
void PrintString(unsigned int base, char *str)
{
    float length = 0;          // the length of the glyph string
    unsigned int idx;

    if ((str == NULL))
        return;

    // center the text
    for (idx = 0; idx < strlen(str); idx++)        // find length of text
    {
                length += gmf[str[idx]].gmfCellIncX;  // increase length
    }
    glTranslatef(-length/2,0.0f,0.0f);             // translate to center text

    // draw the text
    glPushAttrib(GL_LIST_BIT);
        glListBase(base);
        glCallLists(strlen(str), GL_UNSIGNED_BYTE, str);
    glPopAttrib();
}

void CleanUp()
{
    ClearFont(listBase);
    free(texture);
}

void Initialize()
{
    glClearColor(0.0f, 0.0f, 0.0f, 0.0f);        // clear to black

    glShadeModel(GL_SMOOTH);                      // use smooth shading
    glEnable(GL_DEPTH_TEST);                      // hidden surface removal
    glEnable(GL_LIGHT0);                          // enable light0
    glEnable(GL_LIGHTING);                        // enable lighting
    glEnable(GL_COLOR_MATERIAL);                  // enable color for material
    glEnable(GL_TEXTURE_2D);                      // enable texture mapping
```

```
            listBase = CreateOutlineFont("Arial", 14, 0.1f);  // load Arial font

        // set up textures
        LoadAllTextures();
        glBindTexture(GL_TEXTURE_2D, texture->texID);
    }

// Render
// desc: handles drawing of scene
void Render()
{
        // clear screen and depth buffer
        glClear(GL_COLOR_BUFFER_BIT | GL_DEPTH_BUFFER_BIT);
        glLoadIdentity();

        // zoom in/out and rotate the text
        glTranslatef(0.0f, 0.0f, zDepth);
        glRotatef(angle*0.9f, 1.0f, 0.0f, 0.0f);
        glRotatef(angle*1.5f, 0.0f, 1.0f, 0.0f);
        glRotatef(angle, 0.0f, 0.0f, 1.0f);

        // display the text
        PrintString(listBase, "TEXTURE MAPPING!");

        angle += 0.1f;

        SwapBuffers(g_HDC);                         // bring back buffer to foreground
}
...
// this code is from WndProc()
    switch(message)
    {
            ...
            case WM_SIZE:
                    height = HIWORD(lParam);    // retrieve width and height
                    width = LOWORD(lParam);

                    if (height == 0)            // don't want divide by zero
                        height = 1;
```

```
            glViewport(0, 0, width, height);    // reset viewport
            glMatrixMode(GL_PROJECTION);         // set projection matrix
            glLoadIdentity();                    // reset projection

            // calculate aspect ratio of window
            gluPerspective(54.0f, (GLfloat)width/(GLfloat)height, 1.0f, 1000.0f);

            glMatrixMode(GL_MODELVIEW);           // set modelview matrix
            glLoadIdentity();

            return 0;
        ...
    }
...
// this code is from WinMain()
done = false;
Initialize();

while (!done)
{
    PeekMessage(&msg, hwnd, NULL, NULL, PM_REMOVE);

    if (msg.message == WM_QUIT)        // do we receive a WM_QUIT message?
    {
        done = true;                   // if so, time to quit the application
    }
    else
    {
        if (keyPressed[VK_ESCAPE])
            done = true;
        else
        {
            if (keyPressed['A'])
                zDepth += 0.1f;
            if (keyPressed['Z'])
                zDepth -= 0.1f;

            Render();
```

```
            TranslateMessage(&msg);      // translate and dispatch to event queue
            DispatchMessage(&msg);
        }
    }
}

Cleanup();
```

Doesn't look too bad, does it? As you can see, the only real difference between texture-mapped fonts and outline fonts is that you tell OpenGL to automatically calculate the texture coordinates, which you do with these lines:

```
// we want OpenGL to automatically generate the texture coordinates for the text
glTexGeni(GL_S, GL_TEXTURE_GEN_MODE, GL_OBJECT_LINEAR);
glTexGeni(GL_T, GL_TEXTURE_GEN_MODE, GL_OBJECT_LINEAR);
glEnable(GL_TEXTURE_GEN_S);
glEnable(GL_TEXTURE_GEN_T);
```

You first saw the glTexGeni() function when we discussed environment mapping. Here you'll look at this function in a little more detail. The first parameter for this function tells OpenGL which texture coordinate you're going to generate. It can be equal to either GL_S or GL_T for 2D textures.

The second parameter tells OpenGL that you're going to specify the texture-mapping mode that you want to use when it generates the texture coordinates. The last parameter can be one of the following from Table 11.1.

Table 11.1 Texture-Generation Parameters

Value	Description
GL_EYE_LINEAR	The texture is set in a fixed position on the screen. Objects that pass over it are mapped with the section of the texture map over which they are passing.
GL_OBJECT_LINEAR	The texture is fixed to the object.
GL_SPHERE_MAP	The texture is an environment map (sphere map).

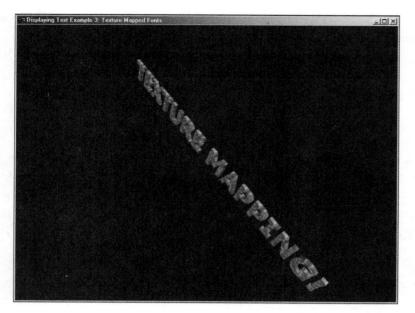

Figure 11.3

A screenshot of the texture-font example.

You're ready to draw the text after you bind the texture object for the texture you want to use. Using the water texture that you have results in the image shown in Figure 11.3.

SUMMARY

Bitmap fonts are probably the cleanest and best looking for displaying text. To create them, you use the wglUseFontBitmaps() function, which generates bitmaps from font files loaded on the system.

Outline fonts are very similar to bitmap fonts. For instance, you can move outline-font text around the screen in 3D, give the font text some thickness, and essentially turn any font on the current system into a 3D font with all the functionality of other 3D objects. You use the wglUseOutlineFonts() function to generate the polygons for the outline-font text.

Because outline fonts are composed of polygons and treated as regular 3D objects by OpenGL, you can enhance their look by applying a texture to them to get texture-mapped fonts. You don't even need to worry about calculating or determining the texture coordinates on the polygon text, because you can get OpenGL to do that through automatic texture-coordinate generation.

CHAPTER 12

OpenGL Buffers

e've been discussing buffers in some form for quite some time now but haven't really taken the time to discuss them in detail. For instance, we've used the color and depth buffers in nearly every example thus far for functions such as double-buffering and hidden-surface removal. In this chapter, we'll extend beyond these basic functionalities while also looking at two more buffers called the stencil buffer and the accumulation buffer.

In this chapter, you'll learn:

- What OpenGL buffers are
- How to use the color buffer
- How to use the depth buffer
- How to use the stencil buffer
- How to use the accumulation buffer

WHAT IS AN OpenGL BUFFER?

There are several buffers in OpenGL that you can use and manipulate, but just what exactly is a buffer? Well, first consider how you generate images on the computer screen. The screen is divided into a rectangular array of pixels, or a *buffer*, where color data is stored for each pixel. Essentially, whenever you store data for pixels, the buffer is the set of all those pixels that are storing the same data. In OpenGL, the color buffer stores RGBA and color-index data for each pixel on the screen or window.

A *frame buffer* is composed of all the buffers in a system. So with OpenGL, the color buffer, depth buffer, stencil buffer, and accumulation buffer combine to give you a single frame buffer. When you operate on any OpenGL buffer, you are operating on the frame buffer.

Setting Up the Pixel Format

You've been setting up the OpenGL buffers since you first started exploring OpenGL, but you haven't really taken a deeper look at what's happening. In almost all of our examples, we've used the function SetupPixelFormat() to configure the OpenGL window's device context for the buffers and pixel format that you want. Here's the function you've been using:

```
void SetupPixelFormat(HDC hDC)
{
    int nPixelFormat;                          // the pixel format index

    static PIXELFORMATDESCRIPTOR pfd = {
        sizeof(PIXELFORMATDESCRIPTOR),    // size of structure
        1,                                // default version
        PFD_DRAW_TO_WINDOW |              // window-drawing support
        PFD_SUPPORT_OPENGL |              // OpenGL support
        PFD_DOUBLEBUFFER,                 // double-buffering support
        PFD_TYPE_RGBA,                    // RGBA color mode
        32,                               // 32-bit color mode
        0, 0, 0, 0, 0, 0,                 // ignore color bits, non-palletized mode
        0,                                // no alpha buffer
        0,                                // ignore shift bit
        0,                                // no accumulation buffer
        0, 0, 0, 0,                       // ignore accumulation bits
        16,                               // 16-bit z-buffer size
        0,                                // no stencil buffer
        0,                                // no auxiliary buffer
        PFD_MAIN_PLANE,                   // main drawing plane
        0,                                // reserved
        0, 0, 0 };                        // layer masks ignored

        // choose best-matching pixel format
        nPixelFormat = ChoosePixelFormat(hDC, &pfd);

        // set pixel format to device context
        SetPixelFormat(hDC, nPixelFormat, &pfd);
}
```

As you can see, you use the PIXELFORMATDESCRIPTOR structure to set up the pixel format. Here is the structure's definition:

```
typedef struct tagPIXELFORMATDESCRIPTOR { // pfd
    WORD  nSize;            // size of data structure
    WORD  nVersion;        // version of data structure
    DWORD dwFlags;         // properties of the pixel buffer
    BYTE  iPixelType;      // type of pixel data
    BYTE  cColorBits;      // size of color buffer
    BYTE  cRedBits;        // number of bits for red
```

```
    BYTE   cRedShift;        // shift count of red bits
    BYTE   cGreenBits;       // number of bits for green
    BYTE   cGreenShift;      // shift count of green bits
    BYTE   cBlueBits;        // number of bits for blue
    BYTE   cBlueShift;       // shift count of blue bits
    BYTE   cAlphaBits;       // number of bits for alpha
    BYTE   cAlphaShift;      // shift count of alpha bits
    BYTE   cAccumBits;       // number of bits for the accumulation buffer
    BYTE   cAccumRedBits;    // number of bits for red in the accumulation buffer
    BYTE   cAccumGreenBits;  // number of bits for green in the accumulation buffer
    BYTE   cAccumBlueBits;   // number of bits for blue in the accumulation buffer
    BYTE   cAccumAlphaBits;  // number of bits for alpha in the accumulation buffer
    BYTE   cDepthBits;       // bit depth of the depth (z axis) buffer
    BYTE   cStencilBits;     // bit depth of the stencil buffer
    BYTE   cAuxBuffers;      // number of auxiliary buffers (not supported in MS OpenGL)
    BYTE   iLayerType;       // ignored; no longer used
    BYTE   bReserved;        // number of overlay and underlay planes
    DWORD  dwLayerMask;      // ignored; no longer used
    DWORD  dwVisibleMask;    // transparent color or color index of underlay plane
    DWORD  dwDamageMask;     // ignored; no longer used
} PIXELFORMATDESCRIPTOR;
```

You set each of these when you initialize the PIXELFORMATDESCRIPTOR structure in the
SetPixelFormat() function. The first important field you should look at is the dwFlags field, which
tells OpenGL the properties of the pixel buffer. Table 12.1 lists the flags you can use for this field
and their descriptions.

The iPixelType field is used to specify the type of pixel data. You can use one of the two values
listed in Table 12.2 for this field, but you'll normally be using the PFD_TYPE_RGBA flag.

Next, the cColorBits, cDepthBits, cAccumBits, and cStencilBits fields define the size of each buffer.
In the default SetPixelFormat() function that you have been using, you set the cAccumBits (accumulation buffer) and cStencilBits (stencil buffer) fields to 0. Setting any four of these fields to 0
will disable that field.

Lastly, you can set the iLayerType field to PFD_MAIN_PLANE, PFD_OVERLAY_PLANE, or PFD_UNDERLAY_PLANE.
You'll normally set this field to PFD_MAIN_PLANE, which specifies the main drawing layer.

After setting all the values in the PIXELFORMATDESCRIPTOR structure, you can send this structure to
the ChoosePixelFormat() function, which attempts to match an appropriate pixel format supported by a device context for the pixel format you specified in the PIXELFORMATDESCRIPTOR structure.
The ChoosePixelFormat() function will return an index to an appropriate pixel format, which you

Table 12.1 Values for `dwFlags`

Flag	Description
PFD_DRAW_TO_WINDOW	The buffer can draw to a window or device surface.
PFD_DRAW_TO_BITMAP	The buffer can draw to a memory bitmap.
PFD_SUPPORT_GDI	The buffer supports GDI drawing.
PFD_SUPPORT_OPENGL	The buffer supports OpenGL.
PFD_DOUBLEBUFFER	The buffer is double buffered.
PFD_STEREO	The buffer is stereoscopic.
PFD_DEPTH_DONTCARE	The requested pixel format can either have or not have a depth buffer. Can only specify when calling `ChoosePixelFormat()`.
PFD_DOUBLEBUFFER_DONTCARE	The requested pixel format can be either single or double buffered. Can only specify when calling `ChoosePixelFormat()`.
PFD_STEREO_DONTCARE	The requested pixel format can be either monoscopic or stereoscopic. Can only specify when calling `ChoosePixelFormat()`.

Table 12.2 Values for `iPixelType`

Flag	Description
PFD_TYPE_RGBA	RGBA pixels. Each pixel has four components in this order: red, green, blue, and alpha.
PFD_TYPE_COLORINDEX	Color-index pixels. Each pixel uses a color-index value.

can then send to the SetPixelFormat() function to set the pixel format for the device context. You accomplish all of this through the following code:

```
...
// set up PIXELFORMATDESCRIPTOR structure

        // choose best matching pixel format
        nPixelFormat = ChoosePixelFormat(hDC, &pfd);

        // set pixel format to device context
        SetPixelFormat(hDC, nPixelFormat, &pfd);
}
```

Now that you know how to get the OpenGL buffers set up in Windows, let's start discussing how you can use these buffers.

Clearing the Buffers

Before we get into detail on each of the available buffers, let's discuss how you can clear any of the buffers. OpenGL provides you with four functions, one for each buffer type, which will allow you to set the current clearing value for that buffer. This way, when you call the glClear() function to clear a buffer, that buffer will be cleared to the value you defined. The four functions you can use include

```
void glClearColor(GLclampf red, GLclampf green, GLclampf blue, GLclampf alpha);
```

```
void glClearDepth(GLclampd depth);
```

```
void glClearStencil(GLint s);
```

```
void glClearAccum(GLfloat red, GLfloat green, GLfloat blue, GLfloat alpha);
```

In order, these functions set the clearing value for the color buffer, depth buffer, stencil buffer, and accumulation buffer. The GLclampf and GLclampd types define variables that must be equal to a value between 0.0 and 1.0. All the default clearing values are equal to 0, except for the depth-buffer clearing value, which is equal to 1.0.

As mentioned, when you actually want to clear a specific buffer you use the glClear() function, which is defined as

```
void glClear(GLbitfield mask);
```

The mask parameter is equal to the bitwise logical OR of a combination of the values listed in Table 12.3.

Table 12.3 glClear() Mask Values

Flag	Buffer
GL_COLOR_BUFFER_BIT	RGBA color buffer
GL_DEPTH_BUFFER_BIT	Depth buffer
GL_STENCIL_BUFFER_BIT	Stencil buffer
GL_ACCUM_BUFFER_BIT	Accumulation buffer

THE COLOR BUFFER

As mentioned, the color buffer stores RGBA and color-index data for each pixel on the screen and is typically the buffer you draw on. You use the color buffer for such functionality as double buffering and stereoscopic viewing.

Double-Buffered Systems

Double-buffered systems are often used for animation through front and back color buffers, with the off-screen back buffer being where you render your scene. After the scene is finished rendering, you swap the back buffer with the front buffer to get a smooth animation effect. Using the back buffer eliminates the flickering effect you get when you try to animate a scene by drawing only on the front buffer. Double-buffered systems are limited to the color buffer, which means that you are not provided with a back buffer for the depth, accumulation, or stencil buffers.

By default, OpenGL selects the back buffer for rendering when you define double buffering in the pixel format; however, by using the glDrawBuffer() function, you can tell OpenGL which buffer to use to render the scene. The glDrawBuffer() function is defined as

```
void glDrawBuffer(GLenum mode);
```

You can select any of the values listed in Table 12.4 for the mode parameter.

The default value for double buffering when calling the glDrawBuffer() function is GL_BACK, while the default value for single buffering is GL_FRONT.

You can also tell OpenGL which buffer to read from when using the glReadPixels(), glCopyPixels(), glCopyTexImage*(), and glCopyTexSubImage*() functions through the glReadBuffer() function:

```
void glReadBuffer(GLenum mode);
```

Table 12.4 glDrawBuffer() Modes

Mode	Description
GL_FRONT	Draw to the front color buffer. Default for single buffering.
GL_BACK	Draw to the back color buffer. Default for double buffering.
GL_FRONT_AND_BACK	Draw to both the front and back color buffers.
GL_NONE	No color buffers are drawn to.

You can use the same values listed in Table 12.4 for the mode parameter of the glReadBuffer() function.

Stereo Buffering

Stereo buffering lets you use the left- and right-eye buffers to create a true three-dimensional image. As with double buffering, you use the glDrawBuffer() function with one of the parameters in Table 12.5 to tell OpenGL whether you want to draw to the left or right buffer. Keep in mind that you can't combine the parameters specified in Table 12.4 with those in Table 12.5.

Table 12.5 Stereo Buffer glDrawBuffer() Modes

Mode	Description
GL_LEFT	Draw to the front-left and back-left color buffers.
GL_RIGHT	Draw to the front-right and back-right color buffers.
GL_FRONT_LEFT	Draw to the front-left color buffer.
GL_FRONT_RIGHT	Draw to the front-right color buffer.
GL_BACK_LEFT	Draw to the back-left color buffer.
GL_BACK_RIGHT	Draw to the back-right color buffer.

THE DEPTH BUFFER

You typically use the *depth buffer* to perform hidden-surface removal on the objects in a scene. The values stored by the depth buffer for each pixel represent the distance between the pixel and the viewpoint. So when you draw one object in front of another in relation to the camera, the depth buffer is manipulated depending on the depth-comparison function you use.

Depth-Comparison Functions

As mentioned, when you draw your scene with OpenGL, the z coordinate of each pixel on the screen is compared with the previous z coordinate already stored in the depth value as a distance. The function to determine what type of comparison you're going to use is set with the glDepthFunc() function:

```
void glDepthFunc(GLenum func);
```

You can use any of the values listed in Table 12.6 for the func parameter.

Table 12.6 Depth-Comparison Functions

Function	Description
GL_NEVER	Never passes.
GL_LESS	Passes if the incoming z value is less than the stored z value. This is the default value.
GL_EQUAL	Passes if the incoming z value is equal to the stored z value.
GL_LEQUAL	Passes if the incoming z value is less than or equal to the stored z value.
GL_GREATER	Passes if the incoming z value is greater than the stored z value.
GL_NOTEQUAL	Passes if the incoming z value is not equal to the stored z value.
GL_GEQUAL	Passes if the incoming z value is greater than or equal to the stored z value.
GL_ALWAYS	Always passes.

OpenGL will compare the current pixel's z value with the z value stored in the pixel's depth buffer. If the depth-comparison function returns true, then the pixel is stored in the color buffer. The default depth-comparison function is GL_LESS, which draws a pixel only if its z value is less than the z value in the depth buffer.

Using the Depth Buffer

As we've already discussed, the most common application of the depth buffer is for hidden-surface removal. You can also use it to cut away parts of a scene so you can view the internal operations of an object (for example, an engine or a computer). So how do you actually use the depth buffer?

Well, first we have a simple example that changes the depth-comparison function from GL_LESS to GL_ALWAYS, and vice versa, when the user presses the space bar. This means that when the program starts with the GL_LESS comparison function, you will see the scene as normal, with hidden surfaces not being drawn. When you press the space bar, and the GL_ALWAYS comparison function is set, the scene will be drawn such that the objects are shown in the order they are drawn. So if you had a sphere sitting behind a cube with the GL_ALWAYS depth-comparison function set, then you would need to draw the sphere first and the cube second in order to get proper hidden-surface removal. If you draw the cube first and the sphere second, then the sphere will appear to be in front of the cube. However, with the GL_LESS depth-comparison function set, you don't need to worry about the order in which you draw the objects because OpenGL will automatically handle the hidden-surface removal through the depth function. Let's take a look at the example.

```
////// Includes
#include <windows.h>          // standard Windows app include
#include <gl/gl.h>            // standard OpenGL include
#include <gl/glu.h>           // OpenGL utilities
#include <gl/glaux.h>         // OpenGL auxiliary functions

////// Global Variables
float angle = 0.0f;          // current rotation angle
HDC g_HDC;                    // global device context
bool fullScreen = false;     // true = full screen; false = windowed
bool keyPressed[256];        // holds true for keys that are pressed

bool depthLess = true;       // true: uses GL_LESS; false: uses GL_ALWAYS

// Initialize
// desc: initializes OpenGL
```

```cpp
void Initialize()
{
    glEnable(GL_DEPTH_TEST);        // enable the depth buffer
    glEnable(GL_CULL_FACE);         // cull hidden faces
    glEnable(GL_LIGHTING);          // enable lighting
    glEnable(GL_LIGHT0);            // enable light0
    glEnable(GL_COLOR_MATERIAL);              // set material to colors
    glShadeModel(GL_SMOOTH);              // enable smooth shading
    glClearColor(0.0f, 0.0f, 0.0f, 0.0f); // clear background to black
}


// Render
// desc: handles drawing of scene
void Render()
{
    // clear screen and depth buffer
    glClear(GL_COLOR_BUFFER_BIT | GL_DEPTH_BUFFER_BIT);
    glLoadIdentity();

    // set the proper depth function
    if (depthLess)
        glDepthFunc(GL_LESS);
    else
        glDepthFunc(GL_ALWAYS);


    angle += 0.3;                        // increase rotation angle

    // move scene back 100 units
    glTranslatef(0.0f, 0.0f, -100.0f);

    // first draw the solid cube
    glPushMatrix();
        glRotatef(angle, 1.0f, 0.0f, 0.0f);
        glRotatef(angle*0.5f, 0.0f, 1.0f, 0.0f);
        glRotatef(angle*1.2f, 0.0f, 0.0f, 1.0f);
        glColor3f(0.2f, 0.4f, 0.6f);
        auxSolidCube(30.0f);
    glPopMatrix();
```

```
        // then draw the solid sphere behind the cube
        glPushMatrix();
                glTranslatef(0.0f, 0.0f, -50.0f);
                glRotatef(angle, 0.0f, 1.0f, 0.0f);
                glColor3f(1.0f, 1.0f, 1.0f);
                auxSolidSphere(30.0f);
        glPopMatrix();

        glFlush();
        SwapBuffers(g_HDC);                       // bring back buffer to foreground
}

// SetupPixelFormat()
// desc: function to set the pixel format for the device context
void SetupPixelFormat(HDC hDC)
{
        int nPixelFormat;                        // our pixel format index

        static PIXELFORMATDESCRIPTOR pfd = {
                sizeof(PIXELFORMATDESCRIPTOR),   // size of structure
                1,                               // default version
                PFD_DRAW_TO_WINDOW |             // window drawing support
                PFD_SUPPORT_OPENGL |             // OpenGL support
                PFD_DOUBLEBUFFER,                // double-buffering support
                PFD_TYPE_RGBA,                   // RGBA color mode
                32,                              // 32-bit color mode
                0, 0, 0, 0, 0, 0,                // ignore color bits, non-palletized mode
                0,                               // no alpha buffer
                0,                               // ignore shift bit
                0,                               // no accumulation buffer
                0, 0, 0, 0,                      // ignore accumulation bits
                16,                              // 16-bit z-buffer size
                0,                               // no stencil buffer
                0,                               // no auxiliary buffer
                PFD_MAIN_PLANE,                  // main drawing plane
                0,                               // reserved
                0, 0, 0 };                       // layer masks ignored

        nPixelFormat = ChoosePixelFormat(hDC, &pfd); // choose best matching pixel format
```

```
        SetPixelFormat(hDC, nPixelFormat, &pfd);      // set pixel format to device context
}


// WndProc()
// desc: the Windows Procedure event handler
LRESULT CALLBACK WndProc(HWND hwnd, UINT message, WPARAM wParam, LPARAM lParam)
{
    static HGLRC hRC;            // rendering context
    static HDC hDC;             // device context
    int width, height;          // window width and height

    switch(message)
    {
        case WM_CREATE:         // window is being created
            hDC = GetDC(hwnd);      // get current window's device context
            g_HDC = hDC;
            SetupPixelFormat(hDC); // call our pixel format setup function

            // create rendering context and make it current
            hRC = wglCreateContext(hDC);
            wglMakeCurrent(hDC, hRC);
            break;

        case WM_CLOSE:          // windows is closing

            // deselect rendering context and delete it
            wglMakeCurrent(hDC, NULL);
            wglDeleteContext(hRC);

            // send WM_QUIT to message queue
            PostQuitMessage(0);
            break;

        case WM_SIZE:
            height = HIWORD(lParam);        // retrieve width and height
            width = LOWORD(lParam);

            if (height==0)                  // don't want a divide by zero
            {
                height=1;
            }
```

```
            glViewport(0, 0, width, height); // reset viewport to new dimensions
            glMatrixMode(GL_PROJECTION);      // set projection current matrix
            glLoadIdentity();                 // reset projection matrix

            // calculate aspect ratio of window
            gluPerspective(54.0f,(GLfloat)width/(GLfloat)height,1.0f,1000.0f);
            glMatrixMode(GL_MODELVIEW);       // set modelview matrix
            glLoadIdentity();                 // reset modelview matrix
            break;

        case WM_KEYDOWN:                          // is a key pressed?
            keyPressed[wParam] = true;
            break;

        case WM_KEYUP:
            keyPressed[wParam] = false;
            break;

        default:
            break;
    }
    return (DefWindowProc(hwnd, message, wParam, lParam));
}

// WinMain()
// the main Windows entry point
int WINAPI WinMain(HINSTANCE hInstance, HINSTANCE hPrevInstance, LPSTR lpCmdLine, int
nShowCmd)
{
    WNDCLASSEX windowClass;     // window class
    HWND        hwnd;           // window handle
    MSG         msg;            // message
    bool        done;           // flag saying when our app is complete
    DWORD       dwExStyle;      // window extended style
    DWORD       dwStyle;        // window style
    RECT        windowRect;

    // 800x600x32 mode
    int width = 800;
    int height = 600;
    int bits = 32;
```

```c
fullScreen = FALSE;

windowRect.left=(long)0;              // set left value to 0
windowRect.right=(long)width;         // set right value to requested width
windowRect.top=(long)0;               // set top value to 0
windowRect.bottom=(long)height;       // set bottom value to requested height

// fill out the windows class structure
windowClass.cbSize        = sizeof(WNDCLASSEX);
windowClass.style         = CS_HREDRAW | CS_VREDRAW;
windowClass.lpfnWndProc   = WndProc;
windowClass.cbClsExtra    = 0;
windowClass.cbWndExtra    = 0;
windowClass.hInstance     = hInstance;
windowClass.hIcon         = LoadIcon(NULL, IDI_APPLICATION); // default icon
windowClass.hCursor       = LoadCursor(NULL, IDC_ARROW); // default arrow
windowClass.hbrBackground = NULL; // don't need background
windowClass.lpszMenuName  = NULL; // no menu
windowClass.lpszClassName = "MyClass";
windowClass.hIconSm       = LoadIcon(NULL, IDI_WINLOGO);

// register the windows class
if (!RegisterClassEx(&windowClass))
    return 0;

if (fullScreen) // full screen?
{
    DEVMODE dmScreenSettings;                   // device mode
    memset(&dmScreenSettings,0,sizeof(dmScreenSettings));
    dmScreenSettings.dmSize = sizeof(dmScreenSettings);
    dmScreenSettings.dmPelsWidth = width;       // screen width
    dmScreenSettings.dmPelsHeight = height;     // screen height
    dmScreenSettings.dmBitsPerPel = bits;       // bits per pixel
    dmScreenSettings.dmFields=DM_BITSPERPEL|DM_PELSWIDTH|DM_PELSHEIGHT;

    if (ChangeDisplaySettings(&dmScreenSettings, CDS_FULLSCREEN) !=
                        DISP_CHANGE_SUCCESSFUL)
    {
        // setting display mode failed, switch to windowed
        MessageBox(NULL, "Display mode failed", NULL, MB_OK);
        fullScreen=FALSE;
```

```
        }
    }

    if (fullScreen)                // still full screen?
    {
        dwExStyle=WS_EX_APPWINDOW;
        dwStyle=WS_POPUP;
        ShowCursor(FALSE);
    }
    else                           // windowed mode
    {
        dwExStyle=WS_EX_APPWINDOW | WS_EX_WINDOWEDGE;
        dwStyle=WS_OVERLAPPEDWINDOW;
    }

    AdjustWindowRectEx(&windowRect, dwStyle, FALSE, dwExStyle);

    // class registered, so now create our window
    hwnd = CreateWindowEx(NULL,         // extended style
                      "MyClass",  // class name
                      "Depth Buffer Example 1: Depth Comparison Functions",
                      dwStyle | WS_CLIPCHILDREN |
                      WS_CLIPSIBLINGS,
                      0, 0,       // x,y coordinate
                      windowRect.right - windowRect.left,
                      windowRect.bottom - windowRect.top,   // width, height
                      NULL,       // handle to parent
                      NULL,       // handle to menu
                      hInstance,  // application instance
                      NULL);      // no extra params

    // check if window creation failed (hwnd would equal NULL)
    if (!hwnd)
        return 0;

    ShowWindow(hwnd, SW_SHOW);          // display the window
    UpdateWindow(hwnd);                 // update the window

    done = false;                       // initialize the loop condition variable
    Initialize();                       // initialize OpenGL
```

```
    // main message loop
    while (!done)
    {
        PeekMessage(&msg, hwnd, NULL, NULL, PM_REMOVE);

        if (msg.message == WM_QUIT)  // do we receive a WM_QUIT message?
        {
            done = true;             // if so, time to quit the application
        }
        else
        {
            if (keyPressed[VK_ESCAPE])
                done = true;
            else
            {
                if (keyPressed[VK_SPACE])
                    depthLess = !depthLess;
                Render();

                TranslateMessage(&msg);  // translate and dispatch to event queue
                DispatchMessage(&msg);
            }
        }
    }

    if (fullScreen)
    {
        ChangeDisplaySettings(NULL,0);    // switch back to desktop
        ShowCursor(TRUE);                 // show mouse
    }

    return msg.wParam;
}
```

This demonstrates the cube and sphere example we discussed prior to the code listing. Figure 12.1 shows the example running when GL_LESS is enabled as the depth-comparison function. You see how changing the depth-comparison function to GL_ALWAYS affects the resulting scene in Figure 12.2.

Figure 12.1

The example with GL_LESS enabled.

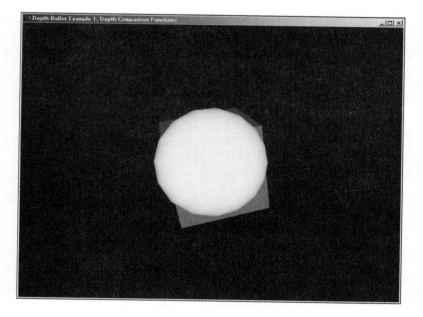

Figure 12.2

The example with GL_ALWAYS enabled.

Another example of using the depth buffer is when looking at a cutout of a scene. For example, if you were rendering an automobile engine on the screen and you wanted to show the internal workings of the engine, you could use the depth buffer to allow you to render the cutout scene. To accomplish this, you draw on what is called a *cutting plane.* The cutting plane is drawn by disabling drawing to the color buffer with the glDrawBuffer() function, drawing the plane itself, and then setting drawing to the back buffer of the color buffer again with the glDrawBuffer() function. Here's a snippet:

```
glDrawBuffer(GL_NONE);              // disable drawing to the color buffer
// DRAW CUTTING PLANE HERE
glDrawBuffer(GL_BACK);
```

The code example that follows doesn't quite use an engine to demonstrate this technique; instead, it uses a solid cube with a sphere inside it. The example starts off with only the cube being seen, but after the user presses the space bar, the cutting plane is enabled and drawn on one side of the cube. When that side of the cube comes into view, the user can see the yellow sphere inside.

```
////// Includes
#include <windows.h>           // standard Windows app include
#include <gl/gl.h>             // standard OpenGL include
#include <gl/glu.h>            // OpenGL utilities
#include <gl/glaux.h>          // OpenGL auxiliary functions

////// Global Variables
float angle = 0.0f;           // current rotation angle
HDC g_HDC;                     // global device context
bool fullScreen = false;       // true = full screen; false = windowed
bool keyPressed[256];          // holds true for keys that are pressed

bool cuttingPlane = true;      // true: cutting plane is enabled

// Initialize
// desc: initializes OpenGL
void Initialize()
{
    glEnable(GL_DEPTH_TEST);       // enable the depth buffer
    glEnable(GL_CULL_FACE);        // cull hidden faces
    glEnable(GL_LIGHTING);         // enable lighting
    glEnable(GL_LIGHT0);           // enable light0
    glEnable(GL_COLOR_MATERIAL);   // set material to colors
```

```
        glShadeModel(GL_SMOOTH);          // enable smooth shading
        glClearColor(0.0f, 0.0f, 0.0f, 0.0f);  // clear background to black
}


// Render
// desc: handles drawing of scene
void Render()
{
        // clear screen and depth buffer
        glClear(GL_COLOR_BUFFER_BIT | GL_DEPTH_BUFFER_BIT);
        glLoadIdentity();

        angle += 0.5;                   // increase rotation angle

        // move scene back 100 units
        glTranslatef(0.0f, 0.0f, -100.0f);

        // first draw the solid sphere inside the cube
        glPushMatrix();
            glRotatef(angle, 0.0f, 1.0f, 0.0f);
            glColor3f(1.0f, 1.0f, 0.0f);
            auxSolidSphere(5.0f);
        glPopMatrix();


        // then draw the solid cube
        glPushMatrix();
            glRotatef(angle, 1.0f, 0.0f, 0.0f);
            glRotatef(angle*0.5f, 0.0f, 1.0f, 0.0f);
            glRotatef(angle*1.2f, 0.0f, 0.0f, 1.0f);

            // draw the cutting plane if cutting is enabled
            // on one side of the cube
            if (cuttingPlane)
            {
                glDrawBuffer(GL_NONE);
                glBegin(GL_QUADS);
                    glVertex3f(-10.0f, -10.0f, 15.1f);
                    glVertex3f(10.0f, -10.0f, 15.1f);
                    glVertex3f(10.0f, 10.0f, 15.1f);
                    glVertex3f(-10.0f, 10.0f, 15.1f);
                glEnd();
```

```
                    glDrawBuffer(GL_BACK);
            }

            glColor3f(0.2f, 0.4f, 0.6f);
            auxSolidCube(30.0f);
        glPopMatrix();

        glFlush();
        SwapBuffers(g_HDC);                    // bring back buffer to foreground
}

void SetupPixelFormat(HDC hDC)
{
        /* ... */
}

LRESULT CALLBACK WndProc(HWND hwnd, UINT message, WPARAM wParam, LPARAM lParam)
{
        /* ... */
}

int WINAPI WinMain(HINSTANCE hInstance, HINSTANCE hPrevInstance, LPSTR lpCmdLine, int
nShowCmd)
{
        /* ... */

        // main message loop
        while (!done)
        {
            PeekMessage(&msg, hwnd, NULL, NULL, PM_REMOVE);

            if (msg.message == WM_QUIT)  // do we receive a WM_QUIT message?
            {
                done = true;                // if so, time to quit the application
            }
            else
            {
                if (keyPressed[VK_ESCAPE])
                    done = true;
                else
                {
```

```
                    if (keyPressed[VK_SPACE])
                        cuttingPlane = !cuttingPlane;
                    Render();

                    TranslateMessage(&msg);  // translate and dispatch to event queue
                    DispatchMessage(&msg);
                }
            }
        }

        if (fullScreen)
        {
            ChangeDisplaySettings(NULL,0);     // switch back to desktop
            ShowCursor(TRUE);                  // show mouse
        }

        return msg.wParam;
}
```

As you can see, first you draw the sphere because it's visible through the cutting plane. Then you draw the cutting plane on one side of the cube before drawing the cube itself. Doing this results in one side of the cube having a hole in it that the user can look through to see the sphere. Figure 12.3 shows the result of the cutting plane on one side of the cube.

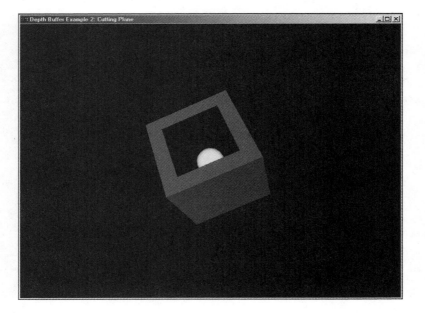

Figure 12.3

The cutting-plane example.

THE STENCIL BUFFER

Like the depth buffer, you can use the *stencil buffer* to block out portions of the screen from view. However, the stencil buffer also gives you more functionality to do things that are otherwise impossible with the depth buffer. An example of an application for the stencil buffer would be a window for a house. You can't see through the wall around the window, but you can see through the window itself and everything within the viewport that the window gives you.

To use the stencil buffer, you first need to set the cStencilBits field for the PIXELFORMATDESCRIPTOR structure when you set up the pixel format, like this:

```
pfd.cStencilBits = 16;
```

This will set up a 16-bit stencil buffer in Windows that you can use with OpenGL. To actually use stencil buffering in OpenGL, you need to enable it with the glEnable() function and the GL_STEN-CIL_TEST parameter:

```
glEnable(GL_STENCIL_TEST);
```

But wait, there's more. Even though you've enabled stencil buffering, you still need to tell OpenGL how to use it. If you don't, the stencil buffer won't affect any rendering you do. You use the functions glStencilFunc() and glStencilOp() to tell OpenGL how to use the stencil buffer. The glStencilFunc() function is defined as

```
void glStencilFunc(GLenum func, GLint ref, GLuint mask)
```

This function takes in the stencil-comparison function, reference value, and stencil mask that you want to use for your stencil buffer. Table 12.7 lists the stencil-comparison functions you can use.

Here's an example of using the glStencilFunc() function to set the stencil-comparison function to always pass, the reference value to 1, and the mask to 1:

```
glStencilFunc(GL_ALWAYS, 1, 1);
```

You also need to specify the stencil operation through the function glStencilOp(), which is defined as

```
void glStencilOp(GLenum fail, GLenum zfail, GLenum zpass);
```

This function specifies the action to take when the stencil test fails (fail), the stencil test passes but the depth test fails (zfail), or both the stencil and depth tests pass (zpass). You can specify any of the values listed in Table 12.8 for each of the three glStencilOp() parameters.

The following line will tell OpenGL to set the value of ref that you defined with the glStencilFunc() function whenever you draw to the stencil buffer:

```
glStencilOp(GL_REPLACE, GL_REPLACE, GL_REPLACE);
```

Table 12.7 Stencil-Comparison Functions

Function	Description
GL_NEVER	Always fails.
GL_LESS	Passes if the reference value is less than the stencil value.
GL_LEQUAL	Passes if the reference value is less than or equal to the stencil value.
GL_GREATER	Passes if the reference value is greater than the stencil value.
GL_GEQUAL	Passes if the reference value is greater than or equal to the stencil value.
GL_EQUAL	Passes if the reference value is equal to the stencil value.
GL_NOTEQUAL	Passes if the reference value is not equal to the stencil value.
GL_ALWAYS	Always passes; the default.

Table 12.8 Stencil Operations

Operation	Description
GL_KEEP	Keeps the current value.
GL_ZERO	Sets the stencil-buffer value to 0.
GL_REPLACE	Sets the stencil-buffer value to ref, as specified by glStencilFunc().
GL_INCR	Increments the current stencil-buffer value.
GL_DECR	Decrements the current stencil-buffer value.
GL_INVERT	Inverts each bit in the stencil-buffer value.

In the example you're going to look at, you use the following code to draw the floor in the example into the stencil buffer:

```
// set up the stencil buffer for drawing
glStencilOp(GL_REPLACE, GL_REPLACE, GL_REPLACE);
glStencilFunc(GL_ALWAYS, 1, 1);

// draw the floor into the stencil buffer
DrawFloor();
```

You can't see the floor, but you've created a sort of hole in the stencil buffer that you can now use to clip objects not drawn in the hole. That's the whole purpose of the stencil buffer! Now let's take a look at the full example.

A Stencil-Buffer Example

The example you're going to look at now shows how you can create reflection in your scene and clip the reflection to the edge of the reflecting object, which is, in this case, a floor. Figure 12.4 shows how the example looks while running.

Figure 12.4

A screenshot of the stencil-buffer example.

At the start of each frame, the first thing you do is turn off depth testing and color modification. You then enable stencil testing and draw the floor into the stencil buffer. After re-enabling depth testing and color modification, you set up the stencil buffer so you can only render where the stencil buffer is equal to 1, which is your reference value. When you set up the stencil buffer this way, you are telling OpenGL not to draw anything that lies outside of the area defined by the ones in the stencil buffer. Because you just rendered the floor into the stencil buffer, hence setting all of the floor's stencil buffer pixels to 1, OpenGL will not draw anything that lies outside the floor's area. This is a perfect time to draw the reflection, because you don't want the reflection to show outside the floor's area. So that's what you do: You perform scaling to invert the coordinate system and draw the torus underneath the floor.

Now that you have the reflection drawn (the important part), you can disable stencil buffering and render the parts of your scene that don't require clipping by the stencil buffer. First you draw the floor with transparency enabled, and next you draw the real torus.

Now that you know what's happening, let's look at the code:

```
////// Defines
#define BITMAP_ID 0x4D42          // the universal bitmap ID
#define PI 3.14195


////// Includes
#include <windows.h>                   // standard Windows app include
#include <stdio.h>
#include <stdlib.h>
#include <math.h>
#include <gl/gl.h>                 // standard OpenGL include
#include <gl/glu.h>                // OpenGL utilities
#include <gl/glaux.h>              // OpenGL auxiliary library


////// Types
typedef struct
{
    int width;                     // width of texture
    int height;                    // height of texture
    unsigned int texID;            // the texture object id of this texture
    unsigned char *data;           // the texture data
} texture_t;


////// Global Variables
HDC g_HDC;                         // global device context
```

```cpp
bool fullScreen = false;              // true = full screen; false = windowed
bool keyPressed[256];                 // holds true for keys that are pressed

float objectAngle = 0.0f;             // object rotation angle
float angle = 0.0f;                   // camera angle
float radians = 0.0f;                 // camera angle in radians

////// Mouse/Camera Variables
int mouseX, mouseY;                   // mouse coordinates
float cameraX, cameraY, cameraZ;      // camera coordinates
float lookX, lookY, lookZ;            // camera look-at coordinates

////// Texture Information
texture_t *envTex;                    // environment map
texture_t *floorTex;                    // floor texture

// vertices for the floor
float floorData[4][3] = { { -5.0, 0.0, 5.0 }, { 5.0, 0.0, 5.0 },
                          { 5.0, 0.0, -5.0 }, { -5.0, 0.0, -5.0 } };

/* The LoadBitmapFile() function is not listed for space purposes. */
/* The LoadTextureFile() function is not listed for space purposes. */


bool LoadAllTextures()
{
    // load the environment map
    envTex = LoadTextureFile("waterenv.bmp");
    if (envTex == NULL)
        return false;

    // load the floor texture
    floorTex = LoadTextureFile("chess.bmp");
    if (floorTex == NULL)
        return false;

    // set up the torus's environment map
    glBindTexture(GL_TEXTURE_2D, envTex->texID);
    glTexParameteri(GL_TEXTURE_2D, GL_TEXTURE_MAG_FILTER, GL_LINEAR);
    glTexParameteri(GL_TEXTURE_2D, GL_TEXTURE_MIN_FILTER, GL_LINEAR);
    glTexParameteri(GL_TEXTURE_2D, GL_TEXTURE_WRAP_S, GL_REPEAT);
```

```
        glTexParameteri(GL_TEXTURE_2D, GL_TEXTURE_WRAP_T, GL_REPEAT);
        glTexEnvi(GL_TEXTURE_ENV, GL_TEXTURE_ENV_MODE, GL_REPLACE);
        gluBuild2DMipmaps(GL_TEXTURE_2D, GL_RGB, envTex->width, envTex->height, GL_RGB,
                          GL_UNSIGNED_BYTE, envTex->data);

        // set up the floor texture
        glBindTexture(GL_TEXTURE_2D, floorTex->texID);
        glTexParameteri(GL_TEXTURE_2D, GL_TEXTURE_MAG_FILTER, GL_LINEAR);
        glTexParameteri(GL_TEXTURE_2D, GL_TEXTURE_MIN_FILTER, GL_LINEAR);
        glTexParameteri(GL_TEXTURE_2D, GL_TEXTURE_WRAP_S, GL_REPEAT);
        glTexParameteri(GL_TEXTURE_2D, GL_TEXTURE_WRAP_T, GL_REPEAT);
        glTexEnvi(GL_TEXTURE_ENV, GL_TEXTURE_ENV_MODE, GL_MODULATE);
        gluBuild2DMipmaps(GL_TEXTURE_2D, GL_RGB, floorTex->width, floorTex->height,
                          GL_RGB, GL_UNSIGNED_BYTE, floorTex->data);

        return true;
}

void CleanUp()
{
    free(envTex);
    free(floorTex);
}

void Initialize()
{
        glClearColor(0.0f, 0.0f, 0.0f, 0.0f);      // clear to black
        glShadeModel(GL_SMOOTH);                    // use smooth shading
        glEnable(GL_CULL_FACE);                     // do not calculate inside of polys
        glFrontFace(GL_CCW);                        // counterclockwise polygons are out
        glEnable(GL_TEXTURE_2D);                    // enable 2D texturing

        LoadAllTextures();
}

// DrawFloor()
// desc: draws the textured floor
void DrawFloor()
{
        glBindTexture(GL_TEXTURE_2D, floorTex->texID);
        glBegin(GL_QUADS);
```

```
            glTexCoord2f(0.0, 0.0); glVertex3fv(floorData[0]);
            glTexCoord2f(0.0, 4.0); glVertex3fv(floorData[1]);
            glTexCoord2f(4.0, 4.0); glVertex3fv(floorData[2]);
            glTexCoord2f(4.0, 0.0); glVertex3fv(floorData[3]);
        glEnd();
}


// DrawTorus()
// desc: draws the environment-mapped torus
void DrawTorus()
{
    glPushMatrix();
        // set up environment mapping
        glTexGenf(GL_S, GL_TEXTURE_GEN_MODE, GL_SPHERE_MAP);
        glTexGenf(GL_T, GL_TEXTURE_GEN_MODE, GL_SPHERE_MAP);
        glEnable(GL_TEXTURE_GEN_S);
        glEnable(GL_TEXTURE_GEN_T);

        // bind the environment texture
        glBindTexture(GL_TEXTURE_2D, envTex->texID);

        // translate and rotate
        glTranslatef(0.0f, 4.0f, 0.0f);
        glRotatef(objectAngle, 1.0f, 1.0f, 0.0f);
        glRotatef(objectAngle, 0.0f, 1.0f, 0.0f);
        glRotatef(objectAngle, 0.0f, 0.0f, 1.0f);

        // draw torus
        auxSolidTorus(1.0f, 2.0f);

        // disable texture-coordinate generation
        glDisable(GL_TEXTURE_GEN_T);
        glDisable(GL_TEXTURE_GEN_S);
    glPopMatrix();
}


// Render
// desc: handles drawing of scene
void Render()
{
```

```
objectAngle += 0.2f;                              // increase object-rotation angle
radians =  float(PI*(angle-90.0f)/180.0f);

// calculate the camera's position
cameraX = lookX + sin(radians)*mouseY;
cameraZ = lookZ + cos(radians)*mouseY;
cameraY = lookY + mouseY / 2.0f;

// point camera at (0,2,0)
lookX = 0.0f;
lookY = 2.0f;
lookZ = 0.0f;

// clear color, depth, and stencil buffer
glClear(GL_COLOR_BUFFER_BIT | GL_DEPTH_BUFFER_BIT | GL_STENCIL_BUFFER_BIT);
glLoadIdentity();

// set the camera position
gluLookAt(cameraX, cameraY, cameraZ, lookX, lookY, lookZ, 0.0, 1.0, 0.0);

// disable depth testing
glDisable(GL_DEPTH_TEST);

// disable modification of all color components
glColorMask(GL_FALSE, GL_FALSE, GL_FALSE, GL_FALSE);

// enable stencil testing
glEnable(GL_STENCIL_TEST);

// set up the stencil buffer for a function-reference value
glStencilOp(GL_REPLACE, GL_REPLACE, GL_REPLACE);
glStencilFunc(GL_ALWAYS, 1, 1);

// draw the floor; this will set the floor pixels in the stencil buffer
// to 1, since we defined 1 as the mask value with the glStencilFunc() command
DrawFloor();

// enable modification of all color components
glColorMask(GL_TRUE, GL_TRUE, GL_TRUE, GL_TRUE);
```

```
// enable depth testing
glEnable(GL_DEPTH_TEST);

// make it so we can only render where the stencil buffer is equal to 1
glStencilFunc(GL_EQUAL, 1, 1);
glStencilOp(GL_KEEP, GL_KEEP, GL_KEEP);

// draw "reflection"
glPushMatrix();

    // reflect (invert) the torus
    glScalef(1.0, -1.0, 1.0);

    // eliminate front of polygons from drawing
    glCullFace(GL_FRONT);

    // draw the reflected torus
    DrawTorus();

    // re-enable back-face culling
    glCullFace(GL_BACK);
glPopMatrix();

// disable stencil testing
glDisable(GL_STENCIL_TEST);

// draw floor with 40% blending so we can see the "reflection"
glEnable(GL_BLEND);
glBlendFunc(GL_SRC_ALPHA, GL_ONE_MINUS_SRC_ALPHA);
glColor4f(1.0f, 1.0f, 1.0f, 0.4f);
DrawFloor();
glDisable(GL_BLEND);

// draw the "real" torus
DrawTorus();

glFlush();
SwapBuffers(g_HDC);             // bring back buffer to foreground
}
```

```c
// SetupPixelFormat()
// function to set the pixel format for the device context
void SetupPixelFormat(HDC hDC)
{
    int nPixelFormat;                           // our pixel format index

    static PIXELFORMATDESCRIPTOR pfd = {
        sizeof(PIXELFORMATDESCRIPTOR),          // size of structure
        1,                                      // default version
        PFD_DRAW_TO_WINDOW |                    // window-drawing support
        PFD_SUPPORT_OPENGL |                    // OpenGL support
        PFD_DOUBLEBUFFER,                       // double-buffering support
        PFD_TYPE_RGBA,                          // RGBA color mode
        32,                                     // 32-bit color mode
        0, 0, 0, 0, 0, 0,                       // ignore color bits
        0,                                      // no alpha buffer
        0,                                      // ignore shift bit
        0,                                      // no accumulation buffer
        0, 0, 0, 0,                             // ignore accumulation bits
        16,                                     // 16-bit z-buffer size
        16,                                     // 16-bit stencil buffer
        0,                                      // no auxiliary buffer
        PFD_MAIN_PLANE,                         // main drawing plane
        0,                                      // reserved
        0, 0, 0 };                              // layer masks ignored

    // choose best-matching pixel format
    nPixelFormat = ChoosePixelFormat(hDC, &pfd);

    // set pixel format to device context
    SetPixelFormat(hDC, nPixelFormat, &pfd);
}

/* The WndProc() function is not listed for space purposes */
/* The WinMain() function is not listed for space purposes */
```

THE ACCUMULATION BUFFER

Let's get this out in the open: At the time of this writing, the accumulation buffer was SLOW! Until hardware supports it, using the accumulation buffer in games is not a very good idea. As such, we're not going to look at this buffer in detail, but we will take a quick look at its basic functionality.

The idea of the accumulation buffer is that you draw multiple images into the color buffer, one at a time, and then *accumulate* each image into the accumulation buffer. After you've accumulated all the images, you put them back onto the color buffer to be displayed on the screen. You can create some cool effects with this buffer, including motion blur, depth-of-field effects, scene antialiasing, and soft shadows.

OpenGL provides a single function to work on the accumulation buffer:

```
void glAccum(GLenum op, GLfloat value);
```

The op parameter specifies the operation you're going to do, and the value parameter specifies a number you're going to use for that operation. Table 12.9 shows the operations you can use.

To use the accumulation buffer for motion blur, you accumulate several images representing the trail of the blur by using the glAccum() function like this:

```
glAccum(GL_ACCUM, 0.1);
```

Table 12.9 Accumulation Buffer Operations

Operation	Description
GL_ACCUM	Obtains RGBA values from the current buffer selected for reading.
GL_LOAD	Same as GL_ACCUM, except new values replace those already in the accumulation buffer instead of being added to them.
GL_ADD	Add the value of each pixel in the accumulation buffer to value.
GL_MULT	Multiply the value of each pixel in the accumulation buffer by value.
GL_RETURN	Multiplies pixel values in the accumulation buffer by value and sends the results in the color buffer.

For motion blur, the `value` parameter is treated as a decay factor between images. Each time this line is called, the object's image will be fainter than the previous image. After you're finished accumulating your images into the accumulation buffer, you call the `glAccum()` function again with the `GL_RETURN` operation:

```
glAccum(GL_RETURN, 1.0);
```

The following code shows how you can combine these two operations to generate a single rendering frame using the accumulation buffer to create motion blur:

```
int idx;

// first draw the object in full
DrawObject();

// now we set up the accumulation buffer with 70% of the rendered object
glAccum(GL_LOAD, 0.7);

// next we start a loop to draw four images for the motion-blur "trail"
for (idx = 1; idx < 5; idx++)
{
    // rotate object around y axis and draw it
    glRotatef(objectAngle - (float)idx, 0.0, 1.0, 0.0);
    DrawObject();

    // now we accumulate 20% of the drawn object
    glAccum(GL_ACCUM, 0.2);
}

// we're all done with the accumulation buffer, now put in on the color buffer
glAccum(GL_RETURN, 1.0);
```

And that concludes our brief introduction to the accumulation buffer! Keep in mind that although the accumulation buffer is in fact very useful to graphics developers, at this point in time it is not very useful for game developers. The speed just isn't good enough to warrant use in games. Regardless, graphics hardware is still improving every six months, so expect hardware support for the accumulation buffer soon!

SUMMARY

The screen is divided into a rectangular array of pixels, or a *buffer*, where color data is stored for each pixel. Essentially, whenever you store data for pixels, the buffer is the set of all those pixels that are storing the same data. In OpenGL, the color buffer stores RGBA and color-index data for each pixel on the screen or window. A *frame buffer* is composed of all the buffers in a system.

You use the PIXELFORMATDESCRIPTOR structure to set up the pixel format for OpenGL under Microsoft Windows.

OpenGL provides you with four functions, one for each buffer type, that will allow you to set the current clearing value for that buffer: glClearColor(), glClearDepth(), glClearStencil(), and glClearAccum().

Double-buffered systems are often used for animation through front and back color buffers, with the off-screen back buffer being where you render your scene. After the scene is finished rendering, you swap the back buffer with the front buffer to get a smooth animation effect. Using the back buffer eliminates the flickering effect you get when you try to animate a scene by drawing only on the front buffer. Double-buffered systems are limited to the color buffer, which means that you are not provided with a back buffer for the depth, accumulation, or stencil buffers.

Stereo buffering lets you use the left- and right-eye buffers to create a true three-dimensional image.

You typically use the *depth buffer* to perform hidden-surface removal on the objects in a scene. The values stored by the depth buffer for each pixel represent the distance between the pixel and the viewpoint. So when you draw one object in front of another in relation to the camera, the depth buffer is manipulated depending on the depth-comparison function you use.

Like the depth buffer, you can use the *stencil buffer* to block out portions of the screen from view. However, the stencil buffer also gives you more functionality to do things that are otherwise impossible with the depth buffer. An example of an application for the stencil buffer would be a window for a house. You can't see through the wall around the window, but you can see through the window itself and everything within the viewport that the window gives you.

The idea of the accumulation buffer is that you draw multiple images into the color buffer, one at a time, and then *accumulate* each image into the accumulation buffer. After you've accumulated all the images, you put them back onto the color buffer to be displayed on the screen. You can create some cool effects with this buffer, including motion blur, depth-of-field effects, scene antialiasing, and soft shadows.

CHAPTER 13

OpenGL
Quadrics

ack in Chapter 4, "OpenGL States and Primitives," we covered primitive types such as points and triangles. Although these are the building blocks you'll use to create most of the objects in your games, there are times when it would be nice to have built-in support for more advanced shapes, such as spheres or cylinders. You could, of course, write your own library to do this, and many people do exactly that. But rather than reinventing the wheel, you can use the support for more advanced shapes that is already included as part of the OpenGL Utility Library.

GLU contains a set of functions and states allowing you to use *quadrics*, which enable you to quickly generate disks, cylinders, cones, and spheres. You'll look at each of these in turn, but first, you need to understand how to use quadrics in general.

In this chapter, you'll learn the following:

- What quadrics are and how to create them
- How to modify the properties of a quadric to control how it is displayed
- Which shapes are available through quadrics

THE BASICS OF OPENGL QUADRICS

To properly understand quadrics, it's helpful to realize that the term *quadric* does not refer to the shape itself, but rather to an object containing state information about how the shape should be drawn. This is important because before you can create a shape using quadrics, you have to create a quadric object. Let's look at how to do that first, and then we can discuss how to use it in greater detail.

A quadric object is created with a call to gluNewQuadric():

```
GLUquadricObj *gluNewQuadric();
```

If a new quadric object is available, this will return a pointer to it. Otherwise, it returns NULL.

After you have a valid quadric object, you can use it to draw any number of shapes, and the same object can be used to draw disks, cylinders, cones, and spheres. So, you may wonder, if a single quadric can be used to draw any shape and as many of each shape as you want, why would you want to create more than one? And for that matter, if you only need one, couldn't OpenGL just manage that behind the scenes, and not require you to create a quadric object?

Well, in truth, you could get away with using a single quadric object, and in some applications, that's perfectly acceptable. But remember that quadric objects are used to store state information about the shapes you want to draw. If you use a single quadric, all shapes drawn with it must use the same states, or else you need to change states between shapes. Because state changes aren't free, unless you really do want all your shapes to share the same state variables, it's probably going to be more efficient to create multiple quadrics.

So, the next obvious question is what are the states controlled by quadrics, and how do you change them? Well, there are four states, each with a function to control it:

- Draw style
- Normals
- Orientation
- Texture coordinates

Draw Style

The draw-style state specifies whether the polygons in the object are drawn filled, as lines, as points, or as a silhouette, which is like the lines mode except that lines between coplanar polygons are not drawn. The draw style is set with

```
void gluQuadricDrawStyle(GLUquadricObj *quadObj, GLenum style);
```

quadObj is a pointer to the quadric object you want to change, and style can be GLU_FILL, GLU_LINE, GLU_POINT, or GLU_SILHOUETTE. GLU_FILL is the default state.

Normal

The normal state controls how the surface normals for the shapes created by this object are generated. You can choose to have no normals generated, or you can choose to have a normal generated for each polygon (thus producing flat shading) or for each vertex (producing smooth shading, which is the default). Essentially, setting the way the normal is generated controls how the shape will be shaded. The normal mode is selected with

```
void gluQuadricNormals(GLUquadricObj *quadObj, GLenum normalMode);
```

quadObj is your quadric object, and normal mode can be GLU_NONE, GLU_FLAT, or GLU_SMOOTH.

Orientation

The exact meaning of this somewhat depends on the type of shape being drawn, but it controls whether the normals that are generated for the object are pointing inward or outward. This is modified via

```
void gluQuadricOrientation(GLUquadricObj *quadObj, GLenum orientation);
```

`orientation` can be either `GLU_OUTSIDE`, which is the default, or `GLU_INSIDE`. The meaning of inside and outside should be fairly obvious for a cone, cylinder, or sphere, but is somewhat ambiguous for a disk. For disks, outside is defined as being the side of the disk facing the positive z axis.

Texture Coordinates

The texture-coordinates state specifies whether texture coordinates should be generated for the shape. The exact method of texture-coordinate generation depends on the type of shape that is drawn, but this state is turned on or off with

```
void gluQuadricTexture(GLUquadricObj *quadObj, GLboolean useTextureCoords);
```

If `useTextureCoords` is `GL_TRUE`, texture coordinates are generated; if it is `GL_FALSE`, they are not. Texture coordinates are turned off by default.

Cleaning Up

The last thing we need to cover is how to clean up when you're finished. Because quadric objects take up memory, you need to free them when you're finished with them. To do this, you simply call `gluDeleteQuadric()`:

```
void gluDeleteQuadric (GLUquadricObj *quadObj);
```

This destroys the object pointed to by `quadObj` and frees memory associated with it.

Now that you know how to create and destroy quadric objects and how to control the states associated with them, you can turn your attention to the reason you want to use them in the first place: drawing shapes.

DISKS

A *disk*, at least as defined by the GLU quadric system, is a flat circle, possibly with a hole in the middle of it, as shown in Figure 13.1. It is drawn around the origin on the z = 0 plane, but of course, you can rotate and translate it to be wherever you want.

To create a disk, use the following call:

```
void gluDisk(GLUquadricObj *quadObj,
             GLdouble innerRadius,
             GLdouble outerRadius,
             GLint slices,
             GLint loops);
```

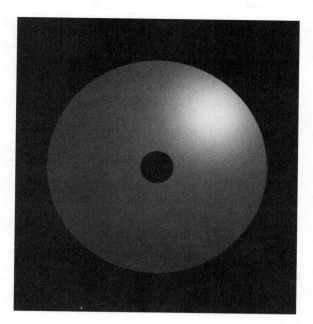

Figure 13.1

A quadric disk.

quadObj is a pointer to a quadric object you have created previously. outerRadius should be fairly self-explanatory; it's the radius of the outside of the circle, or disk. If innerRadius is 0, then the disk is solid; if it is greater than 0, then there is a hole in the center of it. slices and loops are a little less intuitive. They both control how many polygons are drawn to create the disk. slices is the number of subdivisions around the z axis, and loops is the number of rings into which the disk is divided. The higher the values of these two parameters, the more polygons are used to approximate the curved surface, and thus the better it looks. Of course, draw too many and it'll take too long to render, so you need to find a balance between quality and speed. In general, slices needs to be at least 20 for the disc to look round. loops can be as little as 2 without much of a quality sacrifice, unless you want a specular lighting effect to show up.

If texture coordinates are enabled, they are generated linearly around the circle, as shown in Figure 13.2.

In addition to normal disks, GLU supports partial disks, or arcs. These are a slice of a disk you might create with gluDisk(), and they are created using gluPartialDisk():

```
void gluPartialDisk(GLUquadricObj *quadObj,
            GLdouble innerRadius,
            GLdouble outerRadius,
            GLint slices,
            GLint loops,
            GLdouble startAngle,
            GLdouble sweepAngle);
```

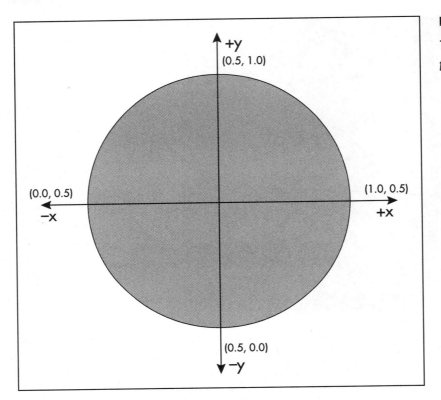

Figure 13.2

*Texture coordinates
for quadric disks.*

The first five parameters here are the same as with gluDisk(). startAngle is the angle at which the partial disk begins, with 0 degrees being along the positive y axis and rotating clockwise from there. sweepAngle is how many degrees the arc extends from startAngle—that is, the arc ends at startAngle + sweepAngle. Thus, with a startAngle of 90 and sweepAngle of 90, an arc would be drawn beginning along the positive x axis and rotating clockwise to the negative z axis.

With regard to orientation and texture coordinate generation, partial disks behave exactly as disks do.

CYLINDERS

Cylinders and cones are drawn with the same function (you'll see how to differentiate them in a moment). For convenience, we'll refer to them collectively as cylinders, understanding that cones are a special type of cylinder. Some examples are shown in Figure 13.3. Cylinders are drawn oriented along the z axis, with the bottom at z = 0, facing the negative z axis, and the top at z = height, facing the positive z axis. Again, you can translate and rotate the cylinder to your heart's content to put it where you want it.

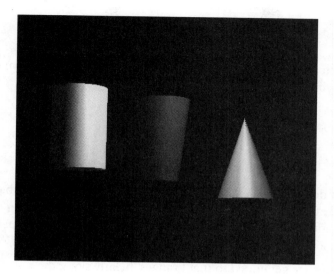

Figure 13.3

Quadric cylinders.

When using cylinders, keep in mind that only the sides are drawn; the top and bottom are not. If you want a top and/or bottom on your cylinder, you'll have to draw them separately using disks (be sure to use the same number of slices so they line up correctly).

Cylinders are created with the `gluCylinder()` function as follows:

```
void gluCylinder(GLUquadricObj *quadObj,
                 GLdouble baseRadius,
                 GLdouble topRadius,
                 GLdouble height,
                 GLint slices,
                 GLint stacks);
```

`quadObj` is, of course, your quadric object. `baseRadius` is the radius of the cylinder at its bottom (that is, z = 0), and `topRadius` is the radius of the cylinder at its top (z = `height`). `height` should thus be fairly obvious. `slices` and `stacks` control how many polygons make up the cylinder. `slices` is how many divisions are made around the z axis, and, as with disks, should be at least 20; `stacks` is how many divisions are made along the z axis, which can be as few as 2 to 4, though higher numbers will show specular highlights better.

Notice that the top and bottom radius don't have to be the same, and so you can create tapered cylinders; if the radius of either is set to 0, you get a cone. Pretty slick.

If texture coordinates are enabled, they are generated linearly with the cylinder's height for the t coordinate, with t ranging from 0.0 at z = 0 and 1.0 at z = height. The s coordinate ranges from 0.0 at the positive y axis, to 0.25 at the positive x axis, to 0.5 at the negative y axis, to 0.75 at the negative y axis, and finally wraps back around to 1.0 at the positive y axis.

SPHERES

Finally, we have spheres, which are probably the easiest to understand. They are drawn centered symmetrically around the origin. To draw a sphere, you use `gluSphere()`:

```
void gluSphere(GLUquadricObj *quadObj,
               GLdouble radius,
               GLint slices,
               GLint stacks);
```

The meaning of `radius` really doesn't need explanation, and by now, you should be able to guess at the meaning of `slices` and `stacks`. They define subdivisions both around and along the z axis, similar to longitude and latitude (respectively). Because both affect how round the surface actually looks, they should both be set to 20 or more.

Texture coordinates for spheres are generated so that t ranges linearly along the z axis from 0.0 at `-radius` to 1.0 at `radius`. s ranges just as it does with cylinders: from 0.0 at the positive y axis, to 0.25 at the positive x axis, to 0.5 at the negative y axis, to 0.75 at the negative y axis, and back around to 1.0 at the positive y axis.

EXAMPLE: A QUADRIC FLY-THROUGH WORLD

It's time to see some quadrics in action. For this example, shown in Figure 13.4, we've created a 3D world filled with a variety of quadric shapes. Each of the drawing modes and normal (shading) modes is used, as well as texturing for some objects, so you can see the effects of all of these. You can move through the world using the up- and down-arrow keys to move forward and backward, and the left- and right-arrow keys to turn. The source and executable can be found on the CD-ROM in the directory for this chapter. The relevant code is presented here.

Before you can use quadrics, you need to create them. This is done in `InitializeScene()`:

```
GLUquadricObj *g_normalObject     = NULL;
GLUquadricObj *g_wireframeObject  = NULL;
GLUquadricObj *g_texturedObject   = NULL;
GLUquadricObj *g_flatshadedObject = NULL;

...


BOOL InitializeScene()
{
   ...
```

Figure 13.4

A world made of quadric objects.

```
  // create a normal quadric (uses default settings)
  g_normalObject = gluNewQuadric();

  // create an object to use with the wire-frame draw style
  g_wireframeObject = gluNewQuadric();
  gluQuadricDrawStyle(g_wireframeObject, GLU_LINE);

  // create an object that generates texture coordinates
  g_texturedObject = gluNewQuadric();
  gluQuadricTexture(g_texturedObject, GL_TRUE);

  // create an object that uses flat shading
  g_flatshadedObject = gluNewQuadric();
  gluQuadricNormals(g_flatshadedObject, GLU_FLAT);
  ...
}
```

This code creates the four quadric objects you'll be using with gluNewQuadric(). It leaves g_normalObject with the default settings; it uses gluQuadricDrawStyle() to set g_wireframeObject to use the line drawing style; it uses gluQuadricTexture() to let g_texturedObject know it needs to generate texture coordinates; and finally, it sets g_flatshadedObject to only generate polygon normals with gluQuadricNormals(), resulting in those objects being rendered with flat shading.

In DisplayScene(), several routines are drawn to create quadrics with each of these objects. Because they are all similar, we'll just look at one here:

```
GLvoid DrawWireframeObjects(GLfloat rotation)
{
  // make sure the random color values we get are the same every time
  srand(300);

  // save the existing color properties
  glPushAttrib(GL_CURRENT_BIT);

  // enable blending to get antialiased lines.
  glEnable(GL_BLEND);

  // a couple of spheres that chase each other around
  glPushMatrix();
    glMateriali(GL_FRONT_AND_BACK, GL_SHININESS, rand() % 128);
    glColor3f(FRAND, FRAND, FRAND);
    glTranslatef(-20.0, 2.0, -20.0);
    glRotatef(rotation * 2.0f, 1.0, 0.0, 0.0);
    glRotatef(rotation * 2.0f, 0.0, 1.0, 0.0);
    glRotatef(rotation * 2.0f, 0.0, 0.0, 1.0);
    glTranslatef(-0.4, 0.0, 0.0);
    gluSphere(g_wireframeObject, 0.3, 16, 10);
  glPopMatrix();

  glPushMatrix();
    glMateriali(GL_FRONT_AND_BACK, GL_SHININESS, rand() % 128);
    glColor3f(FRAND, FRAND, FRAND);
    glTranslatef(-20.0, 2.0, -20.0);
    glRotatef(-rotation * 2.0f, 1.0, 0.0, 0.0);
    glRotatef(-rotation * 2.0f, 0.0, 1.0, 0.0);
    glRotatef(-rotation * 2.0f, 0.0, 0.0, 1.0);
    glTranslatef(0.4, 0.0, 0.0);
    gluSphere(g_wireframeObject, 0.3, 16, 10);
  glPopMatrix();

  // an inverted cone
  glPushMatrix();
    glMateriali(GL_FRONT_AND_BACK, GL_SHININESS, rand() % 128);
    glColor3f(FRAND, FRAND, FRAND);
```

```
   glTranslatef(-150.0, 0.5, 0.0);
   glRotatef(-90, 1.0, 0.0, 0.0);
   gluCylinder(g_wireframeObject, 0.0, 0.5, 3.0, 32, 4);
 glPopMatrix();

 // a filled disk
 glPushMatrix();
   glMateriali(GL_FRONT_AND_BACK, GL_SHININESS, rand() % 128);
   glColor3f(FRAND, FRAND, FRAND);
   glTranslatef(-40.0, 0.5, 20.0);
   glRotatef(45.0, 1.0, 0.0, 0.0);
   gluDisk(g_wireframeObject, 0.0, 0.5, 32, 4);
 glPopMatrix();

 glDisable(GL_BLEND);

 // restore previous attributes
 glPopAttrib();
} // DrawWireframeObjects()
```

Here, the attributes of the quadric objects have already been set, so you just set the material properties, rotate to the orientation you want, translate to where you want the shape to appear, and render the objects using gluDisk(), gluCylinder(), and gluSphere().

Finally, when the program exits, you need to clean up your quadric objects:

```
BOOL Cleanup()
{
  // delete every valid quadric object
  if (g_normalObject)
    gluDeleteQuadric(g_normalObject);
  if (g_wireframeObject)
    gluDeleteQuadric(g_wireframeObject);
  if (g_texturedObject)
    gluDeleteQuadric(g_texturedObject);
  if (g_flatshadedObject)
    gluDeleteQuadric(g_flatshadedObject);

  return TRUE;
} // end Cleanup()
```

As long as the objects are actually valid (not NULL) you can free them safely with gluDeleteQuadric().

SUMMARY

You've now learned how to create quadric objects, how to set up the states associated with them, and how to delete them when you don't need them any more. More importantly, you know how to use them to quickly and easily add more complex shapes to your world.

The shapes provided by the OpenGL Utility Library are useful, but are not all inclusive by any means. However, there are other libraries out there providing additional shapes that you may find useful. GLUT, for example, includes routines to draw a cube, a torus, and even a teapot. If you find that you need additional shapes, don't hesitate to check out GLUT and other support libraries.

CHAPTER 14

CURVES AND SURFACES

Throughout your journey, you've been creating scenes using points, lines, and polygons. These entities are very useful and simple to use, but they do have their limitations. For instance, creating a smooth curved surface is virtually impossible with polygons. You can only approximate a smooth curved surface by using many small polygons, but even then the surface is not truly a smooth curve. Now it's time for you to shift gears and create some scenes using OpenGL's support for curves and surfaces through control points, evaluators, and NURBS.

In this chapter you'll learn about the following:

- Curve and surface basics
- Evaluators
- Texturing surfaces

CURVE AND SURFACE REPRESENTATION

What exactly is a curve? For that matter, what exactly is a surface? Well, a basic definition of a *curve* is a type of line that moves around, as you move from one point to another, in 3D space. Like a line, a curve has a single starting point, length, and endpoint. When we say *surface*, we're talking about an entity with a width and length that is often composed of curves.

When we talked about points, lines, and polygons, we could always show how to represent these entities mathematically. You can, of course, do this with curves and surfaces. However, instead of using the point-slope equation of a line

```
y = m*x + b
```

you use what are called *parametric equations*. But before we dive into parametric equations, let's look at the basic algebra equation in more depth.

Back in algebra class, you would take the equation of a parabola, such as $f(x) = x^2$, and plot the possible x and y values within a certain range to get the graph of the function, as shown in Figure 14.1. Basically this equation says that a function of x equals x^2. So when x equals 2, the function of x (sometimes referred to as y) equals 4. When x equals –5, y equals 25, and so on. You also learned in algebra that when a vertical line is drawn through a graph, that vertical line couldn't touch the graph at more than one place. If this were to occur, then the graph was not a function.

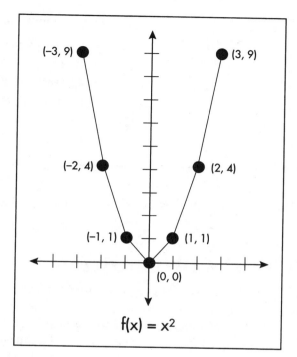

Figure 14.1

The graph of the function f(x) = x².

Parametric Equations

With that in mind, what are parametric equations? Instead of expressing y as some function of x (or vice versa), parametric equations express both x and y together in terms of some other variable. For instance, physics uses parametric equations to define x and y coordinates on a 2D plane according to some function of time in seconds. In 3D graphics, you can use parametric equations to keep track of a particle in 3D space according to a function of virtual time, which you keep track of in your application. You would just define the x, y, and z coordinates of the particle using functions that calculate the position of the particle based on the current time. An example of a parametric equation could be

```
Q(t) = { x(t), y(t) }
```

Knowing the definition of a curve and surface, you can easily see how you can use parametric equations to draw them. For example, with a curve you start at one endpoint, which has 2D coordinates of its own, and move along some parameter (for example, time in physics) until you reach the other endpoint of the curve, which again has its own set of 2D coordinates. We'll call the parameter that you move along s; its domain equals the range of values from one endpoint of the curve to the other endpoint. When we look at surfaces, we'll be using two parametric parameters, s and t, which describe the range of values in the two directions that the surface extends, but

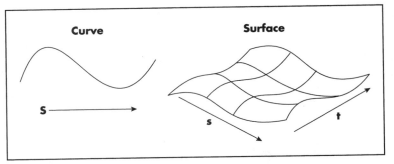

do not represent the actual coordinates. Figure 14.2 illustrates how s and t are used when defining curves and surfaces.

Control Points and Continuity

Control points are used to define the shape of a curve. They can be viewed as magnets that attract the curve toward the control point's position. The first and last control points that you define represent the two endpoints of the curve. All the other control points are used to move and bend the curve. Figure 14.3 shows three curves with a different number of control points for each curve. Notice how each time you add a control point, the curve reacts as though it is attracted to the point.

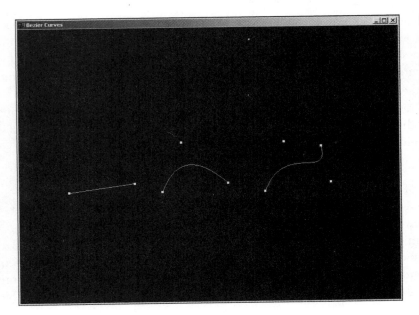

Figure 14.3

The control points of a curve act as mag-nets to move and bend the curve.

The term *continuity* describes how two curves should transition when they are connected by a common control point representing an endpoint for each curve. For instance, if you have two curves and combine an endpoint from each curve into a single control point, then the continuity would define how smoothly the transition should be between the two curves. There are four possible categories of continuity (see Figure 14.4):

- **None.** The two curves do not meet at all (C^0).
- **Positional.** The two curves meet and share a common endpoint (C^1).
- **Tangential.** The two curves meet and have the same tangent at the control point (C^2).
- **Curvature.** The two curves' tangents have the same rate of change as they approach the control point (C^3).

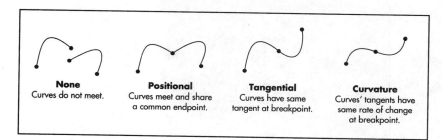

None
Curves do not meet.

Positional
Curves meet and share a common endpoint.

Tangential
Curves have same tangent at breakpoint.

Curvature
Curves' tangents have same rate of change at breakpoint.

Figure 14.4

The categories of curve continuity.

EVALUATORS

Evaluators are what you use with control points to define a curve or surface. They are used to define Bézier curves and surfaces, so if you are using another basis for curves and surfaces, you will need to convert your basis to a Bézier basis before trying to use evaluators. A single Bézier curve can be defined as the parametric function

```
C(u) = [ x(u) y(u) ]
```

In this function, u is the parametric parameter in some domain that you specify, typically between 0 and 1. As you will see, you can extend this function to represent 3D Bézier surfaces by adding the v parameter and the z coordinate:

```
S(u, v) = [ x(u, v) y(u, v) z(u, v) ]
```

We'll discuss the surfaces later, so let's concentrate on the u parameter for now. When calculating C(u), the u parameter defines an interval somewhere in the u domain that is used to calculate a point on the curve. The u parameter starts at the low end of its domain and is incremented at a specific interval each time an evaluator is defined. The interval that you define determines the resolution level of the curve. For example, an interval of 1/30 will create a less detailed curve than an interval of 1/100. So each time you define an evaluator, you are in effect calculating the position of the curve based on the interval defined by the u parameter. You can think of defining an evaluator as analogous to defining the position of a vertex.

So how do you do this in OpenGL? Let's look at the code that draws the curve shown in Figure 14.5.

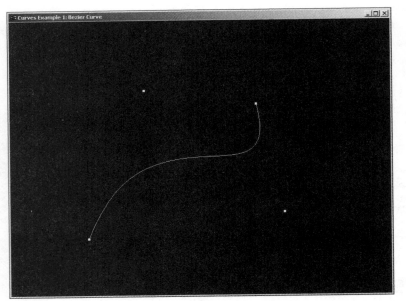

Figure 14.5

A shot of our first Bézier curve example.

First you define the four control points for the curve:

```
float control[4][3] = { { 1.0, -3.0, 0.0 }, { 3.0, 2.5, 0.0 },
                        { 8.0, -2.0, 0.0}, {7.0, 2.0, 0.0 } };
```

The first and last control point that you define, control[0] and control[3], are actually the two endpoints of the curve. The rest of the points, control[1] and control[2], are the control points.

Next is the Initialize() function, which clears the color buffer to black and sets the shade model to flat shading:

```
void Initialize()
{
    glClearColor(0.0f, 0.0f, 0.0f, 0.0f);        // clear to black
    glShadeModel(GL_FLAT);                       // use smooth shading
}
```

Now you use to the Render() function, where you set up and render your curve:

```
void Render()
{
    // clear screen and depth buffer
    glClear(GL_COLOR_BUFFER_BIT | GL_DEPTH_BUFFER_BIT);
    glLoadIdentity();

    // center the scene for the curve
    glTranslatef(-5.0f, 0.0f, -10.0f);

    // set up the Bezier curve
    glMap1f(GL_MAP1_VERTEX_3, 0.0, 1.0, 3, 4, &control[0][0]);
    glEnable(GL_MAP1_VERTEX_3);

    // set color to white
    glColor3f(1.0, 1.0, 1.0);

    // draw the curve using line strips for each interval of evaluators
    glBegin(GL_LINE_STRIP);
        for (int i = 0; i <= 30; i++)
            glEvalCoord1f((float)i/30.0f);
    glEnd();

    // now we draw the control points at their coordinates
    glPointSize(3.0);
    glColor3f(1.0, 1.0, 1.0);
    glBegin(GL_POINTS);
        for (i = 0; i < 4; i++)
            glVertex3fv(&control[i][0]);
    glEnd();

    glFlush();
    SwapBuffers(g_HDC);                 // bring back buffer to foreground
}
```

First you set up the Bézier curve by defining a one-dimensional evaluator through the following line:

```
glMap1f(GL_MAP1_VERTEX_3, 0.0, 1.0, 3, 4, &control[0][0]);
```

The glMap1f() function defines the one-dimensional evaluator and is defined as

```
void glMap1f(GLenum target, float u1, float u2, int stride, int order,
             const float *points);
```

The *u1* and *u2* parameters define the domain range for the u parameter. The *stride* parameter is essentially the distance between each point in the curve (the order should always equal the number of control points). Finally, the *points* parameter is a pointer to the control-point data.

The *target* parameter can be any of the values listed in Table 14.1 and is used to define what the control points represent. In our case, we define the control points as GL_MAP1_VERTEX_3, which tells OpenGL that the control points are (x, y, z) vertex coordinates.

Next you need to enable the control point type that you created by calling

```
glEnable(GL_MAP1_VERTEX_3);
```

Now you're ready to start drawing your curve. You accomplish this with the following code:

```
glBegin(GL_LINE_STRIP);
    for (int i = 0; i <= 100; i++)
        glEvalCoord1f((float)i/100.0f);
glEnd();
```

Table 14.1 Control Point Types

Value	Control Point Format
GL_MAP1_VERTEX_3	Vertex coordinates (x, y, z)
GL_MAP1_VERTEX_4	Vertex coordinates (x, y, z, w)
GL_MAP1_INDEX	Color index
GL_MAP1_COLOR_4	Color values (RGBA)
GL_MAP1_NORMAL	Normal coordinates
GL_MAP1_TEXTURE_COORD_1	Texture coordinates (s)
GL_MAP1_TEXTURE_COORD_2	Texture coordinates (s, t)
GL_MAP1_TEXTURE_COORD_3	Texture coordinates (s, t, r)
GL_MAP1_TEXTURE_COORD_4	Texture coordinates (s, t, r, q)

This code tells OpenGL to draw the Bézier curve with the defined control points using 100 line strips. You create a loop here to calculate the evaluator at 100 specified intervals, or points on the curve. The glEvalCoord1f() function accepts each interval, one at a time, and draws the corresponding point on the curve. This function is defined as

```
void glEvalCoord1f(float u);
```

This function causes evaluation of the current control point map that you defined with glMap1f() and enabled with glEnable(). The u parameter equals the current interval along the domain range for the u parameter, which is from 0 to 100 for this example.

After drawing the curve, you next draw the control points that you used to create the curve. Doing this involves calling the glVertex3fv() function and setting the point size to 3.0:

```
glPointSize(3.0);
glColor3f(1.0, 1.0, 1.0);
glBegin(GL_POINTS);
        for (i = 0; i < 4; i++)
                glVertex3fv(&control[i][0]);
glEnd();
```

And that's it! When executing this code, you get a window similar to the one shown in Figure 14.5.

Evenly Spaced Grids

You can use some other OpenGL functions to make curve drawing even easier than in the previous example. In particular, you can use the glMapGrid1f() function to define an evenly spaced grid that can be defined in a certain number of steps. This function is defined as

```
void glMapGrid1f(int n, float u1, float u2);
```

The n parameter specifies the number of steps into which you want to divide the grid. The grid itself goes from the range of u1 to u2.

After you define the grid, you can call the glEvalMesh1() function to draw your curve using either points or lines. The glEvalMesh1() function is defined as

```
void glEvalMesh1(GLenum mode, int p1, int p2);
```

The mode parameter can equal either GL_POINT or GL_LINE, depending on whether you want OpenGL to draw the curve using points or lines. The p1 and p2 parameters specify the range of steps OpenGL should use when performing evaluation for the curve.

The great thing about using these two functions is that they can replace the code you used in the preceding sample program. For instance, the following code can be used:

```
glMapGrid1f(100, 0.0, 100.0);
glEvalMesh1(GL_LINE, 0, 100);
```

instead of this code from the example:

```
glBegin(GL_LINE_STRIP);
    for (int i = 0; i <= 100; i++)
        glEvalCoord1f((float)i/100.0f);
glEnd();
```

Using these functions can make life easier with OpenGL curves, but their real power comes when you start using them to make surfaces.

SURFACES

The difference between 3D surfaces and 2D curves is the addition of the v parametric parameter to account for the v domain range. So now instead of the C(u) curve function, you have the S(u, v) surface function:

```
S(u, v) = [ x(u, v) y(u, v) z(u, v) ]
```

Just about everything you do to set up surfaces in OpenGL is the same as setting up curves, with the exception of the v parameter and a z coordinate in the control-point vertices. Figure 14.6 illustrates a sample Bézier surface.

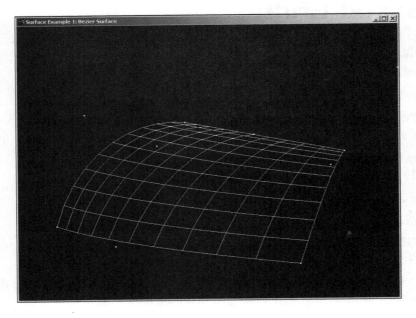

Figure 14.6

A Bézier surface.

So how can you create a simple surface like the one shown in Figure 14.6? Take a look at the following code:

```
float cSurface[3][3][3] = { { { -200.0, 40.0, 200.0 }, { -100.0, 100.0, 200.0 },
                              { 200.0, 0.0, 200.0 } },
                            { { -240.0, 0.0, 0.0 }, { -150.0, 100.0, 0.0 },
                              { 200.0, 0.0, 0.0 } },
                            { { -200.0, -80.0, -200.0 }, { -100.0, 100.0, -200.0 },
                              { 200.0, 0.0, -200.0 } } };

void Render()
{
    // camera code...

    // clear screen and depth buffer
    glClear(GL_COLOR_BUFFER_BIT | GL_DEPTH_BUFFER_BIT);
    glLoadIdentity();

    // camera code...

    glColor3f(1.0f, 1.0f, 1.0f);

    // set up the Bezier surface and enable it
    glMap2f(GL_MAP2_VERTEX_3, 0.0, 10.0, 3, 3, 0.0, 10.0, 9, 3, &cSurface[0][0][0]);
    glEnable(GL_MAP2_VERTEX_3);

    // map a grid and set number of divisions
    glMapGrid2f(10, 0.0f, 10.0f, 10, 0.0f, 10.0f);

    // evaluate the surface grid using lines
    glEvalMesh2(GL_LINE, 0, 10, 0, 10);

    // draw control points in yellow
    glPointSize(3.0);
    glColor3f(1.0, 1.0, 0.0);
    glBegin(GL_POINTS);
        for (int i = 0; i < 3; i++)
            for (int j = 0; j < 3; j++)
                glVertex3fv(&cSurface[i][j][0]);
    glEnd();
    glPointSize(1.0);
```

```
        glFlush();
        SwapBuffers(g_HDC);           // bring back buffer to foreground
}
```

You first define the surface with three sets comprised of three control points per set. What this creates is essentially three Bézier curves (*u* parameter) that are interconnected along the *v* parameter to create the surface.

In the Render() function you use the grid mapping function glMap2f(), which is defined as

```
void glMap2f(GLenum target, float u1, float u2, int ustride, int uorder,
             float v1, float v2, int vstride, int vorder, float points);
```

This function is essentially the same as the glMap1f() function you used for 2D curves with the addition of the *v* parameter. The target parameter for this function can be any of the values listed in Table 14.1, except MAP1 is replaced with MAP2 to denote the two parameters that you're using (*u* and *v*).

After you set up the Bézier curve with the glMap2f() function, you need to enable the curve with glEnable():

```
glEnable(GL_MAP2_VERTEX_3);
```

Now to make your life easier, you used the glMapGrid2() function to define a two-dimensional map grid to be used with evaluators. As with the glMap2f() function, the glMapGrid2() function is essentially an extension of the 2D glMapGrid1f() function:

```
void glMapGrid2f(int nu, float u1, float u2, int nv, float v1, float v2);
```

Lastly, you apply the grid you just created to the evaluators by using the glEvalMesh2() function:

```
void glEvalMesh2(GLenum mode, int i1, int i2, int j1, int j2);
```

The *mode* parameter for this function can be GL_POINT, GL_LINE, or GL_FILL. Using GL_FILL tells OpenGL to generate filled polygons using the GL_QUADS primitive.

If you use the value GL_FILL for the *mode* parameter of glEvalMesh2(), OpenGL will fill the surface solidly with the current color. To get a more realistic look, you need to add lighting and shading. You already know how to add lighting to your scenes, but how do you tell OpenGL what the normals are for the surface so it can properly calculate lighting? The glEnable() function to the rescue:

```
glEnable(GL_AUTO_NORMAL);
```

After setting up the lighting that you're going to use in the scene, you simply call this line and all the surfaces you render will appear shaded and lit. Figure 14.7 shows the sample surface using the GL_FILL value for glEvalMesh2(), with lighting and shading applied to the scene.

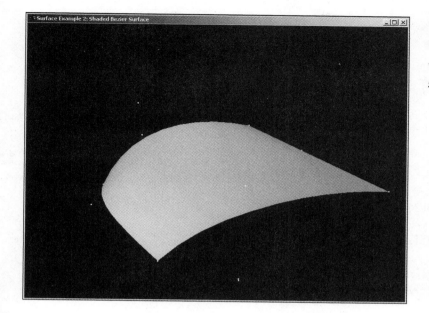

Figure 14.7

The Bézier surface with lighting and shading.

Applying Textures to Surfaces

You can also use evaluators to set up textures for surfaces. To accomplish this, you use the glMap2f() function with the GL_MAP2_TEXTURE_COORD_2 parameter to generate an evaluator for the texture coordinates to use on the surface. In the example that follows, you apply the checkerboard texture to the same surface that you've been using. Let's look at the code:

```
////// Defines
#define BITMAP_ID 0x4D42          // the universal bitmap ID
#define PI 3.14195

// Includes...

////// Types
typedef struct
{
    int width;                    // width of texture
    int height;                   // height of texture
    unsigned int texID;           // the texture object id of this texture
    unsigned char *data;          // the texture data
} texture_t;
```

```
////// Variables
float angle = 0.0f;                 // camera angle
float radians = 0.0f;               // camera angle in radians

float cSurface[3][3][3] = { { { -200.0, 40.0, 200.0 }, { -100.0, 100.0, 200.0 },
                              { 200.0, 0.0, 200.0 } },
                            { { -240.0, 0.0, 0.0 }, { -150.0, 100.0, 0.0 },
                              { 200.0, 0.0, 0.0 } },
                            { { -200.0, -80.0, -200.0 }, { -100.0, 100.0, -200.0 },
                              { 200.0, 0.0, -200.0 } }  };

float sTexCoords[2][2][2] = {{ {0.0, 0.0}, {0.0, 1.0} }, { {1.0, 0.0}, {1.0, 1.0} }};

////// Mouse/Camera Variables
int mouseX, mouseY;                 // mouse coordinates
float cameraX, cameraY, cameraZ;    // camera coordinates
float lookX, lookY, lookZ;          // camera look-at coordinates

////// Textures
texture_t *surfaceTex;              // the surface's texture

// LoadBitmapFile()
// ...

// LoadTextureFile()
// desc: loads the texture "filename" into memory
texture_t *LoadTextureFile(char *filename)
{
    BITMAPINFOHEADER texInfo;
    texture_t *thisTexture;

    // allocate memory for the texture structure
    thisTexture = (texture_t*)malloc(sizeof(texture_t));
    if (thisTexture == NULL)
        return NULL;

    // load the texture data and check validity
    thisTexture->data = LoadBitmapFile(filename, &texInfo);
    if (thisTexture->data == NULL)
    {
        free(thisTexture);
```

```
            return NULL;
    }

    // set width and height info for this texture
    thisTexture->width = texInfo.biWidth;
    thisTexture->height = texInfo.biHeight;

    // generate the texture object for this texture
    glGenTextures(1, &thisTexture->texID);

    return thisTexture;
}

// LoadAllTextures()
// desc: loads all the program's textures into memory
bool LoadAllTextures()
{
    // load the surface texture data
    surfaceTex = LoadTextureFile("chess.bmp");
    if (surfaceTex == NULL)
        return false;

    // set up the surface texture
    glBindTexture(GL_TEXTURE_2D, surfaceTex->texID);
    glTexParameteri(GL_TEXTURE_2D, GL_TEXTURE_MAG_FILTER, GL_LINEAR);
    glTexParameteri(GL_TEXTURE_2D, GL_TEXTURE_MIN_FILTER, GL_LINEAR);
    glTexEnvi(GL_TEXTURE_ENV, GL_TEXTURE_ENV_MODE, GL_REPLACE);
    gluBuild2DMipmaps(GL_TEXTURE_2D, GL_RGB, surfaceTex->width, surfaceTex->height,
                      GL_RGB, GL_UNSIGNED_BYTE, surfaceTex->data);

    return true;
}

// CleanUp()
// desc: free allocated objects
void CleanUp()
{
    free(surfaceTex);
}
```

```cpp
// Initialize
// desc: initializes OpenGL
void Initialize()
{
    glClearColor(0.0f, 0.0f, 0.0f, 0.0f);        // clear to black

    glShadeModel(GL_FLAT);                        // use flat shading
    glEnable(GL_DEPTH_TEST);                      // hidden surface removal
    glEnable(GL_TEXTURE_2D);                      // enable 2D texturing

    LoadAllTextures();                            // load all the textures
}


// Render
// desc: handles drawing of scene
void Render()
{
    radians =  float(PI*(angle-90.0f)/180.0f);

    // calculate the camera's position
    cameraX = lookX + (float)sin(radians)*mouseY;  // calculate camera's x coordinate
    cameraZ = lookZ + (float)cos(radians)*mouseY;  // calculate camera's z coordinate
    cameraY = lookY + mouseY / 2.0f + 30.0f;       // calculate camera's y coordinate

    // set camera to point at (-20, 20, 0)
    lookX = -20.0f;
    lookY = 20.0f;
    lookZ = 0.0f;

    // clear screen and depth buffer
    glClear(GL_COLOR_BUFFER_BIT | GL_DEPTH_BUFFER_BIT);
    glLoadIdentity();

    // set the camera position
    gluLookAt(cameraX, cameraY, cameraZ, lookX, lookY, lookZ, 0.0, 1.0, 0.0);

    // create evaluator for surface control points
    glMap2f(GL_MAP2_VERTEX_3, 0.0, 1.0, 3, 3, 0.0, 1.0, 9, 3, &cSurface[0][0][0]);

    // create evaluator for texture coordinates
    glMap2f(GL_MAP2_TEXTURE_COORD_2, 0, 1, 2, 2, 0, 1, 4, 2, &sTexCoords[0][0][0]);
```

```
        // enable texture coordinate and vertex evaluators
        glEnable(GL_MAP2_TEXTURE_COORD_2);
        glEnable(GL_MAP2_VERTEX_3);

        // create surface mesh
        glMapGrid2f(10, 0.0f, 1.0f, 10, 0.0f, 1.0f);
        glEvalMesh2(GL_FILL, 0, 10, 0, 10);

        // disable 2D texturing so we can draw the control points
        glDisable(GL_TEXTURE_2D);

        // set point size to 4, color to yellow, and draw points
        glPointSize(4.0);
        glColor3f(1.0, 1.0, 0.0);
        glBegin(GL_POINTS);
            for (int i = 0; i < 3; i++)
                for (int j = 0; j < 3; j++)
                    glVertex3fv(&cSurface[i][j][0]);
        glEnd();

        // set original point size and enable texturing
        glPointSize(1.0);
        glEnable(GL_TEXTURE_2D);

        glFlush();
        SwapBuffers(g_HDC);              // bring back buffer to foreground
}
```

The part in which we're particularly interested is this:

```
// create evaluator for surface control points
glMap2f(GL_MAP2_VERTEX_3, 0.0, 1.0, 3, 3, 0.0, 1.0, 9, 3, &cSurface[0][0][0]);

// create evaluator for texture coordinates
glMap2f(GL_MAP2_TEXTURE_COORD_2, 0, 1, 2, 2, 0, 1, 4, 2, &sTexCoords[0][0][0]);

// enable texture coordinate and vertex evaluators
glEnable(GL_MAP2_TEXTURE_COORD_2);
glEnable(GL_MAP2_VERTEX_3);

// create surface mesh
glMapGrid2f(10, 0.0f, 1.0f, 10, 0.0f, 1.0f);
glEvalMesh2(GL_FILL, 0, 10, 0, 10);
```

In this block of code you start off by creating the vertex evaluator for the surface by using the `glMap2f()` function. Then, you again use the `glMap2f()` function to create the evaluator for the texture coordinates. The texture coordinates you use are specified in the `sTexCoords` variable:

```
float sTexCoords[2][2][2] = {{ {0.0, 0.0}, {0.0, 1.0} }, { {1.0, 0.0}, {1.0, 1.0} }};
```

This variable defines a square with coordinates $(0, 0)$, $(0, 1)$, $(1, 0)$, and $(1, 1)$ for the corners; each of these corners will apply directly to the corners of the surface because of how you set up the texture with the `glMap2f()` function. When you call the `glEvalMesh2()` function to compute the vertices of the surface, OpenGL will automatically calculate the texture coordinates across the surface as well.

Figure 14.8 shows your textured surface.

Figure 14.8

The textured surface.

NURBS

As the number of control points for a Bézier curve increases, the difficulty of creating a smooth, continuous curve increases as well. Bézier curves are classified based on the number of control points they have. For instance, a curve with three control points is called *quadratic*, while a curve with four control points is called *cubic*. As you move up to a total of five, six, seven, and more control points, the smoothness of the Bézier curve starts to break down from the pull of the high number of control points.

To combat this problem, we introduce what are called *NURBS*, short for *non-uniform rational B-splines* (*B-spline* stands for *bi-cubic spline*). B-splines are essentially the same as Bézier curves, except that B-splines are divided into fragments of four control points per fragment. This division of the entire curve into segments essentially produces a combination of cubic Bézier curves that combine to form a single, more-complex curve.

We're not going to get into the heavy details of NURBS theory; instead, we're going to look at some functions to help you get started with rendering basic NURBS. From here, you can move on to other resources created specifically for NURBS.

A *knot* is a sequence of values that control how much influence a control point has on the curve segments created with four control points. This feature is essentially what separates the Bézier curve from the NURB.

Each control point holds two knots, whose values may be equal to any value in the range of the u or v parametric domain. So when you have four control points, you will have eight knot values. You can see this in the following sample program:

```
GLUnurbsObj *myNurb;
float knots[8] = { 0.0, 0.0, 0.0, 0.0, 1.0, 1.0, 1.0, 1.0 };
float nurb[4][4][3];

void CleanUp()
{
    gluDeleteNurbsRenderer(myNurb);
}

void Initialize()
{
    glClearColor(0.0f, 0.0f, 0.0f, 0.0f);       // clear to black

    glEnable(GL_DEPTH_TEST);                     // hidden surface removal
    glEnable(GL_LIGHTING);                       // enable lighting
    glEnable(GL_LIGHT0);                         // enable light0
    glEnable(GL_COLOR_MATERIAL);                 // colors act as materials
    glEnable(GL_AUTO_NORMAL);                    // generate normals for surface
    glEnable(GL_NORMALIZE);                      // automatically calculate normals

    // set up the surface data points; make a "hill"
    int u, v;
    for (u = 0; u < 4; u++)
    {
```

```
            for (v = 0; v < 4; v++)
            {
                nurb[u][v][0] = 3.0*((float)u - 1.5);
                nurb[u][v][1] = 2.0*((float)v - 1.5);

                if ( (u == 1 || u == 2) && (v == 1 || v == 2))
                    nurb[u][v][2] = 3.0;
                else
                    nurb[u][v][2] = -1.0;
            }
        }

    // initialize NURBS object
    myNurb = gluNewNurbsRenderer();

    // set maximum length to use for polygons
    gluNurbsProperty(myNurb, GLU_SAMPLING_TOLERANCE, 50.0);

    // render surface as polygons
    gluNurbsProperty(myNurb, GLU_DISPLAY_MODE, GLU_FILL);
}

void Render()
{
    // clear screen and depth buffer
    glClear(GL_COLOR_BUFFER_BIT | GL_DEPTH_BUFFER_BIT);
    glLoadIdentity();

    // make surface more "visible"
    glTranslatef(0.0, 0.0, -10.0);
    glRotatef(290.0, 1.0, 0.0, 0.0);

    glPushMatrix();
        glRotatef(angle, 0.0, 0.0, 1.0);        // rotate surface

        glColor3f(0.2, 0.5, 0.8);

        // begin defining the NURBS surface
        gluBeginSurface(myNurb);
```

```
            // evaluate the surface
            gluNurbsSurface(myNurb, 8, knots, 8, knots, 4*3, 3, &nurb[0][0][0], 4, 4,
                            GL_MAP2_VERTEX_3);

            // finished
            gluEndSurface(myNurb);

            // draw the control points
            glPointSize(6.0);
            glColor3f(1.0, 1.0, 0.0);
            glBegin(GL_POINTS);
                for (int i = 0; i < 4; i++)
                    for (int j = 0; j < 4; j++)
                        glVertex3fv(&nurb[i][j][0]);
            glEnd();
            glPointSize(1.0);

        glPopMatrix();

        glFlush();
        SwapBuffers(g_HDC);             // bring back buffer to foreground

        angle+=0.3f;                    // increase rotation angle
}
```

As you can see, the amount of code to actually draw a NURBS surface is rather small compared to what one might expect. The GLU library provides a nice set of NURBS functions that present a higher level of functionality than do the Bézier surface functions that you've already looked at.

The first thing you do in this example is declare your NURBS object, which represents the NURBS surface that you're going to render:

```
GLUnurbsObj *myNurb;                  // NURBS object
```

You also define the knots for the control points and a variable to hold the control points:

```
float knots[8] = { 0.0, 0.0, 0.0, 0.0, 1.0, 1.0, 1.0, 1.0 };
float nurb[4][4][3];
```

In the Initialize() function, you turn on the lighting and tell OpenGL to calculate the surface normals for you. You then generate your control points before heading into the functions to set up and define the NURBS object:

```
// initialize NURBS object
myNurb = gluNewNurbsRenderer();

// set maximum length to use for polygons
gluNurbsProperty(myNurb, GLU_SAMPLING_TOLERANCE, 50.0);

// render surface as polygons
gluNurbsProperty(myNurb, GLU_DISPLAY_MODE, GLU_FILL);
```

The first function you have here is the `gluNewNurbsRenderer()` function. Essentially, it allocates memory and initializes your NURBS object pointer.

Next, you call the `gluNurbsProperty()` function to set up the sampling tolerance and to tell OpenGL how you want the NURBS to be rendered. The `GLU_SAMPLING_TOLERANCE` parameter tells OpenGL the maximum length to use when drawing polygons, which in this case equals 50 units. The `GLU_DISPLAY_MODE` parameter tells OpenGL how you want the NURBS surface to be rendered. This parameter can be set to equal one of three values:

- **GLU_FILL.** The `GLU_FILL` value causes the surface to be rendered as filled polygons.
- **GLU_OUTLINE_POLYGON.** The `GLU_OUTLINE_POLYGON` value causes only the outlines of polygons created via tessellation (the breakdown of polygons into smaller polygons) to be rendered.
- **GLU_OUTLINE_PATCH.** The `GLU_OUTLINE_PATCH` value renders the outlines of patches and trimming curves.

Here are the definitions of both the `gluNewNurbsRenderer()` and `gluNurbsProperty()` functions:

```
GLUnurbsObj* gluNewNurbsRenderer(void);
void gluNurbsProperty(GLUnurbsObj *nobj, GLenum property, float value);
```

To finally render the NURBS surface, you only need to make three function calls:

```
// begin defining the NURBS surface
gluBeginSurface(myNurb);

// evaluate the surface
gluNurbsSurface(myNurb, 8, knots, 8, knots, 4*3, 3, &nurb[0][0][0], 4, 4,
                        GL_MAP2_VERTEX_3);

// finished
gluEndSurface(myNurb);
```

The gluBeginSurface() function tells OpenGL that you are going to be rendering a NURBS surface, and, through the NURBS object that you pass to it, which NURBS object attributes you want to use. This function is defined as

```
void gluBeginSurface(GLUnurbsObj *nobj);
```

Next, you evaluate the NURBS surface by calling the gluNurbsSurface() function. This function, like glEvalCoor2f(), determines the vertices that you need to use to properly render the NURBS surface.

```
void gluNurbsSurface(GLUnurbsObj *nobj, int uknot_count, float *uknot,
                     int vknot_count, float *vknot, int u_stride, int v_stride,
                     float *ctlarray, int uorder, int vorder, GLenum type);
```

The first parameter of this function, nobj, is the pointer to your NURBS object. The uknot_count and uknot parameters specify the number of knots and the knot data in the u direction, respectively. Similarly, the vknot_count and vknot parameters specify the number of knots and the knot data in the v direction, respectively. The u_stride and v_stride parameters specify the distance between the control points in the u and v directions, respectively. You pass your control-point data into the ctlarray parameter. The uorder and vorder parameters specify the order of the polynomial for the surface, which is typically equal to the number of control points in each parametric direction. And finally, the type parameter specifies what type of surface you're rendering. In this example, this value equals GL_MAP2_VERTEX_3.

After you finish evaluating the surface and rendering your vertices, you tell OpenGL that you're finished with the surface with a call to gluEndSurface(). You simply pass the object that you're finished with to the function, as it is defined:

```
void gluEndSurface(GLUnurbsObj *nobj);
```

After you finish with your application, you need to call the gluDeleteNurbsRenderer() function to free the NURBS object you used. This function is defined as

```
void gluDeleteNurbsRenderer(GLUnurbsObj *nobj);
```

In the example, you use this function like so:

```
gluDeleteNurbsRenderer(myNurb);
```

And that's all for NURBS! What we covered is merely the basics to get set up and start rendering simple NURBS surfaces. Try changing values and parameters to see what kind of effect they have on the final result for the example. Then try to make your own NURBS programs! Speaking of final results, Figure 14.9 shows the sample program.

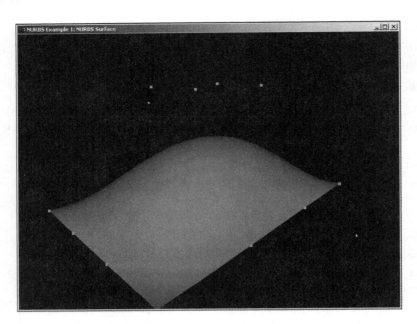

Figure 14.9

The NURBS surface example.

Summary

A *curve* is a type of line that moves around, as you move from one point to another, in 3D space. Like a line, a curve has a single starting point, length, and endpoint. When we say *surface*, we're talking about an entity with a width and length that is often composed of curves.

Parametric equations express both x and y together in terms of some other variable. For instance, physics uses parametric equations to define x and y coordinates on a 2D plane according to some function of time in seconds. In 3D graphics, you can use parametric equations to keep track of a particle in 3D space according to a function of virtual time, which you keep track of in your application.

Control points are used to define the shape of a curve. They can be viewed as magnets that attract the curve toward the control point's position. The first and last control points that you define represent the two endpoints of the curve. All the other control points are used to move and bend the curve.

NURBS stands for *non-uniform rational B-splines* (*B-spline* stands for *bi-cubic spline*). *B-splines* are essentially the same as Bézier curves, except that they are divided into fragments of four control points per fragment. This division of the entire curve into segments essentially produces a combination of cubic Bézier curves that combine to form a single, more-complex curve.

CHAPTER 15

SPECIAL EFFECTS

To this point, we've discussed a variety of graphics techniques that will provide the foundation of your games. Now it's time to use the things you've learned to fill your programming toolbox with techniques to add flash and spice to your games. It's time to learn some special effects. After all, what's a game without explosions, fire, smoke, and all the other eye candy?

Special effects is a fairly broad topic, and we can't cover nearly as many effects as we'd like to, but we'll explain some of the most common effects here. In this chapter, you'll read about

- Using billboarding to reduce the polygon count
- Creating a particle system for a variety of effects from fountains to fireballs
- Using fog, both as an effect and to reduce scene complexity
- Adding reflections to flat surfaces
- Several techniques for creating shadows

No matter what effect you want to achieve, there are usually several commonly known ways to achieve it, each with varying degrees of quality, realism, and performance. Because this is a game-programming book, we'll focus on techniques that can be done at interactive rates.

BILLBOARDING

Billboarding probably isn't the most exciting effect we'll cover in this chapter, but it comes in handy in particle systems, so we'll cover it first. *Billboarding* is the technique of making a polygon always face the viewer. To understand why this is useful, let's look at an example.

Suppose you are working on a terrain engine and included in the terrain are trees. To make these trees look as realistic as possible, you're either generating them from models or creating them procedurally. The problem is, when you're rendering trees that are distant from the viewer, you could be processing dozens or even hundreds of polygons that end up being only a few pixels on the screen. One way to get around this is by using progressive meshes (that is, models with fewer polygons for distant objects). Another popular technique is to replace the 3D representation of the tree with a 2D image—texture-mapped onto a quad—that looks just like the 3D version. When the viewer gets closer, the 2D image can be replaced with the 3D representation (doing this smoothly is tricky, but that's beside the point just now).

What does all this have to do with billboarding? Well, imagine that the player is looking north at a tree image textured onto a polygon facing south. The tree will look exactly the way it should.

Now, the player begins moving in an arc to the east. The tree polygon is still facing south, so as he moves, he'll begin seeing it at an angle. It will appear to narrow, until finally, when he is due east, the tree will disappear because he is viewing the polygon from the side. The illusion has been destroyed.

This comes up in practice in many situations, especially when trying to make a 2D representation seem 3D. Particle systems, which we'll discuss next, often use single texture-mapped quads to simulate 3D particles. Older 3D games, such as *Doom, Duke Nukem' 3D,* and *Daggerfall,* represented enemies as 2D sprites. To maintain the illusion of 3D, billboarding can be used to make sure that these polygons face the viewer, no matter where he is located or which direction he is looking.

Now that you know what billboarding is and why it's used, let's talk about how to achieve it. There are several common approaches to implementing billboarding; we'll choose a method that is fairly straightforward, requires only a few lines of code, and is most appropriate for use in the particle engine you'll be developing later. The basic idea is to align the billboarded polygon so that its surface normal is parallel to and opposite the player's viewing direction. The way to do this is to simply reverse the rotations performed by the view matrix.

The first step is to grab the current modelview matrix, as follows:

```
GLfloat viewMatrix[16];

glGetFloatv(GL_MODELVIEW_MATRIX, viewMatrix);
```

What we are trying to do is, in effect, reverse the operation of this matrix. To reverse the effects of any matrix, you just need to multiply it by its inverse—in our case, however, we won't actually be multiplying by the inverse matrix; we need to find it to get information we need for a shortcut we'll be using instead.

You can simplify finding the inverse of this matrix by recognizing that you only need the upper 3×3 portion of it. If this 3×3 matrix is orthogonal, which it should be, then the inverse is just the transpose, which can be calculated easily. Once you have the transpose, you need to grab two vectors from the first two rows, which represent vectors orthogonal to the viewing direction pointing up and to the right. Note, though, that the rows in the transpose are equivalent to the columns in the original, so you can avoid the transpose step altogether. This is illustrated in Figure 15.1.

The next step, then, is to extract the up and right vectors from the modelview matrix, like this:

```
vector3_t right(viewMatrix[0], viewMatrix [4], viewMatrix [8]);
vector3_t up(viewMatrix [1], viewMatrix [5], viewMatrix [9]);
```

Note that vector3_t is a simple vector class with overloaded operators for most vector operators, which can be found under the *vectorlib* header on the CD.

Figure 15.1

The modelview matrix
and its transpose.

$$
\begin{bmatrix}
m_0 & m_1 & m_2 & m_3 \\
m_4 & m_5 & m_6 & m_7 \\
m_8 & m_9 & m_{10} & m_{11} \\
m_{12} & m_{13} & m_{14} & m_{15}
\end{bmatrix}
\qquad
\begin{matrix}
\text{right ->} \\
\text{up ->} \\
\\
\\
\end{matrix}
\begin{bmatrix}
m_0 & m_4 & m_8 & m_{12} \\
m_1 & m_5 & m_9 & m_{13} \\
m_2 & m_6 & m_{10} & m_{14} \\
m_3 & m_7 & m_{11} & m_{15}
\end{bmatrix}
$$

matrix M · matrix M^T (M transposed)

Next, assume that you have a point in space, and you want to construct a billboarded quad around it that you will then texture map. You'll treat this point as the center of the quad. Each of the corners can be found by scaling the up and right vectors to attain the proper size, and then adding them together. The general formula is

```
newPoint = centerPoint + up * heightScale + right * widthScale;
```

For points to the left of the center point, widthScale should be negative, and for points below the center point, heightScale should be negative. If the quad you're rendering is square (as in the following sample code below), there only needs to be one scalar factor, although you still need to account for left and below points using a negative value.

So, code for an entire square quad, with *point* representing the center and *size* representing the half-size, would look like this:

```
// bottom left corner
glTexCoord2f(0.0, 0.0); glVertex3fv((point + (right + up) * -size).v);
// bottom right corner
glTexCoord2f(1.0, 0.0); glVertex3fv((point + (right - up) * size).v);
// top right corner
glTexCoord2f(1.0, 1.0); glVertex3fv((point + (right + up) * size).v);
// top left corner
glTexCoord2f(0.0, 1.0); glVertex3fv((point + (up - right) * size).v);
```

And there you have it.

Example: Cacti in the Desert

We suppose the standard example for billboarding would be trees on a landscape, so we're going to use something a little different. Instead, we'll show you how to create a desert scene filled with billboarded cacti, as pictured in Figure 15.2.

The relevant code from this demo appears in the DrawCacti() routine, shown here:

Figure 15.2

Look at those saguaros!

```
/****************************************************************************
 DrawCacti()

 Draw cacti as billboarded quads.
 ****************************************************************************/
void DrawCacti()
{
  // make sure the random numbers we generate are the same every time
  srand(100);

  // make sure the transparent part of the texture isn't drawn
  glEnable(GL_BLEND);
  glBlendFunc(GL_SRC_ALPHA, GL_ONE_MINUS_SRC_ALPHA);
  glEnable(GL_ALPHA_TEST);
  glAlphaFunc(GL_GREATER, 0);

  // get the modelview matrix
  float mat[16];
  glGetFloatv(GL_MODELVIEW_MATRIX, mat);
```

```
    // get the right and up vectors
    vector3_t right(mat[0], mat[4], mat[8]);
    vector3_t up(mat[1], mat[5], mat[9]);

    // select the cactus texture
    glBindTexture(GL_TEXTURE_2D, g_cactus);
    glTexEnvf(GL_TEXTURE_ENV, GL_TEXTURE_ENV_MODE, GL_REPLACE);

    // draw all cacti
    glBegin(GL_QUADS);
    for (int n = 0; n < NUM_CACTI; n++)
    {
      // randomly size the cactus
      float size = 5.0f + FRAND + 3.0f;

      // pick a random position on the map
      vector3_t pos(RAND_COORD((MAP_X - 1) * MAP_SCALE), 0.0, -RAND_COORD((MAP_Z - 1) *
MAP_SCALE));
      pos.y = GetHeight(pos.x, pos.z) + size - 0.5f;

      // bottom-left corner
      glTexCoord2f(0.0, 0.0); glVertex3fv((pos + (right + up) * -size).v);
      // bottom-right corner
      glTexCoord2f(1.0, 0.0); glVertex3fv((pos + (right - up) * size).v);
      // top-right corner
      glTexCoord2f(1.0, 1.0); glVertex3fv((pos + (right + up) * size).v);
      // top-left corner
      glTexCoord2f(0.0, 1.0); glVertex3fv((pos + (up - right) * size).v);
    }
    glEnd();
    glDisable(GL_ALPHA);
    glDisable(GL_BLEND);
} // end DrawCacti()
```

To control the demo, use the forward and back keys to move, the left and right keys to turn, and press and hold the Shift key to run.

USING PARTICLE SYSTEMS

Before we get into the details of creating a particle system, we need to talk about what a particle system is. A *particle system* is a collection of a number of individual elements, or *particles*. Each particle has individual attributes, such as velocity, color, life span, and so on. Each particle acts in mostly an autonomous way—that is, it doesn't care about what other particles are doing. The particles within a given particle system generally share a common set of attributes, so that even though the individual particles act independently, together they create a common effect. An easy-to-visualize example of a particle system is a shower of sparks coming from a firecracker, where each spark is an individual particle. Through the clever use of textures and other properties, particle systems can also be used to create effects like fire, smoke, explosions, liquid (such as water or blood) spraying, snow, star fields, vapor trails, and more. Clearly, you want to create a powerful and versatile system capable of simulating any of these effects.

Due to the self-contained nature of the elements of particle system, they lend themselves to an object-oriented design, so that's what we'll use here. There are two ways you can go using C++ classes: You can create a base particle-system class and then derive a new child class for each type of particle system you want (for example, a smoke particle system, a fire particle system, and so on), or you can create a single generic particle-system class with a set of attributes that you can change to·determine the particle-system type. Which you choose is really a matter of personal preference. We'll be taking the former approach, mainly because it seems a little more flexible, and considerably cleaner.

Before we get into implementation specifics, let's look at each component of the particle system and discuss the methods and attributes each one could possess.

Particles

We'll start at the most basic element: the individual particle. To begin, you need to decide what attributes a particle should possess. Possible attributes include

- Position
- Velocity
- Life span
- Size
- Weight
- Representation
- Color
- Owner

> **NOTE**
>
> There may be other attributes you want to add to your particles, but this list provides a good place to start and should be sufficient for most applications. As always, feel free to experiment and find what works best for you.

Position

You need to know where the particle is in 3D space so that you can render it correctly. This is an attribute that will almost certainly belong to the particle, not the particle system. You may also want to track the particle's last position to achieve effects such as trails. Note that the particle's position will be affected by the particle's velocity.

Velocity

Your particles are probably going to be moving, so you need to store their velocity. It's most convenient to store this as a vector representing both speed and direction so that you can use this value to update the position.

CAUTION

Although some attributes would seem to belong to the particle, they should in fact be stored in the particle-system class because all the particles in that system are working together to achieve the same effect. For example, if all the particles have the exact same weight, there is no point in making hundreds of copies of that data in each particle; you can just have the particle system keep track of it.

Velocity will likely be affected by such factors as wind and gravity, which we'll discuss later in this chapter in the "Forces" subsection under "Particle Systems." If the particle is capable of accelerating itself, that could affect the velocity as well, and you'd want to create an additional attribute to store the acceleration. More often, though, factors that affect the velocity of a particle are external.

Life Span

For most effects, particles are going to be emitted from their source, and, after some period of time, are going to disappear. For this reason, you need to either keep track of how long a particle has been alive or how long it has left to live (the latter can be thought of as the amount of energy left in the particle). The life span may affect other attributes, because a particle will often grow, shrink, fade, and so on over time.

Size

Size is an attribute that may not need to be handled by individual particles. In fact, unless the size of a particle changes over its life span or if there is variation in the sizes of particles within a system, there is no need to store size with the particle. However, in practice, you'll probably find that there are many situations in which you will want variation in particle sizes, so you may want to include it as a particle attribute. You may also want to have another attribute to store how the size should change over time.

Weight

Weight is a lot like size in terms of whether it should be included as a particle attribute. *Weight* probably isn't the most accurate term for the purpose this attribute serves, but it conveys the idea: It determines how much of an effect external forces will have on the particle.

Representation

To have the particles produce some kind of effect, you're going to have to be able to see them. The question is, how are you going to represent them on the screen? There are three commonly used alternatives:

- **Points.** Points can be used for a number of effects, especially those that aren't viewed closely. Each particle is simply a 3D point.
- **Lines.** These can be used to create a trailing effect, which is often useful. The line connects the particle's current position with its last position.
- **Texture-mapped quads.** These offer the greatest flexibility, and are thus probably the most widely used. The particle itself is a quad or pair of triangles, upon which a texture is drawn, usually with some degree of alpha blending. One example of this would to be to use an image of an actual spark as the texture for a spark particle.

In most cases, all the particles within a system will share the same representation, including the same texture if quads are used, so this is something you'll likely want to handle on the particle-system level (discussed in the section titled "Particle System.")

> **NOTE**
>
> If quads are used, you'll probably want to use billboarding so that they always face the user, as we discussed in the first section of this chapter.

Color

If you choose the point or line representation discussed in the preceding section, you'll also want to give each particle a color. Even if you're using texture-mapped quads, there may be times when you want to blend the color of the particle with the texture (such as in a multi-colored spark shower). Color is something that may change over time, so a color delta attribute may be used—for example, to have the particle fade out as it ages.

Owner

Each particle might need to know which particle system it belongs to so that it can access methods in the particle-system class.

Methods

In addition to attributes, your particle class is going to need some methods. As it turns out, the only method your particle class needs in this case is a method to update its attributes. This method will take as a parameter the amount of time that has passed since the last call. Other operations on particles (such as initialization or shutdown) will be handled directly by the particle system.

Particle Systems

Each particle system will control a set of particles, each of which act autonomously but share some common attributes. It is the job of the particle system to assign these attributes in such a way that, collectively, the particles create the desired effect. Some of the things a particle system should handle include

- Particle list
- Position
- Emission rate
- Forces
- Default particle attributes and ranges
- Current state
- Blending
- Representation

Particle List

First and foremost, the particle system needs to be able to access the particles its managing, so it needs a list of all of them. It should also know the maximum number of particles it's allowed to generate.

> **NOTE**
>
> If the particle system can move, then you may want to include a velocity vector as well rather than modifying the position directly from your host program.

Position

The particle system must be located somewhere to determine where particles start. Although this is usually modeled as a single point in space, it doesn't have to be. You could represent it as a two-dimensional rectangle, and then emit particles from random positions within the rectangle. This would be useful for a snow particle system, where the rectangle is some region in the sky from which snow is falling.

Emission Rate

The emission rate determines how often a new particle is created. To maintain a regular emission rate, the particle system will also need to keep track of how much time has elapsed since the last particle was emitted and reset that value each time a new particle is emitted.

CAUTION

The emission rate will have to interact with the maximum number of particles and thus the average life span of particles. If particles are living for too long, you'll reach the maximum number of particles—when you try to emit a new one, you won't be able to, creating a spurting effect. (Of course, a spurting effect may be what you're after, but if not, then you'll have to either better balance the emission rate and life span or possibly kill old particles prematurely when it's time to emit new ones.)

NOTE

Not all particle systems will require an emission rate. Some, such as the explosion used in the game at the end of this book, emit all their particles in a single burst.

Forces

Adding one or more external forces acting on a particle system can create a greater degree of realism, so you'll want at least one force vector as part of your particle system. It's preferable to assign a unique force vector to each particle system instead of assigning a single value shared by all particle systems in your world.

Default Particle Attributes and Ranges

When the system creates a new particle, it will initialize the values within the particle, so the system needs to know which values are valid. Some particles have attributes that change over time, so the system will need to know both the initial and final values.

When initializing particles, you'll also want to introduce some variation in these default attributes so that your particles don't all look and act the same. To achieve this, include a variable for each value that holds the maximum acceptable variation from the default value. When creating the particle, you'll multiply this value by a random floating-point value ranging between −1 and 1, and add the result to the default value to set the particle's attributes.

Current State

You may want your particle system to change its behavior over time; in the system we're building, that change simply involves turning the system on or off. There are a couple of cases in which you'll want to do this—one is when the particle system involves a limited-time effect, such as an explosion. After a while, you'll want the system to stop emitting new particles. Another is if the system is temporarily outside the viewing frustum; there's no point in updating the particles every frame if the player can't see them.

When the particle system is turned off, you may want the system to stop emitting new particles but let existing particles live out their normal life span, or you may want to kill them all immediately. In order to be able to do all this and to invoke any other changes beyond simply turning the system on or off, you'll need to include a variable to track which state the particle system is in.

Blending

Most particle systems use some form of alpha blending. Because the exact form of blending is likely going to be specific to the system, you need to include the source and destination blend settings to pass to OpenGL's blend function.

Representation

In most cases, all particles within a system are going to be represented in the same way, whether that be points, lines, or texture-mapped quads. You can store information about that representation within the particle system itself. For example, if you're using texture maps, you can store the name of the texture in the particle-system class rather than in each particle.

NOTE

Here you must make a design decision: Do you make a general-purpose particle-system class that can support points, lines, or quads, which you can specify through function calls? Or do you create a base particle-system class and then derive new classes that differ in the form of representation? For that matter, do you even need all three representations, or are you using only one? There's no right answer, because everyone has his own preferences and needs. For the particle system you're implementing here, however, you'll use the base class with inheritance approach, primarily because it leaves room to easily add alternative representations.

Methods

The particle system will have to *do* things. The following is a list of some of the functions you'll need:

- **Initialize.** You'll need to set up the particle system to produce a desired effect; you do this by setting the properties listed previously with an initialize function. Because there are numerous parameters, you might want to pass them all to the function in a single structure containing all the values rather than passing them individually.

- **Update.** This function will use a time delta to update the particles managed in the system. It will also determine whether it's time to release one or more new particles.
- **Render.** The particle system knows how its particles are represented, so this function will just need to loop through its particles and use their position, size, and color to render them.
- **Move.** Even if you have set up the particle system on its own, there may be times when you want to explicitly relocate it in your world. This is done with a move function. You'll also add a function that returns the system's current position.
- **Change State.** This function simply changes the system's state, as mentioned previously. A corresponding function to determine the current state will be helpful as well.
- **Get/Set Force.** You'll use these to modify the force acting on the system, because it may change over time, and because the particles themselves will need to access this information when they update themselves.

As always, you may want to add or remove functions to fit your needs.

Particle-System Managers

So you have individual particles, which mostly handle themselves; and you have particle systems, which generate, update, and kill particles, and which can move and otherwise change themselves. If you have multiple particle systems within a game, which is usually the case, you might consider adding another layer to this—something that is to particle systems what particle systems are to particles: a particle-system manager. A *particle-system manager* could do things like move particle systems around; change the forces acting on particle systems, which would be influenced by some global values, such as wind; and create and kill particle systems, either as they are generated by happenings in the game world or as they move beyond the field of view of the player(s).

Particle-system managers can be fairly application specific, and for that reason, we're not going to provide an implementation here. However, the ideas suggested here and the implementation of the particles and particle systems should provide the basis you need to write your own.

Implementation

To this point, we've been focusing on design issues involved with the creation of a particle system. It's very important to think about the design, because you want your particle system to be as flexible and powerful as possible. To that end, the approach you'll take will be to first create a set of base classes that provide a bare minimum of the functionality common to any type of particle effect you want to create. These classes are not intended to be used directly for particle effects; instead you'll derive new classes from them, each new class implementing a specific type of effect.

First let's look at the individual particle class. Because you only have data members that will be accessed directly, you'll make it a struct:

```
struct particle_t
{
  vector3_t  m_pos;              // current position of the particle
  vector3_t  m_prevPos;          // last position of the particle
  vector3_t  m_velocity;         // direction and speed
  vector3_t  m_acceleration;     // acceleration

  float    m_energy;             // determines how long the particle is alive

  float    m_size;               // size of particle
  float    m_sizeDelta;          // amount to change the size over time

  float    m_weight;             // determines how gravity affects the particle
  float    m_weightDelta;        // change over time

  float    m_color[4];           // current color of the particle
  float    m_colorDelta[4];      // how the color changes with time
};
```

You'll notice that this implementation doesn't include many of the attributes discussed earlier. That's because this is a base class. You want to include only those attributes that will be useful in most particle effects. The alternative, which is to include all the attributes you think you'll ever need, has the advantage that you likely won't have to ever derive a new particle class. However, it also means that you'll have a lot of wasted memory because for any given effect at least a few fields will go unused. When dealing with effects that use thousands of particles, the wasted space can add up, so we'll take a minimalist approach here.

You've probably also noticed that this class has no methods. There's no need for anything other than the default constructor or destructor; the particle system will handle initializing the particles' attributes because some fields are dependent on values known only to the particle system. Also, although we discussed having a function that updates the particles' attributes based on a time delta, there is no such function. Again, the particle system will handle this. We decided to do this because the particle system needs to be fast, and, because there is some overhead involved in every function call, we wanted to avoid calling an update function possibly thousands of times every frame.

Moving on, you have the particle system itself:

```
class CParticleSystem
{
public:
    CParticleSystem(int maxParticles, vector3_t origin);
```

```cpp
  // abstract functions
  virtual void  Update(float elapsedTime)     = 0;
  virtual void  Render()                      = 0;

  virtual int   Emit(int numParticles);

  virtual void  InitializeSystem();
  virtual void  KillSystem();

protected:
  virtual void  InitializeParticle(int index) = 0;
  particle_t *m_particleList;     // particles for this emitter
  int         m_maxParticles;     // maximum number of particles in total
  int         m_numParticles;     // indices of all free particles
  vector3_t   m_origin;           // center of the particle system

  float       m_accumulatedTime;  // used to track how long since the last particle
was emitted

  vector3_t   m_force;                    // force (gravity, wind, etc.) acting on the
particle system
};

// Particles.cpp
/**************************************************************************
  CParticleSystem::Constructor

  Store initialization values and set defaults.
**************************************************************************/
CParticleSystem::CParticleSystem(int maxParticles, vector3_t origin)
{
  m_maxParticles = maxParticles;
  m_origin = origin;
  m_particleList = NULL;
} // end CParticleSystem::Constructor


/**************************************************************************
  CParticleSystem::Emit()
```

```
   Creates the number of new particles specified by the parameter, using
   the general particle system values with some random element. Note that
   only initial values will be randomized. Final values will not. This may
   be changed in the future.
***************************************************************************/
int CParticleSystem::Emit(int numParticles)
{
   // create numParticles new particles (if there's room)
   while (numParticles && (m_numParticles < m_maxParticles))
   {
      // initialize the current particle and increase the count
      InitializeParticle(m_numParticles++);
      --numParticles;
   }
   return numParticles;
} // end CParticleSystem::Emit




/**************************************************************************
  CParticleSystem::InitializeSystem()

  Allocate memory for the maximum number of particles in the system
***************************************************************************/
void CParticleSystem::InitializeSystem()
{
   // if this is just a reset, free the memory
   if (m_particleList)
   {
      delete[] m_particleList;
      m_particleList = NULL;
   }

   // allocate the maximum number of particles
   m_particleList = new particle_t[m_maxParticles];

   // reset the number of particles and accumulated time
   m_numParticles = 0;
   m_accumulatedTime = 0.0f;
} // end CParticleSystem::InitializeSystem
```

```
/**************************************************************************
CParticleSystem::KillSystem()

Tells the emitter to stop emitting. If the parameter is true, all live
particles are killed as well. Otherwise, they are allowed to die off on
their own.
**************************************************************************/
void CParticleSystem::KillSystem()
{
  if (m_particleList)
  {
    delete[] m_particleList;
    m_particleList = NULL;
  }

  m_numParticles = 0;
} // end CParticleSystem::KillSystem
```

This is an abstract base class, so it can't be used directly, but it provides a common framework from which you can easily derive to create a new particle class. It provides functions to initialize and kill the system, which are responsible for allocating and deleting an array large enough to hold the maximum number of particles. From 0 to (m_numParticles - 1), this array contains active particles, and m_numParticles to (m_maxParticles -1) contains particles that the Emit() function helps manage this array.

Particle-System Effects

With a base particle system implemented, you can now derive new particle systems from it to create specific effects. The trick is in knowing what attributes and behaviors to add to simulate a particular effect. As it turns out, it usually takes a bit of work and experimentation to get the effect you're after. We'd like nothing more than to give you an extensive list of popular effects and how to achieve them, but there are too many variables that come into play to make that possible. Instead, we can provide you with tips to get you started on the right track:

- **Think about it.** Most of the attributes in your particle system are meant to represent properties in the physical world. Because of this, common sense should give you a good starting point for implementing them. For example, you know that smoke rises, possibly affected by wind, so the initial velocity vector should be roughly up, with an orthogonal force affecting the particle if you want wind. Smoke also dissipates as it rises, gradually fading, suggesting that you have the size of the particle grow while its color fades.

- **Use physics.** So far, we've discussed only basic physics. If you want your particles to behave as closely to their physical counterparts as possible, consider using more advanced physics modeling (that is, if you have the CPU cycles for it). You'll still have to come up with a good way to represent them visually, but getting them to move correctly is a big part of the challenge.
- **Look at what others have done.** A lot of people have released particle-system demos on the Web, many of which have source code included. If you're stumped, looking at what's out there can give you ideas for things to try. We've listed several sites focusing on particle systems in Appendix A, "Online Resources."
- **Experiment.** The CD packaged with this book includes a particle-system demo called "Particle Sim" by Brian Tischler (based on a Direct3D-based project by Rich Benson) that will allow you to change settings in realtime to see the effects of most of the attributes we've discussed here. This is a great way to learn how particle-system effects are attained.

Example: Snowstorm

A discussion of particle systems wouldn't be complete without a program demonstrating some effects, so we put together an example, which you'll find on the CD in the directory for this chapter. There are also several particle systems in the game you develop in Chapter 21, "Making a Game: A Time to Kill."

This example is a simple snowstorm effect, shown in Figure 15.3. The class derived for this effect, CSnowstorm, uses textured quads to represent individual snowflakes and emits the particles from a rectangular area (the "sky").

We've included the implementation of CSnowstorm here for your convenience; the full program is, of course, included on the CD.

```
const vector3_t SNOWFLAKE_VELOCITY   (0.0f, -3.0f, 0.0f);
const vector3_t VELOCITY_VARIATION   (0.2f, 0.5f, 0.2f);
const float     SNOWFLAKE_SIZE     = 0.02f;
const float     SNOWFLAKES_PER_SEC = 2000;


/*************************** Data structures ***************************/
class CSnowstorm : public CParticleSystem
{
public:
  CSnowstorm(int maxParticles, vector3_t origin, float height, float width, float
depth);
```

Figure 15.3

Snow on a foggy terrain.

```
    void  Update(float elapsedTime);
    void  Render();

    void  InitializeSystem();
    void  KillSystem();

protected:
    void     InitializeParticle(int index);
    float    m_height;
    float    m_width;
    float    m_depth;

    GLuint  m_texture;      // snowflake texture
};

// snowstorm.cpp
/***********************************************************************
  CSnowstorm::Constructor

  Nothing to do
 ***********************************************************************/
```

```cpp
CSnowstorm::CSnowstorm(int numParticles, vector3_t origin, float height, float width,
float depth)
  : m_height(height), m_width(width), m_depth(depth), CParticleSystem(numParticles,
origin)
{
} // end CSnowstorm::Constructor


/******************************************************************************
  CSnowstorm::InitializeParticle()

  Sets the initial particle properties for the snowstorm
******************************************************************************/
void CSnowstorm::InitializeParticle(int index)
{
  // start the particle at the sky at a random location in the emission zone
  m_particleList[index].m_pos.y = m_height;
  m_particleList[index].m_pos.x = m_origin.x + FRAND * m_width;
  m_particleList[index].m_pos.z = m_origin.z + FRAND * m_depth;

  // set the size of the particle
  m_particleList[index].m_size = SNOWFLAKE_SIZE;

  // give the particle a random velocity
  m_particleList[index].m_velocity.x = SNOWFLAKE_VELOCITY.x + FRAND *
VELOCITY_VARIATION.x;
  m_particleList[index].m_velocity.y = SNOWFLAKE_VELOCITY.y + FRAND *
VELOCITY_VARIATION.y;
  m_particleList[index].m_velocity.z = SNOWFLAKE_VELOCITY.z + FRAND *
VELOCITY_VARIATION.z;
} // end CSnowstorm::InitializeParticle


/******************************************************************************
  CSnowstorm::Update

  Update the existing particles, killing them and creating new ones as needed
******************************************************************************/
void CSnowstorm::Update(float elapsedTime)
{
```

```cpp
    for (int i = 0; i < m_numParticles; )
    {
        // update the particle's position based on the elapsed time and velocity
        m_particleList[i].m_pos = m_particleList[i].m_pos + m_particleList[i].m_velocity *
elapsedTime;

        // if the particle has hit the ground plane, kill it
        if (m_particleList[i].m_pos.y <= m_origin.y)
        {
            // move the last particle to the current position, and decrease the count
            m_particleList[i] = m_particleList[--m_numParticles];
        }
        else
        {
            ++i;
        }
    }

    // store the accumulated time
    m_accumulatedTime += elapsedTime;

    // determine how many new particles are needed
    int newParticles = SNOWFLAKES_PER_SEC * m_accumulatedTime;

    // save the remaining time for after the new particles are released.
    m_accumulatedTime -= 1.0f/(float)SNOWFLAKES_PER_SEC * newParticles;

    Emit(newParticles);
} // end CSnowstorm::Update()


/*********************************************************************
  CSnowstorm::Render()

  Draw the snowflake particles as textured quads
*********************************************************************/
void CSnowstorm::Render()
{
    // enable alpha blending and texturing
    glEnable(GL_BLEND);
    glEnable(GL_TEXTURE_2D);
```

```cpp
    // set the blend mode
    glBlendFunc(GL_SRC_ALPHA, GL_ONE);

    // select the snow texture
    glBindTexture(GL_TEXTURE_2D, m_texture);
    glTexEnvf(GL_TEXTURE_ENV, GL_TEXTURE_ENV_MODE, GL_MODULATE);

    // to avoid constant dereferencing...
    vector3_t partPos;
    float size;

    // draw the quads
    glBegin(GL_QUADS);
    for (int i = 0; i < m_numParticles; ++i)
    {
      partPos = m_particleList[i].m_pos;
      size = m_particleList[i].m_size;
      glTexCoord2f(0.0, 1.0);
      glVertex3f(partPos.x, partPos.y, partPos.z);
      glTexCoord2f(1.0, 1.0);
      glVertex3f(partPos.x + size, partPos.y, partPos.z);
      glTexCoord2f(1.0, 0.0);
      glVertex3f(partPos.x + size, partPos.y - size, partPos.z);
      glTexCoord2f(0.0, 0.0);
      glVertex3f(partPos.x, partPos.y - size, partPos.z);
    }
    glEnd();

    glDisable(GL_BLEND);
    glDisable(GL_TEXTURE_2D);
} // end CSnowstorm::Update


/*****************************************************************************
  CSnowstorm::InitializeSystem

  Load the snow texture
*****************************************************************************/
void CSnowstorm::InitializeSystem()
{
    // get a texture object
```

```cpp
    glGenTextures(1, &m_texture);
    glBindTexture(GL_TEXTURE_2D, m_texture);

    // load the bitmap
    BITMAPINFOHEADER bitmapInfoHeader;
    unsigned char *buffer = LoadBitmapFileWithAlpha("snowstorm.bmp", &bitmapInfoHeader);

    // set up the texture
    glTexParameteri(GL_TEXTURE_2D, GL_TEXTURE_WRAP_S, GL_REPEAT);
    glTexParameteri(GL_TEXTURE_2D, GL_TEXTURE_WRAP_T, GL_REPEAT);
    glTexParameteri(GL_TEXTURE_2D, GL_TEXTURE_MAG_FILTER, GL_LINEAR);
    glTexParameteri(GL_TEXTURE_2D, GL_TEXTURE_MIN_FILTER, GL_LINEAR_MIPMAP_NEAREST);
    glTexImage2D(GL_TEXTURE_2D, 0, 4, bitmapInfoHeader.biWidth,
bitmapInfoHeader.biHeight, 0, GL_RGBA, GL_UNSIGNED_BYTE, buffer);
    gluBuild2DMipmaps(GL_TEXTURE_2D, 4, bitmapInfoHeader.biWidth,
bitmapInfoHeader.biHeight, GL_RGBA, GL_UNSIGNED_BYTE, buffer);

    // we're done with the bitmap data
    free(buffer);

    // let parent do remaining initialization
    CParticleSystem::InitializeSystem();
} // end CSnowstorm::InitializeSystem


/**************************************************************************
  CSnowstorm::KillSystem

  Free the texture
**************************************************************************/
void CSnowstorm::KillSystem()
{
    // if we have a valid texture object, free it
    if (glIsTexture(m_texture))
    {
        glDeleteTextures(1, &m_texture);
    }

    // let parent do remaining shutdown
    CParticleSystem::KillSystem();
} // end CSnowstorm::KillSystem
```

Fog

Adding fog to your world has more than one purpose. Besides trying to give the player the impression of actual fog, it can be used to obscure objects in the distance and have them gradually become clearer as the player gets closer. This is beneficial both in reducing the amount of geometry on the scene at one time (thus improving performance) and in preventing objects from suddenly popping into view as they enter the view frustum.

There is more than one way to implement fog, but because OpenGL provides native support for it, that's the approach we'll cover here.

OpenGL Fog

OpenGL's built-in fog support works by blending each pixel with the color of the fog using a blend factor dependent on the distance from the viewer, the density of the fog, and the currently selected fog mode (more on that momentarily). To turn on fog, you first have to enable it, which, not surprisingly, is done with a call to glEnable():

```
glEnable(GL_FOG);
```

Fog has several states associated with it, which you can control with calls to glFog():

```
glFogf(GLenum pname, GLfloat param);
glFogi(GLenum pname, GLint param);
glFogfv(GLenum pname, GLfloat *params);
glFogiv(GLenum pname, GLint *params);
```

In these prototypes, param represents a single parameter, and params represents an array of one or more parameters. The meanings of these parameters depend on the value of pname, which can be any of the values in Table 15.1.

The blending factor used to combine the fog color with geometry and pixels in the scene is determined by one of three functions, which is selected with the GL_FOG_MODE parameter. The three equations are as follows:

GL_LINEAR

$$blendFactor = (end-z) / (end-start)$$

GL_EXP

$$blendFactor = e^{(-density \times depth)}$$

GL_EXP2

$$blendFactor = e^{(-density \times depth)^2}$$

Table 15.1 Fog Parameters

Parameter	Description
GL_FOG_MODE	This parameter can be GL_LINEAR, GL_EXP, or GL_EXP2, specifying which of the three equations is used to calculate the blend factor. The default is GL_EXP.
GL_FOG_DENSITY	This parameter is a single value representing the density of the fog used in the three previous equations. The value must be positive, and the default is 1.0.
GL_FOG_START	This parameter is a single value defining the start, or near distance, used in the three fog equations.
GL_FOG_END	This parameter is a single value defining the end, or far distance, used in the three fog equations.
GL_FOG_INDEX	This parameter specifies the color index to use for fog when using 8-bit color.
GL_FOG_COLOR	This specifies the color to be used for fog. It is an array—and so requires one of the array versions of glFog()—representing color values. The default fog color is black.

You don't really need to know these, except to understand how the values are used. Note that the start and end values matter only if you are using GL_LINEAR mode, and density matters only when you are using GL_EXP or GL_EXP2 mode.

And that's it! As you can see, adding OpenGL's native fog to your game is really quite simple. You may have to tweak the parameters to get it to look the way you want, but with a little experimentation, you should soon be quite comfortable with OpenGL's fog support.

NOTE

You can turn fog on and off at will so that you can have it affect only some of the objects in your scene.

Volumetric Fog

Although OpenGL's fog is easy to use and looks pretty good in most cases, it's far from perfect. Its most notable shortcoming is that the fog color calculated for each vertex is based on the z distance from the plane perpendicular to the viewer's line of sight. This becomes evident if there are objects in the player's peripheral vision that are far away but that are close in the z direction. These objects won't appear as heavily fogged as they should be.

Ideally, rather than having fog effects appear based on distance alone, the fog could be represented as a physical entity in your world. There are several common ways to represent fog in this way, including as spheres, particles, or as fog maps (similar in concept to lightmaps). Collectively, these methods are known as *volumetric fog*. Whichever method is used, the effect is that you're defining volumes of fog filling your world. These volumes aren't drawn directly, but rather, as you draw other objects, you determine how much fog the object is being viewed through and adjust the lighting and coloring of the object accordingly.

Unfortunately, we don't have the space to cover the technical details of volumetric fog, but there are several good articles online describing it. Check Appendix A for URLs.

REFLECTIONS

In Chapter 9, "Advanced Texture Mapping," we discussed using environment maps to make objects appear to reflect the room around them. Although environment maps can offer impressive results, there are other ways to simulate reflections that can be coded very quickly. In this section, we're going to cover casting reflections in a plane.

If you've looked at the sample programs included with the book, you've already seen the technique we'll be discussing in action. The only difference is that in the sample programs, we were able to take advantage of some scene-specific details to simplify the process.

Let's start off with a simple situation to get an idea of how the technique works, and then we'll look at other factors you need to account for to apply the technique in general. Imagine a scene with an infinite plane at $y = 0$ with an object suspended in the air above it. How do you get the object to cast a reflection on the surface? You simply draw the plane and the object normally once, and then draw the object a second time after reversing the sign on its y coordinates:

```
DrawGround();
DrawObject();
glScale(1.0, -1.0, 1.0);
DrawObject();
```

Reflecting Lights

That's the basic concept, but to get the reflections to look right, there's a lot more that needs to be done. First of all, if you're using lights, then the reflected objects will be shaded incorrectly unless you reflect the light position along with the positions of the reflected objects. Let's assume that the lights are positioned in a function called PositionLights(), in which case, the code can be changed to the following:

```
PositionLights();
DrawGround();
DrawObject();
glScale(1.0, -1.0, 1.0);
PositionLights();
DrawObject();
```

Handling the Depth Buffer

There are still numerous significant problems that need to be fixed. For starters, if you're using a depth buffer (and you probably are), then the reflected object isn't going to show up at all because the plane is closer to the eye. The obvious solution is to turn off the depth test when rendering the reflected object, and in this simple example, that would work. However, if you have multiple objects being reflected, you can run into problems if some of them are close together. You still want them to obscure each other just as the non-reflected versions do. The answer is to not write to the depth buffer when you're drawing the plane. You still perform the depth test because you don't want the plane to obscure anything that's in front of it, but by not updating the depth buffer, anything that's behind it (for example, the reflections) will show up. Let's take a gander at how this might look:

```
// draw original object
PositionLights();
DrawObjects();
glDepthMask(GL_FALSE);
DrawGround();
// draw the reflected object
glScale(1.0, -1.0, 1.0);
PositionLights();
DrawObject();
```

Handling Finite Planes Using Stencil Buffers

Thus far, we've assumed that the plane is infinite, which, in practice, isn't going to be the case. If the ground plane isn't infinite, then the player may be able to move into a position where he can see under it, seeing more of the reflected image than he should, thus spoiling the illusion (see Figure 15.4). A similar problem occurs if the plane is surrounded by non-reflective surfaces, as is the case with a mirror hanging on a wall. You don't want the reflection showing up in the wall next to the mirror!

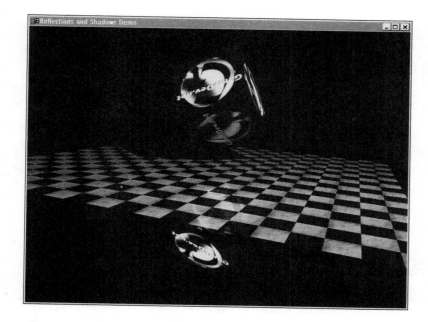

Figure 15.4

The reflection illusion falling apart.

In the demos that used reflections, this wasn't a problem because it wasn't possible for the player to be in a position to see behind the reflective surface. Ultimately, though, you need a solution that works in all situations. What you want to do is tell OpenGL to not render the reflections anywhere other than the reflective plane. Fortunately for you, OpenGL provides the stencil buffer for exactly this kind of application. Your algorithm will be modified so that first you set the stencil buffer wherever the surface appears. At this point, you don't want to actually draw the surface, so you'll disable the color and depth buffers and just write to the stencil buffer. Then you draw the reflected object, only drawing where the stencil buffer is set. Finally, you draw the surface and the object normally. The new code follows:

```
// use the surface to set the stencil buffer wherever it appears
glColorMask(GL_FALSE, GL_FALSE, GL_FALSE, GL_FALSE);
glDepthMask(GL_FALSE);
glEnable(GL_STENCIL_TEST);
glStencilFunc(GL_ALWAYS, 1, 0xFFFFFFFF);
glStencilOp(GL_REPLACE, GL_REPLACE, GL_REPLACE);
DrawSurface();

// draw the reflection only where the stencil buffer is set
glColorMask(GL_TRUE, GL_TRUE, GL_TRUE, GL_TRUE);
glDepthMask(GL_TRUE);
glStencilFunc(GL_EQUAL, 1, 0xFFFFFFFF);
glStencilOp(GL_KEEP, GL_KEEP, GL_KEEP);

glPushMatrix();
  glScalef(1.0, -1.0, 1.0);
  PositionLights();
  DrawObject();
glPopMatrix();

PositionLights();
DrawSurface();
DrawObject();
```

Addressing Irregular Reflective Surfaces

The method we've used so far assumes the use of a perfectly reflective surface—the reflected object looks exactly like the original. That works great for mirrors, but what about other reflective surfaces, such as metal? In the latter case, the reflection should be blended with the surface, so the image becomes a combination of both. Naturally, you can use OpenGL's blending functions to accomplish this. When blending, the reflected objects should be drawn normally first, and then the plane should be drawn with blending enabled. The only change required in the previous code is to enable blending the second time DrawSurface() is called.

Handling Arbitrarily Oriented Planes

The reflective plane you've been using is the xz plane, which makes the reflection transformation itself simple. In practice, you'll want to be able to use arbitrarily oriented planes for reflection. All that this requires is some additional transformation steps:

1. Translate and rotate the reflective plane and the reflected objects so that the plane lies in the xz plane, centered about the origin.
2. Perform the reflection transformation by inverting the coordinate corresponding to the plane you're reflecting through (that is, y for the xz plane, z for the xy plane, and x for the yz plane).
3. Reverse the transformation performed in step 1 to move everything back to its proper position.

Assuming that the xz plane is being used, if the matrix that performs step 1 is represented as mat, and the inverse of mat is matInverse, the complete reflection transformation is as follows:

```
glMultMatrixf(matInverse);
glScalef(1.0, -1.0, 1.0);
glMultMatrixf(mat);
```

That should be all you need to perform realistic-looking planar reflections. You can use this technique to create multiple reflective surfaces just by repeating the process for each plane. You could even create complex surfaces that are reflective by treating each polygon of the surface as a plane. Just because you can, however, doesn't mean you should. Remember that for each reflective plane, you're making an additional pass through much of your geometry. More than a handful of reflective planes will quickly bring your game to a crawl, so use reflections with moderation.

This is the part where we'd normally present a demo. However, since reflections have been used in sample programs from previous chapters, we'll instead combine reflections into the sample program for the next section, "Shadows."

SHADOWS

Look around you right now. Chances are, there are shadows all over the place. Because shadows are a common part of the world you see around you, shadows in your games will add a greater degree of realism. In addition, they serve a role in establishing spatial relationships between objects, further enhancing the illusion of 3D. Over the years, numerous techniques have been developed to create realistic-looking shadows.

Creating a shadow for a sphere floating over a flat plane with a single light source is conceptually fairly easy; you can simply determine which region of the plane is blocked from the view of the light by the sphere. But what if the surface on which the shadow is being cast is not flat? What if, instead of a sphere or other simple geometric object, you have an irregularly shaped object, which shades portions of itself? What about multiple objects in the scene that can cast shadows on each other? What about multiple light sources? Then there is the issue of hard shadows versus soft shadows. Hard shadows are of (relatively) uniform darkness with a distinct edge. Soft shadows, on the other hand, have a soft edge and get gradually darker as you move toward the center. Hard shadows result from a single, fairly focused light source, while soft shadows are the result of multiple light sources, area light sources, and/or ambient light. Both exist in nature, but soft shadows require more work (with most methods) than do hard shadows.

As you can see, modeling of shadows is fairly complex, which is why there are so many ways to do it. Most methods don't correctly address all the issues we've just mentioned, although a few cover the majority of them. There are, however, only a handful of methods that result in a realistic-looking shadow and that also can be rendered at interactive speeds; those are the techniques covered here.

Static Shadows

This approach avoids the issue of having to calculate shadows in realtime altogether. Instead, the shadows are calculated in advance, generally using the most realistic model available (which is usually too expensive to do in realtime), and then added to the scene at runtime, usually as a texture. This method is by far the cheapest, since you aren't adding any additional processing at runtime. The problem is that they don't look very real. Even if you move shadows with objects as they move, they won't change in shape, and they don't change position in relation to light sources. In some cases, though, they look good enough, especially in 2D games or when realism isn't the goal. Because using static shadows is really just a matter of manipulating your game data rather than doing anything programmatically, we won't cover the technique here.

Projective Shadows

Projective shadows, which have been in use for a few years in a number of demos and games, is the method used in the sample program at the end of this section. Projective shadows provide a means to quickly cast shadows onto a plane, with very good-looking results. The idea behind the algorithm is to project the object casting the shadow onto a plane from the perspective of the light. This has the effect of flattening the object, similar to the way objects are flattened onto your 2D screen from the perspective of the viewer. All you have to do is draw the flattened object in black, and you have a shadow!

The Shadow-Projection Matrix

Now that you know the basic concept, let's look at the details of how to implement projective shadows. First of all, you'll need a matrix that performs the projection. The matrix will depend on the position of the light source and the plane onto which you're projecting. Rather than going through the complete matrix derivation, let's just look at the result, shown in Figure 15.5.

Figure 15.5

*Shadow-
projection
matrix.*

$$
\begin{bmatrix}
dot - lightPos[0] * plane.a & - lightPos[1] * plane.a & - lightPos[2] * plane.a & - lightPos[3] * plane.a \\
- lightPos[0] * plane.b & dot - lightPos[1] * plane.b & - lightPos[2] * plane.b & - lightPos[3] * plane.b \\
- lightPos[0] * plane.c & - lightPos[1] * plane.c & dot - lightPos[2] * plane.c & - lightPos[3] * plane.c \\
- lightPos[0] * plane.d & - lightPos[1] * plane.d & - lightPos[2] * plane.d & dot - lightPos[3] * plane.d
\end{bmatrix}
$$

In this equation, dot is the dot product of lightPos and plane. lightPos is an array where elements 0, 1, and 2 correspond to the x, y, and z coordinates of the light's position, and element 3 is set to 0 or 1 depending on whether the light is directional or positional (respectively). plane is a structure in which a, b, c, and d come from the plane equation $ax + by + cz + d = 0$. To find a, b, c, and d for any plane, you need the plane's normal vector and any point on the plane. Given those, a, b, and c are just the x, y, and z components of the normal, and d can be found by plugging the coordinates of the point into the plane equation. We discuss this more completely in Chapter 19, "Physics Modeling with OpenGL."

Once you've created the shadow-projection matrix, you just need to apply it to the vertices of the objects that you want to cast shadows, and the shadows will be drawn on the plane you specify. Unless you take additional steps, however, what gets drawn on the plane will look like a flattened version of the object, and not like a shadow at all. This is illustrated in Figure 15.6.

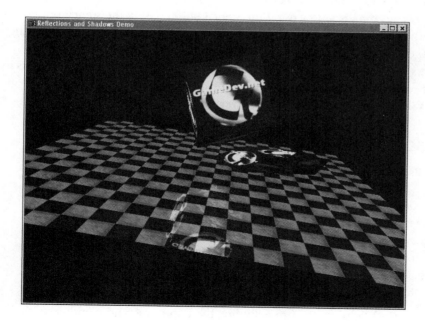

Figure 15.6

*Something's definitely
wrong here.*

Fixing this problem is pretty easy. You just need to draw the shadow as completely black, which can be done by disabling lighting and textures and setting the current color to black before drawing the object. In addition, you should blend the shadow with the surface on which it's being cast for the best-looking results.

Handling Problems with the Depth Buffer

Another problem creeps up in that the shadow will be co-planar with the surface it is on. Although that is your intent, it creates a problem with the depth buffer. Because you can't represent depth values with infinite precision, the shadow won't always have depth values exactly equal to those of the surface. Sometimes, they'll be closer, and other times, they'll be farther away, and the end result is that the shadow can have holes in it. There are a few solutions to this, including using polygon offsets, but the solution we'll use here is to simply disable the depth test while drawing the shadow. Then, you just have to be sure to draw the shadow before anything that might appear in front of it (otherwise, the shadow will appear in front of objects that it shouldn't).

Restricting the Shadow with the Stencil Buffer

Finally, because the surface on which you're drawing the shadow probably isn't infinite, you should restrict the shadow so that it's not drawn outside this surface. As with reflections in the previous section, this can be accomplished by using the stencil buffer. Using the stencil buffer allows you to defeat another problem that occurs when using blending: Unless the object casting a shadow is a single polygon or some other very simple shape, there will be some pixels on the surface that have shadows drawn on them more than once. The blending will cause these spots to appear darker. For a nice, even shadow, each pixel should be drawn exactly once. To do this, you just have to change the value in the stencil buffer whenever the stencil test passes as you're drawing the shadow.

The entire process can be summarized in the following steps:

1. Use the surface to set the stencil buffer, and limit the rendering of the shadow to this area only.
2. Create a shadow-projection matrix using the position of the light and plane equation and multiply it by the modelview matrix.
3. Disable lighting and texture mapping, and set the current color to black.
4. Disable the depth test.
5. Enable blending.
6. Draw the object that is casting a shadow.

After you're done, be sure to set lighting, texture mapping, the depth test, and blending to their original states. The sample program at the end of this section shows this process in action, including the code corresponding to the preceding steps.

Handling Multiple Light Sources and Multiple Planar Surfaces

Thus far, you've assumed a single light source and a single planar surface. If you want more than one light source, you can just repeat the preceding process for each one of them. You can do the same for each surface, and even use this approach to create complex surfaces by repeating the process for each polygon, just as with reflections. Of course, the cost of doing this will soon become prohibitive. Overall, you will have to make one pass through your geometry per light per surface, which adds up quickly, so use this technique sparingly.

Problems with Projective Shadows

Projective shadows look good, but they aren't perfect. First of all, they don't really allow concave objects to cast shadows on themselves or objects to cast shadows on each other unless you treat every polygon in your scene as a shadowed surface—which isn't practical at all. Second, they produce hard shadows. You can create soft shadows with projective shadows by moving the light source slightly as you make multiple passes (a process known as *jittering*) and blending the results, but the overhead this adds offsets the benefit you'll gain from it. Third, because you're blending the shadow with the surface, any specular highlights on that surface in the shadowed area will still show up, which they shouldn't (how can there be a highlight in an area that's not illuminated by the light?). Despite their limitations, however, projective shadows work well in a wide variety of situations. As you can see from the sample program, they produce results that are quite satisfactory.

Stenciled Shadow Volumes

Stenciled shadow volumes have been around for a while but haven't been used as widely as other methods because they require more processing time. With the rapid advances in hardware in general and graphics accelerators in particular over the past several years, however, we are now at the point where stenciled shadow volumes can be used in complex scenes at interactive rates. The advantage they offer over projective shadows is that they correctly shadow every surface in the scene, allowing objects to cast shadows on other objects and even to self shadow. They also avoid the appearance of specular highlights in shadowed areas. Because they provide more realistic-looking shadows and are available now in realtime, they are worth mentioning here, although we'll just describe the algorithm and not provide implementation details.

The idea behind shadow volumes is that you cast lines from the light source through the edges of the objects in your world, which then define infinite volumes on the opposite side of the object, as illustrated in Figure 15.7. After all of your shadow volumes are defined, you just need to determine whether objects or portions of objects lie within the boundaries of one of them. That leaves you with two challenges: how to find the shadow volumes and how to determine whether or not any given point is located within one.

Figure 15.7

*A simple shadow
volume.*

Much of the cost involved with shadow volumes relates to determining what the volumes are. To do this, you need to find the silhouette edge of every object in the scene from the perspective of the light source. The *silhouette edge* is any edge where one adjacent polygon is front facing and the other is back facing. Although we won't go into implementation details, this essentially requires that you test every edge on every object in the scene to see if it qualifies. Once you have found all the silhouette edges, you take the vertices that define them and cast lines through them from the light source, thereby creating infinite quads that collectively comprise enclosed shadow volumes.

To determine whether a point lies within a shadow volume, you just need to cast a ray from the eye to the point and count each time you enter or leave a shadow volume. You can tell if you are entering a shadow volume if the quad you are intersecting is front facing. If it is back facing, you are leaving the shadow volume. All you need to do, then, is increment the count every time you intersect a front-facing shadow quad and decrement the count when you intersect a back-facing quad. The counting can be handled easily using the stencil buffer (hence *stenciled* shadow volumes) by using the following steps:

1. Render the scene normally using ambient and emissive lighting.
2. Make a second pass, this time rendering only the shadow volumes. Because we don't actually want to see the shadow volumes as if they were objects in the scene, disable writes to the depth and color buffers and write only to the stencil buffer. This time through, you're counting how many times a shadow volume is entered, so cull back-facing polygons and set the stencil buffer to increment every time the depth test passes.

3. Make a third pass, similar to the second, but this time cull front-facing polygons, and decrement the value of the stencil buffer when the depth test passes.
4. Make another pass through the geometry, this time rendering with diffuse and specular lighting, but only where the stencil buffer is equal to 0.

There are a few disadvantages to this approach. Because four passes are required, it requires a great deal of processing power, although, as mentioned earlier, this is becoming less of an issue. Another complication is caused by the near viewing plane intersecting a shadow volume, in which case the count is thrown off because you're starting inside a shadow volume and the steps above assume that you don't. There are ways to deal with this, but it further complicates the algorithm. All in all, though, shadow volumes provide impressive results and are beginning to be used in games, so they are worth exploring further on your own.

Other Methods

There are other methods for creating shadows that we can't cover here, including shadow maps, hybrid methods, and even radiosity. For more information on these methods, as well as on the methods presented here, check Appendix A.

Example: Reflections and Shadows

To illustrate reflection and projective shadow methods, we've revisited the rotating cube example from Chapter 1, "The Exploration Begins: OpenGL and DirectX." Although the demo itself is similar, the code has been updated to use the stencil buffer to ensure that the reflection and shadow are not drawn outside the reflective surface. The full source for the project, called *refshad*, is included on the CD in the directory for this chapter, so we'll just look at the relevant portions here.

At initialization, the following is done to create the shadow-projection matrix:

```
float plane[4] = { 0.0, 1.0, 0.0, 0.0 };
SetShadowMatrix(g_shadowMatrix, g_lightPos, plane);
```

g_shadowMatrix is a global array of 16 floats, and g_lightPos is a global array holding the light position. SetShadowMatrix() creates the matrix we described earlier, as follows:

```
void SetShadowMatrix(GLfloat destMat[16], float lightPos[4], float plane[4])
{
  GLfloat dot;
```

```
  // dot product of plane and light position
  dot = plane[0] * lightPos[0] + plane[1] * lightPos[1] + plane[1] * lightPos[2] +
plane[3] * lightPos[3];

  // first column
  destMat[0] = dot - lightPos[0] * plane[0];
  destMat[4] = 0.0f - lightPos[0] * plane[1];
  destMat[8] = 0.0f - lightPos[0] * plane[2];
  destMat[12] = 0.0f - lightPos[0] * plane[3];

  // second column
  destMat[1] = 0.0f - lightPos[1] * plane[0];
  destMat[5] = dot - lightPos[1] * plane[1];
  destMat[9] = 0.0f - lightPos[1] * plane[2];
  destMat[13] = 0.0f - lightPos[1] * plane[3];

  // third column
  destMat[2] = 0.0f - lightPos[2] * plane[0];
  destMat[6] = 0.0f - lightPos[2] * plane[1];
  destMat[10] = dot - lightPos[2] * plane[2];
  destMat[14] = 0.0f - lightPos[2] * plane[3];

  // fourth column
  destMat[3] = 0.0f - lightPos[3] * plane[0];
  destMat[7] = 0.0f - lightPos[3] * plane[1];
  destMat[11] = 0.0f - lightPos[3] * plane[2];
  destMat[15] = dot - lightPos[3] * plane[3];
} // end SetShadowMatrix()
```

And finally, the bulk of the work is done in the DisplayScene() function:

```
BOOL DisplayScene()
{
  // set up the view orientation
  glLoadIdentity();
  gluLookAt(0.0, 3.0, 10.0,
            0.0, 0.0, 0.0,
            0.0, 1.0, 0.0);

  // clear the screen
  glClear(GL_COLOR_BUFFER_BIT | GL_DEPTH_BUFFER_BIT | GL_STENCIL_BUFFER_BIT);
```

```
// rotate the scene
g_rotationAngle += (DEGREES_PER_SECOND * g_timer.GetElapsedSeconds());
glRotated(-g_rotationAngle/8.0, 0.0, 1.0, 0.0);
glRotated(10.0 * sin(g_rotationAngle/45.0), 1.0, 0.0, 0.0);

// prepare to write to the stencil buffer by turning off writes to the
// color and depth buffer
glColorMask(GL_FALSE, GL_FALSE, GL_FALSE, GL_FALSE);
glDepthMask(GL_FALSE);

// set up the stencil func and op to place a 1 in the stencil buffer
// everywhere we're about to draw
glEnable(GL_STENCIL_TEST);
glStencilFunc(GL_ALWAYS, 1, 0xFFFFFFFF);
glStencilOp(GL_REPLACE, GL_REPLACE, GL_REPLACE);

// render the surface. Since the depth and color buffers are disabled,
// only the stencil buffer will be modified
DrawSurface();

// turn the color and depth buffers back on
glColorMask(GL_TRUE, GL_TRUE, GL_TRUE, GL_TRUE);
glDepthMask(GL_TRUE);

// from this point until the stencil test is disabled, only draw where
// the stencil buffer is set to 1
glStencilFunc(GL_EQUAL, 1, 0xFFFFFFFF);

// don't modify the contents of the stencil buffer
glStencilOp(GL_KEEP, GL_KEEP, GL_KEEP);

// draw the reflected cube first
glPushMatrix();
  glScalef(1.0, -1.0, 1.0);
  glLightfv(GL_LIGHT0, GL_POSITION, g_lightPos);
  DrawCube();
glPopMatrix();

// draw the surface normally, blending it with the reflected cube
glLightfv(GL_LIGHT0, GL_POSITION, g_lightPos);
glEnable(GL_BLEND);
```

```
      DrawSurface();
      glDisable(GL_BLEND);

      // draw the shadow
      glPushMatrix();
        // draw the shadow as black, blended with the surface, with no lighting, and not
        // performing the depth test
        glDisable(GL_TEXTURE_2D);
        glDisable(GL_LIGHTING);
        glDisable(GL_DEPTH_TEST);
        glEnable(GL_BLEND);
        // make sure that we don't draw at any raster position more than once
        glStencilOp(GL_KEEP, GL_KEEP, GL_INCR);
        glColor4f(0.0, 0.0, 0.0, 0.5f);

        // project the cube through the shadow matrix
        glMultMatrixf(g_shadowMatrix);
        DrawCube();

        glEnable(GL_TEXTURE_2D);
        glEnable(GL_DEPTH_TEST);
        glDisable(GL_BLEND);
        glEnable(GL_LIGHTING);
      glPopMatrix();
      glDisable(GL_STENCIL_TEST);

      // draw the cube normally
      glPushMatrix();
        DrawCube();
      glPopMatrix();

      return TRUE;
    } // end DisplayScene()
```

The product of all of this is shown in Figure 15.8.

Figure 15.8

Shadows and reflections in action.

SUMMARY

In this chapter, you learned how to create a number of commonly used special effects. You learned how to use billboarding to fake true 3D. You learned how particle systems can be used to create a wide variety of effects and have foundation classes you can build on to create your own effects. You saw how fog is used not only as a special effect, but also as a tool to reduce scene complexity by gradually obscuring objects as they approach the far end of the view frustum. You learned about a simple technique for creating fast planar reflections. Finally, you saw several alternatives to adding realtime shadows to your game.

You don't need to use all these techniques in your games, and you definitely don't want to overdo it by throwing every possible special effect in. That said, judicious use of these and other special effects can greatly add to the realism and make the game much more interesting.

Part III

Building a Game

CHAPTER 16

USING DIRECTX: DIRECTINPUT

ost of the demos we've created for this book have involved some kind of user input, and naturally, for any kind of interesting game, input is going to be necessary. In this chapter, we're going to cover the preferred method of handling game input under Windows, which is using the component of DirectX known as DirectInput. In the process, we'll do the following:

- Examine some of the alternatives to DirectInput, including Windows messages and the Win32 API, and discuss the advantages and disadvantages of each.
- Learn what DirectInput is and how to start using it.
- Create DirectInputDevice objects to represent the keyboard, mouse, and other input devices.
- Cover the various methods for obtaining data from these devices.
- Create a simple DirectInput-based input system that can easily be added to new or existing projects and create a sample program illustrating this system's use.

WHY USE DIRECTINPUT?

None of the sample programs we've shown so far has used DirectInput. Because these programs seem to handle user input quite well, you may be wondering why you need to bother learning DirectInput. So that you can understand the advantages of it, we should first discuss what some of the alternatives are and where they fall short.

Windows Messages

As you probably know, Windows constantly sends messages to your application, notifying it of certain events. Included in these messages are ones generated by input devices. Any time a user presses a key, moves the mouse, clicks a mouse button, and so on, Windows automatically generates a message and sends it to your message handler. There are several dozen input-related message types, but we'll only look at the most relevant ones, which are listed in Table 16.1.

You can use these messages to get input for your games, but doing so will require a few tricks. Let's look at a couple of the challenges involved with this approach.

In your game, you'll probably have many commands that are executed when the player presses a single key one time. For example, the user might press a number key to change weapons, press a key to pull up a configuration message, press a key to jump to a unit, and so on. In these cases, Windows messages work pretty well. From the message loop, you call some routines that initiate a series of animations, change state settings, or some other appropriate action. Coming up with a means of doing this elegantly will require some work, but it's not too bad.

Now consider capturing input that requires the player to hold down a key for an extended period of time, such as moving, or altering the way he moves (for example, holding down the Shift key to run). This doesn't work well with messages for two reasons. First, when a key is pressed and held, Windows initially sends a single message to your application. Then, after a brief pause, it begins to re-send the message repeatedly. The repeated messages are good, but the pause is bad; it will cause the onscreen animation to jerk every time the player starts to move or change direction. The second problem with this approach is that it's not very intuitive. The player is probably moving all the time; rather than having Windows inform you of movement changes through messages, it would be better if you could poll the state of the keyboard every frame to see how the player is moving and update the view matrix accordingly. This second issue isn't just keyboard specific; it comes into play with the mouse as well.

To make Windows messages more usable, you need to come up with some way to store the input information that Windows sends you in a place that your game loop can then access when it's ready. Taking keyboard input as an example, you could create an array of 256 boolean values, set to `false` by default. Any time a `WM_KEYDOWN` message is received, the entry in this array for the key that was pressed is set to `true`. When a `WM_KEYUP` message is received, the value is reset to `false`. Then, the game loop can check this array to see whether a particular key is being pressed. The only down side of this approach is that if a user presses and releases a key quickly enough (that is, so that both the `WM_KEYDOWN` and `WM_KEYUP` messages arrive without a game loop iteration between them), you might not catch it. Since you're hopefully rendering more than 20 frames per second, though, this will rarely be an issue.

Overall, using Windows messages for input isn't a bad approach, and we've seen it used in a number of demos. However, it does have one other drawback that lessens its value in full-blown games, a drawback that is associated with Windows messages in general—lag. Depending on what processes are running on the machine and how many other messages are waiting for your application, there may be a noticeable delay between when the user presses a key or moves the mouse and when your game receives the message and processes it. Because players expect an immediate response, this is something you need to avoid.

Table 16.1 Windows Input Messages

Message	Comments
WM_CHAR	This message is generated any time a WM_KEYDOWN message is processed by TranslateMessage(). *wParam* contains the character code of the key that was pressed. *lParam* is a bit field containing additional information, including the repeat count, previous key state, whether the Alt key was also pressed, and so on. In general, this message is best used when you want to handle text input from the user and isn't as useful for real-time input; for this reason, we won't cover it any further here.
WM_KEYDOWN	This message is generated when a non-system (that is, not pressed in combination with the Alt key) key is pressed. *wParam* contains the virtual key code of the key that was pressed (these are represented in the form VK_*keyname*; see your Win32 documentation for a complete list). *lParam* contains additional information about the current keyboard state. The nice thing about this is that it simply tells you which key was pressed; no translation occurs and no distinction is made between lowercase and uppercase letters, which makes it better suited for game control.
WM_KEYUP	This message serves a purpose similar to WM_KEYDOWN, the only difference being that this message is generated when a key is released.
WM_LBUTTONDOWN	This message is generated when the left mouse button is pressed. *wParam* indicates which buttons or keys were also down at the time and can be one or more of the following:

MK_CONTROL	The Ctrl key was down
MK_SHIFT	The Shift key was down
MK_LBUTTON	The left mouse button was down
MK_MBUTTON	The middle mouse button was down
MK_RBUTTON	The right mouse button was down

Message	Comments
	The high-order word of *lParam* specifies the y coordinate of the mouse pointer at the time the button was clicked, and the low-order word specifies the x coordinate. These coordinates are relative to the top-left corner of the client area (or screen, for full-screen apps). If you're not familiar with how to extract the high- and low-order words from an integer, don't worry. Passing *lParam* to the `GET_X_LPARAM` and `GET_Y_LPARAM` macros can easily retrieve these values, or passing *lParam* to the `MAKEPOINTS` macro can retrieve a `POINT` structure.
WM_MBUTTONDOWN	Generated when the middle mouse button (usually the mouse wheel on PCs) is pressed. Otherwise the same as `WM_LBUTTONDOWN`.
WM_RBUTTONDOWN	Generated when the right mouse button is pressed. Otherwise the same as `WM_LBUTTONDOWN`.
WM_LBUTTONUP	Generated when the left mouse button is released. Otherwise the same as `WM_LBUTTONDOWN`.
WM_MBUTTONUP	Generated when the middle mouse button (usually the mouse wheel on PCs) is released. Otherwise the same as `WM_LBUTTONDOWN`.
WM_RBUTTONUP	Generated when the right mouse button is released. Otherwise the same as `WM_LBUTTONDOWN`.
WM_MOUSEMOVE	This message is posted every time the mouse cursor moves. *wParam* can be any of the key indicators listed above under `WL_LBUTTONDOWN`. *lParam* is the new position of the cursor, stored and retrieved in the same way as with the other mouse messages.
WM_MOUSEWHEEL	This message is posted any time the mouse wheel is rolled. The low-order word of *wParam* is the key indicator, just as with other mouse messages, and the high-order word is the distance the wheel was rotated, represented in multiples or divisions of `WHEEL_DELTA` (defined to be 120). If the number is positive, the wheel was rotated away from the user. If it is negative, the wheel was rotated toward the user. *lParam* contains the position of the mouse cursor.

Win32

As we just mentioned, in many cases, we'd rather poll the state of input devices when it's convenient for us to do so rather than having the devices notify us when the user has done something. We found a way around this when using Windows messages, but in many cases, it would be much easier to just circumvent the Windows message process and instead, directly query the state of input devices. Fortunately, Win32 provides functions to do just that for the keyboard, and even for joysticks. There are a number of functions that interact directly with the mouse as well, but it's generally easier to just use Windows messages instead. In any case, let's look at Win32 keyboard and joystick support.

Win32 Keyboard Input

Win32 contains a couple dozen functions related to keyboard input, but we are interested in only one: GetAsyncKeyState().

```
SHORT GetAsyncKeyState(int vKey);
```

The value returned by this function represents two things: If the most significant bit is set, then the key indicated by *vKey* is currently down. Alternatively, if the least significant bit is set, then the key wasn't down the last time GetAsyncKeyState() was called. Most of the time, you only care about whether or not the key is currently down, so it's convenient to create macros to just test the most significant bit, such as the following:

```
#define KEY_DOWN(vKey)   (GetAsyncKeyState(vKey) & 0x8000) ? true : false
#define KEY_UP(vKey)     (GetAsyncKeyState(vKey) & 0x8000) ? false : true
```

The value passed to GetAsyncKeyState() (or to either of these macros) is one of the 256 possible virtual key codes (actually, some values aren't used, so there are fewer than 256). The most common virtual key codes are listed in Table 16.2. Note that the alpha-numeric values (0–9 and A–Z) are not listed; that's because their virtual key code values are equivalent to their ASCII values, so you can just use the corresponding characters (1, 2, 3..., and A, B, C...). For the alphabetic characters, you should use only uppercase because the ASCII values of lowercase characters map to different virtual key codes.

A related function, GetKeyState(), serves the same purpose on a high level; however, it determines the current state based on information gained from processing and receiving the keyboard messages listed previously, so it can suffer from the same lag problem.

Armed with GetAsychKeyState(), you can now query the keyboard at your leisure to see if the user is pressing any of the keys you care about. Because it allows for an almost immediate response to user input (assuming you're checking every frame), it may be all you need for keyboard input.

Win32 Joystick Input

Windows provides some basic support for joysticks (up to two) through a small number of functions. To use these functions, you must include *mmsystem.h* and link to *winmm.lib*. The provided functions allow you to either query the status of the joystick directly or to have the joystick send messages to your window as events occur. Although the Win32 joystick API is fairly simple, it lacks the performance requirements and flexibility to deal with the myriad input devices available today. So rather than exploring this API extensively here, we'll look briefly at the direct query method and move on.

You can determine the present state of the joystick using the following:

```
MMRESULT joyGetPos(UNIT joyID, LPJOYINFO pji);
```

If successful, this function returns JOYERR_NOERROR; otherwise it returns an error code. *joyID* indicates which joystick you are querying and must be either JOYSTICKID1 or JOYSTICKID2. *pji* is a pointer to a JOYINFO structure, which is defined as follows:

```
typedef struct
{
  UINT wXpos;      // x coordinate
  UINT wYpos;      // y coordinate
  UINT wZpos;      // z coordinate
  UINT wButtons;   // set of flags indicating which buttons are down
} JOYINFO;
```

wButtons will be a combination of any of the following, corresponding to which buttons are currently pressed: JOY_BUTTON1, JOY_BUTTON2, JOY_BUTTON3, or JOY_BUTTON4. For basic functionality, this method works well enough, but it obviously can't account for the massive number of controls available in many joysticks. Win32 provides another function, joyGetPosEx(), which can obtain information from more complex devices; but DirectInput, which we'll discuss next, is much better suited to this task.

DirectInput

The two methods of obtaining input that we've discussed so far are fairly straightforward, are fairly easy to use, and will work well enough for many applications. If that's so, then why do you need DirectInput? Well, DirectInput offers several advantages that the other methods can't:

- It allows full access to any input device and any special device capabilities, such as force feedback.

Table 16.2 Common Virtual Key Codes

Code	Key
VK_BACK	Backspace key
VK_TAB	Tab key
VK_CLEAR	Clear key
VK_RETURN	Enter key
VK_SHIFT	Shift key (either)
VK_CONTROL	Ctrl key (either)
VK_MENU	Alt key (either)
VK_PAUSE	Pause key
VK_CAPITAL	Caps Lock key
VK_ESCAPE	Esc key
VK_SPACE	Spacebar
VK_PRIOR	Page Up key
VK_NEXT	Page Down key
VK_END	End key
VK_HOME	Home key
VK_LEFT	Left-arrow key
VK_UP	Up-arrow key
VK_RIGHT	Right-arrow key
VK_DOWN	Down-arrow key
VK_SNAPSHOT	Print Screen key
VK_INSERT	Ins key
VK_DELETE	Del key
VK_HELP	Help key
VK_LWIN	Left Windows key

Code	Key
VK_RWIN	Right Windows key
VK_APPS	Applications key
VK_NUMPAD0	Numeric keypad 0 key
VK_NUMPAD1	Numeric keypad 1 key
VK_NUMPAD2	Numeric keypad 2 key
VK_NUMPAD3	Numeric keypad 3 key
VK_NUMPAD4	Numeric keypad 4 key
VK_NUMPAD5	Numeric keypad 5 key
VK_NUMPAD6	Numeric keypad 6 key
VK_NUMPAD7	Numeric keypad 7 key
VK_NUMPAD8	Numeric keypad 8 key
VK_NUMPAD9	Numeric keypad 9 key
VK_MULTIPLY	Multiply key
VK_ADD	Add key
VK_SEPARATOR	Separator key
VK_SUBTRACT	Subtract key
VK_DECIMAL	Decimal key
VK_DIVIDE	Divide key
VK_F*xx*	F*xx* key (that is, F1, F12, and so on)
VK_NUMLOCK	Num Lock key
VK_SCROLL	Scroll Lock key
VK_LSHIFT	Left Shift key
VK_RSHIFT	Right Shift key
VK_LCONTROL	Left Ctrl key
VK_RCONTROL	Right Ctrl key

- It allows direct access to the hardware, allowing the fastest possible interaction and greatest degree of control. It even lets you retrieve data from devices while your game is running in the background.
- With DirectX 8, you now don't have to know what type of input device is connected to obtain data from it. This helps reduce or eliminate device-specific code.

As much as we'd like to, we're not going to try to cover all of DirectInput in this chapter. As it turns out, it's a fairly large API, both because it contains many advanced features and because it attempts to support almost any input device you can imagine. Instead of spending a lot of time and space covering things you'll likely never use, we'll focus on the most important aspects of it. Accordingly, most of the tables in this chapter will contain only partial listings of the flags and options available. You can always refer to the SDK documentation for the full details on things not covered here.

INITIALIZING DIRECTINPUT

DirectInput, like the rest of DirectX, is based on the Component Object Model, or *COM* for short. COM is a rather complex programming paradigm that is heavily used by Microsoft. You don't really need to know COM to use DirectX, and in any case, we don't have the space for a complete treatment of it. The most important thing to be aware of is that some of the terminology and methods used in DirectX are due to the underlying COM architecture, so they may seem a little odd at first.

As we discussed at the beginning of this book, DirectX is broken down into a number of sub-components. Most of these high-level components correspond to some physical piece of hardware in your PC. For example, a Direct3D object represents your video card, and a DirectSound object represents your sound card. DirectInput is an exception to that rule, because a DirectInput object has nothing to do with any specific piece of hardware on your machine. Instead, it provides an interface to create DirectInputDevice objects, which represent your mouse, keyboard, joystick, and so on. Before you can create any of those things, though, you need to create and initialize a DirectInput object, so that's where we'll start.

In order to use any DirectInput code in your game, you need to do two things. The first is to include the *dinput.h* header in any files using DirectInput functions. The second is to link your project to *dinput8.lib*, as well as *dxguid.lib* (which is needed for all DirectX components).

To initialize DirectInput, you must first obtain an interface to the DirectInput object. This is done through DirectInput8Create():

```
HRESULT WINAPI DirectInput8Create(
    HINSTANCE hinst,
    DWORD dwVersion,
```

```
REFIID riidltf,
LPVOID *ppvOut,
LPUNKNOWN punkOuter);
```

Oh yeah, we forgot to warn you: DirectX interfaces can be ugly, at least compared to the OpenGL interfaces you've been dealing with. This isn't even the worst you'll see. Oh well, at least it's better now than it was with previous releases.

hinst is the handle to your application (or DLL, as the case may be). dwVersion will be DIRECTINPUT_VERSION, which is defined within *dinput.h* to indicate the current version number. If you want to use an older version of DirectInput, you can define this value yourself prior to including *dinput.h*, but for new applications, you'll probably want the current version anyway. riidltf is a unique identifier indicating the DirectInput interface you want, and it should be IID_IDirectInput8. ppvOut is a pointer to a variable that will point to the requested interface if this call is successful. This should be of type LPDIRECTINPUT8 for the latest interface, which you'll be using to create DirectInput objects. The last parameter, punkOuter is used for aggregation, which you probably won't use and which we're not going to cover, so you can just set it to NULL.

DirectInput Return Values

The return values of most of the DirectInput functions we'll be covering serve the same purpose, so rather than going over it again with every function, let's cover the return values once here and be done with it.

When DirectInput function calls succeed, they will return the value DI_OK. Otherwise, they return one of several error codes, which you can find listed in the DirectX SDK. Rather than checking for specific codes, many DirectX programmers used the FAILED macro, which is set to true if any error code is returned and to false if DI_OK is returned. The code to get a DirectInput interface will look something like this:

```
HRESULT result;
LPDIRECTINPUT8 pDirectInput;

if (FAILED(result = DirectInput8Create(g_hInstance, DIRECTINPUT_VERSION,
                                       IID_IDirectInput8,
                                       (void **)&pDirectInput, NULL)))
{
  // appropriate error processing
}
```

Not too bad. There are a couple of things worth mentioning here. The first is that casting pDirectInput to a pointer to a void pointer is necessary, and something you'll have to do with a few other DirectX functions. The function uses a pointer to a void pointer in order to be compatible with other versions of DirectX. Although it might seem like the function should accept an LPDIRECTINPUT pointer without a problem, failing to cast it to void ** will result in a compiler error.

Amazingly, that's all you need to do to get an interface to a DirectInput object. Of course, by itself, the interface object doesn't really do anything interesting, but you need it to be able to create DirectInputDevice objects, which represent the keyboards, mice, and such from which you'll be getting input. We'll discuss how to do that next.

USING DIRECTINPUT

Once you have a valid interface to a DirectInput object, you can begin to create new objects that represent physical input devices. These are called DirectInputDevice objects, and you'll need one for every type of input device you intend to support in your game.

Adding Devices

A DirectInputDevice is an abstraction of a specific type of input device, providing methods to interact with and obtain data from the device. The nice thing about this approach is that if you create a DirectInputDevice for, say, a joystick, you don't have to know or care about what specific joystick your players are using and thus don't have to write special case code for the many types of joysticks available. Instead, you can just use the interface to find out how many buttons the joystick has, whether it has a hat switch, whether it supports force feedback, and so on.

There are a lot of steps involved with creating a DirectInputDevice object, and some of them are fairly involved, so before we get into it, here's a list of the steps you need to take. Each will be explained as we go.

1. Enumerate available devices (optional).
2. Create a device.
3. Verify device capabilities (optional).
4. Enumerate objects (optional).
5. Set the device data format.
6. Set the cooperative level.
7. Modify device properties (optional).
8. Acquire the device.

Creating Devices

Creating a device is done with the following, which is a method of the DirectInput object interface:

```
HRESULT IDirectInput8::CreateDevice(
    REFGUID rguid,
    LPDIRECTINPUTDEVICE *ppDirectInputDevice,
    LPUNKNOWN punkOuter);
```

rguid is a unique identifier indicating the device for which this interface is being created. ppDirectInputDevice is a pointer to a pointer that will point to this interface if the call is successful. punkOuter is used for aggregation and can be set to NULL.

The first parameter requires a little bit more explanation. To obtain an interface for a specific device, you need to obtain a GUID for it to pass in as this parameter. Fortunately, DirectInput has defined some of these for us:

- GUID_SysKeyboard is used to select the default system keyboard.
- GUID_SysMouse is used to select the default system mouse.

These can be used for any keyboard or mouse the user has connected, and if the user happens to have more than one mouse or keyboard attached, input from each will be combined into a single system device.

So how do you get the GUID for joysticks and other more esoteric input devices? You just have to let DirectInput determine which devices are connected to the user's system and give you a list of everything that's available. You do this by creating a device enumeration.

Enumerating Devices

The DirectInput object interface includes a method that is used to create a device enumeration, which has the following form:

```
HRESULT IDirectInput8::EnumDevices(
    DWORD dwDevType,
    LPDIENUMCALLBACK lpCallback,
    LPVOID pvRef,
    DWORD dwFlags);
```

This function is going to take a while to explain, mainly because it brings up a lot of new things, so brace yourself.

dwDevType

The first parameter, `dwDevType`, is used to specify the type of device you would like to have included in the enumeration. Devices not matching this type will not be listed. Some of the most useful types and subtypes are listed in Table 16.3 (see the DirectX SDK for a complete list).

Table 16.3 DirectInput Device Types

Type	Description
DI8DEVTYPE_1STPERSON	Devices best suited to a first-person action game. The following subtypes are also supported:
	DI8DEVTYPE1STPERSON_LIMITED: Doesn't have enough device objects for action mapping
	DI8DEVTYPE1STPERSON_SHOOTER: For first person shooters
	DI8DEVTYPE1STPERSON_SIXDOF: Has six degrees of freedom
	DI8DEVTYPE1STPERSON_UNKNOWN: Unknown subtype
DI8DEVTYPE_DEVICE	Any device that doesn't fit into one of the other types
DI8DEVTYPE_DRIVING	Any steering device. There are also the following subtypes:
	DI8DEVTYPEDRIVING_COMBINEDPEDALS: Treats acceleration and braking as a single axis
	DI8DEVTYPEDRIVING_DUALPEDALS: Acceleration and braking are separate axes
	DI8DEVTYPEDRIVING_HANDHELD: Hand-held driving device
	DI8DEVTYPEDRIVING_LIMITED: Doesn't have enough device objects for action mapping
	DI8DEVTYPEDRIVING_THREEPEDALS: Acceleration, braking, and clutch pedal values are from separate axes

Type	Description
DI8DEVTYPE_FLIGHT	Devices used for flight simulation. You can also use one of the following subtypes:
	DI8DEVTYPEFLIGHT_LIMITED: Doesn't have enough device objects for action mapping
	DI8DEVTYPEFLIGHT_RC: Device based on a model airplane remote control
	DI8DEVTYPEFLIGHT_STICK: Flight joystick
	DI8DEVTYPEFLIGHT_YOKE: Flight yoke
DI8DEVTYPE_GAMEPAD	Game-pad device. Can also be one of the following:
	DI8DEVTYPEGAMEPAD_LIMITED: Doesn't have enough device objects for action mapping
	DI8DEVTYPEGAMEPAD_STANDARD: Normal game pad with enough device objects for action mapping
	DI8DEVTYPEGAMEPAD_TILT: Can report x- and y-axis data if the controller is tilted
DI8DEVTYPE_JOYSTICK	Standard joystick devices, with the following subtypes:
	DI8DEVTYPEJOYSTICK_LIMITED: Doesn't have enough device objects for action mapping
	DI8DEVTYPEJOYSTICK_STANDARD: Normal joystick with enough device objects for action mapping
DI8DEVTYPE_KEYBOARD	Any keyboard or keyboard-like devices
	DI8DEVTYPEKEYBOARD_UNKNOWN: Unknown keyboard
	DI8DEVTYPEKEYBOARD_PCXT: IBM PC/XT 83-key keyboard
	DI8DEVTYPEKEYBOARD_OLIVETTI: Olivetti 102-key keyboard
	DI8DEVTYPEKEYBOARD_PCAT: IBM PC/AT 84-key keyboard

(continued)

Table 16.3 (Continued)

Type	Description
DI8DEVTYPE_KEYBOARD	**DI8DEVTYPEKEYBOARD_PCENH**: IBM PC Enhanced 101/102-key or Microsoft Natural keyboard
	DI8DEVTYPEKEYBOARD_NOKIA1050: Nokia 1050 keyboard
	DI8DEVTYPEKEYBOARD_NOKIA9140: Nokia 9140 keyboard
DI8DEVTYPE_MOUSE	A mouse or similar device
	DI8DEVTYPEMOUSE_ABSOLUTE: Mouse that returns absolute axis data
	DI8DEVTYPEMOUSE_FINGERSTICK: Fingerstick
	DI8DEVTYPEMOUSE_TOUCHPAD: Touchpad
	DI8DEVTYPEMOUSE_TRACKBALL: Trackball
	DI8DEVTYPEMOUSE_TRADITIONAL: Traditional mouse
	DI8DEVTYPEMOUSE_UNKNOWN: Subtype could not be determined
DI8DEVTYPE_SCREENPOINTER	Any screen-pointer device
	DI8DEVTYPESCREENPTR_UNKNOWN: Unknown subtype
	DI8DEVTYPESCREENPTR_LIGHTGUN: Light gun
	DI8DEVTYPESCREENPTR_LIGHTPEN: Light pen
	DI8DEVTYPESCREENPTR_TOUCH: Touch screen
DI8DEVTYPE_SUPPLEMENTAL	A device meant to be used in conjunction with the main control device
	DI8DEVTYPESUPPLEMENTAL_2NDHANDCONTROLLER: Secondary handheld controller
	DI8DEVTYPESUPPLEMENTAL_COMBINEDPEDALS: Uses a single axis to report acceleration and braking
	DI8DEVTYPESUPPLEMENTAL_DUALPEDALS: Uses separate axes to report acceleration and braking

Type	Description
	DI8DEVTYPESUPPLEMENTAL_HANDTRACKER: Tracks hand movement
	DI8DEVTYPESUPPLEMENTAL_HEADTRACKER: Tracks head movement
	DI8DEVTYPESUPPLEMENTAL_RUDDERPEDALS: Rudder pedals
	DI8DEVTYPESUPPLEMENTAL_SHIFTER: Reports gear selection from an axis
	DI8DEVTYPESUPPLEMENTAL_SHIFTSTICKGATE: Reports gear selection from buttons
	DI8DEVTYPESUPPLEMENTAL_SPLITTHROTTLE: Reports two or more throttle values
	DI8DEVTYPESUPPLEMENTAL_THREEPEDALS: Uses separate axes to report acceleration, braking, and clutch
	DI8DEVTYPESUPPLEMENTAL_THROTTLE: Reports a single throttle value
	DI8DEVTYPESUPPLEMENTAL_UNKNOWN: Unknown subtype

Some of the values in this table might not make sense yet, but you'll be using them in several other places as you move on. In addition to the types listed here, you can use one of the following device classes, each of which encompasses some of these types:

- **DI8DEVCLASS_ALL.** All device types
- **DI8DEVCLASS_DEVICE.** Devices that do not fit into any of the following classes
- **DI8DEVCLASS_GAMECTRL.** Game controllers
- **DI8DEVCLASS_KEYBOARD.** All keyboards (this is actually equivalent to DI8DEVTYPE_KEYBOARD)
- **DI8DEVCLASS_POINTER.** All mouse and pointer devices (for example, types DI8DEVTYPE_MOUSE and DI8DEVTYPE_SCREENPOINTER)

The Callback Function

The second parameter EnumDevices() expects is a pointer to a callback function, which is defined by you. This function will be called one time for every device found matching dwDevType. Within the function, you'll usually fill up a data structure with information about each device found so that you can select the one you want or allow the user to make that selection (more on that in a bit). The callback function must have the following form:

```
BOOL CALLBACK MyDIDevicesCallback(LPCDIDEVICEINSTANCE lpddi, LPVOID pvRef);
```

lpddi points to a DIDEVICEINSTANCE structure, which contains information about the device, including the GUID. pvRef is actually whatever you passed to EnumDevices() for the pvRef parameter (normally a pointer to some data structure, such as a linked list or an array, which you'll use to store the information from the DIDEVICEINSTANCE structure). This callback function should return DIENUM_CONTINUE to move on to the next device or DIENUM_STOP to explicitly terminate enumeration (which is what you'd do if you were looking for a specific device and found it).

Device-Enumeration Flags

The last parameter passed to EnumDevices() is a set of flags that can limit the scope of the enumeration. It can be one or more of the partial list of flags in Table 16.4.

You'll look at a code example of using enumerations in a minute, but you should now at least have a general idea of how they work. The point of all this enumeration business is to get the GUID of an input device other than the system mouse or keyboard. Now that you can create a device for anything attached to the user's system, it's time to move on to the next step.

Verifying Device Capabilities

Enumerating devices enables you to be really selective about what properties the devices returned by it possess. There may be times, however, when you want to verify a device's capabilities, especially if you use a generic device. After you create a device, you might want to verify that it possesses the capabilities you need, including whether the device is currently attached to the computer. This is done with IDirectInputDevice8::GetCapabilities() like so:

```
HRESULT IDirectInputDevice8::GetCapabilities(LPDIDEVCAPS pDIDevCaps);
```

pDIDevCaps points to a DIDEVCAPS structure, which will be filled with valid information about the device if this call is successful. The DIDEVCAPS structure contains the following fields:

- **dwSize.** The size of the DIDEVCAPS structure in bytes (this must be set before the call to GetCapabilities()).
- **dwFlags.** A combination of flags, the most common of which are listed in Table 16.5.
- **dwDevType.** The type of device. Can be any of the values in Table 16.3.
- **dwAxes.** Number of axes on the device.
- **dwButtons.** Number of buttons on the device.
- **dwPOVs.** Number of point-of-view controllers on the device.
- **dwFFSamplePeriod.** For force-feedback capable devices, the minimum number of microseconds between consecutive force commands.

- **dwFFMinTimeResolution.** For force-feedback capable devices, the resolution of the timer in microseconds.
- **dwFirmwareRevision, dwHardwareRevision, dwFFDriverVersion.** Version numbers.

You can use the information returned in this structure to verify that the device supports the capabilities to which you want access.

Table 16.4 Device-Enumeration Flags

Flag	Meaning
DIEDFL_ALLDEVICES	Enumerate all devices. This is the default.
DIEDFL_ATTACHEDONLY	Enumerate devices that are attached and installed.
DIEDFL_FORCEFEEDBACK	Enumerate devices capable of force feedback.

Table 16.5 Device-Capability Flags

Flag	Meaning
DIDC_ALIAS	The device is just an alias for another device.
DIDC_ATTACHED	The device is connected physically to the PC.
DIDC_FORCEFEEDBACK	The device is capable of force feedback. There are also a number of other force feedback–related flags that we won't be discussing, namely DIDC_DEADBAND, DIDC_FFFADE, DIDC_FFATTACK, DIDC_POSNEGCOEFFICIENTS, DIDC_POSNEGSATURATION, DIDC_SATURATION, and DIDC_STARTDELAY.
DIDC_POLLEDDATAFORMAT	One or more of the objects in the current format must be polled to obtain data.
DIDC_POLLEDDEVICE	One or more of the device's objects must be polled to obtain data.

Enumerating Objects

Devices are further broken down into objects representing buttons, keys, axes, sliders, and so on. Keyboards and mice are all pretty standard, so you don't usually have to worry about these objects with them, but joysticks and other input devices are another story. If you want to assign responses to the various controls on these devices, you need to enumerate the objects to see what's available. This is done with EnumObjects():

```
HRESULT IDirectInputDevice8::EnumObjects(LPDIENUMDEVICEOBJECTSCALLBACK lpCallback,
                                         LPVOID pvRef,
                                         DWORD dwFlags);
```

lpCallback is a pointer to a callback function. pvRef is a pointer to an object that you want to have passed to the callback. dwFlags is used to specify which types of objects you want to have enumerated; a partial list of valid flags appear in Table 16.6.

Table 16.6 EnumObjects() Flags

Flag	Meaning
DIDFT_ABSAXIS	Absolute axis
DIDFT_ALL	All objects
DIDFT_AXIS	Any axis (relational or absolute)
DIDFT_BUTTON	Buttons (toggle or push)
DIDFT_NODATA	Objects that don't generate data
DIDFT_OUTPUT	Object that data can be sent to (using SendDeviceData())
DIDFT_POV	Point-of-view controller
DIDFT_PSHBUTTON	Push button (reported as down when it is pressed and up otherwise)
DIDFT_RELAXIS	Relative axis
DIDFT_TGLBUTTON	Toggle button (toggles between down and up every time the user presses the button)

Microsoft has provided a prototype for the callback function for convenience, so you just have to implement it. The prototype is as follows:

```
BOOL CALLBACK DIEnumDeviceObjectsCallback(LPCDIDEVICEOBJECTINSTANCE lpddoi,
                                          LPVOID pvRef);
```

lpddoi is a pointer to a DIDEVICEOBJECTINSTANCE structure (see the SDK for more details). pvRef is whatever you passed to EnumObjects().

Setting the Device Data Format

A required step in preparing the device is to set its data format (unless you're using action mapping). DirectInput offers a great deal of flexibility in how data from the input device is reported. To set the data format, use the following:

```
HRESULT IDirectInputDevice::SetDataFormat(LPCDIDATAFORMAT lpdf);
```

lpdf points to a DIDATAFORMAT structure defining the data format you want to use. For convenience, DirectX provides several predefined global variables containing the data format for the most common input devices:

- **c_dfDIKeyboard.** An array of 256 characters, each representing a key. If the high bit of a character is set, the key was down; otherwise, it was up. DirectInput defines a series of constants representing each key, in the form DIK_*key*. (See the DirectX SDK under "Keyboard Device Constants" for a complete listing of keys.)
- **c_dfDIMouse.** A mouse with three axes and four buttons, associated with the DIMOUSESTATE structure:

```
typedef struct DIMOUSESTATE
{
  LONG lX;               // X-axis (relative)
  LONG lY;               // Y-axis (relative)
  LONG lZ;               // Z-axis (relative)
  BYTE rgbButtons[4];    // buttons; high bit is set when the button is down
} DIMOUSESTATE, *LPDIMOUSESTATE;
```

- **c_dfDIMouse2.** A mouse with three axes and eight buttons, associated with the DIMOUSESTATE2 structure, which is identical to DIMOUSESTATE except that rgbButtons has eight elements.
- **c_dfDIJoystick.** A joystick with three positional axes, three rotational axes, two sliders, four POV controllers, and 32 buttons, associated with the DIJOYSTATE structure:

```
typedef struct DIJOYSTATE
{
```

```
     LONG 1X;              // X-axis (usually left-right)
     LONG 1Y;              // Y-axis (usually forward-back)
     LONG 1Z;              // Z-axis (usually a throttle control, if present)
     LONG 1Rx;             // rotation around X-axis
     LONG 1Ry;             // rotation around Y-axis
     LONG 1Rz;             // rotation around Z-axis
     LONG rglSlider[2];    // u- and v-axis
     DWORD rgdwPOV[4];     // directional controllers
     BYTE rgbButtons[32];  // buttons; high bit is set when the button is down
   } DIJOYSTATE, *LPDIJOYSTATE;
```

- **c_dfDIJoystick2.** Associated with the DIJOYSTATE2 structure, which is too large to document here. As always, you can see the DirectX SDK for information about this structure.

The vast majority of games will get by using one of these values, and for that reason, we won't go into an in-depth discussion of the DIDATAFORMAT structure and the options it provides. Full documentation for the structure is provided in the DirectX SDK.

Setting the Cooperative Level

Because Windows is a multitasking operating system, you will almost always have to share input devices with other applications. Therefore, you need to specify how your game behaves with regard to control of these devices; you do so by setting the cooperative level:

```
HRESULT IDirectInputDevice::SetCooperativeLevel(HWND hwnd, DWORD dwFlags);
```

hwnd needs to be the handle to your top-level window. dwFlags is a set of flags that specify how you want your application's control of the device to behave with other applications. Valid values appear in Table 16.7.

All applications must select either DISCL_BACKGROUND or DISCL_FOREGROUND, and either DISCL_EXCLUSIVE or DISCL_NONEXCLUSIVE. In most cases, you'll want to use DISCL_FOREGROUND and DISCL_EXCLUSIVE. Also, adding DISCL_NOWINKEY for the keyboard is a good idea for games.

Modifying Device Properties

DirectInput offers you the option of modifying device properties such as the range, granularity, and other axis data, input buffer sizes, and so on. This is done through the IDirectInputDevice8::SetProperty() method:

```
HRESULT IDirectInputDevice8::SetProperty(REFGUID rguidProp, LPCDIPROPHEADER pdiph);
```

Table 16.7 Cooperative-Level Flags

Flag	Meaning
DISCL_BACKGROUND	This flag allows your application to acquire the device even when it is not the active application.
DISCL_EXCLUSIVE	This flag sets exclusive access for this device, meaning that as long as it is acquired, no other application can gain exclusive access—although nonexclusive access can always be gained.
DISCL_FOREGROUND	This flag grants foreground access for this device. If the window associated with it moves from the foreground, the device will be unacquired.
DISCL_NONEXCLUSIVE	This flag allows your application to access the devices without interfering with other applications using it.
DISCL_NOWINKEY	This flag disables the Windows logo key on keyboards that have it, preventing unintended program interruption.

rguidProp is an identifier for the property you want to modify. For the purposes of this discussion, the only property you care about is DIPROP_BUFFERSIZE, which allows you to change the size of the input buffer from the default of 0 when using buffered-data mode (see the section titled "Buffered Data" later in this chapter). The other properties mostly deal with joysticks; see the DirectX SDK for a complete list. pdiph is a pointer to a DIPROPHEADER structure, which we'll discuss in greater detail in the section titled "Getting Input" later in this chapter.

Acquiring the Device

Finally, to use any device, you must gain access to it, because most devices will be shared across all currently running applications. This is done through the Acquire() method:

```
HRESULT IDirectInputDevice8::Acquire();
```

This function can return several values. If the device was acquired successfully, DI_OK is returned. If called when the device has already been acquired by your application, S_FALSE is returned. Otherwise, one of the following error codes is returned:

- **DIERR_INVALIDPARAM.** SetDataFormat() or SetActionMap() wasn't called prior to the call to Acquire().
- **DIERR_NOTINITIALIZED.** Acquire() was called before the necessary steps above were taken.
- **DIERR_OTHERAPPHASPRIO.** This error occurs when you are attempting to acquire a device from the background when you have only foreground access.

Note that if your device has foreground access, it will automatically be unacquired when your application is minimized or otherwise loses foreground status. You should watch for this by handling the WM_ACTIVATE message and reacquire your devices as needed.

Once you have successfully acquired a device, you can begin to get data from it, as described next.

Getting Input

Finally, the part you really care about: getting data from the input device. How you do this depends on whether you're using immediate or buffered data.

Immediate Data

Simply put, immediate data reflects the state of the device at any particular moment in time. This is useful when you want to know what the player is doing at that particular moment. For example, if the user is currently pressing the key to move forward, then you want to move the character in that direction; you don't really care about which keys the user pressed previously. To obtain immediate data, use the following call:

```
HRESULT IDirectInputDevice8::GetDeviceState(DWORD cbData, LPVOID lpvData);
```

cbData is the size of lpvData in bytes. lpvData is a pointer to a structure that will store the device data. The format of this structure depends on the value passed to SetDataFormat().

Buffered Data

Immediate data works well in many cases, but it's not ideal for all situations, and it suffers from the fact that it may miss input. For example, if the user presses and releases a key between calls to GetDeviceState(), you'll never know about it. If you have a good frame rate and are querying the device state every frame, you can minimize the likelihood of this happening, but if it happens at all, it can be frustrating for the player. Fortunately, buffered input is provided as an alternative. With buffered data, a sequence of device states is stored, so you can process and handle them all. It is also useful for tracking such things as mouse movement. Buffered data is accessed through the following function:

```
HRESULT IDirectInputDevice8::GetDeviceData(DWORD cbObjectData,
                                           LPDIDEVICEOBJECTDATA rgdod,
                                           LPDWORD pdwInOut,
                                           DWORD dwFlags);
```

cbObjectData is the number of bytes in the DIDEVICEOBJECTDATA structure, which is fully document-ed in the DirectX SDK. rgdod is a pointer to an array of these structures. pdwInOut serves two pur-poses: When you call the function, it should be set to the number of elements in the array; when the function returns, it will be set to the number of array elements that were actually filled. Finally, dwFlags can be either 0, which will cause the data to be removed from the buffer, or DIGDD_PEEK, in which case the data will remain in the buffer. The former will normally be used.

Whether you use buffered or immediate mode for a device depends entirely upon the needs of your game. For the most part, immediate data will suffice, and it's simpler, so that's what we'll use in the examples here.

Polling Devices

The two methods we just discussed return the data most recently reported by the device to DirectInput. Most devices behave well and report changes as they happen, but some do not; for this reason, it may be necessary to poll the device before obtaining data from it. Some devices even require polling. This can be done using IDirectInputDevice8::Poll():

```
HRESULT IDirectInputDevice8::Poll();
```

This will cause DirectInput to update everything associated with the device, if it requires polling. If polling is not necessary, the function simply has no effect.

Shutting Down

To properly clean up when using DirectInput, several steps must be taken. First of all, you must unacquire any devices that are currently acquired. This is done with the following:

```
HRESULT IDirectInputDevice8::Unacquire();
```

Note that calling this function on a device that is not currently acquired has no affect, so you may want to simply unacquire all devices at shut down. Also, shutdown is not the only time you'll use this function. In general, you should unacquire all devices whenever your application becomes inactive, and reacquire them when it is reactivated.

The next step is to release the interface for each device, which can be done with the following:

```
HRESULT IDirectInputDevice8::Release();
```

Finally, after all the devices have been freed, you must free the DirectInput object itself with

```
HRESULT IDirectInput8::Release();
```

That's all there is to it!

ACTION MAPPING

Remember earlier when we said that you need a DirectInputDevice for every device type you want to support? As of DirectX 8, that's not necessarily true. A new technology, called *action mapping*, has been added to DirectInput to provide an additional layer of abstraction for physical input devices.

The idea behind action mapping is that you define a set of controls that your game might need. If, for example, you are writing a flight-combat game, the controls might include yaw, pitch, roll, throttle, fire weapons, and so on. Then, you tell DirectInput that your game belongs to the air-combat genre, and register each of these control types with it. When the game is running, DirectInput detects all the input devices that are currently attached and allows the user to select and configure whichever ones they like to use. It then matches data received from these devices and maps them to the controls you have defined. This benefits you because you don't have to write device-specific code, and the player because he can easily choose whichever device he prefers.

The only downside to action mapping is that it's fairly complex to set up, and because of that, we don't have space to go into the details of it here. For now, we can get by with vanilla DirectInput, and there's always time for you to explore action mapping on your own later. The DirectX SDK provides a great reference, and Microsoft's developer site (listed in Appendix A) has several articles covering it as well.

BUILDING THE INPUT SUB-SYSTEM

Now that you understand the basics of DirectInput, it's time to put it all together in a system into which you can easily drop any game. This system will consist of an input layer to manage everything, and a keyboard, mouse, and object to handle those devices. You won't be adding joystick support; it's simple enough to do, but the fact is that most PC games use the mouse and keyboard, so it'll probably be a while before you need to use the joystick.

For the input layer, you'll create a thin class wrapper for DirectInput, and then you'll create classes for each of the device types for it to manage. You'll keep things as simple as possible; most games aren't going to need a great deal of complexity, and you can always add to the system later to suit your own purposes.

The design we've chosen gives the client application the option of handling all input functionality through the input system itself. It also provides the option to request interfaces to the keyboard and mouse objects directly, if such is required. To use the input system, declare a variable of type CInputSystem. At program startup, Initialize() should be called to set up the system properly.

Once the input system is initialized, you should call Update() every frame before requesting data from the input devices, which can be done through KeyUp(), KeyDown(), ButtonUp(), GetMouseMovement(), and so on. When your application window loses focus, you should call UnacquireAll(), and then AcquireAll() when it regains focus. At program termination, you should call Shutdown() to make sure all interfaces are released properly and that dynamically allocated memory is freed.

Let's look at the declaration and implementation of this class:

> **NOTE**
>
> We've chosen to explicitly initialize the class this way rather than having initialization done in the constructor. This is because the input system variable may be created as a global variable, and constructors for global objects are called before any other functions, which may produce undesirable side effects.

> **NOTE**
>
> If you're new to Windows programming, you might not be familiar with the term "focus" as it's being used here. Simply put, having the focus means that your application is the one that the user is actively interacting with. You can use several Windows messages, such as WM_ACTIVATE, to determine whether or not your application has the focus.

```
// in InputSystem.h
#define IS_USEKEYBOARD  1
#define IS_USEMOUSE     2


class CInputSystem
{
public:
   bool   Initialize(HWND hwnd, HINSTANCE appInstance, bool isExclusive = true, DWORD
flags = 0);
   bool   Shutdown();

   void   AcquireAll();
   void   UnacquireAll();

   CKeyboard   *GetKeyboard() { return m_pKeyboard; }
   CMouse      *GetMouse()    { return m_pMouse; }
```

```cpp
  bool   Update();

  bool   KeyDown(char key) { return (m_pKeyboard && m_pKeyboard->KeyDown(key)); }
  bool   KeyUp(char key) { return (m_pKeyboard && m_pKeyboard->KeyUp(key)); }

  bool   ButtonDown(int button) { return (m_pMouse && m_pMouse->ButtonDown(button)); }
  bool   ButtonUp(int button) { return (m_pMouse && m_pMouse->ButtonUp(button)); }
  void   GetMouseMovement(int &dx, int &dy) { if (m_pMouse) m_pMouse->GetMovement(dx,
dy); }
  int    GetMouseWheelMovement() { return (m_pMouse) ? m_pMouse->GetWheelMovement() :
0; }

private:
  CKeyboard   *m_pKeyboard;
  CMouse      *m_pMouse;

  LPDIRECTINPUT8 m_pDI;
};


// in InputSystem.cpp
/************************************************************************
 CInputSystem::Initialize()

 Initializes the input system. isExclusive should be set to true for exclusive
 mouse access, false otherwise. Flags should be a combination of
 IS_USEKEYBOARD and/or IS_USEMOUSE.
 ************************************************************************/
bool CInputSystem::Initialize(HWND hwnd, HINSTANCE appInstance, bool isExclusive,
DWORD flags)
{
  // create the DI object
  if (FAILED(DirectInput8Create(appInstance,
                                DIRECTINPUT_VERSION,
                                IID_IDirectInput8,
                                (void **)&m_pDI,
                                NULL)))

    return false;

  if (flags & IS_USEKEYBOARD)
  {
```

```cpp
    m_pKeyboard = new CKeyboard(m_pDI, hwnd);
    if (m_pKeyboard == NULL)
      return false;
  }
  if (flags & IS_USEMOUSE)
  {
    m_pMouse = new CMouse(m_pDI, hwnd, isExclusive);
    if (m_pMouse == NULL)
      return false;
  }


  return true;
} // end CInputSystem::Initialize()



/****************************************************************************
 CInputSystem::Shutdown()

 Releases all objects and frees memory.
 ****************************************************************************/
bool CInputSystem::Shutdown()
{
  UnacquireAll();
  if (m_pKeyboard)
  {
    delete m_pKeyboard;
    m_pKeyboard = NULL;
  }

  if (m_pKeyboard)
  {
    delete m_pMouse;
    m_pMouse = NULL;
  }

  if (FAILED(m_pDI->Release()))
    return false;

  return true;
} // end CInputSystem::Shutdown()
```

```
/*************************************************************************
 CInputSystem::Update()

 Queries the current state of all devices.
*************************************************************************/
bool CInputSystem::Update()
{
  if (m_pKeyboard)
    m_pKeyboard->Update();
  if (m_pMouse)
    m_pMouse->Update();

  return true;
} // end CInputSystem::Update()


/*************************************************************************
 CInputSystem::AcquireAll()

 Makes sure all input devices are acquired
*************************************************************************/
void CInputSystem::AcquireAll()
{
  if (m_pKeyboard)
    m_pKeyboard->Acquire();
  if (m_pMouse)
    m_pMouse->Acquire();
} // end CInputSystem::AcquireAll()



/*************************************************************************
 CInputSystem::UnacquireAll()

 Unacquires all devices
*************************************************************************/
void CInputSystem::UnacquireAll()
{
  if (m_pKeyboard)
    m_pKeyboard->Unacquire();
  if (m_pMouse)
    m_pMouse->Unacquire();
} // end CInputSystem::UnacquireAll()
```

The keyboard and mouse classes are both thin wrappers providing basic functionality. Both do all their initialization within their constructors, creating device objects, setting the data format and cooperative levels, and acquiring the device. They each maintain data structures containing their most recently requested state information. This data is refreshed through the Update() function, which the input system will take care of unless you choose to access these devices directly. The keyboard allows you to check the state of any key, and the mouse provides you with the relative change in position, relative change of the mouse wheel, and the current state of up to four buttons. These classes are shown here:

```cpp
class CKeyboard
{
public:
  CKeyboard(LPDIRECTINPUT8 pDI, HWND hwnd);
  ~CKeyboard();

  bool  KeyDown(char key) { return (m_keys[key] & 0x80) ? true : false; }
  bool  KeyUp(char key) { return (m_keys[key] & 0x80) ? false : true; }

  bool  Update();

  void  Clear() { ZeroMemory(m_keys, 256 * sizeof(char)); }

  bool  Acquire();
  bool  Unacquire();

private:
  LPDIRECTINPUTDEVICE8  m_pDIDev;

  char     m_keys[256];
};


/**************************************************************************
  CKeyboard::Constructor

  Initializes the DI device
 **************************************************************************/
CKeyboard::CKeyboard(LPDIRECTINPUT8 pDI, HWND hwnd)
{
```

```
   if (FAILED(pDI->CreateDevice(GUID_SysKeyboard, &m_pDIDev, NULL)))
   {
     // error processing
   }

   if (FAILED(m_pDIDev->SetDataFormat(&c_dfDIKeyboard)))
   {
     // error processing
   }

   if (FAILED(m_pDIDev->SetCooperativeLevel(hwnd, DISCL_FOREGROUND |
 DISCL_NONEXCLUSIVE)))
   {
     // error processing
   }

   if (FAILED(m_pDIDev->Acquire()))
   {
     // error processing
   }

   Clear();
} // end CKeyboard::Constructor


/*************************************************************************
 CKeyboard::Destructor

 Releases the DI device
 *************************************************************************/
CKeyboard::~CKeyboard()
{
   if (m_pDIDev)
   {
     m_pDIDev->Unacquire();
     m_pDIDev->Release();
   }
} // end CKeyboard::Destructor
```

```
/***************************************************************************
  CKeyboard::Update()

  Queries the current state of the keyboard and stores it in the member
  variables.
***************************************************************************/
bool CKeyboard::Update()
{
  if (FAILED(m_pDIDev->GetDeviceState(sizeof(m_keys), (LPVOID)m_keys)))
  {
    if (FAILED(m_pDIDev->Acquire()))
    {
      return false;
    }
    if (FAILED(m_pDIDev->GetDeviceState(sizeof(m_keys), (LPVOID)m_keys)))
    {
      return false;
    }
  }
  return true;
} // end CKeyboard::Update()


/***************************************************************************
  CKeyboard::Acquire()

  Acquires the keyboard
***************************************************************************/
bool CKeyboard::Acquire()
{
  Clear();
  return (!FAILED(m_pDIDev->Acquire()));
} // end CKeyboard::Acquire()


/***************************************************************************
  CKeyboard::Unacquire()

  Unacquires the keyboard
***************************************************************************/
```

```cpp
bool CKeyboard::Unacquire()
{
  Clear();
  return (!FAILED(m_pDIDev->Unacquire()));
} // end CKeyboard::Unacquire()




class CMouse
{
public:
  CMouse(LPDIRECTINPUT8 pDI, HWND hwnd, bool isExclusive = true);
  ~CMouse();

  bool  ButtonDown(int button) { return (m_state.rgbButtons[button] & 0x80) ? true :
false; }
  bool  ButtonUp(int button) { return (m_state.rgbButtons[button] & 0x80) ? false :
true; }
  int   GetWheelMovement() { return m_state.lZ; }
  void  GetMovement(int &dx, int &dy) { dx = m_state.lX; dy = m_state.lY; }

  bool  Update();

  bool  Acquire();
  bool  Unacquire();

private:
  LPDIRECTINPUTDEVICE8  m_pDIDev;
  DIMOUSESTATE          m_state;
};

/*************************************************************************
  CMouse::Constructor

  Initializes the DI device
*************************************************************************/
CMouse::CMouse(LPDIRECTINPUT8 pDI, HWND hwnd, bool isExclusive)
{
```

```
    if (FAILED(pDI->CreateDevice(GUID_SysMouse, &m_pDIDev, NULL)))
    {
      // error processing
    }


    if (FAILED(m_pDIDev->SetDataFormat(&c_dfDIMouse)))
    {
      // error processing
    }


    DWORD flags;
    if (isExclusive)
      flags = DISCL_FOREGROUND | DISCL_EXCLUSIVE | DISCL_NOWINKEY;
    else
      flags = DISCL_FOREGROUND | DISCL_NONEXCLUSIVE;


    if (FAILED(m_pDIDev->SetCooperativeLevel(hwnd, flags)))
    {
      // error processing
    }


    if (FAILED(m_pDIDev->Acquire()))
    {
      // error processing
    }


    if (FAILED(m_pDIDev->GetDeviceState(sizeof(DIMOUSESTATE), &m_state)))
    {
      // error processing
    }
} // end CMouse::Constructor


/*************************************************************************
  CMouse::Destructor

  Releases the DI device
*************************************************************************/
```

```cpp
CMouse::~CMouse()
{
  if (m_pDIDev)
  {
    m_pDIDev->Unacquire();
    m_pDIDev->Release();
  }
} // end CMouse::Destructor


/***************************************************************************
 CMouse::Update()

 Queries the current state of the mouse and stores it in the member
 variables.
 ***************************************************************************/
bool CMouse::Update()
{
  if (FAILED(m_pDIDev->GetDeviceState(sizeof(DIMOUSESTATE), &m_state)))
  {
    if (FAILED(m_pDIDev->Acquire()))
    {
      return false;
    }
    if (FAILED(m_pDIDev->GetDeviceState(sizeof(DIMOUSESTATE), &m_state)))
    {
      return false;
    }
  }

  return true;
} // end CMouse::Update()


/***************************************************************************
 CMouse::Acquire()

 Acquires the mouse
 ***************************************************************************/
bool CMouse::Acquire()
{
```

```
  return (!FAILED(m_pDIDev->Acquire()));
} // end CMouse::Acquire



/***************************************************************************
 CMouse::Unacquire()

 Unacquires the keyboard
 ***************************************************************************/
bool CMouse::Unacquire()
{
  return (!FAILED(m_pDIDev->Unacquire()));
} // end CMouse::Unacquire()
```

INPUT SAMPLE PROGRAM

To illustrate the use of the input system, we've created a simple application that uses it, shown in Figure 16.1. The program tracks mouse activity and uses it to display a mouse pointer on the screen. Pushing either mouse button or rolling the wheel will cause the application to rotate through several pointer images. In addition, the program monitors the function keys and displays whichever was pressed last in the middle of the screen.

Figure 16.1

DirectInput in action.

The full source code is available on the CD, but the relevant portion, from the `ProcessInput()` function, is included here for your convenience. Note that in order to get the mouse image to change only once every time a mouse button is pressed, you can't just call `ButtonDown()` by itself. This is because you're updating at dozens of frames per second; in the time it takes to perform a single mouse click, this function will return `true` many times. The approach used here is to keep track of when each button was pressed, and then not do anything until the button is released, thus ensuring only one change per click. Alternatively, you could update the first time `ButtonDown()` returns `true`, and then set a state so that another update won't be permitted until `ButtonUp()` returns `true` at least once.

```cpp
void ProcessInput()
{
  static bool leftButtonDown = false;
  static bool rightButtonDown = false;

  // rotate through mouse cursors on mouse clicks or wheel movement
  if (g_input.ButtonDown(0))
    leftButtonDown = true;

  if (g_input.ButtonDown(1))
    rightButtonDown = true;

  if (g_input.GetMouseWheelMovement() < 0 || (leftButtonDown && g_input.ButtonUp(0)))
  {
    leftButtonDown = false;
    g_textureIndex--;
    if (g_textureIndex < 0)
      g_textureIndex = NUM_TEXTURES - 1;
  }

  if (g_input.GetMouseWheelMovement() > 0 || (rightButtonDown && g_input.ButtonUp(1)))
  {
    rightButtonDown = false;
    g_textureIndex++;
    if (g_textureIndex == NUM_TEXTURES)
      g_textureIndex = 0;
  }

  // update the mouse position
  int dx, dy;
  g_input.GetMouseMovement(dx, dy);
```

```
    // keep the cursor within the window
    g_mouseX += dx;
    if (g_mouseX >= g_screenWidth)
      g_mouseX = g_screenWidth - 1;
    if (g_mouseX < 0)
      g_mouseX = 0;
    g_mouseY -= dy;
    if (g_mouseY >= g_screenHeight)
      g_mouseY = g_screenHeight - 1;
    if (g_mouseY < 0)
      g_mouseY = 0;

    // check to see if one of the function keys was pressed
    if (g_input.KeyDown(DIK_F1))
      strcpy(g_lastKey, "F1");
    if (g_input.KeyDown(DIK_F2))
      strcpy(g_lastKey, "F2");
    if (g_input.KeyDown(DIK_F3))
      strcpy(g_lastKey, "F3");
    if (g_input.KeyDown(DIK_F4))
      strcpy(g_lastKey, "F4");
    if (g_input.KeyDown(DIK_F5))
      strcpy(g_lastKey, "F5");
    if (g_input.KeyDown(DIK_F6))
      strcpy(g_lastKey, "F6");
    if (g_input.KeyDown(DIK_F7))
      strcpy(g_lastKey, "F7");
    if (g_input.KeyDown(DIK_F8))
      strcpy(g_lastKey, "F8");
    if (g_input.KeyDown(DIK_F9))
      strcpy(g_lastKey, "F9");
    if (g_input.KeyDown(DIK_F10))
      strcpy(g_lastKey, "F10");
    if (g_input.KeyDown(DIK_F11))
      strcpy(g_lastKey, "F11");
    if (g_input.KeyDown(DIK_F12))
      strcpy(g_lastKey, "F12");

    // check for the exit key
    if (g_input.KeyDown(DIK_ESCAPE))
      PostQuitMessage(0);

} // end ProcessInput()
```

SUMMARY

Windows provides you with a number of options for obtaining input from the user. The Windows messaging system and Win32 API both provide methods that are fairly straightforward and appropriate in many situations, but they lack the flexibility and speed that are required by most games. DirectInput provides a robust, flexible, and—most importantly—fast alternative to these other approaches. Although some aspects of DirectInput are not fully covered here, you should now know enough to use it in your own games.

CHAPTER 17

USING DIRECTX AUDIO

ack in the early days of game development, programming the sound system of a game was always considered the hardest part because of the required support for the myriad sound cards on the market. Then Windows came along and handled the sound card–compatibility problems, but we were plagued by poor performance because Windows was not originally intended as a gaming platform. Now we have DirectX Audio with exceptional performance, support for nearly every sound card on the market, and the functionality to do everything you need to do. In this chapter, we'll take a look at how to use DirectX Audio as the backbone of the sound system in your games.

In this chapter, you'll learn about the following:

- The basics of sound in the real world and on the computer
- The basics of DirectX Audio
- Loading and playing audio with DirectMusic
- DirectX Audio audiopaths
- 3D Sound in DirectX Audio

THE BASICS OF SOUND

According to physics people, sound is a mechanical wave emitted from a source that travels through some sort of medium, as seen in Figure 17.1. This means that you can only hear sound in places like our atmosphere, where the medium is air molecules. In contrast, if you were in outer space and witnessed a huge explosion, you wouldn't hear anything because space is a vacuum, and there are no air molecules for the sound wave to travel through. Sound can also travel through a medium like water, and in fact it moves at a much higher velocity in water than in air.

When we talk about sound being a mechanical wave traveling through a medium, we are actually describing the motion of molecules in the medium. Now is a good time for a quick experiment. Go turn on your stereo to your favorite music (or go to an electronics store with one) and watch your bass speakers as you slowly turn up the volume. At some point, probably at a really high volume, you'll notice that the bass speakers start moving in and out of their casing. Now go put your hand up close to one of the bass speakers. Feel the wind? That's the mechanical wave of sound being produced by the bass speaker as it plays your music. As the speaker moves in and out from the bass in your music, it moves the molecules surrounding the speaker, which in turn move the molecules next to those molecules, and so on, until the energy propagating through the molecules reaches your ear, where it is translated into a sound.

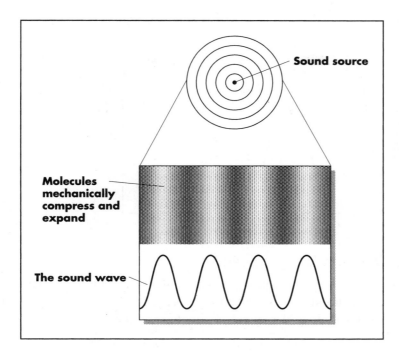

Figure 17.1

Sound is a mechanical wave emitted from a source.

Sound source

Molecules mechanically compress and expand

The sound wave

Essentially, sound travels through the air as a series of collisions from molecule to molecule with each collision representing a transfer of mechanical energy. As a result, sound travels fairly slowly, especially compared to the speed of light. For instance, if you were standing 2,000 feet away from a shooting gun, you would see the gun shoot with a puff of smoke, but you would not hear the shot until approximately two seconds later. In air, sound travels at about 600 miles per hour (mph), or 344 meters per second (m/s).

Sound waves have two primary characteristics that describe them:

- **Amplitude.** Amplitude can be defined as the amount of air volume that the sound wave moves. For instance, if you have big speakers on your stereo, then you have the potential to move a lot of air. You can also think of amplitude as the volume on your stereo system. When looking at the *waveform,* or display of a sound wave's amplitude changes, shown in Figure 17.2, the amplitude is the height of the wave from the base to the crest.
- **Frequency.** Frequency is the number of cycles per second given off by the sound source. A *cycle* is defined as one complete wave, as shown in Figure 17.2. You measure frequency in hertz (Hz). You can think of frequency as the pitch of a sound. For example, the bass speaker that you experimented with emitted a low-frequency sound wave that resulted in the deep bass sounds coming from the speaker. On the other hand, a high frequency produces a higher-pitched sound, such as the whine of a jet fighter.

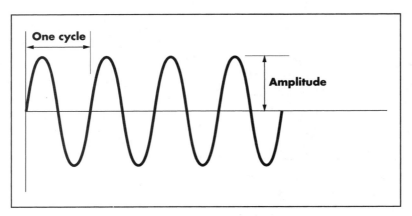

Figure 17.2

*The waveform of
a sine wave.*

Sound on the Computer

It doesn't take a rocket scientist (or a computer programmer, for that matter) to understand that sound from a computer is neither stored nor created as molecules of mechanically compressed air. In fact, this is simply impossible to do in our current technological state.

Computers can, however, make and store both digitized and synthesized sounds. You are creating a digitized sound when you record sounds with a microphone on the computer. Typically, digital sounds are used for sound effects in games (for example, explosions, movement, and speech). Synthesized sounds, on the other hand, are algorithmic reproductions of sounds and are typically used for music.

Digitized Sound

To create digital sound, you must go through the process of *digitization*, or encoding data in binary form. As you talk into the microphone, the microphone's magnetic cone creates an electrical signal from the vibration of your voice. This electrical signal is sent to an analog-to-digital converter, which changes the linear voltages received from the microphone into a digital data stream of ones and zeros. Figure 17.3 outlines the process of digitization.

After the sound is stored in memory, you can play it back into the computer speakers through a digital-to-analog converter, which converts the binary information into electrical signals. These electrical signals are then sent to the computer's speakers where they cause the speaker to vibrate and produce sound.

When recording digital sound, you must keep in mind the following:

- **Sampling rate.** The sampling rate is the number of samples of the sound that get recorded per second, and it must be at least twice the frequency of the original sound (for

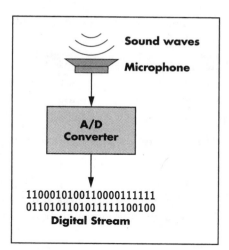

Figure 17.3

The process of digitization.

mathematical reasons). For instance, if you want to record a sound at approximately 10,000Hz, then you need to use a sample rate of 20,000Hz to accurately record the sound.

- **Amplitude resolution.** Amplitude resolution defines the number of values that you can use for the amplitude. If you have an 8-bit recording, then your amplitude can equal any one of 256 values (2^8). Similarly, a 16-bit recording allows for 65,536 values for the amplitude, which equates to professional-quality sounds.

As mentioned, you typically use digitized sound for short recordings and sound effects. You *could* use digitized sound for music, but doing so could result in a lot of extra space being eaten up from the size of the sound files. With the advent of the MP3, however, music as digitized sound may become more of a realistic option, especially because digitized sound produces much better quality than synthesized sound.

Synthesized Sound

Synthesized sound is not recorded sound. It's sound produced mathematically through special algorithms that create the sound based on some sort of description. For instance, because the A note operates at a frequency of 440Hz, you could tell a synthesizer to generate a tone at this frequency, and you would get back an A note.

When computers were starting to make their first beeps, sounds with a single frequency at a time were good enough for most people; however, people soon got bored of the same old single tone tunes (who wouldn't?), and hardware with multiple channels was born. With multiple channels, the synthesizer could play multiple tones at any one time and provide a slightly better experience musically than before. The problem with this approach, however, is that the tones still did not sound "real" because "real" tones have several other frequencies in them like undertones, overtones, and harmonics.

The FM synthesizer (frequency modulation) was created in response to the lack of "real" tones. Instead of providing just a single tone per channel with a single amplitude and frequency, the FM synthesizer alters both the amplitude and frequency of the wave to provide a more rich and full sound through phase shifting and harmonics.

Nowadays there are two more methods of sound synthesis:

- **Wave table.** Wave-table synthesis is actually a mix between synthesis and digital recording. Basically, the wave table holds a number of digital sound samples that are processed by a digital signal processor (DSP). The DSP plays the sample back at the amplitude and frequency that you desire. The result is a near-digital sound at the cost of storing the digital samples in memory.
- **Wave guide.** With wave-guide synthesis, special hardware and DSP chips mathematically generate a model of an instrument and actually play it. The generated model is close to a perfect match to the real model; the human ear cannot tell the difference between a wave-guide instrument and a real instrument.

Although you can create awesome sounds with these synthesizers, you become limited by a special file format for music synthesis called *MIDI*, which stands for *Musical Instrument Digital Interface*. MIDI is used to create music compositions through a series of channels, where each channel represents an instrument or sound. So if you had four channels, you would have four instruments (perhaps piano, flute, guitar, and saxophone), where each instrument is given a sequence of notes to play over a specific time interval. The problem with MIDI is that music created with it has a tendency to sound different on different computers. This fallacy is a result of MIDI leaving the actual synthesis of the music up to the hardware, because it only records the actual musical notes and timing. The advantage to using MIDI is its file size. Several minutes of MIDI music might take up only a few hundred kilobytes, while several minutes of music in digital form would require many, many megabytes.

What Is DirectX Audio?

So what exactly is DirectX Audio? In a nutshell, this component of DirectX enables you to create and implement a fully dynamic soundtrack with hardware acceleration, including the ability for 3D sound positioning. In previous versions, you used DirectX for the DirectSound and DirectMusic components to handle audio playback, but with the introduction of DirectX 8, these two components have been combined into the DirectX Audio API. DirectSound handles wave playback and capture, while DirectMusic is the primary mechanism for loading and playing all sounds.

With DirectX 8, the DirectSound and DirectMusic components are now interfaces for DirectX Audio. With these interfaces, you can

- Load and play sounds from files in MIDI, WAV, or DirectMusic Producer runtime format.
- Play from multiple sources simultaneously.
- Schedule the timing of music events with high precision.
- Use downloadable sounds (DLS). With DLS, developers can make sure that the game music sounds the same on all computers.
- Use 3D sound effects.
- Apply pitch changes, reverb, distortion, and other effects to sounds.
- Capture MIDI data or stream it from one port to another.
- Capture WAV sounds from a microphone or other input.
- Play music that changes subtly each time it repeats.
- Dynamically compose transitions between existing pieces of music.

This list is only a sample of all the features DirectX Audio brings to developers. Before you can go much further, however, you need to get back to the basics and learn about sound.

DirectX Audio Features

Before you can get started with DirectX Audio, you need to understand its basic features:

- Loader
- Segments and Segment States
- Performance
- Messages
- Performance Channels
- DLS Synthesizer
- Instruments and Downloading
- Audiopaths and Buffers

Let's look at each of these features in more detail.

Loader

The *loader* is an object that loads other objects, including all audio content including DirectMusic segment files, DLS collections, MIDI files, and both mono and stereo WAV files. It is typically one of the first objects created when DirectX Audio is used.

Segments and Segment States

Generally, a *segment* is an object encapsulating sequenced sound data representing a piece of music or sound that is played as a unit. The sound data can be a MIDI sequence, a WAV, a piece of music composed at runtime, or a collection of information in a segment file from DirectMusic Producer.

Segments are played as either a primary segment or a secondary segment. Primary segments can only be played one at a time, but secondary segments are typically short musical motifs or sound effects that can be played over the entire primary segment.

Segments can combine different kinds of data such as waves, patterns, chord changes, band changes, and tempo changes. They can also hold information about the audiopath (soon to be discussed) on which they should be played, including special effects.

Performance

The *performance* object handles the flow of data from the source to the synthesizer. It handles timing, mapping of data channels to audiopaths, routing of messages, tool management, notification, and other important tasks. Normally, you only need a single performance.

Messages

Audio data flows through the performance object in the form of messages. A *message* can hold information about a musical note, a wave, a controller change, or even text for lyrics display. Typically, you don't deal directly with messages, because they are generated by tracks when a segment is playing. You can, however, insert messages into the performance or intercept messages. You can also use messages for notifications. For instance, you can request that an event be signaled whenever certain points in the performance are reached, such as every beat of the music.

Performance Channels

A *performance channel* is the route between a part and an audiopath. A *part* can be a MIDI channel, a part in a DirectMusic Producer segment, or a wave. Every playing sound consists of one or more parts, and normally, a part represents a single musical instrument. Performance channels are similar to MIDI channels, except the number of performance channels is virtually unlimited (MIDI is typically limited to 16 channels).

DLS Synthesizer

When you have data that is not already in the form of a wave, such as a MIDI note, it has to be converted by a synthesizer to a wave before the sound card can play the data. Most synthesizers implement the downloadable sounds (DLS) Level 2 standard, but in the absence of a suitable hardware synthesizer, a software synthesizer is used. The synthesizer produces sounds based on wave samples and is capable of producing highly sophisticated musical timbres or any other kind of sound.

Instruments and Downloading

In order to play an instrument, the synthesizer needs information about how the instrument sounds. Instrument data consists of wave samples and articulation data stored in DLS collections and is downloaded by the synthesizer.

A range of notes from an instrument is typically based on one sample that is pitched for each note. With DLS Level 2, however, each note can be based on a different sample or combination of samples. Even the note velocity can trigger use of different samples for an instrument.

Audiopaths and Buffers

An *audiopath* controls the flow of sounds that a DirectMusic segment takes from the performance to the synthesizer, then through the DirectSound buffers where effects are applied, and finally to the primary buffer, where the final output is mixed.

You can create standard audiopaths and play segments on them. For instance, you could create an audiopath for MIDI files with musical reverb, and you could use another audiopath for playing wave files with 3D control. Essentially, an audiopath can be viewed as a chain of objects through which sound data is streamed.

Audio Data Flow

You typically use DirectX Audio to load music or sound data from MIDI files, wave files, DirectMusic Producer segment files, or DirectMusic Producer component files. After the data is loaded, it is encapsulated in segment objects, where each segment object represents data from a single source. You can play one primary segment and any number of secondary segments during a performance.

A segment contains one or more tracks, with each track containing timed data such as notes or tempo changes. The majority of tracks produce time-stamped messages when the segment is played by the performance.

The performance object dispatches messages to tools grouped in the following toolgraphs:

- **The segment toolgraph.** Accepts messages only from particular segments.
- **The audiopath toolgraph.** Accepts messages from all segments playing on the path.
- **The performance toolgraph.** Accepts messages from all segments. Tools can modify, pass, delete, or send new messages.

Lastly, the messages are delivered to the output tool, which converts the data to MIDI format before passing it to the synthesizer. The synthesizer creates sound waves and streams them to a *sink*, which manages the distribution of data through buses to one of three types of DirectSound buffers:

- **Sink-in buffers.** Secondary buffers into which the sink-in streams data. They convert the data format to that of the primary buffer and allow you to control pan, volume, 3D spatialization, and other properties. Sink-in buffers can also pass their sound data through effects modules to add such effects as reverberation, distortion, and echo. The result is passed either directly to the primary buffer or to one or more mix-in buffers.
- **Mix-in buffers.** Receive data from other buffers, apply effects, and then mix the results. Global effects are often applied through the use of mix-in buffers.
- **Primary buffer.** Performs the final mixing on all data and passes it to the output channels.

Figure 17.4 illustrates the flow of data from files to the output speakers.

LOADING AND PLAYING AUDIO WITH DIRECTMUSIC

DirectMusic is a purely COM (Component Object Model) component of DirectX. This means that there are no helper functions in an import library to help you create the COM objects—you'll have to create the COM objects yourself with calls to the COM library. Because this also means that there are no import LIB files, you only need to worry about the header files to include: *dmusicc.h* and *dmusici.h*.

After you have the header files included, there are six basic steps you need to follow to play an audio file:

1. **Initialize COM.** Because there are no helper functions for creating DirectMusic objects, you need to call CoInitialize() to initialize COM.
2. **Create and initialize the performance.** You need to create a single performance object by calling CoCreateInstance() and obtaining the IDirectMusicPerformance8 interface. You then call IDirectMusicPerformance8::InitAudio() to set up a default audiopath.

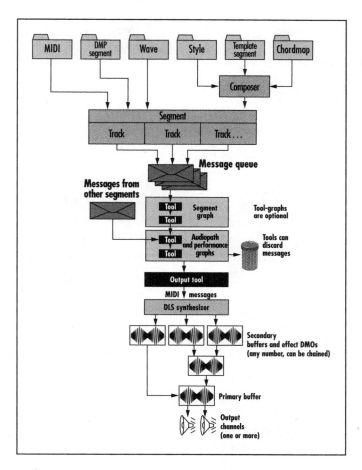

Figure 17.4

The flow of audio data in DirectX Audio.

3. **Create the loader.** You use the CoCreateInstance() function again to obtain an IDirectMusicLoader8 interface.
4. **Load a segment.** You call IDirectMusicLoader8::SetSearchDirectory() to tell the loader where to find the data files. To load a segment from a file or resource and to obtain its IDirectMusicSegment8 interface, you call IDirectMusicLoad8::GetObject().
5. **Download the band.** Download DLS data to the synthesizer so instruments can play by calling IDirectMusicSegment8::Download(). Wave files must also be downloaded.
6. **Play the segment.** You pass the segment pointer to IDirectMusicPerformance8::PlaySegmentEx().

Let's look at each of these steps one at a time.

Initialize COM

This is the most straightforward step in the process of setting up DirectX Audio. You initialize COM with the function CoInitialize():

```
// initialize COM
CoInitialize(NULL);
```

You must place this at the beginning of your application, before any direct COM calls are made.

Create and Initialize the Performance

Next you need to create and initialize the performance object. The performance can be considered the master interface of the DirectX Audio component. To create a performance interface, you use the CoCreateInstance() function with the performance interface identifier, object class identifier, and the storage for the interface pointer as parameters. First, you must define the IDirectMusicPerformance8 object:

```
IDirectMusicPerformance8* dmusicPerformance = NULL;    // the performance object
```

Then you can create the performance:

```
// create the performance
CoCreateInstance(CLSID_IDirectMusicPerformance, NULL, CLSCTX_INPROC,
                 IID_IDirectMusicPerformance8, (void**)&dmusicPerformance);
```

Now you are ready to make calls to the performance interface's functions. The first function you need to call is the IDirectMusicPerformance8::InitAudio() function, which initializes the performance and optionally sets up a default audiopath and is defined as

```
HRESULT InitAudio(
    IDirectMusic**     ppDirectMusic,      // interface pointer to a DMusic object
    IDirectSound**     ppDirectSound,      // interface pointer to a DSound object
    HWND               hWnd,               // window handle
    DWORD              dwDefaultPathType,  // default audiopath type
    DWORD              dwPChannelCount,    // number of performance channels for path
    DWORD              dwFlags,            // flags for synthesizer features
    DMUS_AUDIOPARAMS   pParams);           // specifies parameters for synthesizer
```

Here's an example of using the InitAudio() function:

```
dmusicPerformance->InitAudio(NULL,           // IDirectMusic interface (not needed)
                             NULL,           // IdirectSound interface (not needed)
```

```
                       NULL,                // window handle
                       DMUS_APATH_SHARED_STEREOPLUSREVERB, // default audiopath
                       64,                  // number of performance channels
                       DMUS_AUDIOF_ALL,     // synthesizer features
                       NULL);               // audio parameters (default)
```

Calling the InitAudio() function with these parameters tells DirectX Audio to set up the
DirectMusic and DirectSound interfaces with 64 performance channels allocated for the default
audiopath and all synthesizer features turned on.

Create the Loader

Again, you use the CoCreateInstance() function to obtain an IDirectMusicLoader8 interface, but
first, you must define the IDirectMusicLoader8 object:

```
IDirectMusicLoader8* dmusicLoader = NULL;        // the loader object

// create the loader
CoCreateInstance(CLSID_IDirectMusicLoader, NULL, CLSCTX_INPROC,
                 IID_IDirectMusicLoader8, (void**)&dmusicLoader);
```

Load a Segment

Before you can load a segment, you need to tell the loader object where to find the audio files.
Although you can provide a full path each time you load an audio file, it is much easier to define
a default directory. You accomplish this through the IDirectMusicLoader8::SetSearchDirectory()
function, which is defined as

```
HRESULT SetSearchDirectory(
     REFGUID rguidClass,       // reference to identifier of the class of objects
                               // that the call pertains to
     WCHAR*  pwszPath,         // file path for directory
     BOOL    fClear);          // if TRUE, clears all information about objects
                               // before setting the directory
```

Here's an example of how you set the loader's search directory:

```
WCHAR searchPath[MAX_PATH];                        // the search path in WCHAR format
MultiByteToWideChar(CP_ACP, 0, "c:\\music", -1,  // converts CHAR to WCHAR
                    searchPath, MAX_PATH);
```

```
// set the loader's search directory
dmusicLoader->SetSearchDirectory(GUID_DirectMusicAllTypes,
                                 searchPath, FALSE);
```

Now you can load the segment from a file located in the search directory through one of two functions: IDirectMusicLoader8::LoadObjectFromFile() or IDirectMusicLoader8::GetObject(). The LoadObjectFromFile() function, which you'll normally use to load audio files from disk, is defined as

```
HRESULT LoadObjectFromFile(
     REFGUID rguidClassID,       // unique identifier for class of object
     REFIID  iidInterfaceID,     // unique identifier of the interface
     WCHAR   *pwzFilePath,       // name of the file that contains the object
     void    **ppObject);        // pointer to desired interface of the object
```

To use this function, you simply need to specify the filename of the segment you want to load and the segment object as parameters. The segment object is defined as

```
IDirectMusicSegment8* dmusicSegment = NULL;        // the segment object
```

Now you can load the segment from the directory previously set by IDirectMusicLoader8::SetSearchDirectory():

```
// the segment filename
WCHAR filename[MAX_PATH] = "testsound.wav";

// load the segment from the file
if (FAILED(dmusicLoader->LoadObjectFromFile(CLSID_DirectMusicSegment,
                                            IID_IDirectMusicSegment8,
                                            filename,
                                            (void**)&dmusicSegment)))
{
     MessageBox(NULL, "Could not find audio media! Press OK to exit.",
                "Error!", MB_OK);
     return  0;
}
```

Download the Band

Before you can play the segment you just loaded, its band must be downloaded to the synthesizer. As long as the band isn't unloaded, you need to download the band only once for each segment. You perform this step by calling the IDirectMusicSegment8::Download() function, which is defined as

```
HRESULT Download(
     Iunknown *pAudioPath          // pointer to the Iuknown interface of the performance
);                                 // or audiopath that receives the data
```

So to load a segment into the performance, you simply call

```
dmusicSegment->Download(dmusicPerformance); // download the segment to the performance
```

Play the Segment

Finally, you play the audio file you've loaded by passing the segment to
IDirectMusicPerformance8::PlaySegmentEx(), which is defined as

```
HRESULT PlaySegmentEx(
     IUnknown* pSource,            // address of IUknown interface of the object to play
     WCHAR     pwzSegmentName,     // set to NULL (not implemented in DX8)
     IUknown*  pTransition,        // template segment pointer for transition to segment
     DWORD     dwFlags,            // flags that modify the method's behavior
     __int64   i64StartTime,       // performance time at which to begin playing
     IDirectMusicSegmentState** ppSegmentState, // segment state
     IUnknown* pFrom,              // object to stop when segment begins playing
     IUnknown* pAudioPath          // audiopath on which to play (NULL is default)
);
```

Although you can alter the playback of the segment, to play the segment immediately on the
default audiopath, you set all the parameters except the first to NULL or 0:

```
dmusicPerformance->PlaySegmentEx(dmusicSegment,  // segment to play
                       NULL,          // used for songs; not implemented
                       NULL,          // for transitions
                       0,             // flags
                       0,             // start time (0 is immediate)
                       NULL,          // pointer - receives segment state
                       NULL,          // object to stop
                       NULL);         // audiopath, if not default
```

After this function is called, your program will continue execution, but the audio file you have
loaded will continue playing until you tell it to stop.

Stopping a Segment

Speaking of stopping, you can stop a segment from playing by calling the IDirectMusicPerformance8::Stop() function, which is defined as

```
HRESULT Stop(
    IDirectMusicSegment*      pSegment,        // segment to stop playing
    IDirectMusicSegmentState* pSegmentState,   // segment state to stop playing
    MUSIC_TIME mtTime,                         // time to stop segment
    DWORD dwFlags                              // when the stop should occur
);
```

To use the stop function, you do the following:

```
dmusicPerformance->Stop(dmusicSegment,  // segment to stop playing (NULL is all audio)
                        NULL,           // segment state to stop playing
                        0,              // time to stop the segment (0 is immediately)
                        0);             // when the stop should occur (0 immediately)
```

Another option is to use the IDirectMusicPerformance8::StopEx() function, which is defined as

```
HRESULT StopEx(
    IUnknown *pObjectToStop,       // interface to stop playing
    __int64   i64StopTime,         // time to stop
    DWORD     dwFlags              // when stop should occur
);
```

This new addition to the DirectMusic component stops a segment, segment state, or audiopath. In your case, you'd call the StopEx() function like this:

```
dmusicPerformance->StopEx(dmusicSegment, // interface to stop playing
                          0,             // time to stop
                          0);            // when stop should occur
```

Is the Segment Playing?

You can find out if a segment or segment state is currently being heard from the speakers through the IDirectMusicPerformance8::IsPlaying() function, which is defined as

```
HRESULT IsPlaying(
    IDirectMusicSegment*      pSegment,
    IdirectMusicSegmentState* pSegState
);
```

In your case, you would want to see if the segment was still playing, so you'd set *pSegState* to NULL and *pSegment* to your segment:

```
if (dmusicPerformance->IsPlaying(dmusicSegment, NULL) == S_OK)
{
    // segment is still playing
}
else
{
    // segment is not playing
}
```

Controlling Segment Loops

You can control the number of times a segment loops by using the IDirectMusicSegment8::SetRepeats() function, defined as

```
HRESULT SetRepeats(
    DWORD dwRepeats            // number of times to loop
);
```

This function sets the number of times the looping portion of the segment is to repeat. By default, the entire segment is looped, but you can change this with the IDirectMusicSegment8::SetLoopPoints() function. If you set the *dwRepeats* parameter to DMUS_SEG_REPEAT_INFINITE, then the segment will repeat until you explicitly stop it. Likewise, if you set the *dwRepeats* parameter to 0, the segment will play only once.

The IDirectMusicSegment8::SetLoopPoints() function allows you to set the start and end points of the part of the segment that repeats and is defined as

```
HRESULT SetLoopPoints(
    MUSIC_TIME mtStart,        // point at which to begin the loop
    MUSIC_TIME mtEnd           // point at which to end the loop (0 - entire segment)
);
```

When you play the segment, it will play from the segment start time until *mtEnd*. Then it will loop to *mtStart*, and continue playing the loop portion the number of times set by IDirectMusicSegment8::SetRepeats().

Cleaning Up

After you're finished playing with audio and are ready to exit the application, you need to release the COM objects and close down the performance. First, though, you need to stop any playing segments with the IDirectMusicPerformance8::Stop() function just mentioned. Then you can close down the performance with the IDirectMusicPerformance8::CloseDown() function, which is defined as

```
HRESULT CloseDown();
```

and called as

```
dmusicPerformance->CloseDown();
```

Next, you release all interfaces that have been allocated, such as the loader, performance, and segment:

```
dmusicLoader->Release();
dmusicPerformance->Release();
dmusicSegment->Release();
```

And finally, you close COM with the CoUninitialize() function:

```
CoUninitialize();
```

A SIMPLE EXAMPLE

Now that you know how to load audio files and play them, let's look at a simple example that loads a MIDI music file and plays it while some basic OpenGL graphics are rendered to the window. Pay attention to the comments to get a better understanding of what's happening.

```
#define WIN32_LEAN_AND_MEAN       // trim the excess fat from Windows
#define INITGUID                  // we use GUID's with DMusic
                                  // must either #define this or include
                                  // dxguid.lib when linking


////// Includes
#include <windows.h>              // standard Windows app include
#include <dmusicc.h>              // DirectMusic includes
#include <dmusici.h>
#include <stdio.h>
#include <stdlib.h>
#include <math.h>
```

```
#include <gl/gl.h>                    // standard OpenGL include
#include <gl/glu.h>                   // OpenGL utilities

////// Global Variables
HDC g_HDC;                            // global device context
bool fullScreen = false;             // true = full screen; false = windowed
bool keyPressed[256];                // holds true for keys that are pressed

float angle = 0.0f;                   // angle of rotation
unsigned int listBase;               // display list base
GLYPHMETRICSFLOAT gmf[256];          // holds orientation and placement
                                      // info for display lists

////// DirectMusic variables
IDirectMusicLoader8 *dmusicLoader = NULL;            // the loader
IDirectMusicPerformance8 *dmusicPerformance = NULL; // the performance
IDirectMusicSegment8 *dmusicSegment = NULL;          // the segment

/********************************************************
*    DirectMusic Interfaces
********************************************************/


// InitDirectXAudio()
// desc: initializes the DirectX Audio component for playback
bool InitDirectXAudio(HWND hwnd)
{
    char pathStr[MAX_PATH];      // path for audio file
    WCHAR wcharStr[MAX_PATH];

    // create the loader object
    if (FAILED(CoCreateInstance(CLSID_DirectMusicLoader, NULL, CLSCTX_INPROC,
                        IID_IDirectMusicLoader8, (void**)&dmusicLoader)))
    {
        MessageBox(hwnd, "Unable to create the IDirectMusicLoader8 object! Press OK
                        to exit", "ERROR!", MB_OK);
        return false;
    }
```

```cpp
        // create the performance object
        if (FAILED(CoCreateInstance(CLSID_DirectMusicPerformance, NULL, CLSCTX_INPROC,
                            IID_IDirectMusicPerformance8, (void**)&dmusicPerformance)))
        {
            MessageBox(hwnd, "Unable to create the IDirectMusicPerformance8 object!
                            Press OK to exit", "ERROR!", MB_OK);
            return false;
        }

        // initialize the performance with the standard audiopath
        dmusicPerformance->InitAudio(NULL, NULL, hwnd,
                                DMUS_APATH_SHARED_STEREOPLUSREVERB, 64,
                                DMUS_AUDIOF_ALL, NULL);

        // retrieve the current directory
        GetCurrentDirectory(MAX_PATH, pathStr);

        // convert to unicode string
        MultiByteToWideChar(CP_ACP, 0, pathStr, -1, wcharStr, MAX_PATH);

        // set the search directory
        dmusicLoader->SetSearchDirectory(GUID_DirectMusicAllTypes, wcharStr, FALSE);

        return true;
}

// LoadSegment()
// desc: load a segment from a file
bool LoadSegment(HWND hwnd, char *filename)
{
        WCHAR wcharStr[MAX_PATH];

        // convert filename to unicode string
        MultiByteToWideChar(CP_ACP, 0, filename, -1, wcharStr, MAX_PATH);

        // load the segment from file
        if (FAILED(dmusicLoader->LoadObjectFromFile(CLSID_DirectMusicSegment,
                                            IID_IDirectMusicSegment8,
                                            wcharStr,
                                            (void**)&dmusicSegment)))
```

```cpp
        {
            MessageBox(hwnd, "Audio file not found! Press OK to exit",
                        "ERROR!", MB_OK);
            return false;
        }


        // download the segment's instruments to the synthesizer
        dmusicSegment->Download(dmusicPerformance);


        return true;
}


// PlaySegment()
// desc: start playing a segment
void PlaySegment(IDirectMusicPerformance8* dmPerf, IDirectMusicSegment8* dmSeg)
{
        // play the segment
        dmPerf->PlaySegmentEx(dmSeg, NULL, NULL, 0, 0, NULL, NULL, NULL);
}


// StopSegment()
// desc: stop a segment from playing
void StopSegment(IDirectMusicPerformance8* dmPerf, IDirectMusicSegment8* dmSeg)
{
        // stop the dmSeg from playing
        dmPerf->StopEx(dmSeg, 0, 0);
}


// CloseDown()
// desc: shutdown music performance
void CloseDown(IDirectMusicPerformance8* dmPerf)
{
        // stop the music
        dmPerf->Stop(NULL, NULL, 0, 0);

        // close down DirectMusic
        dmPerf->CloseDown();
}
```

```
/*******************************************************
*    OpenGL Interfaces
*******************************************************/

// CreateOutlineFont()
// desc: creates the outline font using the CreateFont() function
unsigned int CreateOutlineFont(char *fontName, int fontSize, float depth)
{
     HFONT hFont;           // Windows font
     unsigned int base;

     base = glGenLists(256);        // create storage for 96 characters

     if (stricmp(fontName, "symbol") == 0)
     {
          hFont = CreateFont(fontSize, 0, 0, 0, FW_BOLD, FALSE, FALSE, FALSE,
                             SYMBOL_CHARSET, OUT_TT_PRECIS, CLIP_DEFAULT_PRECIS,
                             ANTIALIASED_QUALITY, FF_DONTCARE | DEFAULT_PITCH,
                             fontName);
     }
     else
     {
          hFont = CreateFont(fontSize, 0, 0, 0, FW_BOLD, FALSE, FALSE, FALSE,
                             ANSI_CHARSET, OUT_TT_PRECIS, CLIP_DEFAULT_PRECIS,
                             ANTIALIASED_QUALITY, FF_DONTCARE | DEFAULT_PITCH,
                             fontName);
     }

     if (!hFont)
          return 0;

     SelectObject(g_HDC, hFont);
     wglUseFontOutlines(g_HDC, 0, 255, base, 0.0f, depth, WGL_FONT_POLYGONS, gmf);

     return base;
}

// ClearFont()
// desc: deletes the display list for the font
void ClearFont(unsigned int base)
```

```
{
    glDeleteLists(base, 256);
}


// PrintString()
// desc: displays the text in str from the font indicated by base
void PrintString(unsigned int base, char *str)
{
    float length = 0;

    if ((str == NULL))
        return;

    // center the text
    for (unsigned int loop=0;loop<(strlen(str));loop++) // find length of text
    {
        length+=gmf[str[loop]].gmfCellIncX;  // increase length by character's width
    }
    glTranslatef(-length/2,0.0f,0.0f);                      // translate to center text

    // draw the text
    glPushAttrib(GL_LIST_BIT);
        glListBase(base);
        glCallLists(strlen(str), GL_UNSIGNED_BYTE, str);
    glPopAttrib();
}


// CleanUp()
// desc: application cleanup
void CleanUp()
{
    ClearFont(listBase);
    dmusicLoader->Release();
    dmusicPerformance->Release();
    dmusicSegment->Release();
}


// Initialize
// desc: initializes OpenGL
void Initialize()
```

```cpp
{
    glClearColor(0.0f, 0.0f, 0.0f, 0.0f);              // clear to black

    glShadeModel(GL_SMOOTH);                           // use smooth shading
    glEnable(GL_DEPTH_TEST);                           // hidden surface removal
    glEnable(GL_LIGHT0);                               // enable light0
    glEnable(GL_LIGHTING);                             // enable lighting
    glEnable(GL_COLOR_MATERIAL);                       // enable color for material

    listBase = CreateOutlineFont("Arial", 10, 0.25f);  // load 10pt Arial font
}

// Render
// desc: handles drawing of scene
void Render()
{
    // clear screen and depth buffer
    glClear(GL_COLOR_BUFFER_BIT | GL_DEPTH_BUFFER_BIT);
    glLoadIdentity();

    // move 15 units into the screen and rotate along all axes
    glTranslatef(0.0f, 0.0f, -15.0f);
    glRotatef(angle*0.9f, 1.0f, 0.0f, 0.0f);
    glRotatef(angle*1.5f, 0.0f, 1.0f, 0.0f);
    glRotatef(angle, 0.0f, 0.0f, 1.0f);

    // set color to blueish color
    glColor3f(0.3f, 0.4f, 0.8f);

    // display the text
    PrintString(listBase, "DirectX Audio!");

    // yellow-green color
    glColor3f(0.6f, 0.8f, 0.5f);

    // display text
    glPushMatrix();
        glTranslatef(-3.0f, -1.0f, 0.0f);
        PrintString(listBase, "P - Play");
    glPopMatrix();
```

```c
    glPushMatrix();
        glTranslatef(-3.0f, -2.0f, 0.0f);
        PrintString(listBase, "S - Stop");
    glPopMatrix();
    glPushMatrix();
        glTranslatef(-3.0f, -3.0f, 0.0f);
        PrintString(listBase, "ESC - Quit");
    glPopMatrix();

    angle += 0.4f;

    SwapBuffers(g_HDC);             // bring back buffer to foreground
}


// function to set the pixel format for the device context
void SetupPixelFormat(HDC hDC)
{
    int nPixelFormat;                  // our pixel-format index

    static PIXELFORMATDESCRIPTOR pfd = {
        sizeof(PIXELFORMATDESCRIPTOR),  // size of structure
        1,                              // default version
        PFD_DRAW_TO_WINDOW |            // window-drawing support
        PFD_SUPPORT_OPENGL |            // OpenGL support
        PFD_DOUBLEBUFFER,               // double-buffering support
        PFD_TYPE_RGBA,                  // RGBA color mode
        32,                             // 32-bit color mode
        0, 0, 0, 0, 0, 0,               // ignore color bits, non-palletized mode
        0,                              // no alpha buffer
        0,                              // ignore shift bit
        0,                              // no accumulation buffer
        0, 0, 0, 0,                     // ignore accumulation bits
        16,                             // 16 bit z-buffer size
        0,                              // no stencil buffer
        0,                              // no auxiliary buffer
        PFD_MAIN_PLANE,                 // main drawing plane
        0,                              // reserved
        0, 0, 0 };                      // layer masks ignored
```

```
        // choose best-matching pixel format
        nPixelFormat = ChoosePixelFormat(hDC, &pfd);
        SetPixelFormat(hDC, nPixelFormat, &pfd);    // set pixel format to device context
}

// the Windows Procedure event handler
LRESULT CALLBACK WndProc(HWND hwnd, UINT message, WPARAM wParam, LPARAM lParam)
{
        static HGLRC hRC;               // rendering context
        static HDC hDC;                 // device context
        int width, height;             // window width and height

        switch(message)
        {
            case WM_CREATE:             // window is being created

                hDC = GetDC(hwnd);      // get current window's device context
                g_HDC = hDC;
                SetupPixelFormat(hDC);  // call our pixel-format setup function

                // create rendering context and make it current
                hRC = wglCreateContext(hDC);
                wglMakeCurrent(hDC, hRC);

                return 0;
                break;

            case WM_CLOSE:                    // Windows is closing

                // deselect rendering context and delete it
                wglMakeCurrent(hDC, NULL);
                wglDeleteContext(hRC);

                // send WM_QUIT to message queue
                PostQuitMessage(0);

                return 0;
                break;

            case WM_SIZE:
                height = HIWORD(lParam);       // retrieve width and height
                width = LOWORD(lParam);
```

```
                    if (height==0)                  // don't want a divide by zero
                    {
                        height=1;
                    }

                    // reset the viewport to new dimensions
                    glViewport(0, 0, width, height);

                    // set projection matrix to current matrix
                    glMatrixMode(GL_PROJECTION);
                    glLoadIdentity();                // reset projection matrix

                    // calculate aspect ratio of window
                    gluPerspective(54.0f,(GLfloat)width/(GLfloat)height,1.0f,1000.0f);

                    glMatrixMode(GL_MODELVIEW);       // set modelview matrix
                    glLoadIdentity();                // reset modelview matrix

                    return 0;
                    break;

            case WM_KEYDOWN:                          // is a key pressed?
                    keyPressed[wParam] = true;
                    return 0;
                    break;

            case WM_KEYUP:
                    keyPressed[wParam] = false;
                    return 0;
                    break;

            default:
                    break;
        }

    return (DefWindowProc(hwnd, message, wParam, lParam));
}

// the main Windows entry point
int WINAPI WinMain(HINSTANCE hInstance, HINSTANCE hPrevInstance, LPSTR lpCmdLine,
                int nShowCmd)
```

```
{
        WNDCLASSEX windowClass; // window class
        HWND       hwnd;        // window handle
        MSG        msg;         // message
        bool       done;        // flag saying when our app is complete
        DWORD      dwExStyle;   // Window Extended Style
        DWORD      dwStyle;     // Window Style
        RECT       windowRect;

    // screen resolution
    int width = 800;
    int height = 600;
    int bits = 16;

    windowRect.left=(long)0;                   // set left value to 0
    windowRect.right=(long)width;              // set right value to requested width
    windowRect.top=(long)0;                    // set top value to 0
    windowRect.bottom=(long)height;            // set bottom value to requested height

    // fill out the window class structure
    windowClass.cbSize            = sizeof(WNDCLASSEX);
    windowClass.style             = CS_HREDRAW | CS_VREDRAW;
    windowClass.lpfnWndProc       = WndProc;
    windowClass.cbClsExtra        = 0;
    windowClass.cbWndExtra        = 0;
    windowClass.hInstance         = hInstance;
    windowClass.hIcon             = LoadIcon(NULL, IDI_APPLICATION); // default icon
    windowClass.hCursor           = LoadCursor(NULL, IDC_ARROW);     // default arrow
    windowClass.hbrBackground     = NULL;                      // don't need background
    windowClass.lpszMenuName      = NULL;                      // no menu
    windowClass.lpszClassName     = "MyClass";
    windowClass.hIconSm           = LoadIcon(NULL, IDI_WINLOGO);

    // register the windows class
    if (!RegisterClassEx(&windowClass))
        return 0;

    if (fullScreen)                                    // fullscreen?
    {
        DEVMODE dmScreenSettings;                          // device mode
        memset(&dmScreenSettings,0,sizeof(dmScreenSettings));
```

```
dmScreenSettings.dmSize = sizeof(dmScreenSettings);
dmScreenSettings.dmPelsWidth = width;          // screen width
dmScreenSettings.dmPelsHeight = height;        // screen height
dmScreenSettings.dmBitsPerPel = bits;          // bits per pixel
dmScreenSettings.dmFields=DM_BITSPERPEL|DM_PELSWIDTH|DM_PELSHEIGHT;

if (ChangeDisplaySettings(&dmScreenSettings, CDS_FULLSCREEN) !=
                          DISP_CHANGE_SUCCESSFUL)
{
    // setting display mode failed, switch to windowed
    MessageBox(NULL, "Display mode failed", NULL, MB_OK);
    fullScreen=FALSE;
}
}

if (fullScreen)                         // are we still in full-screen mode?
{
    dwExStyle=WS_EX_APPWINDOW;          // window extended style
    dwStyle=WS_POPUP;                   // Windows style
    ShowCursor(FALSE);                  // hide mouse pointer
}
else
{
    dwExStyle=WS_EX_APPWINDOW | WS_EX_WINDOWEDGE;  // window extended style
    dwStyle=WS_OVERLAPPEDWINDOW;                    // Windows style
}

// adjust window to true requested size
AdjustWindowRectEx(&windowRect, dwStyle, FALSE, dwExStyle);

// class registered, so now create our window
hwnd = CreateWindowEx(NULL,             // extended style
                 "MyClass",             // class name
                 "DirectX Audio Example 1 - Playing Audio", // app name
                 dwStyle | WS_CLIPCHILDREN |
                 WS_CLIPSIBLINGS,
                 0, 0,                  // x,y coordinate
                 windowRect.right - windowRect.left,
                 windowRect.bottom - windowRect.top,   // width, height
                 NULL,                  // handle to parent
                 NULL,                  // handle to menu
```

```cpp
                          hInstance,         // application instance
                          NULL);             // no extra params

    // check if window creation failed (hwnd would equal NULL)
    if (!hwnd)
        return 0;


    // initialize COM
    if (FAILED(CoInitialize(NULL)))
        return 0;                            // if unable to initialize COM, exit


    // initialize DirectX Audio
    if (!InitDirectXAudio(hwnd))
        return 0;


    // load the segment
    if (!LoadSegment(hwnd, "canyon.mid"))
        return 0;


    // play the segment
    PlaySegment(dmusicPerformance, dmusicSegment);


    ShowWindow(hwnd, SW_SHOW);               // display the window
    UpdateWindow(hwnd);                      // update the window


    done = false;                            // initialize the loop condition variable
    Initialize();                            // initialize OpenGL


    // main message loop
    while (!done)
    {
        PeekMessage(&msg, hwnd, NULL, NULL, PM_REMOVE);

        if (msg.message == WM_QUIT)          // do we receive a WM_QUIT message?
        {
            done = true;                     // if so, time to quit the application
        }
        else
        {
            // play the segment
            if (keyPressed['P'] || keyPressed['p'])
```

```
                    {
                        if (dmusicPerformance->IsPlaying(dmusicSegment, NULL) != S_OK)
                            PlaySegment(dmusicPerformance, dmusicSegment);
                    }

                    // stop the segment
                    if (keyPressed['S'] || keyPressed['s'])
                    {
                        if (dmusicPerformance->IsPlaying(dmusicSegment, NULL) == S_OK)
                            StopSegment(dmusicPerformance, dmusicSegment);
                    }

                    // exit the app
                    if (keyPressed[VK_ESCAPE])
                        done = true;
                    else
                    {
                        Render();                    // render a frame

                        TranslateMessage(&msg); // translate and dispatch to event queue
                        DispatchMessage(&msg);
                    }
                }
        }

        // close down the performance
        CloseDown(dmusicPerformance);

        // clean up application
        CleanUp();

        // close down COM
        CoUninitialize();

        if (fullScreen)
        {
            ChangeDisplaySettings(NULL,0);          // if so switch back to the desktop
            ShowCursor(TRUE);                       // show mouse pointer
        }

        return msg.wParam;
}
```

This example displays the rotating text seen in Figure 17.5 while playing *canyon.mid* in the background. The music stops playing if you press the S key on the keyboard. Although the music is stopped, if you press the P key on the keyboard, the music will begin playing again. You exit the application by pressing the Esc key.

Figure 17.5

The DirectX Audio example.

USING AUDIOPATHS

Audiopaths manage the flow of sound data through various objects from the audio file itself to the output lines for the speakers. An audiopath can include the performance to which it belongs, a segment, toolgraphs, the synthesizer, and DirectSound buffers. As we just discussed, if you're only looking to do basic 2D sound effects or play MIDI files, then you can set up a standard default audiopath and play everything on it. But if you really want to use the full power of DirectX Audio, then you need to be able to control the audiopath.

There are four ways you can set up an audiopath:

- You can create one or more standard audiopaths by using
  `IDirectMusicPerformance8::CreateStandardAudioPath()`.
- You can create a default standard audiopath for the performance in the call to
  `IDirectMusicPerformance8::InitAudio()`.

- You can obtain an audiopath configuration from a file authored in DirectMusic Producer and pass the configuration object to `IDirectMusicPerformance8::CreateAudioPath()`.
- You can use DirectMusic to create an audiopath from the segment's audiopath configuration when the segment is played.

You can use the `IDirectMusicLoader8::GetObject()` or `IDirectMusicLoader8::LoadObjectFromFile()` functions to load an audiopath configuration object just like any other object. To retrieve an audiopath configuration from a segment, you use `IDirectMusicSegment8::GetAudioPathConfig()`.

Audiopath configurations do not have a unique interface or any methods, so after you have an audiopath object, you cannot alter the configuration in any way. All you can do is pass it to `IDirectMusicPerformance8::CreateAudioPath()`.

The Default Audiopath

The default audiopath is used when you play a segment with the `IDirectMusicPerformance8::PlaySegment()` or `IDirectMusicPerformance8::PlaySegmentEx()` functions. To create an audiopath and make it the default, you specify a standard type for the *dwDefaultType* parameter of the `IDirectMusicPerformance8::InitAudio()` function.

To set an existing audiopath to the default audiopath, you use the `IDirectMusicPerformance8::SetDefaultAudioPath()` function, which is defined as

```
HRESULT SetDefaultAudioPath(
    IDirectMusicAudioPath *pAudioPath        // interface of the default audiopath
);
```

To retrieve the default audiopath, you use the `IDirectMusicPerformance8::GetDefaultAudioPath()` function:

```
HRESULT GetDefaultAudioPath(
    IDirectMusicAudioPath **ppAudioPath      // receives the default audiopath
);
```

Standard Audiopaths

Unless you exclusively use audiopaths created from audiopath configuration objects, you need to create one or more standard audiopaths with the `IDirectMusicPerformance8::CreateStandardAudioPath()` function:

```
HRESULT CreateStandardAudioPath(
        DWORD dwType,                          // type of the path
        DWORD dwPChannelCount,                 // number of performance channels
        BOOL  fActive,                         // true activates the audiopath on creation
        IDirectMusicAudioPath **ppNewPath      // address of audiopath interface pointer
);
```

You can also create a standard audiopath through the *dwDefaultPathType* parameter of
IDirectMusicPerformance8::InitAudio().

The *dwType* parameter of the CreateStandardAudioPath() function identifies the type of audiopath
that you are creating. Table 17.1 lists the standard audiopaths and the standard buffers they contain. Shared buffers can be used by more than one audiopath.

The following code creates a 3D audiopath through the CreateStandardAudioPath() function:

```
IDirectMusicAudioPath8 *dmusic3DaudioPath = NULL;       // the audiopath interface

if (FAILED(dmusicPerformance->CreateStandardAudioPath(DMUS_APATH_DYNAMIC_3D, 128,
                                                TRUE, &dmusic3DAudiopath)))
{
        // audiopath not created
}
else
        // audiopath created
```

Table 17.1 Standard Audiopaths

Audiopath Type	Standard Buffers	Buffer Shared?
DMUS_APATH_DYNAMIC_3D	3D Dry	No
DMUS_APATH_DYNAMIC_MONO	Mono	No
DMUS_APATH_DYNAMIC_STEREO	Stereo	No
DMUS_APATH_SHARED_STEREOPLUSREVERB	Stereo; Reverb	Yes; Yes

Playing Sound on Audiopaths

You've already seen how to play a segment on the default audiopath by using the `IDirectMusicPerformance8::PlaySegmentEx()` function and passing `NULL` for the *pAudioPath* parameter. When you're playing a segment on another audiopath, you use the `PlaySegmentEx()` function again, but you can specify the audiopath in two ways:

- You can supply a pointer to an audiopath interface object in the *pAudioPath* parameter.
- You can include `DMUS_SEGF_USE_AUDIOPATH` in *dwFlags*. This flag causes the segment to create an audiopath from a configuration embedded in the segment object.

Table 17.2 lists all the possible values for the *dwFlags* parameter of the `PlaySegmentEx()` function.

Table 17.2 PlaySegmentEx() dwFlags Values

Value	Definition
DMUS_SEGF_REFTIME	Time parameter is in reference time.
DMUS_SEGF_SECONDARY	This is a secondary segment.
DMUS_SEGF_QUEUE	Put at end of primary segment queue (primary segments only).
DMUS_SEGF_CONTROL	Play as control segment (secondary segments only).
DMUS_SEGF_AFTERPREPARETIME	Play after the prepare time.
DMUS_SEGF_GRID	Play on a grid boundary.
DMUS_SEGF_BEAT	Play on a beat boundary.
DMUS_SEGF_MEASURE	Play on a measure boundary.
DMUS_SEGF_DEFAULT	Use the segment's default boundary.
DMUS_SEGF_NOINVALIDATE	Causes the new segment not to cause an invalidation.
DMUS_SEGF_ALIGN	The beginning of the segment can be aligned with a boundary that has already passed.

(continued)

Table 17.2 (continued)

Value	Definition
DMUS_SEGF_VALID_START_BEAT	Allow the start to occur on any beat.
DMUS_SEGF_VALID_START_GRID	Allow the start to occur on any grid.
DMUS_SEGF_VALID_START_TICK	Allow the start to occur at any time.
DMUS_SEGF_AUTOTRANSITION	Compose and play a transition segment, using the transition template.
DMUS_SEGF_AFTERQUEUETIME	Play after the queue time. This is default for primary segments.
DMUS_SEGF_AFTERLATENCYTIME	Play after the latency time. This is true for all segments (no effect at this time).
DMUS_SEGF_SEGMENTEND	Play at the end of the primary segment that is playing at the start time. Any segments already queued after the currently playing primary segment are flushed.
DMUS_SEGF_MARKER	Play at next marker in the primary segment.
DMUS_SEGF_TIMESIG_ALWAYS	Align start time with current time signature, even if there is no primary segment.
DMUS_SEGF_USE_AUDIOPATH	Use the audiopath embedded in the segment. Automatic downloading of bands must be enabled to ensure that the segment plays correctly.
DMUS_SEGF_VALID_START_MEASURE	Allow the start to occur at the beginning of a measure.

To play a segment with an audiopath and without any flags specified, you do the following

```
dmusicPerformance->PlaySegmentEx(dmusicSegment, NULL, NULL, 0, 0, NULL, NULL,
                                 dmusic3DaudioPath);
```

One thing we've failed to mention so far is how to play sound effect–type audio. Sound effects should be played through secondary segments by specifying the `DMUS_SEGF_SECONDARY` value for the `dwFlags` parameter in the `PlaySegmentEx()` function, as seen in this code:

```
dmusicPerformance->PlaySegmentEx(dmusicSegment, NULL, NULL,
                      DMUS_SEGF_DEFAULT | DMUS_SEGF_SECONDARY, 0, NULL,
                      dmusic3DaudioPath);
```

Granted, you don't need to specify an audiopath to use a secondary segment, so the last parameter of this function could also equal `NULL`.

You can also change the volume on the performance channels playing through an audiopath through the function `IDirectMusicAudioPath8::SetVolume()`:

```
HRESULT SetVolume(
    long lVolume,    // Specifies the attenuation, in hundredths of decibel.
                     // Ranges from -9600 to 0, with 0 being full volume.
    DWORD dwDuration  // Specifies the time, in milliseconds, over which volume
                      // change takes place. A value of 0 ensures maximum efficiency.
);
```

So to set the volume to full volume over a period of 500 milliseconds, you do the following:

```
dmusic3DaudioPath->SetVolume(0, 500);
```

Keep in mind that this volume is not the global volume, but rather the volume for the performance channels playing through an audiopath.

Retrieving Objects from Audiopaths

There are times you may need to retrieve an interface to an object within the audiopath. For instance, you may want to alter the 3D properties of sounds, set global 3D sound properties, or apply sound effects to sound.

To retrieve an object from an audiopath, you call `IDirectMusicAudioPath8::GetObjectInPath()` on the segment state that is playing on the audiopath, which is defined as the following:

```
HRESULT GetObjectInPath(
    DWORD dwPChannel,         // performance channel to search, with 0 being the first
                             // DMUS_PCHANNEL_ALL for all
    DWORD dwStage,           // stage in the path
    DWORD dwBuffer,          // index of the buffer, if dwStage is DMO or mixing buffer
    REFGUID guidObject,      // class identifier
    DWORD dwIndex,           // index of the object in list of matching; 0 for first
    REGUID iidInterface,     // identifier of the desired interface, such as
                             // IID_IDirectMusicGraph
    void **ppObject          // address of a variable that receives a pointer to the
                             // requested interface
);
```

The following code shows how you can retrieve a buffer from a standard audiopath:

```
IDirectMusicAudioPath *dmusicAudioPath;
IdirectSoundBuffer8    *dmusicSoundBuff;

// create a standard audiopath with a source and environment reverb buffer
// no activation
dmusicPerformance->CreateStandardAudioPath(DMUSIC_APATH_DYNAMIC_3D, 64, FALSE,
                                    &dmusicAudioPath);

// get the sound buffer from the audiopath
dmusicAudioPath->GetObjectInPath(DMUS_PCHANNEL_ALL, DMUS_PATH_BUFFER, 0, GUID_NULL,
                        0, IID_IdirectSoundBuffer8,
                        (void**)&dmusicSoundBuff);
```

3D SOUND

3D effects are easily applied to any sound by retrieving a DirectSound buffer from an audiopath and applying the 3D effect to the buffer. Adding 3D sound effects to your games can greatly increase the realism effect by immersing the player even more than beautiful graphics can.

3D Sound Coordinates

Before you start applying 3D effects, you need to understand how 3D sound coordinates work with DirectX Audio. As you should expect, the position, velocity, and orientation of sound sources and listeners are defined in Cartesian coordinates along the x, y, and z axes. The axes are relative to the viewpoint, or camera, and are the same as those used in OpenGL with one exception: The z axis is flipped. Instead of the negative z axis going *into* the screen, the negative z axis comes out of the screen. In DirectX Audio, the positive z axis goes into the screen.

Position is measured in meters by default, but this can be changed by setting a distance factor, which is a value representing meters per unit defined by the application. Velocity is measured in application units per second.

Orientation is measured in application units and is relative to the world orientation. For instance, if the world's orientation is pointing along the negative z axis (due south in DirectX Audio), and the orientation of the listener is (1, 0, 0), then the listener is facing due west.

Also, the 3D vectors that DirectX Audio uses are from the 3D graphics component of DirectX, Direct3D. This means that the 3D vector type is defined as

```
typedef struct {
    float x;
    float y;
    float z;
} D3DVECTOR;
```

Perception

One's perception of a sound's position in the world is influenced by several factors, including sight. Factors that come from the sounds themselves include

- **Overall loudness.** As a sound source moves away from a listener, the sound's perceived volume decreases at a fixed rate. This is known as *rolloff.*
- **Interaural intensity difference.** A sound that comes from a source to the right of the listener's sounds louder in the listener's right ear than in the listener's left ear.
- **Interaural time difference.** A sound emitted by a source to the right of the listener will arrive at the right ear slightly before it arrives at the left ear. The time difference is usually a millisecond.
- **Muffling.** The shape and orientation of the ears guarantee that sounds coming from behind the listener will be slightly muffled compared to sounds coming from the front. Also, a sound coming from the right of the listener will be muffled for the left ear because of the mass of the listener's head and orientation of the left ear.

These are not the only factors that help you determine the position of a sound, but they are the primary factors and the ones that have been implemented in DirectX Audio.

The DirectSound 3D Buffer

Every sound source you have in the world will be represented by an IDirectSound3DBuffer8 interface. The sound itself must be monaural, meaning the sound is created with a single channel (not stereo). You will receive an error if you attempt to use a 3D sound source with two channels.

To create a 3D sound, the first thing you need to do is create an IDirectSound3DBuffer8 interface. As you saw with audiopaths, you can extract one of these interfaces by using the IDirectMusicPerformance8::GetObjectInPath() function, like this:

```
IDirectMusicAudioPath8 *dmusic3DaudioPath;    // the audiopath
IDirectSound3DBuffer8  *dmusic3DSoundBuff;     // the 3D sound buffer

// create the audiopath (not necessary if we already have one)
if (FAILED(dmusicPerformance->CreateStandardAudioPath(DMUS_APATH_DYNAMIC_3D, 64, TRUE,
                                                &dmusic3DaudioPath)))

    return 0;

// retrieve the 3D sound buffer
if (FAILED(dmusic3DaudioPath->GetObjectInPath(DMUS_PCHANNEL_ALL, DMUS_PATH_BUFFER, 0,
                                       GUID_NULL, 0, IID_IDirectSound3DBuffer8,
                                       (void**)&dmusic3DsoundBuff)))

    return 0;
```

Setting 3D Parameters

There are two ways you can set the 3D parameters of a sound: individually or in batches. Setting individual values simply involves using the proper IDirectSound3DBuffer8 interface method, all of which are listed in Table 17.3.

All these methods are described in detail in the DirectX 8 documentation.

Usually, you'll need to retrieve or set these values all at once. You do this through IDirectSound3DBuffer8::GetAllParameters() and IDirectSound3DBuffer8::SetAllParameters(). SetAllParameters() is defined as

```
HRESULT SetAllParameters(
    LPCDS3DBUFFER pcDs3dBuffer, // DS3DBUFFER structure describes 3D characteristics
    DWORD dwApply               // specifies when setting should be applied
                                // typically DS3D_IMMEDIATE for immediate application

);
```

Table 17.3 IDirectSound3DBuffer8 Methods

Classification	Method
Distance	GetMaxDistance
	GetMinDistance
	SetMaxDistance
	GetMaxDistance
Operation mode	GetMode
	SetMode
Position	GetPosition
	SetPosition
Sound projection cones	GetConeAngles
	GetConeOrientation
	GetConeOutsideVolume
	SetConeAngles
	SetConeOrientation
	SetConeOutsideVolume
Velocity	GetVelocity
	SetVelocity

To use this function, all you need to do is specify values for a DS3DBUFFER structure:

```
typedef struct {
    DWORD     dwSize;              // size of the DS3DBUFFER structure
    D3DVECTOR vPosition;          // position of the sound
    D3DVECTOR vVelocity;          // velocity of the sound
    DWORD     dwInsideConeAngle;  // angle of inside sound-projection cone
    DWORD     dwOutsideConeAngle; // angle of outside sound-projection cone
    D3DVECTOR vConeOrientation;   // orientation of sound-projection cone
    LONG      lConeOutsideVolume; // cone outside volume
    D3DVALUE  flMinDistance;      // minimum distance
    D3DVALUE  flMaxDistance;      // maximum distance
    DWORD     dwMode;             // 3D sound-processing mode to be set
} DS3DBUFFER, *LPDS3DBUFFER;

typedef const DS3DBUFFER *LPCDS3DUFFER;
```

The dwMode field of the DS3DBUFFER structure can be set to one of the following:

- **DS3DMODE_DISABLE.** 3D sound processing is disabled. The sound will appear to originate from the center of the listener's head.
- **DS3DMODE_HEADRELATIVE.** Sound parameters are relative to the listener's parameters. In this mode, the absolute parameters of the sound are updated automatically as the listener's parameters change so that the relative parameters remain constant.
- **DS3DMODE_NORMAL.** Normal processing. This is the default.

Let's look at how the fields of the DS3DBUFFER structure can alter the way a sound is perceived.

The Minimum and Maximum Distances

The minimum distance can be defined as the distance from the listener at which the maximum volume of a sound is heard. For example, as you approach a sound source, the sound gets louder. When you reach the halfway point to the source, the volume doubles. After you reach the minimum distance, however, the volume stops increasing.

This is particularly useful when you need to compensate for the difference in absolute volume between two sounds. For instance, consider a jet engine and an air conditioner. Even though a jet engine is much louder than an air conditioner, you'd need to record these two sounds at similar absolute volume levels. To achieve realistic results with your application, however, you could use a minimum distance of 100 meters for the jet engine and 1 meter for the air conditioner. That way, when the listener is 200 meters away from the jet engine, the engine volume will be halved; when the listener is 2 meters away from the air conditioner, its volume will be halved. The default minimum distance value is DS3D_DEFAULTMINDISTANCE, or 1 unit (1 meter at the default distance factor). So unless you change the value of the minimum distance, your sounds will be at full volume when the sound is 1 meter away from the listener, half volume at 2 meters away, a quarter as loud at 4 meters, and so on.

The maximum distance, on the other hand, is the distance at which the sound does not get any quieter. The default maximum distance is DS3D_DEFAULTMAXDISTANCE, or 1 billion meters. This means that the sound attenuation will continue to be calculated for quite some time, even when the sound has moved out of normal hearing range.

The difference between the maximum and minimum distance can have an effect on the degree of attenuation as a sound source moves within the range. For instance, when the difference is very large, a sound source's volume will not change as much as when the difference is very small.

Processing Mode

You can specify three processing modes:

- **Normal.** Normal is the default mode, and specifies that the sound source is positioned and oriented absolutely in the world.
- **Head-relative.** Head-relative mode specifies that the buffer is automatically repositioned in world space as the listener moves and turns.
- **Disabled.** Disabled mode specifies that 3D sound process is disabled and the sound appears to originate from the center of the listener's head.

Position and Velocity

The position of a sound source is expressed as a vector that is relative to either the world or the listener, depending on the processing mode. Velocity is used to calculate the effects of Doppler shift and does not have to equal the actual velocity of the sound source.

Sound Cones

Sound cones define the loudness of an oriented sound, where the sound is loudest in its direction of orientation. A sound with no orientation has the same amplitude at a given distance in all directions. Sound cones consist of an inside cone and an outside cone, as shown in Figure 17.6.

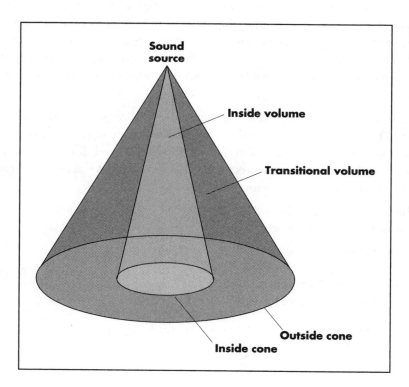

Figure 17.6

A sound cone.

Within the confines of the inner cone, the sound volume is the same as it would be if there was not a cone in the first place. Beyond the outer cone, the normal volume is attenuated by a factor that you define. The outside cone volume is a negative value expressed in hundredths of decibels, because it represents attenuation from the default volume of 0.

Between these two cones is a transitional zone, where the volume decreases as the cone angle increases.

One possible use of sound cones is to simulate a sound coming out of a room through a door. For instance, if you position a sound source in the room and set its orientation toward the open door with the inside cone equal to the approximate width of the door and the outer cone slightly bigger, then when the listener walks by the door, the sound will be heard. When the listener is walking along the outside of the room and not in front of the door, the sound volume will be faint until the listener gets close to the doorway.

The DirectSound 3D Listener

The 3D sound effects that you create are not only affected by the position, orientation, and velocity of sound sources, but also by the position, orientation, and velocity of the listener, or the point of sound reception. The listener by default is not moving at the origin of the world and points toward the positive z axis of the world. By changing the values of the listener's position, orientation, and velocity, you can effectively control the parameters of the acoustic environment, including the Doppler shift and rate of volume attenuation over distance. Also, there is only one listener object, which makes sense because you cannot hear in two different places of the world at once anyway.

The listener's orientation is defined by two vectors that start at the center of the listener's head: the *front* and *top* vectors. The front vector points forward from the listener's face and is at a right angle to the top vector, which points straight up through the top of the head. If you define a front vector that is not at a right angle to the top vector, then DirectX Audio will alter the front vector so that it is at a right angle to the top vector.

To obtain a listener object, you must use IDirectMusicAudioPath8::GetObjectInPath(), as you did before for the IDirectSound3DBuffer interface:

```
IDirectSound3DListener8 *dmusicListener;    // the listener object

// retrieve the listener object from the audiopath
if (FAILED(dmusic3DaudioPath->GetObjectInPath(DMUS_PCHANNEL_ALL,
                              DMUS_PATH_PRIMARY_BUFFER, 0, GUID_NULL,
                              0, IID_IDirectSound3DListener8,
                              (void**)&dmusicListener)))
    return 0;
```

Table 17.4 IDirectSound3DListener8 Methods

Classification	Method
Distance factor	GetDistanceFactor
	SetDistanceFactor
Doppler factor	GetDopplerFactor
	SetDopperFactor
Orientation	GetOrientation
	SetOrientation
Position	GetPosition
	SetPosition
Rolloff Factor	GetRolloffFactor
	SetRolloffFactor
Velocity	GetVelocity
	SetVelocity

Now you can use the listener object in much the same way as the IDirectSound3DBuffer object. For instance, you can use any of the methods listed in Table 17.4, or you can use IDirectSound3DListener8::SetAllParameters() and IDirectSound3DListener8::GetAllParameters() to define and retrieve the 3D parameters of the listener.

As you can see from the definition of SetAllParameters(), you need to set the values for your 3D listener in a DS3DLISTENER structure:

```
HRESULT SetAllParameters(
    LPCDS3DLISTENER pcListener,      // contains 3D listener information
    DWORD dwApply                    // when the setting should be applied
);
```

The DS3DLISTENER structure is defined as

```
typedef struct {
    DWORD dwSize;                    // size of the DS3DLISTENER structure in bytes
    D3DVECTOR vPosition;             // listener's position
```

```
       D3DVECTOR vVelocity;              // listener's velocity
       D3DVECTOR vOrientFront;           // listener's front orientation
       D3DVECTOR vOrientTop;             // listener's back orientation
       D3DVECTOR flDistanceFactor;       // current distance factor
       D3DVECTOR flRolloffFactor;        // rolloff factor
       D3DVECTOR flDopplerFactor;        // Doppler factor
} DS3DLISTENER, *LPDS3DLISTENER;

typedef const DS3DLISTENER *LPCDS3DLISTENER;
```

Now all you do is set the values in the DS3DLISTENER and pass them to the SetAllParams() function from the IDirectSound3DListener interface, and the listener object's 3D parameters will be set.

3D Clicking Text Example

The sample code that follows illustrates how you can use basic 3D sound effects with DirectX Audio. You use the same outline font rendering as before, except this time the text is moving away from and toward the camera and making a clicking sound as it moves. When you give the IDirectSound3DBuffer the same position as the text in the 3D world, the volume of the sound that you loaded decreases as the text moves further away, increases as the text gets closer, and becomes muffled when the text goes behind the camera. Speaking of the camera, you associate the IDirectSound3DListener interface as having the same position as the camera (0, 0, 0). Also, the text changes to let you know if it is moving toward the camera or away from the camera. Figure 17.7 shows a screenshot of the example.

Here's the entire listing of the program. Be sure to pay attention to the comments!

```
#define WIN32_LEAN_AND_MEAN        // trim the excess fat from Windows
#define INITGUID                   // we use GUID's with DMusic

////// Includes
#include <windows.h>               // standard Windows app include
#include <dmusicc.h>               // DirectMusic includes
#include <dmusici.h>
#include <d3d8types.h>             // for D3DVECTOR
#include <cguid.h>                 // for GUID_NULL
#include <stdio.h>
#include <stdlib.h>
#include <math.h>
#include <gl/gl.h>                 // standard OpenGL include
#include <gl/glu.h>                // OpenGL utilities
```

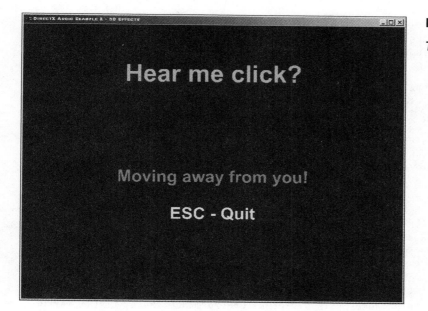

Figure 17.7

The 3D clicking text.

```
////// Global Variables
HDC g_HDC;                                  // global device context
bool fullScreen = false;                    // true = full screen; false = windowed
bool keyPressed[256];                       // holds true for keys that are pressed
unsigned int listBase;                      // display list base
GLYPHMETRICSFLOAT gmf[256];                 // holds orientation and placement
                                            // info for display lists


////// DirectMusic variables
IDirectMusicLoader8 *dmusicLoader = NULL;              // the loader
IDirectMusicPerformance8 *dmusicPerformance = NULL;    // the performance
IDirectMusicSegment8 *dmusicSegment = NULL;            // the segment
IDirectMusicAudioPath *dmusic3DAudioPath = NULL;       // the audiopath
IDirectSound3DBuffer *ds3DBuffer = NULL;               // 3d buffer
IDirectSound3DListener *ds3DListener = NULL;           // 3d listener

DS3DBUFFER dsBufferParams;                              // 3d buffer properties
DS3DLISTENER dsListenerParams;                         // 3d listener properties

/*******************************************************
*     DirectMusic Interfaces
*******************************************************/
```

```cpp
// InitDirectXAudio()
// desc: initializes the DirectX Audio component for playback
bool InitDirectXAudio(HWND hwnd)
{
    char pathStr[MAX_PATH];          // path for audio file
    WCHAR wcharStr[MAX_PATH];

    // create the loader object
    if (FAILED(CoCreateInstance(CLSID_DirectMusicLoader, NULL, CLSCTX_INPROC,
                                IID_IDirectMusicLoader8, (void**)&dmusicLoader)))
    {
        MessageBox(hwnd, "Unable to create the IDirectMusicLoader8 object!",
                    "ERROR!", MB_OK);
        return false;
    }

    // create the performance object
    if (FAILED(CoCreateInstance(CLSID_DirectMusicPerformance, NULL, CLSCTX_INPROC,
                                IID_IDirectMusicPerformance8,
                                (void**)&dmusicPerformance)))
    {
        MessageBox(hwnd, "Unable to create the IDirectMusicPerformance8
                        object!", "ERROR!", MB_OK);
        return false;
    }

    // initialize DirectMusic and DirectSound
    if (FAILED(dmusicPerformance->InitAudio(NULL, NULL, NULL,
                                            DMUS_APATH_DYNAMIC_STEREO, 64,
                                            DMUS_AUDIOF_ALL, NULL)))
    {
        MessageBox(hwnd, "Unable to initialize audio!", "ERROR!", MB_OK);
        return false;
    }

    // create a standard 3D audiopath
    if (FAILED(dmusicPerformance->CreateStandardAudioPath(DMUS_APATH_DYNAMIC_3D,
                                                        64, TRUE,
                                                        &dmusic3DAudioPath)))
```

```cpp
    {
        MessageBox(hwnd, "Unable to create standard 3D audiopath! Press OK to exit",
                   "ERROR!", MB_OK);
        return false;
    }


    // get the 3D buffer in the audiopath
    if (FAILED(dmusic3DAudioPath->GetObjectInPath(0, DMUS_PATH_BUFFER, 0, GUID_NULL,
                                                  0, IID_IDirectSound3DBuffer,
                                                  (void**)&ds3DBuffer)))
    {
        MessageBox(hwnd, "Unable to retrieve 3D buffer from audiopath!",
                   "ERROR!", MB_OK);
        return false;
    }


    // get the 3D buffer parameters
    dsBufferParams.dwSize = sizeof(DS3DBUFFER);
    ds3DBuffer->GetAllParameters(&dsBufferParams);


    // set the new 3D buffer parameters
    dsBufferParams.dwMode = DS3DMODE_HEADRELATIVE;    // relative to the listener
    ds3DBuffer->SetAllParameters(&dsBufferParams, DS3D_IMMEDIATE);


    // retrieve the listener from the audiopath
    if (FAILED(dmusic3DAudioPath->GetObjectInPath(0, DMUS_PATH_PRIMARY_BUFFER, 0,
                                                  GUID_NULL, 0,
                                                  IID_IDirectSound3DListener,
                                                  (void**)&ds3DListener)))
    {
        MessageBox(hwnd, "Unable to retrieve the listener! Press OK to exit",
                   "ERROR!", MB_OK);
        return false;
    }


    // get the listener parameters
    dsListenerParams.dwSize = sizeof(DS3DLISTENER);
    ds3DListener->GetAllParameters(&dsListenerParams);
```

```cpp
        // set position of listener
        dsListenerParams.vPosition.x = 0.0f;
        dsListenerParams.vPosition.y = 0.0f;
        dsListenerParams.vPosition.z = 0.0f;
        ds3DListener->SetAllParameters(&dsListenerParams, DS3D_IMMEDIATE);

        // retrieve the current directory
        GetCurrentDirectory(MAX_PATH, pathStr);

        // convert to unicode string
        MultiByteToWideChar(CP_ACP, 0, pathStr, -1, wcharStr, MAX_PATH);

        // set the search directory
        dmusicLoader->SetSearchDirectory(GUID_DirectMusicAllTypes, wcharStr, FALSE);

        return true;
}

// LoadSegment()
// desc: load a segment from a file
bool LoadSegment(HWND hwnd, char *filename)
{
        WCHAR wcharStr[MAX_PATH];

        // convert filename to unicode string
        MultiByteToWideChar(CP_ACP, 0, filename, -1, wcharStr, MAX_PATH);

        // load the segment from file
        if (FAILED(dmusicLoader->LoadObjectFromFile(CLSID_DirectMusicSegment,
                                                    IID_IDirectMusicSegment8,
                                                    wcharStr,
                                                    (void**)&dmusicSegment)))

        {
            MessageBox(hwnd, "Audio file not found! Press OK to exit",
                    "ERROR!", MB_OK);

            return false;
        }

        // set the number of repeats for the segment to infinite
        dmusicSegment->SetRepeats(DMUS_SEG_REPEAT_INFINITE);
```

```cpp
        // download the segment's instruments to the audiopath
        dmusicSegment->Download(dmusic3DAudioPath);

        return true;
}


// PlaySegment()
// desc: start playing a segment
void PlaySegment(IDirectMusicPerformance8* dmPerf, IDirectMusicSegment8* dmSeg)
{
        // play the segment on the next beat
        dmPerf->PlaySegmentEx(dmSeg, NULL, NULL, DMUS_SEGF_DEFAULT, 0,
                              NULL, NULL, dmusic3DAudioPath);
}


// StopSegment()
// desc: stop a segment from playing
void StopSegment(IDirectMusicPerformance8* dmPerf, IDirectMusicSegment8* dmSeg)
{
        // stop the dmSeg from playing
        dmPerf->StopEx(dmSeg, 0, 0);
}


// CloseDown()
// desc: shut down music performance
void CloseDown(IDirectMusicPerformance8* dmPerf)
{
        // stop the music
        dmPerf->Stop(NULL, NULL, 0, 0);

        // close down DirectMusic
        dmPerf->CloseDown();
}


// Set3DSoundParams()
// desc: sets the 3d buffer parameters
void Set3DSoundParams(float doppler, float rolloff, float minDist, float maxDist)
{
        // set doppler and rolloff parameters
        dsListenerParams.flDopplerFactor = doppler;
        dsListenerParams.flRolloffFactor = rolloff;
```

```
        if (ds3DListener)
            ds3DListener->SetAllParameters(&dsListenerParams, DS3D_IMMEDIATE);


        // set minimum and maximum distances
        dsBufferParams.flMinDistance = minDist;
        dsBufferParams.flMaxDistance = maxDist;


        if (ds3DBuffer)
            ds3DBuffer->SetAllParameters(&dsBufferParams, DS3D_IMMEDIATE);
}


// Set3DSoundPos()
// desc: updates position of sound source (accepts OpenGL coordinates)
void Set3DSoundPos(IDirectSound3DBuffer* dsBuff, float x, float y, float z)
{
        // we use -z because DirectX and OpenGL z-axes are flipped
        if (dsBuff != NULL)
        {
            dsBuff->SetPosition(x, y, -z, DS3D_IMMEDIATE);
        }
}


/*******************************************************
*     OpenGL Interfaces
*******************************************************/

// CreateOutlineFont()
// desc: creates the outline font using the CreateFont() function
unsigned int CreateOutlineFont(char *fontName, int fontSize, float depth)
{
        HFONT hFont;             // windows font
        unsigned int base;

        base = glGenLists(256);          // create storage for 96 characters

        if (stricmp(fontName, "symbol") == 0)
        {
            hFont = CreateFont(fontSize, 0, 0, 0, FW_BOLD, FALSE, FALSE, FALSE,
                               SYMBOL_CHARSET, OUT_TT_PRECIS, CLIP_DEFAULT_PRECIS,
                               ANTIALIASED_QUALITY, FF_DONTCARE | DEFAULT_PITCH,
                               fontName);
```

```
        }
        else
        {
            hFont = CreateFont(fontSize, 0, 0, 0, FW_BOLD, FALSE, FALSE, FALSE,
                               ANSI_CHARSET, OUT_TT_PRECIS, CLIP_DEFAULT_PRECIS,
                               ANTIALIASED_QUALITY, FF_DONTCARE | DEFAULT_PITCH,
                               fontName);
        }

        if (!hFont)
            return 0;

        SelectObject(g_HDC, hFont);
        wglUseFontOutlines(g_HDC, 0, 255, base, 0.0f, depth, WGL_FONT_POLYGONS, gmf);

        return base;
}


// ClearFont()
// desc: deletes the display list for the font
void ClearFont(unsigned int base)
{
        glDeleteLists(base, 256);
}


// PrintString()
// desc: displays the text in str from the font indicated by base
void PrintString(unsigned int base, char *str)
{
        float length = 0;

        if ((str == NULL))
            return;

        // center the text
        for (unsigned int loop=0;loop<(strlen(str));loop++)     // find length of text
        {
            length+=gmf[str[loop]].gmfCellIncX;  // increase length by character's width
        }
        glTranslatef(-length/2,0.0f,0.0f);              // translate to center text
```

```
        // draw the text
        glPushAttrib(GL_LIST_BIT);
            glListBase(base);
            glCallLists(strlen(str), GL_UNSIGNED_BYTE, str);
        glPopAttrib();
}


// CleanUp()
// desc: application cleanup
void CleanUp()
{
        ClearFont(listBase);

        dmusic3DAudioPath->Release();        // release DirectX Audio objects
        dmusicLoader->Release();
        dmusicPerformance->Release();
        dmusicSegment->Release();
}


// Initialize
// desc: initializes OpenGL
void Initialize()
{
        glClearColor(0.0f, 0.0f, 0.0f, 0.0f);         // clear to black

        glShadeModel(GL_SMOOTH);                      // use smooth shading
        glEnable(GL_DEPTH_TEST);                      // hidden surface removal
        glEnable(GL_LIGHT0);                          // enable light0
        glEnable(GL_LIGHTING);                        // enable lighting
        glEnable(GL_COLOR_MATERIAL);                  // enable color for material

        listBase = CreateOutlineFont("Arial", 10, 0.25f);  // load 10pt Arial font
}


// Render
// desc: handles drawing of scene
void Render()
{
        static float zpos = 0.0f;       // the position along the z axis
        static bool zDir = false;       // false = negative, true = positive
```

```cpp
// move text forward and backward
if (zDir)
    zpos += 0.08f;
else
    zpos -= 0.08f;

if (zpos > 30.0f)
    zDir = false;
if (zpos < -30.0f)
    zDir = true;

// clear screen and depth buffer
glClear(GL_COLOR_BUFFER_BIT | GL_DEPTH_BUFFER_BIT);
glLoadIdentity();

glPushMatrix();
    glColor3f(0.5f, 0.5f, 0.5f);
    glTranslatef(0.0f, 3.0f, -10.0f);
    PrintString(listBase, "Hear me click?");
glPopMatrix();

// move the text along the z axis
glTranslatef(0.0f, 0.0f, zpos);

// update sound source position to reflect text
Set3DSoundPos(ds3DBuffer, 0.0, 0.0, zpos);

// set color to blueish color
glColor3f(0.3f, 0.4f, 0.8f);

// display the text
glPushMatrix();
    glTranslatef(0.0f, -1.0f, 0.0f);
    if (zDir)
        PrintString(listBase, "Coming at you!");
    else
        PrintString(listBase, "Moving away from you!");
glPopMatrix();

// yellow-green color
glColor3f(0.6f, 0.8f, 0.5f);
```

```
          // display text
          glPushMatrix();
               glTranslatef(0.0f, -3.0f, 0.0f);
               PrintString(listBase, "ESC - Quit");
          glPopMatrix();

          SwapBuffers(g_HDC);                  // bring back buffer to foreground
     }

     // function to set the pixel format for the device context
     void SetupPixelFormat(HDC hDC)
     {
          int nPixelFormat;                    // our pixel format index

          static PIXELFORMATDESCRIPTOR pfd = {
               sizeof(PIXELFORMATDESCRIPTOR),    // size of structure
               1,                                // default version
               PFD_DRAW_TO_WINDOW |              // window-drawing support
               PFD_SUPPORT_OPENGL |              // OpenGL support
               PFD_DOUBLEBUFFER,                 // double-buffering support
               PFD_TYPE_RGBA,                    // RGBA color mode
               32,                               // 32-bit color mode
               0, 0, 0, 0, 0, 0,                 // ignore color bits, non-palletized mode
               0,                                // no alpha buffer
               0,                                // ignore shift bit
               0,                                // no accumulation buffer
               0, 0, 0, 0,                       // ignore accumulation bits
               16,                               // 16-bit z-buffer size
               0,                                // no stencil buffer
               0,                                // no auxiliary buffer
               PFD_MAIN_PLANE,                   // main drawing plane
               0,                                // reserved
               0, 0, 0 };                        // layer masks ignored

          // choose best matching pixel format
          nPixelFormat = ChoosePixelFormat(hDC, &pfd);

          // set pixel format to device context
          SetPixelFormat(hDC, nPixelFormat, &pfd);
     }
```

```c
// the Windows Procedure event handler
LRESULT CALLBACK WndProc(HWND hwnd, UINT message, WPARAM wParam, LPARAM lParam)
{
    static HGLRC hRC;                       // rendering context
    static HDC hDC;                         // device context
    int width, height;                      // window width and height

    switch(message)
    {
        case WM_CREATE:                     // window is being created

            hDC = GetDC(hwnd);              // get current window's device context
            g_HDC = hDC;
            SetupPixelFormat(hDC);          // call our pixel-format setup function

            // create rendering context and make it current
            hRC = wglCreateContext(hDC);
            wglMakeCurrent(hDC, hRC);

            return 0;
            break;

        case WM_CLOSE:                      // Windows is closing

            // deselect rendering context and delete it
            wglMakeCurrent(hDC, NULL);
            wglDeleteContext(hRC);

            // send WM_QUIT to message queue
            PostQuitMessage(0);

            return 0;
            break;

        case WM_SIZE:
            height = HIWORD(lParam);        // retrieve width and height
            width = LOWORD(lParam);

            if (height==0)                  // don't want a divide by zero
            {
```

```
                    height=1;
             }

             glViewport(0, 0, width, height);      // reset the viewport
             glMatrixMode(GL_PROJECTION);
             glLoadIdentity();                     // reset projection matrix

             // calculate aspect ratio of window
             gluPerspective(54.0f,(GLfloat)width/(GLfloat)height,1.0f,1000.0f);

             glMatrixMode(GL_MODELVIEW);           // set modelview matrix
             glLoadIdentity();                     // reset modelview matrix

             return 0;
             break;

      case WM_KEYDOWN:                             // is a key pressed?
             keyPressed[wParam] = true;
             return 0;
             break;

      case WM_KEYUP:
             keyPressed[wParam] = false;
             return 0;
             break;

      default:
             break;
      }

   return (DefWindowProc(hwnd, message, wParam, lParam));
}

// the main Windows entry point
int WINAPI WinMain(HINSTANCE hInstance, HINSTANCE hPrevInstance, LPSTR lpCmdLine,
                   int nShowCmd)
{
      WNDCLASSEX windowClass;   // window class
      HWND    hwnd;             // window handle
      MSG     msg;              // message
      bool    done;             // flag saying when our app is complete
```

```
    DWORD    dwExStyle;            // window extended style
    DWORD    dwStyle;             // window style
    RECT     windowRect;

    // screen resolution
    int width = 800;
    int height = 600;
    int bits = 16;

    windowRect.left=(long)0;                    // set left value to 0
    windowRect.right=(long)width;               // set right value to requested width
    windowRect.top=(long)0;                     // set top value to 0
    windowRect.bottom=(long)height;             // set bottom value to requested height

    // fill out the window class structure
    windowClass.cbSize              = sizeof(WNDCLASSEX);
    windowClass.style               = CS_HREDRAW | CS_VREDRAW;
    windowClass.lpfnWndProc         = WndProc;
    windowClass.cbClsExtra          = 0;
    windowClass.cbWndExtra          = 0;
    windowClass.hInstance           = hInstance;
    windowClass.hIcon               = LoadIcon(NULL, IDI_APPLICATION); // default icon
    windowClass.hCursor             = LoadCursor(NULL, IDC_ARROW);     // default arrow
    windowClass.hbrBackground       = NULL;
    windowClass.lpszMenuName        = NULL;                            // no menu
    windowClass.lpszClassName       = "MyClass";
    windowClass.hIconSm             = LoadIcon(NULL, IDI_WINLOGO);

    // register the windows class
    if (!RegisterClassEx(&windowClass))
        return 0;

    if (fullScreen)                                 // full screen?
    {
        DEVMODE dmScreenSettings;                   // device mode
        memset(&dmScreenSettings,0,sizeof(dmScreenSettings));
        dmScreenSettings.dmSize = sizeof(dmScreenSettings);
        dmScreenSettings.dmPelsWidth = width;       // screen width
        dmScreenSettings.dmPelsHeight = height;     // screen height
        dmScreenSettings.dmBitsPerPel = bits;       // bits per pixel
        dmScreenSettings.dmFields=DM_BITSPERPEL|DM_PELSWIDTH|DM_PELSHEIGHT;
```

```cpp
        //
        if (ChangeDisplaySettings(&dmScreenSettings, CDS_FULLSCREEN) !=
                            DISP_CHANGE_SUCCESSFUL)
        {
            // setting display mode failed, switch to windowed
            MessageBox(NULL, "Display mode failed", NULL, MB_OK);
            fullScreen=FALSE;
        }
    }

    if (fullScreen)                             // are we still in full-screen mode?
    {
        dwExStyle=WS_EX_APPWINDOW;              // window extended style
        dwStyle=WS_POPUP;                       // Windows style
        ShowCursor(FALSE);                      // hide mouse pointer
    }
    else
    {
        dwExStyle=WS_EX_APPWINDOW | WS_EX_WINDOWEDGE;    // window extended style
        dwStyle=WS_OVERLAPPEDWINDOW;                     // Windows style
    }

    AdjustWindowRectEx(&windowRect, dwStyle, FALSE, dwExStyle);

    // class registered, so now create our window
    hwnd = CreateWindowEx(NULL,                          // extended style
                    "MyClass",                  // class name
                    "DirectX Audio Example 1 - Playing Audio",// app name
                    dwStyle | WS_CLIPCHILDREN |
                    WS_CLIPSIBLINGS,
                    0, 0,                               // x,y coordinate
                    windowRect.right - windowRect.left,
                    windowRect.bottom - windowRect.top,  // width, height
                    NULL,                               // handle to parent
                    NULL,                               // handle to menu
                    hInstance,                          // application instance
                    NULL);                              // no extra params

    // check if window creation failed (hwnd would equal NULL)
    if (!hwnd)
        return 0;
```

```
// initialize COM
if (FAILED(CoInitialize(NULL)))
    return 0;                          // if unable to initialize COM, exit

// initialize DirectX Audio
if (!InitDirectXAudio(hwnd))
    return 0;

// load the segment
if (!LoadSegment(hwnd, "start.wav"))
    return 0;

// set the 3D sound parameters
Set3DSoundParams(0.0, 0.1f, 1.0f, 100.0f);

// start the segment (infinitely loops)
PlaySegment(dmusicPerformance, dmusicSegment);

ShowWindow(hwnd, SW_SHOW);             // display the window
UpdateWindow(hwnd);                    // update the window

done = false;                          // initialize the loop condition variable
Initialize();                          // initialize OpenGL

// main message loop
while (!done)
{
    PeekMessage(&msg, hwnd, NULL, NULL, PM_REMOVE);

    if (msg.message == WM_QUIT)        // do we receive a WM_QUIT message?
    {
        done = true;                   // if so, time to quit the application
    }
    else
    {
        // exit the app
        if (keyPressed[VK_ESCAPE])
            done = true;
        else
        {
            Render();                  // render a frame
```

```
                    TranslateMessage(&msg);    // translate and dispatch to event queue
                    DispatchMessage(&msg);
            }
        }
}

    // close down the performance
    CloseDown(dmusicPerformance);

    // clean up application
    CleanUp();

    // close down COM
    CoUninitialize();

    if (fullScreen)
    {
        ChangeDisplaySettings(NULL,0);        // if so switch back to the desktop
        ShowCursor(TRUE);                     // show mouse pointer
    }

    return msg.wParam;
}
```

SUMMARY

That's all for the basics of DirectX Audio! Some of the topics we did not discuss include how to add sound effects like reverb, echo, chorus, and distortion to the sounds, and how to dynamically compose music using DirectMusic. Also, if you're interested in learning how to load and play the MP3 file format, then browse through the DirectShow documentation. It includes an entire MP3 player example.

Computers can make and store both digitized and synthesized sounds. You are creating a digitized sound when you record sounds with a microphone on the computer. Typically, digital sounds are used for sound effects in games (for example, explosions, movement, and speech). On the other hand, synthesized sounds are algorithmic reproductions of sounds and are typically used for music.

The DirectX Audio component of DirectX provides for the ability to create and implement a fully dynamic soundtrack with hardware acceleration, including the ability for 3D sound positioning.

To load and play audio with DirectMusic, you initialize COM, create and initialize the performance, create the loader, load a segment, download the band, and play the segment.

Audiopaths manage the flow of sound data through various objects from the audio file itself to the output lines for the speakers. An audiopath can include the performance to which it belongs, a segment, toolgraphs, the synthesizer, and DirectSound buffers.

You can easily apply 3D effects to any sound by retrieving a DirectSound buffer from an audiopath and applying the 3D effect to the buffer. Adding 3D sound to your games can greatly increase their realism by immersing the player even more than beautiful graphics can.

CHAPTER 18

WORKING WITH 3D MODELS

early every game nowadays stores its characters and objects in some sort of 3D model file format. In fact, most of today's hit games enable players to edit and add new 3D models for expansions and more customizability. In this chapter, you'll look at one of the more popular 3D model file formats, the *Quake 2* MD2 format, and we'll discuss how you can load, display, and animate this format for use in your games.

In this chapter, you'll learn about the following:

- 3D file formats
- The MD2 model format
- PCX texture loading

3D MODEL FILE FORMATS

Putting object information in the source code of your programs can be tedious to type and limits you to using only the objects you put in the program. This means you can't change how an object looks or even add a new object without typing all the object information in the source code. To combat this problem, you can create your objects with some sort of modeling tool (or sometimes just type the information in a text file) that will then export the object model into a file format of your choice to be loaded by your game.

Most games today use some sort of file format for their object models, with the majority of games using their own customized format. Figure 18.1 illustrates this notion. For example, many game-development studios have a 3D modeler whose job is basically to create 3D models for their current game project using such tools as Discreet's 3D Studio MAX, NewTek's Lightwave, Caligari's trueSpace, and Alias|Wavefront's Maya. After they are created, these models are saved in the game's own internal format. As a result, the game can load the models, display them, and animate them in the game world.

We're not concerned with how to make the models. Instead, we're interested in how to display a model from a file on the screen, or even animate those models that have animations. Model formats can range anywhere from plain-text files that specify the vertices of an object to a complex binary that holds vertex, texture-coordinate, and skeletal animation information. One great file format that we're going to look at is called *MD2*. This format is what *Quake 2*, the first-person shooter by id Software, used for its character models. It combines a great feature set with an easy-to-use format and is a great starting point for anybody interested in creating a good model file format.

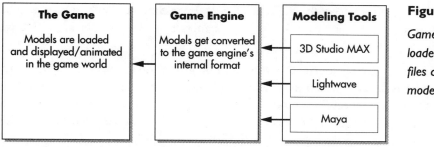

THE MD2 FILE FORMAT

At its highest level, the MD2 format is broken into two parts: the header and the data. The header itself holds the model's basic dimensional information, such as the number of vertices and triangles, but it also holds the location in the file of each type of model data. Here is the structure of the header:

```
typedef struct
{
    int ident;          // identifies as MD2 file "IDP2"
    int version;        // should be equal to 8
    int skinwidth;      // width of texture
    int skinheight;     // height of texture
    int framesize;      // number of bytes per frame
    int numSkins;       // number of textures
    int numXYZ;         // number of points
    int numST;          // number of texture coordinates
    int numTris;        // number of triangles
    int numGLcmds;      // number of OpenGL command types
    int numFrames;      // total number of frames
    int offsetSkins;    // offset to skin names (64 bytes each)
    int offsetST;       // offset of texture s-t values
    int offsetTris;     // offset of triangle mesh
    int offsetFrames;   // offset of frame data (points)
    int offsetGLcmds;   // type of OpenGL commands to use
    int offsetEnd;      // end of file
} modelHeader_t;
```

Let's tear this structure apart. First you have *ident*, which identifies the model you're loading as an MD2 file. When you're loading the model and you want to check that the file you're loading is in fact an MD2 model, you check *ident* for the value "IDP2". If you have a match, then you can continue loading; otherwise, you need to spit out an error message to let the user know that you cannot load the file.

The *skinwidth* and *skinheight* fields specify the width and height of the textures you'll be using to skin the model. *Skinning* is the term often used when applying or building a texture map for an object. When you say you have a skin for a model, you're saying you have a texture that is for that model. The *skinwidth* and *skinheight* fields specify the size for all the textures used by the model.

The *framesize* field tells you the size of each frame in bytes. A *frame* is like a picture, or a snapshot, of any given moment, much like a frame in a movie film or a cell in a cartoon. The MD2 format holds the frames that you will use to create a smooth animation. Each frame holds a snapshot of the model in a particular position. We'll discuss animation shortly, but for now remember that you can use the *framesize* field to calculate how much memory you need to allocate for all the frame data.

Next is the *numSkins* field, which tells you how many skins are available for the model. When most models are packaged together for use in *Quake 2*, they include several different types of textures that the player can choose among for the model. This field tells you how many of these textures will be listed in the file at the location specified by *offsetSkins*. Although this is a great idea for use in your own model formats, you won't be loading this parameter from the file because the skin names listed at the location pointed to by *offsetSkins* typically includes file paths that are specific to *Quake 2*.

The *numXYZ* field specifies the total number of vertices of the model, which is the sum of the number of vertices in each frame. For example, suppose you have a model with 100 frames, and each frame has 100 vertices for the model. Well, if you multiply these amounts, you find that there are 10,000 total possible vertices in all the frames of the model. That's quite a bit!

Next you have *numST*, which stores the number of texture coordinates. You use this field to calculate the amount of memory you need to allocate to store the texture coordinates of the model.

The *numTris* field tells you how many faces, or triangles, are in the model. In modeling terms, this value is referred to as the *polygon count*. A higher polygon count generally results in a more-detailed model, while a lower polygon count generally results in a less-detailed model. Although you want smooth detail in your games, the problem is that higher polygon counts risk higher system specs because you're increasing the number of polygons on the screen at any one time. Game developers must find a reasonable polygon count while not sacrificing too much detail for their game models.

The *numGLcmds* field specifies the number of OpenGL commands that are stored at the location *offsetGLcmds* in the data section of the MD2 file. What do we mean by storing OpenGL commands? Well, stored in *offsetGLcmds* is an array of integers that can be used to help determine how you should draw the model. For instance, you might draw the first nine vertices of a model using GL_TRIANGLE_STRIP, and then check the next integer in the offsetGLcmds buffer and determine that you need to use GL_TRIANGLE_FAN for the next 20 vertices. Drawing the models this way is not absolutely necessary, but it can be a useful feature for some.

The last dimensional field you have in the header is numFrames. This specifies the number of frames of animation that the model has available. Each of these frames is what modelers refer to as *keyframes*, which are frames of animation taken from discrete time intervals. Each keyframe is like a snapshot of the model at specific points in time. Figure 18.2 illustrates how keyframes can create an animation of a stick figure walking.

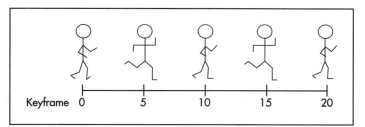

Figure 18.2

Keyframes are frames located at discrete time intervals in an animation.

Keyframes are useful for keeping storage space at a minimum, because you don't need to store every frame of animation in the MD2 file. In order to get smooth animation, however, you will need to calculate the position of the model for the frames in between each keyframe. We'll discuss how to do this soon.

Finally, you get to the final block of data in the header file: the offset values for the model's data. The first offset, offsetSkins, points to the location in the file where the skin texture names are stored. Each skin name takes up 64 bytes of data, so if you have five skins, then this offset will point to a data block that is 64 bytes * 5 bytes, or 320 bytes long.

Next you have the data offset value, offsetST, which points to the location in the file that stores the texture coordinates of the model. When you load the model, you use the numST field to calculate the number of texture coordinates you need to read in at this offset.

The offsetTris field points to the location of the triangle mesh that tells you the orientation of the triangles in the model. Similarly, the offsetFrames field points to the location of the vertices for the model. The vertices here are for every frame.

The last two fields, offsetGLcmds and offsetEnd, tell the locations of the OpenGL commands and the end of the file, respectively.

Our MD2 Implementation

Now that you know what the MD2 header looks like and the data inside the model file, it's time to tie everything together to see how it works. The first action you need to take is to create a representation of the most basic entity in the world: the vector. In reality, if you're developing a game, then you really *should* have a representation of this entity already, but you're just developing an example here. The following code defines a vector_t type and several operations you'll need to use between two vectors:

```
// a single vector
typedef struct
{
    float point[3];
} vector_t;

// vector subtraction
vector_t operator-(vector_t a, vector_t b)
{
    vector_t c;

    c.point[0] = a.point[0] - b.point[0];
    c.point[1] = a.point[1] - b.point[1];
    c.point[2] = a.point[2] - b.point[2];

    return c;
}

// Vector multiplication
vector_t operator*(float f, vector_t b)
{
    vector_t c;

    c.point[0] = f * b.point[0];
    c.point[1] = f * b.point[1];
    c.point[2] = f * b.point[2];

    return c;
}

// vector division
vector_t operator/(vector_t a, vector_t b)
```

```
{
    vector_t c;

    c.point[0] = a.point[0] / b.point[0];
    c.point[1] = a.point[1] / b.point[1];
    c.point[2] = a.point[2] / b.point[2];

    return c;
}

// Vector addition
vector_t operator+(vector_t a, vector_t b)
{
    vector_t c;

    c.point[0] = a.point[0] + b.point[0];
    c.point[1] = a.point[1] + b.point[1];
    c.point[2] = a.point[2] + b.point[2];

    return c;
}
```

Next you define a structure to hold a single texture coordinate and a structure that holds the index value for a texture coordinate in the texture-coordinate array:

```
// texture coordinate
typedef struct
{
    float s;        // s coordinate
    float t;        // t coordinate
} texCoord_t;

// texture coordinate index
typedef struct
{
    short s;
    short t;
} stIndex_t;
```

You also need to define a structure to hold the information for a single frame point. This structure includes an index value to a light normal array, but you will not be using this in your implementation. You just need to include it so your model loads correctly.

```
// info for a single frame point
typedef struct
{
    unsigned char v[3];              // the point info
    unsigned char normalIndex;       // not used
} framePoint_t;
```

You use framePoint_t in the following structure, which holds the information for a single frame:

```
// information for a single frame
typedef struct
{
    float scale[3];          // scaling for frame vertices
    float translate[3];      // translation for frame vertices
    char name[16];           // name of model
    framePoint_t fp[1];      // beginning of frame vertex list
} frame_t;
```

When you load the MD2 model, you'll need to calculate the position of each frame's vertices by using the scale and translate fields of the frame_t structure. The fp field defines the starting point in memory for the frame's vertices.

Because the MD2 model mesh is composed entirely of triangles, it seems logical that you should store the list of triangles in the model. If you're storing the model as a list of triangles, you can determine the structure of the model through a list of triangle indices. The following structure holds both the indices for the triangle's three vertices (meshIndex) and the indices for the three texture coordinates needed to texture the triangle (stIndex):

```
// data for a single triangle
typedef struct
{
    unsigned short meshIndex[3];     // vertex indices
    unsigned short stIndex[3];       // texture-coordinate indices
} mesh_t;
```

You define this structure as the generic mesh_t for two reasons. The first is for extensibility later on in case you decide to extend the basic polygon of the model from triangles to, say, quadrilaterals. The second reason is because a single triangle can be one part of a mesh.

And finally, you bring all these structures together to form a single structure that defines a model:

```
// the model data for a single model
typedef struct
{
    int numFrames;            // number of frames
    int numPoints;            // number of vertices
    int numTriangles;         // number of triangles
    int numST;                // number of texture coordinates
    int frameSize;            // size of each frame in bytes
    int texWidth, texHeight;  // texture width, height
    int currentFrame;         // current frame # in animation
    int nextFrame;            // next frame # in animation
    float interpol;           // percent through current frame
    mesh_t *triIndex;         // triangle list
    texCoord_t *st;           // texture coordinate list
    vector_t *pointList;      // vertex list
    texture_t *modelTex;      // texture data
} modelData_t;
```

Inside this structure you have several of the fields from the true MD2 header, such as the number of frames, vertices, texture coordinates, and triangles, and the size of each frame in bytes. You also store some of the values you'll be using for animation, such as the current keyframe, the next keyframe, and the interpolation to use between the two keyframes. Finally, the modelData_t structure stores the list of triangles for the model, the texture coordinates, and the vertex list. To finish off the modelData_t, you use the texture_t structure, which stores the model's current texture, or skin. For reference, the texture_t structure is defined as

```
// types of texture files we support
enum texTypes_t
{
    PCX, BMP, TGA
};

// a texture
typedef struct
{
    texTypes_t textureType;   // the type of image file this texture is

    int width;                // width of texture
    int height;               // height of texture
```

```
        long int scaledWidth;        // scaled width and height for PCX images
        long int scaledHeight;
        unsigned int texID;          // the texture object id of this texture
        unsigned char *data;         // the texture data
        unsigned char *palette;      // palette for texture (if it exists)
} texture_t;
```

You'll be using all these structures. Because looking at all these structures together can become rather confusing, Figure 18.3 shows the overall architecture of your MD2 model representation.

Now you might be wondering how all these structures actually interact with each other. Well, given the modelData_t structure, Figure 18.4 illustrates how you branch through the model data to get to the vertex coordinates and texture coordinates of the model.

Starting with the modelData_t structure, you have the following:

■ A list of triangles defined by triIndex
■ A list of vertex coordinates defined by pointList
■ A list of texture coordinates defined by st

You iterate through the list of triangle meshes, where each triangle holds indices to three vertices and three texture coordinates. You use these indices to look up the vertices of the current triangle in the pointList and the texture coordinates of the current triangle in the st texture coordinate list. Now you can both draw and texture the current triangle, and because you're iterating through the entire list of triangles, you eventually realize the full model.

So now that you know how the MD2 is structured and works, let's look at how you're going to implement some functions on the model format.

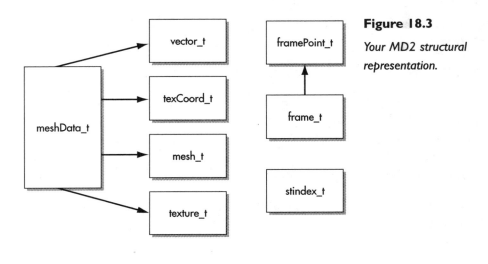

Figure 18.3

Your MD2 structural representation.

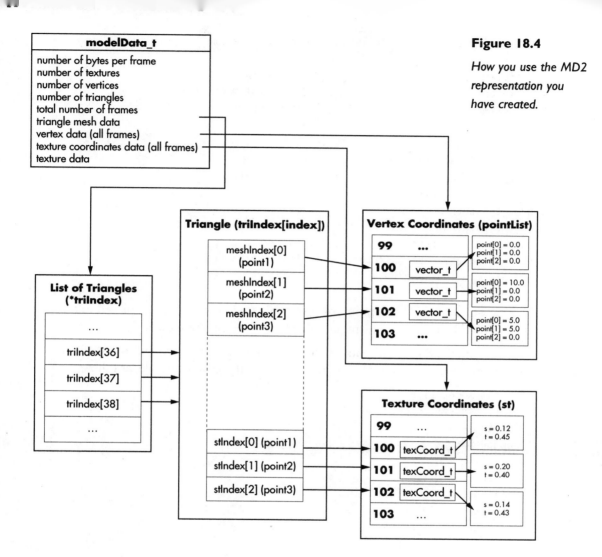

Figure 18.4

How you use the MD2 representation you have created.

Loading the MD2

Obviously the first thing you need to do is load the model into memory. Here you have a function, LoadMD2Model(), that will load and return a model structure given the model filename and the model's skin or texture filename:

```c
modelData_t *LoadMD2Model(char *filename, char *textureName)
{
    FILE *filePtr;                      // file pointer
    int fileLen;                        // length of model file
    char *buffer;                       // file buffer

    modelData_t *model;                 // the model
    modelHeader_t *modelHeader;         // model header
    texture_t *md2Texture;              // model texture

    stIndex_t *stPtr;                   // texture indices
    frame_t *frame;                     // frame data
    vector_t *pointListPtr;             // index variable
    mesh_t *triIndex, *bufIndexPtr;     // index variables
    int i, j;                           // index variables
```

Most of these variables are used to temporarily store data until it is ready to be placed in the model variable, which the function returns after you finish loading the model.

Next you open the model file and find its length. Because you know the length of the file, you can allocate enough memory to load the entire model into the buffer variable, as follows:

```c
    // open the model file
    filePtr = fopen(filename, "rb");
    if (filePtr == NULL)
        return NULL;

    // find length of file
    fseek(filePtr, 0, SEEK_END);
    fileLen = ftell(filePtr);
    fseek(filePtr, 0, SEEK_SET);

    // read entire file into buffer
    buffer = (char*)malloc(fileLen + 1);
    fread(buffer, sizeof(char), fileLen, filePtr);
```

Next you extract the model header from the buffer so you can determine the model's attributes. You then allocate memory for the model data as you prepare to store the model into memory.

```c
    // extract model file header from buffer
    modelHeader = (modelHeader_t*)buffer;
```

```
// allocate memory for model data
model = (modelData_t*)malloc(sizeof(modelData_t));
if (model == NULL)
    return NULL;
```

Using the model header you just extracted from the buffer, you calculate and allocate the amount of memory you need to store all the vertices used in the model. This calculation involves multiplying the number of vertices in the model times the total number of frames that the model uses. The pointList field of the model points to this newly allocated memory, because this field is used to store every vertex from every frame of the model.

After allocating the memory for the vertex list, you store the number of vertices, the number of frames, and the size of each frame in the model variable.

```
// allocate memory for all vertices used in model, including animations
model->pointList = (vector_t*)malloc(sizeof(vector_t)*modelHeader->numXYZ *
                   modelHeader->numFrames);

// store vital model data
model->numPoints = modelHeader->numXYZ;      // number of vertices
model->numFrames = modelHeader->numFrames;   // number of frames
model->frameSize = modelHeader->framesize;   // size of each frame
```

Next you load the model vertices into memory by looping through each frame of the model, calculating the offset to the frame's vertex data, and then calculating the position of each vertex in the frame through the translation and scaling factors of the frame:

```
// loop number of frames in model file
for(j = 0; j < modelHeader->numFrames; j++)
{
    // offset to the points in this frame
    frame = (frame_t*)&buffer[modelHeader->offsetFrames +
            modelHeader->framesize * j];

    // calculate the point positions based on frame details
    pointListPtr = (vector_t*)&model->pointList[modelHeader->numXYZ * j];
    for(i = 0; i < modelHeader->numXYZ; i++)
    {
        pointListPtr[i].point[0] = frame->scale[0] * frame->fp[i].v[0] +
                                   frame->translate[0];
        pointListPtr[i].point[1] = frame->scale[1] * frame->fp[i].v[1] +
                                   frame->translate[1];
```

```
                    pointListPtr[i].point[2] = frame->scale[2] * frame->fp[i].v[2] +
                                              frame->translate[2];
            }
    }
```

With all the model's frames and their vertex coordinates loaded, you can now load the model's texture into the md2Texture variable. After you verify that the texture is found and properly loaded into memory, you set the model's texture field, modelTex, to point to the memory location of md2Texture.

```
    // load the model texture
    md2Texture = LoadTexture(textureName);
    if (md2Texture != NULL)
    {
        // set up texture for OpenGL and store it in model data structure
        SetupMd2Texture(md2Texture);
        model->modelTex = md2Texture;
    }
    else
        return NULL;
```

Next you allocate the memory you need for the model's texture coordinates, and then you store the number of texture coordinates allocated in the model data structure:

```
    // allocate memory for the model texture coordinates
    model->st = (texCoord_t*)malloc(sizeof(texCoord_t)*modelHeader->numST);

    // store number of texture coordinates
    model->numST = modelHeader->numST;
```

With the memory for the texture coordinates allocated, you set a temporary pointer to the offset in the file where the model texture coordinates are stored. You then loop through the number of texture coordinates for the model and store their values in the model data structure.

```
    // set texture pointer to texture coordinate offset
    stPtr = (stIndex_t*)&buffer[modelHeader->offsetST];

    // calculate and store the texture coordinates for the model
    for (i = 0; i < modelHeader->numST; i++)
    {
        model->st[i].s = (float)stPtr[i].s / (float)md2Texture->width;
        model->st[i].t = (float)stPtr[i].t / (float)md2Texture->height;
    }
```

Next you allocate the memory for the triangle index data, set the total number of triangles, and set a temporary pointer to the triangle indices in the buffer:

```
// allocate the list of triangle indices
triIndex = (mesh_t*)malloc(sizeof(mesh_t) * modelHeader->numTris);

// set total number of triangles
model->numTriangles = modelHeader->numTris;
model->triIndex = triIndex;

// point to triangle indices in buffer
bufIndexPtr = (mesh_t*)&buffer[modelHeader->offsetTris];
```

Now that you've allocated the memory, you can load and store the triangle indices from the file buffer. You accomplish this by looping through every triangle in every frame of the model and storing the mesh and texture indices in the model data structure.

```
// create a mesh (triangle) list
for (j = 0; j < model->numFrames; j++)
{
    // for all triangles in each frame
    for(i = 0; i < modelHeader->numTris; i++)
    {
        // store the mesh and texture indices
        triIndex[i].meshIndex[0] = bufIndexPtr[i].meshIndex[0];
        triIndex[i].meshIndex[1] = bufIndexPtr[i].meshIndex[1];
        triIndex[i].meshIndex[2] = bufIndexPtr[i].meshIndex[2];
        triIndex[i].stIndex[0] = bufIndexPtr[i].stIndex[0];
        triIndex[i].stIndex[1] = bufIndexPtr[i].stIndex[1];
        triIndex[i].stIndex[2] = bufIndexPtr[i].stIndex[2];
    }
}
```

And that's it! The entire model is loaded. Now you can close the file pointer and free the memory you allocated for the buffer. Then you initialize the variables you'll use for the keyframe animation (we'll discuss these in this chapter), return the model data, and the function is complete!

```
// close file and free memory
fclose(filePtr);
free(buffer);
```

```
// initialize animation variables
model->currentFrame = 0;
model->nextFrame = 1;
model->interpol = 0.0;

return model;
}
```

So how do you use this function? It's very simple, really. Let's say you have a model, myModel, declared as

```
modelData_t *myModel;
```

And you have a model file stored in the current directory as *mymodel.md2* with the texture *mymodel.pcx*. To load the model, you simply call

```
MyModel = LoadMD2Model("mymodel.md2", "mymodel.pcx");
```

Now the model is loaded into memory and ready to be used!

Displaying the MD2

After you've loaded the model data into memory, you can do whatever you want to it. For now, let's display its vertices on the screen and worry about animation later.

Displaying an MD2 file simply involves knowing the current frame to display, looping through all the triangle indices in the model, and using these indices to extract the model's vertices. The function DisplayMD2l() accomplishes just that:

```
void DisplayMD2(modelData_t *model, int frameNum)
{
    vector_t *pointList;      // current frame's vertices
    int i;                    // index counter

    // create a pointer to the frame we want to show
    pointList = &model->pointList[model->numPoints * frameNum];

    // display the model as solid triangles
    glBegin(GL_TRIANGLES);
        for(i = 0; i < model->numTriangles; i++)
        {
            glVertex3fv(pointList[model->triIndex[i].meshIndex[0]].point);
            glVertex3fv(pointList[model->triIndex[i].meshIndex[2]].point);
```

```
            glVertex3fv(pointList[model->triIndex[i].meshIndex[1]].point);
        }
    glEnd();
}
```

This function accepts the model and the frame of the model that you want to draw as parameters. Using the `frameNum` parameter, you calculate the offset in the model's vertex list that references the desired frame's vertices. In this first version of the `DisplayMD2()` function, you're displaying the model as solid triangles, so after telling OpenGL this, you start looping through the triangle index. Because the mesh index refers to the vertices in a frame's vertex list, you reference the current triangle's vertices through the current triangle's mesh indices to get the proper display of the current triangle. When you execute this function with the following line, the `DisplayMD2()` function will display the first frame of the model loaded into `myModel`:

```
DisplayMD2(myModel, 0);
```

Figure 18.5 shows a sample model that is very popular in the *Quake 2* community.

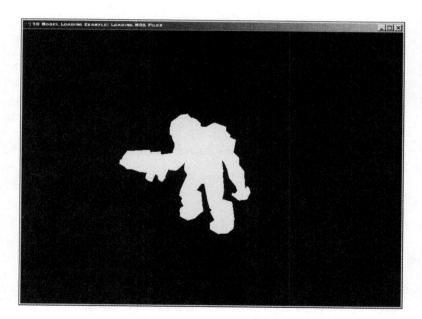

Figure 18.5

The model drawn with `GL_TRIANGLES` *and no lighting from the first* `DisplayMD2()` *function.*

Obviously, something must be wrong if your model just looks like one big blob in the world as it does in Figure 18.5. To produce a more realistic-looking model, you need to add lighting to the scene. Because you're adding lighting, you also need to define a normal for every triangle on the model. You can accomplish this through the `CalculateNormal()` function, defined here:

```
void CalculateNormal( float *p1, float *p2, float *p3 )
{
      float a[3], b[3], result[3];
      float length;

      a[0] = p1[0] - p2[0];
      a[1] = p1[1] - p2[1];
      a[2] = p1[2] - p2[2];

      b[0] = p1[0] - p3[0];
      b[1] = p1[1] - p3[1];
      b[2] = p1[2] - p3[2];

      result[0] = a[1] * b[2] - b[1] * a[2];
      result[1] = b[0] * a[2] - a[0] * b[2];
      result[2] = a[0] * b[1] - b[0] * a[1];

      // calculate the length of the normal
      length = (float)sqrt(result[0]*result[0] + result[1]*result[1] +
                  result[2]*result[2]);

      // normalize and specify the normal
      glNormal3f(result[0]/length, result[1]/length, result[2]/length);
}
```

You then use this function to calculate and set the triangle's normal before you render its vertices:

```
      ...
      glBegin(GL_TRIANGLES);
            for(i = 0; i < model->numTriangles; i++)
            {
                  CalculateNormal(pointList[model->triIndex[i].meshIndex[0]].point,
                              pointList[model->triIndex[i].meshIndex[2]].point,
                              pointList[model->triIndex[i].meshIndex[1]].point);
                  glVertex3fv(pointList[model->triIndex[i].meshIndex[0]].point);
                  glVertex3fv(pointList[model->triIndex[i].meshIndex[2]].point);
                  glVertex3fv(pointList[model->triIndex[i].meshIndex[1]].point);
            }
      glEnd();
      ...
```

The model looks much better with lighting, as shown in Figure 18.6.

Now you can actually display the model on the screen, but it still doesn't look real enough to be used in a game. To get the realism, you need to apply the model's skin as a texture.

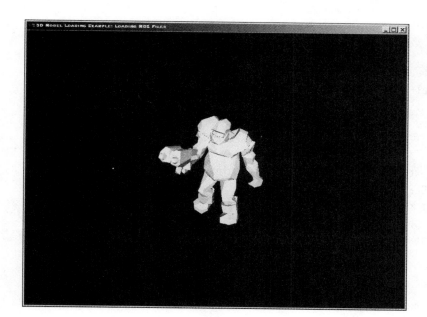

Figure 18.6

The MD2 model again, but with shading and lighting.

Adding the Texture

Adding a texture, or skin, to a model is just like adding a texture to any other 3D object. You load the texture, set it up with OpenGL, and then bind the texture object before defining the texture coordinates for each vertex you draw. Similar to how you extract the vertex data with the mesh indices, you'll use the texture-coordinate indices to extract the texture coordinates for each triangle you draw.

Before you move on, however, understand that most MD2 models (should you choose to use them in your own games) come packaged with their textures as PCX images. We're not going to discuss the PCX image format here for sake of brevity, but you will see some code that you can use to load PCX images as textures into OpenGL, along with some better texture-loading code, when you develop a complete MD2 application. The other alternative is to convert the PCX images into another format, such as the BMP or TGA formats we discussed earlier.

So let's assume that you've already loaded your texture into the model data structure you've defined, and you've come to the `DisplayMD2()` function to display the model. How do you add texture to the model? Well, you've already completed the first few steps of texturing: loading the texture and setting it up with OpenGL. Now you need to bind the texture object and define the texture coordinates. You can easily accomplish this with a new `DisplayMD2()` function:

```c
void DisplayMD2(modelData_t *model, int frameNum)
{
    vector_t *pointList;
    int i;

    // create a pointer to the frame we want to show
    pointList = &model->pointList[model->numPoints * frameNum];

    // set the texture
    glBindTexture(GL_TEXTURE_2D, model->modelTex->texID);

    // display the textured model with proper lighting normals
    glBegin(GL_TRIANGLES);
        for(i = 0; i < model->numTriangles; i++)
        {
            CalculateNormal(pointList[model->triIndex[i].meshIndex[0]].point,
                            pointList[model->triIndex[i].meshIndex[2]].point,
                            pointList[model->triIndex[i].meshIndex[1]].point);

            // define texture coordinates and draw vertices
            glTexCoord2f(model->st[model->triIndex[i].stIndex[0]].s,
                        model->st[model->triIndex[i].stIndex[0]].t);
            glVertex3fv(pointList[model->triIndex[i].meshIndex[0]].point);

            glTexCoord2f(model->st[model->triIndex[i].stIndex[2]].s ,
                        model->st[model->triIndex[i].stIndex[2]].t);
            glVertex3fv(pointList[model->triIndex[i].meshIndex[2]].point);

            glTexCoord2f(model->st[model->triIndex[i].stIndex[1]].s,
                        model->st[model->triIndex[i].stIndex[1]].t);
            glVertex3fv(pointList[model->triIndex[i].meshIndex[1]].point);
        }
    glEnd();
}
```

As you can see, you use the same method of using the texture-coordinate indices to extract the texture coordinates for each vertex as you did to extract the vertices themselves using the mesh indices (Refer to Figure 18.4). The result of this new `DisplayMD2()` function is shown in Figure 18.7.

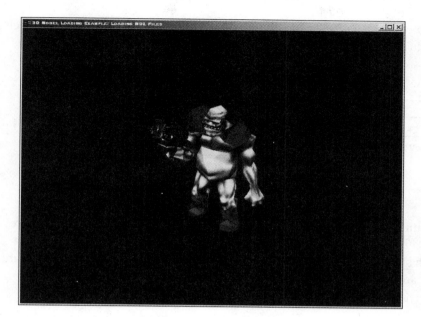

Figure 18.7

The textured MD2 model.

You're off to a great start! Now you have a static, lit, textured model that you *can* use in your games; however, nowadays, static models are not very exciting. You need to animate them so they move in fluid motions to make them look real. We're going to look at one way to accomplish this: *keyframe animation*, or *keyframe interpolation*.

Animating the Model

Remember the *currentFrame*, *nextFrame*, and *interpol* fields of the modelData_t structure? Well, now you get to use them! Animating a model can be one of the most realistic elements you can put in a game and very rewarding at the same time.

The method of animation we're going to look at is called *keyframe interpolation*. Because the MD2 model's frames are actually keyframes, or frames from discrete time intervals in a model's animation, you will need to calculate, or *interpolate*, the animation sequence between each set of keyframes. This method is also commonly known as *blending, morphing,* or *tweening*.

For instance, suppose you have an animation of a bullet model, where the bullet travels from the point (x0, y0, z0) to the point (x1, y1, z1). The modeler can create a keyframe animation sequence of just two frames from the bullet animation: one frame with the bullet located at (x0, y0, z0), and the next frame with the bullet located at (x1, y1, z1). Your job as a programmer would be to then calculate all the points through which the bullet will travel in between (x0, y0, z0) and (x1, y1, z1) for a certain number of frames to produce a smooth animation of the traveling bullet. Figure 18.8 illustrates how you calculate several bullet positions between (x0, y0, z0) and (x1, y1, z1) to get a smooth animation.

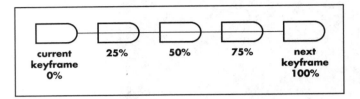

Figure 18.8

Using interpolation to determine the frames between two keyframes.

The key to keyframe animation (no pun intended) is keeping track of the two keyframes you're interpolating and calculating each vertex's position based on the current interpolation percentage. You can accomplish all this through the three fields you defined in the modelData_t structure: currentFrame, nextFrame, and interpol.

The currentFrame and nextFrame fields specify the first and second keyframes, respectively, on which you're performing the interpolation. The interpol field specifies the percentage of the path from one keyframe to another that you should render. For instance, if you take a vertex from the first keyframe with the x coordinate equal to 0.0, and you set the interpol field to 0.5 with the next keyframe's x coordinate equal to 10.0, then the current frame that you render's x coordinate will equal 5.0.

To calculate the value of an interpolated vertex at a defined percentage between two keyframe vertices, you just need to follow one simple formula, which defines linear interpolation:

```
Xᵢ + interpolatePercentage * (Xf - Xᵢ)
```

X_i is equal to the initial keyframe position of the vertex, and X_f is equal to the next keyframe position of the vertex. interpolatePercentage is the percentage between the two keyframes that will define the position at which you want the vertex to be. Figure 18.9 shows an example of this formula.

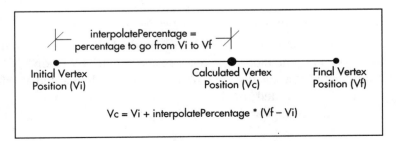

Figure 18.9

The result of using the linear-interpolation formula.

Now let's create a function, `DisplayMD2Interpolate()`, that will animate your models using every frame that the model has available:

```c
void DisplayMD2Interpolate(modelData_t *model)
{
    vector_t *pointList;        // current frame vertices
    vector_t *nextPointList;    // next frame vertices
    int i;                      // index counter
    float x1, y1, z1;           // current frame-point values
    float x2, y2, z2;           // next frame-point values

    vector_t vertex[3];         // temporary vertex

    // if we've reached 100% interpolation, then we need to change the current
    // and next keyframes
    if (model->interpol >= 1.0)
    {
        model->interpol = 0.0f;     // reset the interpolation percentage to 0%
        model->currentFrame++;      // increase current frame

        if (model->currentFrame >= model->numFrames)
            model->currentFrame = 0;

        // increase next frame
        model->nextFrame = model->currentFrame + 1;

        if (model->nextFrame >= model->numFrames)
            model->nextFrame = 0;
    }

    // extract current keyframe vertices
    pointList = &model->pointList[model->numPoints*model->currentFrame];

    // extract next keyframe vertices
    nextPointList = &model->pointList[model->numPoints*model->nextFrame];

    // set up the model texture and set rendering to triangles
    glBindTexture(GL_TEXTURE_2D, model->modelTex->texID);
    glBegin(GL_TRIANGLES);
        for (i = 0; i < model->numTriangles; i++)
        {
```

```c
// get first points of each keyframe
x1 = pointList[model->triIndex[i].meshIndex[0]].point[0];
y1 = pointList[model->triIndex[i].meshIndex[0]].point[1];
z1 = pointList[model->triIndex[i].meshIndex[0]].point[2];
x2 = nextPointList[model->triIndex[i].meshIndex[0]].point[0];
y2 = nextPointList[model->triIndex[i].meshIndex[0]].point[1];
z2 = nextPointList[model->triIndex[i].meshIndex[0]].point[2];

// store first interpolated vertex of triangle
vertex[0].point[0] = x1 + model->interpol * (x2 - x1);
vertex[0].point[1] = y1 + model->interpol * (y2 - y1);
vertex[0].point[2] = z1 + model->interpol * (z2 - z1);

// get second points of each frame
x1 = pointList[model->triIndex[i].meshIndex[2]].point[0];
y1 = pointList[model->triIndex[i].meshIndex[2]].point[1];
z1 = pointList[model->triIndex[i].meshIndex[2]].point[2];
x2 = nextPointList[model->triIndex[i].meshIndex[2]].point[0];
y2 = nextPointList[model->triIndex[i].meshIndex[2]].point[1];
z2 = nextPointList[model->triIndex[i].meshIndex[2]].point[2];

// store second interpolated vertex of triangle
vertex[2].point[0] = x1 + model->interpol * (x2 - x1);
vertex[2].point[1] = y1 + model->interpol * (y2 - y1);
vertex[2].point[2] = z1 + model->interpol * (z2 - z1);

// get third points of each frame
x1 = pointList[model->triIndex[i].meshIndex[1]].point[0];
y1 = pointList[model->triIndex[i].meshIndex[1]].point[1];
z1 = pointList[model->triIndex[i].meshIndex[1]].point[2];
x2 = nextPointList[model->triIndex[i].meshIndex[1]].point[0];
y2 = nextPointList[model->triIndex[i].meshIndex[1]].point[1];
z2 = nextPointList[model->triIndex[i].meshIndex[1]].point[2];

// store third interpolated vertex of triangle
vertex[1].point[0] = x1 + model->interpol * (x2 - x1);
vertex[1].point[1] = y1 + model->interpol * (y2 - y1);
vertex[1].point[2] = z1 + model->interpol * (z2 - z1);
```

```
                // calculate the normal of the triangle
                CalculateNormal(vertex[0].point, vertex[2].point, vertex[1].point);

                // render properly textured triangle
                glTexCoord2f(model->st[model->triIndex[i].stIndex[0]].s,
                            model->st[model->triIndex[i].stIndex[0]].t);
                glVertex3fv(vertex[0].point);

                glTexCoord2f(model->st[model->triIndex[i].stIndex[2]].s,
                            model->st[model->triIndex[i].stIndex[2]].t);
                glVertex3fv(vertex[2].point);

                glTexCoord2f(model->st[model->triIndex[i].stIndex[1]].s,
                            model->st[model->triIndex[i].stIndex[1]].t);
                glVertex3fv(vertex[1].point);
        }
    glEnd();

    // increase percentage of interpolation between frames
    model->interpol += 0.05f;
}
```

As you can see from the function, you calculate the interpolated position of each vertex in the model and draw every three vertices as a textured triangle. You also keep track of the interpolation percentage you're currently drawing so you know when to change the values of the current keyframe and next keyframe variables.

Although the function is useful for demonstrating how to perform keyframe interpolation for animation, it's not very useful for implementing model animation in games. The drawback to this function is that you can't control what frames to show, and at what rate to show them. You can easily change this, however, by adding three more parameters to the function: the startFrame, the endFrame, and the interpolation percent to increase per frame. When you add these parameters, you get a new DisplayMD2Interpolate() function:

```
void DisplayMD2Interpolate(modelData_t *model, int startFrame, int endFrame,
                            float percent)
{
    vector_t *pointList;        // current frame vertices
    vector_t *nextPointList;    // next frame vertices
    int i;                      // index counter
```

```
    float x1, y1, z1;          // current frame-point values
    float x2, y2, z2;          // next frame-point values
    vector_t vertex[3];        // temporary vertex

    if (model == NULL)
        return;

    if ( (startFrame > currentFrame) )
        currentFrame = startFrame;

    // verify parameters
    if ( (startFrame < 0) || (endFrame < 0) )
        return;

    // verify parameters
    if ( (startFrame >= model->numFrames) || (endFrame >= model->numFrames) )
        return;

    // if we've reached 100% interpolation, change the current keyframe
    if (model->interpol >= 1.0)
    {
        model->interpol = 0.0f;
        model->currentFrame++;
        if (model->currentFrame >= endFrame)
            model->currentFrame = startFrame;

        model->nextFrame = model->currentFrame + 1;

        if (model->nextFrame >= endFrame)
            model->nextFrame = startFrame;
    }

    pointList = &model->pointList[model->numPoints*model->currentFrame];
    nextPointList = &model->pointList[model->numPoints*model->nextFrame];

    glBindTexture(GL_TEXTURE_2D, model->modelTex->texID);
    glBegin(GL_TRIANGLES);
    for (i = 0; i < model->numTriangles; i++)
    {
```

```
        // calculate interpolated vertices and render triangle
        ...
    }
    glEnd();

    // increase percentage of interpolation between frames
    model->interpol += percent;
}
```

To use this function, you would do something like

```
DisplayMD2Interpolate(myModel, 0, 40, 0.005);
```

With this new version of the `DisplayMD2Interpolate()` function, not only can you specify the start and end frames of the model's animation that you want to render, you can also specify what percentage to increase the interpolation each frame. This will come in handy when you start to apply more timing functionality to your applications, because you can calculate the percentage you need to show the full animation between two keyframes in a certain time interval (for example, 1 second).

Although you can't see the model moving, Figure 18.10 shows the `DisplayMD2Interpolate()` function.

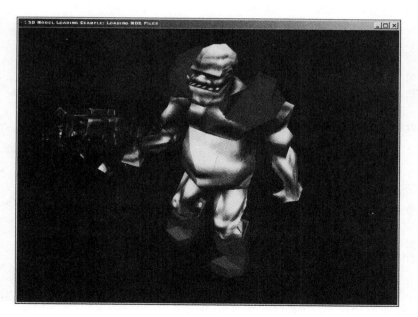

Figure 18.10

The animated model rendered using the `DisplayMD2Interpolate()` function.

Developing a *CMD2Model* Class

You know how to load, display, and animate an MD2 model, and you've even looked at some source code that tells you how to do all that. You have a basic set of structures that you use to represent the MD2 format and allow for ease of use when rendering the models. The problem, however, is that you can't easily plug all this code into a game.

So now what we're going to do is develop a C++ class called CMD2Model. This class will be useful for when you develop games in the future, while also allowing for extensibility not possible through the examples you've seen previously in this chapter. Using the structures we've already defined, here is the class definition:

```
class CMD2Model
{
private:

    int numFrames;          // number of model frames
    int numVertices;        // number of vertices
    int numTriangles;       // number of triangles
    int numST;              // number of skins
    int frameSize;          // size of each frame in bytes
    int currentFrame;       // current frame # in animation
    int nextFrame;          // next frame # in animation
    float interpol;         // percent through current frame
    mesh_t *triIndex;       // triangle list
    texCoord_t *st;         // texture-coordinate list
    vector_t *vertexList;   // vertex list
    texture_t *modelTex;    // texture data

    void SetupSkin(texture_t *thisTexture);

public:

    CMD2Model();            // constructor
    ~CMD2Model();           // destructor

    // load model and skin/texture at the same time
    int Load(char *modelFile, char *skinFile);

    // load model only
    int LoadModel(char *modelFile);
```

```
        // load skin only
        int LoadSkin(char *skinFile);

        // set model's texture/skin
        int SetTexture(texture_t *texture);

        // render model with interpolation to get animation
        int Animate(int startFrame, int endFrame, float percent);

        // render a single frame
        int RenderFrame(int keyFrame);

        // free memory of model
        int UnLoad();
};
```

This class basically encapsulates all the functionality that you have created so far for the MD2 model. The private attributes of the class should all be rather familiar at this point. You do replace the SetupMd2Texture() function with the private SetupSkin() method of the CMD2Model class.

In the public section of the class, you have a few different methods, although their functionality is nearly the same as the functions you developed before. For instance, the Load() method loads the model and its texture into memory to be ready for use. You also include the LoadSkin(), LoadModel(), and SetTexture(), all of which perform some sort of initialization on the model object. LoadSkin() loads and applies a texture to the model given the texture filename. LoadModel() does essentially the same thing as LoadSkin(), except it loads a new model into memory. SetTexture() applies to the model a texture_t object that has already been loaded into memory.

You also have the Animate() method, which renders the model with animation (assuming it's called each frame) between the startFrame and endFrame keyframes, with a percent interpolation between each keyframe. Then you have the RenderFrame() method to render just a single, still keyframe. Lastly, you have the UnLoad() method to free all the memory that this model object has allocated. So really, changing the MD2 model functionality to a class hasn't changed the base functionality. You can still load, display, and animate the model, but now you're encapsulating all its data while providing a little more flexibility for your software design.

Because we've already discussed how each basic function works on the MD2 model, we won't be discussing much of the following code. Instead, be sure to look at the differences and changes that needed to be made to incorporate the basic functions into the CMD2Model class. Without further ado, here's the implementation of the CMD2Model class:

```cpp
CMD2Model::CMD2Model()
{
    numVertices = 0;       // vertices
    numTriangles = 0;      // triangles
    numFrames = 0;         // frames
    numST = 0;             // texture coordinates
    frameSize = 0;         // needed?
    currentFrame = 0;      // current keyframe
    nextFrame = 1;         // next keyframe
    interpol = 0.0;        // interpolation percent
    triIndex = NULL;       // triangle indices
    st = NULL;             // texture-coordinate indices
    vertexList = NULL;     // vertices
    modelTex = NULL;       // skin/texture
}

CMD2Model::~CMD2Model()
{
}

void CMD2Model::SetupSkin(texture_t *thisTexture)
{
    // set the proper parameters for an MD2 texture
    glGenTextures(1, &thisTexture->texID);
    glBindTexture(GL_TEXTURE_2D, thisTexture->texID);
    glTexParameteri(GL_TEXTURE_2D,GL_TEXTURE_WRAP_S,GL_CLAMP);
    glTexParameteri(GL_TEXTURE_2D,GL_TEXTURE_WRAP_T,GL_CLAMP);
    glTexParameteri(GL_TEXTURE_2D,GL_TEXTURE_MIN_FILTER,GL_LINEAR);
    glTexParameteri(GL_TEXTURE_2D,GL_TEXTURE_MAG_FILTER,GL_LINEAR);

    switch (thisTexture->textureType)
    {
    case BMP:
        gluBuild2DMipmaps(GL_TEXTURE_2D, GL_RGB, thisTexture->width,
                        thisTexture->height, GL_RGB, GL_UNSIGNED_BYTE,
                        thisTexture->data);
        break;
    case PCX:
        gluBuild2DMipmaps(GL_TEXTURE_2D, GL_RGBA, thisTexture->width,
                        thisTexture->height, GL_RGBA, GL_UNSIGNED_BYTE,
                        thisTexture->data);
```

```cpp
        case TGA:
            break;
        default:
            break;
        }
}


int CMD2Model::Load(char *modelFile, char *skinFile)
{
    FILE *filePtr;                          // file pointer
    int fileLen;                            // length of model file
    char *buffer;                           // file buffer

    modelHeader_t *modelHeader;             // model header

    stIndex_t *stPtr;                       // texture data
    frame_t *frame;                         // frame data
    vector_t *vertexListPtr;                // index variable
    mesh_t *bufIndexPtr;                    // index variables
    int i, j;                               // index variables

    // open the model file
    filePtr = fopen(modelFile, "rb");
    if (filePtr == NULL)
        return FALSE;

    // find length of file
    fseek(filePtr, 0, SEEK_END);
    fileLen = ftell(filePtr);
    fseek(filePtr, 0, SEEK_SET);

    // read entire file into buffer
    buffer = new char [fileLen+1];//(char*)malloc(fileLen + 1);
    fread(buffer, sizeof(char), fileLen, filePtr);

    // extract model file header from buffer
    modelHeader = (modelHeader_t*)buffer;

    vertexList = new vector_t [modelHeader->numXYZ * modelHeader->numFrames];
```

```c
numVertices = modelHeader->numXYZ;
numFrames = modelHeader->numFrames;
frameSize = modelHeader->framesize;

for (j = 0; j < numFrames; j++)
{
    frame = (frame_t*)&buffer[modelHeader->offsetFrames + frameSize * j];

    vertexListPtr = (vector_t*)&vertexList[numVertices * j];
    for (i = 0; i < numVertices; i++)
    {
        vertexListPtr[i].point[0] = frame->scale[0] * frame->fp[i].v[0] +
                                    frame->translate[0];
        vertexListPtr[i].point[1] = frame->scale[1] * frame->fp[i].v[1] +
                                    frame->translate[1];
        vertexListPtr[i].point[2] = frame->scale[2] * frame->fp[i].v[2] +
                                    frame->translate[2];
    }
}

modelTex = LoadTexture(skinFile);
if (modelTex != NULL)
    SetupSkin(modelTex);
else
    return FALSE;

numST = modelHeader->numST;
st = new texCoord_t [numST];

stPtr = (stIndex_t*)&buffer[modelHeader->offsetST];
for (i = 0; i < numST; i++)
{
    st[i].s = (float)stPtr[i].s / (float)modelTex->width;
    st[i].t = (float)stPtr[i].t / (float)modelTex->height;
}

numTriangles = modelHeader->numTris;
triIndex = new mesh_t [numTriangles];

// point to triangle indexes in buffer
bufIndexPtr = (mesh_t*)&buffer[modelHeader->offsetTris];
```

```
        // create a mesh (triangle) list
        for (j = 0; j < numFrames; j++)
        {
            // for all triangles in each frame
            for(i = 0; i < numTriangles; i++)
            {
                triIndex[i].meshIndex[0] = bufIndexPtr[i].meshIndex[0];
                triIndex[i].meshIndex[1] = bufIndexPtr[i].meshIndex[1];
                triIndex[i].meshIndex[2] = bufIndexPtr[i].meshIndex[2];
                triIndex[i].stIndex[0] = bufIndexPtr[i].stIndex[0];
                triIndex[i].stIndex[1] = bufIndexPtr[i].stIndex[1];
                triIndex[i].stIndex[2] = bufIndexPtr[i].stIndex[2];
            }
        }

        // close file and free memory
        fclose(filePtr);
        free(buffer);

        currentFrame = 0;
        nextFrame = 1;
        interpol = 0.0;

        return TRUE;
}

int CMD2Model::LoadModel(char *modelFile)
{
        FILE *filePtr;                          // file pointer
        int fileLen;                            // length of model file
        char *buffer;                           // file buffer

        modelHeader_t *modelHeader;             // model header

        stIndex_t *stPtr;                       // texture data
        frame_t *frame;                         // frame data
        vector_t *vertexListPtr;                // index variable
        mesh_t *bufIndexPtr;                    // index variables
        int i, j;                               // index variables
```

```
// open the model file
filePtr = fopen(modelFile, "rb");
if (filePtr == NULL)
    return FALSE;

// find length of file
fseek(filePtr, 0, SEEK_END);
fileLen = ftell(filePtr);
fseek(filePtr, 0, SEEK_SET);

// read entire file into buffer
buffer = new char [fileLen+1];//(char*)malloc(fileLen + 1);
fread(buffer, sizeof(char), fileLen, filePtr);

// extract model file header from buffer
modelHeader = (modelHeader_t*)buffer;

if (vertexList != NULL)
    delete [] vertexList;

vertexList = new vector_t [modelHeader->numXYZ * modelHeader->numFrames];

numVertices = modelHeader->numXYZ;
numFrames = modelHeader->numFrames;
frameSize = modelHeader->framesize;

for (j = 0; j < numFrames; j++)
{
    frame = (frame_t*)&buffer[modelHeader->offsetFrames + frameSize * j];

    vertexListPtr = (vector_t*)&vertexList[numVertices * j];
    for (i = 0; i < numVertices; i++)
    {
        vertexListPtr[i].point[0] = frame->scale[0] * frame->fp[i].v[0] +
                                    frame->translate[0];
        vertexListPtr[i].point[1] = frame->scale[1] * frame->fp[i].v[1] +
                                    frame->translate[1];
        vertexListPtr[i].point[2] = frame->scale[2] * frame->fp[i].v[2] +
                                    frame->translate[2];

    }
}
```

```cpp
numST = modelHeader->numST;

if (st != NULL)
    delete [] st;

st = new texCoord_t [numST];

stPtr = (stIndex_t*)&buffer[modelHeader->offsetST];
for (i = 0; i < numST; i++)
{
    st[i].s = 0.0;
    st[i].t = 0.0;
}

numTriangles = modelHeader->numTris;

if (triIndex != NULL)
    delete [] triIndex;

triIndex = new mesh_t [numTriangles];

// point to triangle indexes in buffer
bufIndexPtr = (mesh_t*)&buffer[modelHeader->offsetTris];

// create a mesh (triangle) list
for (j = 0; j < numFrames; j++)
{
    // for all triangles in each frame
    for(i = 0; i < numTriangles; i++)
    {
        triIndex[i].meshIndex[0] = bufIndexPtr[i].meshIndex[0];
        triIndex[i].meshIndex[1] = bufIndexPtr[i].meshIndex[1];
        triIndex[i].meshIndex[2] = bufIndexPtr[i].meshIndex[2];
        triIndex[i].stIndex[0] = bufIndexPtr[i].stIndex[0];
        triIndex[i].stIndex[1] = bufIndexPtr[i].stIndex[1];
        triIndex[i].stIndex[2] = bufIndexPtr[i].stIndex[2];
    }
}

// close file and free memory
fclose(filePtr);
```

```cpp
        ///free(buffer);

        delete [] buffer;

        currentFrame = 0;
        nextFrame = 1;
        interpol = 0.0;

        return 0;
}

int CMD2Model::LoadSkin(char *skinFile)
{
        int i;

        modelTex = LoadTexture(skinFile);

        if (modelTex != NULL)
            SetupSkin(modelTex);
        else
            return -1;

        for (i = 0; i < numST; i++)
        {
            st[i].s /= (float)modelTex->width;
            st[i].t /= (float)modelTex->height;
        }

        return 0;
}

int CMD2Model::SetTexture(texture_t *texture)
{
        int i;

        if (texture != NULL)
            modelTex = texture;
        else
            return -1;

        SetupSkin(modelTex);
```

```cpp
        for (i = 0; i < numST; i++)
        {
                st[i].s /= (float)modelTex->width;
                st[i].t /= (float)modelTex->height;
        }

        return 0;
}

int CMD2Model::Animate(int startFrame, int endFrame, float percent)
{
        vector_t *vList;                // current frame vertices
        vector_t *nextVList;            // next frame vertices
        int i;                          // index counter
        float x1, y1, z1;               // current frame-point values
        float x2, y2, z2;               // next frame-point values

        vector_t vertex[3];

        if ((startFrame > currentFrame))
                currentFrame = startFrame;

        if ((startFrame < 0) || (endFrame < 0))
                return -1;

        if ((startFrame >= numFrames) || (endFrame >= numFrames))
                return -1;

        if (interpol >= 1.0)
        {
                interpol = 0.0f;
                currentFrame++;
                if (currentFrame >= endFrame)//model->numFrames)
                        currentFrame = startFrame; //0;

                nextFrame = currentFrame + 1;

                if (nextFrame >= endFrame)
                        nextFrame = startFrame;

        }
```

```
vList = &vertexList[numVertices*currentFrame];
nextVList = &vertexList[numVertices*nextFrame];

glBindTexture(GL_TEXTURE_2D, modelTex->texID);
glBegin(GL_TRIANGLES);
for (i = 0; i < numTriangles; i++)
{
    // get first points of each frame
    x1 = vList[triIndex[i].meshIndex[0]].point[0];
    y1 = vList[triIndex[i].meshIndex[0]].point[1];
    z1 = vList[triIndex[i].meshIndex[0]].point[2];
    x2 = nextVList[triIndex[i].meshIndex[0]].point[0];
    y2 = nextVList[triIndex[i].meshIndex[0]].point[1];
    z2 = nextVList[triIndex[i].meshIndex[0]].point[2];

    // store first interpolated vertex of triangle
    vertex[0].point[0] = x1 + interpol * (x2 - x1);
    vertex[0].point[1] = y1 + interpol * (y2 - y1);
    vertex[0].point[2] = z1 + interpol * (z2 - z1);

    // get second points of each frame
    x1 = vList[triIndex[i].meshIndex[2]].point[0];
    y1 = vList[triIndex[i].meshIndex[2]].point[1];
    z1 = vList[triIndex[i].meshIndex[2]].point[2];
    x2 = nextVList[triIndex[i].meshIndex[2]].point[0];
    y2 = nextVList[triIndex[i].meshIndex[2]].point[1];
    z2 = nextVList[triIndex[i].meshIndex[2]].point[2];

    // store second interpolated vertex of triangle
    vertex[2].point[0] = x1 + interpol * (x2 - x1);
    vertex[2].point[1] = y1 + interpol * (y2 - y1);
    vertex[2].point[2] = z1 + interpol * (z2 - z1);

    // get third points of each frame
    x1 = vList[triIndex[i].meshIndex[1]].point[0];
    y1 = vList[triIndex[i].meshIndex[1]].point[1];
    z1 = vList[triIndex[i].meshIndex[1]].point[2];
    x2 = nextVList[triIndex[i].meshIndex[1]].point[0];
    y2 = nextVList[triIndex[i].meshIndex[1]].point[1];
    z2 = nextVList[triIndex[i].meshIndex[1]].point[2];
```

```cpp
            // store third interpolated vertex of triangle
            vertex[1].point[0] = x1 + interpol * (x2 - x1);
            vertex[1].point[1] = y1 + interpol * (y2 - y1);
            vertex[1].point[2] = z1 + interpol * (z2 - z1);

            // calculate the normal of the triangle
            CalculateNormal(vertex[0].point, vertex[2].point, vertex[1].point);

            // render properly textured triangle
            glTexCoord2f(st[triIndex[i].stIndex[0]].s,
                         st[triIndex[i].stIndex[0]].t);
            glVertex3fv(vertex[0].point);

            glTexCoord2f(st[triIndex[i].stIndex[2]].s ,
                         st[triIndex[i].stIndex[2]].t);
            glVertex3fv(vertex[2].point);

            glTexCoord2f(st[triIndex[i].stIndex[1]].s,
                         st[triIndex[i].stIndex[1]].t);
            glVertex3fv(vertex[1].point);
        }
        glEnd();

        interpol += percent;   // increase percentage of interpolation between frames

        return 0;
    }


int CMD2Model::RenderFrame(int keyFrame)
{
        vector_t *vList;
        int i;

        // create a pointer to the frame we want to show
        vList = &vertexList[numVertices * keyFrame];

        // set the texture
        glBindTexture(GL_TEXTURE_2D, modelTex->texID);

        // display the textured model with proper lighting normals
        glBegin(GL_TRIANGLES);
```

```
        for(i = 0; i < numTriangles; i++)
        {
                CalculateNormal(vList[triIndex[i].meshIndex[0]].point,
                        vList[triIndex[i].meshIndex[2]].point,
                        vList[triIndex[i].meshIndex[1]].point);
                glTexCoord2f(st[triIndex[i].stIndex[0]].s,
                                st[triIndex[i].stIndex[0]].t);
                glVertex3fv(vList[triIndex[i].meshIndex[0]].point);

                glTexCoord2f(st[triIndex[i].stIndex[2]].s ,
                                st[triIndex[i].stIndex[2]].t);
                glVertex3fv(vList[triIndex[i].meshIndex[2]].point);

                glTexCoord2f(st[triIndex[i].stIndex[1]].s,
                                st[triIndex[i].stIndex[1]].t);
                glVertex3fv(vList[triIndex[i].meshIndex[1]].point);
        }
        glEnd();

        return 0;
}


int CMD2Model::UnLoad()
{
        if (triIndex != NULL)
                free(triIndex);
        if (vertexList != NULL)
                free(vertexList);
        if (st != NULL)
                free(st);

        return 0;
}
```

That's quite a bit of code you have there! Now you can easily implement MD2 model functionality. For instance, to load, animate, and shut down a model, you simply need these lines of code:

```
CMD2Model *myModel;           // the model instance
...
myModel = new CMD2Model;      // allocate memory for object
...
```

```
myModel->Load("mymodel.md2", "mymodel.pcx");
...
myModel->Animate(0, 40, percentage);
...
myModel->UnLoad();
...
delete myModel;
```

Controlling the Model Animation

It's great that you can show frames of a model's animation, but to get more realism, you need to be able to control what model animations are shown and when they are shown. One way you can do this is through *states*, where each state defines an animation or action of the model. For example, you can define an idle state, which occurs when the model is not doing anything. Other examples include running, walking, jumping, crouching, and dying states.

Typically, model states are specific to the game for which the models have been created. As an example, Table 18.1 shows how the animation frames of an MD2 model relate to its animation states.

Suppose you wanted to keep track of the animation states idle, running, jumping, and crouching. You can set up an enumerated type like this:

```
enum modelState_t
{
     MODEL_IDLE,    // idle animation
     MODEL_CROUCH,  // crouching animation
     MODEL_RUN,     // running animation
     MODEL_JUMP     // jumping animation
};
```

Then, you can add two methods to the CMD2Model class. One method is to keep track of which state the model is in, and the other is to retrieve the model's current state:

```
// set animation state of model
int SetState(modelState_t state);

// retrieve animation state of model
modelState_t GetState();
```

Table 18.1 MD2 Animation States

Frame Number	Action State
0–39	Idle
40–46	Running
47–60	Shot, not falling down
61–66	Shot in shoulder
67–73	Jump
74–95	Idle
96–112	Shot, falling down
113–122	Idle
123–135	Idle
136–154	Crouching
155–161	Crouching crawl
162–169	Idle crouching
170–177	Kneeling dying
178–185	Falling back dying
186–190	Falling forward dying
191–198	Falling back slowly dying

You also add a private member variable to the class to hold the model's current state:

```
modelState_t modelState;        // current model animation state
```

Typically, you will want to control the model state based on the player's actions through an input device such as the keyboard. So how do you do this? Well, the simple (and definitely not best) solution is to keep a global state of the model and change this state when the user presses a key. For simplicity, you'll keep track of the global state in the message loop of the `WinMain()` function. Here's the definition of the global model state:

```
modelState_t modelState;        // global model state
```

Here's the modified message loop from WinMain():

```
// main message loop
while (!done)
{
    PeekMessage(&msg, hwnd, NULL, NULL, PM_REMOVE);

    if (msg.message == WM_QUIT)              // do we receive a WM_QUIT message?
    {
        done = true;                         // if so, time to quit the application
    }
    else
    {
        if (keyPressed[VK_ESCAPE])
            done = true;
        else
        {
            if (keyPressed[VK_UP])
                modelState = MODEL_RUN;
            else if (keyPressed[VK_CONTROL])
                modelState = MODEL_CROUCH;
            else if (keyPressed[VK_SHIFT])
                modelState = MODEL_JUMP;
            else
                modelState = MODEL_IDLE;

            Render();     // render frame

            TranslateMessage(&msg);           // translate and dispatch to event queue
            DispatchMessage(&msg);
        }
    }
}
```

As you can see, you simply change the model state based on the keys that the user presses. This model state then carries over to the Render() function, where you draw the correct animation for the current model state:

```
void Render()
{
    float percent;
    ...
    percent = 0.07f;
```

```
glPushMatrix();
        glRotatef(90.0f, -1.0f, 0.0f, 0.0f);
        glColor3f(1.0, 1.0, 1.0);

        // set current model animation state
        myModel->SetState(modelState);
        gunModel->SetState(modelState);

        // perform animation based on model state
        // NOTE: Not the best way to do this!!!
        switch (myModel->GetState())
        {
        case MODEL_IDLE:
            myModel->Animate(0, 39, percent);
            gunModel->Animate(0, 39, percent);
            break;
        case MODEL_RUN:
            myModel->Animate(40, 46, percent);
            gunModel->Animate(40, 46, percent);
            break;
        case MODEL_CROUCH:
            myModel->Animate(136, 154, percent);
            gunModel->Animate(136, 154, percent);
            break;
        case MODEL_JUMP:
            myModel->Animate(67, 73, percent);
            gunModel->Animate(67, 73, percent);
            break;
        default:
            break;
        }
    glPopMatrix();
    ...
}
```

And that's basically all you have to do! When you press the up-arrow key on the keyboard, the model will be running, and when no keys are being pressed, the model will perform its idle animation. Similarly, the Ctrl and Shift keys initiate the crouch and jumping animations, respectively.

Now that we've discussed the MD2 format, feel free to experiment and develop your own formats for your own games and game engines. The MD2 is merely a good example of basic 3D model formats, and it may not be the best format for you to use in your own games. Also, be sure to research other model formats to get exposed to other methods used for 3D models.

ONE LAST TIDBIT

Because a large majority of *Quake 2* models come with textures stored in the PCX image format, following is some code that you might find useful to load the PCX image into a texture object. We're not going to discuss the ins and outs of this code, so feel free to explore the PCX image format on your own.

```
// LoadPCXFile()
// desc: loads a PCX file into memory
unsigned char *LoadPCXFile(char *filename, PCXHEADER *pcxHeader)
{
    int idx = 0;                    // counter index
    int c;                          // used to retrieve a char from the file
    int i;                          // counter index
    int numRepeat;
    FILE *filePtr;                  // file handle
    int width;                      // pcx width
    int height;                     // pcx height
    unsigned char *pixelData;       // pcx image data
    unsigned char *paletteData;     // pcx palette data

    // open PCX file
    filePtr = fopen(filename, "rb");
    if (filePtr == NULL)
        return NULL;

    // retrieve first character; should be equal to 10
    c = getc(filePtr);
    if (c != 10)
    {
        fclose(filePtr);
        return NULL;
    }

    // retrieve next character; should be equal to 5
    c = getc(filePtr);
```

```c
if (c != 5)
{
    fclose(filePtr);
    return NULL;
}

// reposition file pointer to beginning of file
rewind(filePtr);

// read 4 characters of data to skip
fgetc(filePtr);
fgetc(filePtr);
fgetc(filePtr);
fgetc(filePtr);

// retrieve leftmost x value of PCX
pcxHeader->xMin = fgetc(filePtr);        // loword
pcxHeader->xMin |= fgetc(filePtr) << 8; // hiword

// retrieve bottom-most y value of PCX
pcxHeader->yMin = fgetc(filePtr);        // loword
pcxHeader->yMin |= fgetc(filePtr) << 8; // hiword

// retrieve rightmost x value of PCX
pcxHeader->xMax = fgetc(filePtr);        // loword
pcxHeader->xMax |= fgetc(filePtr) << 8; // hiword

// retrieve topmost y value of PCX
pcxHeader->yMax = fgetc(filePtr);        // loword
pcxHeader->yMax |= fgetc(filePtr) << 8; // hiword

// calculate the width and height of the PCX
width = pcxHeader->xMax - pcxHeader->xMin + 1;
height = pcxHeader->yMax - pcxHeader->yMin + 1;

// allocate memory for PCX image data
pixelData = (unsigned char*)malloc(width*height);

// set file pointer to 128th byte of file, where the PCX image data starts
fseek(filePtr, 128, SEEK_SET);
```

```c
// decode the pixel data and store
while (idx < (width*height))
{
    c = getc(filePtr);
    if (c > 0xbf)
    {
        numRepeat = 0x3f & c;
        c = getc(filePtr);

        for (i = 0; i < numRepeat; i++)
        {
            pixelData[idx++] = c;
        }
    }
    else
        pixelData[idx++] = c;

    fflush(stdout);
}

// allocate memory for the PCX image palette
paletteData = (unsigned char*)malloc(768);

// palette is the last 769 bytes of the PCX file
fseek(filePtr, -769, SEEK_END);

// verify palette; first character should be 12
c = getc(filePtr);
if (c != 12)
{
    fclose(filePtr);
    return NULL;
}

// read and store all of palette
for (i = 0; i < 768; i++)
{
    c = getc(filePtr);
    paletteData[i] = c;
}
```

```c
        // close file and store palette in header
        fclose(filePtr);
        pcxHeader->palette = paletteData;

        // return the pixel image data
        return pixelData;
}

// LoadPCXTexture()
// desc: loads a PCX image file as a texture
texture_t *LoadPCXTexture(char *filename)
{
        PCXHEADER texInfo;              // header of texture
        texture_t *thisTexture;        // the texture
        unsigned char *unscaledData;   // used to calculate pcx
        int i;                         // index counter
        int j;                         // index counter
        int width;                     // width of texture
        int height;                    // height of texture

        // allocate memory for texture struct
        thisTexture = (texture_t*)malloc(sizeof(texture_t));
        if (thisTexture == NULL)
            return NULL;

        // load the PCX file into the texture struct
        thisTexture->data = LoadPCXFile(filename, &texInfo);
        if (thisTexture->data == NULL)
        {
            free(thisTexture->data);
            return NULL;
        }

        // store the texture information
        thisTexture->palette = texInfo.palette;
        thisTexture->width = texInfo.xMax - texInfo.xMin + 1;
        thisTexture->height = texInfo.yMax - texInfo.yMin + 1;
        thisTexture->textureType = PCX;

        // allocate memory for the unscaled data
        unscaledData = (unsigned char*)malloc(thisTexture->width*thisTexture->height*4);
```

```c
// store the unscaled data via the palette
for (j = 0; j < thisTexture->height; j++)
{
    for (i = 0; i < thisTexture->width; i++)
    {
        unscaledData[4*(j*thisTexture->width+i)+0] =
                    (unsigned char)thisTexture->palette[3*
                    thisTexture->data[j*thisTexture->width+i]+0];
        unscaledData[4*(j*thisTexture->width+i)+1] =
                    (unsigned char)thisTexture->palette[3*
                    thisTexture->data[j*thisTexture->width+i]+1];
        unscaledData[4*(j*thisTexture->width+i)+2] =
                    (unsigned char)thisTexture->palette[3*
                    thisTexture->data[j*thisTexture->width+i]+2];
        unscaledData[4*(j*thisTexture->width+i)+3] = (unsigned char)255;
    }
}

// find width and height's nearest greater power of 2
width = thisTexture->width;
height = thisTexture->height;

// find width's
i = 0;
while (width)
{
    width /= 2;
    i++;
}
thisTexture->scaledHeight = (long)pow(2, i-1);

// find height's
i = 0;
while (height)
{
    height /= 2;
    i++;
}
thisTexture->scaledWidth = (long)pow(2, i-1);
```

```
// clear the texture data
if (thisTexture->data != NULL)
{
    free(thisTexture->data);
    thisTexture->data = NULL;
}

// reallocate memory for the texture data
thisTexture->data = (unsigned char*)malloc(thisTexture->scaledWidth*
                    thisTexture->scaledHeight*4);

// use the GL utility library to scale the texture to the unscaled dimensions
gluScaleImage (GL_RGBA, thisTexture->width, thisTexture->height,
               GL_UNSIGNED_BYTE, unscaledData, thisTexture->scaledWidth,
               thisTexture->scaledHeight, GL_UNSIGNED_BYTE, thisTexture->data);

    return thisTexture;
}
```

SUMMARY

At its highest level, the MD2 format is broken into two parts: the header and the data. The header itself holds the model's basic dimensional information, such as the number of vertices and triangles, and holds the location in the file of each type of model data.

Keyframes are frames of animation taken from discrete time intervals, which means that each keyframe is like a snapshot of the model at specific points in the time of an animation.

Using *keyframe interpolation,* you can calculate the frames in between two keyframes to get a smooth animation. By storing only the keyframes of model animations, you can reduce the amount of storage space necessary for a model.

One method, although not the best, of controlling the animation of a model is through states. By changing the model's state when the user presses a key or an event occurs, you can create a more realistic and controllable character in your worlds.

CHAPTER 19

PHYSICS
MODELING WITH
OPENGL

One of the most important elements of a game is how realistic its world seems. Besides making the game appealing to the eye with beautiful, realistic graphics, you must make the game world and the interactions within it as realistic as possible to truly immerse the player. Although there was once a time when developers could get away with making games whose objects moved around the world in non-realistic manners, times have changed. These days, objects in games must move and interact with each other much like they do in the real world.

In this chapter, you're going to take a look at how you can simulate the real world through simple physics modeling with Newtonian physics and collision-detection techniques.

A PHYSICS REVIEW

Before we can really discuss how to simulate the real world in your games, we must make sure you have a solid understanding of basic physics concepts. We won't be able to discuss every minute detail of physics, simply because we don't have enough room, but the concepts we discuss should be enough to help you develop a physics model for anything you might need in your games.

Time

Even though we can't easily define it, everyone knows what time is. Our entire society is based on clocks and watches. We use these devices to measure time in seconds, minutes, hours, days, and years. In science, when you need to be more accurate, you might measure time in milliseconds (10^{-3} seconds), microseconds (10^{-6} seconds), or nanoseconds (10^{-9} seconds).

Physics uses time to describe how objects move around in space. For instance, consider the term *40 miles per hour* to describe the speed of an object. What this term is saying is that the object moves 40 miles (a distance) for every time interval that spans one hour.

The great thing about time is that you can easily incorporate it into your games to simulate the real world. One option would be to use a sort of *virtual time* where every frame that you render equals one second of the game world. The problem with this approach, however, is that if you do not keep a constant frame rate, then the objects in the world will not physically model the real world very well. For example, suppose you start with a frame rate of 30 frames per second with an object moving across the world at 30 feet per frame, and shortly thereafter, the frame rate drops to 20 frames per second. What happens to the object's movement? Well, even though you never slow down the speed of the object, it will appear to have slowed down because the number of frames, or seconds, that have elapsed has decreased.

The other option you have is to simulate the world by using real time. With real time, you can closely approximate the physical model of the real world, because you're not bound to the limitations of the frame-based approach. The motion of the objects in the world changes independently from the frame rate, so your objects will move the same distance whether you are getting five frames per second or 80 frames per second. Because our goal is realism, we're going to use the real-time approach by measuring time in seconds in our physics model.

Distance, Displacement, and Position

Distance and displacement, although seemingly the same thing, are two quantities with different definitions and meanings. *Distance* is a scalar quantity that defines the amount of "ground" an object has covered while moving. Alternatively, *displacement* is a vector quantity that defines the object's change in position. To get a better understanding, let's look at an example.

Say you have an object moving in a rectangular path, as shown in Figure 19.1. As you can see, the object starts at the origin (0,0) and moves north to (0,5). It then moves east to (10,5), south to (10,0), and finally west back to the origin.

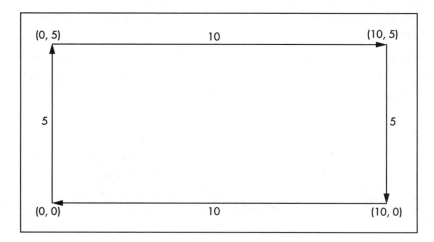

Figure 19.1

An object moving in a rectangular path moves a distance but has no displacement.

If you think about the amount of "ground" the object has covered while moving, you calculate a distance of

```
Distance = North Distance + East Distance + South Distance + West Distance
Distance = 5 + 10 + 5 + 10
Distance = 30
```

When you think in terms of vectors, however, and how much the object has changed its position during its movement, you find that the displacement equals 0:

```
Displacement = North Vector + East Vector + South Vector + West Vector
Displacement = (0,5) + (10,0) + (0,-5) + (-10,0)
Displacement = (0 + 10 + 0 - 10, 5 + 0 - 5 + 0)
Displacement = (0,0)      or no change
```

Why does displacement equal zero when you know that the object moved? You must remember that displacement is a vector quantity, meaning it has both a magnitude and direction. So for this example, the North Vector cancels out the South Vector, and the East Vector cancels out the West Vector to give you zero displacement.

To determine the distance an object travels or the displacement of an object's movement, you must be able to keep track of the object through the object's *position*. Every object has a position in 3D space defined by the notation (x,y,z); 2D is (x,y) and 1D is (x). Typically, the position you define for an object is actually the center of the object. For instance, if you have a baseball, then you would probably use the center of the baseball to represent its location. Using the center-oriented approach is fine for most applications, but what happens if you have an irregularly shaped object, such as a baseball bat?

Looking at Figure 19.2, you can see that a baseball bat has more mass on one end than on the other. Although you could use the center of the baseball bat's dimensions as the position of the bat, most physicists would use the bat's *center of mass* to reference the center of the bat in the

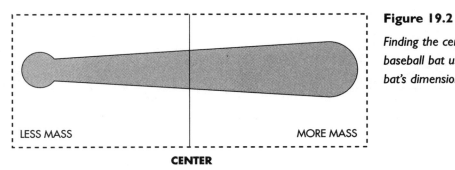

Figure 19.2

Finding the center of a baseball bat using the bat's dimensions.

LESS MASS   MORE MASS

CENTER

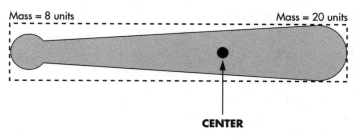

Mass = 8 units   Mass = 20 units

CENTER

Figure 19.3

Finding the center of a baseball bat using the bat's center of mass.

world. You can think of the center of mass as the balancing point of the object, as you see with the baseball bat shown in Figure 19.3.

By using an object's center of mass, you can get more accurate results from the physics equations that you use on the object. Keep in mind, however, that you need not always use an object's center of mass for the physics calculations in your games. Typically, the more advanced the physics are of a game, the more likely it is that the game's physics calculations use the object center of mass.

So what if you decide to use the center of mass in your calculations? How do you calculate it? Well, because you use objects that are created from vertices, you can assign weights to each vertex, where each weight represents the mass of the object at that vertex. To calculate the center of mass, you take the sum of each component of each vertex, multiply the component by its mass, and then divide the sum by the sum of all vertex masses. Sound complicated? Maybe some code will help:

```
float centerOfMass[3];              // (x = 0,y = 1,z = 2)
float object[NUM_VERTICES][3];      // object vertices
float objectMass[NUM_VERTICES];     // vertex weights
int i;                              // index counter
float totalMass = 0.0;
...
centerOfMass[0] = 0.0;
centerOfMass[1] = 0.0;
centerOfMass[2] = 0.0;

// calculate the total mass
for (i = 0; i < NUM_VERTICES; i++)
    totalMass += objectMass[i];

// calculate the total center of mass for all components
for (i = 0; i < NUM_VERTICES; i++)
{
```

```
        centerOfMass[0] += object[i][0] * objectMass[i];
        centerOfMass[1] += object[i][1] * objectMass[i];
        centerOfMass[2] += object[i][2] * objectMass[i];
}

// now divide the total mass for each component by the total mass of all vertices
centerOfMass[0] /= totalMass;
centerOfMass[1] /= totalMass;
centerOfMass[2] /= totalMass;

// center of mass in (x,y,z) form is
// (centerOfMass[0], centerOfMass[1], centerOfMass[2])
```

As mentioned, you don't *have* to use the center of mass in your calculations to maintain realism in your game. But if you are aiming for a higher degree of realism than that achieved by using the dimensional center of an object, then you will want to use the center of mass. In the examples that you'll be looking at, we will just keep things simple by using the dimensional center of objects.

Velocity

Velocity is how quickly an object is moving in a certain direction. More specifically, it is the change in position per change in time. Velocity is a vector because it has both magnitude (how fast) and direction. There are two types of velocity:

- Instantaneous velocity
- Average velocity

Instantaneous velocity is the velocity of an object at a specific point in time. For example, if you're in a car that is traveling at 20 meters per second (m/s), then the instantaneous velocity of the car at that moment equals 20 meters per second.

Average velocity is the average velocity of an object over a period of time. To calculate the average velocity of an object, you divide the displacement of the object by the total time that the object took to move that displacement. If you have displacement s, and time t, then the equation for velocity v looks like this:

$v = \Delta s / \Delta t = (s_f - s_i) / (t_f - t_i)$

So let's say you move an object 10 meters in one second. What is the velocity of the object? With the displacement equal to 10 meters, and the change in time equal to 1 second, you get

$v = \Delta s / \Delta t = 10 / 1 = 10 \text{ m/s}$

But how do you apply velocity to games? Although you might perform a bunch of other physics calculations on objects in the game world, everything boils down to how quickly the objects are moving, or their velocity. After determining an object's velocity, you can then proceed to calculate the new position of the object with respect to the change in time since the object last moved by using this equation:

$$X_f = X_i + v*\Delta t$$

which means

```
new position = old position + (velocity * change in time)
```

This equation says that an object starting at the position defined by X_i , with the velocity v, will be at the location defined by X_f after the time interval Δt has passed. Essentially, you're just adding the initial position of the object to the object's displacement after Δt has passed. Figure 19.4 attempts to illustrate this equation more clearly.

Acceleration

So far we've talked only about objects that move around at a constant velocity. Alas, very few, if any, objects move around in the real world this way. *Acceleration* is a vector that measures the rate of change in velocity.

To understand acceleration, look at the graphs shown in Figure 19.5. The first graph shows the plotting of velocity versus time when acceleration equals zero (a=0). When this occurs, you get a constant velocity, as shown through the horizontal line graph. Suppose, however, that you have a constant, positive, non-zero acceleration. In this case, you get a sloped line for the velocity because it steadily increases; if you were to measure the slope of the line, you would find that the slope equals the acceleration (remember, the slope is constant and acceleration is constant). The final graph shows a non-constant acceleration that continuously increases. This case results in the velocity increasing as a function of acceleration and resulting in a curve on the graph. You can find the acceleration at any point on the graph by finding the tangent slope of the curve at that point.

In physics, you define acceleration as the rate of change of velocity divided by the change in time:

$$a = \Delta v / \quad \Delta t = (v_f - v_i) / (t_f - t_i)$$

Because the unit meters per second (m/s) is used for velocity, the unit meters per second squared (m/s^2) is used for acceleration. This may seem confusing at first, but try to think of acceleration as the change in velocity per second, so you're getting meters per second, per second. If you apply this idea to determining the final velocity of an object v_f over a time period Δt, given its initial velocity v_i and the object's acceleration a, you get the following:

$$v_f = v_i + a*\Delta t$$

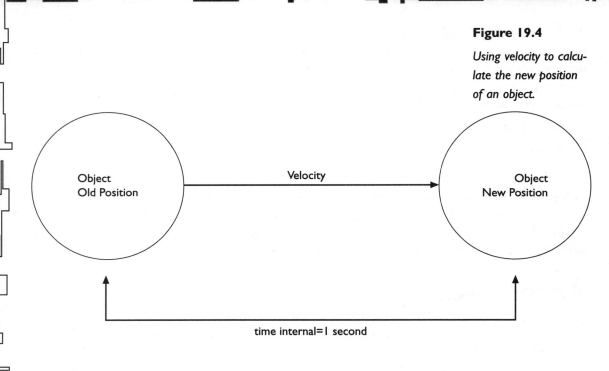

Figure 19.4

*Using velocity to calcu-
late the new position
of an object.*

Object
Old Position

Velocity

Object
New Position

time internal=1 second

which means

```
new velocity = old velocity + (acceleration * change in time)
```

You can then plug this new velocity into the equation you use to calculate an object's new position to move your object by using acceleration. As you can see, you've reached a point where you
can create a very basic physics model for your game; however, it's not time to do that yet. We still
have some more fun topics to cover!

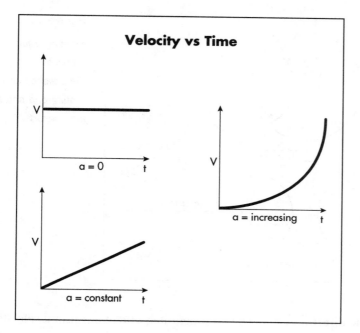

Figure 19.5

Graphs of velocity versus time with different acceleration cases.

Force

Force is probably the most important discovery in physics. It opens up a whole new physics world through which it is impossible to journey with regular kinematics equations of velocity and acceleration. Essentially, a *force* is a push or pull on an object. It can be defined as something that accelerates objects. For example, when you throw a baseball, you exert a force on the ball, as shown in Figure 19.6.

To understand force, you must understand Newton's Laws of Motion. There are three of them, and they define the basis for everything dealing with forces in the classical physics world.

Newton's First Law of Motion

Newton's First Law of Motion states the following: "Every object in a state of uniform motion tends to remain in that state of motion unless an external force is applied to it." In other words, if an object is at rest, meaning *it's not* moving, then that object will stay at rest unless a force is applied to it. If an object is in motion, meaning *it is* moving, then that object will stay in motion unless a force is applied to it. This law is also known as the *Law of Inertia*.

Suppose, for example, that you were in outer space, where there is no friction, no wind resistance, and nobody to interrupt your little experiment, and you pushed an object away from you.

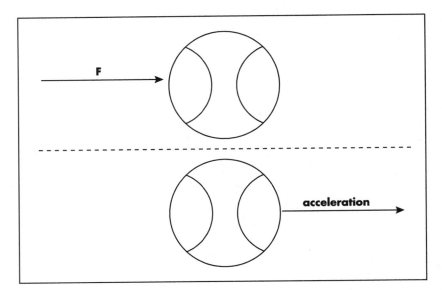

Figure 19.6

Exerting a force on a baseball results in the baseball accelerating and obtaining a velocity.

That object would travel in the direction you pushed it indefinitely and at a constant velocity (unless it ran into the moon or an asteroid or was sucked into a black hole). If you were to push an object on Earth away from you, chances are that the object would stop moving from external forces such as friction, wind resistance, gravity, and the like.

Newton's Second Law of Motion

Newton's Second Law of Motion states the following: "The relationship between an object's mass m, its acceleration a, and the applied force F is F = ma." The equation F = ma is essentially saying that force causes a change in velocity, because acceleration changes velocity.

Because mass is a scalar, and acceleration is a vector, then force is also a vector (scalar * vector = vector). This means that force has both a direction and a magnitude, with the force vector direction in the same direction as the acceleration vector. Lastly, you measure force in kg m/s^2, or Newtons (N).

Newton's Third Law of Motion

Newton's Third Law of Motion states the following: "For every action there is an equal and opposite reaction." This law seems to be the most remembered of the three, perhaps because it is one commonly witnessed in everyday life. For example, when you apply a force on a door, the door reacts by opening. Similarly, when you step off a boat onto a dock, the boat moves away from the dock in response to the force you exert on the boat as you step off.

Momentum

Momentum is the property of moving objects that measures both the velocity and mass of an object. It is defined as the product of velocity and mass:

```
momentum = mass * velocity
```

or

```
p = m*v
```

Both the equation for force and the equation for momentum can be related, because both force and momentum involve mass. If you solve for m in the equation for momentum, you get

```
m = p / v
```

If you take the equation for force and substitute p for m, you get

```
F = m*a
F = (p / v)*a
F = (p*a) / v
```

When you substitute a for dv/dt, or the rate of change of velocity with respect to time, you find that force equals the rate of change of momentum with respect to time, or

```
F = Δp / Δt
```

This means that when the momentum of an object changes, the force acting on the object changes as well. For example, if you throw a 1kg ball at a wall at a velocity of 3m/s, then the momentum equals

```
p = m*v = 3*1 = 3 kg m/s
```

You can then calculate the force of the ball hitting the wall. Suppose the ball takes 1 second to reach the wall, and you know that the final momentum of the ball at the point of impact equals 0, because the velocity of the ball equals 0. You then calculate:

```
F = Δp / Δt
F = (3 - 0) / (1 - 0)
F = 3 N
```

Conservation of Momentum

The beauty of momentum, however, is not just calculating it and knowing how much momentum an object has. Your use of momentum lies in what is known as the *conservation of momentum*, which you use when calculating the velocity of objects during collisions.

There are two types of collisions: perfectly elastic collisions and inelastic collisions. With perfectly elastic collisions, an object bounces off of a wall at the same velocity at which it hit the wall. In other words, the momentum of the object was conserved and the collision was perfectly elastic. Although this is great for keeping things simple, the real world normally doesn't work this way. Most collisions are inelastic collisions, which means that when the object strikes a wall, it loses some of the velocity it started with. The lost velocity, or energy, might be converted into heat from friction or into work if the object or wall gets deformed.

For now, we'll keep things simple and talk about perfectly elastic collisions in one dimension.

Let's start with two blocks that collide with each other in a perfectly elastic collision. Suppose you have blocks, A and B, each with its own mass and velocity. You can determine what happens after these two objects collide through the conservation of momentum:

$$m_a * v_{ai} + m_b * v_{bi} = m_a * v_{af} + m_b * v_{bf}$$

Your goal is to find the final velocities v_{af} and v_{bf}, but how do you do this when you have two unknown variables in the same equation? The answer: the *conservation of kinetic energy*. Kinetic energy measures the amount of total energy that a physical system has. You can compute it with this equation:

$$KE = [1/2] * m * v^2$$

You measure kinetic energy in Joules, or $kg * m^2 * v^2$. So how do you use kinetic energy? Well, the kinetic energy stays the same both before and after a collision, so in a perfectly elastic collision, you get

$$KE_{ai} + KE_{bi} = KE_{af} + KE_{bf}$$

$$[1/2] * m_a * v_{ai}^2 + [1/2] * m_b * v_{bi}^2 = [1/2] * m_a * v_{af}^2 + [1/2] * m_b * v_{bf}^2$$

Now you combine the equation for conservation of momentum with the equation for conservation of kinetic energy, and after some algebraic manipulation, you get the final velocities of each object:

$$v_{af} = (2 * m_b * v_{bi} + v_{ai} * (m_a - m_b)) / (m_a + m_b)$$

$$v_{bf} = (2 * m_a * v_{ai} - v_{bi} * (m_a - m_b)) / (m_a + m_b)$$

Looks like fun, eh? As you can see, you can calculate velocities of objects during collisions by using momentum and kinetic energy. You'll look at more of this when we discuss how to handle collisions, but for now, let's move on to another force you must deal with: friction.

Friction

Friction is any force acting on an object that causes the object to lose energy. You see and use friction everywhere in the world around you; in fact, chances are you couldn't hold this book if it weren't for friction.

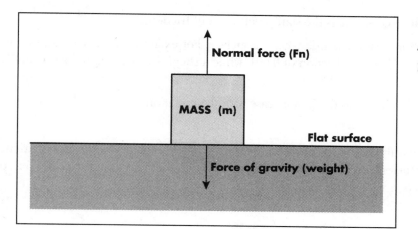

Figure 19.7

A basic model of friction.

To model friction, you use a frictional force on an object, which acts as a resistance in the opposite direction of motion to the object. Figure 19.7 shows the basic model of friction on a flat plane.

There are two cases of friction with which you must concern yourself:

- **Static.** The static case of friction occurs when the object is not moving. You use the static case to calculate the amount of force that you must overcome to move the object on the surface.
- **Kinetic.** The kinetic case occurs when the object is moving. The kinetic case is used to calculate the amount of force you must overcome to keep the object moving on the surface.

Before you can go much further with friction, you must understand the *normal force*. The normal force acts on any object that touches a surface. For example, a box sitting on the ground would have a normal force applied to it, but a box falling through the air would not. Going along with the definition of a normal, the normal force always acts perpendicular to the surface. You calculate the normal force with the equation

$F_N = -m*g$

where m is the mass of the object and g is the acceleration due to gravity, which on Earth is $-9.8m/s^2$. The calculation $m*g$ is also known as the *weight* of an object.

Friction on a Flat Surface

When you slide an object on a flat surface, a *friction force* acts on the object, eventually slowing it down to a stop. For static objects, you can use the friction force to determine how much force you must use to get the object moving. In this case, you use the equation

$F_f = \mu_s * F_N$

where F_N is the normal force and μ_s is the static coefficient of friction.

The coefficient of friction varies depending on the surface. For example, a surface without much friction might have a coefficient of friction of 0.001, while a rough surface might have a coefficient of friction of 0.9.

You calculate the frictional force in the kinetic case with the equation

$$F_f = \mu_k * F_N$$

Look familiar? Yep, the only difference between the static frictional force and the kinetic frictional force is that the coefficient of friction for moving objects is slightly less than the coefficient of friction for static objects.

Friction on an Inclined Plane

Calculating friction on a flat surface seems simple enough, but what about calculating friction on an inclined plane? Well, this gets a little more complex, and Figure 19.8 shows why.

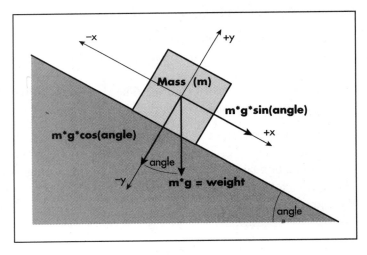

Figure 19.8

Friction on an inclined plane.

As you can see, you have your object with mass m on an inclined plane. Obviously, gravity is going to cause the object to slide. The inclined plane has the static and kinetic friction coefficients μ_s and μ_k, respectively, as well as a normal force that is perpendicular to the plane and acting on the object.

You also change the coordinate system so that the x axis is parallel to the inclined plane, and the y axis is perpendicular to the inclined plane (or parallel to the normal force). The positive x axis extends downward along the plane, in the direction that the object will move after it's released. The positive y axis extends outward from the plane.

To calculate the force of friction on the object on the inclined plane, you must calculate the sum of the forces along each axis. Along the positive x axis, you find that the force of gravity pushing the object equals

$F_g = m*g*sin [gt]$

Along the negative x axis, the force of friction pulling the object, or keeping it from sliding easily is

$F_f = -F_N*\mu_s$

You use the negative sign because the force of friction is working in the opposite direction of the force of gravity. With the object at equilibrium (not moving), the sum of the forces along the x axis equals 0, or

$\sigma Fx = m*g*sin [gt] - F_N*\mu_s = 0$

Calculating the forces along the y axis is similar. First you have the force of gravity along the y axis, equal to

$F_{g_.} = m*g*cos [gt]$

And then you have the normal force pushing on the object:

$F_f = F_N$

So the sum of the forces along the y axis equals

$\sigma Fx = F_N - m*g*sin [gt]$

Because the sum of the forces along the y axis is 0, you find that the normal force, F_N, equals the force due to gravity, or

$F_N = m*g*sin [gt]$

From here, you find

$(m*g*cos [gt])*\mu_s = m*g*sin [gt]$

$\mu_s = (m*g*sin [gt]) / (m*g*cos [gt])$

If you cancel out the m*g in the fraction, you get

$\mu_s = sin [gt] / cos [gt] = tan [gt]$

Now if you rearrange the equation and do a little substitution, you get an angle called the *critical angle*:

$[gt]_{critical} = tan^{-1} \mu_s$

The critical angle tells you the angle of the incline plane at which the object will start sliding. If there is a large amount of friction between the object and the surface, then the object will not slide when the surface incline is small.

So you have all these equations, but how do you use them in your game? Well, your final equation to calculate the force acting on an object as it slides down an incline is

```
F = m*g*sin [gt] - (m*g*cos [gt])*μₖ
```

Because $F = m*a$, you can find the acceleration of the object as

```
a = g*(sin [gt] - μₖ*cos [gt])
```

Almost there! Keep in mind that this acceleration is in the rotated coordinate system, so in order to use it in the "real" coordinate system, you must make a simple adjustment with sin and cos:

```
acceleration in x direction = cos [gt]*g*(sin [gt] - μₖ*cos [gt])
acceleration in y direction = sin [gt]*g*(sin [gt] - μₖ*cos [gt])
```

Then you just use these values for acceleration to calculate the velocity of the object as you did earlier, and voilà! You have friction.

MODELING THE REAL WORLD

If your goal is to simulate the real world, then just how do you do it? Well, presented here is one of many techniques that you can use to simulate in your games what happens in the real world.

You first must make a few assumptions. For one, you're going to use an object-oriented design (OOD) approach to modeling the real world. So if you're not familiar with C++ and object-oriented programming, now is a good time to learn it.

Also, be ready for some fun math! We're not going to go into heavy detail on the mathematical topics we cover, but if you're having trouble with any of the concepts presented, then be sure to search for more information on the Internet at the sites listed in Appendix A, "Online Resources."

Although the techniques we're going to cover may not be the best for performing certain functions, our goal is simplicity and flexibility combined into one.

Breaking Things Up

When trying to determine how to design a system, the first action you should take is to break every component into small parts so you can see all the pieces you have to work with. For instance, look at a football team. A football team is composed of many players, each of whom is supposed to accomplish a specific task. You have the kicker, quarterback, wide receiver, running back, and so on. Each player wears various pieces of equipment, such as a helmet, kneepads, and shoulder pads. If you were trying to model a football team, then you might use all these objects, as shown in Figure 19.9.

When modeling the world, you simply divide objects into smaller components, which in turn are divided into even smaller components, until the most basic component is found. Every object you create in your 3D world can be defined with three entities: a vector, a plane, and the object itself. We're going to look at each of these entities, but first we must discuss how to keep time in your virtual world.

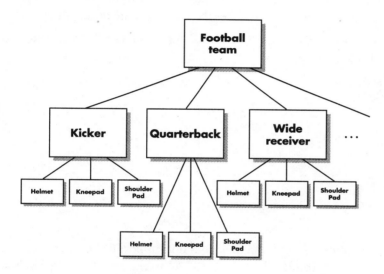

Figure 19.9

Modeling a football team by breaking things down into components.

Timing

Because time is an attribute of the real world, you should keep track of time in your game world as well. There are two ways you can keep track of time in your game: by frames or by real time. We're going to keep track of time using real time to get what is called *time-based modeling*.

To keep track of time, you use what is called a *timer* (surprise!). Using a timer enables you to handle more realistic physics calculations and keeps your calculations independent of the frame rate.

There are two types of timers you can use: a high-performance timer or the Windows messaging timer, WM_TIMER. The difference between the two is primarily speed and accuracy, with the high performance timer being better at both. Because speed and accuracy are important to a game, we're going to opt for the high-performance timer. If your computer does not support this type, you'll need to use WM_TIMER instead.

To use the high-performance timer, you first must determine how many ticks are in a second for the machine you're on, and then you must retrieve the current time on the machine and store it in a variable that represents the startup time of your application. You accomplish each of these tasks through the functions QueryPerformanceFrequency() and QueryPerformanceCounter(), which are defined as

```
BOOL QueryPerformanceFrequency(LARGE_INTEGER *lpFrequency);
BOOL QueryPerformanceCounter(LARGE_INTEGER *lpPerformanceCount);
```

The QueryPerformanceFrequency() function retrieves the frequency of the timer in ticks per second, and the QueryPerformanceCounter() function retrieves the current value of the timer.

Both of the functions take a parameter of type LARGE_INTEGER. This type is actually a structure that represents a 64-bit integer and is defined as

```
typedef union _LARGE_INTEGER
{
    struct
    {
        DWORD LowPart;
        DWORD HighPart;
    };
    LONGLONG QuadPart;
} LARGE_INTEGER;
```

As you can see, the structure is a union. If your compiler does not support 64-bit integers, then you can use the LowPart, HighPart fields (much like LOWORD, HIWORD) to retrieve the integer value. If your compiler *does* support 64-bit integers, then you can use the QuadPart field of type LONGLONG (64-bit signed integer).

Now you can declare two variables of type LARGE_INTEGER, which you can then use to retrieve the ticks per second and the current value of the timer:

```
LARGE_INTEGER ticksPerSecond;
LARGE_INTEGER startTime;
```

And then you can use the functions to retrieve the values:

```
if (!QueryPerformanceFrequency(&ticksPerSecond))
{
    // high performance timer not supported
    return false;
}
```

```
    else
    {
        // high performance timer supported
        QueryPerformanceCounter(&startTime);
        return true;
    }
```

Besides being able to keep track of time, you can also maintain a steady frame rate and determine the current frame rate. To provide all this functionality, you create a CHiResTimer class in *HiResTimer.h*, as shown here:

```
#ifndef __TIMER_H_INCLUDED__
#define __TIMER_H_INCLUDED__

#include <windows.h>

class CHiResTimer
{
public:
    CHiResTimer() {}
    ~CHiResTimer() {}

// Init()
// If the hi-res timer is present, the tick rate is stored and the function
// returns true. Otherwise, the function returns false, and the timer should
// not be used.
bool Init()
{
    if (!QueryPerformanceFrequency(&m_ticksPerSecond))
    {
        // system doesn't support hi-res timer
        return false;
    }
    else
    {
        QueryPerformanceCounter(&m_startTime);
        return true;
    }
} // end Init()
```

```cpp
// GetElapsedSeconds()
// Returns the total time in seconds (as a float) that has elapsed since the
// function was last called. elapsedFrames defines the number of frames that
// have elapsed since GetElapsedSeconds() was last called.
float GetElapsedSeconds(unsigned long elapsedFrames = 1)
{
    static LARGE_INTEGER s_lastTime = m_startTime;
    LARGE_INTEGER currentTime;

    QueryPerformanceCounter(&currentTime);

    float seconds = ((float)currentTime.QuadPart - (float)s_lastTime.QuadPart) /
                    (float)m_ticksPerSecond.QuadPart;

    // reset the timer
    s_lastTime = currentTime;

    return seconds;
} // end GetElapsedSeconds()


// GetFPS()
// Returns the average frames per second over elapsedFrames, which defaults to
// one. If this is not called every frame, the client should track the number
// of frames itself, and reset the value after this is called.
float GetFPS(unsigned long elapsedFrames = 1)
{
    static LARGE_INTEGER s_lastTime = m_startTime;
    LARGE_INTEGER currentTime;

    QueryPerformanceCounter(&currentTime);

    float fps = (float)elapsedFrames * (float)m_ticksPerSecond.QuadPart /
                ((float)currentTime.QuadPart - (float)s_lastTime.QuadPart);

    // reset the timer
    s_lastTime = currentTime;

    return fps;
} // end GetFPS
```

```cpp
// LockFPS()
// Used to lock the frame rate to a set amount. This will block until enough
// time has passed to ensure that the fps won't go over the requested amount.
// Note that this can only keep the fps from going above the specified level;
// it can still drop below it. It is assumed that if used, this function will
// be called every frame. The value returned is the instantaneous fps, which
// will be <= targetFPS.
float LockFPS(unsigned char targetFPS)
{

    if (targetFPS == 0)
        targetFPS = 1;

    static LARGE_INTEGER s_lastTime = m_startTime;
    LARGE_INTEGER currentTime;
    float   fps;

    // delay to maintain a constant frame rate
    do
    {

        QueryPerformanceCounter(&currentTime);
        fps = (float)m_ticksPerSecond.QuadPart/((float)(currentTime.QuadPart -
            s_lastTime.QuadPart));
    } while (fps > (float)targetFPS);

    // reset the timer
    s_lastTime = m_startTime;

    return fps;
} // end LockFPS()

private:
    LARGE_INTEGER    m_startTime;
    LARGE_INTEGER    m_ticksPerSecond;
};

#endif // __TIMER_H_INCLUDED_
```

As you can see, you have the methods Init() to initialize the timer, GetElapsedSeconds() to return the total time in seconds since the function was last called, GetFPS() to return the current frames per second, and LockFPS() to "lock" the number of frames that are displayed per second.

Now how do you use this thing? Well, first you must define a timer:

```
#include "HiResTimer.h"

CHiResTimer *timer = NULL;
```

Next, in the initialization of your game, you allocate the timer and initialize it with the CHiResTimer::Init() method:

```
timer = new CHiResTimer;
if (!timer->Init())
{
      // timer initialization failed
}
else
{
      // timer initialized
}
```

There are several ways you can use the other three methods, but we're only going to look at how to use CHiResTimer::GetElapsedSeconds() because you want to keep track of the amount of game time that has passed.

Because you must know how much time has passed every time you move an object, you can call the CHiResTimer::GetElapsedSeconds() method before you perform your physics calculations and render the current frame, as seen in the modified game loop shown in Figure 19.10.

To use the CHiResTimer::GetElapsedSeconds() method, you simply pass the number of frames that have passed since you last called the method and store the result in a variable that we'll call timeElapsed:

```
float timeElapsed;          // elapsed time since previous frame
...
timeElapsed = timer->GetElapsedSeconds(1);     // 1 frame has passed
// calculate physics
// e.g. DoPhysics(timeElapsed);
// render objects
```

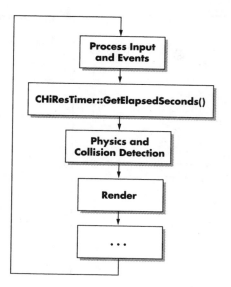

Figure 19.10

A simple game loop with a timer.

The Vector

The next entity you need is the vector. We first mentioned the vector back when we discussed the basics of 3D theory. Now we'll extend that discussion with more operations and ways that you can use a vector for modeling the real world.

What can you use a vector for? Well, remember that a vector defines both a magnitude (length) and a direction; so one use for the vector is as a data type for the entities in your physics equations. You can also use a vector to define a point in 3D space, because a point is essentially a vector that originates at (0,0,0), as illustrated in Figure 19.11.

You know what a vector is, but the important part is how you use it through vector operations. Vector operations can include vector addition, vector subtraction, vector-scalar multiplication, vector-scalar division, normalization, cross product, dot product, length, and vector reflection about a normal. The CVector class we're going to look at has these operations and more.

But before we look at the class, let's first define a scalar type, scalar_t, which we'll use to define a scalar value anywhere in the game code. In this case, we're defining a scalar to be of a float data type:

```
typedef float scalar_t;
```

Now you can use the scalar_t data type in your code for the CVector class. Here is the class in full, placed in *vector.h*:

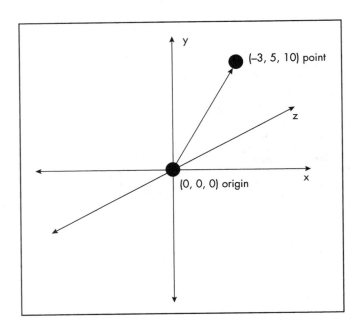

Figure 19.11

A point in 3D space can be defined as a vector.

```
#ifndef __VECTOR_H
#define __VECTOR_H

#include <math.h>

typedef float scalar_t;          // the scalar data type

// class CVector
// Special thanks to Bas Kuenen for some operator symbol ideas

class CVector
{
public:
    scalar_t x;        // x, y, z vector components
    scalar_t y;
    scalar_t z;

public:
    // constructors
    CVector(scalar_t a = 0, scalar_t b = 0, scalar_t c = 0)
    {
        x = a; y = b; z = c;
    }
```

```cpp
CVector(const CVector &vec)
{
    x = vec.x; y = vec.y; z = vec.z;
}

// Vector Assignment
const CVector &operator=(const CVector &vec)
{
    x = vec.x;
    y = vec.y;
    z = vec.z;

    return *this;
}

// Vector Equality
const bool operator==(const CVector &vec) const
{
    return ((x == vec.x) && (y == vec.y) && (z == vec.z));
}

// Vector Inequality
const bool operator!=(const CVector &vec) const
{
    return !(*this == vec);
}

// Vector Addition
const CVector operator+(const CVector &vec) const
{
    return CVector(x + vec.x, y + vec.y, z + vec.z);
}

// Vector Add
const CVector operator+() const
{
    return CVector(*this);
}

// Vector Increment
const CVector& operator+=(const CVector& vec)
```

```cpp
{
    x += vec.x;
    y += vec.y;
    z += vec.z;

    return *this;
}

// Vector Subtraction
const CVector operator-(const CVector& vec) const
{
    return CVector(x - vec.x, y - vec.y, z - vec.z);
}

// Vector Negation
const CVector operator-() const
{
    return CVector(-x, -y, -z);
}

// Vector Decrement
const CVector &operator-=(const CVector& vec)
{
    x -= vec.x;
    y -= vec.y;
    z -= vec.z;

    return *this;
}

// Scalar Multiply
const CVector &operator*=(const scalar_t &s)
{
    x *= s;
    y *= s;
    z *= s;

    return *this;
}
```

```cpp
// Scalar Division
const CVector &operator/=(const scalar_t &s)
{
    const float recip = 1/s;    // for speed

    x *= recip;
    y *= recip;
    z *= recip;

    return *this;
}

// Post Multiply by Scalar
const CVector operator*(const scalar_t &s) const
{
    return CVector(x*s, y*s, z*s);
}

// Pre Multiply by Scalar
friend inline const CVector operator*(const scalar_t &s, const CVector &vec)
{
    return vec*s;
}

// Divide by Scalar
const CVector operator/(scalar_t s) const
{
    s = 1/s;

    return CVector(s*x, s*y, s*z);
}

// Cross Product of This Vector and vec
const CVector CrossProduct(const CVector &vec) const
{
    return CVector(y*vec.z - z*vec.y, z*vec.x - x*vec.z, x*vec.y - y*vec.x);
}

// Cross Product (Thanks to Bas Kuenen for symbol idea!)
const CVector operator^(const CVector &vec) const
{
```

```cpp
        return CVector(y*vec.z - z*vec.y, z*vec.x - x*vec.z, x*vec.y - y*vec.x);
}


// Dot Product
const scalar_t DotProduct(const CVector &vec) const
{
        return x*vec.x + y*vec.x + z*vec.z;
}


// Dot Product
const scalar_t operator%(const CVector &vec) const
{
        return x*vec.x + y*vec.x + z*vec.z;
}


// Length of Vector
const scalar_t Length() const
{
        return (scalar_t)sqrt((double)(x*x + y*y + z*z));
}


// Return the Unit Vector of this Vector
const CVector UnitVector() const
{
        return (*this) / Length();
}


// Normalize this Vector
void Normalize()
{
        (*this) /= Length();
}


// Vector Length Operator
const scalar_t operator!() const
{
        return sqrtf(x*x + y*y + z*z);
}


// Return this Vector with the Specified length
const CVector operator | (const scalar_t length) const
```

```
        {
            return *this * (length / !(*this));
        }

        // Set Length of Vector Equal to length
        const CVector& operator |= (const float length)
        {
            return *this = *this | length;
        }

        // Return Angle Between this Vector and a Normal Vector
        const float inline Angle(const CVector& normal) const
        {
            return acosf(*this % normal);  // return arccos(this vector . normal)
        }

        // Reflect this Vector about a Normal Vector
        const CVector inline Reflection(const CVector& normal) const
        {
            const CVector vec(*this | 1);           // get unit vector
            return (vec - normal * 2.0 * (vec % normal)) * !*this;
        }
};  // end CVector

#endif
```

With the operator-overloading feature of C++, you can simplify the look of your code when performing vector operations. For instance, you can change this code from

```
CVector a, b;
CVector result;
...
result->x = a->x + b->x;        // add x component
result->y = a->y + b->y;        // add y component
result->z = a->z + b->z;        // add z component
```

to

```
CVector a, b;
CVector result;
...
result = a + b;                 // add the two vectors
```

Here are some more examples of using the CVector class operations:

```
CVector a, b;
CVector result;
result = a ^ b;                   // cross product
result = a->CrossProduct(b);      // another cross product
result = a % b;                   // dot product
a |= 10;                          // change vector so its length equals 10
b->Normalize();                   // normalize vector
result = a * 2.0;                 // scale vector by factor of 2 (multiply by 2)
```

The vector provides the basis of measurement and movement for the rest of your virtual world. You'll use it in everything from kinematics calculations to object positions to collision detection.

The Plane

Geometry class taught you that a plane is like a flat surface that extends infinitely in all directions, as seen in Figure 19.12. For example, if you cut a thin slice out of the entire universe, you'd have a plane. In games, a plane can represent a boundary, be part of an object, or be representative of a polygon.

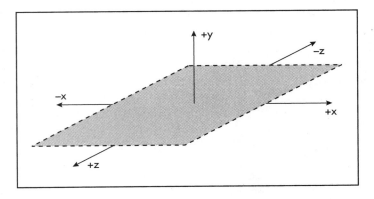

Figure 19.12

A plane extends infinitely in all directions.

The mathematical representation of a plane is defined by the equation

```
A*x + B*y + C*z - D = 0
```

where the vector components <A, B, C> define the normal vector of the plane, and <x, y, z> define points on the plane. The D is a scalar value, called the *plane-shift constant,* that specifies the distance of the plane from the origin of the world. Although this is basically all you must know to work with planes, you should understand where this equation comes from.

Look at the plane equation again, in this configuration:

```
A*x + B*y + C*z = D
```

Does the left side of the equation look familiar? If not, maybe this will help:

```
A . B = A.x*B.x*C.x + A.y*B.y*C.y + A.z*B.z*C.z
```

That's right, the plane equation is essentially the dot product of the plane normal and a point on the plane, which can be defined as a vector from the origin to the point. In this form, the equation looks like:

```
A . N = <Aₓ, A_y, A_z> . <Nₓ, N_y, N_z>
A . N = Aₓ* Nₓ + A_y* N_y + A_z* N_z
```

When you relate this equation to the previous plane equation, you see that

```
<A, B, C> = <Nₓ, N_y, N_z>
<x, y, z> = <Aₓ, A_y, A_z>
```

which, after substitution, results in

```
A*x + B*y + C*z
```

When you take the dot product of the plane's normal vector <A, B, C> and a point on the plane <x, y, z>, you get the plane-shift constant D:

```
A*x + B*y + C*z = D
```

or

```
A*x + B*y + C*z - D = 0
```

which is the plane equation.

Like we did with the vector, we'll implement a plane class called CPlane to represent each plane in the 3D world. This class will also provide several functions that can be used when working with planes, such as determining whether a point is on a plane, finding the distance of a point from a plane, and finding where a ray intersects with a plane.

To find the distance between a point and a plane, add the result of the dot product of the plane normal and the point vector to the plane-shift constant D. If the distance between the point and the plane is 0, then the point is on the plane. To find where a ray intersects with a plane, you must first know the ray's origin and direction. You then calculate the dot product of the normal of the plane and the ray's direction. If the result of the dot product is 0, then the ray is parallel to the plane and will never intersect it. Otherwise, you calculate the distance from the plane to the ray's origin, divide the result by the dot product of the plane normal and the ray's direction, multiply that result by the ray's direction, and then subtract the multiplication from the ray's origin. Sound like fun? Here's the code, as seen in *plane.h*:

```cpp
#ifndef __PLANE_H
#define __PLANE_H

#include "vector.h"

class CPlane
{
public:
    CVector N;        // plane normal
    double  D;        // plane-shift constant

    // constructors

    // Ax + By + Cz - D = 0
    CPlane(double a = 1, double b = 0, double c = 0, double d = 0)
    {
        N = CVector(a, b, c);
        D = d;
    }

    // instantiate a plane with normal Normal and D = d
    CPlane(const CVector& normal, double d = 0)
    {
        N = normal;
        D = d;
    }

    // instantiate a copy of Plane
    CPlane(const CPlane& plane)
    {
        N = plane.N;
        D = plane.D;
    }

    // instantiate a plane with three points
    CPlane(const CVector& vertexA, const CVector& vertexB, const CVector& vertexC)
    {
        CVector normalA((vertexC - vertexA) | 1.0);  // unit normal of C - A
        CVector normalB((vertexC - vertexB) | 1.0);  // unit normal of C - B
```

```cpp
        N = (normalA ^ normalB) | 1.0;      // normalize cross product
        D = -vertexA % N;                   // calculate distance
    }

    // assignment operator
    const CPlane& operator=(const CPlane& plane)
    {
        N = plane.N;
        D = plane.D;

        return *this;
    }

    // equality operator
    const bool operator==(const CPlane& plane) const
    {
        return N == plane.N && D == plane.D;
    }

    // inequality operator
    const bool operator!=(const CPlane& plane) const
    {
        return !(*this == plane);
    }

    // is point on this plane?
    const bool inline PointOnPlane(const CVector& point) const
    {
        return DistanceToPlane(point) == 0;
    }

    // return the distance of point to the plane
    const double inline DistanceToPlane(const CVector& point) const
    {
        return N % point + D;
    }

    // return the intersection point of the ray to this plane
    const CVector inline RayIntersection(const CVector& rayPos,
                                         const CVector& rayDir) const
```

```
        {
            const double a = N % rayDir;
            if (a == 0)
                    return rayPos;        // ray is parallel to plane

            return rayPos - rayDir * (DistanceToPlane(ryPos) / a);
        }
    };    // CPlane

#endif
```

Here are some examples of how you can use the CPlane class:

```
#include "plane.h"
...
CPlane *plane1 = NULL;
CPlane *plane2 = NULL;
...
plane1 = new CPlane(0.0, 1.0, 0.0, 5.0);            // instantiate plane pointing "up"
plane2 = new CPlane(plane1);                        // make plane1 a copy of plane2
plane1 = plane2;                                    // point plane1 to plane2
if (plane1->PointOnPlane(CVector(0.0, 5.0, 0.0))   // see if (0,5,0) is on plane1
{          /* point is on plane */ }
```

Try not to feel overwhelmed about planes at this point. We'll explain them in more depth when we discuss collision detection of objects in the world.

The Object

The most basic and recognizable entity in a world is the object. Objects can be boxes, walls, rooms, monsters, players, cameras, lights, and anything else that might be recognizable to you as an entity of the world. You can move them, interact with them, and allow them to interact with each other. Essentially, objects are what you can see and work with in the world.

When you try to classify what an object is, you find that all objects have a specific set of common attributes. The number of attributes that you define for the basic object normally depends on the application or game you are developing. Typically, however, you'll have a basic set of attributes to allow objects to move around and interact with each other. For instance, if you create a CObject class, you might have the attributes position, velocity, and acceleration. You might also want to store a bounding sphere radius for collision detection (we'll get to this later). The problem you run into, however, is that you can't define attributes to describe your object in detail. For example, if you define a crate with the CObject class, you can't define an attribute to hold the crate's dimensions. What happens if your world also has a door? You can't just create a dimension attribute for a door, because it's considered very poor design to create a single CObject class that has an attribute for every possible object in the world.

To combat this problem, you use the CObject class as a base class for all the objects in the world. For example, as shown in Figure 19.13, you use the functionality of C++ inheritance to derive CCrate and CDoor classes from the CObject class. When you do this, you get the entire base attributes of CObject included in the derived classes, and now you can add customized attributes to each of the derived objects. For instance, the door might have a door-knob location, or swing direction, while the crate can have the crate dimensions or crate textures. Using this approach even allows for different types of crates, such as metal and wood, and different types of doors, such as cloth and stone.

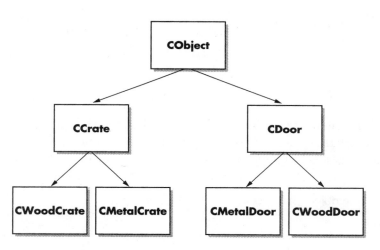

Figure 19.13

Using inheritance to derive crates and doors from CObject.

In your basic implementation of the CObject class, you'll keep track of four attributes: position, velocity, acceleration, and the size of the bounding sphere for collision detection. You'll also have methods to load the object into memory, unload it from memory, draw the object, and animate the object. So with this in mind, the CObject class looks like this (in *object.h*):

```
#ifndef __OBJECT_H
#define __OBJECT_H

#include "vector.h"

class CObject
{
```

```
public:
    CVector position;          // position of object
    CVector velocity;          // velocity of object
    CVector acceleration;      // acceleration of object
    scalar_t size;             // size of bounding sphere

public:
    CObject() {};              // constructor
    ~CObject() {};             // destructor

    virtual void Load() = 0;       // load into memory
    virtual void Unload() = 0;     // unload from memory
    virtual void Draw() = 0;       // draw object

    // animate object (physics calculations)
    virtual void Animate(scalar_t deltaTime) = 0;
};

#endif
```

As you can see, you define the functions Load(), Unload(), Draw(), and Animate() as pure virtual functions in order to force every derived class of CObject to provide its own implementation of these functions. If the derived class does not implement any one of these functions, then a compilation error will occur.

Now you can implement the crate object that we talked about earlier, CCrate:

```
#include "object.h"

class CCrate : public CObject
{
public:
    CCrate() {};
    ~CCrate() {};

    void Load()
    {
        //... load crate data into memory
    }

    void Unload()
    {
```

```
        //... free crate data from memory
    }

    void Draw()
    {
        //... draw the crate
    }

    void Animate(scalar_t deltaTime)
    {
        //... animate the crate; perform time-based physics calculations
    }

};
```

Handling Object Collisions

Collision detection and response is what we're interested in when trying to determine how objects in a world interact with each other. For instance, when you shoot a bullet at an enemy, how do you know if the bullet hits the enemy or the wall behind the enemy? Similarly, how do you keep the player within the walls and boundaries of the world?

Bounding Spheres

One of the easiest and most straightforward approaches to collision detection is by using *object-bounding spheres*. In this case, a hidden "collision sphere" surrounds every object in the world, with each sphere's radius equaling the length from the object's center to the vertex farthest away from the center. Figure 19.14 illustrates an object-bounding sphere.

Depending on the shape of your object, you might need to calculate the radius of the bounding sphere. In such a case, you simply loop through all the object's vertices and find the maximum distance from the center point of the object. During each loop iteration, you check whether the current vertex's distance is greater than the current maximum distance. If it is, you replace the maximum distance with the vertex's distance. Here's some sample code:

```
float FindBoundingSphereRadius(CVector *points, CVector center,
                               int numPoints)
{
    float currDist = 0.0;      // current distance
    float maxDist = 0.0;       // maximum distance
```

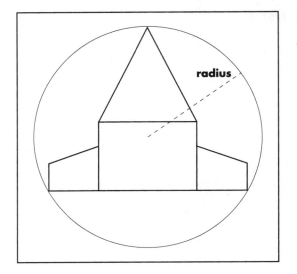

Figure 19.14

An object-bounding sphere.

```
// make sure we have a valid object
if (points == NULL)
    return -1.0;

// loop through all of the points in the object
for (int idx = 0; idx < numPoints; idx++)
{
    // calculate current vertex distance squares
    // with CVertex, could just do currDist = (points[idx] - center).Length()
    currDist = ((points[idx]->x - center.x)*(points[idx]->x - center.x)) +
               ((points[idx]->y - center.y)*(points[idx]->y - center.y)) +
               ((points[idx]->z - center.z)*(points[idx]->z - center.z));

    // check maximum distance
    if (currDist > maxDist)
        maxDist = currDist;
}

// return real distance
return sqrt(maxDist);
}
```

To use the bounding sphere approach, you check whether the distance between two objects is less than the sum of the two bounding sphere radii. For example, suppose you have an asteroid approaching a ship, as shown in Figure 19.15. You'll find that the two objects collide when the sum of the asteroid radius and the ship radius are less than or equal to the distance between the center of the asteroid and the center of the ship. If the sum of the radii is less than the distance, then the objects are not colliding.

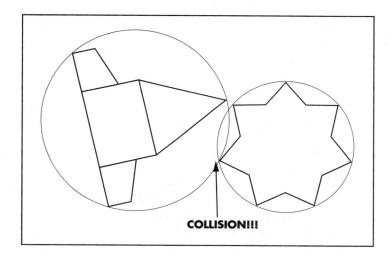

Figure 19.15

Using object-bounding sphere collision detection to determine whether two objects collide.

The bounding sphere approach is not without its limitations, however. For instance, what if you have an irregularly shaped object, where one side of the object is longer than the others, as shown in Figure 19.16? In this case, the bounding sphere would cover a large amount of space that the object does not, and you get imprecise collision detection.

Bounding Boxes

To combat this problem, you can try another approach called *bounding-box collision detection.* Instead of creating a sphere around the object, you create a box that surrounds all the object's extreme points along each axis. Figure 19.17 illustrates a bounding box around an object.

You create the bounding box in a similar manner to the way you created the bounding sphere, except this time you must find the box edges instead of a sphere radius. As shown in Figure 19.17, you can define the box with maximum and minimum vertices that are relative to the center of the object. To find these vertices, you simply check each vertex component with the minimum and maximum vertex component values and update these values as needed. In code, this looks like the following:

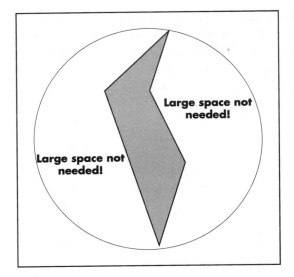

Figure 19.16

Applying a bounding sphere to an irregularly shaped object.

Large space not needed!

Large space not needed!

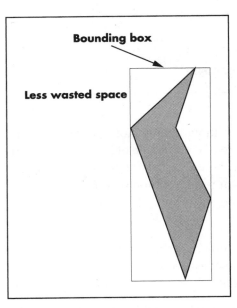

Figure 19.17

A bounding box around an object.

Bounding box

Less wasted space

```
void CalcBoundingBox(CVector *points, int numPoints, CVector *min, CVector *max)
{
    // make sure object is valid
    if (points == NULL)
        return;
```

```
// initialize mins/maxs to zero
min->x = min->y = min->z = 0.0;
max->x = max->y = max->z = 0.0;

// loop through all object vertices
for (int idx = 0; idx < numPoints; idx++)
{
    if (points[idx]->x > max->x)        // max x
        max->x = points[idx]->x;
    if (points[idx]->x < min->x)        // min x
        min->x = points[idx]->x;
    if (points[idx]->y > max->y)        // max y
        max->y = points[idx]->y;
    if (points[idx]->y < min->y)        // min y
        min->y = points[idx]->y;
    if (points[idx]->z > max->z)        // max z
        max->z = points[idx]->z;
    if (points[idx]->z < min->z)        // min z
        min->z = points[idx]->z;
}
}
```

This function will create what is called an *axis-aligned bounding box,* or AABB, which means that the sides of the box are parallel to the world x, y, and z axes. Determining whether an object collides with this type of box is rather simple, fast, and only requires a simple test. If you have an object for which you want to test collision, you simply do the following

```
if ( (object->x >= box.min->x && object->x <= box.max->x) &&
     (object->y >= box.min->y && object->y <= box.max->y) &&
     (object->z >= box.min->z && object->z <= box.max->z) )
{
    // collision occurred
}
```

The problem with bounding boxes is that, like bounding spheres, they are not accurate in many cases. Depending on the application or game you are developing, you might use bounding spheres and boxes as initial tests to see whether two objects even collide. Then, to determine the exact point of collision, you might use a hierarchy of smaller spheres or boxes that reside on the object.

A prime example of this technique would be in a 3D fighting game, where a kick to the face might have a different result than a kick to the abdomen. In the collision hierarchy, you might have a bounding sphere specifically for the face, another for the abdomen, another for the arms, and another for the legs. After first using a large bounding box or sphere on the entire fighter to see if any contact was made, you could then traverse through each of the smaller bounding spheres and boxes to find the "exact" point of collision. If the collision is in the face sphere, then the face is hit; but if the collision is in the abdominal sphere, then the abdomen is hit. The fighter could then react accordingly.

Plane Collisions

What do you do if neither spheres nor boxes are applicable to your situation? For example, how do you keep the camera and objects from moving through walls? You don't want to allow the player to walk through walls, and you *especially* don't want to allow monsters to do that.

To combat this, you must determine when an object has hit a wall and then keep the object from going past the wall (or make it respond as necessary). The trick is in realizing that walls, being made of polygons, are actually just planes with a defined boundary. In order to determine whether an object has collided with a plane, you simply check whether the object will cross the plane of the polygon you're checking against. If the object will cross the plane, then you calculate the exact intersection point on that plane and determine whether that intersection point is within the boundaries of the polygon. If so, then you have a collision.

As you can see, this type of collision detection does not apply strictly to walls, but to all polygons in the world. For instance, if you wanted to know the exact polygon where a laser strikes an enemy, you could apply this collision-detection test between the laser and the polygons of the enemy. Sound cool? Let's see how to do it.

We discussed planes and the plane equation earlier, but we created a few functions for the CPlane class that might have left you feeling a bit overwhelmed. Let's take another look at those:

```
// from CPlane...

// is point on this plane?
const bool inline PointOnPlane(const CVector& point) const
{
      return DistanceToPlane(point) == 0;
}

// return the distance of point to the plane
const double inline DistanceToPlane(const CVector& point) const
{
      return N % Point + D;
}
```

The first function you want to look at is DistanceToPlane(). This function returns the distance of a point that you pass as a parameter to the plane that the CPlane instance defines. To calculate the distance, you add the distance of the plane from the origin (D) to the dot product of the plane normal vector and the point vector. What you're interested in is the float value that this function returns. If this value is less than 0.0, then the point is "behind" the plane (opposite side of the plane normal); if this value is greater than 0.0, then the point is in "front" of the plane (same side as the plane normal). As the PointOnPlane() function determines, if the DistanceToPlane() function returns 0.0, then the point lies on the plane.

Applying these functions to collision detection is merely a matter of changing the context of the situation. For example, what if the point you're dealing with is actually the destination point of an object? First, you can execute the DistanceToPlane() function with the destination point to find the distance of the object from the plane after it has moved. Then, you can compare this value with the object's current distance from the plane. You have a collision with the plane if the current and destination values are opposite in their signed value (for example, 3.0 and –1.0), or if the destination point lies on the plane itself. For example, if the object is currently 5 units from the plane, and executing DistanceToPlane() on the destination point returns –0.05, then the object collides with the plane. If, however, the object is 3 units from the plane, and executing DistanceToPlane() on the destination point returns 0.01, then the object does *not* collide with the plane.

Just because the object collides with a plane does not mean that the object collides with the polygon. All we've discovered so far is that the object's current motion will pass through the polygon's plane. So what you must do now is check whether you hit the plane within the boundaries of the polygon through the RayIntersection() function from the CPlane class:

```
// return the intersection point of the ray to this plane
const CVector inline RayIntersection(const CVector& rayPos,
                                     const CVector& rayDir) const
{
     const double a = N % rayDir;    // plane normal . ray direction

     if (a == 0)
          return rayPos;             // ray is parallel to plane

     return rayPos - rayDir * (DistanceToPlane(rayPos) / a);
}
```

This function will return the point on the current CPlane instance where the ray defined by rayPos (the ray origin) and rayDir (direction of ray) intersect the plane. In your physics modeling, the ray origin can be viewed as the current object position, and the ray direction can be viewed as the object velocity. After you find out where you're going to collide on the plane, you have one final step to make sure you are going to collide with the actual polygon.

There are several methods for determining whether a point is inside a polygon; one involves creating a plane for each edge of the polygon you're testing, where the normals of each of these planes points toward the center of the polygon. You would then calculate the distance of this point from each of these planes. As long as the distance calculation returns values greater than 0.0, the point lies on the polygon. The problem with this approach is that it can be rather slow and requires a good bit of work.

Another method involves computing the sum of the angles between the point you're interested in and every point of the polygon. If the point lies inside the polygon, then the sum of the angles between the point and the polygon vertices will equal (or be very close to) 2*PI radians, or 360°, as shown in Figure 19.18.

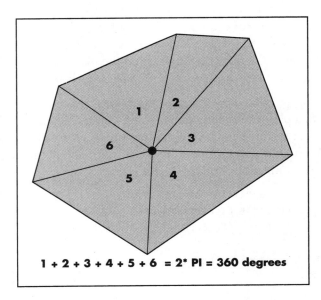

1 + 2 + 3 + 4 + 5 + 6 = 2* PI = 360 degrees

Figure 19.18

Determine whether a point lies in a polygon by calculating the angles between the point and each polygon vertex.

Here is a function that determines whether a point p lies in the polygon defined by points:

```
#define TWOPI 6.283185307179586476925287
#define RADTODEG 57.2957795
#define TOLERANCE 0.0000001
```

```cpp
// PointInPlane()
// desc: returns true if the point p is in the polygon consisting of
//       the points points.
bool PointInPolygon(CVector p, CVector *points, int numPoints)
{
    CVector segment1, segment2;     // vectors from point to boundary points
    double length1, length2;        // length of segments
    double sumAngles = 0.0;         // sum of angles between segments
    double cosAngle = 0.0;          // the cosine of the angle between two segments

    // loop through all points of the polygon
    for (int idx = 0; idx < numPoints; idx++)
    {
        // calculate the length of two segments from the point to the
        // points on the polygon
        segment1 = points[idx] - p;
        segment2 = points[(idx+1)%numPoints] - p;

        // check if point is on boundary
        if (segment1.Length() * segment2.Length() <= TOLERANCE)
        {
            sumAngles = TWOPI;      // we count boundary as "inside"
            break;
        }

        // calculate the cosine of the angle between the two segments
        cosAngle = (segment1 % segment2) / (segment1.Length()*segment2.Length());

        // add the angle to the angle sum
        sumAngles += acos(cosAngle);
    }

    // if sum of the angles is within our tolerance of 2*PI, then point is in polygon
    if ((sumAngles <= (TWOPI + TOLERANCE)) && (sumAngles >= (TWOPI - TOLERANCE)))
        return true;
    else
        return false;
}
```

If this function returns true, then you have a collision with the polygon.

Collision Response

After you know that you have a collision, you can calculate the collision response, which is how the object reacts to the collision. Different objects will respond differently to collisions, so there is no single way to perform collision response. There is, however, a generic method that will be sufficient for most collisions.

For example, think about the physics of the game of pool and how the balls bounce off the rails of a pool table. When a ball moving in a straight line collides with a rail, it will bounce away from the rail at the same angle that it strikes the rail, as shown in Figure 19.19. This angle is called the *angle of incidence* and is the angle between the ball movement vector and the plane of the rail.

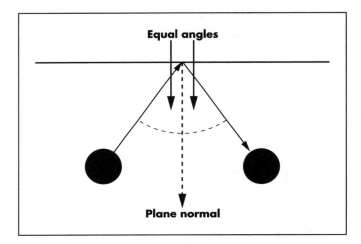

Figure 19.19

When a ball strikes the rail of a pool table, it bounces away from the rail at the same angle that it approached the rail.

Keep in mind that we're not taking into account any rotational forces that may be acting on the ball or any frictional forces between the rail and the ball. All we're concerned about is the general direction of the ball after it strikes the rail. We're also not worrying about the velocity of the ball because it will remain the same after the collision.

By using the ball's velocity vector and the normal vector to the rail, you can calculate the new direction of the ball after the collision has occurred. You can use the `CVector` function `Reflection()` to calculate the new velocity, as demonstrated by this code:

```
reflectedVelocity = velocity.Reflection(plane->normal);
```

Voilà! The object has responded to the collision.

An Example: Air Hockey

Let's apply what we've discussed so far to a game-like example. Shown in Figure 19.20 is a screen-shot of the air-hockey demo program that you are going to create. Although this demo is not a full-blown game, it does illustrate some of the basic concepts of physics modeling that we've been discussing throughout this chapter: basic physics with velocity, acceleration, friction, collision detection, and how to model the world with an object-oriented approach.

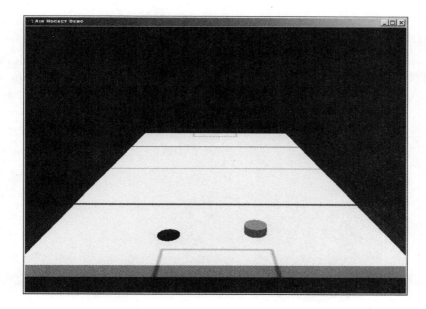

Figure 19.20

The air-hockey example.

The Air-Hockey World

Before we can look at the details of implementing the air-hockey table, we must discuss the design and overall framework of the system. As with most object-oriented systems, you first determine the objects that are in the world, and then you decide the structure that you're going to use to model them. In the case of the air-hockey table, you have the table object, puck object, and player object. We'll create a class for each of these objects and derive these classes from the CObject class that we discussed earlier. Figure 19.21 shows the structure of this system.

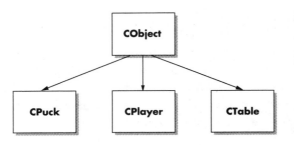

Figure 19.21

*The structure of the
air hockey system.*

The Hockey Table

The first component you're going to look at is the hockey table itself. The table restricts both the player and puck to a 300×500 area of the world through four planes that act as the walls of the table. A texture is also applied to give the table a more realistic look. You create the CTable class to represent the air-hockey table object, as seen here in *TABLE.H*:

```
#ifndef __TABLE_H
#define __TABLE_H

#include <windows.h>
#include <gl/gl.h>
#include <gl/glu.h>
#include <gl/glaux.h>
#include <math.h>
#include "vector.h"
#include "object.h"
#include "texture.h"
#include "plane.h"

/*
  CTable (derived from CObject)

  Description: The air-hockey table. Holds the table corner coordinates,
               table wall planes, and table texture.
*/

class CTable : public CObject
{
private:
    CTexture iceTex;                // table texture
```

```
public:
    float tableCorners[4][3];      // table corner coordinates
    CPlane tableWalls[4];          // table wall planes

    CTable()
    {
        position = CVector(0.0, 0.0, 0.0);
    }

    ~CTable() {}

    void Load();
    void Unload();
    void Draw();
    void Animate(scalar_t deltaTime);
    void SetupTexture();
};

#endif
```

As you can see, the CTable class holds the table-corner coordinates, the CPlanes for the table walls, and the texture (CTexture type) for the table. Because CTable is derived from CObject, it also inherits the position, velocity, acceleration, and size properties that all objects have, but you only end up using the position attribute to position the table in the world (at the 0,0,0 origin).

The first function we're going to look at from the CTable class is the SetupTexture() function, which loads and sets up the table texture for use with OpenGL. It assumes that you've already loaded the texture with the CTexture::LoadTexture() method (you do this in CTable::Load()).

```
// SetupTexture()
// desc: initialize the texture with OpenGL
void CTable::SetupTexture()
{
    // set the proper parameters (wrap repeat, linear filtering)
    glGenTextures(1, &iceTex.texID);
    glBindTexture(GL_TEXTURE_2D, iceTex.texID);
    glTexParameteri(GL_TEXTURE_2D,GL_TEXTURE_WRAP_S,GL_REPEAT);
    glTexParameteri(GL_TEXTURE_2D,GL_TEXTURE_WRAP_T,GL_REPEAT);
    glTexParameteri(GL_TEXTURE_2D,GL_TEXTURE_MIN_FILTER,GL_LINEAR);
    glTexParameteri(GL_TEXTURE_2D,GL_TEXTURE_MAG_FILTER,GL_LINEAR);
```

```
// set up texture based on the file-format type
// see texTypes_t in texture.h
switch (iceTex.textureType)
{
case BMP:              // BMP file format
    gluBuild2DMipmaps(GL_TEXTURE_2D, GL_RGB, iceTex.width, iceTex.height,
                      GL_RGB, GL_UNSIGNED_BYTE, iceTex.data);
    break;
case PCX:              // PCX file format
    gluBuild2DMipmaps(GL_TEXTURE_2D, GL_RGBA, iceTex.width, iceTex.height,
                      GL_RGBA, GL_UNSIGNED_BYTE, iceTex.data);
case TGA:              // no TGA support
    break;

default:
    break;
}
}
```

The SetupTexture() function is rather straightforward, as it only involves generating the texture object and setting the texture parameters before building the texture mipmaps (see Chapter 8, "Texture Mapping"). The mipmaps are built based on the texture's file format type (BMP or PCX), which is defined under texTypes_t in *TEXTURE.H*.

Next is the Load() function to set up and initialize the table corners, table walls, and texture.

```
// Load()
// desc: initialize table info and set up texture
void CTable::Load()
{
    // Initialize table corner coordinates (300x500)
    tableCorners[0][0] = 0.0;
    tableCorners[0][1] = 0.0;
    tableCorners[0][2] = 0.0;

    tableCorners[1][0] = 0.0;
    tableCorners[1][1] = 0.0;
    tableCorners[1][2] = -500.0;

    tableCorners[2][0] = 300.0;
    tableCorners[2][1] = 0.0;
    tableCorners[2][2] = -500.0;
```

```
        tableCorners[3][0] = 300.0;
        tableCorners[3][1] = 0.0;
        tableCorners[3][2] = 0.0;

        // Initialize the table walls (planes)
        // 0 = left, 2 = opposite, 1 = right, 3 = player
        // corners 1,0 left wall
        // corners 3,2 right wall
        // corners 2,1 opposite wall
        // corners 3,0 player wall
        tableWalls[0] = CPlane(
                    CVector(tableCorners[0][0], tableCorners[0][1], tableCorners[0][2]),
                    CVector(tableCorners[1][0], tableCorners[1][1], tableCorners[1][2]),
                    CVector(tableCorners[1][0], 10.0, tableCorners[1][2])
                    );

        tableWalls[1] = CPlane(
                    CVector(tableCorners[2][0], tableCorners[2][1], tableCorners[2][2]),
                    CVector(tableCorners[3][0], tableCorners[3][1], tableCorners[3][2]),
                    CVector(tableCorners[3][0], 10.0, tableCorners[3][2])
                    );

        tableWalls[2] = CPlane(
                    CVector(tableCorners[1][0], tableCorners[1][1], tableCorners[1][2]),
                    CVector(tableCorners[2][0], tableCorners[2][1], tableCorners[2][2]),
                    CVector(tableCorners[2][0], 10.0, tableCorners[2][2])
                    );

        tableWalls[3] = CPlane(
                    CVector(tableCorners[3][0], tableCorners[3][1], tableCorners[3][2]),
                    CVector(tableCorners[0][0], tableCorners[0][1], tableCorners[0][2]),
                    CVector(tableCorners[0][0], 10.0, tableCorners[0][2])
                    );

        // Load and initialize the texture
        iceTex.LoadTexture("table.bmp");
        SetupTexture();
}
```

In this function you define the four table-corner coordinates and build the table-wall planes based on the table corners. The table walls are given a height of 10 units. Lastly, you load the texture and set it up for OpenGL through the SetupTexture() function.

Next up is the Draw() function that performs the actual rendering of the textured air-hockey table:

```
// Draw()
// desc: draws the table at its current position
void CTable::Draw()
{
    // draw hockey table
    glPushMatrix();
        glTranslatef(position.x, position.y, position.z);

        // draw table floor
        glColor3f(1.0, 1.0, 1.0);
        // bind table texture and render table "floor"
        glBindTexture(GL_TEXTURE_2D, iceTex.texID);
        glBegin(GL_TRIANGLE_STRIP);
            glTexCoord2f(1.0, 1.0);
            glVertex3fv(&tableCorners[3][0]);
            glTexCoord2f(0.0, 1.0);
            glVertex3fv(&tableCorners[2][0]);
            glTexCoord2f(1.0, 0.0);
            glVertex3fv(&tableCorners[0][0]);
            glTexCoord2f(0.0, 0.0);
            glVertex3fv(&tableCorners[1][0]);
        glEnd();

        // enable blending for walls
        glEnable(GL_BLEND);
        glDepthMask(GL_FALSE);
        glBlendFunc(GL_SRC_ALPHA, GL_ONE);

        // draw walls in dark bluish color
        glColor4f(0.0, 0.1, 0.3, 1.0);

        // left side
        glBegin(GL_TRIANGLE_STRIP);
            glVertex3fv(&tableCorners[1][0]);
            glVertex3f(tableCorners[1][0], 10.0, tableCorners[1][2]);
```

```
        glVertex3fv(&tableCorners[0][0]);
        glVertex3f(tableCorners[0][0], 10.0, tableCorners[0][2]);
    glEnd();

    // right side
    glBegin(GL_TRIANGLE_STRIP);
        glVertex3fv(&tableCorners[3][0]);
        glVertex3f(tableCorners[3][0], 10.0, tableCorners[3][2]);
        glVertex3fv(&tableCorners[2][0]);
        glVertex3f(tableCorners[2][0], 10.0, tableCorners[2][2]);
    glEnd();

    // opposite side
    glBegin(GL_TRIANGLE_STRIP);
        glVertex3fv(&tableCorners[2][0]);
        glVertex3f(tableCorners[2][0], 10.0, tableCorners[2][2]);
        glVertex3fv(&tableCorners[1][0]);
        glVertex3f(tableCorners[1][0], 10.0, tableCorners[1][2]);
    glEnd();

    // player side (transparent)
    glBlendFunc(GL_SRC_ALPHA, GL_ONE_MINUS_SRC_ALPHA);
    glColor4f(0.0, 0.1, 0.3, 0.6);
    glBegin(GL_TRIANGLE_STRIP);
        glVertex3fv(&tableCorners[3][0]);
        glVertex3f(tableCorners[3][0], 10.0, tableCorners[3][2]);
        glVertex3fv(&tableCorners[0][0]);
        glVertex3f(tableCorners[0][0], 10.0, tableCorners[0][2]);
    glEnd();

    // re-enable depth testing, disable blending
    glDepthMask(GL_TRUE);
    glDisable(GL_BLEND);
    glPopMatrix();
}
```

This function draws the table "floor" (textured) and walls. When drawing the table wall closest to the camera, you enable blending so you can see the puck as it hits the wall; otherwise, a portion of the puck would completely disappear until it hit the wall and came back into view. Not that this is a bad thing, but it's much cooler to have a little transparency!

And finally, you have the Unload() function. All this function does is call the CTexture::Unload() method to free the texture from memory:

```
// Unload()
// desc: free texture
void CTable::Unload()
{
    iceTex.Unload();
}
```

The Puck and Time-Based Collision

Now for the object that is at the heart of the air-hockey demo: the puck. The puck is a cylinder that sits slightly above the table (a representation of the air cushion created by the table) and moves around the table within the restrictions of the table walls. The puck's movement is affected both by these walls and by the player, which we haven't discussed yet. You also apply some friction between the puck and the table so it doesn't move around forever; it should eventually come to a stop.

Besides the normal CObject attributes (position, velocity, acceleration, size), you store the radius of the puck in the CPuck class to help you with collision detection and rendering. You also define the data points for the puck in a variable external to the CPuck class. As they are set up, the data points define two circles with radii of 1.0 and a vertical separation of 0.6 units. When you draw the puck, however, it will be a single, solid cylinder. The data points and the definition of the CPuck class is listed here from *PUCK.H*:

```
#ifndef __PUCK_H
#define __PUCK_H

#include <windows.h>
#include <stdio.h>
#include <stdlib.h>
#include <math.h>
#include <gl/gl.h>
#include <gl/glu.h>
#include <gl/glaux.h>
#include "object.h"
#include "vector.h"
#include "table.h"
```

```cpp
// data points for puck
static float puckData[32][3] =
    // bottom points
    { { 0.0, 0.01, 1.0 }, { 0.3827, 0.01, 0.9239 },
    { 0.7071, 0.01, 0.7071 }, { 0.9239, 0.01, 0.3827 }, { 1.0, 0.01, 0.0 },
    { 0.9239, 0.01, -0.3827 }, { 0.7071, 0.01, -0.7071 }, { 0.3827, 0.01, -0.9239 },
    { 0.0, 0.01, -1.0 }, { -0.3827, 0.01, -0.9239 }, { -0.7071, 0.01, -0.7071 },
    { -0.9239, 0.01, -0.3827 }, { -1.0, 0.01, 0.0 }, { -0.9237, 0.01, 0.3827 },
    { -0.7071, 0.01, 0.7071 }, { -0.3827, 0.01, 0.9239 },

    // top points
    { 0.0, 0.07, 1.0 }, { 0.3827, 0.07, 0.9239 },
    { 0.7071, 0.07, 0.7071 }, { 0.9239, 0.07, 0.3827 }, { 1.0, 0.07, 0.0 },
    { 0.9239, 0.07, -0.3827 }, { 0.7071, 0.07, -0.7071 }, { 0.3827, 0.07, -0.9239 },
    { 0.0, 0.07, -1.0 }, { -0.3827, 0.07, -0.9239 }, { -0.7071, 0.07, -0.7071 },
    { -0.9239, 0.07, -0.3827 }, { -1.0, 0.07, 0.0 }, { -0.9237, 0.07, 0.3827 },
    { -0.7071, 0.07, 0.7071 }, { -0.3827, 0.07, 0.9239 } };


class CPuck : public CObject
{
private:
    float radius;                   // puck radius

public:

    CPuck()
    {
        acceleration = CVector(0.0, 0.0, 0.0);
        velocity = CVector(50.0, 0.0, 100.0);
        position = CVector(150.0, 0.0, -200.0);
        radius = 10.0; size = radius;
    }


    CPuck(float r)
    {
        radius = r; size = r;
        acceleration = CVector(0.0, 0.0, 0.0);
        velocity = CVector(50.0, 0.0, 100.0);
        position = CVector(150.0, 0.5, -200.0);
    }
```

```
        ~CPuck() {}

        void Load();
        void Unload();

        void Draw();
        void Animate(scalar_t deltaTime);
        void Animate(scalar_t deltaTime, CTable *table);
};
```

```
#endif
```

You might notice that there is a second Animate() function in the CPuck class. This function was created with a second parameter, table, which defines the air-hockey table to which this puck belongs and is used in the Animate() function for collision detection.

Because only the Draw() and Animate() functions are actually used by the CPuck class (and because the Draw() function is rather self-explanatory), here is the full listing from *PUCK.CPP*:

```
#include "puck.h"

// Load()
// desc: not used by CPuck
void CPuck::Load()
{
    // override virtual function
}

// Unload()
// desc: not used by CPuck
void CPuck::Unload()
{
    // override virtual function
}

// Draw()
// desc: renders the puck as a solid cylinder
void CPuck::Draw()
{
    glPushMatrix();
        glTranslatef(position.x, position.y, position.z);
```

```
            glScalef(radius, radius, radius);
            glColor3f(0.0, 0.0, 0.0);                    // black

            // draw side ring of puck
            glBegin(GL_TRIANGLE_STRIP);
            for (int i = 0; i < 16; i++)
            {
                    glVertex3fv(&puckData[i+16][0]); // top
                    glVertex3fv(&puckData[i][0]);    // bottom
            }
            glVertex3fv(&puckData[16][0]);
            glVertex3fv(&puckData[0][0]);
            glEnd();

            // draw top and bottom of puck
            glBegin(GL_TRIANGLE_FAN);
                glVertex3f(0.0, puckData[0][1], 0.0);
                for (i = 0; i < 16; i++)
                    glVertex3fv(&puckData[i][0]);
                glVertex3fv(&puckData[0][0]);
            glEnd();
            glBegin(GL_TRIANGLE_FAN);
                glVertex3f(0.0, puckData[31][1], 0.0);
                for (i = 16; i < 32; i++)
                    glVertex3fv(&puckData[i][0]);
                glVertex3fv(&puckData[16][0]);
            glEnd();

    glPopMatrix();
}


// Animate()
// desc: overridable version not used by CPuck
void CPuck::Animate(scalar_t deltaTime)
{
    // just used to override virtual function
}


// Animate()
// desc: handles physics and collision detection
//       within table space defined by table
```

```
void CPuck::Animate(scalar_t deltaTime, CTable *table)
{
      // recursion condition
      if (deltaTime <= 0) return;

      double fastestTime = deltaTime;              // time of collision
      CPlane *planeCollision = NULL;               // the plane to collide with

      // check collision for each table wall
      for (int idx = 0; idx < 4; idx++)
      {
          CPlane *plane = &table->tableWalls[idx];  // set plane to current wall
          double collisionTime;
          double a, b, c;                  // quadratic equation!coefficients

          // dot product - quadratic equation
          a = plane->N % (acceleration * 0.5);
          b = plane->N % velocity;
          c = plane->N % position + plane->D - radius; // radius - bounding sphere

          // no acceleration is a straight line graph
          // a.k.a. first degree (line) equation of the form:
          // 0 = bx + c
          if (a == 0)
          {
              if (b != 0 && c != 0)     // must have velocity (b)
              {
                  // time of collision equals distance (position)
                  // divided by velocity
                  collisionTime = -c/b;
                  if (collisionTime >= 0 && collisionTime < fastestTime)
                  {
                      fastestTime = collisionTime;  // save collision time
                      planeCollision = plane;
                  }
              }
          }
          else
          {
              // if we have acceleration (does not equal 0)
```

```cpp
        // calculate the determinant (b^2 - 4*a*c)
        double D = b*b - 4*a*c;

        // there is a solution if determinant is greater than or equal to zero
        if (D >= 0)
        {
            // solve the quadratic equation. since time cannot be negative,
            // we drop the negative solution
            collisionTime = (- b - sqrt(D)) / (2*a);
            if (collisionTime >= 0.0 && collisionTime < fastestTime)
            {
                fastestTime = collisionTime;
                planeCollision = plane;
            }
        }  // if (D >= 0)
    } // if (a == 0)
} // for

// if we're moving, apply friction (coefficient = 0.2)
if (velocity.Length() > 0.0)
    acceleration = -velocity * 0.2;

// move to collision point & set velocity there
position += velocity * fastestTime +
        acceleration * (fastestTime*fastestTime*0.5);
velocity += acceleration * fastestTime;

// only allow velocity to max out at 800
if (velocity.Length() > 800.0)
    velocity |= 800.0;        // set velocity equal to 800

// if we had a collision, reflect the velocity vector
if (planeCollision)
{
    velocity = velocity.Reflection(planeCollision->N);
}

// recursively call function to find exact moment of collision
Animate(deltaTime - fastestTime, table);
}
```

So, how does all this collision-detection stuff going on in the Animate() function work? Well, you might notice that the approach used here is not the same approach we discussed earlier. In the Animate() function here, you take a time-based approach to collision detection through this second-degree equation:

$x_f = x_0 + v_0*t + [1/2]*a*t^2$

This equation might look a little bit more familiar as

$a*x^2 + b*x + c = 0$

which is the quadratic equation. With substitution, you get

$a = [1/2]*a$

$b = v_0$

$c = x_0 - x_f$

The first equation is actually a two-dimensional, time-based motion equation. So let's extend it to the third dimension with these equations:

$x_t = c_x + b_x*t + a_x*t^2$

$y_t = c_y + b_y*t + a_y*t^2$

$z_t = c_z + b_z*t + a_z*t^2$

If you apply these to the plane equation, you get

$A*x_t + B*y_t + C*z_t + D = 0$

This equation tells you that if there is a collision between the object and the plane, then the point of collision will be located at the point (x_t, y_t, z_t). With a little substitution and algebraic manipulation, you find that

$(A*a_x + B*a_y + C*a_z)*x^2 + (A*b_x + B*b_y + C*b_z)*x + (A*c_x + B*c_y + C*c_z) + D = 0$

which is essentially the quadratic equation with the plane equation terms $(a*x^2 + b*x + c = 0)$. You may recognize the dot product in this equation:

$a*x^2 = (A*a_x + B*a_y + C*a_z)*x^2 = \mathbf{N} . ([1/2]*\mathbf{A})$

With the dot product, you can find the quadratic coefficients:

$a = \mathbf{N} . (\mathbf{A}*0.5)$

$b = \mathbf{N} . \mathbf{V}$

$c = \mathbf{N} . \mathbf{X} + D$

With these quadratic coefficients, you can calculate the time of collision. There are actually two different cases that you must handle for calculating the collision time: when you have acceleration, and when you don't have acceleration.

If you find that the quadratic coefficient for acceleration (a) equals 0.0, then the object has no acceleration, and you can find the time of collision by dividing the position coefficient (c) by the velocity coefficient (b), as seen in this block of code from the `Animate()` function:

```
if (a == 0)
    {
        if (b != 0 && c != 0)      // must have velocity (b)
        {
            // time of collision equals distance (position)
            // divided by velocity
            collisionTime = -c/b;
            if (collisionTime >= 0 && collisionTime < fastestTime)
            {
                fastestTime = collisionTime;  // save collision time
                planeCollision = plane;
            }
        }
    }
}
...
```

You negate the collision time because the position coefficient turns out to be less than zero because of the plane-shift constant. You then make sure that the collision is happening within the current change in time, and if it is you save the time of collision and the plane that the collision will be taking place.

If you do have acceleration, you can use the solution to the quadratic equation to determine the time of collision:

```
x₁,₂ = (-b +/- sqrt(b² - 4*a*c)) / 2*a
```

Before you even attempt to calculate the time of collision using the quadratic equation, however, you can first determine whether there is a solution by calculating the determinant:

```
D = b² - 4*a*c
```

If the determinant, D, is less than 0, then there is no solution. If it equals 0, there is one solution, and if it is greater than or equal to 0, there are two solutions. You're only interested in one time of collision, so you drop the negative solution (there is no negative time of collision) and just calculate the time of collision with one equation, as seen in this block of code:

```
// if we have acceleration (does not equal 0)
// calculate the determinant (b^2 - 4*a*c)
double D = b*b - 4*a*c;
```

```
// there is a solution if determinant is greater than or equal to zero
if (D >= 0)
{
    // solve the quadratic equation; since time cannot be negative,
    // we drop the negative solution
    collisionTime = (-b - sqrt(D)) / (2*a);
    if (collisionTime >= 0.0 && collisionTime < fastestTime)
    {
        fastestTime = collisionTime;
        planeCollision = plane;
    }
}  // if (D >= 0)
```

After determining the time of collision, the force of friction is applied as a deceleration force. Then, you use the normal velocity and position equations to calculate the new velocity and new position of the puck. To keep the puck from moving too quickly for anybody to handle, its velocity is limited to 800 units (via vector length).

Finally, you may have noticed that the Animate() function is recursive. This is done so you find the exact moment of collision. For instance, if the time of collision is less than the amount of time that has passed for the current frame when you get to the recursive call, then you are going to need to calculate the position of the object after the collision has already occurred and before the next frame is drawn—all of which is done by recursively calling the Animate() function. On the other hand, if the collision occurs exactly when the next frame is going to be drawn, then you don't need to worry about calculating the position of the puck after the collision has occurred because the vector has already been reflected.

If this seems confusing, then try stepping through the code by hand and watch how the values change. Although time-based collision detection and response might seem overwhelming at first (and it is), by repeatedly going over it, you'll find that it is actually somewhat easy to work with.

Also note that you treat the four table walls as infinite planes when performing collision detection because you don't check collision with the plane inside a specific boundary (as with a polygon). You do this because the table acts as an enclosed box where each wall prevents the puck from moving beyond the boundaries of the other walls. Hence, you don't need to worry about where the puck hits on each wall's plane—you only need to worry about whether the puck hits the wall.

The Player

The player is the interactive part of the demo and is represented by another cylinder that can be moved around the table with the mouse. Like the puck, you store the radius of the player for use when rendering. You also keep track of the old mouse coordinates so you know how far the player should move and in which direction. Here's the player cylinder data coordinates and the CPlayer class from *PLAYER.H*:

```c
#ifndef __PLAYER_H
#define __PLAYER_H

#include <windows.h>
#include <stdio.h>
#include <stdlib.h>
#include <math.h>
#include <gl/gl.h>
#include <gl/glu.h>
#include <gl/glaux.h>
#include "object.h"
#include "vector.h"
#include "table.h"
#include "puck.h"

static float playerData[32][3] =
     // bottom points
     { { 0.0, 0.01, 1.0 }, { 0.3827, 0.01, 0.9239 },
     { 0.7071, 0.01, 0.7071 }, { 0.9239, 0.01, 0.3827 }, { 1.0, 0.01, 0.0 },
     { 0.9239, 0.01, -0.3827 }, { 0.7071, 0.01, -0.7071 }, { 0.3827, 0.01, -0.9239 },
     { 0.0, 0.01, -1.0 }, { -0.3827, 0.01, -0.9239 }, { -0.7071, 0.01, -0.7071 },
     { -0.9239, 0.01, -0.3827 }, { -1.0, 0.01, 0.0 }, { -0.9237, 0.01, 0.3827 },
     { -0.7071, 0.01, 0.7071 }, { -0.3827, 0.01, 0.9239 },

     // top points
     { 0.0, 0.8, 1.0 }, { 0.3827, 0.8, 0.9239 },
     { 0.7071, 0.8, 0.7071 }, { 0.9239, 0.8, 0.3827 }, { 1.0, 0.8, 0.0 },
     { 0.9239, 0.8, -0.3827 }, { 0.7071, 0.8, -0.7071 }, { 0.3827, 0.8, -0.9239 },
     { 0.0, 0.8, -1.0 }, { -0.3827, 0.8, -0.9239 }, { -0.7071, 0.8, -0.7071 },
     { -0.9239, 0.8, -0.3827 }, { -1.0, 0.8, 0.0 }, { -0.9237, 0.8, 0.3827 },
     { -0.7071, 0.8, 0.7071 }, { -0.3827, 0.8, 0.9239 } };

class CPlayer : public CObject
{
private:
     float radius;
     int oldMouseX;
     int oldMouseY;
```

```
public:
    CPlayer()
    {
        acceleration = CVector(0.0, 0.0, 0.0);
        velocity = CVector(0.0, 0.0, 0.0);
        position = CVector(150.0, 0.0, -110.0);
        oldMouseX = 0;
        oldMouseY = 0;
        radius = size = 10.0;
    }

    ~CPlayer() {}

    void Draw();
    void Load();
    void Unload();
    void Animate(scalar_t deltaTime);

    void Move(scalar_t deltaTime, int mouseX, int mouseY, CTable *table,
            CPuck *puck);
};

#endif
```

Instead of using the Animate() function to move the mouse around, you have a new Move() function that will move the player based on the movements of the mouse and will perform collision detection with the table and puck.

With the exception of the Move() function, the CPlayer class is much like the CPuck class. Here is the implementation of the CPlayer class from *PLAYER.CPP*:

```
#include "player.h"

// Load()
// desc: not used by CPlayer
void CPlayer::Load()
{}

// Unload()
// desc: not used by CPlayer
void CPlayer::Unload()
{}
```

```cpp
// Draw()
// desc: draws the player at its current position
void CPlayer::Draw()
{
     glPushMatrix();
          glTranslatef(position.x, position.y, position.z);
          glScalef(radius, radius, radius);
          glColor3f(0.5, 0.0, 0.0);

          // draw side ring of player
          glBegin(GL_TRIANGLE_STRIP);
          for (int i = 0; i < 16; i++)
          {
               glVertex3fv(&playerData[i+16][0]); // top
               glVertex3fv(&playerData[i][0]);    // bottom
          }
          glVertex3fv(&playerData[16][0]);
          glVertex3fv(&playerData[0][0]);
          glEnd();

          glColor3f(0.5, 0.5, 0.5);
          // draw top and bottom of player
          glBegin(GL_TRIANGLE_FAN);
               glVertex3f(0.0, playerData[0][1], 0.0);
               for (i = 0; i < 16; i++)
                    glVertex3fv(&playerData[i][0]);
               glVertex3fv(&playerData[0][0]);
          glEnd();
          glBegin(GL_TRIANGLE_FAN);
               glVertex3f(0.0, playerData[31][1], 0.0);
               for (i = 16; i < 32; i++)
                    glVertex3fv(&playerData[i][0]);
               glVertex3fv(&playerData[16][0]);
          glEnd();
     glPopMatrix();
}

// Animate()
// desc: not used by CPlayer
void CPlayer::Animate(scalar_t deltaTime)
{}
```

```
// Move()
// desc: moves the player on the table based on the movements of the mouse
//       performs collision detection with puck
void CPlayer::Move(scalar_t deltaTime, int mouseX, int mouseY, CTable *table,
                   CPuck *puck)
{
      int xDiff, yDiff;           // distance mouse has moved in mouse coordinate units

      // calculate distance mouse has moved
      xDiff = (mouseX - oldMouseX)*4.0;
      yDiff = (mouseY - oldMouseY)*4.0;

      // save mouse position
      oldMouseX = mouseX;
      oldMouseY = mouseY;

      // calculate velocity based on mouse movement
      velocity = CVector(xDiff, 0.0, yDiff) * 10.0;

      // calculate position
      position = position + (velocity * deltaTime);

      // collisions with table walls
      if (position.x - radius < table->tableCorners[0][0])
          position.x = table->tableCorners[0][0] + radius;
      if (position.x + radius > table->tableCorners[3][0])
          position.x = table->tableCorners[3][0] - radius;
      if (position.z - radius < table->tableCorners[1][2])
          position.z = table->tableCorners[1][2] + radius;
      if (position.z + radius > table->tableCorners[3][2])
          position.z = table->tableCorners[3][2] - radius;

      // collision with puck
      if ((puck->position - position).Length() <= (puck->size + radius))
      {
          // stationary collision (simple)
          if (velocity.Length() == 0)
          {
              puck->velocity = -puck->velocity;
          }
```

```
        else        // moving collision
        {
                // new puck velocity equals reflection of the cross product of
                // the player velocity and the puck velocity plus the player velocity
                puck->velocity = puck->velocity.Reflection(puck->velocity ^ velocity) +
                                 velocity;
        }
    }
}
```

In the Move() function, you first calculate the amount that the mouse has moved since the last frame and translate that difference into a velocity for the player. The new position of the player is then calculated based on this velocity. Next, simple collision detection is performed with the walls of the table to keep the player within the table boundaries. Finally, you check whether the puck and the player have collided.

To determine whether the puck and player collide, you check the distance between the two objects and see if that distance is less than or equal to the sum of the two object's radii. Again, this is very simple collision detection and is *not* time-based; therefore, the physics between the puck and the player will not be perfect. We're going to leave this as an exercise for you, the reader. Because you've seen how to do time-based collision detection and response between the puck and the table walls, see if you can figure out how to do time-based collision detection between the puck and the player!

Putting It Together

You have all the objects developed, and you're almost ready to put them together with some "glue" from the main program. First, however, you must implement one more important piece in this system: time. Remember that the Animate() functions from all the CObject-derived classes take a delta time as a parameter. This means that the physics calculations that you perform are calculated in real time, so you need a way to keep track of the time as the program executes. Because you've already created the CHiResTimer class, you can use the GetElapsedSeconds() function to return the delta time to be used in your physics calculations.

So now you have four objects: the table, puck, player, and timer. Getting them to work together is actually very simple because you've designed the system well. Let's see how.

Here you have the declarations for the main program from *MAIN.CPP*:

```
#define WIN32_LEAN_AND_MEAN                    // trim the excess fat from Windows
#define WIN32_EXTRA_LEAN
```

```
////// Includes
#include <windows.h>                   // standard Windows app include
#include <gl/gl.h>                     // standard OpenGL include
#include <gl/glu.h>                    // OpenGL utilities
#include <gl/glaux.h>                  // OpenGL auxiliary functions

#include "HiResTimer.h"                // hi-resolution timer
#include "vector.h"                    // vector math
#include "object.h"                    // base object
#include "table.h"                     // table object
#include "puck.h"                      // puck object
#include "player.h"                    // player object


////// Global Variables
HDC g_HDC;                             // global device context
int mouseX, mouseY;                    // mouse coordinates

////// Lighting variables
float ambientLight[] = { 0.5f, 0.5f, 0.5f, 1.0f };        // ambient light
float diffuseLight[] = { 0.5f, 0.5f, 0.5f, 1.0f };        // diffuse light
float lightPosition[] = { 0.0f, -1.0f, 0.0f, 0.0f };      // light position

////// The Air Hockey Objects
CTable *myTable = NULL;                // the table
CPuck *myPuck = NULL;                  // the puck
CHiResTimer *timer = NULL;             // the timer
CPlayer *player = NULL;                // the player
```

The first thing you must do is set up and initialize OpenGL and the world objects with the
Initialize() function:

```
// Initialize()
// desc: initialize OpenGL and allocate objects
void Initialize()
{
     glClearColor(0.0, 0.0, 0.0, 0.0);
     glEnable(GL_DEPTH_TEST);          // enable depth testing
     glShadeModel(GL_SMOOTH);          // smooth shading
     glDepthFunc(GL_LEQUAL);
     glEnable(GL_CULL_FACE);           // cull back faces
     glFrontFace(GL_CCW);              // counterclockwise rendering
```

```
    // Now set up LIGHT0
    glLightfv(GL_LIGHT0, GL_AMBIENT, ambientLight);    // set up the ambient element
    glLightfv(GL_LIGHT0, GL_DIFFUSE, ambientLight);    // the diffuse element
    glLightfv(GL_LIGHT0, GL_POSITION, lightPosition); // place the light in the world

    // Enable the light
    glEnable(GL_LIGHT0);
    glEnable(GL_COLOR_MATERIAL);
    glColorMaterial(GL_FRONT, GL_AMBIENT_AND_DIFFUSE);

    // Enable 2D textures
    glEnable(GL_TEXTURE_2D);

    // Allocate memory for table and load
    myTable = new CTable;
    myTable->Load();

    // Allocate puck object with 10 unit radius
    myPuck = new CPuck(10.0);

    // Allocate the timer and initialize
    timer = new CHiResTimer;
    timer->Init();

    // Allocate the player
    player = new CPlayer;
}
```

In the Initialize() function, you set up OpenGL with lighting and texturing enabled and allocate memory for the objects that you use. Next you have the Render() function:

```
// Render()
// desc: perform physics and draw world
void Render()
{
    // retrieve elapsed seconds since last frame
    float elapsedSec = timer->GetElapsedSeconds(1);

    glClear(GL_COLOR_BUFFER_BIT | GL_DEPTH_BUFFER_BIT);
    glLoadIdentity();
```

```
    // place camera at (150, 150, 200), looking at the center of the table
    gluLookAt(150.0, 150.0, 200.0, 150.0, 0.0, -300.0, 0.0, 1.0, 0.0);

    // do physics/movement for the player and puck
    player->Move(elapsedSec, mouseX, mouseY, myTable, myPuck);
    myPuck->Animate(elapsedSec, myTable);

    // draw objects after performing physics/movement
    player->Draw();
    myTable->Draw();
    myPuck->Draw();

    glFlush();
    SwapBuffers(g_HDC);
}
```

In the Render() function, you first retrieve from the high-resolution timer the amount of time that has elapsed since the last frame. This elapsed time is then used to move the player and puck objects before you render the puck, player, and table objects.

Next is the CleanUp() function, which is used to free the objects from memory when the demo program is terminating:

```
// CleanUp()
// desc: free memory of objects
void CleanUp()
{
    // table object
    myTable->Unload();
    delete myTable;
    myTable = NULL;

    // puck object
    delete myPuck;
    myPuck = NULL;

    // timer object
    delete timer;
    timer = NULL;
```

```
        // player object
        delete player;
        player = NULL;
}
```

And finally, you have the three Windows support functions SetupPixelFormat(), WndProc(), and WinMain():

```
// set up PixelFormat()
// function to set the pixel format for the device context
void SetupPixelFormat(HDC hDC)
{
    int nPixelFormat;                       // our pixel-format index

    static PIXELFORMATDESCRIPTOR pfd = {
        sizeof(PIXELFORMATDESCRIPTOR),      // size of structure
        1,                                  // default version
        PFD_DRAW_TO_WINDOW |                // window-drawing support
        PFD_SUPPORT_OPENGL |                // OpenGL support
        PFD_DOUBLEBUFFER,                   // double-buffering support
        PFD_TYPE_RGBA,                      // RGBA color mode
        32,                                 // 32-bit color mode
        0, 0, 0, 0, 0, 0,                   // ignore color bits, non-palletized mode
        0,                                  // no alpha buffer
        0,                                  // ignore shift bit
        0,                                  // no accumulation buffer
        0, 0, 0, 0,                         // ignore accumulation bits
        16,                                 // 16-bit z-buffer size
        0,                                  // no stencil buffer
        0,                                  // no auxiliary buffer
        PFD_MAIN_PLANE,                     // main drawing plane
        0,                                  // reserved
        0, 0, 0 };                          // layer masks ignored

    nPixelFormat = ChoosePixelFormat(hDC, &pfd); // choose best-matching pixel format

    SetPixelFormat(hDC, nPixelFormat, &pfd);  // set pixel format to device context
}
```

```
// WndProc()
// the Windows Procedure event handler
LRESULT CALLBACK WndProc(HWND hwnd, UINT message, WPARAM wParam, LPARAM lParam)
{
    static HGLRC hRC;                    // rendering context
    static HDC hDC;                      // device context
    int width, height;                  // window width and height
    static int oldMouseX, oldMouseY;    // old mouse coordinates

    switch(message)
    {
        case WM_CREATE:                 // window is being created

            hDC = GetDC(hwnd);          // get current window's device context
            g_HDC = hDC;
            SetupPixelFormat(hDC);      // call our pixel-format setup function

            // create rendering context and make it current
            hRC = wglCreateContext(hDC);
            wglMakeCurrent(hDC, hRC);

            return 0;
            break;

        case WM_CLOSE:                  // Windows is closing

            // deselect rendering context and delete it
            wglMakeCurrent(hDC, NULL);
            wglDeleteContext(hRC);

            // send WM_QUIT to message queue
            PostQuitMessage(0);

            return 0;
            break;

        case WM_SIZE:
            height = HIWORD(lParam);    // retrieve width and height
            width = LOWORD(lParam);
```

```
            if (height==0)                   // don't want a divide by zero
            {
                height=1;
            }

            // reset the viewport to new dimensions
            glViewport(0, 0, width, height);
            glMatrixMode(GL_PROJECTION);    // set projection to current matrix
            glLoadIdentity();               // reset projection matrix

            // calculate aspect ratio of window
            gluPerspective(45.0f,(GLfloat)width/(GLfloat)height,1.0f,1000.0f);

            glMatrixMode(GL_MODELVIEW);     // set modelview matrix
            glLoadIdentity();               // reset modelview matrix

            return 0;
            break;

        case WM_MOUSEMOVE:
            // save old mouse coordinates
            oldMouseX = mouseX;
            oldMouseY = mouseY;

            // get mouse coordinates from Windows
            mouseX = LOWORD(lParam);
            mouseY = HIWORD(lParam);

            break;

        default:
            break;
    }

    return (DefWindowProc(hwnd, message, wParam, lParam));
}

// WinMain()
// the main Windows entry point
int WINAPI WinMain(HINSTANCE hInstance, HINSTANCE hPrevInstance, LPSTR lpCmdLine,
                int nShowCmd)
```

```
{
    WNDCLASSEX windowClass;        // window class
    HWND       hwnd;               // window handle
    MSG        msg;                // message
    bool       done;              // flag saying when our app is complete

    // fill out the window class structure
    windowClass.cbSize           = sizeof(WNDCLASSEX);
    windowClass.style            = CS_HREDRAW | CS_VREDRAW;
    windowClass.lpfnWndProc      = WndProc;
    windowClass.cbClsExtra       = 0;
    windowClass.cbWndExtra       = 0;
    windowClass.hInstance        = hInstance;
    windowClass.hIcon            = LoadIcon(NULL, IDI_APPLICATION); // default icon
    windowClass.hCursor          = LoadCursor(NULL, IDC_ARROW);    // default arrow
    windowClass.hbrBackground    = NULL;                 // don't need background
    windowClass.lpszMenuName = NULL;                          // no menu
    windowClass.lpszClassName    = "MyClass";
    windowClass.hIconSm          = LoadIcon(NULL, IDI_WINLOGO);  // small icon

    // register the windows class
    if (!RegisterClassEx(&windowClass))
        return 0;

    // class registered, so now create our window
    hwnd = CreateWindowEx(NULL,                              // extended style
                          "MyClass",                         // class name
                          "The OpenGL Window Application",   // app name
                          WS_OVERLAPPEDWINDOW | WS_VISIBLE | // style
                          WS_SYSMENU | WS_CLIPCHILDREN |
                          WS_CLIPSIBLINGS,
                          100, 100,                          // x,y coordinate
                          800, 600,                          // width, height
                          NULL,                              // handle of parent
                          NULL,                              // handle to menu
                          hInstance,                         // application instance
                          NULL);                             // no extra params

    // check if window creation failed (hwnd would equal NULL)
    if (!hwnd)
        return 0;
```

```
    ShowWindow(hwnd, SW_SHOW);              // display the window
    UpdateWindow(hwnd);                     // update the window

    done = false;                           // initialize the loop condition variable
    Initialize();                           // initialize the app
    ShowCursor(FALSE);                      // hide the cursor

// main message loop
while (!done)
{
     PeekMessage(&msg, hwnd, NULL, NULL, PM_REMOVE);

     if (msg.message == WM_QUIT)            // do we receive a WM_QUIT message?
     {
          done = true;                      // if so, time to quit the application
     }
     else
     {
          Render();                         // render world

          TranslateMessage(&msg);           // translate and dispatch to event queue
          DispatchMessage(&msg);
     }
}

    CleanUp();              // free objects
    ShowCursor(TRUE);       // show the cursor again

    return msg.wParam;
}
```

One thing new you might notice in the WinMain() function is the ShowCursor() function. By passing a value of FALSE to the ShowCursor() function, you are telling Windows to hide the cursor while this application is running. Hiding the cursor eliminates the problem of having a cursor moving around the application window while the mouse is also controlling the player object. After the application is finished, you can re-enable the cursor by passing a value of TRUE to the ShowCursor() function. If you don't tell Windows to show the cursor again, then you will be without a cursor in a GUI environment. That's not a good thing!

SUMMARY

Physics modeling and collision detection (and response) are such large topics that one measly chapter just is not enough to cover everything you must know. In this chapter we discussed common physics models used in games and a simple approach to modeling the real world in your games.

The air-hockey demo has been started and left as an exercise to be developed into a full-blown game with all the bells and whistles. Also keep in mind the player/puck collision-detection problem that was presented. It may not be as difficult as you think!

CHAPTER 20

BUILDING A GAME ENGINE

Building a game engine is not an easy task. Commercial engines such as the *Quake 3* engine from id Software and the *Unreal* engine from Epic Games are very complex architecturally and can take years to fully develop. Even so, in this chapter, you'll learn how to develop a relatively simple game engine called *SimpEngine* (short for "simple engine"). The full source code for the SimpEngine is readily available on the included CD-ROM.

This chapter covers the following:

- The SimpEngine's overall design
- Handling Windows messages and input
- The game cycle
- The camera and the game world
- Entities and models
- The audio system
- The particle system

DESIGNING THE SIMPENGINE

The SimpEngine is an object-oriented framework that you can use to build games. Because of the relative simplicity of the SimpEngine, it's not meant to be used for the development of large-scale games; you can, however, use it to build simple games quickly and efficiently—with expansion of the engine itself being just as easy.

The SimpEngine (from here on also referred to as *engine*) can be broken down into the subsystems shown in Figure 20.1.

Essentially, the engine receives input through the Input subsystem and sends a message to the Game Logic subsystem, which then handles the message and executes a game cycle. In a single game cycle, the Game Logic subsystem responds to input, performs any physics calculations necessary on the game objects, handles collision detection and response, loads and destroys objects, moves the camera around the world, and plays any sounds needed while the game is executing.

In further detail, the SimpEngine is broken down into the classes shown in Figure 20.2. These are the actual classes that the engine uses.

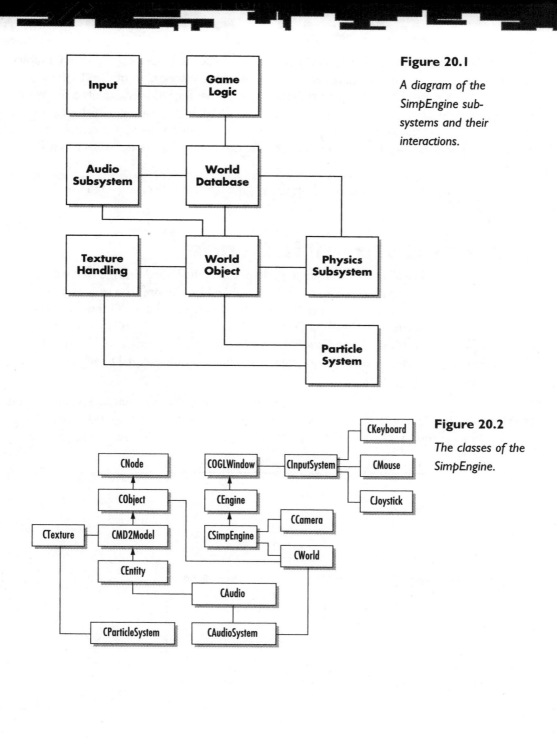

Figure 20.1

A diagram of the SimpEngine sub-systems and their interactions.

Figure 20.2

The classes of the SimpEngine.

At the base of the engine, you have the COGLWindow and CNode classes. COGLWindow handles Windows messages, window creation, some basic input, and is ultimately the base class of the CEngine and CSimpEngine classes. As you will see in the next section of this chapter, CNode is actually a single node of a cyclic linked list tree that you use to build the world object hierarchy, which provides the basis for world object management in the engine. From these two classes, you can build objects, enemies, the engine core, object containers, the camera, and any extensions you wish to add to the engine.

Now let's start things off by taking a look at how the engine handles objects through the CNode and CObject classes.

Managing Data with *CNode*

As mentioned, the CNode class represents a single node of the cyclic linked list tree that you use to maintain the objects in the engine. If you have not used linked lists before, you may want to explore them through another resource, such as those listed in Appendix A, "Online Resources," before moving on much further. As shown in Figure 20.3, a CNode object "links" to a parent node, a child node, a previous node, and a next node. Each link is actually a pointer to the other node. Sometimes, a link might even point to the node itself. If a link pointer is equal to NULL, then that link to another node does not exist.

When you link several CNode objects, you might get something similar to what's shown in Figure 20.4. In this hierarchy, Node 1 is the root node and parent node of Nodes 2, 3, and 4. Also, Node 2 is the child node of Node 1, but Nodes 3 and 4 are not child nodes—they are siblings of Node 2.

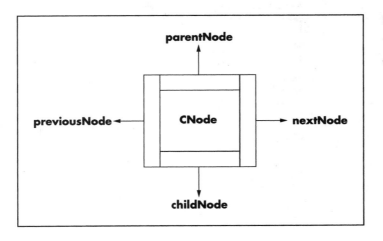

Figure 20.3

The CNode object with links.

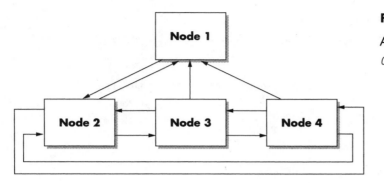

Figure 20.4

A collection of CNode objects.

Each parent node (for example, Node 1) can have only one child node. This child node is actually the head of the parent's linked list of children nodes. To access all of a parent node's children, you must first access the child node, go to the child's next link, and then go to that sibling's next link, and so on—until the last child has been reached.

The following code is the CNode class definition from *tree.h*:

```
class CNode
{
public:
    // data
    CNode *parentNode;   // parent node
    CNode *childNode;    // child node
    CNode *prevNode;     // previous node
    CNode *nextNode;     // next node


    bool HasParent() { return (parentNode != NULL); } // does node have a parent?
    bool HasChild() { return (childNode != NULL); }   // does node have a child?

    // is this node the first child?
    bool IsFirstChild()
    {
        if (parentNode)
            return (parentNode->childNode == this);
        else
            return false;
    }
```

```cpp
// is this node the last child?
bool IsLastChild()
{
    if (parentNode)
        return (parentNode->childNode->prevNode == this);
    else
        return false;
}


// attach this node to a parent node
void AttachTo(CNode *newParent)
{
    // if this node is already attached to another node, then detach
    if (parentNode)
        Detach();

    parentNode = newParent;

    if (parentNode->childNode)
    {
        prevNode = parentNode->childNode->prevNode;
        nextNode = parentNode->childNode;
        parentNode->childNode->prevNode->nextNode = this;
        parentNode->childNode->prevNode = this;
    }
    else
    {
        parentNode->childNode = this;        // this is the first child
    }
}


// attach a child to this node
void Attach(CNode *newChild)
{
    // if the child node is already attached, then detach it
    if (newChild->HasParent())
        newChild->Detach();

    newChild->parentNode = this;
```

```
        if (childNode)
        {
            newChild->prevNode = childNode->prevNode;
            newChild->nextNode = childNode;
            childNode->prevNode->nextNode = newChild;
            childNode->prevNode = newChild;
        }
        else
            childNode = newChild;
    }

    // detach node from parent
    void Detach()
    {
        // if this node is the first child of the parent (first in list)
        // then the parent points to the next child in the list
        if (parentNode && parentNode->childNode == this)
        {
            if (nextNode != this)
                parentNode->childNode = nextNode;
            else
                parentNode->childNode = NULL;        // no next child
        }

        // get rid of links
        prevNode->nextNode = nextNode;
        nextNode->prevNode = prevNode;

        // now this node is not in the list
        prevNode = this;
        nextNode = this;
    }

    // count the number of nodes
    int CountNodes()
    {
        if (childNode)
            return childNode->CountNodes() + 1;
        else
            return 1;
    }
```

```
// constructor
CNode()                                      // set up node
{
     parentNode = childNode = NULL;
     prevNode = nextNode = this;
}

// constructor
CNode(CNode *node)
{
     parentNode = childNode = NULL;       // set up and attach this node to node
     prevNode = nextNode = this;
     AttachTo(node);
}

// destructor
virtual ~CNode()
{
     Detach();                 // detach from hierarchy

     while (childNode)         // delete all children
     {
          delete childNode;
     }
}
};
```

The CNode class gives you the ability to attach nodes to each other, detach nodes from the hierarchy, and check whether a node has children, a parent, and so on. For example, when you attach one node (we'll call it Node A) to another node (say, Node B), you are actually specifying that Node A is a child of Node B.

You may already have begun to see the usefulness of the CNode class at this point, but the real power of this class is more evident in the CObject class, which is derived from CNode.

Working with Objects: *CObject*

The CObject class represents the smallest possible entity in the SimpEngine and is a class derived from the CNode class. The CObject class can represent anything in the SimpEngine that can draw, move, collide, or even "think." And because CObject is derived from CNode, you can attach objects to each other to create an object hierarchy for easier object management in the engine.

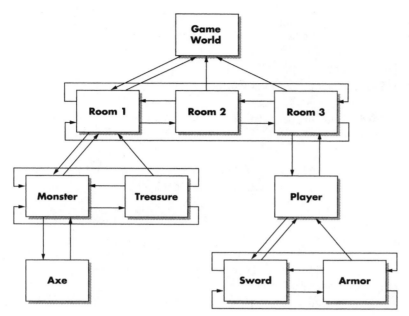

Figure 20.5

A sample object hierarchy from a hypothetical game.

As an example, Figure 20.5 presents an object hierarchy from a hypothetical game world. In this example, the game world is the root object of the hierarchy, with the game world's rooms representing the children objects of the game world. In each of these rooms, you can have any sort of monsters, players, or game objects, all of which can in turn have other objects attached to them. For instance, a monster might have a sword attached to it, and the sword, in turn, might have a handle attached to it.

The real power of the CObject class, however, becomes evident when you want to render, move, and track collisions with an object. Before we discuss how to accomplish these tasks, here is the CObject class definition from *object.h*:

```
class CObject : public CNode
{
protected:

    // perform basic physics on the object
    virtual void OnAnimate(scalar_t deltaTime)
    {
        position += velocity * deltaTime;
        velocity += acceleration * deltaTime;
    }
```

```cpp
        // draw the object given the camera position
        virtual void OnDraw(CCamera *camera) {}

        // collide with other objects
        virtual void OnCollision(CObject *collisionObject) {}

        // perform collision and other preparations for this object
        virtual void OnPrepare()
        {
            ProcessCollisions(FindRoot());      // perform collisions starting with
                                                // root world object

        }

public:
        CVector position;           // object position
        CVector velocity;           // velocity of object
        CVector acceleration;       // acceleration
        scalar_t size;              // size of bounding sphere (radius)

        bool isDead;

        CObject() { isDead = false; }
        ~CObject() {}

        virtual void Load() {}
        virtual void Unload() {}

        // draw object
        void Draw(CCamera *camera)
        {
            // push modelview matrix on stack
            glPushMatrix();
                OnDraw(camera);             // draw this object
                if (HasChild())             // draw children
                    ((CObject*)childNode)->Draw(camera);
            glPopMatrix();

            // draw siblings
            if (HasParent() && !IsLastChild())
                ((CObject*)nextNode)->Draw(camera);
        }
```

```cpp
    // animate object
    void Animate(scalar_t deltaTime)
    {
        OnAnimate(deltaTime);              // animate this object

        // animate children
        if (HasChild())
            ((CObject*)childNode)->Animate(deltaTime);

        // animate siblings
        if (HasParent() && !IsLastChild())
            ((CObject*)nextNode)->Animate(deltaTime);

        if (isDead)
            delete this;
    }


    // perform collision detection
    void ProcessCollisions(CObject *obj)
    {
        // if this object's bounding sphere collides with obj's sphere
        // and obj is not this object
        if (((obj->position - position).Length() <= (obj->size + size)) &&
            (obj != ((CObject*)this)))
        {
            OnCollision(obj);             // perform this object's collision with obj

            // test child collisions with obj
            if (HasChild())
                ((CObject*)childNode)->ProcessCollisions(obj);

            // test sibling collisions with obj
            if (HasParent() && !IsLastChild())
                ((CObject*)nextNode)->ProcessCollisions(obj);
        }

        // if obj has children, check collisions with these children
        if (obj->HasChild())
            ProcessCollisions((CObject*)(obj->childNode));
```

```
            // if obj has siblings, check collisions with these siblings
            if (obj->HasParent() && !obj->IsLastChild())
                ProcessCollisions((CObject*)(obj->nextNode));
        }

        // prepare object
        void Prepare()
        {
            OnPrepare();                                // prepare this object

            if (HasChild())                             // prepare children
                ((CObject*)childNode)->Prepare();

            if (HasParent() && !IsLastChild())          // prepare siblings
                ((CObject*)nextNode)->Prepare();
        }

        // find root object of cyclic linked list tree
        CObject *FindRoot()
        {
            // if this object has a parent node, return the root of the parent node
            if (parentNode)
                return ((CObject*)parentNode)->FindRoot();

            return this;
        }
};
```

In the public section of the CObject class, we have defined the Prepare(), Animate(),
ProcessCollisions(), and Draw() functions. Each of these functions performs the specified function on the object itself, and then performs the specified function on the object's children. As an
example, the following code is the CObject::Animate() function:

```
// animate object
void Animate(scalar_t deltaTime)
{
    OnAnimate(deltaTime);          // animate this object

    // animate children
    if (HasChild())
        ((CObject*)childNode)->Animate(deltaTime);
```

```
    // animate siblings
    if (HasParent() && !IsLastChild())
        ((CObject*)nextNode)->Animate(deltaTime);

    if (isDead)
        delete this;
}
```

What's happening here is that every object has its own set of protected-level virtual On*() functions, such as OnPrepare(), OnAnimate(), OnCollision(), and OnDraw(). Whenever one of the public functions, such as Animate(), is called, the corresponding On*() function is where the customized code for the object is stored. In the preceding code, the Animate() function first animates the current object, then it animates all the object's children and all the object's siblings by recursively calling Animate(). The final block of code provides a way for you to remove the object from the hierarchy from within the Animate() function. Figure 20.6 attempts to illustrate a call to the Animate() function of the root-world object to the hypothetical hierarchy created earlier.

Typically, you use the Animate() function to perform physics calculations on the objects, the Prepare() function for AI and object state changes, the ProcessCollisions() function to perform collision detection, and the Draw() function to render the object.

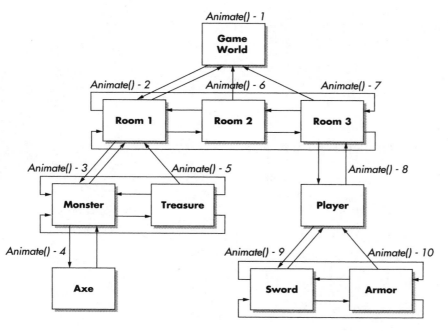

Figure 20.6

A sample trace of the Animate() function from the root-object level.

Because the OnPrepare(), OnAnimate(), OnCollision(), and OnDraw() functions are virtual, you need to override them with customized code when you derive subclasses from CObject. For example, if you were to derive a CBox class from CObject, then the OnDraw() implementation for CBox should be different from the OnDraw() implementation for a CObject-derived CGun. Using these virtual functions allows for simple expansion of the engine with customization of the CObject-derived classes.

When you use the Draw() function, note that you end up using the glPushMatrix() and glPopMatrix() functions for each object that you draw. We first discussed these OpenGL matrix functions back in Chapter 5, "Coordinate Transformations and OpenGL Matrices." In this chapter, we discussed how you could use these functions to create object hierarchies. In an object hierarchy, a child object's coordinates are relative to its parent's coordinate system. For example, your head could be considered a child object of your body (the parent object), with coordinates of (0.0, 5.0, 0.0).

Now let's say you want to draw a car and its four tires. One possible solution is to create the car body as an object and attach each of the four tires to this body. Now all you need to do is specify the tires' locations in relation to the body of the car—for example, left front (2.0, 0.0, 2.0), right front (–2.0, 0.0, 2.0), and so on—and the CObject hierarchy will render the full scene.

With the SimpEngine, it's this easy:

```
CObject *body;
CObject *tire1, *tire2, *tire3, *tire4;
...
tire1->AttachTo(body);          // or body->Attach(tire1)
tire2->AttachTo(body);
tire3->AttachTo(body);
tire4->AttachTo(body);
...
body->Draw(...);
```

The code results in the object hierarchy shown in Figure 20.7.

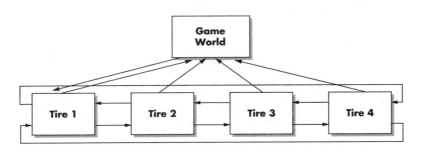

Figure 20.7

The object hierarchy of the car and four tires.

THE ENGINE CORE

At the core of the engine is the COGLWindow class, which creates an OpenGL window and handles the Windows messages that are received from the operating system. You create a virtual function in the COGLWindow class for each message that you want to handle. For instance, if you want to handle the Windows message WM_SIZE, you create the virtual function OnSize(). All these functions are called by the Windows procedure, WndProcOGL, when the corresponding message is received. Here is the COGLWindow class definition:

```
class COGLWindow
{
protected:
     HWND       hWnd;     // window handle
     HDC        hDC;      // device context
     HPALETTE   hPalette; // palette
     HGLRC      hGLRC;    // rendering context

private:

     // the WndProc
     friend LRESULT APIENTRY WndProcOGL(HWND hWnd, UINT uMsg, WPARAM wParam,
                                        LPARAM lParam);

     void SetupPixelFormat();        // set up the pixel format
     void SetupPalette();            // set up the palette

     // Windows message handling functions
     bool Create();                       // WM_CREATE
     void Destroy();                      // WM_DESTROY
     void PaletteChanged(WPARAM wParam);  // WM_PALETTECHANGED
     BOOL QueryNewPalette();              // WM_QUERYNEWPALETTE
     void Paint();                        // WM_PAINT
     void Size();                         // WM_SIZE
     void MouseMove(int x, int y);        // WM_MOUSEMOVE

     int GetMouseX(LPARAM lParam);        // get true mouse coordinates
     int GetMouseY(LPARAM lParam);

     float GetNormalizedPosX(LPARAM lParam); // get normalized mouse coordinates
     float GetNormalizedPosY(LPARAM lParam); // between (-1.0 and 1.0)
```

```cpp
        int iPrevWidth;
        int iPrevHeight;
        void BeginFullScreen(int w, int h, int b);   // go to full-screen mode
        void EndFullScreen();                         // come back from full-screen mode

public:
        int width;                      // window dimensions
        int height;
        int centerX;                    // window center coordinates
        int centerY;
        int bits;                       // bits per pixel
        int aspect;                     // window aspect ratio
        int mouseX;                     // mouse coordinates
        int mouseY;
        bool fullscreen;                // is this a full-screen app
        float mouseSensitivity;         // mouse sensitivity

        bool useDInput;                 // true if dinput is enabled
        CInputSystem *inputSystem;      // the input system object

protected:
        virtual bool OnCreate() { return true; }
        virtual bool OnClose() { return true; }
        virtual void OnSize() { }
        virtual void OnMouseDownL(float x, float y) { }
        virtual void OnMouseDownR(float x, float y) { }
        virtual void OnMouseUpL() { }
        virtual void OnMouseUpR() { }
        virtual void OnMouseMove(int x, int y, int centerX, int centerY) { }
        virtual void OnMouseMove(int deltaX, int deltaY) { }
        virtual void OnMouseDragL(int x, int y, int dx, int dy) { }
        virtual void OnMouseDragR(int x, int y, int dx, int dy) { }
        virtual void OnCommand(WORD wNotifyCode, WORD wID, HWND hWndCtrl) { }
        virtual void OnContextMenu(HWND hWnd, int x, int y) { }
        virtual void OnKeyUp(int nVirtKey) { }
        virtual void OnInitMenu(HMENU hMenu) { }
        virtual void OnKeyDown(int nVirtKey) { }
        virtual void OnChar(char c) { }

public:
        COGLWindow() {}
```

```
    COGLWindow(const char *szName, bool fscreen, int w, int h, int b);
    virtual ~COGLWindow();

    // this must be called before the class is used
    static bool RegisterWindow(HINSTANCE hInst);
};
```

The Input System

The COGLWindow class also holds the input system object, CInputSystem, which uses DirectInput to
retrieve the current keyboard, mouse, and joystick states. The input system object includes functions to determine whether a key has been pressed or released or how much the mouse has
moved, whether a mouse button has been clicked, and whether the joystick has moved or its but-
ton(s) has been pushed. Despite all this functionality, the CInputSystem is only initialized and shut
down in the COGLWindow class. The class definition for CInputSystem is shown here:

```
class CInputSystem
{
public:
    CInputSystem() { }
    ~CInputSystem() { Shutdown(); }
    bool  Initialize(HWND hwnd, HINSTANCE appInstance, bool isExclusive,
                     DWORD flags = 0);
    bool  Shutdown();

    void  AcquireAll();
    void  UnacquireAll();

    CKeyboard  *GetKeyboard() { return m_pKeyboard; }
    CMouse     *GetMouse()    { return m_pMouse; }
    CJoystick  *GetJoystick() { return m_pJoystick; }

    bool  Update();    // update device states

    bool  KeyDown(char key) { return (m_pKeyboard && m_pKeyboard->KeyDown(key)); }
    bool  KeyUp(char key) { return (m_pKeyboard && m_pKeyboard->KeyUp(key)); }

    bool  ButtonDown(int button)
         { return (m_pMouse && m_pMouse->ButtonDown(button)); }
```

```
    bool  ButtonUp(int button) { return (m_pMouse && m_pMouse->ButtonUp(button)); }
    void  GetMouseMovement(int &dx, int &dy)
          { if (m_pMouse) m_pMouse->GetMovement(dx, dy); }

private:
    CKeyboard  *m_pKeyboard;      // the keyboard object
    CMouse     *m_pMouse;         // the mouse object
    CJoystick  *m_pJoystick;      // the joystick object

    LPDIRECTINPUT8 m_pDI;
};
```

The *CEngine* Class

Derived from the COGLWindow class is the CEngine class, which provides the main Windows message loop, the game loop, and a function to handle any input received from the input system. The class definition for the CEngine class is shown here:

```
class CEngine : public COGLWindow
{
private:

protected:
    CHiResTimer *timer;                               // high-performance timer

    virtual void GameCycle(float deltaTime);          // the game cycle

    virtual void OnPrepare() {}                        // set up OpenGL for frame
    virtual CCamera *OnGetCamera() { return NULL; }    // override in derived engine
    virtual CWorld *OnGetWorld() { return NULL; }      // override in derived engine
    virtual void CheckInput(float deltaTime);          // retrieve input

public:
    CEngine() {}
    CEngine(const char *szName, bool fscreen, int w, int h, int b) :
            COGLWindow(szName, fscreen, w, h, b) {}
    ~CEngine() {}
    LRESULT EnterMessageLoop();
};
```

The message loop function, EnterMessageLoop(), contains the typical message loop with the addition of the high-resolution timer, CHiResTimer. Here is the code for the CEngine::EnterMessageLoop() function:

```
LRESULT CEngine::EnterMessageLoop()
{
    MSG msg;                         // the received message
    timer = new CHiResTimer;         // the timer

    timer->Init();                   // initialize the timer
    for (;;)
    {
        // execute a single game cycle
        GameCycle(timer->GetElapsedSeconds(1));

        while (PeekMessage (&msg, NULL, 0, 0, PM_NOREMOVE))
        {
            // we always update if there are any events, even if we're paused
            if (!GetMessage (&msg, NULL, 0, 0))
            {
                delete timer;         // quit message received, delete timer
                return msg.wParam;    // return to operating system
            }

            TranslateMessage (&msg);
            DispatchMessage (&msg);
        }
    }

    delete timer;         // delete the timer
    return msg.wParam;    // return to operating system
}
```

During each loop, you execute one game cycle and check whether a quit message has been sent to the application. The game cycle function, GameCycle(), receives the amount of time that has passed since the last game cycle. The entire engine uses this time to perform physics calculations and other time-based functions.

The Game Cycle

The typical game cycle consists of the following steps:

1. Gather input
2. Move player
3. Perform artificial intelligence (AI)
4. Calculate physics
5. Play sounds
6. Render the scene

The SimpEngine's game cycle, however, is not as clear-cut as the one listed here. Because of the object hierarchy, the game cycle must call the CObject functions Prepare(), Animate(), and Draw(), as seen here in the CEngine::GameCycle() code:

```
void CEngine::GameCycle(float deltaTime)
{
    CCamera *camera = OnGetCamera();   // get the camera
    CWorld *world = OnGetWorld();       // get the world

    // check for input
    CheckInput(deltaTime);

    // set up opengl for frame (clear, identity)
    OnPrepare();

    // prepare objects and perform collisions
    world->Prepare();

    // move/orient camera
    camera->Animate(deltaTime);

    // move/orient objects
    world->Animate(deltaTime);

    // draw objects
    world->Draw(camera);

    // swap buffers
    SwapBuffers(hDC);
}
```

We'll be discussing the camera and world objects shortly; for now, just keep in mind the order in which the functions are executed by the game cycle.

Handling Input

As you've seen in the GameCycle() function, you determine whether any input devices have been used (for example, keys pressed, mouse movement, and such) through the CheckInput() function, which uses the CInputSystem object defined in the COGLWindow class. As shown in the following code listing of CheckInput(), you verify that an input device event has occurred, such as the Esc key being pressed, and call the appropriate function:

```
void CEngine::CheckInput(float deltaTime)
{
    static float buttonDelta = 0.0f;   // the amount of time until the next
                                       // mouse button press is allowed

    int mouseDeltaX, mouseDeltaY;      // changes in the mouse position

    // decrease amount of time until next possible recognized button pressing
    buttonDelta -= deltaTime;

    if (buttonDelta < 0.0f)
        buttonDelta = 0.0f;

    // update devices
    inputSystem->Update();

    // retrieve the latest mouse movements and respond to them
    inputSystem->GetMouseMovement(mouseDeltaX, mouseDeltaY);
    OnMouseMove(mouseDeltaX, mouseDeltaY);

    // if W key has been pressed
    if (inputSystem->KeyDown(DIK_W))
        OnKeyDown(VK_UP);
    // if S key has been pressed
    if (inputSystem->KeyDown(DIK_S))
        OnKeyDown(VK_DOWN);

    // if A key has been pressed
    if (inputSystem->KeyDown(DIK_A))
        OnKeyDown(VK_LEFT);
```

```
        // if D key has been pressed
    if (inputSystem->KeyDown(DIK_D))
        OnKeyDown(VK_RIGHT);

        // if Esc key has been pressed
    if (inputSystem->KeyDown(DIK_ESCAPE))
        OnKeyDown(VK_ESCAPE);

        // if left mouse button has been pressed
    if (inputSystem->ButtonDown(0))
    {
        // if button can be pressed
        if (buttonDelta == 0.0f)
        {
            OnMouseDownL(0,0);
            buttonDelta = 0.5f;   // reset to half second delay
        }
    }
}
```

In this function, you first call the `CInputSystem::Update()` function to update the status of the input devices that the application is currently using (for example, keyboard and mouse). Then, you retrieve the distance the mouse has moved in both the x and y directions and send these distances to the `OnMouseMove()` function, which responds to the mouse movement. Finally, you determine whether certain keys have been pressed or whether any mouse buttons have been clicked by passing the corresponding `DIK_` constant to the `CInputSystem::KeyDown()` and `CInputSystem::ButtonDown()` functions. If a key has been pressed, then you call the `OnKeyDown()` function with the key's corresponding virtual key value passed as the parameter. If the left mouse button has been clicked, then you call the `OnMouseLButton()` function.

The SimpEngine

The `CSimpEngine` class is derived from `CEngine` and represents the entry point into the SimpEngine framework. As shown in the following class definition, the `CSimpEngine` class contains the input response functions, such as `OnKeyDown()`, which can be modified to reflect how you want the engine to respond to certain input events. Also, this class holds the engine's camera and world objects, defined by `CCamera` and `CWorld`, respectively.

```
class CSimpEngine : public CEngine
{
private:
```

```cpp
    CCamera *gameCamera;          // the camera
    CWorld *gameWorld;            // the world

protected:
    CCamera *OnGetCamera() { return gameCamera; }
    CWorld *OnGetWorld() { return gameWorld; }

    void OnPrepare();
    void OnMouseDownL(float x, float y);
    void OnMouseMove(int deltaX, int deltaY);
    void OnMouseMove(int x, int y, int centerX, int centerY);
    void OnKeyDown(int nVirtKey);

public:
    CSimpEngine()
    {
        gameCamera = new CCamera;
        gameWorld = new CWorld;
    }

    CSimpEngine(const char *szName, bool fscreen, int w, int h, int b) :
        CEngine(szName, fscreen, w, h, b)
    {
        gameCamera = new CCamera;
        gameWorld = new CWorld(gameCamera);
    }

    ~CSimpEngine()
    {
        delete gameWorld;
        delete gameCamera;
        gameWorld = NULL;
        gameCamera = NULL;
    }
};
```

You've seen the camera and world objects in several places, so now let's take a look at these important parts of the engine in more detail.

THE CAMERA

As expected, the CCamera class defines the camera viewing system for the engine and is responsible for determining how you view the world. The CCamera class is defined as

```
class CCamera
{
private:
    // these are used for moving and changing camera orientation
    // through the MoveTo/LookTo methods
    CVector initPosition, finalPosition;
    CVector initLookAt, finalLookAt;

    CVector lookAtVel;             // velocity for looking at objects
    CVector lookAtAccel;           // acceleration for looking at objects

    void UpdateLookAt();
    void UpdateMoveTo();

public:
    CVector position;              // position of camera
    CVector velocity;              // velocity of camera
    CVector acceleration;          // acceleration of camera
    CVector lookAt;                // lookat vector

    // up, forward, right vectors
    CVector up;
    CVector forward;
    CVector right;

    // yaw and pitch angles
    float yaw;
    float pitch;

    CCamera();
    CCamera(int width, int height) {}
    CCamera(CVector *look);
    CCamera(CVector *pos, CVector *look);
    ~CCamera();
```

```
        void LookAt(CObject *object);        // look at an object over time
        void LookAtNow(CObject *object);     // look at an object immediately
        void MoveTo(CObject *object);        // move to the location of an object
        void MoveToNow(CObject *object);     // move to an object immediately
        void MoveToNow(scalar_t x, scalar_t y, scalar_t z); // move to location now

        void RotateYaw(scalar_t radians);    // rotation along y axis (yaw)
        void RotatePitch(scalar_t radians);  // rotation along x axis (pitch)
        void RotateRoll(scalar_t radians);   // rotation along z axis (roll)

        // do physics/movement calculations
        void Animate(scalar_t deltaTime);
};
```

The camera is actually very simple to use, especially because most of the time you control it through the input you receive from the input system. The most important function in the CCamera class is the CCamera::Animate() function, which acts very much like the CObject::Animate() function in that it is used to move and orient the camera. Because the camera has a velocity and acceleration, you can use these values to control how the camera moves. You control the camera's orientation through the yaw and pitch angles, which represent the rotation about the y axis and x axis, respectively. You also have a lookAt vector that defines the vector representing the pointing direction of the camera. So if the camera is pointing directly down the negative z axis, then the lookAt vector will be equal to (0.0, 0.0, –1.0). Here's the CCamera::Animate() function code listing:

```
void CCamera::Animate(float deltaTime)
{
    if ((yaw >= 360.0f) || (yaw <= -360.0f))
        yaw = 0.0f;

    if (pitch > 60.0f)              // set boundaries for pitch
        pitch = 60.0f;
    if (pitch < -60.0f)
        pitch = -60.0f;

    float cosYaw = (float)cos(DEG2RAD(yaw));
    float sinYaw = (float)sin(DEG2RAD(yaw));
    float sinPitch = (float)sin(DEG2RAD(pitch));

    float speed = velocity.z * deltaTime;          // forward/backward speed
    float strafeSpeed = velocity.x * deltaTime;    // left/right speed
```

```
        if (speed > 15.0)                // set the speed limit
            speed = 15.0;                // forward
        if (strafeSpeed > 15.0)
            strafeSpeed = 15.0;          // right
        if (speed < -15.0)
            speed = -15.0;               // backward
        if (strafeSpeed < -15.0)
            strafeSpeed = -15.0;         // left

        if (velocity.Length() > 0.0)                     // apply friction
            acceleration = -velocity * 1.5f;

        velocity += acceleration*deltaTime;

        // calculate the new position of the camera based on the forward and
        // strafe speeds
        position.x += float(cos(DEG2RAD(yaw + 90.0)))*strafeSpeed;
        position.z += float(sin(DEG2RAD(yaw + 90.0)))*strafeSpeed;
        position.x += float(cosYaw)*speed;
        position.z += float(sinYaw)*speed;

        // calculate the new lookAt vector
        lookAt.x = float(position.x + cosYaw);
        lookAt.y = float(position.y + sinPitch);
        lookAt.z = float(position.z + sinYaw);

        // use gluLookAt to set the new camera position and orientation
        gluLookAt(position.x, position.y, position.z,
                  lookAt.x, lookAt.y, lookAt.z,
                  0.0, 1.0, 0.0);
}
```

As you can see, at the end of the Animate() function you set the camera's new position and orientation through the gluLookAt() function. If you remember when we discussed the game cycle, the camera was the first object to use the Animate() function. The call to gluLookAt() is the reason. Before you start drawing the world, you need to first set up the camera view so OpenGL knows what to draw and how to draw it.

THE WORLD

The CWorld class defines the game world that the SimpEngine is running, displaying, and interacting with. As you've already seen, the CEngine::GameCycle() function uses the CWorld class to interact with all the objects in the game world through the Prepare(), Animate(), and Draw() functions. Typically, you store the game's level object in the CWorld class, and you might even want to store some sort of object container that manages the objects in the world through the object hierarchy. The CWorld class also stores the engine's audio system object, CAudioSystem, which is used to load and play music and sounds. Here is the class definition for the CWorld class:

```
class CWorld
{
protected:
    void OnAnimate(float deltaTime);
    void OnDraw(CCamera *camera);
    void OnPrepare();

public:

    CTerrain *terrain;          // the terrain
    CCamera *camera;            // the camera
    CAudioSystem *audioSystem;  // the audio system

    CWorld();
    CWorld(CCamera *c);
    ~CWorld();

    void LoadWorld();           // load the world objects, music, sound, etc.
    void UnloadWorld();         // unload the world

    // do movement/orientation calculations for all objects in the world
    void Animate(float deltaTime);

    // render all objects in the world
    void Draw(CCamera *camera);

    // prepare all objects in the world
    void Prepare();
};
```

As an example, we included a CTerrain object, which represents the game-level object. This object represents the world that the player explores, and is typically the root object of the object hierarchy.

ADDING MODELS

You add the capability of loading MD2 models to the SimpEngine through the CMD2Model class, which you derive from the CObject class. This derivation occurs because you want to treat MD2 models as objects of the world through the object hierarchy. Because the entire CMD2Model class is listed in Chapter 18, "Working with 3D Models," we don't need to display it here; however, remember to change the line

```
class CMD2Model
```

to

```
class CMD2Model : public CObject
```

This changes the CMD2Model class from a standalone class to a derived class of CObject.

The CMD2Model class is more of a stepping-stone to greater things, as your real interest in adding MD2 model support to the SimpEngine lies in the CEntity class. The CEntity class represents a game object that has the capability to be animated through keyframes animation. In fact, the CEntity class provides good support for controlling the behavior of an MD2 model, and because the CEntity class is ultimately derived from CObject, you can work with a CEntity object the same way you can work with CObject objects.

The CEntity class holds the entity's direction (rotation about the y axis), any sounds the entity might make through a CAudio object (to be discussed), the current keyframe animation start frame and end frame, and the speed of the model's animation. The CEntity class definition is shown here:

```
class CEntity : public CMD2Model
{
protected:
    void OnAnimate(float deltaTime);
    void OnDraw(CCamera *camera);
    void OnCollision(CObject *collisionObject);
    void OnPrepare();

public:
    float direction;            // angle the entity is facing (in radians)
    CAudio *entitySound;        // the sound the entity makes
                                // currently only supports one sound
                                // per entity
```

```
    CEntity();
    ~CEntity();

    int stateStart, stateEnd;       // state keyframe start/end
    float deltaT;                   // used for keyframe interpolation
    float animSpeed;                // model animation speed

    // load the entity's sound
    void LoadAudio(CAudioSystem *audioSystem, char *filename, bool is3DSound);
};
```

THE AUDIO SYSTEM

The CAudioSystem class is responsible for the creation, playing, and management of DirectX
Audio sounds and music through the CAudio class, which represents a single-sound object such as
a sound effect or music.

The CAudio class definition is listed here:

```
class CAudio
{
private:
    IDirectMusicSegment8 *dmusicSegment;     // the segment

    // The 3D buffer might not be used (e.g. background music).
    // It should only be used for 3D positional sounds.
    IDirectSound3DBuffer *ds3DBuffer;

    bool is3DSound;        // true if this is a 3D sound

protected:

public:
    CAudio() { dmusicSegment = NULL; ds3DBuffer = NULL; is3DSound = false; }
    ~CAudio()
    {
        if (dmusicSegment != NULL)
        {
            dmusicSegment->Release();
            dmusicSegment = NULL;
        }
```

```
            if (ds3DBuffer != NULL)
            {
                ds3DBuffer->Release();
                ds3DBuffer = NULL;
            }
    }

    void SetSegment(IDirectMusicSegment8 *seg) { dmusicSegment = seg; }
    IDirectMusicSegment8 *GetSegment() { return dmusicSegment; }
    void Set3DBuffer(IDirectSound3DBuffer *dsBuff);
    IDirectSound3DBuffer *Get3DBuffer() { return ds3DBuffer; }

    bool Is3DSound() { return is3DSound; }
    void Set3DSound(bool b) { is3DSound = b; }

    void Set3DParams(float minDistance, float maxDistance);
    void Set3DPos(float x, float y, float z);
};
```

The CAudio class provides both an IDirectMusicSegment8 and an IDirectSound3DBuffer8 interface for the audio object. If the sound is just background music, then you would just want to load the segment, but if you have a 3D sound, then you would also want to load the 3D buffer.

You use the CAudioSystem class to load, play, and manage CAudio objects. The class definition is listed here:

```
class CAudioSystem
{
private:
    IDirectMusicLoader8 *dmusicLoader;            // the loader
    IDirectMusicPerformance8 *dmusicPerformance;  // the performance
    IDirectMusicAudioPath8 *dmusic3DAudioPath;    // the audiopath
    IDirectSound3DListener8 *ds3DListener;        // 3D listener

    DS3DLISTENER dsListenerParams;                // 3D listener properties

public:
    CAudioSystem();
    ~CAudioSystem();

    bool InitDirectXAudio(HWND hwnd);
    IDirectSound3DBuffer8 *Create3DBuffer();
```

```
    CAudio *Create(char *filename, bool is3DSound);
    IDirectMusicSegment8 *CreateSegment(char *filename, bool is3DSound);

    void Play(CAudio *audio, DWORD numRepeats);
    void Stop(CAudio *audio);

    void PlaySegment(IDirectMusicSegment8 *dmSeg, bool is3DSound, DWORD numRepeats);
    void StopSegment(IDirectMusicSegment8 *dmSeg);
    void Shutdown();

    void SetListenerPos(float cameraX, float cameraY, float cameraZ);
    void SetListenerRolloff(float rolloff);
    void SetListenerOrientation(float forwardX, float forwardY, float forwardZ,
                                float topX, float topY, float topZ);
    IDirectMusicPerformance8 *GetPerformance() { return dmusicPerformance; }
};
```

THE PARTICLE SYSTEM

The final system of the SimpEngine is the CParticleSystem, which you derive from to produce various particle effects, including explosions, smoke, fire, and precipitation. We discussed how to work with the particle system in Chapter 15, "Special Effects," so we won't be going into specific detail on how to use the CParticleSystem class here.

You should already know how to use the CParticleSystem class, but if not, here's a brief summary. First, the desired particle effect is derived from CParticleSystem—something like CExplosion. Then, the virtual functions Update(), Render(), and InitializeParticle() must be overridden with the physics and rendering needed to achieve the desired effect. To use the particle system, call the Update() function through the appropriate object's OnAnimate() function, and call the Render() function through the appropriate OnDraw() function.

SUMMARY

This chapter presented an overview of the SimpEngine, a simple, yet extensible game engine that you will be using in the next chapter to create a game.

You use the CNode as the base for CObject to create an object hierarchy, which is used for object management in the SimpEngine.

At the core of the engine is the COGLWindow class, which creates an OpenGL window and handles the Windows messages that are received from the operating system. You create a virtual function in the COGLWindow class for each message that you want to handle. The COGLWindow class also holds the input system object, CInputSystem, which uses DirectInput to retrieve the current keyboard, mouse, and joystick states. The input system object includes functions to determine whether a key has been pressed or released or how much the mouse has moved, whether a mouse button has been clicked, and whether a joystick has been moved or its button(s) clicked. Derived from the COGLWindow class is the CEngine class, which provides the main Windows message loop, the game loop, and a function to handle any input received from the input system.

A typical game cycle consists of gathering input, moving the player, performing artificial intelligence (AI), calculating physics, playing sounds, and rendering the scene. The SimpEngine's game cycle is not as clear-cut, however. Because of the object hierarchy, the game cycle must call the CObject functions Prepare(), Animate(), and Draw().

You determine whether any input devices have been used (keys pressed, mouse movement, and so on) through the CEngine::CheckInput() function, which uses the CInputSystem object defined in the COGLWindow class. The CSimpEngine class is derived from CEngine and represents the entry point into the SimpEngine framework.

The CCamera class defines the camera-viewing system for the engine and is responsible for determining how you view the world. The CWorld class defines the game world with which SimpEngine is running, displaying, and interacting. The CEngine::GameCycle() function uses the CWorld class to interact with all the objects in the game world through the Prepare(), Animate(), and Draw() functions.

You derive the CMD2Model class from CObject to enable the ability to treat models as objects in the object hierarchy. You derive CEntity from the CMD2Model class to encapsulate the functionality you need to work with model objects.

The CAudioSystem class is used to manage the creation and playing of music and sounds through the CAudio class. You derive from the CParticleSystem class to create specific particle effects, such as explosions, smoke, fire, and precipitation.

CHAPTER 21

MAKING A GAME! A TIME TO KILL

We've covered many topics throughout this book, and now we're going discuss the creation of a game as the culmination of these topics. This game took about a week to complete through the use of the SimpEngine discussed in Chapter 20, "Building a Game Engine." It includes such features as particle explosion effects, MD2 model loading and animation, bounding-sphere collision detection and response, camera movement and control, sound effects, basic AI, and terrain rendering and generation. The game itself is very simple, so don't expect too much from it—especially because it only took about a week to create. Maybe you'll want to improve upon the game or even write a completely new and better one!

Here's what we are going to cover:

- *A Time to Kill* initial design
- The creation of the game world, in particular the terrain
- The enemies and their AI
- The rockets you fire and the explosions they make
- The graphical user interface (GUI)
- Playing *A Time to Kill*
- Compilation and building the EXE

INITIAL DESIGN

Honestly, we didn't even know what type of game we were going to create when we first started working on *A Time to Kill*. We just wanted to create something where we could run around on a randomly generated terrain and blow things up. No story. No plot. No trophies.

However, as time passed, we came up with the idea of setting a time limit for the player to eliminate all the enemies. This time limit places a restriction on the player and forces him to have a goal to achieve. Next, we decided that the enemies would not be shooting back at the player. Sound easy? Well, the twist is that the enemies would be running away from the player instead of trying to find him, as in a normal "search-and-destroy" game. If the player kills all the enemies within the specified time limit, then he wins; otherwise, he loses. This provided the basis for the game rules of *A Time to Kill*, and we began working toward these goals immediately.

THE GAME WORLD

The first portion of the game we developed was the randomly generated terrain, which we
defined as a CTerrain object derived from the CObject class. The terrain itself is defined by a
height field of values ranging from zero to one (0...1); you multiply these height values by a
height scale value to keep the terrain in proportion with its width. If you want spiky terrain, then
you set a high height scale value; if you want rolling terrain, then you set a low height scale value.
Let's look at the CTerrain class definition:

```
class CTerrain : public CObject
{
private:
    int width;          // terrain is of size width X width
                        // preferably with 2^n = width
    float terrainMul;   // terrain scale value (width)
    float heightMul;    // height scale value
    float scanDepth;    // scan depth for determining amount of visible terrain
    float textureMul;   // terrain texture scale value

    // midpoint displacement algorithm functions from Jason Shankel
    float RangedRandom(float v1,float v2);
    void NormalizeTerrain(float field[],int size);
    void FilterHeightBand(float *band,int stride,int count,float filter);
    void FilterHeightField(float field[],int size,float filter);
    void MakeTerrainPlasma(float field[],int size,float rough);

protected:
    // terrain doesn't move, so no physics animations
    void OnAnimate(scalar_t deltaTime) {}

    void OnDraw(CCamera *camera);                // rendering
    void OnCollision(CObject *collisionObject);  // collisions with terrain

public:
    float *heightMap;        // dynamic heightmap
    CTexture terrainTex[5];  // for multiple textures on the terrain
    float fogColor[4];       // color of the fog/sky
```

```cpp
    CTerrain();
    CTerrain(int width, float rFactor);
    ~CTerrain() { delete [] heightMap; }

    void Load() {}
    void Unload() {}

    void BuildTerrain(int width, float rFactor); // generate the terrain
    float GetWidth() { return width; }           // get terrain width
    float GetMul() { return terrainMul; }        // get terrain multiply value
    float GetScanDepth() { return scanDepth; }   // get viewing scan depth
    float GetHeight(double x, double z);         // get height of terrain at (x,z)
};
```

As you can see, the terrain is actually a rather low-maintenance object because you really only need to render it and check for collisions. The CTerrain::OnDraw() function renders the terrain using the scanDepth member variable to determine the amount of terrain that you need to draw. The key to this function is the CCamera object that you pass as a parameter. Because this object tells you the location of the camera, you can determine what parts of the terrain you need to draw and what parts you don't need to draw. Here is the CTerrain::OnDraw() function:

```cpp
void CTerrain::OnDraw(CCamera *camera)
{
    int z, x;                               // counter variables

    glEnable(GL_DEPTH_TEST);                // enable depth testing

    glFogi(GL_FOG_MODE, GL_LINEAR);         // set up linear fog
    glFogfv(GL_FOG_COLOR, fogColor);
    glFogf(GL_FOG_START, scanDepth * 0.2f);
    glFogf(GL_FOG_END, scanDepth * 2.5);
    glHint(GL_FOG_HINT, GL_FASTEST);
    glEnable(GL_FOG);                       // enable fog

    // set up and enable blending, alpha testing
    glBlendFunc(GL_SRC_ALPHA, GL_ONE_MINUS_SRC_ALPHA);
    glEnable(GL_BLEND);
    glEnable(GL_ALPHA_TEST);
    glAlphaFunc(GL_GREATER, 0.0);
    glDisable(GL_ALPHA_TEST);
```

```
// enable 2D texturing and set texture to base terrain texture
glEnable(GL_TEXTURE_2D);
glBindTexture(GL_TEXTURE_2D, terrainTex[0].texID);
glTexEnvi(GL_TEXTURE_ENV, GL_TEXTURE_ENV_MODE, GL_MODULATE);
glTexParameteri(GL_TEXTURE_2D, GL_TEXTURE_MAG_FILTER, GL_LINEAR);

glColor3f(1.0, 1.0, 1.0);

// draw triangle strips going along the z axis
for (z = (int)(camera->position.z / terrainMul - scanDepth), z=z<0?0:z;
        (z < camera->position.z / terrainMul + scanDepth) && z < width-1;
        z++)
{
    glBegin(GL_TRIANGLE_STRIP);
    for (x = (int)(camera->position.x / terrainMul - scanDepth), x=x<0?0:x;
            (x < camera->position.x / terrainMul + scanDepth) && x < width-1;
            x++)
    {
        glTexCoord2f(textureMul * x, textureMul * z);
        glVertex3f((float)x*terrainMul,
                    (float)heightMap[x + z*width]*heightMul,
                    (float)z*terrainMul);

        glTexCoord2f(textureMul * (x+1), textureMul * z);
        glVertex3f((float)(x+1)*terrainMul,
                    (float)heightMap[x+1 + z*width]*heightMul,
                    (float)z*terrainMul);

        glTexCoord2f(textureMul * x, textureMul * (z+1));
        glVertex3f((float)x*terrainMul,
                    (float)heightMap[x + (z+1)*width]*heightMul,
                    (float)(z+1)*terrainMul);

        glTexCoord2f(textureMul * (x+1), textureMul * (z+1));
        glVertex3f((float)(x+1)*terrainMul,
                    (float)heightMap[x+1 + (z+1)*width]*heightMul,
                    (float)(z+1)*terrainMul);
    }
    glEnd();
}
}
```

Notice at the beginning of the `CTerrain::OnDraw()` function that you set up a linear fog with medium density, and that you also set up the terrain for blending so it helps disappear into the fog more nicely. Using these two methods keeps you from seeing where the terrain stops being rendered because of the `scanDepth` value.

You use the `CTerrain::GetHeight()` function to determine the height of the terrain at any point in the world, even in between vertices. The function accomplishes this by determining the closest four vertices to the (x, z) location that you are looking for and interpolating the heights of these four vertices to produce a final height. All the objects in the world use this function, particularly when checking for collision detection with the `CTerrain` object.

THE ENEMIES

The enemies in *A Time to Kill* can be one of two types: an Ogro or a Sod. Although these names may sound strange, they are simply based on the MD2 models that they represent. The Ogro runs slower and is not as "smart" as the Sod, but both are equally killable.

To create these enemies, you first derive a `CEnemy` class from `CEntity`. The `CEnemy` class allows you to encapsulate everything an enemy might need, such as the AI state, the enemy's distance from the player, and the enemy's running speed. To create each of the actual enemy classes, you derive the `COgroEnemy` and `CSodEnemy` classes from `CEnemy`.

First, here's the `CEnemy` class:

```
class CEnemy : public CEntity
{
private:

protected:
    float distFromPlayer;    // distance this enemy is from player
    float runSpeed;          // speed of enemy when running
    AIState_t aiState;       // state of enemy thought

    // we override this function to have specific enemy AI
    virtual void OnProcessAI() {}

    // handle collisions with other objects
    virtual void OnCollision(CObject *collisionObject) {}

public:
    CPlayer *player;                         // a reference to the player
```

```
    CEnemy()                                  // constructor
    {
        isDead = false;                       // enemy starts off alive
        velocity = CVector(0.0, 0.0, 0.0);    // velocity of enemy
        runSpeed = velocity.z;                // speed of enemy is velocity's 'z'
        SetState(MODEL_IDLE);                 // enemy AI/model state - idle state
        direction = 0.0f;                     // point north
        player = NULL;                        // no player has been set
    }

    ~CEnemy() {}                              // destructor

    void ProcessAI() { OnProcessAI(); }       // process the enemy AI
    void SetPlayer(CPlayer *p)                // set reference to player object
        { player = p; }
};
```

The CEnemy class has two virtual functions that you override for the derived enemies:
OnProcessAI() and OnCollision(). OnProcessAI() is where you will determine how the enemy will
"think." The enemy's AI state is specified by the protected member variable aiState, of the
AiState_t type.

Enemy AI

As mentioned, the enemy AI uses states (a *state machine*) to determine how the enemy acts in the
game. The enemy states are defined by the AiState_t enumeration type, which is shown here:

```
enum AIState_t
{
    AI_UNCARING,    // enemy is not scared and does not care
    AI_SCARED,      // enemy is scared and running away
    AI_DEAD         // enemy is dead
};
```

In *A Time to Kill*, there are only a few enemy states and conditions that you need to worry about:
either the enemy is scared, or it is uncaring (if it's not dead). If the enemy is scared, then you
need to make it run away from the player's current position. If the enemy is uncaring, then it can
either run around on its own, in any direction, or it can remain idle. Table 21.1 illustrates how
the AI states relate to the MD2 model states in *A Time to Kill*.

Table 21.1 AI State Table

AI States	Model States
AI_UNCARING	MODEL_IDLE
	MODEL_RUN
AI_SCARED	MODEL_RUN
AI_DEAD	MODEL_DIE

As you see, the AI_UNCARING state can be one of two model states: MODEL_IDLE or MODEL_RUN. The percentage of time that each model state will be used is directly related to the enemy, which is why you specify the OnProcessAI() function as a virtual function.

The Ogro

The Ogro is a slow-moving, ogre-like creature who is not very smart when trying to run away from the player. When the Ogro is in the AI_UNCARING state, there is a 25-percent chance that it will run around on its own, and a 75-percent chance that it will remain idle. When in the AI_SCARED state, the Ogro will run away at a 45-degree angle (in either direction) from the player when the player is within 100 world units, as illustrated in Figure 21.1.

If the Ogro collides with another Ogro or a Sod enemy, then the Ogro enters the AI_UNCARING state and stops moving. When the Ogro collides with the terrain (as it should always do), you retrieve the height of the terrain at the Ogro's current location and set the Ogro's y position to that height. You also make sure the Ogro doesn't go out of bounds of the terrain by checking the Ogro's x and z position in the world. Finally, if the Ogro collides with a rocket (as we'll discuss), the Ogro enters the AI_DEAD state.

How about some code? Here is the COgroEnemy::OnProcessAI() function:

```
void COgroEnemy::OnProcessAI()
{
    // calculate distance from player
    CVector diff = player->position - position;

    if (aiState != AI_DEAD)
    {
```

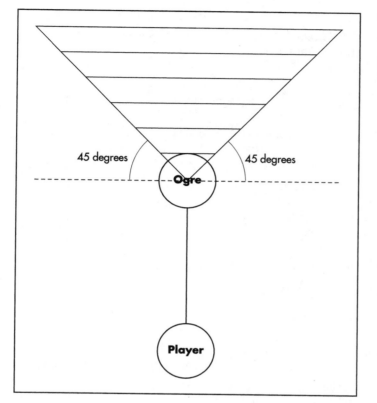

Figure 21.1

The Ogro runs away from the player at a 45-degree angle.

```
        // if the player is close enough, the enemy should become scared
        distFromPlayer = sqrt(diff.x*diff.x + diff.y*diff.y + diff.z*diff.z);
        if (distFromPlayer < 100.0)
            aiState = AI_SCARED;
        else
            aiState = AI_UNCARING;
    }
}
```

And here is the `COgroEnemy::OnPrepare()` function, which sets the model state based on the AI state:

```
void COgroEnemy::OnPrepare()
{
    float dirToPlayer;  // the angle of the enemy-player vector
```

```
CVector diff;         // the vector from the enemy to the player
diff.x = position.x - player->position.x;
diff.z = position.z - player->position.z;
diff.Normalize();

// find the angle in the world of the vector from the enemy to the player
// in relation the negative z axis
dirToPlayer = RAD2DEG(diff.Angle(CVector(0,0,-1)));

// seed random generator
srand((unsigned int)time(NULL));

// perform AI operations
ProcessAI();

// now do Ogro prep
// set modelState based on AIstate
switch (aiState)
{
case AI_SCARED:
    // set the direction of the enemy
    direction = (dirToPlayer - 90) + ((rand()%90)-45);
    modelState = MODEL_RUN;
    velocity = CVector(0.0, 0.0, 13.0);
    break;
case AI_UNCARING:
    direction = float(rand() % 360);       // face any direction
    if ((rand() % 4) != 0)                 // idle 75% of the time
    {
        modelState = MODEL_IDLE;
        velocity = CVector(0.0, 0.0, 0.0);
    }
    else
    {
        velocity = CVector(0.0, 0.0, 13.0);
        modelState = MODEL_RUN;
    }
    break;
case AI_DEAD:
    modelState = MODEL_DIE;
    velocity = CVector(0.0, 0.0, 0.0);
```

```
            if (nextFrame == stateStart)          // remove monster from world
            {                                       // after dying animation ends
                // time to kill the monster
                isDead = true;
            }
        break;
    default:
        break;
    }

    // do prep for MD2 model states
    CEntity::OnPrepare();
}
```

The Sod

The Sod enemy is nearly identical to the Ogro, except that the Sod is faster and slightly "smarter"—that is, the Sod will run away when the player is within 125 world units, in the direction range shown in Figure 21.2. The code for the Sod is essentially the same as the code for the Ogro, with the exception of the "runaway" angle calculation; hence, the Sod code is not displayed here.

ROCKETS AND EXPLOSIONS

The rocket is the projectile that the player shoots at the enemies when the left mouse button is clicked. It is represented by the CRocket class, which loads the rocket MD2 model, renders it, and performs the physics calculations on it. The rocket travels at a crisp 120 world units per second. The CRocket class, whose class definition is shown below, is derived from the CEntity class.

```
class CRocket : public CEntity
{
private:
    void SetupExplosionTexture();    // sets up the texture for OpenGL

protected:
    void OnAnimate(scalar_t deltaTime);       // movement
    void OnCollision(CObject *collisionObject);  // collision
    void OnDraw(CCamera *camera);             // rendering
    void OnPrepare();
```

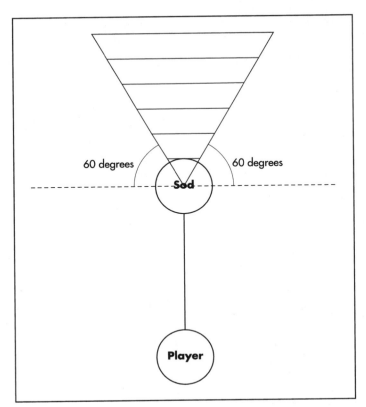

Figure 21.2

The Sod runs away at a 60-degree angle from the player.

```
public:
    float distanceTravel;     // distance rocket has traveled
    CVector forward;          // forward vector of rocket
    bool isExplosion;         // true if the rocket has exploded

    CTexture *explosionTex;   // texture for the explosion
    CExplosion *explosion;    // the explosion particle effect

    CRocket();
    ~CRocket();

    void Load();
    void Unload();
};
```

Whenever the rocket hits an object, it explodes; the CExplosion object (derived from CParticleSystem) is used to create the explosion. This event results in the isExplosion boolean variable being set to true when the rocket collides with the object. The CExplosion class uses the explosionTex specified in the CRocket class as the texture when rendering the explosion. Figure 21.3 shows the rocket explosion.

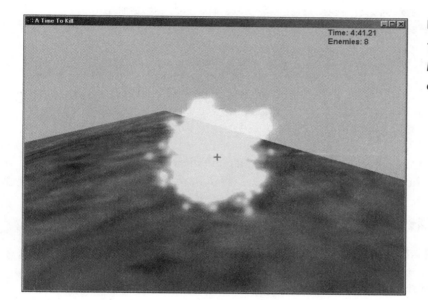

Figure 21.3

The rocket explosion. Notice the blended and textured quads.

THE USER INTERFACE

The game's final class is the CGUI class, which represents the graphical user interface of *A Time to Kill*. This class encapsulates the rendering of the game's countdown timer and the number of enemies left in the game. It also renders the "You win!" and "You lose!" screens, not to mention the crosshair in the center of the screen. Here is the class definition for CGUI:

```
class CGUI
{
private:
    // amount of time left in current game
    int minutesLeft, secondsLeft, millisecondsLeft;
    int enemiesLeft;                        // number of enemies left

    CFont *font;                            // the GUI main font
    CFont *crosshair;                       // the GUI crosshair font
```

```
        CFont *endText;                         // win/lose screen text

public:
        CGUI();
        ~CGUI();

        void SetCurrentTime(float timeLeft);    // sets the current time left
        void SetEnemiesLeft(int eLeft);         // sets the number of enemies left
        void Draw();                            // draws the GUI
        void Animate(float deltaTime);          // not used

        void DrawWinner();                      // the "You win!" screen
        void DrawLoser();                       // the "You lose!" screen
};
```

Sound simple? It is! Be sure to check out the CWorld implementation in *WORLD.CPP* to see how you use the CGUI class in the game.

PLAYING THE GAME

After the game has finished loading, the clock starts ticking, and the player must start searching for the Ogro and Sod enemies in the world. The total number of these enemies is displayed in the upper-right corner of the GUI; whenever the player destroys an enemy, the enemy count decreases to reflect the change. The player wins if all the enemies are destroyed before the clock runs out.

The controls for *A Time to Kill* are listed in Table 21.2.

BUILDING THE EXE

To compile and build the game executable, you need to link with the following LIB files:

- *opengl32.lib.* The base OpenGL LIB
- *glu32.lib.* The GL Utility LIB
- *dxguid.lib.* The DirectX GUID LIB
- *winmm.lib.* The Windows Multimedia LIB
- *dinput8.lib.* The DirectX Input LIB

In Microsoft Visual C++, open the Project menu, select Settings, choose the link tab, and enter these filenames in the Object/Library Modules line.

Figure 21.4 shows the final screenshot of *A Time to Kill.*

Table 21.2 The Controls

Key or Button	Function
W	Move forward
S	Move backward
A	Strafe left
D	Strafe right
Left mouse button	Fire rocket
Move mouse	Look
Numpad +	Increase mouse sensitivity
Numpad –	Decrease mouse sensitivity
Esc	Quit

Figure 21.4

The game A Time to Kill *with the Ogro on the left and the Sod on the right.*

SUMMARY

This chapter has covered only the basics of what you need to know to get started with *A Time to Kill*. The CD-ROM includes the entire source code and media for the game.

In this chapter, we discussed how the game world is created, the enemies and their AI, rockets and explosions, the basics of the user interface, how to play the game, and how to build the executable.

A Time to Kill could greatly be improved and enhanced. Some ideas include a smoke trail on the rockets, enemy sounds, radar, a bigger world, faster rendering, and more world objects. The possibilities are endless, and we look forward to seeing what you can do to improve upon *A Time to Kill*!

The CD-ROM that comes with this book includes all the source code from this book and much, much more. Special thanks to Jeff "NeHe" Molofee for compiling the CD with some of the coolest OpenGL examples and demos around! Also, Bas Kuenen deserves a big thank you for his help and ideas in the design and implementation of the SimpEngine.

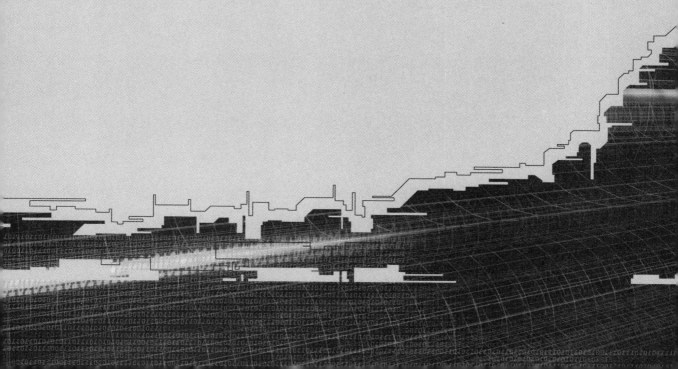

Part IV

Appendixes

APPENDIX A

ONLINE RESOURCES

Although there are many more things we would have liked to have covered in this book, there is no way we could pack all the game-development information you need into a single volume. Fortunately, the Web is full of information that you may find useful when developing games and graphics applications. Here we list some of the best resources to aid you in your research.

In addition, we've created a Web site for this book: **http://glbook.gamedev.net**. There you will find updates, answers to frequently asked questions, and other supplemental information.

GAME DEVELOPMENT

There must be hundreds of sites on the Internet dedicated to making games. We've listed some of the best of them here. None of these sites are OpenGL-specific, but they provide excellent sources of general-purpose information about game development.

GameDev.net

HTTP://WWW.GAMEDEV.NET

This is the leading site for game developers of all levels. Here you'll find more than 1,000 articles covering all aspects of game development, including OpenGL, DirectX, networking, audio, graphics in general, artificial intelligence, and more. In addition, you'll get the most relevant news, source-code samples, a dictionary of game development terms, the largest and most active forums dedicated to game development that you'll find anywhere, and much, much more. GameDev.net also has the coolest Webmasters around.

Game Development Search Engine

HTTP://WWW.GDSE.COM

The GDSE includes news and a handpicked selection of links to hundreds of smaller game-development sites, coupled with a powerful search engine. This is a great way to mine the nuggets of game-development information scattered across the Web.

flipCode

HTTP://WWW.FLIPCODE.COM

flipCode is an impressive site with timely news and articles covering advanced graphics and game-programming topics. One of its nicest features is tech files from some great coders who share their research and methodologies with you.

Gamasutra

HTTP://WWW.GAMASUTRA.COM

Gamasutra is operated by the Gama Network, which also produces *Game Developer Magazine* and the Game Developers Conference. The site features content from the magazine and the conference, as well as original articles and news.

OpenGL

OpenGL boasts an active and enthusiastic online community of game and graphics programmers. A quick search of the Internet will turn up dozens, if not hundreds, of sites dedicated to OpenGL programming. Some of the best of these are listed here.

NeHe Productions

HTTP://NEHE.GAMEDEV.NET

Jeff Molofee has worked hard to make NeHe Productions one of the top OpenGL resources on the Web. In addition to more than 40 original OpenGL tutorials, he's collected an impressive suite of demo programs displaying the capabilities of OpenGL. He also routinely posts links and descriptions of new OpenGL online resources.

OpenGL.org

HTTP://WWW.OPENGL.ORG

OpenGL.org is the official site of the OpenGL ARB. Besides regular OpenGL-related news, they maintain several FAQs full of helpful information.

Additional OpenGL Links

http://reality.sgi.com/mjk/tips/	Way cool, way fast OpenGL rendering techniques
http://glvelocity.gamedev.net	glVelocity
http://romka.demonews.com	Romka Graphics
http://nate.scuzzy.net/	Nate Miller's Programming Page
http://www.gamedev.net/opengl	druid's OpenGL Journal
http://reality.sgi.com/blythe/sig99/	Siggraph '99 Course Notes

DirectX

There are also a number of DirectX-specific sites. A few of the most useful ones are listed here.

DirectX Developer Center

HTTP://MSDN.MICROSOFT.COM/DIRECTX

Here you can download the latest version of the DirectX SDK, read about DirectX-related news and events, and read articles written by members of the Microsoft DirectX team.

The DirectX Mailing List

Archives/Join: HTTP://DISCUSS.MICROSOFT.COM/ARCHIVES/DIRECTXDEV.HTML

FAQ: HTTP://MSDN.MICROSOFT.COM/LIBRARY/TECHART/DXFAQ2.HTM

Now maintained by Microsoft, this mailing list is one of the best sources of information on DirectX around. Participants in the list include members of the DirectX team, developers from leading hardware vendors, and well-known professional game developers. Before joining—and especially before posting to the list—be sure to look over the archives and read the FAQ, and above all: Be courteous.

Miscellaneous Resources

The Internet excels at providing information about subjects that are either too specific or too advanced to cover in books. In this section, we've included links to some of the best sites we've found that supplement or expand upon material presented in this book.

ParticleSystems.com

HTTP://WWW.PARTICLESYSTEMS.COM

A great collection of most of the relevant information on the Web about particle systems. Includes the excellent Particle System API.

Real-Time Rendering

HTTP://WWW.REALTIMERENDERING.COM

This official Web site for the excellent book *Real-Time Rendering* also contains other articles by the authors and links to some of the best information on the Web. There's a lot of advanced information here, which is really worth spending some time exploring.

Developer Pages

NVIDIA: HTTP://WWW.NVIDIA.COM/DEVELOPER.NSF

Intel: HTTP://CEDAR.INTEL.COM/CGI-BIN/IDS.DLL/MAIN.JSP

ATI: HTTP://WWW.ATI.COM/NA/PAGES/RESOURCE_CENTRE/DEV_REL/DEVREL.HTML

NVIDIA, Intel, and ATI maintain Web pages containing white papers and other documents covering advanced topics (primarily graphics related). These are great sources of information.

Fog Articles

HTTP://WWW.GAMEDEV.NET/OPENGL/VOLFOG.HTML

HTTP://WWW.GAMEDEV.NET/REFERENCE/ARTICLES/ARTICLE677.ASP

HTTP://WWW.GAMEDEV.NET/REFERENCE/ARTICLES/ARTICLE672.ASP

We mentioned in Chapter 15, "Special Effects," that we'd provide links to articles describing volumetric fog, and true to our word, that's what these three sites are.

APPENDIX B

USING THE CD

The CD-ROM included with the book contains all the source code listings and demo programs discussed in the book, along with some of the best OpenGL demos, games, and utilities from around the world.

THE CD USER INTERFACE

The CD-ROM menu was written in HTML and can be viewed using Internet Explorer 4.0 or higher, or Netscape Navigator 4.0 or higher. Because of the use of HTML, the menu should run on a wide variety of computers and operating systems.

CD-ROM FILE STRUCTURE

The CD contains five main folders:

- **Book Content.** All the code and examples from each chapter of the book.
- **Contributor Projects.** Demos, games, utilities, and code contributed to the book by extremely talented individuals.
- **Extras.** A collection of extremely useful libraries and utilities that will aid you in developing OpenGL projects of your own.
- **OpenGL Basecode.** OpenGL framework for a wide variety of computers, languages, and operating systems.
- **Web.** The HTML used for the CD menu.

SYSTEM REQUIREMENTS

There are a number of minimum and recommended requirements for your system:

- CD-ROM drive, DVD drive, CD-R drive, or CD-RW drive.
- Web browser: For best results use Internet Explorer 4.0 or higher, or Netscape Navigator 4.0 or higher.
- Memory: 32MB minimum, 64MB or 128MB recommended.

- Video: A very fast video card with hardware support for OpenGL. NVIDIA GeForce or Voodoo3 or higher recommended.
- CPU: To run most of the contributor demos, you should have a Pentium 450 combined with a good video card. The faster your computer, the better!

INSTALLATION

Insert the CD-ROM into your CD-ROM drive. If you are using Windows 95 or higher, and you have the autorun feature enabled, the menu should appear on your screen. If the menu does not appear, you can manually start the menu by going to your CD-ROM drive (for example, D:) under My Computer and double-clicking on the *MENU.HTM* file.

If you are using an operating system other than Windows, you can load the menu by clicking on the *MENU.HTM* file or by opening *MENU.HTM* with your Web browser. In Netscape or Internet Explorer, open the File menu at the top of the browser window, select Open, and then specify *MENU.HTM* as the file you want to open.

MISCELLANEOUS PROBLEMS AND TROUBLESHOOTING INFORMATION

It seems no matter how much testing is done, problems will still occur.

Before publication, all the programs on the CD were scanned for viruses using the latest virus scanners available at the time. The CD passed all testing and was determined to be virus free.

All files on a CD-ROM are marked as read-only, meaning you cannot save or write files to the CD-ROM. To compile code from the CD, you need to copy the code to your hard drive, right-click on the file(s) or folder, and click on Properties. Make sure the Read-Only option is unchecked; otherwise, you may have problems compiling the code!

Much of the contributor code assumes you have a strong understanding of Visual C++ and that you are able to troubleshoot problems on your own. A common problem most new programmers will have when compiling the code is forgetting to include the required libraries. All the code has been tested and does compile as long as the proper libraries have been included. If you are having problems compiling a program, you may be using an old version of Visual C++ or an incompatible compiler. Please make sure you have a good understanding of Visual C++ before you dive into the code.

Although each contributor program has been tested, bugs do slip through the cracks, and you may experience a crash. If this happens, reset your system, and avoid that program in the future. A crash will not damage your computer in any way. Usually a crash occurs when a programmer forgets to free memory used in his program. The system eventually runs out of memory and causes the computer to crash. Resetting the system should return everything to normal.

A common problem you may experience with the contributor code is the error message `Failed to create rendering context`. If you see this message, try setting your desktop color to 16-bit. Usually this will solve the problem, with very little difference in the way your screen looks.

If you experience very slow performance or the program appears to be doing nothing, make sure you have the latest version of OpenGL drivers for your video card, and make sure your video card supports hardware accelerated OpenGL!

STILL NEED HELP?

Try visiting the sites in Appendix A, "Online Resources," specifically GameDev.net at **http://www.gamedev.net** and NeHe Productions at **http://nehe.gamedev.net**. At both sites you will find message forums where you can ask questions about OpenGL, along with links to the e-mail addresses of Kevin Hawkins, Dave Astle, and Jeff Molofee (NeHe).

Enjoy the CD!

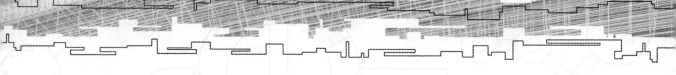

Index